This is the first volume of the first ever comprehensive edition of the works of Immanuel Kant in English translation. The purpose of the Cambridge edition is to offer translations of the best modern German edition of Kant's work in a uniform format suitable for Kant scholars. When complete (fourteen volumes are currently envisaged), the edition will include all of Kant's published writings and a generous selection of his unpublished writings such as the *Opus postumum, handschriftliche Nachlass,* lectures, and correspondence.

The eleven essays in this volume constitute Kant's theoretical, pre-critical philosophical writings from 1755 to 1770. Several of these pieces have never been translated into English before; others have long been unavailable in English. They treat a wide range of issues: the compatibility of science and religious faith, the perfection and harmony of the world, the demonstration of God's existence, causality and its cognition, the mind and its place in nature, the relation of geometry and the world, the nature of space and time, the contrasting methods of mathematics and metaphysics, the origin of metaphysical concepts, and the possibility and limits of metaphysical cognition. We can trace in these works the development of Kant's thought to the eventual emergence in 1770 of the two chief tenets of his mature philosophy: the subjectivity of space and time, and the phenomena-noumena distinction.

The volume has been furnished with substantial editorial apparatus, including a general introduction to the main themes of Kant's early thought, introductions to the individual works and résumés of their contents, linguistic and factual notes, bibliographies, a glossary of key terms, and biographical-bibliographical sketches of persons mentioned by Kant.

THE CAMBRIDGE EDITION OF THE WORKS OF IMMANUEL KANT

Theoretical Philosophy, 1755–1770
The Critique of Pure Reason
Theoretical Philosophy After 1781
Practical Philosophy
Aesthetics and Teleology
Religion and Rational Theology
Anthropology, History, and Education
Natural Science
Lectures on Logic
Lectures on Metaphysics
Lectures on Practical Philosophy
Opus postumum
Notes and Fragments
Correspondence

IMMANUEL KANT
Theoretical philosophy, 1755–1770

THE CAMBRIDGE EDITION OF THE WORKS OF IMMANUEL KANT

IMMANUEL KANT

Theoretical philosophy,
1755–1770

TRANSLATED AND EDITED BY
DAVID WALFORD
Saint David's University College, Lampeter

IN COLLABORATION WITH
RALF MEERBOTE
University of Rochester

CAMBRIDGE
UNIVERSITY PRESS

Published by the Press Syndicate of the University of Cambridge
The Pitt Building, Trumpington Street, Cambridge CB2 1RP
40 West 20th Street, New York, NY 10011–4211, USA
10 Stamford Road, Oakleigh, Victoria 3166, Australia

First published 1992

Printed in the United States of America

Library of Congress Cataloging-in-Publication Data
Kant, Immanuel, 1724–1804.
[Essays. English. Selections]
Theoretical philosophy, 1755–1770 / Immanuel Kant; translated and
edited by David Walford, Ralf Meerbote.
p. cm. – (The Cambridge edition of the works of Immanuel
Kant)
Includes bibliographical references and index.
ISBN 0-521-39214-4
1. Philosophy. I. Walford, David. II. Meerbote, Ralf.
III. Title. IV. Series: Kant, Immanuel, 1724–1804. Works.
English. 1992.
B2758.W35 1992 91-31729
CIP

A catalog record for this book is available from the British Library

ISBN 0-521-39214-4 hardback

Contents

CONTENTS

General editors' preface

Within a few years of the publication of his *Critique of Pure Reason* in 1781, Immanuel Kant (1724–1804) was recognized by his contemporaries as one of the seminal philosophers of modern times – indeed, as one of the great philosophers of all time. This renown soon spread beyond German-speaking lands, and translations of Kant's work into English were published even before 1800. Since then, interpretations of Kant's views have come and gone and loyalty to his positions has waxed and waned, but his importance has not diminished. Generations of scholars have devoted their efforts to producing reliable translations of Kant into English as well as into other languages.

There are four main reasons for the present edition of Kant's writings:

1. Completeness. Although most of the works published in Kant's lifetime have been translated before – the most important ones more than once – only fragments of Kant's many important unpublished works have ever been translated. These include the *Opus postumum*, Kant's unfinished *magnum opus* on the transition from philosophy to physics; transcriptions of his classroom lectures; his correspondence; and his marginalia and other notes. One aim of this edition is to make a comprehensive sampling of these materials available in English for the first time.

2. Availability. Many English translations of Kant's works, especially those that have not individually played a large role in the subsequent development of philosophy, have long been inaccessible or out of print. Many of them, however, are crucial for the understanding of Kant's philosophical development, and the absence of some from English-language bibliographies may be responsible for erroneous or blinkered traditional interpretations of his doctrines by English-speaking philosophers.

3. Organization. Another aim of the present edition is to make all Kant's published work, both major and minor, available in comprehensive volumes organized both chronologically and topically, so as to facilitate the serious study of his philosophy by English-speaking readers.

4. Consistency of translation. Although many of Kant's major works have been translated by the most distinguished scholars of their day, some of these translations are now dated, and there is considerable terminological disparity among them. Our aim has been to enlist some of the most accomplished Kant scholars and translators to produce new translations, freeing readers from both the philosophical and literary preconceptions of previous generations and allowing them to approach texts, as far as possible, with the same directness as present-day readers of the German or Latin originals.

In pursuit of these goals, our editors and translators attempt to follow several fundamental principles:

1. As far as seems advisable, the edition employs a single general glossary, especially for Kant's technical terms. Although we have not attempted to restrict the prerogative of editors and translators in choice of terminology, we have maximized consistency by putting a single editor or editorial team in charge of each of the main groupings of Kant's writings, such as his work in practical philosophy, philosophy of religion, or natural science, so that there will be a high degree of terminological consistency, at least in dealing with the same subject matter.

2. Our translators try to avoid sacrificing literalness to readability. We hope to produce translations that approximate the originals in the sense that they leave as much of the interpretive work as possible to the reader.

3. The paragraph, and even more the sentence, is often Kant's unit of argument, and one can easily transform what Kant intends as a continuous argument into a mere series of assertions by breaking up a sentence so as to make it more readable. Therefore, we try to preserve Kant's own divisions of sentences and paragraphs wherever possible.

4. Earlier editions often attempted to improve Kant's texts on the basis of controversial conceptions about their proper interpretation. In our translations, emendation or improvement of the original edition is kept to the minimum necessary to correct obvious typographical errors.

5. Our editors and translators try to minimize interpretation in other ways as well, for example, by rigorously segregating Kant's own footnotes, the editors' purely linguistic notes, and their more explanatory or informational notes; notes in this last category are treated as endnotes rather than footnotes.

We have not attempted to standardize completely the format of individual volumes. Each, however, includes information about the context in which Kant wrote the works that have been translated, an English–German glossary, an index, and other aids to comprehension. The general introduction to each volume includes an explanation of specific principles of translation and, where necessary, principles of selection of works included in that volume. The pagination of the standard German edition of Kant's works, *Kants gesammelte Schriften,* edited by the Royal Prussian (later German) Academy of Sciences (Berlin: Georg Reimer, later Walter deGruyter & Co., 1900–   ), is indicated throughout by means of marginal numbers.

Our aim is to produce a comprehensive edition of Kant's writings, embodying and displaying the high standards attained by Kant scholarship in the English-speaking world during the second half of the twentieth century, and serving as both an instrument and a stimulus for the further development of Kant studies by English-speaking readers in the century to come. Because of our emphasis on literalness of translation and on information rather than interpretation in editorial practices, we hope our edition will continue to be usable despite the inevitable evolution and occasional revolutions in Kant scholarship.

PAUL GUYER
ALLEN W. WOOD

Preface

The present volume contains the eleven works of theoretical philosophy composed by Kant during the final fifteen years of the pre-critical period of his thought, which comprises the twenty-three years from 1747 to 1770. During this period Kant composed twenty-five works, of which only one – *On Fire* (1755) – was not published and of which fourteen were devoted to a variety of themes not covered by this volume: physics and astronomy, geology and meteorology, aesthetics, ethics, and psychology. These fourteen works include the five scientific works of the first five years of the pre-critical period – the two works on physics *Living Forces* (1747) and *On Fire*, the two short essays on physical geography of 1754, and the important work of Newtonian cosmology, the *Universal Natural History* (1755) – and the nine works published during the period covered by this volume but excluded from it for thematic reasons – the three short earthquake essays of 1756; the two short meteorological essays of 1757; the last of Kant's scientific works, the *Motion and Rest* (1758); an occasional piece of 1760; the essay on morbid psychology, the *Maladies of the Mind* (1764); and an important work on aesthetics and anthropology, the *Observations* (1764).

The eleven pre-critical works of theoretical philosophy included in this volume are: (1) *New Elucidation* (1755), (2) *Physical Monadology* (1756), (3) *Optimism* (1759), (4) *False Subtlety* (1762), (5) *The Only Possible Argument* (1763), (6) *Negative Magnitudes* (1763), (7) *Inquiry* (1764), (8) *Announcement* (1765), (9) *Dreams* (1766), (10) *Directions in Space* (1768), and (11) *Inaugural Dissertation* (1770). The *Physical Monadology* has been included because, although it deals with a scientific theme (atomic theory), it also handles important philosophical themes (such as the distinction between physical space and geometrical space); the *Maladies of the Mind* has been excluded because, although it discusses themes touched on in the *Dreams* (such as madness, religious mania, and sensory hallucination), it does so from a primarily empirical standpoint.

The translations in this volume have been made from the standard edition of those works (to be found in Volumes I and II of *Immanuel Kants gesammelte Schriften*, published by the *Akademie der Wissenschaften zu Berlin* – formerly the *Preussische königliche Akademie der Wissenschaften*). The aim has been to produce translations of the highest possible accuracy couched in the most lucid possible English. Only rarely have the ideals of clarity of style and fidelity to the Kantian text come into conflict; in such cases, the former has been sacrificed in the interest of the latter. Kant's paragraphing and his use of the equivalent of italics (*Sperrschrift*) have always been scrupulously observed. In only one minor respect has Kant's text been modified in the translations: In the interest of greater clarity, employment has occasionally been made of the modern device, unknown to Kant, of quotation marks to indicate that a word or phrase is being *mentioned* rather than used. Latin passages and Greek words have, in conformity with Kant's own practice, been left untranslated in the text itself (the translations are to be found in the Factual Notes, near the end of the book). The pagination of the Academy edition (hereafter abbreviated in the text and notes as AK) has been indicated in the margins of the translations without the letters "AK."

With the exception of the *Inaugural Dissertation,* all the translations (including those of the *Inquiry* and the *Directions in Space,* which were translated previously by the present translator) are new. In the case of the *Inaugural Dissertation,* G. B. Kerferd's translation has been adopted because of its exemplary accuracy. The translation has been revised, not in order to correct it but in order to bring it stylistically and linguistically into line with the other translations in the volume. We should like to express our gratitude to Professor Kerferd both for his courteous advice and ready assistance with the revision and for allowing his name to be associated with the revised edition of his admirable translation. This translation has been reprinted in revised form by permission of the publisher from *Kant: Selected Pre-critical Writings and Correspondence with Beck,* translated and introduced with notes by G. B. Kerferd and D. E. Walford (Manchester: Manchester University Press, 1968), pp. 45–92.

Each of the eleven translations *individually* has been equipped with a set of editorial material consisting of five elements: an *introduction* (the eleven introductions are grouped together and immediately follow the General Introduction), a *résumé* (the eleven résumés are also grouped together and immediately follow the individual introductions), a *bibliography* (the eleven bibliographies have likewise been grouped together, but are located immediately after the Factual Notes towards the end of the volume), *linguistic notes* (which are to be found at the foot of the translations themselves), and *factual notes* (which are located towards the end of the volume immediately after the last translation). The eleven translations *as a whole* have been furnished with a *General Introduction* (immediately following this preface and the Guide to Abbreviations at the front of the volume), a *Glossary, Biographical-Bibliographical Sketches of Persons Mentioned by Kant,* and an *Index* (located in that order at the end of the volume, immediately after the bibliographies). The volume as a whole has also been provided with a *Guide to Abbreviations* (located between this preface and the General Introduction at the front of the volume). Two translations (*Optimism* and *Inquiry*) have been furnished with appendixes (each consisting of supplementary translated material and located immediately after the translation itself). These elements of editorial material require brief explanation.

Introductions.   Each introduction is intended, as far as possible, to furnish the following items of factual and historical information about the work being introduced: (1) the philosophical circumstances surrounding its inception, (2) the biographical circumstances of its composition, (3) the bibliographical details of its publication.

Résumés.   Each résumé contains a brief summary of the argument of the particular work, and is intended to display in concise and schematic form the work's philosophical content and structure.

Bibliographies.   Each bibliography furnishes two elements of information: (1) a list of all the editions and printings of the work to appear during Kant's lifetime and (2) a list of the most important English, French, German (in the case of the three Latin works), Italian, and Spanish translations. Some of the editions and many of the translations appear in collections. For the sake of brevity, these collections have been referred to by the surname of the editor or translator-editor alone. The key to these abbreviated forms of reference is to be found immediately after this preface in the Table of Abbreviations.

Linguistic notes.   Notes on textual and translation matters are indicated by superscript lower-case letters of the alphabet; a new series starts for each translated work. Such notes draw attention to a range of issues of varying degrees of complexity: (1) The simplest and most numerous notes merely cite the original word or phrase; such notes draw attention, without comment, to a philosophically 'sensitive' but otherwise unproblematic term or phrase. (2) More complex notes, relating only to individual words, involve the citation of the original word and a brief comment on it; such a note may, for example, draw attention to Kant's use of a word in a sense which is now obsolete or archaic, or in some other respect deserving of comment. (3) The most complex and least numerous notes involve the citation of the original word or passage, the citation of the relevant word or passage from the most important translations (the range of which has been limited to English, French, German, and Italian), and often, enclosed in parentheses, an explanatory comment analysing the textual or translation problem and specifying the reasons for the solution adopted. The quotations from other translations are identified by the initial letter (occasionally the first two letters) of the surname of the translator. These initials are explained on their first appearance in a particular set of linguistic notes.

Such notes are concerned with substantial textual problems: defective syntax, ambiguity, or obscurity. Provided the reader has at least an elementary knowledge of the languages involved, sufficient data are furnished to understand the problem and to evaluate the relative merits of the various possible solutions represented by the different translations cited. Kant's own footnotes are printed immediately below the text, and thus above the linguistic notes, which are located at the very bottom of the page.

Factual notes.   Notes of a factual or bibliographical character are indicated by superscript Arabic numerals; a new series starts with each new work. The eleven sets of factual notes are grouped together and located immediately after the last translation. The factual notes do *not* furnish philosophical commentary, analysis, or criticism; nor do they contain biographical information about the people mentioned by Kant. (That information is to be found in the Biographical-Bibliographical Sketches.) Most of the factual notes fall into one or another of the following four categories: (1) Cross-references to Kant's other works for earlier formulations, later statements or developments, and criticisms of an idea. (2) References to the works of other philosophers and thinkers, indicating the source of an idea adopted, modified, discussed, or criticised by Kant. In the case of people explicitly mentioned by Kant and therefore included in the Biographical-Bibliographical Sketches, such references contain only a minimum of information sufficient to identify the passage referred to (author's surname, short original title, and date of first publication); for full bibliographical information the reader should consult the Biographical-Bibliographical Sketches of Persons Mentioned by Kant. In the case of writers not explicitly mentioned by Kant and therefore not included in the Biographical-Bibliographical Sketches, full bibliographical information is provided (full name, full original title, full English translation of the title, place and date of first publication). (3) Brief explanations of certain philosophical and scientific ideas mentioned by Kant which may be unfamiliar to the nonspecialist reader (for example, the scientific notion of the *materia medians,* the mathematical notion of *negative magnitudes,* the Leibnizian ideas of the *ars characteristica* and *analysis situs*). (4) Translations of Latin words and phrases cited by Kant which, in conformity with Kant's own practise, have been left untranslated in the texts of the translations themselves. At the beginning of each set of factual notes is a list of acknowledgements, identifying the sources of material which has been adopted or adapted from the notes of other translators and editors.

General Introduction.   Since this volume contains eleven distinct and disparate works published over a fifteen-year period, and since it does not contain all the works published by Kant either during the pre-critical period as a whole or even during the fifteen years of that period covered by this volume, it was considered desirable for the reader to be furnished with some chronological and philosophical orientation. The General Introduction is intended to fulfil that function. It falls into two parts: The first, and shorter, chronological part traces the main outlines of Kant's early life and career during the pre-critical period, especially during the final fifteen years of that period. The second, and longer, thematic part is intended to furnish the reader with philosophical orientation by isolating and examining the central philosophical preoccupations of the eleven works in this volume. Seven such themes have been distinguished: (1) the alleged incompatibility between scientific explanation and religious faith; (2) the seeming incompatibility between the conviction that this is the best of all possible worlds and the occurrence of natural disasters; (3) the possibility of demonstrating the existence of God; (4) the distinctions between the logical and the real and between reasons and causes, as well as the problem of causality itself; (5) the nature and existence of mind, and the problem of its place in nature; (6) the nature and ontological status of space; and (7) the foundations, method, limits, and possibility of metaphysical cognition.

Glossary. The Glossary lists those terms which are the most distinctive and characteristic of each of the works in this collection and which have raised the greatest difficulties in translation. Each entry consists of (1) the English term, (2) its German or Latin equivalent or equivalents, and, when necessary, (3) further comment – specifying, for example, alternative translations which could have been adopted but were not ('alt') or alternative translations which have occasionally been adopted in these translations ('occ'), or, by cross-reference to other English words in the Glossary, alternative translations which have been employed more frequently, or, again by cross-reference, other concepts listed in the Glossary to which the term is related by similarity or contrast. Certain key terms which have raised major translation issues have been further explained in notes (located at the end of the Glossary) specifying the problem and indicating the reasons for the solution adopted. Each such key term is followed by a number which indicates the note containing a discussion of the problems concerned. The reader's attention is drawn, in particular, to the important notes attached to the entries arbitrary-*willkürlich*, concept-*conceptus/notio*, direction-*Gegend*, equal-*gleich*, similar-*ähnlich*, sensible-*sensibilis*, and sensitive-*sensitivus* (notes 1, 4, 7, 8, and 12).

Biographical-Bibliographical Sketches of Persons Mentioned by Kant. These sketches contain an entry for every person explicitly mentioned by Kant in any of the eleven works in this volume. Each entry consists of full name (surname followed by forenames), dates of birth and death, specification of nationality, and general significance, followed by a brief account of the life and publications of the person. Full bibliographical information (full original title, full English translation of that title, place and date of first publication) is furnished for *all* the works either explicitly mentioned or tacitly alluded to by Kant; such information is, in the case of the more important figures, also provided for their other chief works (although no attempt has been made to furnish complete bibliographies). In the case of those writers (chiefly literary figures of the seventeenth century and writers of classical antiquity) to whom Kant alludes only rarely, the entries are brief. In the case of those writers (chiefly philosophers and scientific figures of the seventeenth and eighteenth centuries) whom Kant cites more frequently, the entries are more substantial. Mythical and fictional people are not included in these sketches. (Information about such figures is contained in the factual notes.) Also excluded are the names of the twelve persons involved as respondents or opponents in the three public disputations held in connection with Kant's three Latin dissertations. The reader's attention is drawn to the fact that whenever Kant's personal library contained works by any of the authors included in the sketches, the details are given at the end of the entry concerned. The Biographical-Bibliographical Sketches have rendered possible the simplification of many of the factual notes (which need only furnish the briefest bibliographical information *specifically* relevant to a given passage). The reader is also spared the inconvenience of having to track down earlier notes (containing the fuller information he may need) or of having to pick his way back through a possibly long and discontinuous series of 'loc. cit.' references in order to establish *which* work is being referred to. A reader who needs fuller information about the life or publications of a writer cited in the text can refer *directly* to the Biographical-Bibliographical Sketches. Since *every* name mentioned by Kant is included there, no special indication has been given that an entry for a particular name is to be found in the sketches.

Index.   The eleven translations have been provided with a comprehensive index. This is both an index of names and an analytical index of concepts. It has been compiled by Predrag Cicovacki, to whom we express our gratitude for having performed a difficult, time-consuming, but important task with exemplary thoroughness and accuracy.

Guide to Abbreviations.   Throughout this volume, certain works have been referred to in abbreviated form. Such abbreviated forms of reference have been divided into three groups: (1) *single works by Kant* – (a) pre-critical works (complete) and (b) critical works (selected); (2) *collections of works by Kant* – (a) German editions and collections and (b) collections of translations; (3) *miscellaneous works* – (a) works of reference (dictionaries and encyclopaedias) and (b) historical, biographical, and other works. Works belonging to *Group 1* have been referred to throughout the editorial material by short English title accompanied, at its first occurrence only, by the date of first appearance; the Guide to Abbreviations lists these works chronologically by their short titles and specifies their full German titles, with their full English translations, and their locations in the Academy edition (AK). Works belonging to *Group 2* have been ordered alphabetically and referred to by the surname of the editor or translator or, where this is not known, by the place of publication. Works in *Group 3* have also been ordered alphabetically and referred to chiefly by an acronym, or by the name of the author or editor, but sometimes by the name of the publisher or by means of an abbreviated form of the title. It is to be emphasised that the Guide to Abbreviations is not to be construed as a bibliography (individual bibliographies have been provided for each of the eleven works); it merely lists those works which are referred to most frequently.

Acknowledgements

In the preparation of these eleven translations, in all cases of doubt or difficulty, the translations listed in the bibliography for each work have been consulted. Debts of this nature have been indicated in detail in the linguistic notes. In drawing up the factual notes, the notes with which earlier editions and translations of these works have been equipped have also been consulted, and information has, on occasion, been adopted or adapted from these sources. Debts of this nature have been indicated in detail in the acknowledgements at the beginning of each set of factual notes. (The notes to the three Latin dissertations contain material which has been reprinted by permission of the publisher from Lewis White Beck et al., *Kant's Latin Writings: Translations, Commentaries and Notes* [New York: Peter Lang Publishing, 1986. All rights reserved.], pp. 106–9, 133–4, and 188–92.)

David Walford (who has been responsible for the preparation of the first drafts of all the translations and of all the editorial material – apart from the factual notes to the three Latin dissertations – and then, in the light of Ralf Meerbote's criticisms and suggestions, of the final drafts of all the material) would like to express his gratitude both to his colleagues and friends at Saint David's University College, Lampeter, and to Ralf Meerbote for their endless patience and unstinting generosity in placing their specialist knowledge at his disposal in preparing this volume. In particular, he wishes to express his thanks to A. Bushell, Klaus Fischer, C. J. Lofmark, and R. Woods for their advice on linguistic matters; to A. J. Brothers, Nicole Crossley-Holland, and G. Eatough for their help with matters relating to the three Latin texts; to D. A. Cockburn, G. Overton, and R. R. Rockingham Gill for their advice on the mathematical matters raised by Kant. In addition, Walford would like to express his thanks to H. Harvey and T. Henvey for preparing the typescript of the eleven translations; to L. K. Howells and C. Davies for their endless patience and good humour in preparing the very complicated and repeatedly changed typescript of the editorial material; to the staffs of the British Library, London; the Ryland's Library, Manchester; and the Library of Saint David's University College, Lampeter (particularly to K. Miles for her unfailing equanimity and cheerfulness in handling what must have seemed a never ending series of obscure interlibrary loan requests). Walford also wishes to record his thanks to the Pantyfedwen Fund of Saint David's University College for its assistance with financing the typing of the eleven translations. Finally, he wishes to express his gratitude to Ralf Meerbote for his invaluable assistance in revising all the translations and the whole of the editorial material. His punctilious care has helped to eliminate not a few serious errors. Ralf Meerbote (who has been responsible for the preparation of the three sets of factual notes to the Latin dissertations and for advising on the revision of all the other material) would, in his turn, like to express his gratitude to Lewis W. Beck and Deborah Modrak, of the University of Rochester, for their sound advice on the preparation of the three sets of factual notes to the Latin pieces in this collection. Professor Beck was also extremely helpful with some other matters which arose in the course of revising the various drafts of the works included in the volume. David Walford and Ralf Meerbote would also like to express their gratitude to Helen Wheeler of Cambridge University Press for the exemplary care with which she prepared our long and complex typescript for printing.

Guide to abbreviations

1759   OPTIMISM
        Versuch einiger Betrachtungen über den Optimismus
        (AK 2:27–35)
        ('Attempt at Some Reflections on Optimism')

1760   THOUGHTS
        Gedanken bei dem frühzeitigen Ableben des . . . Herrn Johann Friedrich Funk . . .
        (AK 2:37–44)
        ('Thoughts on the Premature Demise of . . . Herr Johann Friedrich Funk . . .')

1762   FALSE SUBTLETY
        Die falsche Spitzfindigkeit der vier syllogistischen Figuren
        (AK 2:45–61)
        ('The False Subtlety of the Four Syllogistic Figures')

1763   THE ONLY POSSIBLE ARGUMENT
        Der einzig mögliche Beweisgrund zu einer Demonstration des Daseins Gottes
        (AK 2:63–163)
        ('The Only Possible Argument in Support of a Demonstration of the Existence of God')

1763   NEGATIVE MAGNITUDES
        Versuch den Begriff der negativen Grössen in die Weltweisheit einzuführen
        (AK 2:165–204)
        ('Attempt to Introduce the Concept of Negative Magnitudes into Philosophy')

1764   OBSERVATIONS
        Beobachtungen über das Gefühl des Schönen und Erhabenen
        (AK 2:205–56)
        ('Observations on the Feeling of the Beautiful and the Sublime')

1764   MALADIES OF THE MIND
        Versuch über die Krankheiten des Kopfes
        (AK 2:257–71)
        ('Essay on the Maladies of the Mind')

1764   INQUIRY
        Untersuchung über die Deutlichkeit der Grundsätze der natürlichen Theologie und der Moral
        (AK 2:273–301)
        ('Inquiry concerning the Distinctness of the Principles of Natural Theology and Morals')

1765   ANNOUNCEMENT
        Nachricht von der Einrichtung seiner Vorlesungen in dem Winterhalbenjahre von 1763–1766
        (AK 2:303–13)
        ('Announcement of the Organisation of his Lectures in the Winter Semester 1765–1766')

1786   METAPHYSICAL FIRST PRINCIPLES
        Metaphysische Anfangsgründe der Naturwissenschaft
        (AK 4:465–565)
        ('Metaphysical First Principles of Natural Science')

1786   ORIENTATION IN THINKING
        Was heisst: Sich im Denken orientiren
        (AK 8:131–47)
        ('What is Orientation in Thinking?')

1788   CRITIQUE OF PRACTICAL REASON
        Kritik der praktischen Vernunft
        (AK 5:1–163)
        ('Critique of Practical Reason')

1788   TELEOLOGICAL PRINCIPLES
        Über den Gebrauch der teleologischen Principien in der Philosophie
        (AK 8:157–84)
        ('Concerning the Employment of Teleological Principles in Philosophy')

1790   CRITIQUE OF JUDGEMENT
        Kritik der Urtheilskraft
        (AK 5:165–485)
        ('Critique of Judgement')

1790   DISCOVERY
        *Über eine Entdeckung, nach der alle neue Kritik der reinen Vernunft durch eine
        ältere entbehrlich gemacht werden soll*
        (AK 8:185–251)
        ('On a Discovery, according to which all Modern Critique of Pure
        Reason is alleged to be made Superfluous by an Earlier Critique')

1791   THEODICY
        Über das Misslingen aller philosophischen Versuche in der Théodicée
        (AK 8:253–71)
        ('On the Failure of all Philosophical Attempts at Theodicy')

1793   RELIGION
        Die Religion innerhalb der Grenzen der blossen Vernunft
        (AK 6:1–202)
        ('Religion within the Bounds of Unaided Reason')

1795   ETERNAL PEACE
        Zum ewigen Frieden
        (AK 8:341–86)
        ('Towards Eternal Peace')

1797   METAPHYSIC OF MORALS
        Die Metaphysik der Sitten
        (AK 6:203–493)
        ('Metaphysic of Morals')

1798   THE CONFLICT OF THE FACULTIES
Der Streit der Fakultäten
(AK 7:1–116)
('The Conflict of the Faculties')

1798   ANTHROPOLOGY
Anthropologie in pragmatischer Hinsicht
(AK 7:117–333)
('Anthropology from a Pragmatic Standpoint')

1800   LOGIC
Logik. Ein Handbuch zu Vorlesungen
(AK 9:1–150)
('Logic. A Handbook to Lectures')

1802   PHYSICAL GEOGRAPHY
Physische Geographie
(AK 9:151–436)
('Physical Geography')

COLLECTIONS OF WORKS BY KANT

German editions and collections

AK   *Immanuel Kants gesammelte Schriften.* 29 vols. Herausgegeben von der Preussischen Akademie der Wissenschaften (I–XXII), der deutschen Akademie der Wissenschaften zu Berlin (XXIII) und der Akademie der Wissenschaften zu Göttingen (XXIV–XXIX) (Abteilung I: Werke: I–IX; Abteilung II: Briefwechsel: X–XIII; Abteilung III: Handschriftlicher Nachlass: XIV–XXIII; Abteilung IV: Vorlesungen: XXIV–XXIX) Berlin: 1902–

KIRCHMANN   *Immanuel Kants Kleinere Schriften zur Logik und Metaphysik.* Herausgegeben und erläutert von J. H. von Kirchmann. (*Philosophische Bibliothek,* XXXIII) Berlin: 1870.
Immanuel Kants kleinere Schriften zur Naturphilosophie. Herausgegeben und erläutert von J. H. von Kirchmann. (*Philosophische Bibliothek,* XLIX & LX.) 2 vols. Berlin: 1872–7.

RINK   *Sammlung einiger bisher unbekannt gebliebener kleiner Schriften von Immanuel Kant.* Herausgegeben von Friedrich Theodor Rink. Königsberg: 1800. 2nd enlarged edition. Königsberg: 1807.

TIEFTRUNK · *Immanuel Kants vermischte Schriften, Aechte und vollständige Ausgabe.* Herausgegeben von J. H. Tieftrunk. 3 vols. Halle: 1799.
4th volume. *Sammlung einiger bisher unbekannt gebliebener kleiner Schriften von Immanuel Kant.* Königsberg: 1807.

VOIGT · *Immanuel Kants sämmtliche kleine Schriften nach der Zeitfolge geordnet.* 4 vols. Königsberg [really Voigt in Jena]: 1797–8.

VORLÄNDER · *Immanuel Kants sämtliche Werke.* Herausgegeben von Karl Vorländer in Verbindung mit O. Buek, P. Gedan, W. Kinkel, F. M. Schiele, Th. Valentiner und anderen. 10 vols. Leipzig: 1920–9.
Cf. Volume V: *Zur Logik und Metaphysik.* Herausgegeben von Karl Vorländer: Leipzig: 1921 (*Philosophische Bibliothek,* XLVI) and Volume VII: *Schriften zur Naturphilosophie.* Herausgegeben von Otto Buek in 3 parts (part III: *Kleinere Schriften zur Naturphilosophie*). Leipzig: 1922 (*Philosophische Bibliothek* XLIX).

WEISCHEDEL · *Immanuel Kants Werke in Sechs Bänden.* Herausgegeben von Wilhelm Weischedel (Insel-Verlag). Frankfurt: 1960. Reprinted as: *Immanuel Kants Werke in zwölf Bänden* (Theorie-Werk Ausgabe). Frankfurt: 1968; also reprinted as: *Immanuel Kants Werke in sechs Bänden* (*Wissenschaftliche Buchgesellschaft*). Darmstadt: 1968.

ZEITZ · *Immanuel Kants frühere noch nicht gesammelte kleine Schriften.* Lintz [really Zeitz, Webel]: 1795.

Collections of translations

ABBOT · *Kant's introduction to Logic, and his Essay on the Mistaken Subtlety of the Four Figures.* Translated by T. K. Abbot . . . with a few notes by S. T. Coleridge. London: 1885.

ALQUIE · *Emmanuel Kant: Oeuvres philosophiques.* Volume I: *Des premiers écrits à la Critique de la Raison pure.* Edited by F. Alquié with the collaboration of A. J.-L. Delamarre, J. Ferrari, B. Lortholary, F. Marty, J. Rivelaygue & S. Zac. (*Bibliothèque de la Pléiade*) Paris: 1980.

BECK (1798) *Essays and Treatises on Moral, Political and Various Philosophical Subjects by Immanuel Kant* . . . From the German by the Translator of *The Principles of the Critical Philosophy* [J. S. Beck]. 2 vols. London: 1798–9.

BECK (1949) *Kant's Critique of Practical Reason and Other Writings in Moral Philosophy.* Translated and edited with an introduction by L. W. Beck. Chicago: 1949.

BECK (1986) *Kant's Latin Writings: Translations, Commentaries and Notes.* L. W. Beck, in collaboration with M. J. Gregor, R. Meerbote and J. A. Reuscher. New York: 1986.

BORN *Immanuelis Kantii Opera ad philosophiam criticam Latine vertit Fredericus Gottlob Born.* 4 vols. Leipzig: 1796–8.

CARABELLESE *Immanuel Kant: Scritti minori.* Edited and translated with an introduction by P. Carabellese. Bari: 1923. New enlarged edition. *Immanuel Kant: Scritti precritici.* Edited by R. Assunto and R. Hohenemser. Bari: 1953. Further new enlarged edition. *Immanuel Kant: Scritti precritici.* Edited by Angelo Pupi with a new introduction by R. Assunto. Rome: 1982.

FESTUGIERE *Pensées successives sur la théodicée et la religion.* Traduction et introduction par P. Festugière. Paris: 1931. 4th edition. 1980.

FICHANT *Emmanuel Kant: Recherche sur l'évidence des principes de la théologie naturelle et de la morale. Annonce du programme de leçons de M. E. Kant pendant le semestre d'hiver 1765–1766.* Traduction et notes par M. Fichant. Paris: 1966.

HANDYSIDE *Kant's Inaugural Dissertation and Early Writings on Space.* Translated by J. Handyside. Chicago: 1929.

IRVINE *The Metaphysical Rudiments of Liberalism.* David Irvine. London: 1911.

KERFERD *Kant: Selected Pre-Critical Writings and Correspondence with Beck.* Translated and introduced with notes by G. B. Kerferd and D. E. Walford. Manchester: 1968.

RABEL *Kant.* Gabriele Rabel. Oxford: 1963.

RICHARDSON *Metaphysical Works of the Celebrated Immanuel Kant.* Translated from the German, with a sketch of his life by J. Richardson. London: 1836.

ZAC *Emmanuel Kant: Quelques opuscules précritiques.* Introduction, traduction et notes par Sylvie Zac. Paris: 1970.

MISCELLANEOUS WORKS

Works of reference

CAMPE *Wörterbuch der deutschen Sprache.* Veranstaltet und herausgegeben von J. H. Campe. 5 vols. Braunschweig: 1807–11.
Wörterbuch zur Erklärung und Verdeutschung der unserer Sprache aufgedrungenen fremden Ausdrücke Ein Ergänzungsband zu Adelungs und Campes Worterbüchern. Neue starkvermehrte und durchgängig verbesserte Ausgabe von J. H. Campe. Braunschweig: 1813.

GRIMM *Deutsches Wörterbuch.* von Jacob Grimm and Wilhelm Grimm. 16 vols. Leipzig: 1854–1954.

LANGENSCHEIDT *Langenscheidts Enzyklopaedisches Wörterbuch der englischen und deutschen Sprache.* Herausgegeben von Dr. Otto Springer. 2 vols. London: 1974.

LEWIS & SHORT *A Latin Dictionary.* Founded on Andrew's Edition of Freund's Latin Dictionary. Revised, enlarged and in part rewritten by C. T. Lewis and C. Short. Oxford: 1880.

LIDDELL & SCOTT *A Greek-English Lexicon.* Compiled by H. G. Liddell and R. Scott. A new edition revised and augmented throughout by H. S. Jones. 2 vols. Oxford: 1940.

OED *Oxford English Dictionary.* 2nd edition. 20 vols. Oxford: 1989.

OLD *Oxford Latin Dictionary.* Oxford: 1968.

ROBERT *Dictionnaire alphabétique et analogique de la langue francaise.* Paul Robert. Casablanca: 1958–65.

WILDHAGEN — *Englisch-Deutsches und Deutsch-Englisches Wörter-buch.* von K. Wildhagen & W. Héraucourt. 2 vols. Band II: *Deutsch-Englisch.* London: 1972.

Historical, biographical, and other works

BOROWSKI — *Darstellung des Lebens und Charakters Immanuel Kants von Ludwig Ernst Borowski, von Kant selbst genau revidiert und berichtigt,* in *Immanuel Kant: sein Leben in Darstellungen von Zeitgenossen, Die Biographien von L. E. Borowski, R. B. Jachmann und A. Ch. Wasianski.* Königsberg: 1804. Herausgegeben von A. Hoffman. Halle: 1902. 2nd edition. Halle: 1907; auch von F. Gross. Berlin: 1912. Reprinted. *Wissenschaftliche Buchgesellschaft.* Darmstadt: 1980.

CAMPO — *La genesi del criticismo Kantiano* [*Pensiero e storia. Collana di studi e monografie*]. Varese: 1953.

CASSIRER — *Kants Leben und Lehre.* Berlin: 1918. 2nd edition. Berlin: 1921; reprinted. New Haven: 1975; reprinted. *Wissenschaftliche Buchgesellschaft.* Darmstadt: 1977.

GERHARDT (M) — *Leibnizens mathematischen Schriften.* Herausgegeben von C. I. Gerhardt. 7 vols. Berlin: 1849–63.

GERHARDT (P) — *Die philosophischen Schriften von Gottfried Wilhelm Leibniz.* Herausgegeben von C. I. Gerhardt. 7 vols. Berlin: 1875–90.

KIRCHMANN — *Erläuterungen zu Immanuel Kants kleinern Schriften über Logik und Metaphysik.* von J. H. von Kirchmann (*Philosophische Bibliothek,* LVIII). Berlin: 1873.

LOEMKER — *Gottfried Wilhelm Leibnitz: Philosophical Papers and Letters.* A selection translated and edited with an introduction by Leroy E. Loemker. Chicago: 1956. 2nd edition corrected. Dordrecht: 1969.

TONELLI (1957) — *Kant, dall'estetica metafisica all'estetica psicoempirica. Studi sulla genesi del criticismo (1754–1771) et sulle sue fonti.* Turin: 1957.

TONELLI (1959) — *Elementi metodologici e metefisici in Kant dal 1745 al 1768. Saggio di sociologia della conoscenza* [*Studi e ricerche di storia della filosofia*]. Turin: 1959.

VLEESCHAUWER   *La déduction transcendentale dans l'oeuvre de Kant.* 2 vols. Paris: 1934–7. Vol. I: *La déduction transcendentale avant la critique de la raison pure.* Paris: 1934.

VORLÄNDER   *Immanuel Kant: Der Mann und das Werk.* 2 vols. Leipzig: 1924.

WARDA   *Immanuel Kants Bücher . . . Mit einer getreuen Nachbildung des bisher einzigen bekannten Abzuges des Versteigerungskataloges der Bibliothek Kants (Verzeichnis der Bücher des . . . J. F. Gensichen . . . auch die demselben zugefallene Bücher des Professor Kant).* Berlin: 1922.

General introduction

Immanuel Kant was born in Königsberg on 22 April 1724 to Pietist parents of modest means. His precociousness attracted the attention of Franz Albert Schultz (1692–1763), who arranged for the eight-year-old boy to enter the Collegium Fridericianum, of which he was the rector. The young Kant was thus exposed to the powerful spiritual and intellectual influence of Schultz, who was both a Pietist and a follower of Wolff, under whom he had studied at Halle. Kant's eight years at the Fridericianum were devoted largely to the study of classical languages (especially Latin) and religion. His final years at school were overshadowed by the death of his mother in 1737.

In 1740, the sixteen-year-old Kant began his studies at the Herzog Albrecht University in Königsberg. He seems to have read mathematics, natural science, and philosophy. The crucial influence on Kant during this period was that of Martin Knutzen (1713–51). Only eleven years older than Kant, Knutzen likewise was both a Pietist and a follower of Wolff. He was also a Newtonian, and he introduced Kant to the new physics. Kant attended Knutzen's lectures on mathematics, astronomy, and natural science, and it was probably Knutzen who led Kant to the theme of his first work, *Living Forces* (1747).

The death of his father and the completion of *Living Forces* in 1746 marked the end of Kant's six years as a student at Königsberg. Straitened financial circumstances constrained the twenty-four-year-old Kant to interrupt his university career for some eight years to take employment as a tutor with a succession of families in the Königsberg area. He clearly contrived to combine his philosophical and scientific interests with his tutorial duties, for his return to Königsberg in 1754 was marked by the publication of two short works of considerable scientific originality and one major work of indisputable scientific genius, *Universal Natural History* (1755), in which Kant, with characteristic self-assurance, out-Newtoned Newton by offering a purely mechanical account of the structure and motions of the universe. The bankruptcy of the printer, however, prevented this extraordinary work from reaching a wider public.

The year after his return to Königsberg, the thirty-one-year-old Kant set about securing the formal qualifications necessary for appointment as *Privatdozent*. He submitted the first of the two requisite dissertations, *On*

Fire, on 17 April 1755, and the degree of *Magister* was awarded on 12 June 1755. The second dissertation, *New Elucidation* (1755), was submitted *pro venia legendi* and made the object of public disputation on 27 September 1755. This was Kant's first purely philosophical work: Highly critical of Leibniz and Wolff, it displays the strong influence of Crusius. Kant began lecturing that same autumn, offering courses on mathematics, logic, metaphysics and, possibly, natural science. He quickly established a reputation as a successful and exceptionally dedicated teacher.

The start of Kant's career as *Privatdozent* coincided with the Lisbon earthquake in November 1755. Kant, seeking to allay public fears, published three essays on the causes of earthquakes early in 1756, arguing that they were purely geological phenomena which were in no wise incompatible with the goodness and power of God. It was in this year that Kant began lecturing on physical geography, a course he was to conduct annually throughout the forty years of his teaching career.

In April 1756, Kant applied for the position of *professor extraordinarius* in logic and metaphysics, a post which had been occupied by Martin Knutzen until his premature death in 1751. The application required the submission of a third dissertation. The *Physical Monadology* (1756), written in order to satisfy this requirement, was made the object of public disputation on 10 April 1756. Kant's hopes of academic advancement were, however, dashed: The government, bent on economies, made no appointment. Kant's hopes were to be disappointed a second time when, in 1758, he applied for the post of *professor ordinarius* in logic and metaphysics. He was passed over in favour of the more senior Buck. To this period belongs a series of short works: *Theory of Winds* (1756), *West Winds* (1757), *Motion and Rest* (1758), *Optimism* (1759), and *Thoughts* (1760).

Philosophically speaking, the decade and a half stretching from 1747 (the date of Kant's first work) to 1762 was relatively unproductive. In that period, Kant composed only two specifically philosophical works: *New Elucidation* and *Optimism*. It is true that a number of the scientific works written by Kant in this fifteen-year period contain discussions of philosophical issues: *Living Forces,* the issues of space and the limits of mathematical method; *Universal Natural History,* the issue of the compatibility of scientific explanation and religious faith; the three earthquake essays of 1756, the issue of optimism; *Physical Monadology,* the issues of space and the relation of physics and geometry. Nonetheless, all but two of the fifteen works written by Kant between 1746 and 1761 are nonphilosophical in character. By contrast, of the ten works composed by Kant in the eight-year period which culminated with the publication of *Inaugural Dissertation* in 1770, only one – *Maladies of the Mind* (1764) – could be described as other than philosophical in character.

This philosophical silence was suddenly broken in 1762 by the completion, within less than a year and a half, of no fewer than five philosophical works: *False Subtlety* (1762) and *The Only Possible Argument* (1763) (both probably completed by the autumn of 1762), *Inquiry* (1764) (completed by the end of 1762), *Negative Magnitudes* (1763) (completed by mid-June 1763), and *Observations* (1764) (completed by the end of 1763). Of these five works, *False Subtlety* contains a critique of an aspect of the Aristotelian theory of the syllogism, and *Observations*, written under the influence of Rousseau, is devoted to aesthetic, moral, and anthropological themes. Philosophically, the most substantial of these five works are *The Only Possible Argument*, which shows the strong influence of Maupertuis, and contains an *a priori* proof of the existence of God; *Negative Magnitudes*, which articulates the distinction between the ideal and the real; and *Inquiry*, which contrasts the methods of mathematics and metaphysics.

It was in *Dreams* (1766) that Kant expressly addressed for the first time the question of the *possibility* of metaphysics. Ostensibly concerned with Swedenborg's alleged paranormal powers, the work is primarily about the intelligibility of certain kinds of metaphysical claims, such as those relating to pure spirits. Kant's discussion is deeply sceptical and leads to the idea that the human understanding is circumscribed by limits it cannot transcend. *Dreams* was probably composed in the years 1764 and 1765, to which period also belongs the publication of *Maladies of the Mind* and *Announcement* (1765). Also to this period belongs Kant's refusal, in 1764, to be considered for the chair of poetry, and his acceptance, in 1765, of the modest post of sublibrarian of the Royal Palace Library.

Kant's attention during the latter half of this eight-year period had been focused on the thought of Leibniz (in particular the theories of space and of sensibility) by the posthumous appearance in 1765 of his *Nouveaux essais*. The silence of the four and a half years between the completion of *Dreams* at the end of 1765 and the appearance of the *Inaugural Dissertation* in the late summer of 1770 was punctuated only once, early in 1768, by the publication of the brief but deeply significant *Directions in Space*. This work contains a powerful critique of the Leibnizian theory of space and of the *analysis situs;* it also, in effect, prepares the way for the view, articulated two and a half years later, in the *Inaugural Dissertation*, that space is the subjective form of our sensibility.

By the late 1760s, Kant's philosophical reputation was well established. In 1769, he was offered the chair of philosophy at Erlangen, and early in 1770 that at Jena. But he declined both invitations. His patience was eventually rewarded, for, on 31 March 1770, he was offered the chair of logic and metaphysics at Königsberg – the very chair for which he had unsuccessfully applied some twelve years earlier. In accordance with academic tradition, Kant composed a Latin dissertation to inaugurate his professorship, and it was made the object of public disputation on 24 August 1770. Though composed for a formal academic occasion, it represents the culmination of Kant's early philosophical development. It con-

tains a devastating attack on a fundamental tenet of the Leibnizian epistemology: that sensation is a confused form of thought. It also contains a full
statement of the view that space and time are nothing but the *a priori*
forms of our sensibility. The possibility of metaphysical cognition is still
acknowledged, but certain types of metaphysical claims are diagnosed as
involving illegitimate use of the principles of sensibility. The tensions
between the insight into the ideality of space and the as yet unshaken
confidence in the possibility of metaphysical knowledge were eventually,
after a decade of silence, to give birth to the *Critique of Pure Reason* in
1781.

The eleven works in this volume cover a wide variety of philosophical
issues, but certain themes are more dominant, persistent, and important
for an understanding of Kant's mature thought. Such themes include
God, causality, mind, space, and metaphysics.

Among the earliest of Kant's philosophical preoccupations was the theme
of God, although it ceased to be a dominant concern after 1762. Three
religious issues, in particular, absorbed Kant's early attention: the compatibility of scientific explanation with religious faith, the compatibility of
natural disasters with the perfection of the world, and the correct method
of proving the existence of God.

The first of these issues is discussed, albeit briefly, in the preface to
Universal Natural History and, at much greater length, in *The Only Possible
Argument*. Kant was acutely aware that a comprehensive mechanical explanation of the structure and motions of the entire universe might well seem
to render the existence of God a superfluous hypothesis (AK 1:222). Kant
attempts to resolve the conflict in characteristic fashion by arguing that
the defenders and the critics of religion share a mistaken assumption: that
causal necessity is tantamount to blind chance. The defenders of religion
fail to recognise that the harmony and order of nature are *intrinsic* qualities of nature (AK 2:116–23), while the critics of religion fail to recognise
that a multiplicity of independent particulars would be incapable of combining to form a unified harmony (AK 2:95–6, 99–100, 112, 124). Kant
undermines the traditional positions of theists and atheists alike by insisting that it is the very necessity itself with which the unity and harmony of
nature arise from the general properties of matter which proves the existence of a Supremely Intelligent Creator (AK 1:227–8; 2:123–37).

As early as 1753, Kant's attention had been drawn to the second issue,
that of optimism. Kant, in his *Three Manuscript Reflections on Optimism*,
compares the systems of Leibniz and Pope, attacking the former for
undermining the force of the physico-theological argument and for failing
to resolve the problem of the existence of evil in the world. The *New*

Elucidation also briefly discusses this theme (AK 1:403–5). That same year, 1755, the Lisbon earthquake invested the philosophical debate with macabre actuality and seemed to cast doubt on the perfection of God and of the world. In the three earthquake essays of 1756, Kant characteristically sets about reconciling the seemingly irreconcilable by arguing that the supposition that natural disasters are incompatible with the perfection of the world is a product of ignorance, egocentricity, and presumptuousness. In *Optimism*, Kant defends the concept of a maximum degree of perfection against the criticisms of Crusius. In *The Only Possible Argument*, the issue of the reasonableness of optimism is discussed at greater length but in exactly the same terms as in the three earthquake essays. Much later, in the *Theodicy* (1791), Kant will reject all forms of theodicy on the ground that they involve attempts to transcend the necessary limits of our understanding.

The third religious issue to which Kant early addressed himself was that of the proof of the existence of God. At no stage in this period did Kant doubt the possibility of such a proof, although he was already highly critical of the three traditional proofs. Kant adduces two arguments for God's existence: an *a priori* argument from the possibility of things and an *a posteriori* argument from the necessary unity and harmony of nature. Only the former is allowed apodeictic certainty. The earliest statement of the *a priori* proof is to be found, briefly adumbrated, in *Three Manuscript Reflections on Optimism* (AK 17:223–34) of 1753, where it is, rather implausibly, attributed to Pope. A second, somewhat fuller statement of the proof is in the *New Elucidation* (AK 1:395–6). The most elaborate formulation is in *The Only Possible Argument* (AK 2:77–92), where the heart of the proof is expressed as follows:

All possibility presupposes something actual in and through which all that can be thought is given. Accordingly, there is a certain reality, the cancellation of which would itself cancel all internal possibility whatever. But that, the cancellation of which eradicates all possibility, is absolutely necessary. Therefore, something exists absolutely necessarily. (AK 2:83)

This same proof makes a brief final appearance in the *Inquiry*. The *a posteriori* argument is presented for the first time in the preface to *Universal Natural History* (AK 2:222, 225, 227). A version of this same argument is in the discussion of the Principle of Co-existence towards the end of the *New Elucidation* (AK 1:412–15). The most elaborate statement of this argument is to be found in *The Only Possible Argument* (AK 2:92–155), where it appears with a wealth of illustrative material.

Kant's pre-critical writings also contain criticisms of the three traditional proofs of the existence of God which prefigure the critique of rational theology in the *Critique of Pure Reason* (1781/1787) A592–630 / B620–59

(AK 3:397–419). The Cartesian version of the ontological proof is criticised for the first time in the *New Elucidation* (AK 1:394–5), where it is rejected on the ground that it involves the idea of a self-caused being (dismissed as incoherent) and for failing to distinguish between the ideal and the real determination of a concept. This criticism foreshadows but does not actually state the thesis that existence is not a real or determining predicate. That thesis and the corresponding objection are stated for the first time in *The Only Possible Argument* (AK 2:70–7, 156–7). The Leibnizian-Wolffian proof of the existence of God *a contingentia mundi* is also subject to brief criticism in *The Only Possible Argument* (AK 2:157–8) on the ground that it is the ontological argument *incognito* and is thus exposed to the same objection. Kant's objections to the third traditional proof of God's existence – what Kant calls the 'ordinary method of physico-theology' – are outlined in *The Only Possible Argument* (AK 2:116–23). He objects that this method fails to recognise that the order of nature is intrinsic to it, and that, in any case, it establishes, if it establishes anything, the existence not of God but of an Architect only.

The principle of causality makes its first appearance in the *New Elucidation* under the guise of the *ratio antecedenter determinans* ('the antecedently determining ground'). While acknowledging his debt to Crusius and agreeing with him that God is not subject to the principle of the determining ground, Kant attacks Crusius's view that the free will must also be exempted. In Proposition IX (AK 1:398–406), Kant attempts to reconcile the seemingly irreconcilable by arguing that acts of free will may be both antecedently determined and yet free – by virtue of the fact that such acts are *internally*, not externally, determined.

Although Kant, in the *New Elucidation*, is clearly aware of the great importance of Crusius's distinction between real and ideal grounds, his philosophical attention is distracted from the crucial epistemological problems surrounding the issue of causality (the validity of the principle of causality in general and, more particularly, the nature of the relation between a cause and its effect). Indeed, Kant maintains an almost total silence on the issue of causality throughout the period from 1755 to 1763. Not even in the *Inquiry*, which had been completed by the end of 1762, is there any mention of causality, even though there are a number of occasions therein when the issue might naturally have been raised.

In *Negative Magnitudes*, the distinction between the ideal and the real moves to the centre of Kant's attention, and the distinction between logical and real opposition is explored at length. Kant's attention focuses, in particular, on the conflict of forces, both the physical forces of nature and the psychological forces of the mind. In the 'General Remark' (AK 2:201–4) with which the work closes, Kant raises the issue of the relation between cause and effect, or rather, as Kant prefers to express it, between

real ground and consequent. Whereas the logical relation is through identity, the real relation cannot be explained in these terms at all. Nor can the
relation be explained by employing the concepts of cause and effect and of
force and action, for these concepts already presuppose the relation which
is under scrutiny. Kant maintains:

> The relation of a real ground to something, which is either posited or cancelled by
> it, cannot be expressed by a judgement; it can only be expressed by a concept.
> That concept can probably be reduced by means of analysis to simpler concepts of
> real grounds, albeit in such a fashion that in the end all our cognitions of this
> relation reduce to simple, unanalysable concepts of real grounds, the relation of
> which to their consequences cannot be rendered distinct at all. (AK 2:204)

The final chapter of *Dreams* (AK 2:363–73) also contains a brief discussion of causality, and Kant repeats the purely negative thesis of *Negative
Magnitudes* that the relation between cause and effect is not explicable in
terms of identity. But Kant extends the discussion. His concern is to give
content to the notion of the 'limits of human knowledge which are imposed on it by the nature of human reason itself' (AK 2:369). He specifies
two types of such a limit: *metaphysical* forces, relations and beings (such as
disembodied spirits); and *fundamental empirical* forces, relations and beings (such as causes). The former can neither be known (they are not the
possible objects of an experience) nor even understood; their concepts,
not being derived from experience are 'wholly arbitrary . . . and admit of
neither proof nor refutation' (AK 2:370). The latter can be known (are the
possible objects of experience) but cannot be understood. Kant asserts, 'If
one eventually arrives at relations which are fundamental, then the business of philosophy is at an end. It is impossible for reason ever to understand how something can be a cause, or have a force; such relations can
only be derived from experience' (AK 2:370). Kant's attention is still
focused on the specific issue of the cause-effect relation. The *possibility* of
such a relation is, Kant maintains, impenetrably mysterious. But the *existence* of such a relation in a given case can, he claims, be established by
experience, and, specifically, an experience which can be subsumed under
a law of sensation 'which is unanimously accepted by the majority of
people' (AK 2:372). The general issue of the validity of the principle of
causality itself is not raised in these early works. Nor does Kant raise the
crucial question – which he was not to address until after the *Inaugural
Dissertation* – of just how the reality of such fundamental forces could be
established by experience.

Running roughly parallel to his treatment of material substances and
causality is Kant's treatment of immaterial substances (minds or spirits)
and the problem of their existence in space and their relations to each
other and to corporeal beings. In the *New Elucidation*, Kant employs the

Principle of Succession – 'No change can happen to substances except in so far as they are connected with other substances; their reciprocal dependency on each other determines their reciprocal changes of state' (AK 1:410) – to prove the independent existence of an external world, to refute the Leibnizian doctrine of the preestablished harmony, and to establish the conclusion 'that some kind of organic body must be attributed to all spirits whatever' (AK 1:411). The Principle of Co-existence – the interaction between substances, both mental and material, presupposes 'the common principle of their existence . . . the Divine Understanding' (AK 1:412–13) – is used to explain the possibility of interaction between minds and bodies (AK 1:415). In the *New Elucidation*, Kant employs traditional *a priori* arguments to establish and justify the metaphysical positions of Descartes.

A decade later, in *Dreams*, Kant addresses himself to another aspect of Cartesian dualism – the place of minds or spirits in nature. While offering an account of the possibility of such beings' existing in space (in terms of 'occupying' space by virtue of activity but not 'filling space' by means of resistance to material bodies), Kant hastens to add that the possibility of such beings could neither be established nor refuted (AK 1:323). As for the Cartesian issues on which he was so confident in the *New Elucidation*, Kant is now radically agnostic, for they 'far transcend my powers of understanding' (AK 2:328).

In the *Inaugural Dissertation*, Kant employs the notion of the subreptic fallacy (a fallacy in which 'the principles which are native to sensitive cognition transgress their limits, and affect what belongs to the understanding' [AK 2:411]) to dismiss the question about the locus of the mind in nature as a product of the subreptic axiom that 'whatever is, is somewhere and somewhen' (AK 2:413). Kant writes:

But the presence of immaterial things in the corporeal world is a virtual not a local presence. . . . But space contains the conditions of possible reciprocal actions only in respect of matter. But as to what constitutes the external relations of force in the case of immaterial substances, . . . that is quite beyond the human understanding. (AK 2:414)

Kant's early philosophical development culminated in 1770 with the statement in the *Inaugural Dissertation* of the full-fledged critical theory of time and space. It would be in the highest degree misleading to suggest that that theory was the natural product of a long and gradual philosophical evolution. On the contrary, it emerged with rather startling suddenness. Nonetheless, the theme of space continuously preoccupied Kant from the very beginning and from a variety of different perspectives.

In *Living Forces*, Kant presents a version of the Leibnizian thesis that space is a function of the interaction of substances. He writes, 'There would be no space and no extension if substances did not have the power to exercise an external effort. For without this power there would be no connection between substances; without such a connection there would be no order, and without order there would, finally, be no space' (AK 1:23–4). The three dimensions of space are nothing but functions of the laws of motion governing matter. Kant suggestively argues that the laws of motion, and thus the structure of space itself, would have been different had God chosen to create a different kind of matter. The possibility of other types of spaces is thus clearly admitted.

This same Leibnizian view of space appears in both the *New Elucidation* and in *Physical Monadology*. In the former work it is employed to prove the existence of God. Kant argues that the mere existence of substances would not on its own involve their interacting with, or being related to, one another, or even their coexisting in space. That bodies interact and are related to one another and thus exist in space can only be explained in terms of the choice of God (AK 1:414–15). *Physical Monadology* attempts to reconcile the infinite divisibility of space with the indivisibility of physical monads. Limits are thus imposed on the applicability of geometry to nature and physics.

The Only Possible Argument also contains a discussion of space (AK 2:92–6), but the focus of interest has shifted somewhat. Kant's immediate concern is with two new themes: the mysterious paradox that an absolutely homogeneous and thus seemingly simple and unanalysable manifold should be capable of yielding an inexhaustibly rich harvest of geometrical truths (AK 2:94–5), and the strange fact that those same truths should so precisely govern the laws of motion and the interaction of material bodies with one another (AK 2:120–30). By 1763, Kant had abandoned the view that the laws of motion (and hence implicitly the Euclidean character of our space) were contingent. He writes:

And yet the laws of motion are themselves such that matter cannot be thought independently of them. And the necessity of these laws is such that they can be derived from the universal and essential constitution of all matter without the least experiment and with the greatest distinctness. . . . That is to say: If the possibility of matter is presupposed, it would be self-contradictory to suppose it operating in accordance with other laws. This is a logical necessity of the highest kind. (AK 2:99–100)

The brief discussions relating to space in *Negative Magnitudes* (AK 2:168–9) and *Inquiry* (AK 2:280–1) focus on a new issue: the possibility of the *definition* of space. In the latter work, Kant had come to recognise the indefinability of certain fundamental spatial relations (such as 'behind' and 'above'). That Kant's interest should have begun to focus on *these* features of space, and that he should have recognised their indefinability, is of the utmost importance. It suggests that he was beginning to doubt the Leibnizian conception of space; it also suggests that his attention was beginning to shift from the space of geometry and physics to that of ordinary experience. The theme of space makes only a peripheral appearance in the *Dreams*, where it is discussed in connection with the existence of minds in space.

It is clear from *Directions in Space* that Kant's dissatisfaction with Leibnizian relativism had crystalised into open opposition to it. The explicit aim of this short essay was to establish the existence of absolute space. Absolute space is, Kant argues, implied by the directionality of space. Inasmuch as incongruent counterparts differ *only* in respect of directionality (and not in respect of either magnitude or form), they are adduced by Kant as proof of the existence of absolute space. The argument Kant deploys tends, in fact, to establish not the absolute objectivity of space but, rather, its essentially subjectivist nature. In *Living Forces*, the tridimensionality of space had been rooted in the inverse-square law of Newtonian physics; in *Directions in Space*, the three dimensions of space are rooted in our sense of directionality (right and left, above and below, behind and before). But Kant does not yet draw the natural conclusion that spatiality is merely the subjective form of our sensibility. The latter essay may also be understood in terms of Kant's critique of the Leibnizian *analysis situs*. The *analysis situs* was intended to offer an analysis not of spatial *magnitudes* but of spatial *qualities*. The basic concept of the project was that of *congruence* (defined in terms of equality in magnitude and similarity in form). Kant attacks this concept on the grounds that it fails to take account of an essential, fundamental, real, and unanalysable quality of space – its *directionality*. Kant adduces the phenomenon of incongruent counterparts precisely in order to demonstrate that directionality *is* such a quality of space.

At the heart of *Directions in Space* lies an extraordinarily fruitful tension between the professed purpose of the essay and the submerged tendencies of the arguments deployed in it. This conflict was to give birth to the view that space and time are merely the subjective forms of our sensibility and thus only applicable to the phenomena of the empirical world. The submerged tendencies of *Directions in Space* receive their full and systematic statement in the *Inaugural Dissertation*. The theory of time and space there stated (AK 2:398–402, 402–5) is, in substance, identical to that stated in the first *Critique* (1781/1787). Time and space are both described as the grounds of the possibility (not the products) of sensory experience; as singular ideas, not general concepts; as pure intuitions, not substances, accidents, or relations; and as the universal, necessary, and formal conditions of the intuitive representation of all possible objects of the senses. The fact that the reality and objectivity of space and time is denied in the 1770 *Dissertation* and asserted in the 1781 *Critique* is not as significant as it may sound: It marks a shift of emphasis, not a substantive change of view.

It is sometimes suggested that Kant was from the very beginning concerned with the possibility of metaphysics. In fact, this specific problem was to emerge only fairly late, in *Dreams*. It is true that Kant was, from the start, concerned about the general state of metaphysics. As early as 1747, in *Living Forces*, Kant wrote, 'Our metaphysics is . . . only on the threshold of being properly thorough knowledge; God alone knows when it will cross that threshold' (AK 1:30). This general concern was to crystalise into a series of more specific concerns about the foundations, the method, and eventually the limits and possibility of metaphysics.

In the *New Elucidation*, Kant attempts to establish the *foundations* of metaphysical knowledge, and in doing so he betrays no doubts about either its possibility or its method. In addition to establishing the dual principle of identity (the principle of all thought) and distinguishing the two forms of the principle of the determining ground (reasons and causes), Kant isolates the two fundamental principles of metaphysical cognition: the principle of succession and the principle of coexistence. From these two principles a variety of substantive metaphysical conclusions are derived (from the former, the falsity of idealism and the untenability of preestablished harmony; from the latter, the real possibility of a plurality of worlds and of the existence of God).

By the early 1760s, Kant's attention had begun to focus on the problem of the *method* of metaphysics. *The Only Possible Argument* makes it plain that Kant had not yet come to doubt the *possibility* of metaphysical cognition, for, although he rejects the three traditional proofs of God's existence, he constructs a new proof from 'the absolute possibility of all things in general' (AK 2:157). Although this work is not primarily concerned with the problem of the method of metaphysics, allusions to that issue are made in the course of the work: The role of definition in metaphysical enquiry is briefly discussed (AK 2:71), and 'the mania for method and the imitation of the mathematician' are castigated for causing many 'mishaps on the slippery ground of metaphysics' (AK 2:71). In *Negative Magnitudes*, however, Kant also emphasises that metaphysics could greatly benefit from mathematics by adopting certain of its concepts and doctrines (such as the concept of negative magnitudes itself). The issue of the *method* of metaphysics, however, is only alluded to in brief and peripheral fashion.

Inquiry is specifically devoted to the method of metaphysics, which is sharply contrasted with that of mathematics. Mathematics, Kant argues, is based on a small number of stipulative definitions. Metaphysics, by contrast, must start from what is given and from what can be immediately known with certainty about what is given; definitions constitute not its foundation but its ultimate objective. That the object of mathematics (magnitude) is simple, and that mathematics employs signs which display the universal *in concreto*, facilitates its procedure. Metaphysics is far more difficult and far more liable to error: Its objects are far more numerous, and they are given in an obscure and confused fashion; it is also constrained to employ words which can display the universal only *in abstracto*. Both inquiries, however, are in principle capable of the same degree of certainty. The method of metaphysics must, for the present, it is true, be analytic; but Kant does not preclude the possibility of metaphysics's being able to proceed synthetically *more geometrico* ('in a geometrical manner'), once it has eventually established distinct and complete definitions (AK 2:290). Kant adds:

In both sciences, indemonstrable propositions constitute the foundation. . . . But whereas in mathematics the definitions are the first indemonstrable concepts of the things defined, in metaphysics the place of those definitions is taken by a number of indemonstrable propositions which provide the primary data. Their certainty must be just as great as that of the definitions of geometry. (AK 2:296)

In *Dreams*, Kant finally turns to the deeper issue of the *limits* and *possibility* of metaphysical cognition. He approaches the problem by examining the specific issue of the intelligibility of the concept of an immaterial rational substance or spirit. His discussion leads to the notion of the limits of empirical and metaphysical knowledge. Empirical knowledge is constricted by a limit constituted by 'fundamental relations' (such as being the cause of an effect). Although experience acquaints us with such fundamental relations or forces, it does not enable us to understand their possibility, for 'the human understanding has reached its limit here' (AK 2:322). Kant maintains that sensation provides the data of all positive thought (AK 2:351–2), that the senses constitute the 'ultimate foundation of all our judgments' (AK 2:357), and that empirical concepts are the foundation 'upon which all our judgements must at all times be based' (AK 2:367–8). Metaphysical knowledge is constricted by a limit of a much more radical character. Reason cannot understand the possibility of, and experience cannot establish the existence of, the fundamental relations and forces employed in metaphysical claims. Such concepts 'admit of neither proof nor refutation' by either reason or experience (AK 2:370). Towards the end of the work, Kant defines the function of metaphysics in largely negative terms:

It consists both in knowing whether the task has been determined by reference to what one can know, and in knowing what relation the question has to the empirical concepts, upon which all our judgements must at all times be based. To that extent metaphysics is a science of the *limits of human reason*. (AK 2:367–8)

The negative insights of *Dreams* receive sharply focused and positive formulation in the *Inaugural Dissertation*. The realms of the empirical (*phaenomena*) and the metaphysical (*noumena*) are sharply distinguished. The former is characterised in terms of the subjective and the ideal, for its content (sensations) and its form (space and time) are modifications and structures of consciousness; the latter is characterised in terms of the objective and real, for its content (substances) is expressed by the categories of the understanding (concepts of the objective and the real), and its form by the principle of reciprocity (an apodeictic metaphysical principle). The sharp dichotomy between the sensible and the intelligible is rooted in the distinction between two absolutely heterogeneous faculties of the mind: sensibility (which is intuitive and receptive) and understanding (which is conceptual and abstract). The *Inaugural Dissertation* contains two crucial insights – one deriving from arguments deployed in *Directions in Space*, the other from a thesis adumbrated in *Dreams*. The first insight is embodied in the thesis that space and time are the *a priori* forms of our sensibility and thus pure intuitions; the second consists in the recognition that these *a priori* forms can only be the forms of the empirical world of phenomena and *cannot*, therefore, have any application to the metaphysical and intelligible world of *noumena*. The realisation that the sensible world and the intelligible world have each a distinctive form peculiar to itself leads to a third crucially important insight, which relates to the *method* of metaphysics: Metaphysical claims may *never* involve the use of principles (such as the principle 'Whatever is, is somewhere and somewhen') which involve the forms of sensibility. This sharply distinguishes genuine from specious metaphysics.

Kant published almost nothing between 1770 and 1781. The ten-year silence disappointed and exasperated his friends and colleagues. Kant himself in a letter to Herz (24 November 1776 [AK 10:198–200]) says, 'I receive rebukes from all sides because of the inactivity into which I seem long to have fallen' (AK 10:198). His correspondence bears testimony, however, to the systematic and sustained character of his attempts to extend and deepen the insights of the *Inaugural Dissertation* during this period.

The appearance of the *Dissertation* elicited important letters from Herz (11 September 1770 [AK 10:99–102]), Lambert (13 October 1770 [AK 10:98–106]), Sulzer (8 December 1770 [AK 10:106–8]), and Mendelssohn (25 December 1770 [AK 10:108–11]). The last three all object to the view that time is not real. In his letter to Herz (21 February 1772 [AK 10:129–35]), Kant says of this objection that it is 'the most essential objection which could be raised against this theory' (AK 10:134). While not explicitly distinguishing empirical reality and transcendental ideality, Kant's reply to the objection (time *is* real, 'but only in respect of phenomena') prefigures the reply of the *Critique of Pure Reason* (1781/1787) (A36–41 / B53–8 [AK 3:61–4 / AK 4:39–42]).

Kant's important correspondence with Herz (from May 1770 to June 1781) documents the emergence of the first *Critique*. In a letter to Lambert (2 November 1770 [AK 10:96–9]), Kant had expressed the intention of revising and slightly enlarging the *Inaugural Dissertation*, but less than a year later, in a letter to Herz (7 June 1771 [AK 10:121–4]), Kant writes that he is working at 'a book entitled *The Limits of Sensibility and Reason*'. In this important letter – Cassirer says of it that it completes the Copernican revolution – Kant also says, 'I realised that I was still lacking something essential . . . which constituted, indeed, the key to the mystery of metaphysics. . . . I asked myself, namely: What is the foundation of the relation of that which in ourselves we call representation to the object?' Although no positive answer is offered to this crucial question about the validity of the categories, the central question of the *Critique of Pure Reason* had already received clear formulation. Kant adds, 'I am now in a position to present a critique of pure reason. . . . I shall begin by elaborating the first part, which will contain the sources of metaphysics, its method and limits. . . . I shall publish this first part within three months' (AK 10:132).

This wildly optimistic expectation was, of course, to be disappointed. More than two years later, in a letter to Nicolai (25 October 1773 [AK 10:142]), Kant promised that his work of 'transcendental philosophy, which is in fact a critique of pure reason' would be appearing 'shortly'. But towards the end of that same year, in a letter to Herz (AK 10:143–6), we find Kant saying:

Having progressed so far in my project of remodelling a branch of knowledge which has long been worked in vain by half the philosophical world . . . I am now going to adhere strictly to my purpose and not allow myself to be distracted by vanity of authorship into seeking fame in an easier and more popular field until I have levelled my thorny and intractable plot and freed it for general cultivation. (AK 10:144)

He also expresses the hope of publishing the work by Easter, 'or, health permitting, at least shortly after Easter' (AK 10:144–5). Some three years later, however, in another letter to Herz (24 November 1776 [AK 10:198–200]), Kant declares: 'I do not expect to be through with this work before next Easter; and, assuming that my continually interrupted health permits, I intend to devote part of next summer to this purpose' (AK 10:199). In fact, almost two more years were to elapse before Kant, in a famous letter to Herz (1 May 1781 [AK 10:266–7]), was able to announce:

At this Easter Book Fair a work of mine will be published under the title *Critique of Pure Reason*. This book contains the fruit of all the many inquiries which originated from the concepts which we discussed under the name of the *mundus sensibilis* and *mundus intelligibilis*. (AK 10:266)

Introductions to the translations

NEW ELUCIDATION

Although Kant's *New Elucidation* (1755) was his first purely philosophical work, he had already published two major and three minor scientific works. Almost a decade earlier, the twenty-two-year-old Kant, having completed a six-year period of study at the University of Königsberg (devoted in part to the humanities and in part, under the influence of Martin Knutzen, to mathematics and natural science), crowned his studies with *Living Forces* (1747) (AK 1:1–181). Kant had addressed himself to the problem of calculating the magnitude of physical forces, attempting to mediate between and, indeed, reconcile the solution offered by Descartes, who construed force as the product of mass multiplied by velocity (mv), and that of Leibniz, who construed force as the product of mass multiplied by velocity squared (mv^2), arguing that Leibniz's account related to 'living' force whereas that of Descartes related to 'dead' force. The correct account of the matter had been established by Boscovich in 1745, and the correct mathematical formula ($mv^2/2$) was to be published by D'Alembert in the 1758 edition of his *Traité de dynamique*. In spite of its serious scientific shortcomings, the work displays extraordinary flashes of philosophical genius (the discussion of the structure of space and of the possibility of non-Euclidean spaces [AK 1:23–5] is an example). *Living Forces* also strikingly displays features characteristic of Kant's later thought: the predilection for a challenge posed by two cogently argued but incompatible positions; the wish to mediate between and, indeed, reconcile the seemingly irreconcilable by construing the two opposed positions as symptoms of a deeper ground of agreement; and the preoccupation with questions of method and epistemology and, in particular, with the issue of the limits of the applicability of mathematics to nature and physics.

In 1746, Kant was obliged temporarily to abandon his university career – the interruption was to last some eight years – by taking employment as a private tutor in the Königsberg area. His purpose was twofold: to secure for himself a modest financial base from which later to continue his academic career, and, by private study and scientific research, to prepare himself intellectually for such a career. During this eight-year period, Kant clearly contrived to combine the pursuit of his scientific and philosophical interests with the performance of his duties as a tutor, for his return to Königsberg in 1754 was marked by the publication of two short works of considerable scientific originality and one major work of indisputable scientific genius. The two short works (both published in the *Königsbergische wöchentliche Frag- und Anzeigungsnachrichten*) were the *Investigation* (1754) (AK 1:183–91), which maintained the original thesis, confirmed a century later, that the earth's rate of axial rotation was slowing down as a result of the friction caused by tides, and the *Question* (1754) (AK 1:193–213), which was devoted to the concept of the aging of the earth. The major work was the dazzlingly original but ill-fated *Universal Natural History* (1755), which offered a purely mechanical account of the origin of the motions and structure of the solar system (and, indeed, of the entire visible universe) without appealing, as Newton had found himself constrained to appeal, to divine intervention. Lamentably, the bankruptcy of the printer prevented this extraordinary work from reaching a wider public and it remained almost entirely unknown, though it brilliantly anticipated Lambert's *Cosmologische Briefe* (1761), Herschel's discovery of the planet Uranus in 1781, and Laplace's celebrated *Exposition du système du monde* (1798).

The year following his return to Königsberg, the thirty-one-year-old Kant, undeterred by the unsuccess of his two major scientific works, *Living Forces* and the *Universal Natural History*, set about the task of securing the formal academic qualifications necessary for appointment as *Privatdozent*. Kant submitted the first of the two requisite dissertations, *On Fire* (1755) (AK 1:369–84), on 17 April 1755. The *examen rigorosum* took place on 13 May and the degree of *Magister* was awarded to Kant on 12 June 1755. The dissertation contains a statement of the theory of the *materia elastica* or *materia medians* by reference to which Kant attempted to explain a variety of phenomena, such as heat, magnetism, electricity, and the tensile property of metals. *On Fire* was not published during Kant's lifetime and no mention of it is made by Borowski.

The second of the two requisite dissertations, the *New Elucidation*, was submitted *pro venia legendi* and made the object of public disputation on 27 September 1755. The *New Elucidation* met with a kinder fate than the scientific treatises of 1755. Completed in September of 1755, the dissertation was published soon after by J. H. Hartung of Königsberg. It was not reprinted during Kant's lifetime. The respondent on the occasion of Kant's defence was Christoph Abraham Borchard, who was moved to compose a dedication to Johann von Lehwald, Field Marshall of Prussia and Governor of Pillau and Memel. This dedication was printed on the back of the original title page but not included in the text itself of the academy edition of this work (although it is cited by Lasswitz in his introduction to this work [AK 1:565]). The *New Elucidation* received strong praise from Borowski, who says of it: 'This polemical work does not display the mark of the drudgery which one ordinarily encounters in works of this kind'; he detects, indeed, signs that Kant was already planning a revolution in metaphysics 'for the author has subjected the first principles of metaphysics to a mercilessly severe critique'. This work, written under the influence of Crusius, establishes the double principle of all thought (the principle of identity), the double principle of all experience (the principle of the determining ground), and the double principle of metaphysics (the principle of succession and coexistence). Kant boldly establishes a number of substantive metaphysical conclusions – the real existence of an external world, the real possibility of a plurality of worlds, the existence of God, the interaction between mind and body – and attacks a number of contemporary theories – the Leibnizian theory of preestablished harmony, the Leibnizian project of the *ars characteristica*, Wolff's formulation of the principle of sufficient reason, Berkeleyan idealism, and Crusius's theory of freedom. This was the first of Kant's purely philosophical works, and it displays a very comprehensive acquaintance with the dominant issues of his day.

Having received the *venia legendi* and been appointed *Privatdozent*, Kant began lecturing in the winter semester of 1755. In that first term, Kant held courses on logic, metaphysics, mathematics, and possibly physics, basing his lectures, in accordance with the regulations laid down by royal decree, on officially specified texts (in this case, by Meier, Baumeister, Wolff, and Eberhard, respectively). Kant must have already enjoyed a considerable reputation, for his first lecture attracted a large and warmly appreciative audience, among which was Kant's own brother, Johann Heinrich, and Borowski himself, the biographer of Kant. Borowski's report of Kant's first lecture runs as follows: 'At the time, Kant was living in the house of Professor Kypke . . . where he had a spacious lecture-room. This, together with the entrance hall and the staircase, was packed with an incredibly large crowd of students. This seemed to have caused Kant extreme embarrassment. Being a novice, he came near to losing his composure, speaking even more softly than usual and frequently correcting himself.' The warmth of the audience's sympathy for Kant, however, ensured that he recovered his confidence by the time of the second lecture and 'his manner of lecturing was, as it was to remain, not only thorough but also open and pleasant'. In addition to his regular lectures, Kant also held additional meetings devoted to disputations, as well as *privatissima* for individual students. He was regularly lecturing some twenty hours a week (in 1761 he was holding as many as twenty-four hours of instruction each week), and Kant rapidly established a reputation as an exceptionally dedicated teacher (although it ought also to be borne in mind that as *Privatdozent* Kant received no salary from the university and was therefore dependent on the fees payed directly to him by his students for his income).

PHYSICAL MONADOLOGY

Kant's concerns at the beginning of 1756, the year in which *Physical Monadology* was published, were overshadowed by the occurrence, in November 1755, of the great Lisbon earthquake, which wiped out a large part of the Portuguese capital and claimed more than 40,000 lives. The geological effects of the convulsion were felt throughout Europe. The disaster awakened in the mind of the general public widespread religious and moral bewilderment; in more sophisticated circles it aroused the strong suspicion that this could not, after all, be the best of all possible worlds as Leibniz had claimed. Voltaire instantly abandoned optimism and composed his anti-Leibnizian *Sur le désastre de Lisabonne* (1755) and, a few years later, his more celebrated *Candide, ou l'optimisme* (1759). Kant's own philosophical interest in the theme of optimism had, already in 1753, been awakened by the announcement by the Prussian Royal Academy of its 1755 prize-essay theme – Pope's optimism. Kant's three manuscript reflections on optimism (AK 17:229–39) were probably written in 1753 and possibly intended as drafts of an essay he may have considered entering into the competition. The Lisbon earthquake and, in particular, the widespread moral consternation it created, induced Kant to publish *Terrestrial Convulsions* (1756) in numbers 4 and 5 of the *Königsbergische wöchentliche Frag- und Anzeigungsnachrichten* (24 and 31 January 1756). The success of this essay persuaded him to publish the more substantial *Earthquake* (1756); it was submitted to the censor's office by 21 February and shortly thereafter published by J. H. Hartung. A third essay on the same theme, *Further Observation* (1756), was published by Kant in numbers 15 and 16 of the *Königsbergische . . . Nachrichten* (10 and 17 April 1756). Kant's approach to the phenomenon of earthquake is coldly scientific.

It is worth remarking that, when Kant began writing on such matters, geology did not exist as an established branch of enquiry. The scientific claims which Kant makes in this connection are in the highest degree original; more often than not they were confirmed by later research. It is also worth noting that, shortly after the appearance of the three earthquake essays, Kant began to lecture on physical geography – it too a subject which was at the time not recognised as a university discipline. Kant attached considerable importance to the study of physical geography, both for its intrinsic interest and for its pedagogic value, and he lectured on the subject annually for forty years, from the summer semester of 1756 to his retirement in 1796. The first programme of this course was published in the *West Winds* (1757) (AK 2:1–12). Kant's lectures on physical geography were eventually (and with Kant's personal approval) published from carefully collated notes by Rink in 1802 (AK 9:151–436).

In April 1756, Kant wrote to the rector magnificus, to the dean of the Faculty of Philosophy, and, in accordance with established practice, to the government in the person of King Friedrich II, applying for appointment to the position of *professor extraordinarius* in logic and metaphysics. Of the three letters, only that to the king of 8 April 1756 (AK 10:31) is extant. The position for which Kant was applying had been held by the young Martin Knutzen for sixteen years, from his appointment as a young man of twenty-one in 1735 until his premature death at the age of thirty-seven in 1751. The position for which Kant was applying had been vacant for five years, and his appointment to it would have been in the highest degree fitting, for Knutzen (who was only eleven years older than Kant) had exercised a profound and crucial influence on Kant's development, particularly by introducing Kant to the world of astronomy and Newtonian physics, and by placing his library at the disposal of his young student. According to a decree of Friedrich II, admission to the position of *professor extraordinarius* was conditional upon the submission and public defence of *three* dissertations, and Kant thus found himself required to submit a *third* Latin dissertation. *Physical Monadology*, written to satisfy this requirement, was submitted to the censor's office on 23 March and made the subject of public disputation on 10 April 1756, with Borowski, Kant's earliest biographer, acting as one of the three opponents. The dissertation was published by J. H. Hartung that same year, but it was not reprinted during Kant's lifetime. The last half of the title ('of which Sample I contains the Physical Monadology') arouses the expectation that a further sample or samples, illustrating the fruitfulness of the combination of metaphysics and geometry, would later be published. This expectation was to remain disappointed, for no further 'sample' followed. Kant's hopes of academic advancement were also to be disappointed, for the government, bent on economies, was intent on abolishing the position for which Kant had applied. No appointment was made.

Physical Monadology is concerned, as are so many of Kant's works, to reconcile two seemingly incompatible theses; in this case, the theses that space is infinitely divisible but that physical monads (atoms) are indivisible. The reconciliation is effected by the adoption of a dynamic conception of the atom (reminiscent of and possibly influenced by that of Boscovich). Whereas the effect of the activity of the atom (for example, the phenomenon of being solid) is capable of division, and, indeed, division without end, the activity itself which constitutes the being of the atom is not infinitely divisible, indeed, it is not divisible at all. The influence of Knutzen is also evident in the 1756 dissertation: Kant continues the discussion, broached in the *New Elucidation* (1755), of the conditions of interaction and interdependence between finite substances. In adopting Knutzen's theory of physical influence and thus rejecting the doctrine of preestablished harmony, Kant takes issue with the view enunciated by Leibniz in the *Monadology* and outlined by him in a letter to Des Bosses of 16 June 1712: 'It is true that things which happen in the soul must agree with those which happen outside of it. But for this it is enough for the things taking place in one soul to correspond with each other as well as with those happening in any other soul, and it is not necessary to assume anything outside of all souls or monads. According to this hypothesis, we mean nothing else when we say that Socrates is sitting down than what we understand by "Socrates" and by "sitting down" is appearing to us and to others who are concerned'. Later, in the *Monadology* (1714), Leibniz characterised preestablished harmony by holding that each finite substance was a 'perpetual living mirror of the universe, all such substances representing the same universe, each from a different point of view'. In rejecting the Leibnizian preestablished harmony and adopting Knutzen's theory of influence, Kant is contributing to the debate between the Leibnizians and the Newtonians, and doing so on the side of the latter. *Physical Monadology* also manifests the influence of Crusius and Euler, both of whom had, in 1745 and 1746 respectively, presented views on the divisibility of monads or atoms. Furthermore, Crusius held that mathematical entities, in contrast to those which were physical, were imaginary rather than physically real; this conception may have influenced Kant's conception of his problem in Proposition III.

At the end of 1758, Kant was to apply for the position of *professor ordinarius* of logic and metaphysics, which had fallen vacant on the death of Professor Kypke. Shortly after the latter's death, Kant had written letters to the rector magnificus, to the dean of the Faculty of Philosophy, and – the government of Eastern Prussia being, for the moment, in the hands of the Russians (the occupation was to last until 1762) – to Elizabeth, the empress of Russia on, respectively, 11 December 1758, 12 December 1758, and 14 December 1758 (AK 10:4, 5, and 5–6), applying for the vacant professorship. Although Kant's application was supported by his former teacher and patron, F. A. Schultz, who was now rector magnificus of the university, the appointment was granted, on the principle of seniority, to F. J. Buck, who was already *extraordinarius* for philosophy (like Knutzen, having been appointed to the position at the age of twenty-one – which meant that Buck had been *extraordinarius* for fifteen years in 1758). Strangely, Kant would succeed Buck when, as a result of Buck's moving to the chair of mathematics, Kant was belatedly appointed to the chair of logic and metaphysics at the age of forty-six in 1770.

OPTIMISM

Kant's *Optimism* (1759) belongs to a small group of essays (*Theory of Winds* [1756], *West Winds* [1757], *Motion and Rest* [1758], *False Subtlety* [1762], and *Races of Mankind* [1775]) which served as vehicles for announcing his lecture courses (in this case, as can be seen from the final paragraph [AK 2:35], on logic, metaphysics, ethics, physical geography, pure mathematics, and mechanics).

Kant's choice of theme marks his brief entry into what had become a massive European debate on optimism. It was Leibniz who, with the publication of the *Théodicée* (1710), was chiefly responsible for instituting this debate. The Leibnizian thesis that this was the best of all possible worlds was vigorously attacked in France by Bayle and Le Clerc, and in Germany by Wolff, Daries, and Crusius. In England, the optimist thesis had been independently maintained by Shaftesbury in his *Enquiry* (1699) and *The Moralists* (1709). Pope, probably influenced more by Shaftesbury than by Leibniz, presented a popular and philosophically crude version of the optimist thesis in his *Essay on Man* (1733–4). His optimism was savagely attacked by Crousaz and energetically defended by Warburton in his *Vindication* (1740).

The decision of the Prussian Royal Academy in 1753 to adopt the topic of Pope's optimism as the theme for the 1755 prize-essay competition only fed the fires of the debate. The Academy specified the theme in an announcement published in the *Hamburger freyen Urtheilen und Nachrichten* (27 August 1753) as follows: 'An examination of the system of Pope as it is contained in the dictum: Everything is good. The examination shall: (1) specify the true sense of the proposition, according to the hypothesis of the author; (2) compare the author's hypothesis with the system of optimism, or the choice of what is best, with a view to establishing as precisely as possible their particular similarities and to specifying the difference between them; (3) adduce the most important arguments for either establishing or demolishing the system.' The competition attracted submissions from, among others, Mendelssohn, Lessing, Wieland, and Reinhard. Kant himself may have considered entering the competition: The three manuscript reflections on optimism (Reflections 3703–5 [AK 17:229–39]) were doubtless composed with this in mind, although, in the end, Kant did not compete. The prize was awarded to the jurist and theologian, Reinhard, a follower of Crusius. The prize-winning essay was published by the Academy in French (its official language) in 1755. Reinhard privately published his own German translation of his essay in 1757 under the title *Vergleichung des Lehrgebäudes des Herrn Pope von der Vollkommenheit der Welt, mit dem System des Herrn von Leibnitz* ('Comparison of Mr. Pope's Theory of the Perfection of the World with the System of Leibniz') (Leipzig: 1757). Reinhard's essay, which maintained the identity of the systems of Leibniz and Pope, and, following Crusius, attacked optimism, aroused considerable controversy, eliciting from Mendelssohn and Lessing their jointly composed and anonymously published essay, *Pope ein Metaphysiker!* ('Pope a Metaphysician!') (Danzig: 1755).

In 1755, the philosophical debate was invested with vivid and macabre actuality by the Lisbon earthquake, which wiped out most of the town and more than 40,000 of its inhabitants. Voltaire, abandoning his earlier optimism, attacked Leibniz in his poem, *Sur le désastre de Lisbonne*. This provoked Rousseau, in a letter to Voltaire (18 April 1756) to defend optimism. Voltaire returned to the attack with his celebrated *Candide* (1759). The Lisbon earthquake was also the subject of Kant's three short essays on earthquakes which he published in 1756. Although they are primarily scientific in character, it is clear that the essays are also intended to demolish the view that there is an incompatibility between the occurrences of such disasters and the claim that this is the best of all possible worlds.

Both the choice of the theme by the Prussian Royal Academy and the award of the prize to Reinhard occasioned a lively polemic in which Mendelssohn, Lessing, Waser, and Wieland participated. Kant's own essay also helped to fan the flames of controversy. Kant submitted his essay to the official censor on 5 October 1759 and it was published two days later on 7 October. On the preceding day, Daniel Weymann had been awarded a degree for a thesis bearing the title *De mundo non optimo* ('Concerning the World which is not the Best'). Weymann, failing to recognise that Kant's essay was an attack on the views expressed by Crusius in his *Entwurf* (1745) and forgetting that his own thesis was largely a restatement of precisely those views, misconstrued Kant's essay as a personal attack on himself. He accordingly published a reply to Kant a week later on 14 October 1759 under the title *Beantwortung des Versuchs einiger Betrachtungen über den Optimismus* ('Reply to an Attempt at Some Reflections on Optimism'). That Weymann had misunderstood Kant's intentions is clear from a letter written by Kant on 28 October 1759 to Lindner (AK 10:22–3) in which he writes:

A meteor has recently made its appearance above the academic horizon here. M. Weymann has sought, by means of a rather disorganized and unintelligibly written dissertation against optimism, to solemnise his debut on this stage. . . . His notorious immodesty induced me to decline his invitation to act as respondent [on the occasion of the public defence of his dissertation]. However, in an essay announcing my programme of lectures and which I had distributed the day after his dissertation appeared, I briefly defended optimism against Crusius, without giving a thought to Weymann. My defence of optimism, however, aroused his spleen. The following Sunday he published a pamphlet in which he defended himself against my alleged attack – a defence full of immodesties and distortions *etc.* The judgement of the public, and the obvious impropriety of engaging in fisticuffs with a Cyclops, not to mention the saving of a pamphlet which would perhaps already have been forgotten by the time its defence appears – all this obliges me to reply in the most proper manner, namely, by saying nothing.

Kant's later attitude to this short work seems to have been one of embarrassment. Borowski, the earliest biographer of Kant, who had enquired of him about this essay, writes: 'Kant, with genuinely solemn seriousness bade me think no more of this work on optimism, urging me, should I ever come across it anywhere, not to let anyone have a copy but to withdraw it from circulation immediately'.

For a contemporary account of the optimism controversy arising from the Reinhard essay see C. Ziegra, *Sammlung der Streitschriften über die Lehre der besten Welt . . . welche zwischen dem Verfasser der im Jahre 1755 von der Akademie zu Berlin gekrönten Schrift, und einnigen berühmten Gelehrten gewechselt worden* ('Collection of the Polemical Writings concerning the Doctrine of the Best World . . . which passed between the Author of the Essay which was crowned by the Berlin Academy in the Year 1755 and a Number of Celebrated Scholars') (Rostock: 1759).

FALSE SUBTLETY

Kant's *False Subtlety* (1762), *The Only Possible Argument* (1763), *Negative Magnitudes* (1763), and *Inquiry* (1764) constitute a group of four works which were all composed, completed, and published within the same brief time span. These four works have been ordered here in accordance with the dates on the original title pages (although *The Only Possible Argument* was published not in 1763 but in the latter half of December 1762). The order in which these four works were published is not to be taken as a reliable guide to the order of either their completion or their composition.

The order in which these four works were *completed* can be fairly easily established. *False Subtlety* was probably completed by the early autumn of 1762, for Hamann mentions the work in the fourth of his *Hirtenbriefe* ('Pastoral Letters'), which bears the date 17 November 1762; *The Only Possible Argument* had probably also been completed by the early autumn of 1762, for it was already published by mid-December 1762; *Inquiry* had certainly been completed by 31 December 1762, for it was on this date that Kant submitted his essay to Formey, the secretary of the Prussian Royal Academy; *Negative Magnitudes* must have been completed by the early summer of 1763, for the *Acta* of the University of Königsberg contain the record of its registration dated 3 June 1763. It is therefore clear that all four works were probably completed within the nine-month period from October 1762 to June 1763.

As for the order in which these four works were *composed*, there is radical disagreement between scholars. Fischer proposes: *Subtlety, Magnitudes, Argument,* and *Inquiry;* Cohen favours: *Subtlety, Inquiry, Magnitudes,* and *Argument;* Paulsen suggests: *Argument, Inquiry, Magnitudes,* and *Subtlety;* Erdman adopts: *Subtlety, Argument, Inquiry,* and *Magnitudes.* It seems unlikely that this disagreement will ever be resolved by appeal to the internal evidence of the works themselves. The assumption that each work represents a distinct and clearly identifiable phase in Kant's philosophical development is, granted the relative shortness of the time span involved, extremely dubious.

A brief passage towards the end of §5 of *False Subtlety* (1762) (AK 2:57) indicates the purpose of the essay and furnishes a clue to the date of its publication. Kant writes: 'I should be flattering myself too highly if I were to suppose that the labour of a few hours were capable of toppling the colossus, who hides his head in the clouds of antiquity, and whose feet are feet of clay. My intention is simply to explain why, in my course on logic – where I am not permitted to arrange everything in accordance with my own understanding of these things but am often obliged to defer to the prevailing taste – I treat these matters only briefly, so as to devote the time thus saved to the genuine extension of profitable insights'. It is clear from this passage that this essay was intended to serve as a vehicle for announcing his lectures in a manner analogous to that of *Optimism* (1759). The above passage also provides a clue to the date of publication. Kant held courses on logic in each of the following three semesters: winter 1761–2, summer 1762, and winter 1762–3. It is almost certainly this last course which is being announced here. Although the work was certainly available by the end of 1762 – Hamann quotes from the *False Subtlety* in the fourth of his *Hirtenbriefe* ('Pastoral Letters'), which is dated 17 November 1762 – no mention of Kant's work is made in the Book Fair catalogue for October 1762. It seems highly probable, therefore, that the *False Subtlety* appeared at the beginning of the winter semester of 1762–3.

Kant's *False Subtlety* breaks a six-year period of relative philosophical silence and inaugurates an eight-year period of intense philosophical activity which culminated in the *Inaugural Dissertation* (1770). Kant had already touched on logical themes in the *New Elucidation* (1755); he had also already held a dozen courses on logic, all of them based on Meier's *Auszug* (1752). The winter semester of 1761–2 had been particularly burdensome for Kant (he had held courses on logic, metaphysics, mathematics, physics, physical geography, and ethics and had been lecturing twenty-four hours a week); the summer semester of 1762 was much less burdensome (with only two courses, one on logic and one on metaphysics); the winter semester of 1762–3 was also a relatively light one (with courses on logic, metaphysics and mathematics). It was probably during this period, when his teaching commitments were fairly light, that Kant worked on the preparation of the *False Subtlety*, *The Only Possible Argument*, *Negative Magnitudes*, and *Inquiry*.

False Subtlety may be regarded as a contribution to a wider debate on the utility of logic in general and on the validity of the Aristotelian theory of the syllogism in particular. Leibniz was largely alone in maintaining an uncritical attitude to Aristotle's logic. Even Wolff had come to recognise that, from a heuristic point of view, logic was powerless (cf. *Philosophia rationalis* [1728], §5). The passage quoted above from the *False Subtlety* (1762) (AK 2:57) may suggest a higher degree of originality than is justified by the facts. Many of the positions maintained by Kant were already widely accepted: Kant's theory of judgement (AK 2:47) is to be found stated by Meier (*Auszug* [1752], §§292–3); the analysis of clear and distinct ideas offered by Kant (AK 2:58–9) coincides with that maintained by Meier (*Auszug* [1752], §§143–4); Kant's claim that the Aristotelian apparatus of four syllogistic figures was unnecessarily elaborate had already been asserted by Wolff (*Philosophia rationalis* [1728], §5) and by Crusius (*Weg zur Gewissheit* [1747], §54); even the specific thesis that all but the first of the four syllogistic figures are superfluous had already been maintained by Thomasius (*Introductio ad philosophiam aulicam* ['Introduction to Court-Philosophy'] [Leipzig: 1688], pp. 163, 167–8, and 171) and by Crusius (*Weg zur Gewissheit* [1747], §§330–5).

False Subtlety was reviewed by Mendelssohn in *Briefe die neueste Literatur betreffend* ('Letters concerning the Latest Literature') (1765, XXII, 147–58).

THE ONLY POSSIBLE ARGUMENT

Although the title page of the original edition of this work bears the date '1763' it is apparent from Hamann's letter of 21 December 1762 to Nicolai that it was actually published shortly after mid-December 1762, for Hamann speaks of Kant's work's having 'just left the press'. If one allows for a normal and unproblematic process of printing, Kant must have completed *The Only Possible Argument* sometime in October 1762, probably shortly after *False Subtlety* (1762).

The process of composing *The Only Possible Argument* would appear to have been both difficult and time-consuming. In the preface (AK 2:66), Kant tells us, 'The observations which I here present are the fruits of lengthy reflection. But because a variety of commitments has prevented me from devoting the necessary time to it, the manner in which these observations are presented shows the characteristic mark of something incompletely worked out'. A little earlier (AK 2:66), he had said, 'What I am furnishing here is the materials for constructing a building: they have been assembled with great difficulty'. The 'variety of commitments' to which Kant refers is probably an allusion to the completion of the *False Subtlety* for publication, and possibly work on the *Inquiry* (1764), which Kant intended to submit to the Prussian Royal Academy as his entry in the prize-essay competition, and for which the deadline was 31 December 1762. He may also be alluding to the preparation of his courses on logic, metaphysics, and mathematics, which he was about to offer during the winter semester of 1762–3.

How long Kant's 'lengthy reflection' may have lasted is not clear. It is certainly true that a number of the themes and ideas central to *The Only*

Possible Argument had already been either broached or fully developed in earlier works. The *Universal Natural History* (1755) contains a detailed statement of Kant's cosmological theory which is embodied, in abbreviated form, in the Seventh Reflection of Section 2 of *The Only Possible Argument* (AK 2:137–51). The earlier of these two works also broaches the theme, central to the later work, of the relation between scientific explanation and religious faith and their alleged incompatibility, as also that of the nature of the dependency of the world on God. The *New Elucidation* (1755) contains a brief statement of the critique of Descartes's ontological proof of the existence of God and an outline statement of the original proof of the existence of God from the possibility of things in general, which form the heart of *The Only Possible Argument*. It would thus not be implausible to maintain that *The Only Possible Argument* is the product of reflections which extend back to 1755 and, obviously, earlier, for the positions established in the two works of 1755 must themselves have been the product of extended reflection. Indeed, if we may attribute the *Three Manuscript Reflections on Optimism* (AK 17:229–39) to the year 1753, we may say that the argument for the existence of God from the possibility of things dates at least from 1753, for in those reflections Kant attributes this argument, rather implausibly, to Pope.

The views on the concept of Being presented by Kant in *The Only Possible Argument* are very much the product of his critique of the views of Wolff, Baumgarten, and especially of Crusius (cf. in particular, Crusius, *Entwurf* [1745], §§45–61). Kant's views on the relationship between nature and God, as well as his views on the nature of matter, were deeply influenced by two works of Maupertuis: *Essai de Cosmologie* (1751) and the *Examen philosophique* (1758).

The appearance of Kant's *The Only Possible Argument* in the latter half of December 1762 elicited an instant critical response from Daniel Weymann – he had also launched an instant attack on Kant's *Optimism* within a week of its publication – under the title *Bedenklichkeiten über den einzig möglichen Beweisgrund des Herrn M. Kants zu einer Demonstration des Daseyns Gottes* ('Reservations concerning The Only Possible Argument of Herr M. Kant in Support of a Demonstration of the Existence of God') which bore the date '14 January 1763'. (It is dismissed by Adickes as 'a shallow, flimsy and impudent polemic'.) The same year saw the appearance of Ploucquet's *Observationes et commentatio in D. Cant de uno possibili fundamento demonstrationis existentiae Dei* ('Observations by way of Commentary to Kant's Only Possible Foundation to a Demonstration of the Existence of God') (Tübingen: 1763). Most important of all was the very substantial and favourable review published by Mendelssohn (in *Briefe die neueste Literatur betreffend* ['Letters concerning the Latest Literature'] [1764, XVIII, 69–102]). This review, more than any other, was responsible for establishing Kant's reputation in Germany as a major philosopher.

NEGATIVE MAGNITUDES

The official registration of Kant's *Negative Magnitudes* (1763) is recorded in the *Acta Facultatis Philosophiae* of the University of Königsberg (Vol. V, p. 428) for the year 1763. The entry reads: '3rd June: Magister Kant's Attempt to Introduce the Concept of Negative Magnitudes into Philosophy, along with an Appendix containing an Hydrodynamic Exercise'. Nothing is known of the 'hydrodynamic' appendix. Although this work had obviously been completed by June 1763 and published that same year, its publication was not publicly announced until the Easter Book Fair of 1764, which suggests that it must have been published late in 1763, for there is no mention of it in the Autumn Book Fair catalogue.

Although *Inquiry* (1764) was not published until almost a year after *Negative Magnitudes*, the former work had certainly been completed by 31 December 1762 (the closing date for the submission of entries for the 1763 philosophy prize-essay competition), for Kant's letter of 28 June 1763 to Formey, the secretary of the Prussian Royal Academy, informs us that the latter had confirmed the arrival of the manuscript on that date (AK 10:38–9). It would seem almost certain, therefore, that the composition of *Inquiry* must have antedated that of *Negative Magnitudes* by some six months or so.

Negative Magnitudes certainly touches on the central theme of *Inquiry*, namely, the contrasting natures and methods of mathematics and metaphysics. In *Inquiry*, Kant maintains:

One can say with Bishop *Warburton* that nothing has been more damaging to philosophy than mathematics, and in particular the *imitation* of its method in contexts where it cannot possibly be employed. The *application* of the mathematical method in those parts of philosophy involving cognition of magnitudes is something quite different, and its utility is immeasurable. (AK 2:283)

Much the same claim is made at the beginning of the *Negative Magnitudes:*

The use to which mathematics can be put in philosophy consists either in the imitation of its method or in the genuine application of its propositions to the objects of philosophy. With respect to the first of these two uses: it has not been noticed that it has had only one benefit, in spite of the great advantage expected of it to start with. (AK 2:167)

A little later Kant adds:

By contrast, the second use to which mathematics has been put in philosophy has been all the more beneficial to the parts of philosophy affected. These parts of philosophy, by turning the doctrines of mathematics to their own advantage, have attained to heights, to which they would not otherwise have been able to aspire. (AK 2:167)

But although there is this common ground between *Inquiry* and *Negative Magnitudes*, the central themes of the two works are rather different.

Whereas *Inquiry* attacks the use of mathematical method in metaphysics, *Negative Magnitudes* is more opposed to the logicism of Leibniz and the rationalist philosophers. Kant sharply distinguishes logical opposition (contradiction) from real opposition (conflict of forces), maintaining that the product of the former is nothing at all and the product of the latter is something real. Having, in *Optimism* (1759), defended the Leibnizian view of evil as the mere absence of good, Kant, in the *Negative Magnitudes*, insists on the real and irreducible character of pain and evil. The contrast between the ideal and the real, between logic and existence, between concept and being is further emphasised by Kant's insistence on the irreducibility and ultimate incomprehensibility of the cause-effect relation.

Kant's *Negative Magnitudes* was reviewed by Mendelssohn in *Briefe die neueste Literatur betreffend* ('Letters Concerning the Latest Literature') (1765, XXII, 159–76).

INQUIRY

Kant's *Inquiry* (1764) was composed in connection with the philosophy prize-essay competition organised by the Prussian Royal Academy for the year 1763. The theme of the competition, proposed by Professor Johann Georg Sulzer, was approved by the Academy on 28 May 1761 and publicly announced by its secretary on 4 June 1761. The details of the competition were published in the *Berlinische Nachrichten von Staats und Gelehrten Sachen* on 23 June 1761:

The Class of Speculative Philosophy herewith proposes the following question for the year 1763: One wishes to know whether the metaphysical truths in general, and the first principles of *Theologiae naturalis* and morality in particular, admit of distinct proofs to the same degree as geometrical truths; and if they are not capable of such proofs, one wishes to know what the genuine nature of their certainty is, to what degree the said certainty can be brought, and whether this degree is sufficient for complete conviction. Scholars of all countries, ordinary members of the Academy only excepted, are invited to examine this question. The prize, consisting of a memorial medal in gold, *Fifty ducats in weight*, will be awarded to the person whose work, in the *judgement of the Academy*, succeeds best of all. Treatises, written in a clear and very legible hand, shall be submitted to the permanent secretary of the Academy, Herr Professor Formey. Submissions must be made by 1 January 1763; submissions will not be accepted after that date, no matter what excuses may be offered. Authors are requested not to give their names but to choose a motto, attaching a sealed note containing their motto, their name, and their address. The judgement of the Academy will be delivered on 31 May 1763 at the public assembly of the Academy.

Kant's letter of 28 June 1763 to Formey (AK 10:41–2) confirms that the latter, in a letter of 31 December 1762, had acknowledged receipt of the former's submission. That Kant's entry was submitted on the very last possible day suggests that his *Inquiry* was composed and completed at the last moment. A number of things said by Kant confirm this surmise. In the postscript to the *Inquiry* itself, Kant says:

In what concerns the care, precision and elegance of the execution: I have preferred to leave something to be desired in that respect, rather than to allow such matters to prevent my presenting this inquiry for examination at the proper time, particularly since this defect is one which could easily be remedied should my inquiry meet with a favourable reception. (AK 2:301)

In the *Announcement* (1765), Kant alludes to *Inquiry*, describing it as 'a short and hastily composed work' (AK 2:308). In his letter of 28 June 1763 to Formey (AK 10:41–2) Kant speaks of his pleasure at having learned (from the *Berlinische Nachrichten* of 21 June 1763) of the favourable reception accorded his essay by the Academy. He then goes on to say:

My gratitude for this favourable judgement is all the greater in as much as this piece has contributed so little to that favourable judgement by the care of the outer form in which it is couched or of the embellishments with which it is adorned: a somewhat too lengthy hesitation scarcely left me time enough to present, in no special order, some of the most substantial grounds relating to an object which has occupied my thoughts for a number of years, reflections which, I flatter myself, have now brought me close to my goal.

It may therefore be assumed that Kant, having completed *The Only Possible Argument* (1763) by about October 1762, devoted the remaining part of the year to the composition of the *Inquiry*.

The *Acta* of the Prussian Royal Academy contains the following entry, dated 28 May 1763, relating to the award of the 1763 essay-prize: 'The votes were for a while balanced equally between entries No. XX and XXVIII, but agreement was eventually reached in favour of No. XX, the proviso being made that at the public assembly entry No. XXVIII should be declared to have come extremely close to winning and that it merited the highest praise.' The decision to award the prize to Moses Mendelssohn was announced at the public assembly of the Academy on 2 June 1763. On 21 June 1763, the *Berlinische Nachrichten* carried the following report:

At the public assembly of the Academy, the said Academy announced that it had, at its assembly of 31 May, awarded the prize to a certain piece, and that on opening a sealed note, it had transpired that the author of the said piece was the gifted Jew, Moses Mendelssohn, resident of this place. But, at the same time, the Academy declared that the German memoire, bearing the motto: *Verum animo satis haec vestigia parva sagaci / Sunt, per quae possis caetera cognoscere tute*, was almost equal in merit to the work of the Jewish scholar which had won the prize.

Kant, having learned of the outcome of the competition from the above newspaper report, wrote to Formey on 28 June 1763 (AK 10:41–2) both to express his pleasure at the result and to excuse the inadequacies of the outward form of the essay. Kant also hints that the hastiness of its composition was also the cause of its incompleteness. In this connection, Kant writes:

I thus allow myself the liberty of humbly inquiring of you, Noble Sir, whether this piece of mine will be sent to the Royal Academy of Sciences to the press along with the prize-winning essay, and whether, if it will so be sent, a supplement, consisting of substantial enlargements and containing a more detailed explanation would be displeasing to the above excellent Society. (AK 10:41)

Formey's reply to Kant, dated 5 August 1763, contained the following reassurance:

Your dissertation will without doubt be printed in the collection of pieces for the year 1763; they will be four in number. I cannot say when they will be printed, for we are waiting for a new President, named by His Majesty, to succeed the late M. de Maupertuis. All the arrangements will depend on this new President. You thus have the time, good Sir, to prepare a supplement to your essay; if you send it to me when it has been drawn up, I shall see that it is inserted at the appropriate place in the collection.

In spite of Kant's conviction of their importance, the supplements never materialised. The printing of the prize-essays was delayed for the reasons specified in Formey's letter above, and it was not until 24 April 1764 that the *Berlinische Nachrichten* was able to announce that the Mendelssohn and Kant essays would be available for a purchase at the 1764 Leipzig Easter Book Fair. Hamann, in a letter to Lindner of 16 May 1764, confirms that the two works had indeed arrived.

Mendelssohn's prize-winning essay, Kant's *Inquiry* and the two next-best essays were published together under the title: *Dissertation qui a remporté le prix proposé par l'Académie royale des sciences et belles lettres de Prusse, sur la nature, les espèces, et les degrés de l'évidence avec les pièces qui ont concouru. A Berlin chez Haude et Spener, Libraires du Roi et de l'Académie, MDCCLXIV.* The four essays were prefaced by a report which was composed by Merian and written in French (the official language of the Academy) for the benefit of those members who had no German. The report contains an abridgement of Mendelssohn's essay; a translation of that abridgement is to be found attached as an appendix to the translation. It is perhaps worth remarking that, in addition to Mendelssohn and Kant, Lambert also contemplated submitting an entry, but he failed to complete his essay in time. Lambert's manuscript has been published by K. Bopp in *Kant-Studien* (*Ergänzungsheft XLII*) under the title *Über die Methode der Metaphysik, Theologie und Moral richtiger zu beweisen* ('Concerning the Method of Metaphysics, Theology and Morals for Proving more Correctly').

ANNOUNCEMENT

The year 1763 was extraordinarily fruitful for Kant philosophically, for it, in effect, saw either the publication or the completion of four important works: *The Only Possible Argument* (1763) (actually published a couple of weeks before the new year), *Negative Magnitudes* (completed by mid-June 1763), *Inquiry* (1764) (completed by the end of December 1762 but not published until April 1764), and the important work on aesthetics and anthropology *Observations on the Feeling of the Beautiful and the Sublime* (1764) (completed by October 1763 but not published until January 1764).

By contrast, the years 1764 and 1765 were relatively unproductive. In February 1764, Kant, at the invitation of Hamann, published his *Essay on the Maladies of the Mind* in the newspaper edited by Hamann, the *Königsbergsche Gelehrte und Politische Zeitungen*. This work is an examination of a phenomenon belonging to the field of religious psychopathology. A half-crazy religious enthusiast, Jan Pawlikowicz Komarnicki, appeared in the neighbourhood of Königsberg in the company of a young boy and an assorted herd of cows, goats, and sheep. Kant's interest in the bizarre case was partly moral and partly psychological: In the boy, Kant saw a living exemplar of Rousseau's ideal of the noble savage living in the state of nature, uncorrupted by human society or civilisation, whereas Komarnicki aroused Kant's interest in the general issue of madness. His *Maladies of the Mind* (1764) may therefore be regarded as linking the Rousseau-inspired *Observations* and the Swedenborg-inspired *Dreams* (1766), with its submerged themes of madness and sensory delusion.

The year 1765 saw the composition, completion, and publication of only one short work, the *Announcement* (1765). This work – like the *Theory of Winds* (1756), the *West Winds* (1757), *Motion and Rest* (1758), *Optimism* (1759), *False Subtlety* (1762) and, much later, the *Races of Mankind* (1775) – served to announce Kant's forthcoming lectures, in this case his forthcoming lectures on metaphysics, logic, ethics, and physical geography, which he was planning to hold during the winter semester of 1765–6.

The *Announcement* was published in the autumn of 1765. Borowski expresses a high opinion of this little work: 'Under the wholly unassuming title, Kant presents his ideas on school and university instruction in a form which is very much worth reading. For me, this little work was always and still is one of his most important. Anyone from outside Königsberg with no opportunity of attending Kant's courses can see here in the most distinct fashion how Kant lectured on metaphysics, logic, ethics and so forth. He himself, at the end of this work, says that one can form a conception of his method of teaching from it'.

DREAMS

On two occasions before 1766, Kant had written on issues of general popular interest. The three short earthquake essays of 1756, written just after the Lisbon earthquake of 1755, had been intended to allay popular fears and religious doubts by showing that earthquakes are purely natural phenomena with no sinister moral significance. Again, in 1764, wide popular curiosity had been aroused in and around Königsberg by the bizarre appearance in the town and its neighbourhood of the religious enthusiast Jan Pawlikowicz Komarnicki, along with a young boy (who had apparently grown up wild in the forests) and a motley collection of cows, goats, and sheep. Hamann and others prevailed upon Kant to publish his views on 'The Goat Prophet'. Those views were initially published in the Königsberg newspaper edited by Hamann and later published as *Maladies of the Mind* (1764).

Analogous popular interest had also at this period been aroused by certain strange reports which were reaching Königsberg from Sweden, concerning another religious enthusiast, Immanuel Swedenborg. Swedenborg had already published his eight-volume *Arcana coelestia* by 1756, and rumours were circulating that he possessed dramatic paranormal powers. A young friend of Kant's, Charlotte von Knobloch, wrote to him (the letter itself is unfortunately lost) asking him to investigate the strange rumours and enlighten her on their significance. Kant's important reply to her (AK 10:430–48) bears only the date '10 August' but no year. Since Kant refers in that letter to events known to have occurred as late as 1762, it cannot belong to the year 1758 (as Borowski claims); and since Kant addresses his young correspondent by her maiden name, the letter is unlikely to have been written after her marriage (which took place sometime in 1763 or 1764). The general consensus is that Kant's letter was written in 1763; Fräulein von Knobloch's letter was possibly written early in 1762 or somewhat before. Kant's letter of 10 August 1763(?) is an important and interesting document, partly because it contains the stories recounted in *Dreams* (1766) and partly because Kant seems then to have been persuaded of the truth of those stories, for he repeatedly emphasises the veracity and reliability of his informants, insisting that the stories had either been or could in principle be publicly verified. The lost letter from Fräulein von Knobloch may be regarded as the original stimulus to the composition of *Dreams*, for the extensive enquiries in which Kant engaged in order to satisfy the curiosity of his correspondent intrigued and puzzled his friends to such a degree that they importuned him to publish his findings. In his letter to Moses Mendelssohn of 8 April 1766 (AK 10:69–73), Kant has this to say:

I do not know whether, in reading through this book [*Dreams*], which was composed in a rather disorderly fashion, you will have detected any signs of the reluctance with which it was written. For I furnished much matter for talk as a result of the enquiries which I undertook out of curiosity into Swedenborg's visions, partly by interrogating those who had had the opportunity of making Swedenborg's personal acquaintance, partly by the correspondence in which I engaged, and finally by acquiring his works. Having done this, I clearly recognised that I would have no peace from the ceaseless enquiries with which I was bombarded until I had disburdened myself of the knowledge which I was supposed to possess concerning all these anecdotes. (AK 10:69)

If Kant's initial interest in Swedenborg dates from about 1762 (or somewhat earlier), then the composition of *Dreams* belongs to the years 1764–5, which were relatively unproductive. It is true that 1764 saw the publication of *Observations* and *Inquiry;* but both works had been completed before 1764 (the former by the end of 1763 and the latter by the end of 1762). As for 1765 – it saw the publication of only one short work, the *Announcement* (1765). It is evident from the notice found in the *Acta Facultatis Philosophiae* of the University of Königsberg for the year 1766 that *Dreams* already existed in *printed* form by 31 January, for, contrary to regulations – the publishing firm of Johann Jacob Kanter was fined 10 *Reichsthaler* for this contravention of the rules – it was not the manuscript which was submitted to the censor but the already printed work. The publishers defended themselves in the following terms:

The manuscript of Magister Kant was very illegible. . . . The manuscript was sent to the press page by page, with the result that so many revisions had to be made at the proof stage that this treatise only appeared in its present form after it had been finally printed. It was on account of these circumstances that it was, on the one hand, impossible for the professors to censor the treatise, and that, on the other hand, these same professors, had they submitted the work to you before it had been printed, would have censored an entirely different work.

Kant himself, in his letter of 8 April 1766 to Moses Mendelssohn, mentions the disadvantages of the page-by-page manner in which the work was fed to the printer:

I am convinced that your observations will not miss the point which is the focus of all these considerations. It is a point which I would have characterised more clearly had I not had the treatise printed page by page, one after the other; for it was as a result of this procedure that I was not always able to see in advance what ought to be introduced early on in order to facilitate the better understanding of what was to follow at a later stage; and certain elucidations had subsequently to be omitted because they would have otherwise appeared at an inappropriate place. (AK 10:71)

Kant's *Dreams* was published anonymously, though it is clear from his letter to Moses Mendelssohn of 7 February 1766 (AK 10:67–8) that he made no attempt to conceal his authorship from his friends and colleagues, for the letter was accompanied by copies for distribution by Mendelssohn –

one for Mendelssohn himself, and one each for Sack, Spalding, Süssmilch, Lambert, Sulzer, and Formey. The reason for the anonymity was probably the fact that Kant was actually embarrassed at having published on such a theme so lacking in academic respectability. (Mendelssohn's reply to Kant's letter chides him for having so demeaned himself by discussing such a dubious subject.) The measure of Kant's embarrassment is indicated by the fact that, whereas in his letter to Charlotte von Knobloch Kant takes pains to emphasize how thoroughly and reliably the Swedenborg reports had been attested and verified, in *Dreams* Kant constantly refers to these stories in pejorative terms and even characterises his own enquiry into these matters as a 'despicable business', a 'thankless task', and a 'foolish undertaking' (although, of course, he also attempts to justify his enquiry by relating it to the more respectable question of the nature, method, limits and, indeed, possibility of metaphysical cognition).

As can be seen from the Bibliographies of Editions and Translations towards the end of the volume, the original edition of Kant's *Dreams* exists in three typographically distinct impressions, all printed in 1766. The earliest and the most reliable of the three printings is that by Johann Jacob Kanter of Königsberg, which is known as 'A1'. Its title page is without decoration. The impressions known as 'A2' and 'A3' were published by Johann Friedrich Hartknoch in Riga and Mietau. A2 is distinguished by its title page which has a vignette representing the branch of a rose; the title page of A3 is distinguished by a vignette representing a seated figure holding a flower. A3 is more reliable than A2, for it is based directly on A1. Kant's letter to Lambert of 31 December 1765 (AK 10:52) explains the strange change of publisher (Kanter had taken his former employee, Hartknoch, into partnership).

Kant's *Dreams* was reviewed by Herder in the *Königsbergische gelehrte und politische Zeitungen*, No. 18, 3 March 1766.

DIRECTIONS IN SPACE

A period of almost five years elapsed between the completion of *Dreams* (1766) at the end of 1765 and the publication of the *Inaugural Dissertation* (1770) in late September 1770. This five-year period was punctuated by the publication of a single tiny essay, *Directions in Space*, which appeared in numbers 6, 7, and 8 of the *Königsberger Frag- und Anzeigungsnachrichten* early in 1768.

Throughout the early 1760s there were signs that Kant was growing dissatisfied with the Leibnizian theory of space, in particular its epistemological aspects. *The Only Possible Argument* (1763), for example, shows Kant's interest focused on the mysterious paradox of an absolutely homogeneous and thus simple manifold yielding a seemingly inexhaustible harvest of geometrical truths (themselves applying with perfect precision to things in space). In *Inquiry* (1764), Kant's recognition of, and emphasis on, the indefinability of certain fundamental spatial relations is of the utmost philosophical significance, for it prepares the ground for the critique of the Leibnizian *analysis situs.*

Kant's objective in *Directions in Space* is to demonstrate the existence of absolute space (and therefore the falsity of Leibnizian relativism). His strategy consists in the attempt to demonstrate the real existence of a fundamental, essential, and unanalysable spatial *quality*, directionality, in the absence of which certain phenomena would be either unintelligible or impossible. Incongruent counterparts (such as left and right hands) *show* the real existence of the quality of directionality because, although equal in magnitude and similar in form, they cannot be contained within each other's spatial limits (except, of course, by being rotated through an extra dimension). Their congruency is prevented by their differing directionality. Directionality must, therefore, be a real quality of space. The Leibnizian account of congruency, which underlies the *analysis situs*, wholly fails to take account of this essential spatial quality.

A key – perhaps *the* key – to an understanding of *Direction in Space* is to be found in Kant's sceptical attitude towards the Leibnizian project, the *analysis situs*. This was envisaged as a *specifically* geometrical form of analysis entirely different from *mathematical* analysis. The latter was concerned with *magnitudes*, both determinate (arithmetic) and indeterminate (algebra). The *analysis situs* was concerned with the *specifically spatial qualities* of space. Its fundamental operation was not the equation (involving equalities of magnitude) but the relation of congruence (involving similarities of form). Kant's criticism is directed against the Leibnizian concept of congruence which was defined in terms of equality of magnitude and similarity of form. The inadequacy of the Leibnizian notion can be illustrated from Leibniz's own *Studies in the Geometry of Situation* (1679) (Loemker, pp. 249–53):

Instead of using equalities or equations as in algebra, I shall here use relations of congruence, which I shall express by the character ꝏ. For example, in the first figure (Figure 1), ABC ꝏ DEF means that the triangles ABC and DEF are

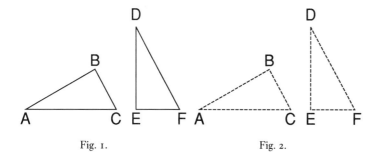

Fig. 1.   Fig. 2.

congruent with respect to the order of their points, that they can occupy exactly the same place, and that one can be applied or placed on the other without changing anything in the two figures except their place. So if one places D upon A, E upon B, and F upon C, the two triangles, which are assumed to be equal and similar, obviously coincide. But without speaking of triangles, one can, in a way, still say the same thing about points, or about ABC ♉ DEF in Figure 2; that is, one can at the same time place A upon D, B upon E, and C upon F without the situation of the three points ABC being changed in relation to each other or that of the three points DEF to each other. (Loemker, p. 251)

Leibniz utterly fails to recognise that the two triangles ABC and DEF are, in fact, not congruent at all. To become so, one of the two triangles, say DEF, has to be rotated, so to speak, through 180° on the axis DE so that the angle EFD is on the left of the axis DE rather than on its right.

The conception of the *qualities* of space underlying the Leibnizian *analysis situs* was manifestly incomplete, and Kant's arguments serve to show as much. It is not so clear that he succeeds in demonstrating the existence of absolute space. Kant suggests that directionality can only be rendered intelligible by appeal to absolute space. He writes: 'The ground of the complete determination of a corporeal form does not depend simply on the relation and position of its parts to each other; it also depends on the reference of that physical form to universal absolute space, as it is conceived by the geometers. This relation to absolute space, however, cannot itself be immediately perceived, though the differences, which exist between bodies and which depend exclusively on this ground alone, can be immediately perceived' (AK 2:381). Kant roots the discrimination of directions in our *sense* of direction, and he grounds the three dimensions of space in our awareness of the asymmetrical character of our physiological structure. Such considerations, however, far from suggesting the absolute existence of space, tend rather to establish its subjective nature. The radical conflict between the explicit intention of the work (establishing the reality of absolute space) and the submerged tendencies of the considerations adduced by Kant (establishing the ideality of space) was peculiarly fruitful, for the resolution of the conflict led to the formulation of the view that space (and thus time) were the *a priori* forms of our sensibility and thus structures of the empirical world of phenomena alone. This view was stated for the first time in the *Inaugural Dissertation.* The importance of *Directions in Space* for an understanding of the development of Kant's views on space and time, and therefore for an understanding of the emergence of the critical philosophy itself, can scarcely be exaggerated.

INAUGURAL DISSERTATION

Kant had been appointed *Privatdozent* in 1755 at the no longer young age of thirty-one, and for a further fifteen years the academic advancement he sought was to elude him. His applications in 1756 and 1758 for the positions, respectively, of *professor extraordinarius* (Knutzen's former position) and *ordinarius* (Kypke's former position) in logic and metaphysics were unsuccessful, in the former case because no appointment was made for reasons of economy and in the latter case because someone more senior, Professor Buck, was appointed. And although he was offered a generously endowed chair at Erlangen in 1769 and a less lucrative chair at Jena early in 1770, Kant declined both invitations, for he had already received assurances from the Königsberg University authorities that a suitable position might soon be available for him. On 15 March 1770, Professor Langhansen, incumbent of the chair of mathematics, died after a long illness. The following day – the almost improper speed of Kant's reaction is indicative of the urgency with which he viewed his position – Kant wrote a letter, dated 16 March 1770 (AK 10:90–2) to the Prussian minister of culture, Freiherr von Fuerst und Kupferberg, suggesting that the vacated chair of mathematics be offered either to Professor Christiani, incumbent of the chair of moral philosophy, or to Professor Buck, incumbent of the chair of logic and metaphysics, and that whichever of the two chairs was thus vacated should be offered to Kant himself. Kant wrote a similar letter, dated 19 March 1770 (AK 10:92–3), to the king of Prussia, Friedrich II, making the same suggestion. The authorities seem to have been persuaded by Kant's arguments, for the vacated chair of mathematics was offered to (and accepted by) Buck, and Kant was appointed to the thus vacated chair of logic and metaphysics – the chair for which he had unsuccessfully applied some twelve years earlier. In accordance with an order in cabinet, the post was formally offered to Kant in a letter from the king, dated 31 March 1770 (AK 10:93–4). Kant was officially installed in his chair at a meeting of the university senate on 2 May 1770.

In accordance with academic tradition, Kant composed a Latin dissertation for public disputation to inaugurate his professorship. The disputation took place on 24 August 1770. It was defended by the twenty-three-year-old Jewish student of medicine and philosophy Marcus Herz, who had attended Kant's lectures, discussed the central themes of the dissertation with Kant, and, having taken up an appointment in Berlin, was to enter into a lengthy correspondence with Kant on medical and philosophical matters. The *Inaugural Dissertation* (1770) was published and distributed by J. J. Kanter of Königsberg, but, as Kant complains in a letter to Herz, dated 7 June 1771 (AK 10:121–4) 'at a rather late stage and in only small numbers and, indeed, without even an announcement in the Autumn Book Fair Catalogue'. Kant adds: 'It annoys me somewhat that this work must so swiftly suffer the fate of all man's efforts, that, namely, of falling into oblivion'. Kant's fears were, however, to prove unduly pessimistic, for the work was reprinted in 1795 (Zeitz, pp. 1–44), translated in 1797 (Voigt, III, 1–63) and reprinted and retranslated in 1799 (Tieftrunk,

II, 435–88 and 488–566). Nor was the work ignored on its publication: It was paraphrased by Herz in 1771 under the title *Betrachtungen aus der speculativen Weltweisheit* ('Reflections drawn from Speculative Philosophy'), and given an important review by Schulz in numbers 94 and 95 of the *Königsbergischen gelehrten und politischen Zeitungen* for 22 and 25 November 1771.

The *Inaugural Dissertation* was probably written between March and August 1770. In an important letter to Lambert dated 2 September 1770 (AK:10 96–9) Kant expresses his dissatisfaction with certain aspects of the work (Sections I and IV are dismissed as 'insignificant', and what Kant regards as the weaknesses of the other sections are attributed to the poor health from which he had been suffering). He was, however, sufficiently satisfied with the work to consider revising it 'by adding a few pages in order to correct the errors which have resulted from the haste with which it was composed and to clarify its meaning' (AK 10:98).

Although written in haste, the *Inaugural Dissertation* was nonetheless the culmination of almost a decade of reflection on the method of metaphysics. The first work in which Kant expressly addresses himself to this problem was the *Inquiry* (1764), which had been completed by the end of 1762. In that work, Kant establishes the negative thesis that the method of metaphysics could not, at least for the foreseeable future, be mathematical in character. Definitions could only be the final product of the analysis of what was *given;* they could not constitute the starting point of metaphysical enquiry.

Very shortly thereafter, Kant seems to have mentioned to J. J. Kanter, the publisher, the possibility of his soon publishing a work to be entitled *The Proper Method of Metaphysics,* for an announcement to that effect had been made in the Autumn Book Fair catalogue for 1765. Lambert mentions it in his letter to Kant, dated 13 November 1765 (AK 10:51–4). But Kant, in his reply, dated 31 December 1765 (AK 10:54–7), explains that he has, for the time being, abandoned the idea. He writes: 'In the process of preparing this work, I came to notice that, although there was no dearth of examples of erroneous judgements illustrating my theses about incorrect procedure, there was a considerable lack of such examples to illustrate the distinctive method of metaphysics *in concreto*'. Nonetheless, Kant makes it plain that he had made significant progress: A link had been established between error and insight in metaphysics and 'the nature of the procedure employed'. More specifically, a method had been discovered for avoiding 'illusion of knowledge' [*das Blendwerk des Wissens*]. Kant does not specify in what the method consists, but his account of 'illusion of knowledge' foreshadows his later concepts of the sure path of a science, transcendental illusion, and the antinomies of metaphysics. Such illusion, he says, 'constantly induces one to suppose that one has arrived at a decision, although one finds oneself just as constantly constrained to retrace one's steps'; furthermore, such illusion is the source of 'the destructive lack of agreement among so-called philosophers, who lack a common standard for harmonising their efforts'.

At this period Kant was working on the *Dreams* (1766). Its theme had preoccupied him since the early 1760s, and its composition was completed by the end of January 1766. Although obliquely concerned with the general problem of the method of metaphysics, it is primarily concerned with an even more fundamental problem: the very possibility of metaphysical knowledge. The issue is approached indirectly by the examination of a very specific metaphysical problem: the possibility and existence of pure spirits, and the nature of their presence in the world. Kant's attention is beginning to focus on the specific issue of the meaning, origin, and validity of metaphysical concepts. The concept of the limits of the human understanding, the distinction between empirical and metaphysical knowledge, the criterion for differentiating between specious and genuine claims to metaphysical cognition, the contrast between sensibility and understanding, are all beginning to assume precise and distinct form.

It is clear from a letter of Kant's to Herder of 9 May 1768 (AK 10:73–4) that the advance to the insights of the *Inaugural Dissertation* was not a smooth one. Kant speaks there in a pessimistic vein 'of feeling no attachment to anything and being profoundly indifferent both to my own ideas and those of others'. It would not be implausible to suggest that further progress was impeded by the lack of the crucial notion of pure intuition or the pure forms of sensible cognition, and that this concept was irresistibly suggested by the inner dynamics of the argument involved in Kant's critique of the Leibnizian concept of the *analysis situs* in *Directions in Space* (1768).

Shortly after its publication, Kant distributed copies of the *Inaugural Dissertation* to Herz, Lambert, Sulzer, and Mendelssohn. Their replies (dated respectively 11 September 1770 [AK:10 99–102], 13 October 1770 [AK 10:103–11], 8 December 1770 [AK 10:111–13] and 25 December 1770 [AK 10:113–17]) are of great philosophical importance. Kant seems not to have replied to Lambert, Sulzer, and Mendelssohn, but his reply to Herz, dated 21 February 1772 (AK 10:120–35) contains a reply to an objection voiced by all three to Kant's theory of time. They objected that because change (at least in our representations) is real, time must be so too. Kant's response was: 'I no more deny that alterations are something real than I deny that bodies are something real, though by that I merely mean that something real corresponds to the appearance'. Kant's reply to this same objection in the *Critique of Pure Reason* (1781/1787) A36–41/B53–58 (AK 3:61–4 / AK 4:39–42) is much more succinctly expressed in terms of the distinction between the empirically real and the transcendentally ideal. Kant's letter to Herz is part of a lengthy and important correspondence between the philosopher and his former student which started in 1770 and continued for over a decade. This exchange of letters is important for the light it throws on the evolution of Kant's thought between 1770 and 1781.

Résumés of the works

NEW ELUCIDATION

Kant's *New Elucidation* (1755) consists of three sections. Section 1, which contains Propositions I–III, rejects the claim that the ultimate principle of all truth is the Law of Contradiction, arguing that affirmative and negative truths require separate principles (What is, is and What is not, is not), which together constitute the Principle of Identity, which takes priority over the Principle of Contradiction. Section 2, which contains Propositions IV–XI, defines the principle of the determining ground (the Principle of Sufficient Reason). Kant distinguishes antecedently and consequentially determining grounds (the former including the ground why, the ground of being, and the ground of becoming; the latter being the ground of knowing). In Proposition V, Kant maintains that nothing is true without a determining ground. In Proposition VI, he attacks the idea that a being can contain the ground of its own being within itself, criticising the Cartesian version of the ontological proof of God's existence (though not on the grounds that existence is not a predicate), and he offers in Proposition VII a proof of God's existence from the possibility both of God Himself and of all other things. All beings which exist contingently (that is to say, all beings apart from God) must have an antecedently determining ground of existence (Proposition VIII). Proposition IX discusses Crusius's objection that the thesis just maintained involves fatalism; Kant's reply consists in a compatibilist defence of freedom. Propositions X and XI, respectively, state the genuine and the spurious corollaries of the principle stated in Proposition VIII, and include an attack on the Leibnizian principle of the Identity of Indiscernibles. Section 3, which contains Propositions XII and XIII, presents a statement of the Principle of Succession (substances are capable of change only in so far as they are dynamically and reciprocally related to one another, from which a proof of the existence of the external world is derived), and of the Principle of Co-existence (such a dynamic and reciprocal relation does not arise from the mere existence of substances alone but is possible only through the common principle of their being, the Divine Intellect, thinking them in a systematic and dynamic schema; from this a proof of the existence of God is derived).

PHYSICAL MONADOLOGY

Kant's *Physical Monadology* (1756) consists of two sections. Section 1, containing Propositions I–VIII, argues the compatibility of two seemingly inconsistent theses: the infinite divisibility of space and the simplicity (or indivisibility) of physical monads (atoms) in space. Kant maintains that monads are not intrinsically spatial but that they occupy space by virtue of an activity (that of attracting and repelling). Both the spatial magnitude and the mass of monads are functions of the forces of repulsion and attraction, which are intrinsic to monads. Space itself is not a substance but an appearance of the external relation of substances. Proposition VIII contains a dynamic account of impenetrability. Section 2, containing Propositions IX–XIII, is less philosophical in character. Proposition IX, touching on the disputed notion of action at a distance through empty space, attempts to clarify the issue by offering a definition of 'touching'; Proposition X maintains that the limits of the extension of a body are a function of both the force of attraction and that of repulsion. Propositions XI and XII touch on the issue of the possibility of the vacuum, and Kant argues that the differing specific density of the simple elements can constitute sometimes less and sometimes more mass. Proposition XIII maintains, on the basis of the dynamic atomic theory, that the elements are 'elastic'.

OPTIMISM

In *Optimism* (1759), Kant defends Leibniz's thesis that God, in creating this world, chose the best or most perfect (or the most real) of all possible worlds. Kant replies to two objections: The first objection maintains that the concept of the most perfect (or most real) world is as incoherent as that of the greatest number; Kant replies that the notion of a perfect world involves a limit, for without such a limit the distinction between the essentially finite world and the essentially infinite God (the sum total of all possible perfections or realities) would be destroyed. The second objection asserts that there could be a plurality of equally perfect worlds, no one of which could be described as the *most* perfect world; Kant replies that distinct and thus different worlds can only differ in respect of degrees of perfection or reality; if they did not, they would be the *same* world. Kant underpins these two theses by arguing that the very notion of divine choice involves the notion of choosing the best or the most perfect. The concept of a world created by an omniscient, omnipotent, and benevolent God necessarily involves the concept of its being the most real and most perfect and thus the best of all possible worlds.

FALSE SUBTLETY

Kant's *False Subtlety* (1762) consists of six sections: Section 1 defines the concepts of judgement and syllogism; Section 2 specifies the rules governing affirmative and negative syllogisms; Section 3 distinguishes pure and mixed syllogisms; Section 4 argues the thesis that only syllogisms in the first figure are pure syllogisms; Section 5 maintains that, whereas syllogisms in the remaining three figures may be valid, they are superfluous and contrary to the ideal of logic, simplicity; Section 6 (philosophically the most substantial) denies (1) that concepts are logically prior to judgements (on the contrary, judgements actualise distinct concepts while syllogisms actualise complete concepts); (2) that understanding and reason are distinct faculties (on the contrary, they are both derived from the faculty of judgement); (3) that animals are capable of distinct concepts (on the contrary, lacking the higher faculties of cognition, they can at best physically differentiate; they cannot logically distinguish). Kant concludes by asserting that there are two ultimate principles of human cognition: the law of identity and the law of contradiction (the central thesis of the *New Elucidation* [1755]).

THE ONLY POSSIBLE ARGUMENT

The Only Possible Argument (1763) consists of a Preface (in which the distinction between a formal demonstration and an argument is drawn) and three unequally long sections. Section 1 contains a statement of the *a priori* argument for the existence of a necessary being, the sum total of all positive realities, from the internal possibility of all things. This Being is unique, simple, immutable, eternal, endowed with understanding and will, and divine. Kant's argument rests on the denial that existence is a real predicate and on the assertion that possibility presupposes existence. Section 2 presents an *a posteriori* argument for the existence of a single principle of all possibility from the unity of space, the simplicity and necessity of the laws of nature, and the perfect harmoniousness of nature as a whole. Kant criticises traditional versions of the physico-theological argument (for attempting to explain too many phenomena in terms of their direct dependency on the choice of God) and offers a revised version of that argument (which eliminates the need for direct divine intervention). This long and discursive section contains a wealth of illustrative material from the fields of geology, meteorology, and astronomy (it also contains a lengthy résumé of the thesis of the *Universal Natural History* [1755]). The extremely brief Section 3, having distinguished four types of proofs of the existence of God, rejects the Cartesian ontological proof from the perfection of God and the Leibnizian argument from the contingency of the world as not proofs at all; the revised physico-theological argument, while acknowledged as powerfully persuasive, is rejected for its lack of rigour. Only the *a priori* argument from the internal possibility of things is allowed to have apodeictic force.

NEGATIVE MAGNITUDES

Kant's *Negative Magnitudes* (1763) consists of a Preface (on the use of mathematics in philosophy) and three sections. Section 1 contrasts logical opposition (contradiction) and real opposition (conflict of forces), and then introduces the concept of negative magnitude, illustrating its use by largely mathematical examples. An important distinction between nothing at all (*nihil negativum*), which results from logical opposition, deprivation (*nihil privativum*), which results from the conflict of forces, and lack (*absentia*), which results from the absence of forces, is made at the end of this section. Section 2 adduces simple examples of deprivations, resulting from the conflict of forces, and contains a discussion of phenomena such as rest, coldness, vice, and omissions of actions. Section 3 applies the concept of negative magnitude to certain problems of psychology (the coming-to-be and the passing-away of thoughts), of physics (the calculation of the sum of positive realities in the world, which is alleged to be constant), and of forces, negative and positive (which is alleged to yield zero). The concluding 'General Remark' emphasises the contrast between the logical grounds of knowing and the real grounds of existence, particularly with reference to the difference between the deductive relation of logic and the causal relation of natural science. The mysteriousness of causality is highlighted.

INQUIRY

Kant's *Inquiry* (1764) consists of four reflections, of which the first two contrast the method of mathematics with that, respectively, of philosophy in general (First Reflection) and of metaphysics in particular (Second Reflection). The certainty and reliability of mathematical method is the product of the following factors: (1) Its object (magnitude) is unique. (2) It presupposes only a few unanalysable concepts or indemonstrable propositions. (3) Its specific objects are not given but *created* definitions, which thus constitute its foundation; they are synthetic and real (not nominal); they are also, and are known to be, distinct and complete. (4) The signs it employs display the universal *in concreto*. None of this is true of philosophy (or, *a fortiori*, of metaphysics): Its objects are numerous and diverse; they are obscurely given and not created by definition; its foundation must therefore be what is given and what can be immediately established with certainty about the given; definitions may not, therefore, constitute its foundation, but only and at best its ultimate objective. Such definitions will be products of analysis and hence neither synthetic nor real (only nominal); their distinctness and completeness will be difficult to establish; the signs they employ (words) can only display the universal *in abstracto;* thus they are liable to generate obscurity, ambiguity, and error. The Third Reflection concludes from these considerations that metaphysical certainty, though the same in kind as geometrical certainty, is vastly more difficult to attain and establish. The Fourth Reflection asserts that natural theology, by virtue of the uniqueness of its object (God), is capable of the greatest certainty; such certainty, though in principle possible for ethics, is, at its present stage of development, beyond its reach.

ANNOUNCEMENT

Kant's *Announcement* (1765) is prefaced by some general remarks on a central and unavoidable problem of all education: the inevitable disparity between teacher and student. Education must always be adapted to the learner's level of maturity. Its aim must, therefore, be to develop first the understanding and the capacity to think independently and then the capacity to reason; only then should education turn to scholarship and the acquisition of learning. As for the teaching of philosophy, its method must be that of enquiry, and its objective the imparting not of philosophical knowledge (which does not exist) but of the capacity to philosophise. The rest of this short essay contains an account of the content of Kant's proposed courses on metaphysics, logic, ethics, and geography, by which we are given an insight into his understanding of the nature of these branches of enquiry.

DREAMS

Kant's *Dreams* (1766) consists of two parts, one dogmatic and the other historical. Part I contains four chapters, of which the first two are analytic and the second two diagnostic. Chapter 1 contains an analysis of the concept of spirit (it is asserted to be a simple, immaterial, and rational substance, occupying space by virtue of its activity but not filling space, for it offers no resistance to material bodies). The chapter concludes with a discussion of the sense in which the human soul, if it is a spirit as thus defined, has a place in the material world. Chapter 2 contains an analysis of the concept of a spirit world consisting of immaterial substances contingently connected with (and thus animating) material substances. The chapter concludes with a discussion of the sense in which spirits might communicate with human beings and with an explanation of why such a phenomenon would be rare. Chapter 3 offers a diagnosis of the visions which might arise from such spirit communications in terms of the derangement of the mechanism of transposition operative in ordinary perception, dreaming, and day-dreaming. Chapter 4 offers a diagnosis of belief in spirits in terms of the mind's natural bias in favour of a future existence. The chapter concludes with a warning: Spirits are not possible objects of knowledge.

Part II contains three chapters, of which the first two are historical and the third philosophical. Chapter 1 contains three stories illustrating Swedenborg's alleged paranormal powers. Chapter 2 contains an account of Swedenborg's visions as they are described in his *Arcana coelestia*, which Kant dismisses as a farrago of nonsense. The chapter ends on a serious philosophical note: The attempt to answer the question about the nature, possibility, and reality of spirits has failed; it has, however, *displayed* the limits of human knowledge. Chapter 3 develops this idea: There are two such limits: (1) that which is fundamental within the empirical world (for example, the fundamental forces of gravitation and causality): such may be *known* but cannot be *understood;* (2) that which transcends the empirical world (for example, pure spirits): Such can neither be known nor understood. Such metaphysical knowledge is not only in principle impossible, it is unnecessary; knowledge of spirit beings is, contrary to popular belief, not even necessary to the moral life.

DIRECTIONS IN SPACE

Kant's *Directions in Space* (1768) contains a short but devastating critique of the Leibnizian view of space as nothing but a system of relations, and of his projected *analysis situs.* The relational view of space implies and the *analysis situs* presupposes that the complete description of the spatiality of a figure would involve the specification of two factors only: magnitude and form (Leibniz defines congruency in terms of equality of size and similarity in form); Kant argues that a third factor, *directionality,* would be necessary. Kant's purpose in this essay is to establish the real and independent existence of absolute physical space. Absolute space cannot itself be immediately perceived (it is not a possible object of perception, although it is the ground of the possibility of outer sensation); its existence can only be *mediately* known through our apprehension of *direction* (above-below, in front-behind, right-left). Directionality is rooted in our physiological structure and is the ground of the three-dimensionality of space. According to Kant, it involves and is ultimately constituted by relatedness to absolute space. Directionality is the fundamental mode of our spatial experience and is the ground of the possibility of familiar activities such as reading a text, interpreting a map, and distinguishing species of plants and animals. More importantly (and devastatingly for Leibniz), directionality (or 'relatedness to absolute space') can alone explain that 'inner difference' which prevents two bodies which are equal in size and similar in form from being congruent. The existence of incongruent counterparts is taken by Kant to prove the existence of absolute physical space.

INAUGURAL DISSERTATION

The *Inaugural Dissertation* (1770) consists of five sections. Section 1 (§§1–2) defines the concept of a world ('a whole which is not a part') and other related notions (analysis and synthesis). The concept of a world involves three factors: matter (substances), form (dynamic interaction between substances), and entirety (absolute completeness). Section 2 (§§3–12) distinguishes the faculties of sensibility and understanding and their respective objects: the sensible (phenomena) and the intelligible (noumena). Sensibility involves intuitions, which are immediate and singular; understanding involves concepts, which are discursive and general; neither can be reduced to the other, their difference being one of origin, not of logical form. Section 3 (§§13–15) specifies the two principles of the form of the sensible world, time and space. Kant asserts of each that: (1) it is not derived from but presupposed by experience; (2) it is a singular representation; (3) it is a pure sensitive intuition; (4) it is not 'objective and real' but 'subjective and ideal'; (5) it is, nonetheless, 'in the highest degree true'; and (6) its parts presuppose the whole. Section 4 (§§16–22) specifies the principle of the form of the intelligible world, reciprocity between substances. Such dynamic interaction between substances is explicable neither in terms of their mere subsistence nor in terms of their being in space, but only in terms of their dependence on the single common principle of their being. Section 5 (§§23–30) discusses an aspect of the method of metaphysics, its illicit employment of certain subreptic axioms which result from the assumption that the subjective principles of the sensitive cognition of phenomena are also the objective principles of the intellectual cognition of noumena. Three classes of such subreptic axioms are distinguished. Kant also discusses certain related principles which the understanding cannot avoid employing if it is to judge at all, but which cannot be objectively validated. Such principles of harmony include the principle of natural causality and the principle of parsimony.

A new elucidation of the first principles of metaphysical cognition (1755)

Principiorum primorum cognitionis metaphysicae
nova dilucidatio (MDCCLV)

PRINCIPIORUM PRIMORUM COGNITIONIS METAPHYSICAE

NOVA DILUCIDATIO,

QUAM

CONSENSU AMPLISSIMAE FACULTATIS PHILOSOPHICAE

DISSERTATIONE PUBLICA

IN AUDITORIO PHIL. DIE 27. SEPTEMBR. HORIS VIII—XII

HABENDA

PRO RECEPTIONE IN EANDEM

DEFENDET

M. IMMANUEL KANT, REGIOM.

RESPONDENTE

CHRISTOPHORO ABRAHAMO BORCHARD, HEILIGENB. BOR.

S. S. THEOL. CULTORE,

OPPONENTIBUS

IOHANNE GODOFREDO MÖLLER, REGIOM.

S. S. THEOL. STUD.,

FRIDERICO HENRICO SAMUELE LYSIO, REGIOM.

I. U. C.

ET

IOHANNE REINHOLDO GRUBE, REGIOM.

I. U. C.

ANNO MDCCLV.

A new elucidation
of the first principles
# of metaphysical cognition

which
with the agreement of the most
distinguished faculty of philosophy,
is to be defended in public disputation
for admission to that faculty
by
M. Immanuel Kant
of Königsberg,
in the philosophical auditorium
on the 27th day of September
between the hours of 8 and 12.
Christoph Abraham Borchard
of Heiligenbeil in Prussia
candidate in sacred theology
will reply to the opponents
Johann Gottfried Möller
of Königsberg,
student of sacred theology;
Friedrich Heinrich Samuel Lysius
of Königsberg,
candidate in ecclesiastical and civil law;
and
Johann Reinhold Grube
of Königsberg,
candidate in ecclesiastical and civil law
in the year 1755[1]

I am about to throw some light, I hope, on the first principles of our cognition, and to expound in as few pages as possible the product of my reflection on the subject. I have thus carefully avoided extensive digressions and only laid bare the muscles and joints of my argument, having put aside all charm and grace of language, like a discarded garment. If I shall anywhere in this undertaking have considered it my duty to dissent from the opinions of celebrated men, and even on occasion to mention them by name, I am so well persuaded of their fair-mindedness that I am confident that my dissent will in no wise detract from the honour which their merits deserve, or that they will in any way resent my criticism. When opinions diverge, each is fully entitled to his own view. Nor is it forbidden to criticise the arguments of others in a modest and balanced fashion, provided that the criticism is free from bitterness and contentiousness. Nor have I ever noticed that impartial judges have deemed such criticism to be contrary to the requirements of either politeness or respect.

Accordingly, I shall, in the first place, attempt to weigh on the scales of a more carefully conducted enquiry the things which are asserted, usually with more confidence than truth, concerning the supreme and undoubted primacy of the principle of contradiction over all truths. I shall then attempt briefly to explain what ought more correctly to be maintained on this head. I shall therupon adduce, in what concerns the law of sufficient reason, whatever may serve to improve both an understanding and the proof of that principle. At the same time, I shall cite the difficulties which seem to beset it, replying to them with all the force of argument at the disposal of my modest mind. Finally, I shall take one further substantial step and establish two new principles of metaphysical cognition which are, it seems at least to me, of an importance which is not to be despised. They are not, it is true, fundamental principles, nor are they the simplest principles. But they are, for that reason, even better adapted for use, and they certainly have as wide an application as any other principles. In an endeavour such as this, one may, in advancing along an untrodden path, very easily fall into error. This being the case, I am convinced that the benevolent and impartial reader will view everything in the most favourable light.

^a *ratio* (alt: plan).

5

Section 1. Concerning the principle of contradiction

WARNING: Since I am particularly concerned to be brief in this treatise, I think it better here not to copy out afresh the definitions and axioms which are firmly established in ordinary knowledge[b] and which are consonant with right reason.[c] Nor do I think it a good idea to follow the example, by imitating their practice, of those who, slavishly bound by I know not what method, only deem themselves to have proceeded in a rational fashion if they have scrutinised from beginning to end whatever they find on the bookshelves of philosophers. I have thought it good to warn the reader of this in advance, lest he take for a fault that which I have done deliberately.

Proposition I. There is no UNIQUE, absolutely first, universal[d]
principle of all truths.[2]

A first and truly unique principle must necessarily be a simple proposition; if it covertly embraced a number of propositions it would merely present the deceptive semblance[e] of a unique principle. If, therefore, a proposition is truly simple, it must be either affirmative or negative. But I maintain that if it is one or the other, it cannot be universal and subsume under itself all truths whatever. For, if you say that it is *affirmative,* it cannot be the absolutely first principle of all negative truths; and if you say that it is *negative* it cannot take command of the positive truths.

Let us suppose, namely, that the proposition is negative. Who is there who does not see that, since the logical derivation of all truths from their principles is either direct or indirect, it is not possible, firstly, to deduce anything from a negative principle by the *direct* method of inference except negative conclusions? If you then go on to insist that affirmative propositions flow from that negative principle *indirectly,* then you will acknowledge that this can only happen by means of the following proposition: *everything of which the opposite is false, is true.* This proposition, since it is itself affirmative, cannot derive from the negative principle by the direct method of argument; still less can it follow indirectly, for it would then be

[b] *pervulgata cognitione.*   [c] *rectae rationi.*   [d] *catholicon.*   [e] *speciem.*

supported by itself. Hence, it will not follow by any method of argument whatever from a negatively formulated principle. Since, therefore, it is not possible for affirmative propositions to issue from a unique and single negative principle, this principle cannot be called *universal*. Likewise, if you set up as your cardinal principle an affirmative proposition, negative propositions will certainly not follow directly from it; but if they are to follow indirectly the following proposition will be necessary: *everything of which the opposite is true, is itself false*. In other words, everything of which the opposite is affirmed, is itself negated. Since this proposition is negative there is, once more, no way in which it can be deduced from an affirmative principle either directly, which is self-evident, or indirectly, unless it presupposes itself. In whatever manner, therefore, you resolve the matter with yourself, you will not reject the proposition which I asserted at the beginning: that there cannot be a unique, ultimate, universal principle of all truths whatever.

1:389

> *Proposition II. There are two absolutely first principles of all truths.*
> *One of them is the principle of affirmative truths, namely the*
> *proposition: whatever is, is; the other is the principle of negative*
> *truths, namely the proposition: whatever is not, is not. These two*
> *principles taken together are commonly called the principle of identity.*[3]

Once more I appeal to the two kinds of method of demonstrating truths, namely the direct and the indirect. The first method of inference arrives at the truth by appealing to the agreement[f] of the concepts of the subject and the predicate. It always has as its foundation this rule: whenever a subject, whether it be viewed in itself or in its connection with other things,[g] either posits those things which embrace the concept of the predicate, or excludes those things which are excluded by the concept of the predicate, it must be concluded that the predicate belongs to the subject. To express the same thing a little more clearly: whenever an identity between the concepts of the subject and the predicate is discovered, the proposition is true. Expressed in the most general terms, as is befitting a first principle, the principle runs: *whatever is, is, and whatever is not, is not*. Accordingly, the principle of identity certainly governs every direct method of argumentation; it is, therefore, the first principle.[h]

If you enquire about the indirect method of inference, you will in the end discover that it is founded on the same twin principle. For appeal is always made to these two propositions: (1) everything of which the oppo-

[f] *convenientia.* [g] *vel in se vel in nexu.*

[h] *q.e. primum* / Bock (hereafter B): *was das erste war* / Carabellese (Assunto) (hereafter C): *che è il primo principio* / England (hereafter E): that is to say, it is a first principle / Ferrari (hereafter F): *qui est le principe premier* / Reuscher (hereafter R): and this makes it a first principle.

7

site is false is true; that is to say: everything of which the opposite is negated must be asserted; (2) everything of which the opposite is true is false. From the first of these two propositions affirmative propositions follow, and from the second there follow negative propositions. If you express the first proposition in the simplest terms you will have: *whatever is not not, is* (for the opposite is expressed by the little word[i] '*not*', and its cancellation[j] is likewise expressed by the little word '*not*'). You will formulate the second proposition in the following manner: *whatever is not, is not* (for here again the expression of the opposite is effected by the little word '*not*', and the expression of its falsity or cancellation is similarly effected by the same little word). Now if, as the law of signs[k] demands, you examine the sense of the signs contained in the first proposition, then, since the one little word 'not' indicates that the other is to be cancelled,[l] when both have been eliminated you will end up with the proposition: *whatever is, is.* Since, however, the second proposition runs: *whatever is not, is not,* it is clear that even in indirect proof the twin principle of identity is supreme. It is, as a result, the ultimate foundation of all cognition whatever.

SCHOLIUM. Here we have a sample – a trifling one, it is true, but not one which is wholly to be despised – of the art of combining signs,[m]4 for the simplest terms, which we have employed in elucidating these principles, scarcely differ from signs at all. I shall take this opportunity to express my opinion of this art. After Leibniz had advertised the merits of his discovery,[n] men of learning all complained that it had been buried along with the great man himself. I confess that the great man's pronouncements on the matter put me in mind of the will of the father in one

1:390 of Aesop's fables.5 On the very point of dying, he revealed to his children that he had hidden a treasure somewhere in his field, but before he could indicate the place he suddenly expired. This induced the sons assiduously to turn up the field and work it over by digging it up, until, their hopes disappointed, they nonetheless found themselves certainly enriched by the fertility of their field. I suspect, at any rate, that this will be the only fruit, to be sure, which an examination of that celebrated art will yield, should there be anyone prepared to devote themselves to the execution of this task. But, if I may be permitted to say plainly what the situation is, I fear that the suspicion, somewhere expressed by the penetrating Boerhaave in his *Chemistry*6 concerning the most celebrated practitioners of the art of alchemy, may have been the fate of that imcomparable man. Boerhaave, namely, suspects that the alchemists, having solved many remarkable mysteries, eventually came to suppose that there would no longer be anything which was not in their power, provided only that they put their hands to it. By a certain precipitate anticipation, they talked

---

[i] *per particulam.* [j] *remotio.* [k] *lege characteristica.* [l] *tollendam.*
[m] *in arte characteristica combinatoria.* [n] *inventam venditabat.*

of those things as achieved which they inferred might, indeed, *must* happen provided only that they addressed their minds to the realisation of these things.7 For my own part, I do not deny that, once one has arrived at absolutely first principles, a certain use of the art of signs may be legitimate, for one has the opportunity there of employing the concepts and consequently the simplest terms, as well, as signs. However, when compound cognition is to be expressed by means of signs, all the mind's perspicacity finds itself suddenly stranded, so to speak, on a reef, and impeded by difficulties from which it is unable to extricate itself. I even find that one philosopher of great renown, the celebrated Daries, has attempted to elucidate the principle of contradiction by means of signs, representing the affirmative concept by the sign '$+A$' and the negative concept by the sign '$-A$', which yields the equation '$+A - A = 0$'.8 In other words, affirming and negating the same thing is impossible or nothing. With all due respect to the great man, I would nonetheless say that I detect an indubitable begging of the question in this attempt. For if you invest the sign of the negative concept with the power of cancelling the affirmative concept, when the former is combined with the latter, you are obviously presupposing the principle of contradiction, which maintains that concepts which are the opposite of each other reciprocally cancel out each other. However, our explanation of the proposition *everything of which the opposite is false is true,* is free from this defect. For since, when expressed in the simplest terms, it runs as follows: *everything which is not not, is,* it follows that by removing the little word '*not*' we do nothing other than follow up their simple meaning. The result is inevitably the principle of identity: *everything which is, is.*

Proposition III. To establish more securely the priority of the principle of identity over the principle of contradiction as the supreme principle in the hierarchy of truths.°

The proposition which arrogates to itself the title of the absolutely supreme and most general principle of all truths must be formulated, firstly, in the simplest terms, and, secondly, in the most general terms. It seems to me beyond doubt that the twin principle of identity satisfies these two conditions. For of all affirmative terms the simplest is the little expression '*is*', and of all negative terms the simplest is the little expression '*is not*'. And then there is nothing which can be conceived which is more universal than the simplest concepts. The reason for this is that the concepts which are more complex*ᵖ* borrow their light from those which are simple; and since the complex concepts are more determinate than the simple concepts, it follows that the former cannot be as general as the latter.

The principle of contradiction, which is expressed by the proposition: *it*   1:391

° in veritatum subordinatione.   *ᵖ magis compositae.*

9

is impossible that the same thing should simultaneously be and not be, is in fact nothing but the definition of the *impossible.* For everything which contradicts itself, that is to say, everything which is thought of as simultaneously being and not being, is called impossible. But in what way is it possible to establish that all truths ought to be referred to this definition as to a touchstone?[9] For it is neither necessary that every truth be guaranteed by the impossibility of its opposite, nor, if the truth be told, is it in itself sufficient, either. For the transition from the impossibility of its opposite to the assertion of its truth can only be effected by means of the maxim: *Everything, of which the opposite is false, is true.* And thus, as we have already shown above, this proposition shares power with the principle of contradiction.

Finally, to confer in the realms of truths the highest rank of all on a negative proposition in particular, and to hail it as the head and foundation of all things, will surely strike everyone[10] as rather harsh and, indeed, as considerably worse even than a paradox, for it is not clear why a negative truth should be invested with this authority in preference to an affirmative truth.

SCHOLIUM. This investigation may, perhaps, appear to some as subtle and elaborate, and even as superfluous and lacking in all utility. And if you are thinking of its fruitfulness in generating corollaries,[q] you have my agreement. For the mind, even if it is not instructed as to the existence of such a principle, cannot but employ it everywhere, doing so spontaneously and in virtue of a certain necessity of its nature. But is it not for that reason the case that tracing the chain of truths to its final link is a subject which deserves to be investigated? And certainly an investigation such as this, which enquires more deeply into the law which governs the reasoning of our mind, is not to be despised. For to mention just one point: since all our reasoning amounts to uncovering the identity between the predicate and the subject, either in itself or in relation to other things, as is apparent from the ultimate rule of truths, it can be seen that God has no need of reasoning,[r] for, since all things are exposed in the clearest possible way to his gaze, it is the same act of representation which presents to his understanding the things which are in agreement and those which are not. Nor does God need the analysis which is made necessary for us by the night which darkens our intelligence.

[q] *corollariorum fecunditatem.*   [r] *ratiocinatione.*

Section 2. *Concerning the principle of the determining ground, commonly called the principle of the sufficient ground*

DEFINITION

Proposition IV. To determine is to posit^s a predicate while excluding its opposite.

That which determines a subject in respect of any of its predicates, is called the *ground.^t Grounds* may be differentiated into those which are antecedently^u determining and those which are consequentially^v determin- 1:392
ing. An *antecedently* determining ground is one, the concept of which precedes that which is determined. That is to say, an antecedently determining ground is one, in the absence of which that which is determined would not be intelligible.* A *consequentially* determining ground is one which would not be posited unless the concept which is determined by it had not already been posited from some other source. You can also call the former the reason *why*, or the ground of being or becoming,^w while the latter can be called the ground *that*, or the ground of knowing.^x

Proof^y of the reality of our definition.   The concept of a ground, as it is commonly understood, establishes a connection and a conjunction^z between the subject and some predicate or other. A ground thus always

---

* It is legitimate to include in this the *identical* ground, where the concept of the subject determines the predicate by means of its own complete identity with the predicate. Take for example: a triangle has three sides. Here, the concept of that which is determined neither follows nor precedes the determining concept.

^s *ponere.*
^t *ratio* / B: *Grund* / C: *ragione (ratio)* / E: reason / F: *raison* / R: reason (*ratio*) / (cf. Glossary).
^u *antecedenter* / B: *vorgängig* / C: *antecedentemente* / E: *antecedenter* / F: *anterieurment* / R: antecedently.
^v *consequenter* / B: *nachträglich* / C: *consequente* / E: *consequenter* / F: *posterieurment* / R: consequently (*consequenter*).
^w *rationem cur s. rationem essendi vel fiendi.*   ^x *rationem quod s. cognoscendi.*   ^y *Adstructio.*
^z *nexum . . . et colligationem.*

11

requires a subject; and it also requires a predicate, which it can unite with the subject. If you ask for the ground of a circle I shall not at all understand what you are asking for unless you add a predicate, for example, that it is, of all the figures which have a perimeter of the same length,[a] the one which embraces the greatest area. For example, suppose we seek for the ground of all evils in the world. We thus have the proposition: the world contains a number of evils. What is being sought is not the ground *that*, in other words, not the ground of knowing, for experience takes its place. What has to be specified is the ground *why*, that is to say, the ground of becoming. In other words, the ground which has to be specified is the ground, the positing of which renders intelligible the fact that the world is not antecedently indeterminate in respect of this predicate. By contrast, once the ground is posited, the predicate of evils is posited to the exclusion of its opposite.[b] A ground, therefore, converts things which are indeterminate into things which are determinate.[c] And since all truth is generated by the determination of a predicate in a subject, it follows that the determining ground is not only the criterion of truth; it is also its source. And if one abandoned it, one would indeed discover a great deal which was possible, but nothing at all which was true. Thus, it is indeterminate for us whether the planet Mercury revolves on its axis, or not, for we lack a ground which would posit one of the two predicates to the exclusion of its opposite. Each of the two predicates remains possible, neither being established as true in respect of our knowledge.

In order to illustrate the difference between *antecedently* and *consequentially* determining grounds, I shall take as an example the eclipses of the satellites of Jupiter. I maintain that they furnish *the ground of knowing* that light is propagated successively and with a specifiable[d] velocity. But this ground determines this truth only consequentially. For if Jupiter had no satellites at all, or if no occultation were produced by their successive revolutions, light would, nonetheless, still move in time in exactly the same way, although this might not, perhaps, be known to us. Or, to rely more heavily on the given definition: the phenomena of the satellites of Jupiter, which demonstrate the successive motion of light, presupposes precisely that very property[e] of light, without which these phenomena could not occur in the way in which they do occur. It follows, therefore, that they determine this truth only consequentially. However, the ground of becoming, that is to say, the ground why the motion of light involves a specifiable expenditure of time is to be found (if you adopt the view of Descartes)[11] in the elasticity of the elastic globules of the atmosphere. According to the laws governing elasticity, these elastic globules of the atmosphere yield a little to impact: when the moments of time taken up by

1:393

[a] *isoperimetrarum.* [b] *praedicatum malorum ponitur cum exclusione oppositi.*
[c] *ex indeterminatis efficit determinata.* [d] *assignabili.* [e] *ingenium.*

each globule to absorb and transmit the impact are added together throughout the enormously long and connected series they eventually yield a perceptible lapse of time. This would be a ground which determines antecedently. In other words, it would be a ground such that, were it not posited, that which was determinate would not occur at all. For if the globules of the atmosphere were perfectly hard, no interval of time would be perceived between the emission and the arrival of the light, no matter how immense the distance traversed.

Since the definition offered by the celebrated Wolff[12] suffers from a notable defect, it seemed to me to require correction here. For he defines a ground in terms of that by reference to which it is possible to understand why something should rather be than not be. And in this he certainly conflates the thing defined with its own definition.[f] For although the little expression *why* may seem sufficiently adapted to common sense to be deemed capable of inclusion in a definition,[g] it, nonetheless, in its turn, tacitly involves the concept of a ground. For if you correctly examine the term, you will find that it means the same as *for which ground*. Thus, once the substitution has been duly made, Wolff's definition runs: a ground is that by reference to which it is possible to understand *for which ground* something should be rather than not be.

Likewise, I thought it better to replace the locution '*sufficient ground*' by the expression '*determining ground*'. And, in making this substitution, I have the support of the celebrated Crusius.[13] For, as he makes abundantly plain, the expression '*sufficient*' is ambiguous, for it is not immediately clear how much is sufficient. Since, however, to determine is to posit in such a way that every opposite is excluded, the term 'determine' designates that which is certainly sufficient to conceive the thing in such and such a way, and in no other.

Proposition V. Nothing is true without a determining ground.

Every true proposition indicates that the subject is determinate in respect of a predicate. That is to say, the predicate is posited to the exclusion of its opposite. Thus, in every true proposition it is necessary that the opposite of the predicate in question should be excluded. However, a predicate is excluded if it is incompatible with another concept which has already been posited, and it is excluded in virtue of the principle of contradiction. Therefore, no exclusion occurs if no concept is present which conflicts with the opposite which is to be excluded. Accordingly, there is something in every truth which determines the truth of the proposition by excluding the opposite predicate. Since this is what is called the determining

---

[f] *definitum immiscuit definitionis.*

[g] *satis videatur communi intelligentiae accommodata, ut in definitione sumi posse censenda.*

13

ground, it is established that nothing is true without a determining ground.

The same argument differently expressed.   From the concept of a ground it is possible to understand which of the opposed predicates is to be ascribed to the subject and which is to be denied. Suppose that something were true without a determining ground: there would be nothing from which it would be apparent which of the two opposed predicates was to be ascribed to the subject, and which of the two was to be denied of it. Thus, neither 1:394 would be excluded, and the subject would be indeterminate in respect of each of the predicates. Hence, there would be no room for truth. But, since it was assumed that the thing was true, a manifest contradiction is apparent.

SCHOLIUM. It has been established by the common opinion of all mortals that knowledge of the truth is always based upon an intuition of the ground.[h] However, when we are only concerned with certainty, we very frequently rest satisfied with a consequentially determining ground. But if one takes the theorem adduced above along with the definition and considers them together, it can easily be seen that there is always an antecedently determining ground, or if you prefer, a genetic or at least an identical ground; for, of course, a consequentially determining ground does not bring the truth into being; it only explains it. But let us proceed to the grounds which determine *existence.*

Proposition VI. To say that something has the ground of its existence within itself is absurd.

For whatever contains within itself the ground of the existence of something is the cause of that thing. Suppose, therefore, that there is something which has within itself the ground of its own existence, then it will be the cause of itself. Since, however, the concept of a cause is by nature prior to the concept of that which is caused, the latter being later than the former, it would follow that the same thing would be simultaneously both earlier and later than itself, which is absurd.

COROLLARY. If anything, therefore, is said to exist absolutely necessarily, that thing does not exist because of some ground; it exists because the opposite cannot be thought at all. This impossibility of the opposite is the ground of the knowledge of existence, but an antecedently determining ground is completely absent. *It exists;* and in respect of the thing in question, to have said and to have conceived this of it is sufficient.

SCHOLIUM. I find, indeed, the view repeatedly expressed in the teach-

[h] *rationis semper intuitu niti.*

14

ings of modern philosophers[14] that God has the ground of His existence posited in Himself. For my part, I find myself unable to support this view. To these good men it seems, namely, somehow rather hard to deny that God, the ultimate and most complete principle both of grounds and of causes, should contain within Himself the ground of Himself. Thus they maintain that, since one may not assert that there is a ground of God which is external to Him, it follows that He contains concealed within Himself the ground of Himself. But there could scarcely be anything more remote from sound reason than this. For when, in a chain of grounds, one has arrived at the beginning, it is self-evident that one comes to a stop and that the questioning is brought to an end by the completeness of the answer. Of course, I know that appeal is made to the concept itself of God; and the claim is made that the existence of God is determined by that concept. It can, however, easily be seen that this happens ideally, not really.[i] Form for yourself the concept of some being or other in which there is a totality of reality.[j] It must be conceded that, given this concept, existence also has to be attributed to this being. And, accordingly, the argument proceeds as follows: if all realities, without distinction of degree,[k] are united together in a certain being, then that being exists. But if all those realities are only conceived as united together, then the existence of that being is also only an existence in ideas.[l] The view we are discussing ought, therefore, rather to be formulated as follows: in framing the concept of a certain Being, which we call God, we have determined that concept in such a fashion that existence is included in it. If, then, the concept which we have conceived in advance[m] is true, then it is also true that God exists. I have said these things, indeed, for the sake of those who support the Cartesian argument.[15]

1:395

Proposition VII. There is a Being, the existence of which is prior to[n] the very possibility both of Itself and of all things. This Being is, therefore, said to exist absolutely necessarily. This Being is called God.[16]

Possibility is only definable in terms of there not being a conflict[o] between certain combined concepts; thus the concept of possibility is the product of a comparison.[p] But in every comparison the things which are to be compared[q] must be available for comparison, and where nothing at all is given there is no room for either comparison or, corresponding to it, for the concept of possibility. This being the case, it follows that nothing can be conceived as possible unless whatever is real in every possible concept exists and indeed exists absolutely necessarily. (For, if this be denied,

---

[i] *idealiter . . . non realiter.*   [j] *omnitudo realitatis.*   [k] *sine gradu.*   [l] *in ideis.*
[m] *praeconcepta notio.*   [n] *praevertit.*   [o] *non repugnantia.*   [p] *collatione.*   [q] *conferenda.*

nothing at all would be possible; in other words, there would be nothing but the impossible.)[17] Furthermore, it is necessary that this entire reality[r] should be united together in a single being.

For suppose that these realities,[s] which are, so to speak, the material of all possible concepts, were to be found distributed among a number of existent things; it would follow that each of these things would have its existence limited in a certain way. In other words, the existence of each of these things would be combined with certain deprivations.[t] Absolute necessity is not compatible with deprivations as it is with realities. Deprivations, however, belong to the complete determination of a thing, and without this complete determination a thing could not exist. This being the case, it follows that the realities which are limited in this way will exist contingently. It is, accordingly, a requirement for their absolute necessity that they should exist without any limitation, in other words, that they should constitute an Infinite Being. Since the plurality of this being, should you wish to imagine such a thing, would be a repetition made a number of times and hence a contingency opposed to absolute necessity, it must be concluded that only one such Being exists absolutely necessarily. Thus, there is a God, and only one God, the absolutely necessary principle of all possibility.[18]

SCHOLIUM. Such is the demonstration of the existence of God. It is, as far as possible, a proof based on essence.[u] And, although properly speaking, there is no room for a genetic proof, nonetheless the proof is based upon a most fundamental consideration, namely, the possibility itself of things. It is plain from this, therefore, that if you deny the existence of God, you instantly abolish not only the entire existence of things but even their inner possibility itself. For although essences (which consist in inner possibility)[v] are ordinarily called absolutely necessary,[19] nonetheless, it would be more correct to say that *they belong*[w] *to things absolutely necessarily.* For the essence of a triangle, which consists in the joining together of three sides, is not itself necessary. For what person of sound understanding would wish to maintain that it is in itself necessary that three sides should always be conceived as joined together? I admit, however, that this is necessary for a triangle. That is to say: if you think of a triangle, then you necessarily think of three sides. And that is the same as saying: if something is, it is.[20] But how it comes about that the concepts of sides, of a space to be enclosed, and so forth, should be available for use by thought;

---

[r] *omnimoda haec realitas* / B: *diese Realität durchgängig* / C: *questa realtà, che attua tutti i possibili modi dell' essere* / E: this complete reality / F: *cette realité, qui existe de toutes les manières* / R: this total reality.

[s] *realia.* [t] *privationibus.* [u] *demonstrationem . . . essentialem.*

[v] *quae consistunt in interna possibilitate.*

[w] *competere* / B: *zukommen* / C: *competeno* / E: coincide / F: *appartiennent* / R: standing in . . . agreement.

how, in other words, it comes about that there is, in general, something which can be thought, from which there then arises, by means of combination, limitation and determination, any concept you please of a thinkable thing – how that should came about is something which cannot be conceived at all, unless it is the case that whatever is real in the concept exists in God, the source of all reality. We know, of course, that Descartes advanced an argument for the existence of God drawn from the inner concept itself of God.[21] But the scholium of the preceding paragraph[22] shows how he was deluded in this matter. Of all beings, God is the only one in which existence is prior to, or, if you prefer, identical with possibility. And as soon as you deny the existence of God, every concept of possibility vanishes.[x]

Proposition VIII. Nothing which exists contingently can be without a ground which determines its existence antecedently.

Suppose that something which existed contingently were to lack an antecedently determining ground. There will be nothing which determines it to exist, except the very existence of the thing itself. But existence is, notwithstanding, determined. That is to say, existence is posited in such a way that whatever is opposed to its complete determination is excluded altogether. It follows from this, therefore, that there will be no other exclusion of the opposite than that which issues from the positing of existence. Since this exclusion, however, is identical (for nothing prevents a thing from not existing apart from the fact of not being non-existent),[y] it follows that the opposite of existence is excluded by itself; in other words, the opposite of existence will be absolutely impossible. In other words, the thing exists absolutely necessarily. But that contradicts our hypothesis.

COROLLARY. It is, therefore, clear from these proofs that it is only the existence of contingent things which requires the support of a determining ground, and that the unique and absolutely necessary Being is exempt from this law. It is hence clear that the principle is not to be admitted in such a general sense that it embraces within its dominion the totality of everything which is possible.

SCHOLIUM. Such is the demonstration of the principle of the determining ground, which has now been finally fully illuminated by all the light of certainty, or so at least I am convinced for my part. It has been sufficiently noticed that the most penetrating philosophers of our age, among whom I mention the celebrated Crusius[23] for special honour, have always complained that the demonstration of this principle, as we find it hawked around in all the books written on the subject, has lacked solidity. The

---

[x] *Et huius nulla manet notio, simulatque ab exsistentia eius discesseris.*

[y] *(quippe nihil aliud vetat rem non exsistere, quan quod non exsistentia remota sit).*

great man so despaired of a cure for this malady that he seriously maintained that this proposition was altogether incapable of demonstration, even if it were admitted to be in the highest degree true.[z] However, I must explain why I did not find the discovery and execution of this demonstration so easy that I was able to complete the entire proof in a single argument, as people ordinarily try to do, but rather found it necessary to adopt a somewhat circuitous route in order, finally, to attain full certainty.

First of all, namely, I had carefully to distinguish between the ground of truth and that of existence, although it might have seemed that the universality of the principle of the determining ground, which holds in the realm of truths, might equally extend over existence as well. For if nothing is true without a determining ground; that is to say, if a predicate does not belong to a subject, unless there is a determining ground, it would also follow that there would be no predicate of existence, either, if there were no determining ground. It is, however, agreed that there is no need for an antecedently determining ground to establish a truth: the identity which exists between the predicate and the subject is sufficient for the purpose. But, in the case of existing things, it is necessary to search for the antecedently determining ground. If there be no such ground, then the being in question exists absolutely necessarily. If existence be contingent, then, as I have already irrefutably demonstrated, the antecedently determining ground cannot fail to precede existence. Hence, the truth, having been drawn from its very sources, emerges, in my opinion at least, all the purer.

1:397

The celebrated Crusius thinks, indeed, that certain existent things are determined by their actuality in such a way that it would be futile to demand anything else in addition.[24] Titus acts of his own free will. I ask: why did he do this rather than not do it? He replies: because he willed it. But why did he will it? He maintains that asking this is foolish. If you ask: why did he not rather do something else? he will reply: because he is already doing this. He therefore thinks that the free will is actually determined[a] by its existence, not antecedently by grounds which are prior to its existence. He maintains that all opposite determinations are excluded by the mere positing of actuality alone, and, hence, that there is no need for a determining ground. But I shall now employ another argument, if you will permit me to do so, to prove again that a contingent thing is never sufficiently determined, if you abandon the antecedently determining ground, and, hence, that a contingent thing cannot exist without such a determining ground. The act of free will exists, and this existence excludes the opposite of this determination. But since at one time it did not exist, and since its existence does not itself determine whether or not it existed at some earlier time, it follows that the existence of this volition leaves the question whether it already existed beforehand or not indeterminate. How-

[z] *maxime vera.*   [a] *actu determinatam.*

ever, since in a thorough determination,[b] the determination whether a being has begun to exist or not is also one question among all the others,[c] it follows that a being will remain indeterminate and, indeed, incapable of being determined, until, in addition to that which belongs to its inner existence, concepts are deployed which are capable of being thought independently of its existence. But that which determines the earlier non-existence of the existing being precedes the concept of existence. It is, however, the same thing which determines that the existent being did not exist beforehand which also determined it to pass from non-existence to existence. (After all, the propositions: Why did that which now exists once not exist? and: Why does that which once did not exist now exist? are, in fact, identical.) That is to say, there is a ground which antecedently determines its existence. It follows from this with complete clarity that, without an antecedently determining ground, there can be no kind of determination of a being, which is conceived of as having come into being; and, hence, there can be no existence. If this demonstration should strike anyone as somewhat obscure on account of the analysis of the concepts which goes too deeply into the matter, he can rest content with what was said earlier.

Finally, I should like to offer a brief explanation for my declining to accept the demonstration frequently employed by the celebrated Wolff[25] and his followers. The demonstration offered by this famous man, as it is to be found expounded more distinctly by the penetrating Baumgarten,[26] amounts, when it is reduced to essentials, to this: if something does not have a ground, then nothing would be its ground; nothing would therefore be something, which is absurd. But the method of arguing ought rather to be formulated as follows: if a being is without a ground, the ground of that being is nothing, that is to say, a non-being.[d] But this I readily[e] concede, for if there is no ground, the concept corresponding to it will be that of a non-being. Hence, if the only ground which can be attributed to the being is one to which no concept corresponds at all, then that being will com-   1:398 pletely lack a ground; and that is tantamount to what we supposed to start with. Hence, the absurdity, which was supposed to follow, does not follow at all. Let me offer an example in support of my view. According to this method of inference I shall venture to prove that even the first human being was begotten by a father. For suppose that he was not begotten. Then it would be nothing which would have begotten him. He would, therefore, have been begotten by nothing. But since this is contradictory, it must be admitted that he was begotten by someone. It is not difficult to escape the sophistry of the argument.[f] If he has not been begotten, noth-

---

[b] *in determinatione omnimoda.*
[c] *haec quoque una omnium* / B: *auch eine von allen* / C: _____ / E: this is the main question of all / F: *parmi toutes les autres la question de savoir* / R: the most important question of all.
[d] *non ens.*   [e] *ambabus manibus.*   [f] *captionem argumenti.*

ing has begotten him. That is to say, the person who is supposed to have begotten him is nothing or a non-being, and that is as certain as certain can be. But if the proposition is converted in the wrong fashion, it yields a distorted sense in the worst way.

Proposition IX. An enumeration and resolution of the difficulties which seem to beset the principle of the determining ground, or, as it is commonly called, the principle of the sufficient ground.

Among those who attack this principle, the most distinguished[g] and pene-trating Crusius is to be regarded, and rightly so, as leading the assault.*[29] He alone of all those involved is able to bear the brunt of the battle. I maintain that Crusius scarcely has an equal among all those who are, I shall not say philosophers, but rather advocates of philosophy in Germany. If my discussion of his doubts[30] turns out well (and the defense of a good cause seems to guarantee a successful outcome), I shall regard myself as having overcome every difficulty. First of all, he criticises the formulation of this principle for its ambiguity and the vagueness of its meaning. For he rightly remarks that the ground of knowing, and likewise the moral ground, and other ideal grounds, are repeatedly mistaken for real and antecedently determining grounds, so that it is often only with difficulty that one can tell which of the two is meant. We do not need to parry this blow because it does not strike at our assertions. Anyone who examines our various claims will find that I carefully distinguish the ground of truth from the ground of actuality. All that is involved in the former case is the positing of a predicate. Such a positing is effected by means of the identity which exists between the concepts which are contained in the subject, whether it be viewed absolutely or in connection with other things, and the predicate; the predicate, which already attaches to the subject, is merely disclosed. In the latter case, those predicates which are posited as inhering in the subject are examined in respect of the question, not *whether* their existence is determined, but *whence* it is determined. If there is nothing present, apart from the absolute positing of the thing itself, which excludes the opposite, it must be deemed to exist in itself and with

---

* I do not wish to dispute the merit of the celebrated Daries.[27] His arguments, and those advanced by some others as well, are, I maintain, of great moment in increasing the difficul-ties which beset the principle of the determining ground. But since they seem to be closely related to the arguments adduced by the excellent Dr Crusius[28] I think that I can limit my reply to the difficulties by concentrating chiefly on the points made by Crusius, without incurring the displeasure of those otherwise great men.

[g] *S. R.* / B: *sehr ehrenwerte* / C: *riveritissimo* / F: *celebre* / E & R: _____ / (*S. R.*: abbreviation for *subrectus:* celebrated, distinguished).

absolute necessity. But if it is assumed to exist contingently, then there must be other things present which, by determining it thus and not otherwise, antecedently exclude the opposite of its existence. So much, then, for our demonstration in general.

Certainly, a greater danger threatens the defenders of the principle from the objection put forward by that most illustrious man:[31] he accuses us, with an eloquence and indeed with a vigour of argument which is not to be despised, of restoring to their ancient rights the immutable necessity of all things and the fate of the Stoics,[32] and, furthermore, of impairing all freedom and morality. His argument, although not entirely new,[33] is, nonetheless, stated by him in greater detail and with greater force. I shall restate his argument as concisely as possible but without diminishing its vigour.   1:399

If it is the case that whatever happens can only happen if it has an antecedently determining ground, it follows that *whatever does not happen could not happen either,* for obviously no ground is present, and without a ground it could not happen at all. And this is something which has to be admitted in the case of all grounds of grounds[h] taken in retrogressive order. It follows, therefore, that all things happen in virtue of a natural conjunction, and in such a connected and continuous fashion that, if someone were to wish the opposite of some event or even of a free action, his wish would involve the conception of something impossible, for the ground necessary to produce the opposite of what happened or was done is simply not present. And thus, by tracing one's way along the inexorable chain of events which, as Chrysippos[34] says, once and for all snakes its way along and weaves its path through the eternal series of consequences,[i] one eventually arrives at the first state of the world.[35] And this state immediately reveals God, the Creator, the ultimate ground of events, and the fertile ground of so many consequences. Once this ultimate ground is posited, other grounds follow, and others from them, down through the ages which follow, in accordance with an ever constant law. The illustrious Crusius attacks the often used distinction between absolute and hypothetical necessity,[36] his opponents thinking that, by means of this distinction, they would be able to escape him, as through a crack. But the distinction obviously has no power at all to break the force and effective power of necessity.[j] For of what avail is it if the opposite of an event, which is precisely determined by antecedent grounds, can be conceived when it is regarded in itself, since the opposite still cannot occur in reality, for the grounds necessary for its existence are not present: indeed, it is the grounds necessary for the reverse which are present. The opposite of an

---

[h] *de omnibus rationum rationibus.*   [i] *voluit et implicat per aeternos consequentiae ordines.*
[j] *necessitatis vim et efficacitatem.*

21

event which is assumed to exist in isolation can, nonetheless, you say, be thought, and thus it is possible. But what then? It still cannot come to be, for the grounds which already exist are sufficient to ensure that it can never come to be in fact. Consider an example: Caius has made a fraudulent claim. Honesty is not incompatible with Caius in virtue of his fundamental determinations; in other words, honesty is not imcompatible with Caius in so far as he is a human being. This I grant. But honesty is certainly incompatible with him as he is determined now. For there are present within him grounds which posit the opposite, and honesty cannot be ascribed to him without overthrowing the entire series of interconnected grounds*k* which stretch right back to the first state of the world. Let us now hear what this celebrated philosopher goes on to infer from this. The determining ground not only brings it about that this action in particular should take place: it also brings it about that no other actions could happen instead of it. Therefore, whatever happens within us has been foreseen by God in its orderly sequence in such a way*l* that nothing else at all could happen. Thus, the charging to our account of the things we have done is charging us with what does not belong to us. But God is the one cause of all things: He has so bound us by those laws that we accomplish the fate to which we are destined, no matter what the circumstances. Does it not follow from this that no sin can be displeasing to God? For when a sin is committed, it also testifies to the fact that the series of interwoven events established by God admits of nothing else. Why then does God reproach sinners for actions which they were ordained to commit from the very seed and womb of the world?

1:400

Refutation of objections. When we distinguish hypothetical necessity, and in particular moral necessity, from absolute necessity, what is at issue here is not the force or the effective power of the necessity. We are not concerned, namely, whether a thing is, in some case or other, more or less necessary. What is at issue is the necessitating principle: namely, *whence* the thing is necessary. I readily admit that here some of the adherents of the Wolffian philosophy deviate somewhat from the truth of the matter.[37] They are convinced that that which is posited by the chain of grounds which hypothetically determine each other still falls a little short of complete necessity, because it lacks absolute necessity. But in this matter I agree with their illustrious opponent:[38] the distinction, which everyone recites parrot-fashion, does little to diminish the force of the necessity or the certainty of the determination. For just as nothing can be conceived which is *more true* than *true,* and nothing *more certain* than *certain,* so nothing can be conceived which is *more determined* than *determined.* The events which occur in the world have been determined with such certainty

k *omni rationum implicitarum ordine.*   *l* *eius consecutione ita a Deo prospectum est.*

that divine foreknowledge, which is incapable of being mistaken, apprehends, both their futurition[m] and the impossibility of their opposites. And
He does so in conformity with the connection of their grounds[n] and as
certainly as if the opposite were excluded by their absolute concept. But
here the question hinges not upon *to what extent* but upon *whence* the
necessary futurition of contingent things derives. Who is there who would
doubt that the act of creation is not indeterminate[o] in God, but that it is so
certainly determinate[p] that the opposite would be unworthy of God, in
other words that the opposite could not be ascribed to Him at all. Nonetheless, however, the action is free, for it is determined by those grounds,
which, in so far as they incline His will with the greatest possible certainty,
include the motives of His infinite intelligence, and do not issue from a
certain blind power of nature to produce effects.[q] So, too, in the case of
the free actions of human beings: in so far as they are regarded as determinate,[r] their opposites are indeed excluded; they are not, however, excluded
by grounds which are posited as existing outside the desires and spontaneous inclinations of the subject, as if the agent were compelled to perform
his actions against his will, so to speak, and as a result of a certain
ineluctable necessity. On the contrary, it is in the very inclination of his
volitions and desires, in so far as that inclination readily yields to the
blandishments of his representations, that his actions are determined by a
fixed law and in a connection which is most certain but also free. It is not a
difference in the nature of the connection or the certainty which constitutes the distinction between physical actions and those possessed of
moral freedom, as if these actions alone, subject to doubt in respect of
their futurition and exempt from the chain of grounds, had a vague and
indeterminate ground of coming to be. For, if that were the case, such
actions would scarcely deserve to figure among the prerogatives of intelligent beings. But the way in which the certainty of their actions is determined by their grounds gives us all the room we need[s] to affirm that they
bear the characteristic mark of freedom. For such actions are called forth
by nothing other than motives of the understanding applied to the will,
whereas in the case of brute animals or physico-mechanical actions everything is necessitated in conformity with external stimuli[t] and impulses and

---

[m] *futuritionem* / B: *künftiges Bestehen* / C: *il loro futuro corse* / E & R: future occurrence / F:
l'existence future / (Leibnizian term; cf. *Théodicée* §§36–7).

[n] *nexu rationum conformiter.*   [o] *ambiguum.*

[p] *determinatum* / (this term, like the German *bestimmt*, is ambiguous and may mean either
'determinate' or 'determined'; this ambiguity infects the whole passage).

[q] *a caeca quadam naturae efficacia.*   [r] *determinatae.*

[s] *omnem paginam facit* / B: *kommt alles auf die Art an* / C: *fa di ogni pagina un argumento a difesa*
/ E: makes every instance stand out as a record / F: *donne toute latitude* / R: _____ / (the
phrase *utramque paginam facere* is to be found in Pliny and has the force of: 'gives us the
upper hand' or 'gives us the freedom to fulfil all the requirements').

[t] *sollicitationibus.*

1:401

without there being any spontaneous inclination of the will. It is, indeed, generally admitted that the power to perform an action is suspended in a state of indifference relative to each of the two directions in which it could realise itself,[u] and that it is determined exclusively by a pleasurable inclination towards the blandishments which arise from our representations. The more certainly the nature of man is bound by this law, the greater is the freedom which he enjoys. The exercise of freedom does not consist in being carried away in all directions towards objects by some vacillating impulse. He acts, you say, for no other reason than the fact that *it pleased*[v] him thus most of all. I now already hold you prisoner by this confession of yours. For what is being pleased[w] if it is not the inclination of the will in one direction rather than another, according to the attraction exercised by the object. Thus, your '*it pleases*' or 'it causes pleasure'[x] signifies that the action is determined by inner grounds. For it is the being pleased[y] which, according to your opinion, determines the action. But that is nothing other than the satisfaction of the will by the object, according to the nature of the attraction exercised by that object on the will. Therefore, the determination is relative. And in the case of such a relative determination, to say that the will is equally attracted in two directions and that one direction is more pleasant[z] is tantamount to saying that there is a pleasure[a] which is at once equal and unequal. But that involves an inconsistency. But the case can arise where the grounds which incline the will in one of two directions completely escape our consciousness, but where, nonetheless, one alternative is chosen in preference to the other. But in that case, the thing passes from a higher faculty of the mind to a lower, and the mind is directed in one direction or another by the preponderance of an obscure representation[b] in one direction rather than the other. (We shall be discussing this at greater length at a later stage.)[39]

If the reader has no objections, I should like to illustrate this well-known dispute by means of a short dialogue between Caius, the advocate of the indifference of equilibrium,[c] and Titius, the champion of the determining ground.

Caius: The course of my past life does, it must be admitted, cause me pangs of conscience. There is one consolation left to me, however, if one may believe what you say: responsibility for the misdeeds committed does not fall on me, for, bound as I was by the connected series[d] of grounds which have determined each other from the very beginning of the world, I could not have failed to have done whatever I did do. And if anyone should reproach me now for my vices or vainly chide me for not having adopted a different way of life, that person would be behaving as foolishly

---

[u] *Potestatem quidem actionis ad utramvis partem indifferenter se habere.*   [v] *lubuit.*   [w] *lubitus.*
[x] *libet s. volupe.*   [y] *lubitus.*   [z] *magis volupe.*   [a] *placere.*
[b] *repraesentationis obscurae . . . suprapondium.*   [c] *indifferentiae aequilibrii.*   [d] *nexu.*

as he would be behaving if he were to rebuke me for not having brought the flow of time to a standstill. *Titius:* Let us see! What is this series of grounds by which you complain you were bound? Is it not the case that whatever you did, you did willingly? Is it not the case that when you were about to sin the silent exhortation of conscience and the fear of God, chiding you within, vainly raised their voices in loud admonition? Is it not the case that nonetheless you preferred to drink, to game, to sacrifice to Venus, and to do other things of the same kind? Were you ever constrained, against your will, to sin? *Caius:* I do not in the least dispute the truth of what you are saying. I know perfectly well that it was not a case of my having been, so to speak, seized by the scruff of the neck and carried off, struggling and energetically resisting what was attracting me, in a direction in which I did not wish to go.[e] It was knowingly, and with pleasure that I surrendered myself to vice. But whence did I acquire this inclination of the will towards baseness? Was it not the case that beforehand, when laws, both human and divine, were inclining me in their direction while I was still undecided, it was already determined by a totality of grounds[f] that I should incline towards the bad rather than towards the good? Is it not the case that positing a ground which is complete in all respects and then blocking its consequences is tantamount to making undone what has been done? But on your view, every inclina-   1:402
tion of my will has been completely determined by an antecedent ground and that, in its turn, by another antecedent ground, and so on right back to the beginning of all things. *Titius:* Well now, then, let me remove your misgivings. At any given juncture, the series of interconnected grounds furnishes motives for the performance of the action which are equally attractive in both directions: you readily adopted one of them because acting thus rather than otherwise was more pleasurable to you. But you say: it was already determined by the totality of grounds that I should incline in one particular direction.[g] I should, however, like you to consider whether it is not the case that the spontaneous inclination[h] of your will, according to the attractions of the object, is not required if there is to be a complete ground of action. *Caius:* Beware of saying 'spontaneous'. The will could not have failed to incline in this direction. *Titius:* But this inclination of the will, far from eliminating spontaneity, actually makes spontaneity all the more certain, provided that 'spontaneity' is taken in the right sense. For *spontaneity is action which issues from an inner principle. When this spontaneity is determined in conformity with the representation of what is best it is called freedom.*[40] The more certainly it can be said of a person that he submits to the law, and thus the more that person is

---

[e] *me non renitentem et allectamentis strenue obluctantem velut obtorto collo in transversum abreptum esse.*

[f] *rationum consummatione.*   [g] *in partem destinatam.*   [h] *spontanea propensio.*

determined by all the motives posited for willing, the greater is that person's freedom. It does not follow from your line of argument that the power belonging to antecedently determining grounds impairs freedom. For your confession that you do not act unwillingly but with pleasure is sufficient to confute you. Hence your action was not *unavoidable,*[i] as you seem indeed to think, for you did not seek to avoid it; it was, however, *bound to happen,*[j] given the inclination of your desire relative to the situation as it was constituted.[k] And this, indeed, increases your guilt. For the eagerness of your desire was such that you were not to be distracted from your purpose. But I shall despatch you with your own weapon. Tell me: in what manner, do you think, is the concept of freedom to be formulated so that it is more consonant with your opinion? *Caius:* Personally, I should think that if you eliminate everything which is in the nature of a connected series of reciprocally determining grounds occurring in a fixed order, and if you admit that in any free action whatever a person finds himself in a state of indifference relative to both alternatives,[l] and if that person, even though all the grounds which you have imagined as determining the will in a particular direction have been posited, is nonetheless able to choose one thing over another, no matter what – if all that is conceded, then I should finally admit that the act had been freely performed. *Titius:* Heavens above! If any deity granted you this wish, how unhappy you would be at every moment of your life. Suppose that you have decided to follow the path of virtue. And suppose that your mind is already sustained by the precepts of religion and whatever else is effective in strengthening your motivation. And suppose that now the occasion for acting arrives. You will immediately slide in the direction of what is less good, for the grounds which solicit you do not determine you. I seem to hear you expressing still more complaints. Ah! What baleful fate has driven me from my sound decision? Of what use are precepts for performing the work of virtue? Actions are the product of chance; they are not determined by grounds. I do not, it is true, you say, complain of the constraint of fate which sweeps me along against my will; but I loathe the unknown something which makes me favourably disposed towards my fall into what is worst. The shame of it! What is the source of this hateful desire for what is precisely the worst course? – this desire which could just as easily have inclined me in the opposite direction. *Caius:* It is, therefore, all over with freedom of every kind. *Titius:* You see how I have driven your forces into a corner. Do not conjure up spectres of ideas; you feel that you are free; but do not fabricate a concept of freedom which is not in agreement with sound reason. To act freely is to act in conformity with one's desire and to do so, indeed, with consciousness. And that is

1:403

---

[i] *inevitabilis.*   [j] *infallibilis.*   [k] *ad circumstantias ita informatas.*
[l] *versus utramque partem indifferenter se habere.*

26

certainly not excluded by the law of the determining ground. *Caius:* Although I have scarcely anything I can say in reply to you, it nonetheless seems to me that inner sense contradicts what you say.*m* For take a case of no great importance: if I pay attention to myself, I am aware that I am free to incline in either direction, so that I am sufficiently convinced that the direction of my action was not determined by an antecedent series of grounds. *Titius:* I am going to show you the silent deception which creates in you the illusion of the indifference of equilibrium. The natural force of desire, inherent in the human mind, directs itself not only towards objects but also towards the various representations which are to be found in the understanding. Accordingly, in so far as we feel that we are ourselves the authors of the representations which contain the motives for choice in a given case, so that we are eminently able either to focus our attention on them, or to suspend our attention, or turn it in another direction, and are consequently conscious of being able not only to strive towards the objects in conformity with our desire but also to interchange the reasons themselves in a variety of ways and as we please – in so far as all that is the case we can scarcely refrain from supposing that the addressing of our will in a given direction is not governed by any law nor subject to any fixed determination. But suppose that we make an effort to arrive at a correct understanding of the fact that the inclination of the attention towards a combination of representations is in this direction rather than in a different direction. Since grounds attract us in a certain direction, we shall, in order at least to test our freedom, turn our attention in the opposite direction, and thus make it preponderant so that the desire *is directed thus and not otherwise.* In this way, we shall easily persuade ourselves that determining grounds must certainly be present. *Caius:* You have involved me, I must confess, in a great number of difficulties. But I am convinced that you are faced by difficulties which are equally great. In what way, do you suppose, can the determinate futurition*n* of evils, of which God is in the last analysis the ultimate determining cause, be reconciled with his goodness and holiness? *Titius:* In order to avoid fruitlessly wasting our time in futile disputes, I shall offer a brief account of the difficulties which prevent you from reaching a decision, and I shall then untie the knot of your doubts. The certainty of all events, both physical occurrences and

---

m Quamquam vix habeam, quod tibi regeram, tamen internus sensus sententiae tuae mihi videtur obloqui / B: *Obwohl ich kaum weiss, was ich dir entgegenhalten könnte, scheint mir doch der innere Sinn deiner Meinung zu widersprechen* / C: *Quantunque ben poco abbia da contrapporti, mi pare tuttavia che a rivoltarsi contro di te sia l'intimo significato della tua stessa tesi* / E: yet the inner meaning of your view seems to me to jar / F: *et pourtant un sentiment intérieur me parait aller a l'encontre de ton opinion* / R: although I have scarcely anything to urge against what you are saying, its inner meaning seems to me to be not quite right / (the word *obloqui* could not be employed in the manner suggested by the translations of B, C, and R; only F has construed the grammar of the sentence [and understood the logic of the argument] correctly).
n determinatam . . . futuritionem (alt: determinate futurition).

free actions, is determined, the consequent being determined by the antecedent, and the antecedent being determined by antecedents which are
still earlier, and so on by grounds which are ever more remote and extend
backwards in a continuous series to the first state of the world. This state,
which reveals God immediately as the Creator, is, so to speak, the well or
bubbling spring from which all things flow with infallible necessity down
an inclined channel. For this reason, you think that God is clearly indicated as the one who engineered[o] evil. For this reason, too, you think that
He cannot hate the web which He Himself began to weave, and which will
continue to be woven, in accordance with the initial design, throughout
the future centuries of times to come. It seems that He cannot persecute
the sins, which have been interwoven into the tapestry, with all the anger
to which the holiness of His nature entitles Him, since the blame for all
these evils eventually redounds upon God Himself, as the one who first
engineered[p] their occurrence. These are the doubts which weigh upon
your mind. I shall now dissipate the clouds. In instituting the origin of the
totality of things, God initiated a sequence of events.[q] This sequence, in
the fixed connected series of interlinked, interconnected and interwoven
grounds,[r] embraced even moral evils, as well as the physical evils corresponding to them. From this, however, it does not follow that God can be
accused of being the Author of morally corrupt actions. If, as happens in
the case of machines,[s] intelligent beings were to comport themselves pas-
sively in relation to those things which impel towards certain determinations and changes, I should not deny that the blame for all things could be
shifted to God as the Architect of the machine. But those things which
happen through the will of beings endowed with understanding and the
spontaneous power itself of self-determination[t] obviously issue from an
inner principle, from conscious desires and from a choice of one of the
alternatives according to the freedom of the power of choice.[u] Hence, no
matter how much the state of things prior to the free acts has been
determined by some ground, and no matter to what degree the intelligent
being is entangled in a connected series of circumstances which is such
that it is certain that moral evils will result and that their occurrence can
be foreseen, nonetheless, this futurition is determined by grounds which
are so constituted that voluntary inclination towards what is base is the
hinge upon which everything turns. And thus it is these grounds which
must be called the causes of those things which it gave sinners the greatest
pleasure to perform. And that they should pay the penalty for their illicit
pleasure corresponds as perfectly as can be with justice. But as for the
aversion with which God turns away from sins and which is indubitably

1:404

---

[o] *machinatorem.* [p] *primum molitorem.* [q] *seriem.*
[r] *quae stabili rationum conserte contexteque colligatarum nexu.* [s] *in mechanicis.*
[t] *semet ipsa sponte determinandi potestate.* [u] *electione . . . secundum arbitrii licentiam.*

worthy of His holiness but which seems scarcely compatible with the decree which established the world and which included the futurition of these evils – even here the difficulty which surrounds the question is not insuperable. For that is how things stand.[v]

The infinite goodness of God strives towards the greatest possible perfection of created things and towards the happiness of the spiritual world.[w] With the same infinite striving to reveal Himself, God addressed Himself to creating not only a more perfect sequence of events, which was later destined to spring from the order of grounds, but in addition to that, and with a view to ensuring that no good, not even goods of a lesser degree, should be missing, and that the totality of things in its immensity should embrace everything from the highest degree of perfection possible for finite things, down to all the lower degrees of perfection, even including, so to speak, nothing itself, God also allowed things to creep into his scheme which, in spite of the admixture of many evils, would yield something which was good and which the wisdom of God would elicit from them, in order to embellish with infinite variety the manifestation of His divine glory. It was perfectly consonant with the wisdom, power and goodness of God that this whole should include the history of the human race; sad as that history is, it would contain, even in the turmoil of evils, numberless testimonies of the divine goodness. One may not, however, for that reason suppose that God was bent upon and deliberately produced the evils themselves which were interwoven into the work which He had begun. For it was the good upon which His eyes were focused: He knew that, once the balance of grounds had been drawn up, the good would nonetheless remain. He knew that the elimination of this good, along with the wretched tares, would not be worthy of His supreme wisdom. For the rest, mortals commit sins voluntarily and as a result of an inmost state of mind, for the chain of antecedent grounds does not hurry them along or sweep them away against their will; it attracts them. And although it was known in advance that they would certainly respond to the spur, nonetheless, since the origin of evils is to be found in the inner principle of self-determination, it is clearly apparent that the evils have to be attributed to the sinners themselves. Nor, for this reason, may one suppose that the divine power abhors sins the less on the grounds that, by having admitted them, God has in a way given His approval to them. For the real end which the Divine Artist had in view was to compensate for the evils, which had been permitted and which were to be remedied by strenuous effort. And this end He strives to attain by warnings, threats, encour-

1:405

---

[v] *Sic enim habeto* / B: *Denn man muss das so nehmen* / C: *Sta a sentire!* / E: Let us put it this way / (transferred to the beginning of the next paragraph) / F: *Sois-en sûr* / R: ———— / (this is a phrase often used by Cicero).

[w] *mundi spiritualis.*

agements and furnishing the means. By thus pruning away the branches which yield an abundant harvest of evils, and, in so far as it is compatible with human freedom, eliminating them, He has in this way shown Himself to be someone who hates all wickedness, but also to be someone who loves the perfections which can nonetheless be extracted from that source. But let me return to my path, for I have wandered rather further than I ought from the purpose of my undertaking.

Supplements to Problem IX

Divine foreknowledge is only possible in respect of free actions if it is conceded that their futurition is determined by their own grounds. Those who endorse our principle have always energetically urged this argument against those who have attacked the principle. I shall therefore spare myself the effort, for I shall have my hands full merely replying to the objections which the penetrating *Crusius* urges against our principle.[41] He criticises those who think in this way for entertaining an opinion of God which is unworthy of Him, for it is as if they were convinced that God makes use of reasoning.^{x} And, indeed, in the case of this opinion, if there are any who think otherwise, I shall happily pass to the side of my illustrious opponent. For I admit that the winding course of reasoning^y is scarcely becoming to the measurelessness of the divine understanding. Nor does the infinite understanding need to abstract^z universal concepts, or combine them together^a, or, in order to establish conclusions, to compare them.^{b} But here we assert that God cannot foresee those things of which the futurition is not antecedently determined, not for the want of the means to do so, for we admit that He has no need of them, but because foreknowledge of a futurition is in itself impossible; for, if its existence is in itself and antecedently altogether indeterminate, it is nothing at all. For the fact that it is in itself indeterminate follows from its contingency. That it is likewise antecedently indeterminate is maintained by our opponents. It is, therefore, both in itself and as it must of necessity be represented by the divine understanding, completely free of determination, that is to say, of futurition.^{c}

Finally, our celebrated opponent candidly admits that there are still some things which we cannot understand. But that this should be so here, when our contemplation is extended to the infinite, is, he maintains, entirely in keeping with the sublimity^d of the object. However, it does not matter how willing I may be to admit that, in our eagerness to plumb the depths of knowledge,^{e} certain sanctuaries, containing knowledge of a more

---

^{x} *ratiociniis.* ^{y} *anfractus ratiociniorum.* ^{z} *abstractione.* ^{a} *combinatione.* ^{b} *collatione.*
^{c} *ergo plane determinationis h.e. futuritionis expers et in se est et a divino intellectu repraesentare necesse est.*
^{d} *eminentia.* ^{e} *se in interiorem cognitionem descendere aveas.*

abstruse character, will forever remain inaccessible[f] to the human understanding. What does matter here is not how but whether the thing itself, namely, an antecedently indeterminate event, occurs. For it is not difficult for human knowledge to see that there is a conflict between it and the opinion of the opposite side.

Refutation of the arguments adduced by the defenders of the indifference of   1:406
equilibrium to support their view.   The supporters of the opposite party challenge us to give a satisfactory account of those cases which seem to witness to the indifference of the human will in respect of all free actions whatever, and to witness with such clarity that it seems scarcely possible that anything could be more obvious. If one plays *odd* or *even* and the beans held hidden in the hand are to be won by guessing, we say one or the other without any deliberation at all and without having any reason for our choice. Something similar to this is recounted about a prince, I know not which, who gave a free choice to someone between two caskets which were exactly alike in weight, form and appearance,[g] and of which one contained lead and the other gold. Here, the determination to take one or the other cannot be the product of prior reasoning. Similar things are said about the freedom of indifference[h] to move forward either with the right or left foot. I shall reply to all these points in a single word and, indeed, in a fashion which, it seems to me, will afford complete satisfaction. When our principle speaks of determining grounds, it is not to be understood to refer to some specific kind of ground, for example, the grounds which present themselves to the conscious understanding in the case of free actions. Our principle, on the contrary, maintains that, in whatever way an action is determined, it must be determined by some ground if it is to occur at all. Objective grounds may be completely absent from the determination of the power of choice,[i] and there may be present a complete balance between the conscious representations of the motives. And yet, nonetheless, it is still possible for there to be a great many grounds which may determine the mind. For all that is brought about by such irresolute uncertainty[j] is that the thing is transferred from a higher faculty to a lower, transferred from a representation which is conjoined with consciousness to representations which are obscure. And in their case, it can scarcely be maintained that everything on both sides is perfectly identical. The striving of an innate desire towards more and more perceptions[k] does not permit the mind to persist for long in the same state. Accordingly, if the state of the inner representations is altered, the mind must incline in some direction or other.

---

[f] *reseranda.*   [g] *speciei.*   [h] *indifferenti . . . libertate.*   [i] *in arbitrii determinatione.*
[j] *ancipiti tali dubitatione.*   [k] *Tendentia appetitus insiti in ulteriores perceptiones.*

*Proposition X. Exposition of certain genuine corollaries of the principle
of the determining ground.*

(1) *There is nothing in that which is grounded^l which was not in the ground
itself.* For nothing is without a determining ground; accordingly, there is
nothing in that which is grounded which does not reveal its determining
ground.

The objection might be raised that, since limits attach to created things,
it follows that these limits likewise attach to God, who contains the ground
of those limits. I reply as follows: the limits which attach to finite things
show that their ground is likewise limited in the act of divine creation. For
the creative act of God is limited according to^m the nature of the limited
being which is to be produced. But since this act is only a relative determination of God which must correspond to the things to be produced, not an
inner determination which is absolutely intelligible in itself, it is clear that
these limitations do not belong internally to God.

1:407   (2) *Of things which have nothing in common, one cannot be the ground of the
other.* This derives from the preceding proposition.

(3) *There is no more in that which is grounded than there is in the ground
itself.* This follows from the same rule.

IMPLICATION. The quantity of absolute reality in the world does not
change *naturally,* neither increasing nor decreasing.[42]

ELUCIDATION. The obviousness of this rule is clearly apparent in the
changes of bodies. If, for example, body A moves another body B by
striking it, a certain force and therefore a certain reality* is imparted to
the latter body. However, an equal quantity of motion is taken from the
body which imparts the blow, so that the sum total of the forces in the
effect is equal in magnitude to the forces of the cause. However, in the
case of the collision of a smaller elastic body with one which is larger the
law we have adduced seems to be false. But this is not at all the case. For
the smaller elastic body in striking the larger is repelled by it, thereby
acquiring a certain force in the opposite direction. This force, when
added to the force which has been transmitted to the larger body, yields, it
is true, a total which is greater than the quantity of force possessed by the
body which strikes the blow, as is established in mechanics. However, the
sum total, which in this case is ordinarily called absolute, ought, more
strictly speaking, to be called relative. For these forces strive in different
directions. Accordingly, the sum total of the forces is calculated from the
effects which operate in conjunction with each other and are thus viewed

---

* In this case we may, in accordance with the usual sense of the term, conceive the imparted
force as if it were a transmitted reality, although strictly speaking it is merely a certain
limiting or directing of an inherent reality.

^l *in rationato.*   ^m *pro ratione* (alt: proportionately to).

in general as a totality.[n] The calculation is performed by subtracting from each other the motions which strive in different directions; for these motions will, of course, in virtue of the fact that they are opposed to each other, somehow eventually cancel each other out. What remains is the motion of the centre of gravity.[o] And, as we know from statics, that motion is the same after impact as it was before.[43] As for the complete destruction of motion by the resistance offered by matter: far from cancelling the aforesaid rule it actually serves to confirm it the more strongly. For the force which arises from rest as a result of the conjunction of several causes will return to rest by expending in its resistance to obstacles as much force as it has acquired, and the situation remains the same as it was before.[44] Hence, the inexhaustible duration[p] of mechanical motion is impossible. Since mechanical motion always expends a certain part of its force in resisting impediments, the supposition that its power to renew itself should nonetheless remain undiminished would equally contradict not only this rule but also sound reason, as well.

Very frequently we see enormous forces issue from an infinitely small initiating cause.[q] How measureless is the explosive force produced when a spark is put to gunpowder?[45] Or, again, to take another case, how great are the conflagrations, how extensive the destructions of cities, how vast the long-lasting devastations of immense forests which result from a spark when it is nourished by highly inflammable materials. How extensive is the structure of the bodies[r] which may be destroyed by the tiny stimulus of a single spark. In these cases, however, the efficient cause of the enormous forces is a cause which lies hidden within the structure of bodies. I refer, namely, to the elastic matter[s] either of air, as in the case of gunpowder (according to the experiments of Hales),[46] or of the igneous matter,[t][47] as is 1:408
the case with all inflammable bodies whatever. The efficient cause is, in these cases, unleashed,[u] rather than actually produced, by the tiny stimulus. Elastic forces which are compressed together are stored within; and if these forces are stimulated just a little, they will release forces which are proportionate to the reciprocal pressure[v] exercised in attraction and repulsion.

Certainly, the forces exercised by spirits and the perpetual advances of those forces to higher perfections seem not to be governed by this law. But they are, in my opinion at least, nonetheless subject to that law. Without doubt, the infinite perception of the entire universe,[w] which is always internally present to the soul, albeit only obscurely, already contains

[n] *ideoque ex effectibus, quos machinae coniunctim applicatae adeoque et in universo summatim spectatae exserere possunt, aestumatae, summa virium cognoscitur.*

[o] *motus centri gravitatis.* [p] *perpetuitas inexhausta.* [q] *ex infinite parvo causae principio.*

[r] *corporum compagen* / B: *Gefüge von Körpern* / C: *gigantesche strutture corporee* / E: a structure of bodies / F: *assemblage de corps* / R: corporeal structure.

[s] *materia . . . elastica.* [t] *materia igneae.* [u] *manifestatur.* [v] *nisui.*

[w] *infinita . . . totius universi perceptio.*

within itself all the reality which must inhere in the thoughts, which are later to be illuminated by a stronger light.[48] And the mind, at a later stage, by merely turning its attention to certain of these thoughts, illuminates them with a stronger light, while withdrawing an equal degree of illumination from certain others; in so doing, it daily acquires greater knowledge. It does not, it is true, extend the realm of absolute reality (for the material element[x] of all ideas, which derives from connection with the universe, remains the same). But the formal element,[y] which consists in the combination of concepts and in the application of attention either to their difference or agreement, certainly changes in a variety of ways. In exactly the same way, we notice something similar in the case of the force inherent in bodies. For motions, if they are rightly considered, are not realities but appearances.[z] And the inherent force, modified by the impact of the external body, resists collision in virtue of an inner principle of action, doing so with as much force as it had acquired in the direction of the forces of the impinging body which collides with it. It follows that all the reality to be found in the forces present in the phenomenon of motion[a] is equal to that which already inheres in the body when it is at rest, even though the inner power, which was indeterminate in respect of direction when it was at rest, is merely directed by the external impulse.

What has been adduced so far concerning the immutable quantity of absolute reality in the universe is to be understood in terms of the fact that everything happens in accordance with the order of nature. For who would dare to doubt that the flagging perfection of the material world could be restored by God's intervention,[b] or that it was possible for intelligent beings to be illuminated by heaven with a light of greater purity than nature allows, and that all things could be raised to a higher peak of perfection?

Proposition XI. In which certain spurious corollaries, which have been incorrectly derived from the principle of the determining ground, are adduced and refuted.

1. *Nothing exists which does not have something which is grounded,* in other words, whatever is has its consequence.[c] This principle is known as the principle of consequence. As far as I know, its originator was *Baumgarten,* chief of the metaphysicians.[49] Since he proved this principle in the same way in which he demonstrated the principle of the sufficient ground,[d] the former is involved in the ruin of the latter. If we are only concerned with the grounds of knowing, then the truth of this principle is saved. For the concept of any being whatever is either general or individual. If the con-

---

[x] *materiale.*   [y] *formale.*   [z] *phaenomenon.*   [a] *omne in phaenomeno motus virium reale.*
[b] *Per Dei . . . operam.*   [c] *sui habere consequentiam.*   [d] *principium rationis.*

cept of a being is general, then it has to be admitted that whatever is established of the generic concept applies[c] to all the lower concepts which are subsumed under it, and hence that the former contains the ground of the latter concepts which are subsumed under it. If the concept of a being is individual, one may conclude that the predicates which belong[f] to this subject in a certain connection must always belong to it, given the same conditions.[g] And, starting out from a given case, the concept determines the truth in similar cases; and hence the concept has that which is conditioned by a ground of knowing.[h] But if we understand by this that which is conditioned by a ground of existence,[i] beings will not be infinitely productive in this respect,[j] as may be seen from the final section of this treatise. We shall there prove by incontestable arguments that the state of any substance, which has no connection with other substances, will be free from all change.[50] 1:409

2. *That there is no substance in the entire totality of things which is in all respects like any other substance.* This principle is called the principle of indiscernibles.[51] Taken in its widest sense, as it usually is, it could not be further from the truth. There are two ways, in particular, in which this principle is demonstrated. The first method of proof scarcely deserves close scrutiny, for it is precipitate to a degree, leaping over the object with a light spring. These are the sophistries employed: all things which agree perfectly in all characteristic marks and are not distinguished by any difference must, it seems, be taken for one and the same thing. Hence, all the things which are perfectly alike are nothing but one and the same thing, to which a number of different places are ascribed. Because this view conflicts with sound reason, it is alleged that it is self-contradictory. But is there anyone who does not notice the trickery of these sophistries? The complete identity of two things demands the identity of all their characteristic marks or determinations, both internal and external.[52] Is there anyone who has excluded place from this complete determination? Accordingly, no matter how great the agreement of things in respect of their internal characteristic marks, things which are distinguished at least in virtue of place are not one and the same thing at all. However, the demonstration which we must examine in particular here, is the demonstration which is erroneously supposed to derive from the principle of the sufficient ground.

It is constantly being said that if two substances agree completely in all other respects, then there is no reason why God should assign different places to them.[53] What nonsense! It amazes me that grown men of the greatest gravity should take a delight in such frivolous arguments. Let the one substance be called A and the other B. Let A occupy the place of τοῦ

---

[c] *competere.* [f] *competunt.* [g] *iisdem positis rationibus.* [h] *rationata cognoscendi.*

[i] *rationata exsistendi* / B: *im Dasein Begründetes* / C: *i razionati a livello di esistenza* / E: *rationata exsistendi* / F: *les effets de l'existence* / R: existential consequences.

[j] *entia hisce in infinitum feracia non esse.*

B.*k* Since A does not differ from B at all in respect of internal characteristic marks, it follows that in occupying its place, it will be identical with it in all respects, and what was previously called A will now have to be called B; and that which bore the name B beforehand will now, having been transferred to the place of τou A,*l* have to be called A. For this difference of characteristics indicates a difference only of places. Tell me, therefore, whether God would have done anything different if he had determined the places in accordance with your opinion. The two are exactly the same; accordingly, the change invented by you is nothing; but it harmonises very well with my own view that for nothing there is no ground.*m*

This spurious law is admirably refuted by the entire totality of things*n* and also by what is appropriate to the divine wisdom. For that bodies which are said to be similar, such as water, mercury, gold, the simplest salts, and so forth, should agree completely in their primitive parts in respect of their homogeneous and internal characteristic marks, corresponds to the identity of the use and function which they are destined to fulfil. This is to be seen from their effects, which we observe issuing from those same things, always the same and never with any discernible difference. Nor is it proper here to suppose that there is some hidden difference which escapes the senses, so that God should have something, by reference to which, so to speak, he can distinguish the parts of his work, for that would be to search for knots in a bullrush.*o*

1:410

We admit that Leibniz, the originator of this principle, always detected a discernible difference in the structure of organic bodies or in the organisation of other bodies of extreme complexity,[54] and we admit that one may with justification assume that there is such a discernible difference in all cases of this kind. For, in cases where it is necessary that a number of different factors have to harmonise together in a very high degree before something can be produced, it is obvious that they cannot always yield the same determinations. Thus among the leaves of the same tree, you will scarcely find two which are completely alike. However, what we are rejecting here is only the metaphysical universality of this principle. Besides it seems that one can scarcely dispute the fact that an identity of type*p* is often to be found in the forms of natural bodies. Is there anyone who would venture to deny that, in the case of the formation of crystals, for example, one could not find, among the infinite diversity of crystals, one or two which were the exact copies of another?

---

k τou B / (Kant employs the Greek definite article to make good the absence of the definite article in Latin, which he needs to identify the first positing of B).

l τou A. See note k above.   *m* *nihil nullam esse rationem.*   *n* *tota rerum universitate.*

o *nodos in scirpo quaerere* / B: *Knoten an eine Binse suchen* / C: *andare a cercare il pelo nell'uovo* / E: to find a difficulty where there is none / F: *chercher les difficultés là où il n'y en a pas* / R: to launch an investigation into problems that do not exist.

p *identitatem exemplaris.*

Section 3. Presentation of the two principles of metaphysical cognition, both of which are extremely rich in consequences and derive from the principle of the determining ground

I. THE PRINCIPLE OF SUCCESSION

Proposition XII. No change can happen to substances except in so far as they are connected with other substances; their reciprocal dependency on each other determines their reciprocal changes of state.[55]

Hence, a simple substance, which is free from every external connection and which is thus abandoned to itself and left in isolation, is completely immutable in itself.

Furthermore, even were this simple substance to be included in a connection with other substances, if this relation did not change, no change could occur in it, not even a change of its inner state. Thus, in a world which was free from all motion (for motion is the appearance of a changed connection[q]), nothing at all in the nature of succession would be found even in the inner states of substances.

Hence, if the connection of substances were cancelled altogether, succession and time would likewise disappear.

Demonstration. Suppose that some simple substance, the connection of which with other substances had been cancelled, were to exist in isolation. I maintain that it could undergo no change of its inner state. The inner determinations, which already belong to the substance, are posited in virtue of inner grounds which exclude the opposite. Accordingly, if you want another determination to follow, you must also posit another ground. But since the opposite of this ground is internal to the substance, and since, in virtue of what we have presupposed, no external ground is added to it, it is patently obvious that the new determination cannot be introduced into the being.

The same differently. It is necessary that whatever is posited by a deter-   1:411

---

[q] *nexus permutati phaenomenon.*

37

mining ground be posited simultaneously with that determining ground. For, having posited the determining ground, it would be absurd if that which was determined by the determining ground were not posited as well. Thus, whatever determining factors[r] exist in some state of a simple substance, it is necessary that all factors whatever which are determined[s] should exist simultaneously with those determining factors. But since change is the succession of determinations, that is to say, since a change occurs when a determination comes into being which was not previously present, and the being is thus determined to the opposite of a certain determination which belongs to it, it follows that the change cannot take place by means of those factors which are to be found within the substance. If, therefore, a change occurs it must be the case that it arises from an external connection.

The same again somewhat differently. Suppose that a change takes place under the conditions specified. Since it begins to exist when it was not present previously, that is to say, when the substance was determined to the opposite, and since no grounds, apart from those which are internal, are supposed to be involved in determining the substance from any other source, it follows that the same grounds, by which the substance is supposed to be determined in a certain way, will determine it to the opposite, and that is absurd.

Elucidation.   This truth depends on an easily understood and infallible chain of grounds. Nonetheless, those who give to the Wolffian philosophy its renown, have paid so little attention to this truth that they maintain, on the contrary, that a simple substance is subject to constant change in virtue of an inner principle of activity.[56] Although I for my part am thoroughly familiar with their arguments, I am, nonetheless, convinced of their sterility.[t] For once they have constructed an arbitrary definition[u] of force so that it means that which contains the ground *of changes,* when one ought to declare that it contains the ground of *determinations,* they were bound to fall headlong into error.

Again, suppose that someone wished to know how, in the final analysis, the alterations, of which the succession is apparent in the universe, take place, granted that they do not issue from the internal factors[v] of a substance considered in isolation. I would have that person turn his attention to things which follow as a consequence in virtue of the connection of things, in other words, in virtue of the reciprocal dependence of their determinations. For the rest, to offer a more detailed explanation of these

---

[r] *determinantia.*   [s] *omnia omnino determinata.*

[t] *ficulnea* / B: *unfruchtbar* / C: *fasulli* / E & R: trivial / F: *sterilité* / (*ficulneus:* lit: pertaining to a fig tree; transf: sterile, unfruitful: an allusion to the fact that fig trees, being sexed, cannot bear fruit in isolation).

[u] *arbitrarium definitionem.*   [v] *ex internis.*

matters here would take us rather beyond the limits of our treatise. Accordingly, our demonstration establishing that the matter certainly could not be otherwise will have to suffice.

Application. 1. Firstly, I find that the real existence of bodies, which a more sensible philosophy has hitherto only been able to defend against the idealists by appealing to probability, follows with the greatest clarity from what is asserted in our principle.[57] For the soul is subject (in virtue of the inner sense) to inner changes. Since, as we have proved, these changes cannot arise from its nature considered in isolation and as disconnected from other things, it follows that there must be a number of things present outside the soul with which it stands in a reciprocal connection.[w] It is likewise apparent from the same considerations that the change of perceptions also takes place in conformity with external motion. It follows from this that we could not have a representation, which was a representation of a body and which was capable of being determined in a variety of ways, unless there was a real thing present to hand, and unless its interaction with the soul induced in it a representation corresponding to that thing. For this reason, it can easily be inferred that the compound, which we call our body, exists.

2. Our proof utterly overthrows the Leibnizian pre-established harmony,[58] not, as is generally the case, by means of final causes, which are thought to be unworthy of God and which not infrequently supply only an unreliable support, but by means of the internal impossibility of the thing itself. For it follows immediately from what we have demonstrated that, if the human soul were free from real connection with external things, the internal state of the soul would be completely devoid of changes.

3. Our demonstration furnishes the opinion that some kind of organic body must be attributed to all spirits whatever with powerful evidence of its certainty.

4. Our proof deduces the essential immutability of God, not from a ground of knowing deriving from His infinite nature, but from a principle which is peculiar to the nature of the Supreme Divinity.[x] The Supreme Divinity is completely free from all dependency whatever, and, since the determinations which belong to Him are not based upon any external relation at all, it is abundantly clear from what we have said that the state of God is completely free from change.

SCHOLIUM. It might perhaps seem to some that the principle we have adduced may be suspected of wrong-headedness on account of the indissolubility of the connection with which the human soul is thus bound with matter in carrying out its internal functions of thought, a view which

1:412

---

[w] *quibus mutuo nexu complexa est.*

[x] *sed e genuino sui principio* / (*genuinus:* from *ingenuus;* alt: innate, natural).

seems not that remote from the pernicious opinion of the materialists. But I do not deprive the soul of its representational state,^{y} even though I openly admit that the soul's state would be immutable and constantly like itself if it were completely released from external connection. And should anyone, perchance, seek to provoke a dispute with me, I should refer the matter to the modern philosophers who unanimously and as if with one voice openly declare that the connection of the soul with an organic body is necessary. I shall call only one witness from their number, the celebrated Crusius.[59] He is, I notice, so completely of my opinion that he frankly asserts that the mind is bound by a law, according to which its striving to produce^z representations is always united with a striving of its substance to produce a certain external motion, so that if the latter is hindered the former is also impeded. But although he does not regard this law as so necessary that it could not be suspended, if God so willed, nonetheless, since he concedes that the nature of the mind is governed by that law, it would have to be admitted that the nature of the mind would also have to be transcreated,^{a} if that law were suspended.

II. THE PRINCIPLE OF CO-EXISTENCE

1:413

Proposition XIII. Finite substances do not, in virtue of their existence alone, stand in a relationship with each other,^{b} nor are they linked together by any interaction at all,^{c} except in so far as the common principle of their existence, namely the divine understanding, maintains them in a state of harmony in their reciprocal relations.[60]

Demonstration.   Individual substances, of which none is the cause of the existence of another, have a separate existence, that is to say, an existence which can be completely understood independently of all other substances. If, therefore, the existence of some substance or other is posited simply, there is nothing inhering in it which proves the existence of other substances distinct from itself. But since a relation is a relative determination, that is to say, a determination which cannot be understood in a being considered absolutely, it follows that a relation and its determining ground can neither of them be understood in terms of the existence of a substance, when that existence is posited in itself. If, therefore, nothing further than this were admitted, no substance would stand in relation to any other substance, and there would be no interaction at all between substances.

---

^{y} *statum repraesentationum.* ^{z} *conatus in.*

^{a} *transcreari* / (Leibniz coined the term to designate the supernatural act by which the animal soul is endowed with reason; cf. *Théodicée* § 91.)

^{b} *nullis se relationibus respeciunt.* ^{c} *nulloque plane commercio contineantur.*

^{d} *mutuis respectibus conformatae* / (*conformare:* cf. OLD *conformo* (3): to make to correspond or agree; to bring into harmony with).

Since, therefore, in so far as each individual substance has an existence which is independent of other substances, no reciprocal connection occurs between them; and since it certainly does not fall to finite beings to be the causes of other substances, and since, nonetheless, all the things in the universe are found to be reciprocally connected with each other – since all this is the case, it has to be admitted that this relation depends on a communality of cause,[e] namely on God, the universal principle of beings. But it does not follow from the fact that God simply established the existence of things that there is also a reciprocal relation between those things, unless the self-same scheme of the divine understanding,[f] which gives existence, also established the relations of things to each other, by conceiving their existences as correlated with each other. It is most clearly apparent from this that the universal interaction of all things is to be ascribed to the concept alone of this divine idea.[g]

Elucidation.   I think that I am the first to have established, by means of reasons which are in the highest degree certain, that the co-existence of the substances of the universe is not sufficient to establish a connection between them. There is required, in addition, a certain community of origin and, arising therefrom, an harmonious dependence.[h] For, to repeat briefly the main line of my demonstration: if substance A exists, and if, in addition, B exists, then this latter can be considered as positing nothing in A. For suppose that it determined something in A, that is to say, suppose that it contained the ground of a determination C. Since this is a kind of relative predicate and hence not intelligible unless A is present, in addition to B, it follows that substance B will, in virtue of those factors which are the reason of τοῦ C, presuppose the existence of substance A. But since, if substance B existed alone, its existence would leave it completely indeterminate whether a certain substance A would have to exist or not, it will be impossible to understand from the existence of B alone that it posits anything in other substances distinct from itself. Hence there is no relation and no interaction at all. If, therefore, God had created, in addition to substance A, other substances B, D, E, and so on to infinity, their reciprocal dependency on each other in respect of their determinations would, nonetheless, not immediately follow from the fact of their existence.[i] Nor, since, in addition to A, there also exist B, D, and E, and A is somehow determined in itself, does it follow that B, D, E have determinations of existence consonant with A.[j] Accordingly, the ground of their reciprocal dependence upon each other must also be present in the manner of their common dependence on God. How that is brought about is   1:414

---

[e] *communione causae.*   [f] *idem . . . intellectus divini schema.*   [g] *divinae ideae conceptui soli.*
[h] *communionem quandam originis et harmonicam ex hoc dependentiam.*
[i] *e data ipsarum exsistentia.*   [j] *huic conformes . . . exsistendi determinationes.*

easy for the understanding to comprehend. The schema of the divine understanding, the origin of existences, is an enduring act (it is called preservation); and in that act, if any substances are conceived by God as existing in isolation and without any relational determinations, no connection between them and no reciprocal relation would come into being. If, however, they are conceived as related[k] in God's intelligence, their determinations would subsequently, in conformity with this idea, always relate to each other for as long as they continued to exist. That is to say, they would act and react; and the individual substances would have a certain external state. But if you abandoned this principle, no such state could exist in virtue of their existence alone.

Application. 1. Since place, position, and space are relations of substances, in virtue of which substances, by means of their reciprocal determinations, relate to other substances which are really distinct from themselves and are in this way connected together in an external connection,[61] and since, furthermore, our demonstration has shown that the mere existence of substances does not in itself involve connection with other substances, it is obvious that, if you posit a number of substances, you do not at the same time and as a result determine place, position, and space, this last being compounded[m] of all these relations. But, since the reciprocal connection of substances requires that there should be, in the effective representation[n] of the divine intellect, a scheme conceived in terms of relations,[o] and since this representation is entirely a matter of choice for God,[p] and can therefore be admitted or omitted according to His pleasure, it follows that substances can exist in accordance with the law which specifies that *they are in no place* and that they stand in no relation at all in respect of the things of our universe.

2. There could be, if God so willed, a number of such substances, free from any connection with our universe, but, nonetheless, linked with each other by means of a certain connection of their determinations so as to produce place, position, and space: they would constitute a world banished beyond the limits of the world, of which we are parts, that is to say, they would constitute a solitary world. For this reason, the possibility that there might be, had it so pleased God, a number of worlds, even in the metaphysical sense, is not absurd.[62]

3. Since, therefore, the existence of substances is completely insufficient on its own to establish their reciprocal interaction or any relation between their determinations; and since, accordingly, their external con-

---

[k] *respective.*

[l] *hacque ratione nexu externo continentur* / (*continentur:* cf. OLD *contineo* (1): to join together, link, connect).

[m] *conflatur.* [n] *in efficaci repraesentatione.* [o] *respective conceptam delineationem.*

[p] *Deo plane arbitraria.*

nection proves that there is a common cause of all things, in which their existence has been conceived as standing in relation to other existences, and since, too, it is not possible, without this communality of principle,[q] to conceive a universal connection, it follows that it is possible to infer with the greatest certainty that there is a supreme cause of all things, and, indeed, only one, that is to say, God. Indeed, this proof, in my opinion, seems to be far superior to the proof from contingency.[63]

4. Our principle also utterly overthrows the extravagant opinion of the Manicheans, who set up two principles which are equally primary and independent of each other, and which exercise dominion over the world.[64] For a substance can only interact with the things of the universe either if it is their common cause or if it has issued from the same cause as the things in the universe. Accordingly, if you declare that one of these two principles is the cause of all things, it follows that the other can in no wise determine anything in them. If you declare that one of the two principles is the cause of at least some things in the universe, it follows that these things will not be able to interact at all with the remaining things in the universe. Alternatively, you must either declare that one of the two principles depends on the other, or that they both depend on a common cause. But both positions are equally incompatible with the hypothesis.

1:415

5. Furthermore, since the determinations of substances are reciprocally related to each other, that is to say, since substances which are distinct from each other reciprocally act on each other (for one substance determines certain things in the other substance), it follows that the concept of space is constituted[r] by the interconnected actions of substances, reaction always being of necessity conjoined with such interconnected actions.[65] If the external appearance[s] of this universal action and reaction throughout the whole realm of the space in which bodies stand in relation to one another consists in their reciprocally drawing closer together, it is called *attraction*. Since it is brought about by co-presence alone, it reaches to all distances whatever, and is *Newtonian attraction* or universal gravity. It is, accordingly, probable that this attraction is brought about by the same connection of substances, by virtue of which they determine space. It is also probable that it is the most fundamental[t] law of nature governing matter, remaining constantly in force only in virtue of God's immediately sustaining it, according to the opinion itself of those who declare themselves to be followers of Newton.

6. All substances, in so far as they are connected with each other[u] in the same space, reciprocally interact with each other, and thus they are dependent on each other in respect of their determinations. It is, hence, possible to understand the universal action of spirits on bodies and of bodies on

---

[q] *sine hac principii communione.*   [r] *absolvitur.*   [s] *phaenomenon.*   [t] *maxime primitivam.*
[u] *continentur.*

spirits.^{v} But no substance of any kind has the power of determining other substances, distinct from itself, by means of that which belongs to it internally (as we have proved). It follows from this that it only has this power in virtue of the connection, by means of which they are linked together in the idea entertained by the Infinite Being.^{w} It follows that, whatever determinations and changes are to be found in any of them, they always refer, indeed, to what is external. Physical influence^x, in the true sense of the term,[66] however, is excluded. There exists a universal *harmony* of things. Nonetheless, this does not give rise to the well-known *Leibnizian pre-established harmony,*[67] which is properly speaking *agreement*^{y} between substances, not their reciprocal *dependency* on each other. For God does not make use of the craftsman's cunning devices, carefully fitted into a sequence of suitably arranged means designed^z to bring about a concord^a between substances. Nor, moreover, is there an ever special influence of God, that is to say, an influence through which the interaction of substances is here established by means of *Malebranche's occasional causes.*[68] For the same indivisible^b act, which brings substances into existence and sustains them in existence, procures their reciprocal and universal dependence, so that the divine act does not need to be determined, now one way, now another, according to circumstances. There is rather a real reciprocal action between substances; in other words, there is interaction between substances by means of truly efficient causes. For the same principle, which establishes the existence of things, also brings it about that they are subject to this law. And, hence, reciprocal interaction is established by means of those determinations which attach to the origin of their existence. For this reason, one is equally justified both in saying that external changes may be produced in this way by means of efficient causes, and also in saying that the changes which occur within the substance are ascribed to an internal force of the substance, although the natural power of this force to produce an effect^c rests, no less than the foundation of the external relations just mentioned, on divine support.

However, the system of the universal interaction of substances, constituted in this way, is certainly somewhat superior to the popular system of *physical influence,* for the former, to be sure, reveals the origin itself of the reciprocal connection of things; and this origin is to be sought outside the

1:416

---

^{v} *Cum substantiarum omnium, quatenus spatio eodem continentur, sit mutuum commercium, hinc dependentia mutua in determinationibus, actio universales spirituum in corpora corporumque in spiritus inde intelligi potest* / (F & B construe *dependentia mutua* as governed by *intelligi potest;* C, E, and R, with whom the present translator agrees, construe *dependentia mutua* as governed by *cum . . . hinc*).

^{w} *in idea entis infiniti.* ^{x} *influxus physicus.* ^{y} *consensum.*

^{z} *in rationum concinnatarum serie adaptatis.* ^{a} *conspirationem.* ^{b} *individua.*

^{c} *huius . . . efficacia.*

principle of substances, considered as existing in isolation. And, in this respect, that threadbare system of efficient causes could not be further from the truth.

SCHOLIUM. Here, kind reader, you have the two principles of a deeper metaphysical cognition. By their means you may acquire no inconsiderable power in the realm of truths. Indeed, if this science be thus carefully cultivated, its soil will be found not to be so barren. The objection of futile and obscure subtlety, raised against it by those who scorn it, will be refuted by an ample harvest of more remarkable knowledge.[d] There are, it is true, certain people who are passionate in their hunting down fallacious conclusions in the writings of others, and who are adepts at invariably extracting a kind of venom from the opinions of others. I do not wish to dispute that they may, perhaps, be able to twist some of what we say, even in this work of ours, in an unfavourable sense. But I shall allow them to indulge their opinions, for I do not think that it is incumbent on me to worry about what someone may happen wrong-headedly to think. My concern is rather to proceed along the straight path of enquiry and knowledge.[e] And I ask, with due respect, that whoever looks with favour on proper scholarship[f] may be well-disposed towards my efforts.

[d] *nobilioris.*

[e] *indaginis atque doctrinae* / B: *der Forschung und Lehre* / C: *dell'indagine e dell'insegnamento* / E: investigation and speculation / F: *de la recherche et de la science* / R: investigation and in a way appropriate to science.

[f] *litteris ingenuis* / B: *echte Wissenschaft* / C: *delle patrie lettere* / E: unfettered enquiry / F: *arts libéraux* / R: liberal letters.

The employment in natural philosophy of metaphysics combined with geometry, of which sample I contains the physical monadology (1756)

Metaphysicae cum geometria junctae usus in philosophia naturali, cuius specimen 1. continet monadologiam physicam
(MDCCLVI)

METAPHYSICAE CUM GEOMETRIA IUNCTAE USUS
IN PHILOSOPHIA NATURALI,

CUIUS

SPECIMEN I.

CONTINET

MONADOLOGIAM PHYSICAM,

QUAM

CONSENTIENTE AMPLISSIMO PHILOSOPHORUM ORDINE

DIE X. APRILIS HORIS VIII—XII

IN AUDITORIO PHIL.

DEFENDET

M. IMMANUEL KANT,

RESPONDENTE

LUCA DAVIDE VOGEL,

REG. BOR. S. THEOL. CULTORE,

OPPONENTIBUS ADOLESCENTIBUS INGENUIS AC PERPOLITIS

LUDOVICO ERNESTO BOROWSKI,

REGIOM. BOR. S. THEOL. CULTORE,

GEORGIO LUDOVICO MUEHLENKAMPF,

TREMPIA AD DARKEHMIAM BORUSSO S. THEOL. CULTORE.

ET

LUDOVICO IOANNE KRUSEMARCK,

KYRIZENSI MARCHICO S. THEOL. CULTORE.

ANNO MDCCLVI.

The employment in natural philosophy of
metaphysics combined with geometry, of
which sample I contains the PHYSICAL
MONADOLOGY,

which,
by consent of the most eminent faculty of philosophers,
will be defended by
Magister Immanuel Kant
on April 10th, in the philosophical auditorium,
between the hours of eight and twelve.
The respondent: Lucas David Vogel,
of Königsberg in Prussia,
candidate in sacred theology,
The opponents:
the honourable and accomplished young gentlemen
Ludwig Ernst Borowski
of Königsberg in Prussia,
candidate in sacred theology;
Georg Ludwig Mühlenkampf
of Trempen near Darkehmen in Prussia,
candidate in sacred theology;
and
Ludwig Johann Krusemark
of Kyritz in the Mark,
candidate in sacred theology,
in the year 1756

The president and respondent
wish in humblest submission
to dedicate this offering
to the most celebrated, noble and excellent,
The Lord
WILHELM LUDWIG VON DER GRÖBEN
Privy Counsellor and Minister of War
to
The Most Powerful King of Prussia,
Most Distinguished President
of the Supreme Court of Appeal in Prussia,
Tireless Protector of our Albertina,
as also
Most August Director of the College of Stipends,
Hereditary Lord of the Domains
Tharau, Karschau etc.,
Peerless Patron of the Muses,
Most Favourably and Benevolently Disposed Hero

Clear-headed philosophers, who seriously engage in the investigations of nature, unanimously agree, indeed, that punctilious care must be taken lest anything concocted with rashness or with a certain arbitrariness of conjecture[a] should insinuate itself into natural science, or lest anything be vainly undertaken in it without the support of experience and without the mediation of geometry.[1] Certainly, nothing can be thought more useful to philosophy, or more beneficial to it, than this counsel. However, hardly any mortal can advance with a firm step along the straight line of truth without here and there turning aside in one direction or another. For this reason there have been some who have observed this law to such a degree that, in searching out the truth, they have not ventured to commit themselves to the deep sea but have considered it better to hug the coast, only admitting what is immediately revealed by the testimony of the senses. And, certainly, if we follow this sound path, we can exhibit the laws of nature though not the origin and causes of these laws. For those who only hunt out the phenomena of nature are always that far removed from the deeper understanding of the first causes. Nor will they ever attain knowledge of the nature itself of bodies, any more than those who persuade themselves that, by climbing higher and higher up the pinnacles of a mountain they will at last be able to reach out and touch the heavens with their hands.

Metaphysics, therefore, which many say may be properly absent from physics is, in fact, its only support; it alone provides illumination. For bodies consist of parts; it is certainly of no little importance that it be clearly established of which parts, and in what way they are combined together, and whether they fill space merely by the co-presence of their primitive parts or by the reciprocal conflict of their forces. But how, in this business, can metaphysics be married to geometry, when it seems easier to mate griffins with horses[2] than to unite transcendental philosophy with geometry? For the former peremptorily denies that space is infinitely divisible, while the latter, with its usual certainty, asserts that it is infinitely divisible. Geometry contends that empty space is necessary for free motion, while metaphysics hisses the idea off the stage.[b] Geometry holds universal attraction or gravitation to be hardly explicable by mechanical

---

[a] *coniectandi quadam licentia.* [b] *illa explodit.*

51

1:476   causes but shows that it derives from the forces which are inherent in bodies at rest and which act at a distance, whereas metaphysics dismisses the notion as an empty delusion of the imagination.

Although the settlement of this argument appears to involve no small labour, I have resolved to devote at least some effort to the matter. Others, whose powers are more adapted to this business, are invited to complete that which has stretched my powers to the full, even though I have merely touched upon the problem.

I would merely add the following remarks by way of conclusion. Since the principle of all internal actions, in other words, the force which is inherent in the elements, must be a moving force, and one, indeed, which operates in an outward direction,^{c} since it is present to what is external; and since we are unable to conceive of any other force for moving that which is co-present than one which endeavours to repel or attract; and since, furthermore, if we posit only the repulsive force, we shall not be able to conceive of the conjunction of elements so that they form compound bodies, but only their diffusion, whereas if we posit only an attractive force we shall only be able to understand their conjunction, but not their determinate^d extension and space – since all this is the case, we can already in a way understand that anyone who is able to deduce these two principles from the very nature and fundamental properties^e of the elements will have made a substantial contribution towards explaining the inner nature of bodies.

^{c} *extrinsicus* / Beck (1986) (hereafter B): _____ / Carabellese (hereafter C): *all'esterno* / Hinske (hereafter H): *von aussen* / Nicolovius (Tieftrunk) (hereafter N): *nach aussen zu* / Zac (hereafter Z): *a l'extérieur.*
^{d} *definita.* ^{e} *affectionibus.*

SECTION I. SHOWING THAT THE EXISTENCE OF PHYSICAL MONADS IS IN AGREEMENT WITH GEOMETRY

PROPOSITION I. DEFINITION. A simple substance, which is also called a monad,* is one which does not consist of a plurality of parts, any one of which could exist separately from the others.

PROPOSITION II. THEOREM. Bodies consist of monads.

Bodies consist of parts, each of which separately has an enduring existence. Since, however, the composition of such parts is nothing but a relation, and hence a determination which is in itself contingent, and which can be denied without abrogating the existence of the things having this relation, it is plain that all composition of a body can be abolished, though all the parts which were formerly combined together nonetheless continue to exist. When all composition is abolished, moreover, the parts which are left are not compound at all; and thus they are completely free from plurality of substances, and, consequently, they are simple. All bodies, whatever, therefore, consist of absolutely simple fundamental parts, that is to say, monads.

SCHOLIUM. I have deliberately omitted the celebrated principle of the sufficient ground*f*4 from the present demonstration. In omitting it, I have accomplished my purpose by means of the ordinary combination of concepts to which all philosophers subscribe, for I was apprehensive that those who do not accept the principle of the sufficient ground5 would be less convinced by an argument which was based upon it.

---

* Since the purpose of my undertaking is only to treat of the class of simple substances which are the primitive parts of bodies, I give advance warning that in what follows I shall use the following terms as if they were synonymous: *simple substances, monads, elements of matter,* and *fundamental parts of body.*3

f rationis principium.

53

PROPOSITION III. THEOREM. *Space which bodies fill is divisible to infinity; space does not, therefore, consist of primitive and simple parts.*[6]

Let there be given a line *ef* which is indefinitely extended, that is to say, a line which is such that it can always be extended further; and let there be given another line *ab*, a physical line, that is to say, a line which, if the

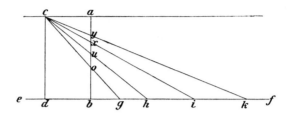

reader will permit, is composed of the fundamental parts of matter,[7] and which intersects *ef* at a right angle. To the side of *ab* let another line *cd* be erected, which is equal to *ab* and parallel to it. This, it will not be disputed, can be done not only in the geometrical sense but also in the physical sense. Let arbitrary[g] points *g*, *h*, *i*, *k*, and so on indefinitely, be marked on the line *ef*. First of all, no one will dispute that between any two points, or, if you will, between any two given monads, it is possible to draw a physical straight line. Thus, let a line *cg* be drawn, and let the point where it intersects the perpendicular *ab* be called *o*. Now imagine another physical line drawn between points *c* and *h*: the place[h] *u*, which is common to both *ch* and *ab*, will be closer to point *a*. Continuing in this way, let there be drawn from the same point *c* lines to whatever points you wish on line *ef* extended indefinitely, such as *i*, *k*, etc. Their points of intersection get closer and closer to the point *a*, as is self-evident even to those who are completely ignorant of geometry. And if you suppose that these physical lines will eventually be too close together, so that they will no longer be able to continue to exist next to each other, the lower lines can be removed. Nonetheless, it is obvious that the points of intersection must get closer and closer to *a*,* the further and further along the line *ef* you place the point. Since this distance[i] can be extended to infinity, the point of intersection can be moved closer and closer to *a* by the addition of infinitely many parts.[j] But the intersection will never coincide with *a* in this way. For, in fact, since the points *c* and *a* are equidistant from *ef*, no matter how far you extend the line which joins points *c* and *a*, it will always be the

---

* Nor can points *y* and *x* ever coincide, for otherwise lines *cy* and *cx* would likewise coincide, and line *ck* would coincide with *ci*; and that is contrary to what has been presupposed.

    [g] *quaelibet.*   [h] *locus.*   [i] *longinquitas.*   [j] *infinitis incrementis partibus.*

same distance from the line *ef* beneath it; nor can they ever meet, for this would be against the hypothesis. Thus, by continuously dividing the line *oa*, we shall never arrive at simple parts, which cannot be divided further. That is to say, space is divisible to infinity and it does not consist of simple parts.

SCHOLIUM. I have adduced this demonstration, which has already been employed by many physicists,[8] and I have adapted it, as clearly as I could, to physical space, so that those who employ a general distinction, based upon the difference between geometrical and natural space,[k] should not escape the force of my argument by means of an exception. There are, it is true, other demonstrations of this proposition available. To mention only one: imagine, if you will, an equilateral triangle constructed from monads. If two sides of the triangle are extended indefinitely, so that you have distances which are twice, thrice, five or a hundred times greater than the sides of the given triangle, the extremities of these lines can be joined by physical lines. These physical lines will be longer than the third side in the same ratio as in the original triangle, and they will consist of a proportionately greater number of simple particles. But, between any of these monads and the one which is situated at the apex of the triangle it is possible to imagine physical lines being drawn which divide the base of the triangle in question to infinity.[l] This provides an excellent defence of the infinity of space. But anyone who is free from the impediments of prejudiced opinion and who has understood the demonstration adduced above, will be able, in my opinion, to dispense with all the other proofs.

1:479

PROPOSITION IV. THEOREM. A compound which is divisible to infinity does not consist of primitive or simple parts.

In the case of an infinitely divisible compound, we never, in the process of dividing it, arrive at parts which are free from composition; composition which cannot be removed by division cannot be removed at all, unless the compound is deprived of all existence; for the parts which are left in the compound when all composition has been eliminated are, according to Proposition I, called simple. It follows that an infinitely divisible compound cannot consist of such parts.

SCHOLIUM. It was my opinion that, having established that the primitive parts of any body whatsoever were simple, and having asserted the infinite division of the space occupied by any such body, it would not be inconsistent with the purpose of this undertaking to take care that no one should take monads to be the infinitely small particles of a body. For it is abundantly plain that space, which is entirely free from substan-

---

[k] *qui generali de diversitate spatiorum geometrici et naturalis discrimine utuntur.*   [l] *infinities.*

tiality and which is the appearance of the external relations of unitary monads,[m] will not at all be exhausted by division continued to infinity. However, in the case of any compound whatever, where composition is nothing but an accident and in which there are substantial subjects of composition, it would be absurd if it admitted infinite division.[9] For if a compound were to admit infinite division, it would follow that all the fundamental parts whatever of a body would be so constituted that, whether they were combined with a thousand, or ten thousand, or millions of millions – in a word, with no matter how many – they would not constitute particles of matter. This would certainly and obviously deprive a compound of all substantiality; it cannot, therefore, apply to the bodies of nature.[10]

COROLLARY. *All bodies therefore consist of a determinate number of simple elements.*

1:480   *PROPOSITION V. THEOREM. Each simple element of a body, that is to say, each monad, is not only in space; it also fills[n] a space, though it does not, for that reason, forfeit its simplicity.*

Since all bodies whatever are compounded of[o] a determinate number of simple elements, whereas the space which it fills admits of infinite division, it follows that each of these elements will occupy a part of space which admits of yet further division; that is to say, a body will fill some specifiable[p] space.

The division of space, however, is not the separation of things,[q] of which one is set apart from another and has a self-sufficient existence of its own. It rather displays a certain plurality or quantity in an external relation. Since this is the case, it is obvious that a plurality of substantial parts does not follow from the division of space. Since it is this plurality alone which would be opposed to the substantial simplicity of the monad, it is sufficiently clear that the divisibility of space is not at all opposed to the simplicity of the monad.

SCHOLIUM. In an inquiry into elements there is certainly no opinion which constitutes a greater impediment to the marriage of geometry and metaphysics than the preconceived but insufficiently examined opinion that the divisibility[r] of the space which an element occupies demonstrates the division[s] of the element itself into substantial parts. This view has been commonly asserted to be so far beyond any possible doubt that those who asserted the infinite division[t] of real space have had an absolute horror of monads, as well;[11] while those who supported monads regarded it as their

---

[m] *relationis externae unitarum monadum phaenomenon.*   [n] *implet.*   [o] *conflatum.*   [p] *assignabile.*
[q] *divisio spatii non sit separatio eorum.*   [r] *divisibilitas.*   [s] *divisionem.*   [t] *divisionem infinitam.*

duty to maintain that the properties[u] of geometrical space were imaginary.[12] But it is clearly apparent from what has been demonstrated above that it is neither the case that the geometer is mistaken nor that the opinion to be found among metaphysicians deviates from the truth. It hence follows that the opinion which divides them both, namely, that an element, which is absolutely simple in respect of its substance, cannot fill a space without losing its simplicity, must be false. The line or surface which divides a small space into two parts certainly indicates that one part of the space exists outside the other. But since space is not a substance but a certain appearance of the external relation of substances, it follows that the possibility of dividing the relation of one and the same substance into two parts is not incompatible with the simplicity of, or if you prefer, the unity of the substance. For what exists on each side of the dividing line is not something which can be so separated from the substance that it preserves an existence of its own, apart from the substance itself and in separation from it, which would, of course, be necessary for real division which destroys simplicity. What exists on each side of the dividing line is an action which is exercised on both sides of one and the same substance; in other words, it is a relation, in which the existence of a certain plurality does not amount to tearing the substance itself into parts.

PROPOSITION VI. THEOREM. *The monad does not determine the little space of its presence by the plurality of its substantial parts, but by the sphere of the activity,[v] by means of which it hinders the things which are external to it and which are present to it on both sides from drawing any closer to each other.*

Since there is no plurality of substances to be found in the monad, though any[w] monad, when posited on its own, fills a space, it follows from what has been said that the ground for the filled space is not to be sought in the mere positing[x] of a substance but in its relation with respect to the substances external to it. But, by filling the space, it prevents the monads immediately present to it on each side from drawing closer to each other, and thus it determines something in their position, doing so, namely, by limiting the degree of proximity to which they are able to approach it. It is, hence, clear that a monad exercises an action, and does so, indeed, in a space which is determinate in all directions. It must, therefore, be granted that the monad fills the space by the sphere of its activity.

1:481

[u] *affectiones.*

[v] *Monas spatiolum praesentiae suae definita non pluralitate partium suarum substantialium, sed sphera activitatis.*

[w] *quaevis* / B: no (following Adickes to avoid an alleged contradiction) / C: *ogni* / H: *eine jede* / Z: *n'importe quelle.*

[x] *positio.*

PROPOSITION VII. PROBLEM. To secure further from difficulties the view that every monad occupies a space by means of the sphere of its activity and without losing its simplicity.

If a monad fills a determinate space, as we have argued, that space can be expressed by any other limited space.[y] Let, therefore, the circle *ABCD* represent the little space which a monad occupies by its activity. *BD* will

be the diameter of the sphere of its activity, that is to say, the diameter at which it prevents other monads present to it at *B* and at *D* from drawing closer to each other. But take care lest you say for that reason that this is the diameter of the monad itself; for that would, of course, be absurd. Nor is anything further from our meaning. For since space can be described only in terms of[z] external relations, it follows that whatever is internal to substance, that is to say, substance itself or the subject of external determinations, is not strictly speaking defined by space.[a] It is only those determinations which stand in relation to something external which may legitimately be sought in space. But, you say, substance is to be found in this little space and is everywhere present within it; so, if one divides space, does not one divide substance? I answer: this space itself is the orbit of the external presence of its element. Accordingly, if one divides space, one divides the extensive quantity of its presence. But, in addition to external presence, that is to say, in addition to the relational determinations of substance, there are other, internal determinations; if the latter did not exist, the former would have no subject in which to inhere. But the internal determinations are not in space, precisely because they are internal.[13] Accordingly, they are not themselves divided by the division of the external determinations. And therefore the subject itself, that is to say, the substance, is not divided in this way. It is as if one were to say that God was internally present to all created things by the act of preservation; and that thus someone who divides the mass of created things divides God, since that person divides the orbit of His presence – and than this there is nothing more absurd which could be said. The monad, therefore, which is the fundamental element of a body, in so far as it fills space, certainly has a certain extensive quantity, namely, an orbit of activity.[14] You will not find in

[y] *illud quaevis alio finito exprimi poterit.*   [z] *absolvatur.*
[a] *proprie non definitur spatio* / (alt: 'is not limited by').

this orbit of activity a plurality of things, of which each one, existing on its own and in isolation from the others, would have its own permanence. For what is found in the space *BCD* cannot be separated from what is present in the space *BAD* so that each existed on its own, for each is nothing but an external determination of one and the same substance; but accidents do not exist independently of their substances.*

> *PROPOSITION VIII. THEOREM. The force by which the simple element of a body occupies its space is the same as that which others call* impenetrability. *If the former force is denied, the latter would not be possible.*

Impenetrability is that property*c* of a body, in virtue of which a thing in contact with it is excluded from the space which the body occupies. But since it is clear from what has been said above that the space which a body occupies (if you conceive the parts of that body as being united together as closely as possible without there being any empty space between)*d* is composed of the little spaces which the individual simple elements fill; since, furthermore, a resistance*e* and, therefore, a certain force is necessary to prevent external bodies penetrating the space it fills; since, in other words, impenetrability is required, but since, finally, it has already been demonstrated above that elements fill their determinate space by a certain activity which prevents other bodies from penetrating it – since all this is the case, it is obvious that the impenetrability of bodies depends on no other force than that same natural force of the elements. That was the first point.

The next thing is this. Let the line *ag* be composed of the primitive elements of matter, that is to say, of monads. If some element or other *d*, by the presence of its substance, merely indicated a place and did not occupy a space, the place *d* would bisect the given line *ag*. And since it

* Of all the difficulties which could be raised against our view, the one which seems to be the most serious is the one which derives from the positing outside each other*b* of the determinations of one and the same substance. For the action of the monad which is in the space *BCD* is external to the action which is in the space *BDA*; they thus seem to be really different from each other and to be found outside the substance. But relations are always both outside each other and outside substance, for those beings, to which the substance is related, are really different from the substance and from one another. And this does not show a substantial plurality.

b extrapositione / B: externalisation / C: *disporre al di fuori* / H: *Heraussetzung* / N: *Aussereinanderseyn* / Z: *sont posées les unes en dehors des autres.*
c affectio. *d* absque vacuo intermisto. *e* renitentia.

thus marks where one half of the line ceases and the other half begins, it would be common to both halves of the line. But physical lines are only equal if they consist of an equal number of elements; but the number of elements in the two halves is only equal in the lines *ac* and *eg*. Therefore the place of the monad *d* is common to the lines *ac* and *eg*. That is to say, the lines in question will meet each other immediately at the place denoted. Accordingly, the element *d* will not prevent *c* and *e* from coming into immediate contact with each other; that is to say, *d* will not be impenetrable. Thus, if you deny that the place occupied by the monad *d* is common to lines *ac* and *eg*, it will be point *x* where lines *ad* and *eg* immediately meet each other and point *o* at which the lines *ad* and *eg* meet each other. Since, therefore, the place of the monad *d* is different from the place *x* and likewise from the place *o* – for otherwise *d* would always be the common place of immediate contact, as we said before – you will have

1:483 three different places, *x*, *d*, and *o*, and they, without any doubt, define a certain line. Consequently, a determinate*ᶠ* line is defined*ᵍ* by the immediate presence of the monad *d*; that is to say, *d* is present in a determinate space. And since, by the mere positing of a substance, the monad can occupy, not a space, but only a place,*ʰ* it necessarily follows that there will be something else present in the substance which determines both the degree of the proximity*ⁱ* of the elements touching it on both sides and the force which prevents the elements *c* and *e* from moving closer together.*ʲ* But on both sides force can only be opposed by force. It is, therefore, the same force in virtue of which an element of a body occupies its space, and which causes impenetrability. That was the second point.

SECTION 2. EXPLAINING THE MOST GENERAL PROPERTIES*ᵏ* OF PHYSICAL MONADS, IN SO FAR AS THEY ARE DIFFERENT IN DIFFERENT THINGS AND CONTRIBUTE TO THE UNDERSTANDING OF THE NATURE OF BODIES

PROPOSITION IX. DEFINITION. Contact is the reciprocal application of the forces of impenetrability of several elements.

SCHOLIUM. Contact is commonly defined in terms of immediate presence.[15] But even if you insisted on adding *external* (for without this addition, God, who is immediately present to all things, albeit *internally* present, would have to be thought of as touching them), the definition will hardly be thought to be complete in all respects. For since others have

---

ᶠ *definita.* *ᵍ* *definitur* / ('defined' in the sense of 'define the limits of').
ʰ *per solam substantiae positionem non spatium, sed locum occupare posset.*
ⁱ *propinquitatis . . . mensuram.* *ʲ* *et vim quamlibet a propriori accessu elementorum c et e arcet.*
ᵏ *Affectiones.*

succeeded in satisfactorily establishing that bodies separated by empty space can nevertheless coexist and can therefore be immediately present to each other, though without reciprocal contact, this definition will doubtless be found to have its weaknesses. The Newtonian School, not without a great show of truth, defended the immediate attraction of bodies, even at a distance from each other, their co-presence, nonetheless, occurring in the absence of reciprocal contact.[16] Furthermore, if one defends the definition which attempts to substitute immediate co-presence for the notion of contact itself, one ought first to explain the notion of this presence. If, as is usual, it is explained in terms of reciprocal action, in what, I ask, does the action consist? Undoubtedly, bodies act by moving each other. But the moving force,[l] which is exerted from a given point, either repels other bodies from that point, or attracts them to it. It is obvious which of the two actions is to be understood as involved in contact. For, in moving one body closer and closer to another, we say that they are touching each other when the force of impenetrability, that is to say, of repulsion, is felt. Thus, the action and reaction of the different elements against each other constitutes the genuine notion of contact.

PROPOSITION X. THEOREM. Bodies would not have a determinate volume[m] in virtue of the force of impenetrability alone; there must be another force, which is likewise inherent in them, the force of attraction. The two forces together define the limit[n] of the extension of bodies.

The force of impenetrability is a repulsive force, which prevents anything external from approaching more closely. Since this force is innate[o] in all elements whatever, one can, it is true, understand from its nature why the intensity of its action diminishes as the distance over which its influence extends increases. But why, at any given distance,[p][17] it should cease altogether – that is something which cannot be understood from its nature at all.[18] Thus, if it were this force alone which existed, bodies would have no cohesive structure[q] at all, for the particles would only repel each other, and no body would have a volume which was circumscribed by a determinate limit. It is, therefore, necessary that there be opposed to this striving another striving which is opposed to it and which is equal to it at a given distance, and which, by occupying a space, determines its limit. But that which acts in the opposite direction to repulsion is attraction. Accordingly, in addition to the force of impenetrability, every element needs another

1:484

---

[l] *vis motrix.*   [m] *definito volumine.*   [n] *limitem definiens.*   [o] *ingenita.*

[p] *in distantia quavis data* / B: at a certain (reading *quadam* for *quavis*) given distance / C: *ad una qualsiasi distanza* / H: *in einer beliebigen gegebenen Entfernung* / Z: *à une distance donnée quelconque.*

[q] *corporum compages plane nulla foret.*

force, that of attraction. If the force of attraction did not exist, then the bodies of nature would have no determinate volume.

SCHOLIUM. To inquire into the laws governing the two forces in the elements, the repulsive and the attractive forces, is an investigation of high importance, and worthy of exercising the most acute minds. It suffices me here to have proved the existence of these forces, and to have done so with the greatest of certainty, and within the limits prescribed by the law of brevity. But if someone wished to look forwards, as from a great distance, to what belongs to this question,ʳ would he not think that, since the repulsive force is exercised in an outward direction from the central pointˢ of the space occupied by an element, its intensity would diminish in inverse proportion to the increase of the space through which it is extended?¹⁹ For the force spreading from the point can only be seen to exercise an effectᵗ in a definite sphere if, by its action, it fills the whole space embraced by the given diameter. This will be clear from the following consideration. If one imagines a force emanating in straight lines from a given surface, as light does, or even, in Keill's view,²⁰ the attractive force itself, the force exercised in this way will be in proportionᵘ to the number of the lines which can be drawn from this surface, that is to say, in proportion to the surface of the active being. Thus, if the surface is infinitely small, the force will be infinitely small, as well; and if, finally, it is a point, the force will be nothing at all. A force spreading along lines diverging from a point cannot, therefore, have a specifiable value at a certain specifiable distance. And, therefore, its exercising an effect can only be ascertained if it fills the whole space in which it acts. But spherical spaces are in proportion to the cube of their radii.ᵛ Therefore, since the same force diffused throughout a larger sphere is diminished in a ratio which is the inverse of the volume of their spaces, the force of impenetrability will be in inverse ratio of the cubes of the distances from the centre of their presence.²¹

On the other hand, since attraction is, of course, the action of the same element, albeit in the opposite direction, the spherical surface towards which the attraction is exercised at a given distance will be the limit from which it is exercised.ʷ²² Since the multitude of the points, from which lines extending to the centre can be drawn, is determinate, and since, therefore, the magnitude of the attraction is also determinate, it follows that the attractive force can be assigned a definite value:ˣ it will decrease in the

---

ʳ *Sed si veluti e longinquo quaedam ad hanc quaestionem pertinentia prospicere arridet.*

ˢ *e puncto intimo.* ᵗ *efficax.* ᵘ *hac ratione exercita in ratione.*

ᵛ *Sed spatia sphaerica sunt, ut cubi distantiarum.*

ʷ *terminus a quo* / B: _____ / C: *il termine di partenza* / H: *der Ausgangspunkt* / Z: *terminus a quo.*

ˣ *assignabilis.*

inverse ratio of the spherical surfaces, that is to say, with the inverse square of the distances.[y][23]

If, therefore, it is established that the repulsive force decreases according to the inverse cube[z] and thus at a far greater rate than the attractive force,[a] there must be some point on the diameter where attraction and repulsion are equal. This point will determine the limit of impenetrability and the orbit of external contact; that is to say, it will determine the volume; for the repulsive force, once it has been overcome by attraction, ceases to act any further.

1:485

COROLLARY. If you consider this law of inherent forces to be valid, you will also acknowledge that all elements will be equal in volume, no matter how different in kind they may be. For, although it is clear that the forces of repulsion, no less than those of attraction, each having a definite degree of intensity, will be entirely different in different elements, sometimes being more intense, sometimes less so; but since, nevertheless, the doubled force of repulsion is doubled at the same distance, and likewise the attractive force; and since it is reasonable to expect that all the moving forces of an element, which is by nature twice as strong, will be stronger in the same proportion, it follows that both the named forces will always be equal to each other at the same distance, and thus that they will necessarily determine an equal volume of elements, no matter how greatly their forces may differ in degree from the like-named forces of other elements.[24]

PROPOSITION XI. THEOREM. The force of inertia[b] has a fixed magnitude in any element whatever and it can differ enormously in different elements.

A body in motion, which collided with another body, would exercise no effect on it,[c] and it would be reduced to a state of rest by any infinitely small obstacle, if it had no force of inertia, in virtue of which it would strive to persevere in the state of motion. The force of inertia of a body (which is, of course, called its mass) is, however, the sum of the forces of inertia of all the elements of which it is composed. Therefore, any element which moved with a certain velocity would only have the power to produce[d] motion if its velocity were multiplied by the force of inertia. But any factor whatever which, in being multiplied by another factor, yields a magnitude[e] which is larger than that other factor, is itself a quantity,[f] to which another quantity, sometimes greater, sometimes smaller, may be assigned. Accordingly, in the case of elements of different kinds, a different quantity, which may be either greater or smaller, can be assigned to the force of inertia of any given element.

[y] *in inversa duplicata distantiarum.*   [z] *in subtriplicata.*   [a] *adeoque longe maiori ratione.*
[b] *vis inertiae.*   [c] *nulla polleret efficacia.*   [d] *nulla . . . polleret . . . efficacia.*   [e] *quantum.*
[f] *quantitas.*

63

COROLLARY I. Any element whatever having been given, other elements can also be given, of which the force of inertia (or, what is in another respect the same, the moving force) is two or three times greater. That is to say, they would resist a certain velocity with a force which was two or three times greater; and, moved with the same velocity, they would be invested with an impetus which was also two or three times greater.

COROLLARY II. From the corollary of the preceding proposition it follows that all elements whatever, no matter how different in kind they may be, have the power to fill the same volume. It also follows, therefore, that, if the same space is completely filled, it will always contain the same number of elements. Hence, it may be validly concluded that, even if you completely deny that there is any admixture of a vacuum and assume that the whole space is completely filled, bodies of the same volume may, nonetheless, contain entirely different masses, the elements being endowed with a force of inertia which may be greater or smaller. For the mass of a body is simply the quantity of the force of inertia, in virtue of which it either resists a motion, or, having been moved with a certain velocity, is invested with a certain impetus of motion.

1:486 Hence, from the fact that a given volume contains a smaller quantity of matter, we cannot always reliably infer that the matter has a lower density and that the empty spaces in the interstices between its elements are greater.[g] Each of two bodies may either possess the same interstitial vacua, or they may both be perfectly dense; and yet one of them may, nonetheless, have a far greater mass than the other, and that simply because of the inherent difference in the nature itself of the elements.[25]

PROPOSITION XII. THEOREM. The specific difference of the density of bodies, which are able to be observed in the world, cannot be fully explained without reference to the specific difference in the inertia of their elements.

If all elements had an equal force of inertia and an equal volume, then an absolute vacuum interposed between their parts would be necessary to explain the difference in the density of bodies. For, according to the proofs given by Newton,[26] Keill,[27] and others, free motion is not possible in a medium which is completely filled in this fashion. Therefore, to explain the infinite diversity of densities, each specific to a kind of medium, for example, aether, air, water, and gold, one would have to indulge an exaggerated passion for conjecture. One would have to fabricate a rash and arbitrary[h] account of the structure itself of the elements – than which nothing is less accessible to the understanding – imagining it to have the form sometimes of the thinnest bubbles,[28] sometimes of branches and

---

[g] *ad maiora interstita vacua intercepta.*   [h] *pro lubitu.*

winding coils.[29] For, in this way, matter can be thought of as distended in a wondrous fashion, and an immense space as filled with very little matter. But consider what reasons militate against such views.

These tiny fibres which are of immeasurable slenderness, or the minute bubbles which, under immeasurably thin skins, contain a vacuum which is, relative to the matter which they contain, enormous, must eventually be ground down by the continuous collision and friction of the bodies. In this way, the minutely ground particles would eventually fill the interstitial empty spaces; and thus the space of the world would everywhere become paralysed[i] by an overwhelming inertia, and all motions would in a short time be brought to rest.[30]

Furthermore, according to a view such as this, media which are by specific nature less dense would have to consist of parts which were extended to the highest degree and endowed with great volume. But, if this were the case, how would it be possible that the interstices of denser bodies, which, according to this same opinion, are narrower, should be accessible to less dense bodies, as can easily be seen to happen in the case of fire and the magnetic or electric fluid[j] penetrating bodies.[31] For how particles which are endowed with greater volume are able to penetrate interstices which are narrower than themselves – this I understand no better than the most ignorant.

Thus, unless it be granted that there exists a specific difference between the simplest elements, and that it is in virtue of this specific difference that it is possible to construct masses which are sometimes smaller and sometimes much greater, though they exactly fill the same space – unless, I say, this be granted, physics will always founder on the rock, so to speak, of this difficulty.

PROPOSITION XIII. THEOREM. The elements of a body, even when they are posited on their own, possess a perfect elastic force which is different in different things; and they constitute a medium which is, in itself and without the admixture of a vacuum, primitively elastic.[k]

Individual simple elements occupy the space of their presence with a certain determinate force, which excludes external substances from the same space. But since any finite force whatever has a degree which can be surpassed by another greater force, it is clear that to this repulsive force another stronger force can be opposed. And since the force which is innate in the element is not sufficient to keep this stronger force at the same distance,[l] it is clear that this other stronger force will in some

1:487

---

[i] *obtorpescet.*   [j] *ignem, fluidum magneticum, electricum.*   [k] *primitive elasticum.*
[l] *in eadem distantia arcendae.*

measure penetrate the space occupied by the element. But all forces whatever spread out into space from a determinate point, becoming weaker as the distance from the point increases. It is thus clear that this repulsive force will react the more strongly, the closer the other force approaches to the centre. And since the repelling force, which is finite at any given distance from the centre of repulsion, will increase in a determinate proportion as one approaches this centre, and will necessarily be infinite at the central point itself, it is obvious that by no conceivable force can an element be penetrated in its inmost part.[m] It will be, therefore, perfectly elastic, and a number of them will, in virtue of their combined elasticities, constitute a medium which is primitively elastic. That this elasticity will vary from element to element follows from Proposition X, Corollary, lines 4–5.[32]

COROLLARY. Elements are completely impenetrable, that is to say, they cannot be wholly excluded from the space they occupy by any external force, no matter how great that force be. They can, however, be compressed, and they constitute bodies which can also be compressed, since, of course, they yield a little to an external force pressing upon them. This is the origin of the bodies or media which are elastic. And among such bodies one may already legitimately include aether, that is to say, the matter of fire.[n][33]

FINIS

[m] *penitus.*   [n] *in quibus aetherem s. materiam ignis in antecessum profiteri liceat.*

*An attempt at some reflections on optimism
by M. Immanuel Kant, also containing an
announcement of his lectures for the coming
semester 7 October 1759 (1759)*

*Versuch einiger Betrachtungen über den Optimismus
von M. Immanuel Kant, wodurch er zugleich seine
Vorlesungen auf das bevorstehende halbe Jahr ankündigt
den 7 October 1759 (1759)*

Versuch

einiger Betrachtungen

über den

Optimismus

von

M. IMMANUEL KANT,

wodurch er zugleich seine Vorlesungen
auf das bevorstehende halbe Jahr ankündigt.

———

Den 7. October 1759.

by
Immanuel Kant
also containing an announcement
of his lectures for the coming
semester
7th October 1759

Now that an appropriate concept of God has been formed, there is perhaps nothing more natural than the thought: if God chooses, he chooses only what is best. It was said of Alexander that he thought that he had done nothing as long as there was still something left for him to do. The same thing can be said with infinitely greater propriety[a] about the most benevolent and most powerful being of all. *Leibniz* did not think that he was saying anything new when he maintained that this world was the best of all possible worlds, or, which amounts to the same thing, that the totality of all that God has created outside Himself[b] was the best which could possibly have been created.[1] What was new was the employment to which Leibniz put this principle. He employed it, namely, to cut the knot, so difficult to untie, of the difficulties relating to the origin of evil. An idea which is so easy and so natural, and which is eventually repeated so often as to become a common platitude[c] and a source of disgust to people of more refined taste, cannot continue an object of respect for long. Where is the honour in thinking like the common herd, or in maintaining a proposition which is so easy to prove? Subtle errors are a stimulus to one's self-love,[d] which takes delight in the sense of its own strength. Obvious truths, on the other hand, are apprehended with such ease and with an understanding so common that in the end their fate is the fate of those songs which become intolerable as soon as they start to ring out from the mouths of the common masses. To put the matter briefly: it is often the case with some of the things we know that they are highly esteemed, not because they are right, but because they have been gained at a cost. We do not care for truth at bargain price.[e] In accordance with this sentiment, it was first found extraordinary, then beautiful and finally correct[f] to assert that it had pleased God to choose this of all possible worlds, not because it was better than the other worlds which lay within his power to choose, but quite simply because it so pleased him. 'And why', I ask in all humility, 'did it please Thee, Eternal Being, to prefer the inferior to the superior?' And man places in the mouth of the All-Highest Being the answer: 'It pleased me thus. Let that suffice.'

I shall now, in some haste, outline some remarks which may make it easier for us to form a judgement about the dispute which has arisen in this connection.[2] The members of my audience may, perhaps, find these remarks of use in better understanding and placing in context what I shall have to say on this matter in my lectures. Accordingly, therefore, I begin my argument.

If no world can be thought, beyond which a still better world cannot be imagined, the Supreme Understanding could not possibly have cognition

---

[a] *Richtigkeit.*   [b] *der Inbegriff alles desseen, was Gott ausser sich hervor gebracht hat.*
[c] *gemein wird.*   [d] *Eigenliebe.*   [e] *die Wahrheit gutes Kaufs.*
[f] *erstlich ausserordentlich, dann schön und endlich richtig.*

of all possible worlds. Now, this latter claim is false, so the former claim must be false as well. The correctness of the major premise[g] becomes apparent in the following way: if I can assert of any particular idea whatever, which can be made of a world, that the representation of a still better world is possible, then the same thing can also be said of all the ideas of worlds in the Divine Understanding. Therefore, there are possible worlds which are better than those known by God, and God has not had knowledge of all possible worlds. I imagine that the minor premise will be admitted by every orthodox believer.[h] My conclusion is that it is false to assert that no world can be thought, beyond which a still better world cannot be thought. Or, to express the same idea differently: there is a possible world, beyond which no better world can be thought. Admittedly, it does not, of course, follow from this that one among all the possible worlds must be the most perfect, for if two or more such possible worlds were equal in respect of perfection, then, although no world could be thought which was better than either of the two, neither of them would be the best, for they would both have the same degree of goodness.[3]

In order to be able to draw this second conclusion, I offer the following reflection, which seems to me to be new. First of all, permit me to equate
2:31 the absolute perfection* of a thing with its degree of reality, absolute perfection being regarded in and for itself and independently of any intention.[k] In making this assumption, I have the agreement of most philosophers on my side, and I could very easily justify this concept. I now assert that reality and reality as such can never be distinguished from each other. For if things differ from each other, then they differ in virtue of something which is present in the one thing and not in the other. If, however, one looks at realities as such, then every characteristic mark[l] which is to be found in them is positive. Now, if these same realities were to differ from each other as realities, then there would have to be something positive in the one which was not in the other. Therefore, something negative would be thought in the one which enabled us to distinguish it from the other. That is to say: the realities are not being compared with each other as realities, though this was what was required. Accordingly,

---

* Perfection in the relative sense[i] consists in the harmony of a manifold with a certain rule,[j] no matter what that rule may be.[4] In this sense, there are many frauds, many gangs of thieves, which are perfect in their fashion. But in the absolute sense, a thing is only perfect in so far as its manifold contains within itself the ground of a reality. The magnitude of this reality determines the degree of the perfection. And since God is the supreme reality, this concept would agree with the concept, according to which a thing is perfect in so far as it harmonises with the divine properties.[5]

[g] *die Richtigkeit des Obersatzes.*   [h] *von jedem Rechtgläubigen.*
[i] *Die Vollkommenheit im respectiven Verstande.*
[j] *Die Zusammenstimmung des Mannigfaltigen zu einer gewissen Regel.*
[k] *wenn man sie ohne irgend eine Absicht für sich selbst betrachtet.*   [l] *Merkmal.*

reality and reality differ from each other only in virtue of the negations, the absences and limits[m] attaching to one of them.[7] In other words, reality and reality differ from one another, not in respect of their quality (*qualitate*) but in respect of their magnitude[n] (*gradu*).

Accordingly, if things differ from one another, they always do so through the degree of their reality. Different things can never have the same degree of reality. Therefore, two different worlds can never have the same degree of reality either. In other words, it is not possible for there to be two worlds which are equally good and equally perfect. *Reinhard* says in his prize essay on optimism:[8] one world could well have precisely the sum of realities, albeit of a different kind, as the other. If that were right, then there would be different worlds which were nonetheless equally perfect. But he errs in supposing that realities of equal degree can be distinguished from each other in respect of their quality[o] (*qualitate*). For, to repeat what I have said before: suppose it were so, then there would be something in the one world which was not in the other. They would thus differ from each other in virtue of the determinations A and not-A, one of the two determinations always being a genuine negation. The two worlds would, accordingly, differ in virtue of their limits and degree, but not in virtue of their quality,[p] for negations can never be numbered among the qualities[q] of a reality; negations rather limit that reality and determine its degree. This observation is abstract and may well be in need of further elucidation; but I shall reserve that for another occasion.[9]

The ground we have now covered enables us thoroughly to understand that, of all possible worlds, one is the most perfect, so that it is neither surpassed nor equalled in excellence by any other world. Now, whether this most perfect of all possible worlds is the real world or not we shall consider in a moment. For the present, it is our wish to put what we have established so far under a more powerful light. 2:32

There are magnitudes such that a still greater magnitude can always be thought.[r] The greatest number, the fastest motion, are magnitudes of this type. Not even the Divine Understanding thinks them, for they are, as Leibniz remarks, deceptive concepts (*notiones deceptrices*): these concepts are such that it seems as if something is being thought by their means, whereas, in fact, they represent nothing at all. Now, the opponents of optimism[10] maintain that the concept of the most perfect of all worlds is, like that of the greatest of all numbers, a self-contradictory concept. For, just as to the sum of units in a number further units can be added without ever producing the greatest number, so also to the sum of reality in a world further reality can be added without ever producing the greatest reality.[11]

[m] *Negationen, Abwesenheiten, Schranken.*   [n] *Grösse.*   [o] *Beschaffenheit.*   [p] *Beschaffenheit.*
[q] *Qualitäten.*
[r] *Es giebt Grössen, von denen sich keine denken lässt, dass nicht eine noch grössere könnte gedacht werden.*

Apart from the fact that the degree of reality of a thing compared with a lesser reality cannot properly be construed on the analogy of a number compared with its units, I would merely adduce the following consideration in order to show that the above example is not very appropriate. No greatest number is possible at all, but a greatest degree of reality is possible, and it is to be found in God. Let us examine the first reason why, in the argument under consideration, the concept of number is erroneously employed. The concept of a greatest finite number is the abstract concept of multiplicity as such.[s] Multiplicity is finite, though additions can nonetheless be made to it in thought without its thereby ceasing to be finite. In this case, therefore, the finitude of the magnitude does not impose any determinate limits, but only such as are general. For this reason, the predicate 'greatest' cannot belong to any such finite number, for no matter what determinate plurality[t] one thinks, every such finite number can be increased by addition without its finitude being thereby diminished. The degree of reality of a world is, on the other hand, something which is completely determinate. The limits which are set upon the greatest possible perfection of a world are not merely general but fixed by a degree which must, of necessity, be lacking to it. Independence, self-sufficiency, presence in all places, the power to create, and so on, are perfections which no world can possess. This present case is not like that of mathematical infinity, where the finite is connected, in accordance with the law of continuity, with the infinite by means of a constantly continued and ever possible augmentation. In this present case, the disparity[u] between infinite reality and finite reality is fixed by means of a determinate magnitude, which constitutes their difference. The world, which finds itself at that point on the scale of beings which marks the start of the chasm containing the measureless degrees of perfection which elevate the Eternal Being above every creature – this world, I repeat, is, of all which is finite, the most perfect.

2:33

It seems to me that the degree of certainty with which the following truth can be understood is so great that our opponents cannot offer anything by way of objection to it which is, at any rate, more powerful. I refer to the truth that, among all that is finite and possible, one world of the greatest excellence was the highest finite good, alone worthy of choice by the Being who is the supreme among all beings,[v] if it is to constitute, in combination with the infinite, the greatest possible sum.[w]

[s] *Begriff der Vielheit schlechthin.*
[t] *Menge* / Carabellese (Assunto) (hereafter C): *molteplicità* / Festugière (hereafter F): *nombre* / Ferrari (hereafter Fe): *quantité* / (alt: amount, quantity, number).
[u] *Abstand.*
[v] *es sei unter allem Endlichen, was möglich war, eine Welt von der grössten Vortrefflichkeit das höchste endliche Gut.*
[w] *um mit dem Unendlichen zusammengenommen die grösste Summe, die sein kann, auszumachen.*

If what has been proved above is conceded, and if it is agreed that, of all possible worlds, one is necessarily the most perfect, then I do not wish for a further continuation of the dispute. Not every extravagance of opinion deserves the trouble of a careful refutation. If anybody[12] were so bold as to assert that the Supreme Wisdom could find the worse better than the best, or that the Supreme Goodness should prefer a lesser good to a greater, which was equally within its power, I should not waste my time in attempting a refutation.[13] Philosophy is put to a poor use if it is employed in overturning the principles of sound reason, and it is little honoured if it is found necessary to mobilise her forces in order to refute such attempts.

There may be someone who finds the detailed examination of all the subtle questions which we have so far raised and answered too elaborate an undertaking. To such a person I would suggest a much easier method of arriving at the same truth. The method is, admittedly, less scholarly in character,[x] but it is, perhaps, equally valid. The alternative argument runs as follows: a most perfect world is possible because it is real, and it is real because it has been produced by the wisest and most benevolent choice. Either I can form no concept of choice at all, or one chooses according to one's pleasure. However, that which is according to one's pleasure pleases. But to be pleased with, to find good, to be particularly according to one's pleasure, to be especially pleased by, to find particularly good, are, in my opinion, expressions which differ only in verbal form.[y] Since God chose this world and this world alone of all the possible worlds of which He had cognition, He must for that very reason, have regarded it as the best. And since God's judgement never errs, it follows that this world is also in fact the best. Even if it had been possible for the Supreme Being to have been able to choose according to the fictitious notion of freedom which some have put into circulation, and to have preferred the worse to much that was better as a result of I know not what absolute whim,[z] He would never have acted in that fashion. One may dream up for oneself something in the nature of a demi-god of fable, but the only handiwork[a] which is proper to the God of gods is that which is worthy of Him, and that is the handiwork which is the best of all that is possible.[14] The reason, perhaps, for the choice[b] which gave existence to this world was not its particular inner superiority but rather its harmonising to a higher degree with the divine properties. Very well! Even then it is still certain that it is more perfect than any other possible world. It is clear from the effect that all other worlds would harmonise to a lesser degree with the properties of the will of God. But in God everything is reality, and nothing harmonises

2:34

---

[x] *mit etwas weniger Schulgelehrsamkeit.*

[y] *Entweder ich kann mir gar keinen Begriff von einer Wahl machen, oder man wählt nach Belieben: was aber beliebt, das gefällt; gefallen aber und für gut halten, vorzüglich belieben, sich vorzüglich gefallen lassen und für vorzüglich gut halten, sind meiner Meinung nach nur Unterschiede der Worte.*

[z] *unbedingtes Belieben.* [a] *Werk.* [b] *des Rathschlusses.*

to a greater degree with that reality than that which itself contains a greater reality. It follows from this that the greatest reality which can belong to a world is to be found in no other world than this present world. Furthermore, not being able to choose other than that which one distinctly and rightly recognises as the best constitutes, perhaps, a constraint which limits the will,^c and a necessity which cancels freedom. Certainly, if freedom is the opposite of this, and if there are at this point two divergent paths within a labyrinth of difficulties, and if, at the risk of getting lost, I am obliged to choose one of them, then I do not deliberate for long.^d Thanks for the freedom which banishes into eternal nothingness the best which it was possible to create, merely in order to command evil so that it should be something, in spite of all the pronouncements of wisdom. If I am positively to choose between errors, then I prefer to praise the benevolent necessity,^e which is so favourable to us, and from which there can arise nothing but the best. I am, accordingly, convinced, and perhaps some of my readers are convinced, too. I am also happy to find myself a citizen of a world which could not possibly have been better than it is. Unworthy in myself but chosen for the sake of the whole by the best of all beings to be a humble member of the most perfect of all possible plans, I esteem my own existence the more highly, since I was elected to occupy a position in the best of schemes. To all creatures, who do not make themselves unworthy of that name,^f I cry: 'Happy are we – we exist!' And the Creator is well pleased with us. Measureless spaces and eternities will probably only disclose the wealth of the creation in all its extent to the eye of the Omniscient Being alone. I, however, from my viewpoint and armed with the insight which has been conferred upon my puny understanding, shall gaze around me as far as my eye can reach, ever more learning to understand that *the whole is the best, and everything is good for the sake of the whole.*

In the coming semester, I shall, as usual, be lecturing on logic using Meier,[15] and on metaphysics and ethics, using Baumgarten.[16] In physical geography I shall be lecturing from my own notes.[17] On pure mathematics, which I am starting, I shall lecture at a special hour; but on mechanical sciences I shall lecture at a separate time. Both of these courses will be based on *Wolff.*[18] The distribution of the hours will be announced separately. As is already known, I shall complete each of these courses in one semester. Should this, however, prove insufficient, I shall make up what is outstanding in a few hours at the beginning of the following semester.

---

^c *ein Zwang des Willens.*

^d *wenn hier zwei Scheidewege in einem Labyrinth von Schwierigkeiten sind, wo ich auf die Gefahr zu irren mich zu einem entschliessen soll, so besinne ich mich nicht lange.*

^e *gütige Nothwendigkeit.*   ^f *welches sich nicht selbst unwürdig macht so zu heissen.*

Appendix: Three manuscript reflections on optimism (Reflections 3703–5: AK 17:229–39)

[The composition of these three reflections was doubtless occasioned by the announcement (published in the *Hamburger freyen Urtheilen und Nachrichten* for 27 July 1753) of the theme proposed by the Prussian Royal Academy of Sciences for its 1755 prize-essay competition. The theme was to be Pope's optimism as it was expressed in the dictum 'Everything is good.' The competition attracted entries from, among others, Mendelssohn, Lessing, Wieland, and Reinhard, to which last the prize was awarded. Kant may himself have considered competing for the prize, but he did not in the end submit an entry. These three reflections were probably composed in 1753 or 1754. They are of philosophical interest for a number of reasons: They contain an anticipation of Kant's proof of the existence of God from the possibility of things – an argument attributed rather implausibly to Pope himself; they also contain a criticism of an aspect of Leibnizian optimism (the 1759 *Optimism* itself containing a defence of a different aspect of Leibnizian optimism). Reflection 3703 contains an outline of an argument in Pope's *Essay on Man* (1733–4), Epistle IV; Reflection 3704 presents a statement of Leibnizian optimism (based on the *Théodicée* [1714]) and a comparison of the positions of Leibniz and Pope; Reflection 3705 contains a criticism of the Leibnizian version of optimism. A French translation by François Marty was published in 1980 under the title *Premières réflexions sur l'optimisme* (in Alquié, 1980, vol. I, pp. 25–34). The text of the three manuscript reflections is fragmentary; breaks in the manuscript are indicated by four dots enclosed in square brackets.]

REFLECTION 3703

You ask: who is happier in the world, the virtuous person or the vicious? If the matter is investigated, it will be found that there is always something intermingled with the advantages enjoyed by the wrong-doer which the virtuous person does not desire and on account of which he would not wish to change his state with that of the other. The virtuous person is therefore actually more content with himself than is supposed. The evils which affect the virtuous person do not really affect his virtue but are common to everybody. If the universal laws are supposed to be limited in their application to the relation of the pious and the ungodly, then tell me this: Who then are the pious? Will not one person regard this individual as deserving punishment, whereas someone else will regard another person as culpable? And would God's justice then be acknowledged by everybody? Bread is the reward, not of virtue, but of toil. And if, eventually, you furnish man with everything good, then tell me: Will you then be satisfied? Will you not desire more and more? And will God be able, do you suppose, to discover the aim of your wishes? The true reward of virtue is inner peace of soul; other goods destroy that peace or corrupt it. Learning, fame, wealth – none of them contains the true good. Thus, virtue alone constitutes the true good. Virtue finds something to satisfy it both in plenty and in need, in laughter and in tears. Since virtue, therefore, finds no lack, wishing is worthless.

Self-love, when combined with the love of God and the love of one's neighbours, constitutes man's happiness. The greater the love and the further it extends, the greater the happiness. God starts with love of the whole and extends it to the parts, whereas human love starts with itself and gradually extends to the whole. Earth smiles upon such a one from all sides, and the Divinity itself beholds its own image in the soul of such a person.

REFLECTION 3704: OUTLINE OF OPTIMISM

Optimism is the doctrine which justifies the existence of evil in the world by assuming that there is an infinitely perfect, benevolent and omnipotent original Being. This justification is furnished by establishing that, in spite of all the apparent contradictions, that which is chosen by this infinitely perfect Being must nonetheless be the best of all that is possible. The presence of evil is attributed, not to the choice of God's positive approval, but to the inescapable necessity that finite beings will have essential defects. These defects have been introduced into the scheme of creation without guilt on God's part by his decision to permit them. God's wisdom and goodness nonetheless turns them to the advantage of the whole, so that the displeasure which they arouse when they are viewed in isolation is completely outweighed in the whole by the compensation which the divine goodness is able to institute. Since, therefore, this world is the best of all the worlds which are possible through the divine power, and since that world which could be better in parts would not, in virtue of [. . . .]

If one carefully examines the outline which Leibniz gives of his principles, it will be found that this summary expresses his view in the most precise manner possible. One may consider the following classification of evils: those which are necessary or metaphysical, and those which are contingent, and are either hypothetical and physical or hypothetical and moral. One only needs to consider his distinction of evils from the point of view of the will which precedes and of the will which follows; the former endeavours to exclude all evils, while the latter includes them within its scheme as the inescapable consequences of the eternal nature of things – one only needs to consider this distinction to be persuaded of the truth of our account. Leibniz represents the goodness of God, which extends without limits, as the current of a river which, with even force, sweeps along everything to be found within it, except that the heavy cargo vessels, which have more natural inertia than those vessels of smaller mass, are carried along more slowly than these latter.

He represents God as He is ready to reveal Himself with all the infinity of all His properties in the works of creation and as feeling a true displeasure at the evils, the sight of which so much upsets people of good disposition. But, appealing to the goodness, wisdom and power of God, which are sufficiently well-known from other indisputable reasons, he gives such people reason to hope that the defects will be balanced by benefits in the whole; he also gives them reason to believe that, though evils may in the end spoil even the best plan, they could not be eliminated from the totality without producing an even greater irregularity. Needless to say, freely acting beings might have avoided many evil actions, and they would have greatly pleased God had they done so. However, the choice of the lesser of two evils, of which one was the lack of freedom and the other of the morally best, was an unavoidable necessity. And even in the best plan there were other impediments which could have induced God, from fear of even greater irregularities, not to institute certain motive causes, which might have been able to prevent some kinds of evil. In a word: nothing else was possible; evil had to be. Gratitude is due to the Eternal Wisdom for having admitted only the smallest amount of evil, and for having executed everything in the whole to His glory in the most magnificent fashion. It is true, it seems to me, that we do not yet see what the real effect will be of the substitution, which is intended to compensate the whole for its partial defects. But do you not have the assurance that God is as He must be if we are to be able to expect all that is good from Him? And, in that case, you could not expect anything other than an eventual perfect satisfaction, or at least a complete justification of God's justice and goodness.

Comparison of Pope's system with optimism; superiority of former

Leibniz admitted that the irregularities and imperfections, which upset those who are of good disposition as if they were true imperfections, were indeed true imperfections. But he reserves the right to excuse the Supreme Wisdom, which he acknowledges for other reasons, for the responsibility of admitting such imperfections. Thus, the properties of God are placed in safety to the satisfaction of those who have enough understanding and sufficient submissiveness to applaud the metaphysical proofs of the Divine Existence. As for the rest of those who are willing to acknowledge that contemplating the world reveals traces of God – they remain troubled. Pope chooses a path which, when it comes to rendering the beautiful proof of God's existence accessible to everyone, is the best suited of all possible paths. This path – and it is precisely this which constitutes the perfection of his system – even subjects every possibility to the dominion of an all-sufficient original Being; under this Being things can have no other properties, not even those which are called essentially necessary, apart from those which harmonise together to give complete expression to His perfection. Pope subjects the creation to detailed scrutiny, particularly where it most seems to lack harmony; and yet he shows that each thing, which we might wish to see removed from the scheme of greatest perfection, is also, when considered in itself, good. He also shows that we should not beforehand entertain an advantageous prejudice in favour of the wisdom of the Organising Being, in order to win applause for Him. The essential and necessary determinations of things, the universal laws which are not placed in relation to each other by any forced union into a harmonious scheme, will adapt themselves as if spontaneously to the attainment of purposes which are perfect. Self-love, which has as its only purpose one's own pleasure, and which seems to be the manifest cause of the moral disorder which we observe, is the origin of that beautiful harmony which we admire. Everything which is of use to itself also finds itself constrained to be of use to other things, as well. The universal bond, which links the whole together in a fashion which has not been examined, ensures that individual advantages always relate to the advantage of other things, and do so in a perfectly natural sequence. Thus, a universal law of nature firmly establishes the love which maintains the whole, and it does so by means of the motive causes which also naturally produce that evil, the sources of which we would happily see destroyed.

When one sees essential characteristics in such universal harmony, can one very well suppose that what is thus adapted to the excellent whole should also be the cause of such evil [. . . .]

Concerning the universal perfection of the constitution of the world,
both in the physical and in the moral sense of the term

The chief rule of the perfection of the world is that it be in the highest degree complete, that everything exist which is possible, and that nothing which is at all capable of existence be lacking either in the chain of beings or in the multiplicity of the changes they undergo; for there is nothing at all which constitutes a greater defect for the world in general than for there to be a nothingness in some part or other of it. Hence it is that the field of revelation of the Divine Power embraces all species of finite things; it extends with a kind of wealth even to defects, and it only vanishes by a process or diminution through all the stages from the highest degrees of perfection down to nothingness.

With this established as an assumption, let us listen with contempt to the lamentations of those to whom, so they think, heaven has not granted a satisfactory share of perfections. I wish, says one, that my understanding were less clouded, and that my sensible desires were less violent; if only I had been fortunate enough to have no other inclinations than those towards virtue. If most people were to remember that, in wishing for such properties for themselves as presuppose a change in their nature, they are, in effect, wishing that they did not exist at all, and that another being with the required constitution should exist in their place, they would think better of it, for self-love has a horror of annihilation, and prefers to rest satisfied with the state which has been conferred upon it, than [. . . .]

REFLECTION 3705: DEFECTS OF OPTIMISM

Leibniz was right to call his system a theodicy, or a defence of God's good cause. For, on the assumption that God may perhaps be the author of evil, the assurance that, as far as it is within his power, everything is good, and that at least it is not his fault if not everything turns out as perfectly as it ought, if it is to accord with what honest people would wish – that assurance is, indeed, nothing but a justification of God.

The errors of this theory are indeed too serious for us to be able to accept it. Leibniz presents the rules, which aim at perfection, as conflicting with each other in their application. He regards exceptions as necessary defects, and he recognises the action appropriate to the Supreme Wisdom by the fact that it chooses on the side of the best, just as a sailor sacrifices part of his cargo in order to save his ship and the rest of the cargo. It is true, the wisdom and goodness of God triumph here over all objections. But what is one to say of infinity and independence? What is it which causes the essential determinations of things to conflict with each other when they are combined together, so that the perfections, each of which on its own would increase God's pleasure, become incompatible with each other? What is the nature of the unfathomable conflict which exists between the general will of God, which aims only at the good, and the metaphysical necessity which is not willing to adapt itself to that end in a general harmony which knows no exceptions? If evils, by I know not what kind of necessary fatality, constrain God to permit them without having aroused any pleasure within Him, then they cause this Supremely Blessed Being a certain kind of displeasure; that displeasure may, it is true, be to a certain extent diminished, though not eliminated, by the defense that God, for his part, is innocent. If everything in the whole was good, or if everything in the parts is still good, then the view on all sides will infallibly be a source of true pleasure. Why is it necessary that everything in the parts should be unpleasant so that pleasure in the whole alone should be awakened? If God abhors vices and torments, if God does not desire them but merely permits them: why then was it necessary that they should have to exist, assuming always that they cannot be excluded, without their making way for still greater defects. This excuse serves, it is true, to free God of guilt, but it will never serve to banish the serious question why the essential necessity should have something about it which conflicts with the will of God, and constrains Him to admit evils without their having won His approval. The whole mistake consists in the fact that Leibniz identifies the scheme of the best world on the one hand with a kind of independence, and on the other hand with dependence on the will of God. All possibility is spread out before God. God beholds it, considers it, and examines it. He is inclined in one direction by the determinations inhering in the possibilities, in accordance with the criterion of their particular perfections, and he is inclined in the other direction according to the effect produced by their combination. It is this comparison which occasions his decision.

The being of the world is not as it is simply because God wishes to have it so, but because it was not possible in any other way, only [. . . .]

The second chief mistake of optimism consists in the fact that the evils and irregularities which are perceived in the world are only excused on the assumption that God exists; the mistake consists, therefore, in having first to believe that an Infinitely Benevolent and Infinitely Perfect Being exists, before one can be assured that the world, which is taken to be His work, is beautiful and regular, instead of believing that the universal agreement of the arrangements of the world, if they can be acknowledged to exist in and for themselves, itself furnishes the most beautiful proof of the existence of God and of the universal dependency of all things on Him. The most reliable and the easiest proof, therefore, of the reality of an All-Sufficient, Infinitely Benevolent and Infinitely Wise Being, something which is acknowledged as a result of contemplating the excellent arrangements which the world everywhere displays, is undermined by Leibniz's system. It seems to me that an Epicurus would reply to someone building on this proof: If the agreement, which you perceive in the world, seems to you to prove the existence of an organising wisdom as its Creator, then you must admit that most of the world does not depend on that wisdom, for it everywhere contains within it, and that in more than half the cases, absurdities and abhorrent irregularities. I do not accept your subterfuge, according to which it is to be supposed of this wisdom that it has, for example, organised some parts for wise purposes, while using other parts to conceal the evidences of its supervision. I prefer, therefore, to conclude as follows: if the wise first cause was not able to bring all things into a scheme of harmonious beauty, then it follows that not all things, at least, are subject, in respect of their properties, to the pleasure of that first cause. Eternal fate, which so much limits the power of the potent cause, and which extorts from it the agreement to the existence of crude evils, thereby deprives that power of its all-sufficiency, and makes it subject to the necessity of those very evils.

The false subtlety of the four syllogistic figures demonstrated by M. Immanuel Kant (1762)

Die falsche Spitzfindigkeit der vier syllogistischen Figuren erwiesen von M. Immanuel Kant (1762)

Die falsche Spitzfindigkeit

der

vier syllogistischen Figuren

erwiesen

von

M. Immanuel Kant.

demonstrated
by
M. Immanuel Kant

To compare something as a characteristic mark[b2] with a thing is *to judge.*
The thing itself is the subject; the characteristic mark is the predicate.
The comparison is expressed by means of the copula *is* or *are.*[3] When used
absolutely,[c] the copula designates the predicate as a characteristic mark of
the subject. If, however, it is combined with the sign for negation, the
copula then signifies that the predicate is a characteristic mark which is
incompatible with the subject.[d] In the former case, the judgement is affirmative, whereas in the latter case the judgement is negative. Obviously, in
calling the predicate a characteristic mark, we are not saying that it is a
characteristic mark of the subject, for that is only the case with affirmative
judgements. What we are saying is that the predicate is regarded as a
characteristic mark of some thing or other, though, in the case of a
negative judgement, it contradicts[e] the subject of the judgement. Thus, let
it be a *mind*[f] of which I am thinking; and let *compound*[g] be the characteristic
mark of something or other. The judgement: *A mind is not compound*
represents this characteristic mark as conflicting with the thing itself.

That which is a characteristic mark of a characteristic mark of a thing is
called a *mediate*[h] characteristic mark of that thing. Thus, *necessary* is an
immediate[i] characteristic mark of God, whereas *immutable* is a characteristic mark of what is necessary, and a mediate characteristic mark of God.
Obviously, the immediate characteristic mark occupies the position of an
intermediate characteristic mark (*nota intermedia*) between the remote[j] characteristic mark and the thing itself, for it is only by its means that the
remote characteristic mark is compared with the thing itself. But it is also
possible to compare a characteristic mark with a thing negatively, by
means of an intermediate characteristic mark, namely, by recognising that   2:48
something conflicts with the immediate characteristic mark of the thing.
Contingent,[k] as a characteristic mark, conflicts with what is *necessary;* but

---

[a] *Vernunftschlüsse* / Abbot (hereafter A): ratiocination / Ferrari (hereafter F) & Zac (hereafter
Z): *syllogismes.*
[b] *Merkmal* / A: mark (or attribute) / F & Z: *caractère.*   [c] *schlechthin.*
[d] *dem Subject entgegen gesetztes Merkmal.*   [e] *widerspricht.*   [f] *Geist.*   [g] *Zusammengesetzt.*
[h] *mittelbares.*   [i] *unmittelbares.*   [j] *entfernte.*   [k] *zufällig.*

89

necessary is a characteristic mark of God; thus, by means of an intermediate characteristic mark, one recognises that being contingent contradicts God.

I am now going to set up my real definition[l4] of the syllogism. *Every judgement which is made by means of a mediate characteristic mark is a syllogism.*[5] In other words, a syllogism is the comparison of a characteristic mark with a thing by means of an intermediate characteristic mark. This intermediate characteristic mark (*nota intermedia*) in a syllogism is also normally called the *middle term*[m] (*terminus medius*); what the other terms are is sufficiently well known.

In order clearly to recognise the relation of the characteristic mark to the thing in the judgement: *the human soul is a mind,* I employ the intermediate characteristic mark *rational,* so that, by its means, I regard *being a mind* as a mediate characteristic mark of the human soul. In this case, three judgements must necessarily occur:

1. Being a mind is a characteristic mark of that which is rational;
2. Rational is a characteristic mark of the human soul;
3. Being a mind is a characteristic mark of the human soul.

Three judgements are necessary because the comparison of a remote characteristic mark with the thing itself is only possible by means of these three operations.[n]

Cast in the form of judgements, the three operations would run: all that is rational is a mind; the soul of man is rational; therefore, the soul of man is a mind. Now, this is an affirmative syllogism. As for negative syllogisms: it is equally obvious that, since I do not always recognise the conflict of a predicate and a subject with sufficient clarity, I must, whenever possible, employ something to help me in order to facilitate my understanding by means of an intermediate characteristic mark. Suppose that I am presented with the negative judgement: the duration of God[o] cannot be measured by any time. And suppose that I do not find that this predicate, compared immediately in this way with the subject, furnishes me with a sufficiently clear idea[p] of the conflict. In such a case, I shall make use of a characteristic mark which I can imagine immediately in the subject, and compare the predicate with it and, by its means, with the thing itself. *Being measurable by time* conflicts with whatever is *immutable;* but *immutable* is a characteristic mark of *God;* therefore *etc.* Expressed formally, this would run: nothing immutable is measurable by time; the duration of God is immutable; therefore, *etc.*

2:49

l *Realerklärung* / A: real definition / F: *définition réele* / Z: *explication réelle.*
m *der mittlere Hauptbegriff.* *n* *Handlungen.* *o* *die Dauer Gottes.* *p* *eine genugsam klare Idee.*

§2. *Concerning the supreme rules governing all syllogisms*

The considerations which have been adduced show that the first general rule of all affirmative syllogisms is this: *A characteristic mark of a characteristic mark is a characteristic mark of the thing itself* (*nota notae est etiam nota rei ipsius*).[6] And the first general rule of all negative syllogisms is this: *that which contradicts*[q] *the characteristic mark of a thing, contradicts the thing itself* (*repugnans notae repugnat rei ipsi*).[7] Neither of these rules is capable of further proof. For a proof is only possible by means of one or more syllogisms, so that attempting to prove the supreme formula of all syllogisms would involve arguing in a circle. That these rules, however, contain the universal and ultimate ground of every kind of syllogism[r] is apparent from the following fact: the principles which all logicians have hitherto regarded as the first rules of all syllogisms have to borrow the only ground of their truth from our two rules. The *dictum de omni*,[8] the ultimate ground of all affirmative syllogisms, runs thus: that which is universally affirmed of a concept, is also affirmed of everything subsumed under that concept. The proof[s] of this principle is clear. A concept, under which other concepts are subsumed, is always abstracted,[t] as a characteristic mark, from those subordinate concepts. Now, that which belongs to this concept is a characteristic mark of a characteristic mark, and thus it is also a characteristic mark of the things themselves from which it has been abstracted. That is to say, that which belongs to the concept belongs to the lower concepts which are subsumed under it. Anybody with even a moderate knowledge of logic can easily see that the *dictum de omni*[9] is true simply for this reason, and that it therefore is governed by our first rule. The *dictum de nullo*[10] stands in exactly the same relation to our second rule. That which is universally denied of a concept is also denied of all that which is subsumed beneath that concept. For that concept, under which these other concepts are subsumed, is simply a characteristic mark which has been abstracted from them. But that which contradicts the characteristic mark also contradicts the things themselves; consequently, that which contradicts the higher concepts, must also conflict with the lower concepts which are subsumed under it.

---

[q] *widerspricht.*   [r] *aller vernünftigen Schlussart.*   [s] *Beweisgrund.*   [t] *abgesondert.*

§3. *Concerning pure and mixed syllogisms*[u]

Everybody knows that there are immediate inferences,[11] where from one judgement the truth of another judgement is cognised immediately without an intermediate concept. For this reason, such inferences are not syllogisms. For example, from the proposition: All matter is changeable, there immediately follows the proposition: that which is not changeable is not matter. The logicians enumerate different types of such immediate inferences.[v] Without doubt, the most important immediate inferences are those which are based upon logical conversion,[w][12] and likewise those which are based upon contraposition.[x][13]

Now, if a syllogism is the product of three propositions only, and if it is in accordance with the rules which have just been explained and which are valid of every syllogism, then I call it a pure syllogism[y] (*ratiocinium purum*).[14] If, however, it is only possible by combining more than three judgements, it is a mixed syllogism[z] (*ratiocinium hybridum*).[15] Suppose, namely, that between the three main propositions there has to be inserted an inference which has been derived immediately from them, and that, therefore, an extra proposition is added, over and above what is allowed in a pure syllogism, the syllogism is a *ratiocinium hybridum*.[16] For example, suppose that someone were to argue as follows:

Nothing which is perishable is simple;
Consequently, nothing simple is perishable;
The soul of man is simple;
Therefore, the soul of man is not perishable.

Anyone who argued in this fashion would, it is true, not have a genuinely compound syllogism, for that would have to consist of a number of syllogisms.[17] But this syllogism[18] contains, in addition to what is required of a syllogism, an extra inference, arrived at immediately by contraposition; the syllogism thus contains four propositions.

But even if only three judgements were really expressed, the conclusion could only be drawn from these judgements by means of legitimate logical conversion, or by contraposition or some other logical transformation of one of these premises, so that the syllogism would, notwithstanding, still

---

[u] *vermischten Vernünftschlüssen.* [v] *unmittelbare Schlüsse.* [w] *logische Umkehrung.*
[x] *Contraposition.* [y] *einen reinen Vernunftschluss.* [z] *vermengter Vernunftschluss.*

be a *ratiocinium hybridum.*[19] For what is important here is not what one says but what is indispensably necessary to thought if a valid inference is to be present.[a] Take the following syllogism:

Nothing perishable is simple;
The soul of man is simple;
Therefore, the soul of man is not perishable.

Suppose for a moment that the conclusion is valid only as a result of my being able to assert, in virtue of a completely valid conversion of the main premiss: nothing perishable is simple, so nothing simple is perishable; the syllogism is still a mixed inference, for its power to establish a conclusion[b] depends upon the tacit addition of this immediate inference, which has to be present if only in thought.

[a] *denn es kommt hier gar nicht darauf an was man sagt, sondern was man unumgänglich nöthig hat, dabei zu denken, wenn eine richtige Schlussfolge soll vorhanden sein.*
[b] *Schlusskraft.*

93

§4. In the so-called first figure only pure syllogisms are possible. In the remaining three figures nothing but mixed syllogisms is possible.[20]

If a syllogism is constructed immedately[c] in accordance with one of the two supreme rules which we have introduced above, then it is always in the first figure. The first rule is, therefore, this: a characteristic mark B of a characteristic mark C of a thing A is a characteristic mark of the thing A itself.[21] Three propositions follow from this:

C has the characteristic mark B	That which is rational (C) is a mind (B);
A has the characteristic C	The human soul (A) is rational (C);
Therefore,	Therefore,
A has the characteristic mark B	The human soul (A) is a mind (B).[22]

It is very easy to adduce other similar propositions as examples, and among them propositions governed by the rule of negative inferences, to convince oneself that if they agree with these rules then they are always in the first figure. My attempt to avoid tedious long-windedness[d] is thus justified. It will also be easily realised that these syllogistic rules do not require that, in addition to these judgements, there must be inserted between them some immediate inference which has been drawn from one or other of them, if the argument is to be valid. It follows that the syllogism in the first figure is of a pure kind.

IN THE SECOND FIGURE ONLY MIXED SYLLOGISMS ARE POSSIBLE

The rule of the second figure is this: Whatever is contradicted by the characteristic mark of a thing contradicts the thing itself.[e23] This proposi-

---

[c] *wenn ein Vernunftschluss unmittelbar . . . geführt wird.*   [d] *eine ekelhafte Weitläufigkeit.*
[e] *Wem ein Merkmal eines Dinges widerspricht, das widerspricht dem Dinge selber.*

tion is only true because that which is contradicted by a characteristic mark also contradicts this characteristic mark; but what contradicts a characteristic mark conflicts with the thing itself; so, that which is contradicted by a characteristic mark of a thing, conflicts with the thing itself. Now, it is obviously the case that an inference by means of the minor premiss to the conclusion is only possible because I can subject the major premiss, as a negative proposition, to a simple conversion. This conversion must, therefore, be tacitly thought*f* in making the inference, for otherwise my propositions do not form a valid inference.*g* The proposition generated by the conversion is, however, a consequence immediately deriving from the first proposition and interpolated between it and the second; the syllogism thus has four judgements and is a *ratiocinium hybridum*.[24] For example, suppose that I say:

No mind is divisible;
All matter is divisible;
So, no matter is a mind.[25]

My inference is valid,*h* but what gives it its power to establish the conclusion*i* is this: from the first proposition: *no mind is divisible,* there follows by means of an immediate inference the proposition: *so nothing divisible is a mind;* after that everything validly follows in accordance with the universal rule governing all syllogisms. But, since the capacity of the argument to establish a conclusion*j* depends exclusively on the inference which is to be drawn immediately from the major premiss, that inference belongs to the argument and it has four judgements:

No mind is divisible;
Hence, nothing divisible is a mind;
All matter is divisible;
Consequently, no matter is a mind.

IN THE THIRD FIGURE ONLY MIXED
SYLLOGISMS ARE POSSIBLE

The rule of the third figure is as follows: that which belongs to or contradicts a thing, also belongs to or contradicts some of the things which are subsumed under another characteristic mark of this thing.*k*[26] This proposition is itself only true because it is possible (*per conversionem logicam*)[27] to convert the judgement, which maintains that another characteristic mark

2:53

---

f geheim gedacht werden.   *g sonst schliessen meine Sätze nicht.*   *h so schliesse ich recht.*
i Schlusskraft.   *j Schlussfähigkeit.*
k was einer Sache zukommt oder widerspricht, das kommt auch zu oder widerspricht einigen, die unter einem andern Merkmal dieser Sache enthalten sind.

belongs to this thing; by this means it comes to agree with the rule of all syllogisms. For example, the argument runs:

All human beings are sinners;
All human beings are rational;
So, some rational beings are sinners.[28]

This conclusion only follows[l] because I can infer from the minor premiss, by means of a conversion *per accidens*: therefore, some rational beings are human beings. After that the concepts are compared in accordance with the rule of all syllogisms, but only by means of an interpolated immediate inference. And what one has is the following *ratiocinium hybridum:*[29]

All human beings are sinners;
All human beings are rational beings;
Consequently, some rational beings are human beings;
Therefore, some rational beings are sinners.

Exactly the same thing can be shown with great ease in the negative mode of this figure; but I shall omit it for the sake of brevity.[30]

IN THE FOURTH FIGURE ONLY MIXED SYLLOGISMS ARE POSSIBLE

The mode of inference in this figure[m] is highly unnatural and depends upon a large number of intermediate inferences which have to be supposed to be interpolated. So much so, indeed, that the general account of the rule governing this mode of syllogistic reasoning which I might offer would be very obscure and difficult to understand.[n][31] For this reason, I shall only specify the conditions under which a valid conclusion may be drawn in this figure of the syllogism. A valid inference is possible in the negative modes of this syllogism because I change the positions of the terms either by means of logical conversion or by means of contraposition. I am thus enabled to think after each premiss its immediate implication. In this way, the sequences of inferences acquire the relation which they must have in a syllogism, according to the general rule. I shall, however, show that in the affirmative mode syllogisms are not possible in the fourth figure at all. The negative syllogism in this figure, the form in which it must really be thought, takes the following form:

2:54   No fool is learned;
So, no learned person is a fool;

[l] *Dieses schliesst nur.*
[m] (The translator has adopted Lasswitz's emendation of *Form* ['form'] to read *Figur* ['figure'].)
[n] *dunkel und unverständlich.*

Some learned people are pious;
So, some pious people are learned;
Therefore, some pious people are not fools.[32]

A syllogism of the second kind[33] would run:

Every mind is simple;
Everything simple is imperishable;
Therefore, some of what is imperishable is a mind.[34]

In this case it is obvious that the conclusion, as it is presented here, cannot follow from the premises at all. This is instantly apparent when one compares the middle term with the conclusion. To be specific: I cannot say that some of what is imperishable is a mind because it is simple; for it is not the case that something is a mind simply in virtue of its being simple.[o] Furthermore, it is not possible, no matter what logical transformations[p] are employed, so to arrange the premises that the conclusion, or, indeed, even another proposition from which the conclusion follows as an immediate consequence, can be derived from them. Such a derivation is impossible, namely, if the terms of the syllogism are to have the positions prescribed by the rule which governs all the figures of the syllogism and which has been established once and for all, and in virtue of which the major term occurs in the major premiss and the minor in the minor premiss.* It is true that, if I completely reverse the positions of the main terms, so that what was previously the major now becomes the minor, and conversely, what was previously the minor now becomes the major, a consequence can be drawn from which the given conclusion follows. But in that case, a complete transposition[r] of the premises is then necessary. The so-called syllogism in the fourth figure which is thus obtained, contains, it is true, the materials for a conclusion, but it does not have the form, in accordance with which the conclusion is to be drawn. From the point of view of the logical order, in which alone the division of the four figures is possible, the fourth syllogism is not a syllogism at all. The situation in the case of the negative mode of

2:55

---

* This rule is based upon the synthetic order according to which the remote attribute is compared with the subject first, and then the nearer attribute is compared with the subject. Although this may, at first sight, look as if it were merely arbitrary,[q] it nonetheless turns out to be indispensably necessary if one is to have four figures. For, as soon as it is a matter of indifference whether the predicate of the conclusion is put in the major premiss or the minor premise, the first figure cannot be distinguished at all from the fourth. A similar mistake is to be found in Crusius's *Logik*,[35] note on page 600.

[o] *denn darum, weil etwas einfach ist, ist es nicht sofort ein Geist.*   [p] *logische Veränderung.*
[q] *willkürlich.*   [r] *eine gänzliche Versetzung.*

inference in the same figure is entirely different. Such a negative mode of inference would have to run, namely, as follows:

Every mind is simple;
Everything simple is imperishable;
So, every mind is imperishable;
Therefore, some of what is imperishable is a mind.

This is a perfectly valid inference.⁵ But such a syllogism differs from a syllogism in the first figure, not in virtue of the middle term having a different position, but only in virtue of a change of the order of the premisses in the syllogism* and of the order of the main terms' in the consequence. But that in no wise amounts to a change of figure. A mistake of this kind is to be found in the passage referred to above in Crusius's *Logik:* he supposes that one is reasoning in the fourth figure and doing so, indeed, with greater naturalness, because one is free to change the order of the premisses. It is a pity that a great mind should have taken this trouble to improve something which is of no value. The only useful thing to do is to do away with it."

* For if the proposition, in which the predicate of the conclusion occurs, is the major premise, then, speaking of the proper conclusion which here follows from the premises, the second proposition is the major premise, and the first proposition is the minor premise. But then everything is inferred in accordance with the first figure, except that the proposed conclusion is drawn by means of logical conversion from that which follows immediately from the judgements mentioned above.

⁵ *Dieses schiesst ganz richtig.*   ' *Hauptbegriffe.*
ᵘ *Man kann nur was Nützliches thun, wenn man sie vernichtigt.*

§5. The logical division of the four syllogistic figures is a piece of false subtlety.[v][36]

One cannot deny that valid inferences may be drawn in all these four figures. But it is indisputable that all four figures, with the exception of the first, determine the conclusion only indirectly by means of interpolated intermediate inferences.[w] It is further indisputable that exactly the same conclusion can be inferred, in pure and undiluted form, from the same middle term employing the first figure. Now, it might at this point occur to someone to suppose that, if such were the case, then the three other figures would, at worst, be useless, but not actually false. But if one considers the intention which inspired their invention and continues to inspire their presentation, one will come to a different view of the matter. Suppose that one wished to bring about the following situation. A number of inferences and the main judgements, all intermingled together, are to be entangled with each other in such a fashion that, some being explicitly stated and others suppressed,[x] a great deal of skill will be required to determine whether or not they conform to the laws of inference. If this were one's objective, one might invent, not, indeed, new figures, but new and puzzling inferences capable of causing headaches enough. The purpose of logic, however, is not to confuse but to clarify;[y] its aim is not to obscure but clearly to reveal.[z] Hence, these four modes of inference ought to be simple, unmixed and free from concealed supplementary inferences.[a] If they do not satisfy these conditions they are not to be granted the freedom of appearing in a logical discourse as the formulae which represent the syllogism in clearest form. It is also certain that hitherto all logicians have regarded them as simple syllogisms, not requiring the interpolation of additional judgements. Had they not been regarded in this light, they would never have received their citizenship.[b][37] Thus, the remaining three modes of inference, construed as syllogistic rules in general, are correct; but construed as containing a simple and pure inference, they are

2:56

---

[v] *falsche Spitzfindigkeit.*   [w] *eingemengte Zwischenschlüsse.*

[x] *Wenn es darauf ankäme, eine Menge von Schlüssen, die unter die Haupturtheile gemengt wären, mit diesen so zu verwickeln, dass, indem einige ausgedrückt, andere verschwiegen würden.*

[y] *nicht zu verwickeln, sondern aufzulösen.*

[z] *nicht verdeckt, sondern augenscheinlich etwas vorzutragen.*   [a] *ohne verdeckte Nebenschlüsse.*

[b] *dieses Bürgerrecht.*

99

mistaken. This mistake turns the confusing of the understanding into a positive right, and it deprives logic of its distinctive purpose, namely that of reducing everything to the simplest mode of cognition.*c* And the magnitude of the mistake increases with the number of the special rules (and each figure has a number of such rules peculiar to itself) which are necessary if one is not to trip over oneself when performing these capers.*d* If ever there was a case of great ingenuity being squandered on something utterly futile, or a case of great apparent learning being wasted, then this is it. The so-called *modi* which are possible in each figure and which are designated by strange words, also contain, very artfully concealed, letters which facilitate their transformation into the first figure. These *modi* will one day come to be regarded as a precious curiosity*e* representative of a way of thinking employed by the human understanding. And that will occur when the venerable rust of antiquity shall teach a better instructed posterity to look with amazement and regret on the eager and futile efforts of their ancestors preserved in these relics.

It is easy to discover what initially led to this subtlety. The person who first wrote down a syllogism in three lines arranged one above the other, and looked at it as one would look at a chess-board, and who then attempted to establish what would happen if one changed the positions of

2:57   the middle term – that person, when he discovered that the transposition yielded good sense was as much taken aback as someone detecting an anagram in a name. To delight in either of these things was equally childish, particularly since it was not noticed that it produced nothing new in respect of distinctness,*f* but only served to increase the obscurity.*g* However, when all is said and done, the fate of the human understanding is such that it is either given to brooding over deep matters and falls into bizarre ideas,*h* or it audaciously chases after objects too great for its grasp and builds castles in the air. Among the common herd of thinkers,*i* there is one who chooses the number 666, another the origin of animals and plants, or the mysteries of providence. The error into which they each fall is very different in character, and that difference corresponds to the difference between their mental constitutions.

Ours is an age in which the things which are worth knowing are increasing in number. It will not be long before our ability grows too weak and our lives too short for us to be able to understand even the most useful of these things. Riches offer themselves to us in such superabundance that, in order to take possession of them, we find ourselves constrained to

---

c *die einfachste Erkenntnisart.*
d *um bei diesen Seitensprungen sich nicht selbst ein Bein unterzuschlagen.*
e *eine schatzbare Seltenheit.* *f* *Deutlichkeit.* *g* *Undeutlichkeit.*
h *grüblerisch und geräth auf Fratzen.* *i* *von dem grossen Haufen der Denker.*

abandon a great deal of useless rubbish,[j] it would have been better had we never been burdened with it in the first place.

I should be flattering myself too highly if I were to suppose that the labour of a few hours were capable of toppling the colossus, who hides his head in the clouds of antiquity, and whose feet are feet of clay. My intention is simply to explain why, in my course on logic[k] – where I am not permitted to arrange everything in accordance with my own understanding of these things but am often obliged to defer to the prevailing taste – I treat these matters only briefly, so as to devote the time thus saved to the genuine enlargement of useful knowledge.[l]

Syllogistic has another certain utility, namely that of enabling one to carry off the victory over a careless opponent in a learned dispute. However, since this belongs to academic athleticism[m] – an art which may well be of great use, though it does not contribute greatly to the advancement of truth – I shall pass it over in silence.

[j] *unnützen Plunder.* [k] *in dem logischen Vortrag.* [l] *nützlicher Einsichten.*
[m] *Athletik der Gelehrten.*

§6. Concluding reflection

Our discussions have established the following points: that the supreme rules governing all syllogisms lead directly to that order of concepts which is called the first figure; that all other transpositions of the middle term only yield valid inferences if, by means of easy and immediate inferences, they lead to such propositions as are connected in the simple order of the first figure; that it is impossible to draw simple and unmixed inferences in more than one figure, for it is only ever the first figure which, concealed in a syllogism by means of covert inferences, has the power to generate the conclusion, with the changed position of the terms merely occasioning a deviation, shorter or longer as the case may be, which has to be followed if one is to understand how the conclusion has been reached; and that the division of the figures in general, in so far as they are supposed to contain inferences which are pure, unmixed and free from interpolated inferences, is false and impossible. It is easy to see from our explanations – and for that reason I do not propose to dwell on it – that the universal fundamental rules which govern all syllogisms contain the special rules of the so-called first figure; it is also easy to see that, given the conclusion and the middle term, one can instantly convert any syllogism belonging to one of the other figures into the first simple figure, without the futile tediousness of the formulae of reduction,[n] so that either the conclusion itself or a proposition from which the conclusion follows by immediate inference, can be inferred.

I do not wish to conclude this reflection without adding some remarks which may be of some considerable use in other connections.

Firstly, then I would say: a *distinct* concept[o] is only possible by means of a *judgement,* while a *complete* concept[p] is only possible by means of a *syllogism.*[38] A distinct concept demands, namely, that I should clearly recognise[q] something as a characteristic mark of a thing; but this is a judgement. In order to have a distinct concept of body, I clearly represent to myself impenetrability as a characteristic mark of it. This representation, however, is nothing other than the thought: *a body is impenetrable.* The only thing which needs to be remarked upon in this connection is the fact that this judgement is not the distinct concept itself, but rather the action,[r] by

[n] *Reductionsformulae.*   [o] *ein deutlicher Begriff.*   [p] *ein Vollständiger.*   [q] *klar erkenne.*
[r] *die Handlung.*

means of which the distinct concept is actualised, for the representation of the thing which comes into being after the operation is distinct. It is easy to show that a complete concept is only possible by means of a syllogism; one needs only to look at the first numbered section[39] of this treatise. For this reason one could also call a distinct^s concept one which is clear,^{t} in virtue of a judgement, while a complete concept could be called one which is distinct^u in virtue of a syllogism. If the completeness is of the first degree, then the syllogism is simple; if the completeness is of the second or third degree, then it is only possible by means of a series of chain-syllogisms,^{v} which the understanding condenses in the manner of a sorites.[40] These considerations also plainly reveal a fundamental mistake of logic, as logic is commonly treated: it discusses distinct and complete concepts before it discusses judgements and syllogisms, although the former are only possible in virtue of the latter.

2:59

Secondly, it is equally obvious that the completeness of a concept and its distinctness do not require different fundamental faculties of the soul (for the capacity which immediately recognises something as a characteristic mark of a thing, and which represents another characteristic mark as contained in the first characteristic mark, and which thus thinks the thing by means of a remote characteristic mark, is in all these cases exactly the same). It is equally obvious that *understanding* and *reason*, that is to say, the faculty of cognising distinctly and the faculty of syllogistic reasoning, are not different *fundamental faculties*.^{w} Both consist in the capacity to judge; but when one judges mediately, one draws an inference.

Thirdly, it can also be concluded from the above considerations that the higher faculty of cognition^x rests absolutely and simply on the capacity to judge. Accordingly, if a being can judge, then it possesses the higher faculty of cognition.^{y} If one has cause to deny of this being that it possesses this faculty, then that being is incapable of judgement. The failure to reflect on these matters has induced a man of renown and learning[41] to attribute distinct concepts to animals. This argument runs like this: an ox's representation of its stall includes the clear representation of its characteristic mark of having a door; therefore, the ox has a distinct concept of its stall. It is easy to prevent the confusion here. The distinct-ness of a concept does not consist in the fact that that which is a character-istic mark of the thing is clearly represented,^{z} but rather in the fact that it is recognised^a as a characteristic mark of the thing. The door is something which does, it is true, belong to the stall and can serve as a characteristic mark of it. But only the being who forms the judgement: *this door belongs to this stable* has a distinct concept of the building, and that is certainly beyond the powers of animals.

---

^{s} *deutlichen.* ^{t} *klar.* ^{u} *deutlich.* ^{v} *eine Reihe von Kettenschlüssen.* ^{w} *Grundfähigkeiten.*
^{x} *die obere Erkenntnisskraft.* ^{y} *die obere Erkenntnissfähigkeit.* ^{z} *klar vorgestellt.* ^{a} *erkannt.*

I would go still further and say: it is one thing *to differentiate*[b] things from each other, and quite another thing *to recognise* the difference between them.[c] The latter is only possible by means of judgements and cannot occur in the case of animals, who are not endowed with reason. The

2:60 following division may be of great use. *Differentiating logically*[d] means recognising[e] that a thing A is not B; it is always a negative judgement. *Physically differentiating*[f] means being driven to different actions by different representations. The dog differentiates the roast from the loaf, and it does so because the way in which it is affected by the roast is different from the way in which it is affected by the loaf (for different things cause different sensations); and the sensations caused by the roast are a ground of desire in the dog which differs from the desire caused by the loaf,* according to the natural connection which exists between its drives and its representations. This consideration may induce us to think more carefully about the essential difference between animals endowed with reason and those not so endowed. If one succeeds in understanding what the mysterious power[g] is which makes judging possible, one will have solved the problem. My present opinion tends to the view that this power or capacity[h] is nothing other than the faculty of inner sense,[i] that is to say, the faculty of making one's own representations the objects of one's thought. This faculty cannot be derived from some other faculty. It is, in the strict sense of the term, a fundamental faculty,[j] which, in my opinion, can only belong to rational beings. But it is upon this faculty that the entire higher faculty of cognition is based. I conclude with a thought which will be bound to be a source of pleasure to those who are able to delight in the unity which is to be found in human cognition. All affirmative judgements are subsumed under a common formula, the law of agreement:[k] *cuilibet subjecto competit praedicatum ipsi identicum;*[42] all negative judgements are subsumed under the law of contradiction: *nulli subjecto competit praedicatum ipsi oppositum.*[43] All affirmative syllogisms are subsumed under the rule; *nota notae est nota rei ipsius;*[44] all negative syllogisms are subsumed under this rule: *oppositum notae opponitur rei ipsi.*[45] All judgements, which are directly subsumed

---

* It is, indeed, of the greatest importance, when considering the nature of animals, to take account of this. In observing them, we only notice external actions; the differences between those actions are indicative of the differing determinations of their appetites. It by no means follows from this that there occurs within them that action of the faculty of cognition in which they have an awareness of the agreement or conflict between what is in one sensation and what is in another, and hence that they judge in accordance with that awareness.

[b] *unterscheiden.*
[c] *den Unterschied der Dinge erkennen* / (alt: to know or cognise the difference between things).
[d] *Logisch unterscheiden.*   [e] *erkennen.*   [f] *physisch unterscheiden.*   [g] *geheime Kraft.*
[h] *Kraft oder Fähigkeit.*   [i] *Vermögen des innern Sinnes.*   [j] *Grundvermögen.*
[k] *Der Satz der Einstimmung.*

under the laws of identity or contradiction, that is to say, all judgements in the case of which identity or contradiction are apprehended immediately, not through an intermediate attribute (and consequently not by means of the analysis of concepts), are indemonstrable propositions; those in which   2:61
identity or contradiction can be cognised mediately are demonstrable. Human knowledge^l is full of such indemonstrable^m judgements. Every definition^n is preceded by a number of such indemonstrable judgements, for in order to arrive at a definition, one represents as a characteristic mark of the thing that which one immediately cognises in a thing before anything else.[46] Those philosophers are mistaken who proceed as if there were only one unprovable fundamental truth and no others.[47] But those philosophers are no less mistaken who, with excessive generosity and inadequate guarantees,^{o} confer this distinction upon a variety of their propositions.[48]

^{l} *Erkenntniss.* ^{m} *unerweisliche.* ^{n} *Definition.*
^{o} *ohne genugsame Gewährleistung zu freigebig sind.*

The only possible argument in support of a demonstration of the existence of God, by M. Immanuel Kant (1763)

Der einzig mögliche Beweisgrund zu einer Demonstration des Daseins Gottes, von M. Immanuel Kant (1763)

Der

einzig mögliche Beweisgrund

zu einer

Demonstration

des

Daseins Gottes

von

M. Immanuel Kant.

The only possible argument in support of a demonstration of the existence of God

by
M. Immanuel Kant

Ne mea dona tibi studio disposta fideli, Intellecta prius quam sint, contempta relinquas.
                                                                    LUCRETIUS[1]

I do not esteem the use of an endeavour, such as this present one, so highly as to suppose that the most important of all our cognitions, *there is a God,* would waver or be imperilled if it were not supported by deep metaphysical investigations. It was not the will of Providence that the insights so necessary to our happiness should depend upon the sophistry of subtle inferences.[a] On the contrary, Providence has directly transmitted these insights to our natural common sense.[b] And, provided that it is not confused by false art, it does not fail to lead us directly to what is true and useful, for we are in extreme need of these two things. Thus, that employment of sound reason,[c] which still lies within the limits of ordinary insights, yields sufficiently convincing proofs[d] of the existence and properties of this Being, though the subtle scholar will everywhere feel the lack of demonstration[e2] and of the exactitude of precisely determined concepts and regularly connected syllogisms. Nonetheless, one cannot refrain from searching for this demonstration, in the hope that it may present itself somewhere. For, without mentioning the reasonable desire to achieve, in cognition of such importance, something which is complete and distinctly understood, – and no understanding which is accustomed to investigation can renounce this desire – it is to be hoped that such an insight, once it has been attained, will be able to illuminate much else in this object. To achieve this purpose, however, one must venture the bottomless abyss of metaphysics. Metaphysics is a dark and shoreless ocean, marked by no beacons. One must proceed as the mariner proceeds on an unnavigated sea: as soon as he makes a landing, he subjects his voyage to scrutiny, with a view to determining whether undetected currents, for example, may not have carried him off course, in spite of all the care, prescribed by the art of navigation, which he has taken.

2:66

This demonstration, however, has not yet been discovered, and this failure has already been noticed by other writers. And, indeed, what I am

---

[a] *Spitzfindigkeit feiner Schlüsse.*   [b] *dem natürlichen gemeinen Verstande.*
[c] *der gesunden Vernunft.*   [d] *genugsam überführende Beweistümer.*   [e] *Demonstration.*

offering here is merely an argument in support of a demonstration.ᶠ³ What I am furnishing here is the materialsᵍ for constructing a building; they have been assembled with great difficulty and they are now offered to the critical scrutiny of the expert in the hope that what is serviceable among them may be used to erect an edifice which accords with the rules of durability and harmoniousness.ʰ I no more wish that the analyses of the conceptsⁱ which I employ should be taken for definitions⁴ than I wish that what I offer here should be held for the demonstration itself. The analyses which I offer furnish correct characteristic marks of the things of which I am treating: they enable us to arrive at precise definitions,ʲ and they are serviceable in themselves for the attainment of truth and distinctness. But they still await the finishing hand of the artist, and until they receive it they cannot be regarded as definitions. In a science such as metaphysics there are times when one confidently undertakes to defineᵏ and demonstrate everything; and then, again, there are times when one ventures upon such undertakings only with fear and trepidation.

The observations which I here present are the fruits of lengthy reflection. But, because a variety of commitments has prevented me from devoting the necessary time to it, the manner in which these observations are presented shows the characteristic mark of something incompletely worked out. However, to plead the reader's indulgence for only being able to wait upon him with something of inferior quality, no matter for what cause, would be a very futile piece of ingratiation. The reader will never grant his pardon, no matter what the excuse may be. In my own case, the incomplete form of the work is to be attributed less to negligence than to deliberate omission. My sole intention has been to sketch the rough outlines of a main draft. It is my belief that an edifice of no mean excellence could be erected on the basis of that draft, provided that hands more practised than my own were to give it greater accuracy in the parts and perfected regularity in the whole. This having been my intention, the 2:67 expenditure of excessive and anxious care on the precise painting in of all the lineaments in the individual parts would have been superfluous effort, for the outline in general must first await the strict judgement of the specialists in the field.ˡ For this reason, I have often adduced argumentsᵐ without presuming to claim to be able, for the moment, to show distinctly their connection with the conclusion. I have, on occasion, advanced common judgements of the understanding without giving them that form of

---

ᶠ *Beweisgrund* / Beck (1798) (hereafter B): argument / Carabellese (hereafter C): *argomento* / Festugière (hereafter F) & Zac (hereafter Z): *fondement* / Treash (hereafter T): basis.

ᵍ *Baugeräth.*

ʰ *Wohlgereimtheit* / B: congruity / C: *armonia* / F. *bon appareillage* / T: harmonious adaptation / Z: *harmonie.*

ⁱ *Auflösungen der Begriffe.*   ʲ *abgemessenen Erklärungen.*   ᵏ *erklären.*

ˡ *der Meister in der Kunst.*   ᵐ *Beweisthümer.*

rigour, through the art of logic, which the elements of a system ought to have. The reason for this omission has either been the fact that I found the task difficult, or the fact that the extent of the preparation which would have been necessary was out of proportion to the intended size of the work, or the fact, indeed, that I regarded myself, not having promised a demonstration, as freed from the requirements which are legitimately made of systematic authors. Of those who presume to judge works of the mind, it is a minority which boldly looks at the attempt as a whole and which gives particular consideration to the possible relation of its main parts to a soundly constructed edifice, once certain defects have been remedied and certain errors corrected. The judgement of this kind of reader is particularly beneficial to human cognition. As for the other kind of reader: incapable of apprehending a connection in the whole, he rivets his brooding attention on some one detail or other, indifferent as to whether a reproach, which is perhaps merited by a part, does not also affect the value of the whole, and as to whether detailed improvements of individual parts may save the general scheme, which is only partially defective. Readers of this kind, whose sole and constant concern is to reduce any building which they find started to ruins before it is completed, might, it is true, be feared on account of their number. However, their judgement is of slight significance to reasonable people when it comes to deciding the true value of a work.

I have, perhaps, in places, not explained myself in sufficient detail to deprive those who wish only for a specious pretext for casting the bitter reproach of heterodoxy[n] upon a book, of all opportunity of doing so. But, then, what precaution could be taken to prevent this? I think, however, that I have spoken distinctly enough for those whose sole wish is to find in a work that which the author intended to put into it. I have involved myself as little as possible with objections, even though my claims differ so much from those of others. Such disagreement I shall leave to the consideration of the reader who has understood both sides of the question. If the judgements of unbiased reason held by different thoughtful people were examined with the frankness of an uncorrupted advocate – an advocate who so weighed the grounds of the two disputed positions that he was able   2:68
to imagine himself in the position of the two proponents, so as to be persuaded as strongly as possible of their respective views, and who only then decided to which side he wished to commit himself – if the judgements of unbiased reason were examined in this way, philosophers would disagree far less than they do. Unfeigned fairness[o] in adopting as far as possible the opposite opinion would soon unite enquiring minds on a single path.

In a reflection as difficult as the present one, I can, I suppose, resign

[n] *Vorwurf des Irrglaubens.*   [o] *ungeheuchelte Billigkeit.*

myself in advance to the fact that many of the things I shall say will be incorrect, that many of the elucidations I shall offer will be inadequate, and that many of the positions I shall develop[p] will prove frail and defective. I lay no claim to the reader's unconditional agreement; I should scarcely concede such unqualified support to an author myself. I shall not, therefore, be taken aback if I am corrected by others on many points. I shall, indeed, be found amenable to such instruction. If, at the beginning, when one is laying the foundations of one's argument, one confidently claims not to be mistaken, it is difficult to withdraw such a claim later on; it is less difficult to withdraw a claim which has been advanced with moderation, diffidence and modesty. Even the most subtle vanity, provided that it understands itself, will notice that allowing oneself to be convinced by others deserves as much credit as convincing others oneself, and that perhaps the former action, in so far as it requires greater self-denial and more self-examination, is more truly creditable than the other. It might seem that the periodic occurrence of fairly detailed physical explanations[q] in a work would be damaging to the unity which one must observe in reflecting upon one's subject. However, since my intention in these cases has been especially focused on the method of using natural science to attain cognition of God, I could scarcely have achieved this purpose without deploying such examples. For that reason the Seventh Reflection of the Second Section requires greater indulgence. This is particularly so since its content is drawn from a book which I once pub-

2:69 lished anonymously* and in which I treated of the same topic in greater detail, though in connection with various hypotheses of a somewhat daring character. Nonetheless, the affinity which exists between at least the freedom permitted to venture upon such explanations and my main intention, and likewise the wish to see certain aspects of the hypothesis subjected to criticism by the experts, have occasioned the inclusion of this reflection. For those wishing to understand all its arguments, it is, perhaps, too short. And for those expecting nothing but metaphysics it is, perhaps, too long. These latter readers may conveniently skip this reflec-

---

* The title of the book is *Allgemeine Naturgeschichte und Theorie des Himmels* (Königsberg and Leipzig: 1755). This work, which has remained little known,[5] cannot have come to the attention of, among others, the celebrated *J. H. Lambert*. Six years later, in his *Kosmologische Briefe* (*1761*),[6] he presented precisely the same theory of the systematic constitution of the cosmos in general, the Milky Way, the nebulae, and so forth, which is to be found in my above-mentioned theory of the heavens, the first part, and likewise in the preface to that book. Something of this theory is also indicated in the brief outline on pages 154 to 158 of the present work.[7] The agreement between the thoughts of this ingenious man and those presented by myself at that time almost extends to the finer details of the theory, and it only serves to strengthen my supposition that this sketch will receive additional confirmation in the course of time.

> [p] *manche Ausführung.*   [q] *ziemlich ausführliche physische Erläuterungen.*

tion. It will, perhaps be necessary, before reading the work, to correct certain printing errors which could affect the sense of my words. A list of such errors is to be found at the end of the book.[8]

The work itself consists of three sections: the *first* presents the argument itself; the *second* explains its extensive usefulness; the *third* offers reasons which are intended to show that no other argument in support of a demonstration of the existence of God is possible.

Section 1. In which is furnished the argument in support of a demonstration of the existence of God

FIRST REFLECTION: OF EXISTENCE^r IN GENERAL

Even in the profoundest of treatises, the rule of thoroughness does not always demand that every concept employed should be developed or defined.[59] No such requirement exists, namely, if one is assured that the clear and ordinary concept by itself can occasion no misunderstanding in the context in which it is employed. Such is the case with the geometer who with the greatest certainty uncovers the most secret properties and relations of that which is extended, even though in doing so he merely makes use of the ordinary concept of space. And such is also the case in the deepest science of all, where the word 'representation' is understood with sufficient precision and employed with confidence, even though its meaning can never be analysed by means of definition.[110]

Hence, in these reflections I should not aspire to analyse the very simple and well-understood concept of existence, were it not for the fact that the present case is one in which such an omission could occasion confusion and lead to serious errors. It is certain that anywhere else in philosophy the concept could confidently be employed in the undeveloped form in which it occurs in ordinary usage. The one exception is the question concerning absolutely necessary existence and contingent exis-

tence. In this one case, an investigation of a subtler sort has drawn errone-ous conclusions from an unhappily contrived^u but otherwise very pure concept. These erroneous conclusions have extended themselves over one of the most sublime parts of philosophy.

It is not to be expected that I shall begin by offering a formal definition^v of existence. Such a procedure is always undesirable when the correctness of the suggested definition is so uncertain.^w This situation arises more frequently than one perhaps realises. My procedure will be like that of

---

^r *Dasein.*   ^s *erklärt.*   ^t *niemals durch eine Erklärung kann aufgelöset werden.*
^u *unglücklich gekünstelten.*   ^v *mit einer förmlichen Erklärung.*
^w *wo es so unsicher ist, richtig erklärt zu haben.*

someone who is searching for a definition and who first of all assures himself of what can be said with certainty, either affirmatively or negatively, about the object of the definition,[x] even though he has not yet established the concept of the object in detail.[y] Long before one ventures a definition of one's object,[z] and even when one lacks the courage to offer a definition at all, there is still a great deal which can be asserted with the highest degree of certainty about the object in question. I doubt whether anyone has ever correctly defined[a] what space is. But, without getting involved in such a definition, I am certain that where space exists external relations must also exist, that it cannot have more than three dimensions, and so on. Whatever a desire may be, it is based upon some representation or other, it presupposes pleasure in the object of the desire, and so on. From that which is known with certainty and prior to the definition of a thing, it is frequently possible to infer with complete certainty that which is relevant to the purpose of our investigation. To aspire to a definition is to venture upon unnecessary difficulties. The mania for method and the imitation of the mathematician, who advances with a sure step along a well-surfaced road, have occasioned a large number of such mishaps on the slippery ground of metaphysics.[11] These mishaps are constantly before one's eyes, but there is little hope that people will be warned by them, or that they will learn to be more circumspect as a result. By this method alone I hope to arrive at the enlightenment which I have vainly sought in others. As for the flattering idea that one's own greater perspicacity will secure one the success which has been denied to others: it is well to remember that this has always been the style of those whose wish it has been to lead us from the errors made by others to errors of their own devising.

1. Existence is not a predicate or a determination[b] of a thing   2:72

This proposition seems strange and absurd, but it is indubitably certain. Take any subject you please, for example, Julius Caesar. Draw up a list of all the predicates which may be thought to belong to him, not excepting even those of space and time. You will quickly see that he can either exist with all these determinations,[c] or not exist at all. The Being who gave existence to the world and to our hero within that world could know every single one of these predicates without exception, and yet still be able to regard him as a merely possible thing which, in the absence of that Being's decision to create him, would not exist. Who can deny that millions of things which do not actually exist are merely possible from the point of view of all the predicates they would contain if they were to exist.

---

[x] *Erklärung.*   [y] *ausführlich.*   [z] *Erklärung von seinem Gegenstande.*   [a] *richtig erklärt.*
[b] *Determination.*   [c] *Bestimmungen.*

Or who can deny that in the representation which the Supreme Being has of them there is not a single determination*d* missing, although existence is not among them, for the Supreme Being cognises them only as possible things. It cannot happen, therefore, that if they were to exist they would contain an extra predicate; for, in the case of the possibility of a thing in its complete determination, no predicate at all can be missing. And if it had pleased God to create a different series of things, to create a different world, that world would have existed with all the determinations, and no additional ones, which He cognises it to have, although that world was merely possible.

Nonetheless, the expression 'existence' is used as a predicate. And, indeed, this can be done safely and without troublesome errors, provided that one does not insist on deriving existence from merely possible concepts, as one is accustomed to doing when one wants to prove absolutely necessary existence. For then one seeks in vain among the predicates of such a possible being;*e* existence is certainly not to be found among them. But when existence occurs as a predicate in common speech, it is a predicate not so much of the thing itself as of the thought which one has of the thing. For example: existence belongs to the sea-unicorn (or narwal) but not to the land-unicorn.*f* This simply means: the representation of a sea-unicorn (or narwal) is an empirical concept; in other words, it is the representation of an existent thing. For this reason, too, one does not examine the concept of the subject in order to demonstrate the correctness of the proposition about the existence of such a thing. The concept of the subject only contains predicates of possibility. If one wishes to demon-
2:73 strate the correctness of such a proposition, one examines the source of one's cognition of the object. One says: 'I have seen it' or 'I have heard about it from those who have seen it'. The expression 'A sea-unicorn (or narwal) is an existent animal' is not, therefore, entirely correct. The expression ought to be formulated the other way round to read 'The predicates, which I think collectively when I think of a sea-unicorn (or narwal), attach to a certain existent sea-animal'. One ought not to say: 'Regular hexagons exist in nature' but rather: 'The predicates, which one thinks collectively when one thinks of an hexagon, attach to certain things in nature, such as the cells of the honeycomb and root crystal'. All human languages have certain ineradicable defects which arise from the contingent circumstances surrounding their origins. It would be pedantic and futile to over-refine language and impose limits upon it in those cases where, in ordinary usage, no misunderstandings could arise. It is suffi-

---

d Bestimmung.   e Wesen (alt: entity).
f The German word for 'unicorn' is *Einhorn:* the word *Landeinhorn* is not listed by Grimm; it is probably Kant's neologism, invented to establish a parallel with *Seeeinhorn,* which is the regular word for 'narwal'. In order to preserve the parallel, *Landeinhorn* has been translated by the neologism 'land-unicorn' and *Seeeinhorn* by the phrase 'sea-unicorn (or narwal)'.

cient that these distinctions should be made in those rarer cases where one is engaged in reflection of a subtler and deeper kind, where such distinctions are necessary. What is being said here can only be judged adequately in the light of what follows.

2. Existence is the absolute positing of a thing. Existence is thereby also distinguished from any predicate; the latter is, as such, always posited only relative to some other thing.

The concept of positing or setting[g] is perfectly simple: it is identical with the concept of being in general.[i] Now, something can be thought as posited merely relatively, or, to express the matter better, it can be thought merely as the relation (*respectus logicus*)[12] of something as a characteristic mark[j13] of a thing. In this case, being, that is to say, the positing of this relation, is nothing other than the copula[k] in a judgement. If what is considered is not merely this relation but the thing posited in and for itself, then this being is the same as existence.[l14]

This concept is so simple that it is not possible to say anything further by way of elaboration,[m] except only to note the caution which must be exercised in not confusing it with the relations which things have to their characteristic marks.

Once it is appreciated that the whole of our cognition ultimately re-solves itself into unanalysable concepts, it will also be understood that there will be some concepts which are almost unanalysable; in other words, there will be some concepts where the characteristic marks are only to a very small degree clearer and simpler than the thing itself.[15] Such is the case with our definition of existence.[n] I readily admit that it is only in a very small degree that our definition renders distinct the concept of that which is defined. But the nature of the object in relation to the faculty of our understanding does not admit of a higher degree of distinctness.

2:74

If I say: 'God is omnipotent' all that is being thought is the logical relation between God and omnipotence, for the latter is a characteristic mark of the former. Nothing further is being posited here. Whether God is, that is to say, whether God is posited absolutely or exists, is not contained in the original assertion at all. For this reason, 'being' is also correctly employed even in the case of the relations which absurdities[o] have to each other. For example: 'The God of Spinoza is subject to continuous change.'[16]

---

[g] *die absolute Position.*
[h] *Position oder Setzung* / (the two terms are synonymous; elsewhere they have both been translated by 'positing').
[i] *Sein überhaupt.* [j] *Merkmal.* [k] *Verbindungsbegriff.*
[l] *Wird nicht bloss diese Beziehung, sondern die Sache an und für sich selbst gesetzt betrachtet, so ist dieses Sein so viel als Dasein.*
[m] *zu seiner Auswicklung.* [n] *Erklärung von der Existenz.* [o] *Undinge.*

If I imagine God uttering His almighty *'Let there be'*[p] over a possible world, He does not grant any new determinations to the whole which is represented in His understanding. He adds no new predicate to it. Rather, He posits the series of things absolutely and unconditionally, and posits it with all its predicates; everything else within the series of things is posited only relatively to this whole. The relations of predicates to their subjects never designate anything existent; if they did, the subject would then have to be already posited as existent. The proposition 'God is omnipotent' must remain true even for someone who does not acknowledge the existence of God, provided that he understands how I construe the concept of God. But His existence must belong directly to the manner in which His concept is posited,[q] for His existence will not be found among the predicates themselves. If the existence of the subject is not already presupposed, every predicate is always indeterminate in respect of whether it belongs to an existent or to a merely possible subject. Existence cannot, therefore, itself be a predicate. If I say: 'God is an existent thing' it looks as if I am expressing the relation of a predicate to a subject. But there is an impropriety in this expression. Strictly speaking, the matter ought to be formulated like this: 'Something existent is God'. In other words, there belongs to an existent thing those predicates which, taken together, we designate by means of the expression 'God'. These predicates are posited relative to the subject, whereas the thing itself, together with all its predicates, is posited absolutely.[17]

My fear is that by offering too elaborate an explanation of such a simple idea, I shall become unintelligible. I might also be afraid of offending the tender sensibilities of those who complain especially of dullness of exposition. However, although I have no wish to dismiss this criticism as trivial, I must, on this occasion, crave indulgence. I have as little taste as the next man for the fastidious wisdom of those who spend so much time in their logic-laboratories subjecting sound and serviceable concepts to excessive analysis, distilling and purifying them until they evaporate altogether in vapours and volatile salts. However, the object of this present reflection is of such a kind that one must either abandon all hope of ever arriving at demonstrative certainty[r] in the matter, or one must patiently accept an analysis of one's concepts into these atoms.

3. Can it properly be said that there is more in existence than there is in mere possibility?

In order to answer this question let me merely remark in advance that a distinction must be drawn between what is posited and how it is posited.

---

[p] *sein allmächtiges Werde.*

[q] *Allein sein Dasein muss unmittelbar zu der Art gehören, wie sein Begriff gesetzt wird.*

[r] *demonstrative Gewissheit.*

2:75

As far as the former is concerned: no more is posited in a real thing than is posited in a merely possible thing, for all the determinations and predicates of the real thing are also to be found in the mere possibility of that same thing. However, as far as the latter is concerned: more is posited through actuality.[s] For if I ask: 'How is all this posited in the case of mere possibility?', I realise that the positing only occurs relative to the thing itself. That is to say, if a triangle exists, then three sides, an enclosed space, three angles, and so forth, also exist. Or, to express the matter better: the relations of these determinations to something such as a triangle are merely posited; but if the triangle exists, then all this is posited absolutely. In other words, the thing itself is posited together with these relations; and consequently, more is posited. In order, therefore, to sum up everything in a representation which is sufficiently subtle to avoid confusion, I maintain that nothing more is posited in an existent thing than is posited in a merely possible thing (for then one is speaking of the predicates of that thing). But more is posited through an existent thing than is posited through a merely possible thing, for positing through an existent thing involves the absolute positing of the thing itself as well. Indeed, in mere possibility it is not the thing itself which is posited; it is merely the relations of something to something which are posited in accordance with the law of contradiction. And it remains certain that existence is really not a predicate of a thing at all. Although it is no part of my present intention to engage in polemics, and although in my opinion an author, if he has read the ideas of others with an impartial mind and made them his own by dint of reflecting on them, can with a reasonable degree of certainty entrust the assessment of his new and heterodox[t] doctrines to the judgement of his reader – although all this is true, I shall, nevertheless, say a few brief words in this connection.

2:76

Wolff's definition of existence,[18] that it is a completion of possibility,[u] is obviously very indeterminate. If one does not already know in advance what can be thought about possibility in a thing, one is not going to learn it from *Wolff's* definition. *Baumgarten* introduces the concept of thoroughgoing internal determination,[v19] and maintains that it is this which is more in existence than in mere possibility, for it completes that which is left indeterminate by the predicates inhering in or issuing from the essence. But we have already seen that the difference between a real thing and a merely possible thing never lies in the connection of that thing with all the predicates which can be thought in it. Furthermore, the proposition that a possible thing, regarded as such, is indeterminate[w] with respect to many of its predicates, could, if taken literally, lead to serious error. For such indeterminacy is forbidden by the law of excluded middle which main-

---

[s] *Wirklichkeit.*   [t] *abweichende.*   [u] *Ergänzung der Möglichkeit.*
[v] *die durchgängige innere Bestimmung.*   [w] *unbestimmt.*

tains that there is no intermediate between two predicates which contradict each other. It is for example impossible that a man should not have a certain stature, position in time, age, location in space, and so forth. Our proposition must rather be taken in the following sense: the predicates which are thought together in a thing in no way determine the many other predicates of that thing. Thus, for example, that which is collected together in the concept of a human being as such specifies nothing with respect to the special characteristics of age, place, and so forth. But then this kind of indeterminacy is to be found as much in an existent thing as it is in a merely possible thing. For this reason, it cannot be used to distinguish the two. The celebrated *Crusius* regards the *somewhere* and the *somewhen* as belonging to the unmistakable determinations of existence.[20] But, without involving ourselves in an examination of the proposition itself that everything which exists must be somewhere and somewhen, these predicates still belong to merely possible things as well. There could thus exist many persons at many determinate places at a given time. The Omniscient certainly knows all the determinations which would inhere in such a person, if he were to exist, even though he does not actually exist. Without doubt, the eternal Jew, *Ahasuerus*,[21] is, in respect of all the countries through which he is to wander and all the times through which he is to live, a possible person. I hope that no one is going to insist that the somewhere and the somewhen are sufficient characteristic marks of existence only when the thing really is then and there. For that would be to demand that one should concede in advance that which one aims to render clear by means of a suitable characteristic mark.[x]

2:77

SECOND REFLECTION: OF INTERNAL POSSIBILITY,[y] IN SO FAR AS IT PRESUPPOSES EXISTENCE

1. Necessary distinction in the concept of possibility

Anything which is self-contradictory is internally impossible. This is a true proposition, even if it is left undecided whether it is a true definition.[z] In the case of a contradiction,[a] however, it is clear that something must stand in logical opposition to something else; that is to say, something is denied which is being affirmed in the same proposition. *Crusius* does not locate this conflict merely in an internal contradiction; he asserts that it is perceived by the understanding, in accordance with a law which is natural

[x] *denn da würde man fordern, dass dasjenige schon eingeräumt werde, was man sich anheischig macht, durch ein taugliches Merkmal von selber kenntlich zu machen.*
[y] *Von der innern Möglichkeit.*   [z] *Erklärung.*
[a] *Bei diesem Widerspruch* / (the *diesem* ['this'] has been translated by 'a' since there is no specific contradiction to which the 'this' could refer).

to it. But even according to him, the impossible always contains the combination of something posited with something which also cancels it.[22] I call this repugnancy the formal element[b] in inconceivability or impossibility. The material element[c] which is given here as standing in such a conflict is itself something and can be thought. A quadrangular triangle is absolutely impossible. Nonetheless, a triangle is something, and so is a quadrangle. The impossibility is based simply on the logical relations which exist between one thinkable thing and another, where the one cannot be a characteristic mark of the other. Likewise, in every possibility we must first distinguish the something which is thought, and then we must distinguish the agreement of what is thought in it with the law of contradiction. A triangle which has a right angle is in itself possible. The triangle and the right angle are the data or the material element in this possible thing. The agreement, however, of the one with the other, in accordance with the law of contradiction, is the formal element in possibility. I shall also call this latter the logical element[d] in possibility, for the comparison of the predicates with their subjects, according to the rule of truth, is nothing other than a logical relation. The something, or that which stands in this agreement, is sometimes called the real element of possibility. Incidentally, I would draw attention to the fact that what I shall be discussing here will always be internal or so-called absolute and unconditional possibility and impossibility, and no other.

2:78

2. The internal possibility of all things presupposes some existence or other.

It is clear from what has now been adduced that possibility disappears not only when an internal contradiction, as the logical element of impossibility, is present, but also when there exists no material element, no *datum*, to be thought. For then nothing is given which can be thought. But everything possible is something which can be thought, and the logical relation pertains to it in accordance with the principle of contradiction.

Now, if all existence is cancelled,[e] then nothing is posited absolutely, nothing at all is given, there is no material element for anything which can be thought; all possibility completely disappears.[23] Admittedly, there is no internal contradiction in the negation of all existence. For, in order that there should be an internal contradiction it is necessary that something should be posited and at the same time cancelled. But there is nothing whatever here which is posited. Consequently, of course, it cannot be said that the negation of all existence involves an internal contradiction. On the other hand, to say that there is a possibility and yet nothing real at all is self-contradictory. For if nothing exists, then nothing which could be

---

[b] *das Formale.*   [c] *das Materiale.*   [d] *das Logische.*   [e] *aufgehoben.*

thought is given either, and we contradict ourselves if we still wish to say that something is possible. In our analysis of the concept of existence we saw that being or being absolutely posited,^{f} provided that these words are not employed to express logical relations between predicates and subjects, mean exactly the same as existence. Accordingly, the assertion 'Nothing exists' means the same as the assertion 'There is nothing whatever'. And it is obviously self-contradictory to add, in spite of this, 'Something is possible'.

3. It is absolutely impossible that nothing at all should exist.

That, by means of which all possibility whatever is cancelled, is absolutely impossible,^{g} for the two expressions are synonymous. Now, to start with, the formal element of all possibility, namely, agreement with the law of contradiction, is cancelled by that which contradicts itself. Hence, that which is self-contradictory in itself is absolutely impossible. This, however, is not the case where we have to consider the complete elimination of all existence. For, as we have proved, the complete cancellation of all existence whatever involves no internal contradiction. However, the means by which the material element, the data, of all that is possible is cancelled, is also the means by which all possibility itself is negated. Now, this is effected by the cancellation of all existence. Thus, when all existence is denied, then all possibility is cancelled as well. As a consequence, it is absolutely impossible that nothing at all should exist.

4. All possibility is given in something actual, either as a
determination existing within it or as a consequence arising from it.

What has to be shown of all possibility in general and of each possibility in particular is that it presupposes something real, whether it be one thing or many. Now, this relation of all possibility to some existence or other can be of two kinds. Either the possible can only be thought in so far as it is itself real, and then the possibility is given as a determination existing within the real; or it is possible because something else is real; in other words, its internal possibility is given as a consequence through another existence. Elucidatory examples cannot yet be suitably furnished here. The nature of the only subject which could serve as an example in this reflection ought to be considered first of all. In the meantime, I would merely add the following remark: the actuality,^{h} by means of which, as by means of a ground, the internal possibility of other realities is given, I shall call the

---

^{f} *das Sein oder das schlechthin Gesetzt sein.*
^{g} *Wodurch alle Möglichkeit überhaupt aufgehoben wird, das ist schlechterdings unmöglich.*
^{h} *dasjenige Wirkliche.*

first real ground of this absolute possibility,[24] the law of contradiction being in like manner its first logical ground, for the formal element of possibility consists in agreement with it. In the same way, that which is real furnishes the data or material element of that which can be thought. 2:80

I am fully aware that propositions of the kind presented in this reflection are in need of considerably more elucidation if they are to acquire the illumination necessary to make them obvious. However, the so very abstract nature of the object itself obstructs every effort at greater clarification, just as the employment of microscopic devices for seeing[i] both enlarges the image of the object so that its minute parts can be discerned but it also proportionately diminishes the brightness and vivacity of the impression. Nonetheless, I shall, as far as I am able, attempt to bring the idea of existence, which is always fundamental even to internal possibility, somewhat closer to the more ordinary concepts of sound understanding.

You know that a fiery body, a cunning person, and such like, are possible things. And if I ask for nothing more than internal possibility, you will not find it at all necessary that a body, or a fire, and so on, should have to exist as their data: they can be thought, and that is sufficient. But the agreement of the predicate, fiery, with the subject, body, in accordance with the law of contradiction, is inherent in the concepts themselves, irrespective of whether the things themselves be real or merely possible. I also concede that neither bodies nor fire need be real things: and yet, nonetheless, a fiery body is internally possible. But I proceed to ask: is then a body itself possible in itself? Not being permitted to appeal to experience here, you will enumerate the data of its possibility, namely extension, impenetrability, force, and I know not what else; and you will add that there is no internal contradiction here. I still concede everything. You must, however, give me an account of what entitles you so readily to accept the concept of extension as a datum. For suppose that it signified nothing: your alleged account of the possibility of the body would then be an illusion. It would also be highly improper to appeal to experience in connection with this datum, for what is at issue is precisely whether an internal possibility of the fiery body would occur even if nothing at all were to exist. Suppose that you can now no longer break up the concept of extension into simpler data in order to show that there is nothing self-contradictory in it – and you must eventually arrive at something whose possibility cannot be analysed[25] – then the question will be whether space 2:81 and extension are empty words, or whether they signify something. The lack of contradiction does not decide the present issue; an empty word never signifies anything self-contradictory. If space did not exist, or if space was not at least given as a consequence through something existent, the word 'space' would signify nothing at all. As long as you prove possibili-

---

[i] *so wie die mikroscopischen Kunstgriffe des Sehens.*

ties by means of the law of contradiction, you are depending upon that which is thinkable in the thing and which is given to you in it, and you are only regarding the relation in accordance with this logical rule. But in the end, when you consider how this is then given to you, the only thing to which you can appeal is an existence.[j]

But we must await the development of this reflection. A concept which one can scarcely explain to oneself without over-reaching oneself, since it treats of the first grounds of what can be thought, can be rendered more intelligible by applying it.

THIRD REFLECTION: OF ABSOLUTELY
NECESSARY EXISTENCE

1. The concept of absolutely necessary existence in general

That of which the opposite is impossible in itself is absolutely necessary. This is a certainly correct nominal definition.[k26] But if I ask: upon what does the absolute impossibility of the non-being of a thing depend? then what I am looking for is the real definition;[l27] this alone can serve our purpose. All our concepts of internal necessity in the properties of possible things of whatever kind they may be amount to this: the opposite is self-contradictory. If, however, it is absolutely necessary existence which is at issue, one would not have much success if one tried to arrive at some understanding of it by means of the above characterisation. Existence is not a predicate at all, nor is the cancellation of existence the negation of a predicate,[m] by means of which something in a thing is cancelled and through which an internal contradiction could arise. The cancellation of an

2:82   existent thing is a complete negation of all that is posited unconditionally or absolutely by its existence. Notwithstanding, the logical relations between the thing, as something possible, and its predicates remain. But these relations are quite different from the absolute positing of a thing along with its predicates, which is what existence is. Accordingly, what is cancelled by non-being is not the same as what is posited in the thing but something else; as a result there is never a contradiction here. The final reflection of this work will make all this more plausible; it will do so by clearly explaining the untenability of the view being examined in the case where it has been genuinely though mistakenly thought that absolutely necessary existence could be explained by means of the law of contradiction.[28] Nonetheless, the necessity in the predicates of merely possible concepts may be called logical necessity. But the necessity, for which I am seeking the ultimate

---

[j] *ein Dasein.*   [k] *Nominal-Erklärung.*   [l] *Realerklärung.*
[m] *Das Dasein ist gar kein Prädikat und die Aufhebung des Daseins keine Verneinung eines Prädikats.*

foundation,[n] namely, the necessity of existence, is absolute real necessity.[o] What I find to start with is this: that which I am supposed to regard as absolutely nothing and impossible must eliminate everything which can be thought. For if there were still something left to be thought, then it would not be completely unthinkable or absolutely impossible.

If I now consider for a moment why that which contradicts itself should be absolutely nothing and impossible, I find that through the cancellation of the law of contradiction, the ultimate logical ground of all that can be thought,[p] all possibility vanishes, and there is nothing left to think. The conclusion immediately follows that, when I cancel all existence whatever and the ultimate real ground of all that can be thought therewith disappears, all possibility likewise vanishes, and nothing any longer remains to be thought. Accordingly, something may be absolutely necessary either when the formal element of all that can be thought is cancelled by means of its opposite, that is to say, when it is self-contradictory; or, alternatively, when its non-existence eliminates the material element and all the data of all that can be thought. The former, as has been said, never occurs in the case of existence. It follows that, since there is no third possibility, either the concept of absolutely necessary existence is a deceptive and false concept,[q] or it must rest on the fact that the non-being of a thing is at the same time the negation of all the data of all that can be thought. That this concept, however, is not imaginary but something true is apparent from the following consideration.

2. *There exists an absolutely necessary being.*[r] 2:83

All possibility presupposes something actual[s] in and through which all that can be thought is given. Accordingly, there is a certain reality, the cancellation of which would itself cancel all internal possibility whatever. But that, the cancellation of which eradicates all possibility, is absolutely necessary. Therefore, something exists absolutely necessarily. Thus far it is apparent that the existence of one or more things itself lies at the foundation of all possibility, and that this existence is necessary in itself. From this it is also easy to derive the concept of contingency. That of which the opposite is possible is, according to the nominal definition,[t][29] contingent. However, in order to find the real definition[u][30] of the contingent, it is necessary to make the following distinction. In the logical sense, that which, as predicate, is contingent in a subject is that, the opposite of which does not contradict the subject. For example: it is contingent in a triangle in general that it be

[n] *Hauptgrund.* [o] *die absolute Realnothwendigkeit.* [p] *der letzte logische Grund alles Denklichen.*
[q] *ein täuschender und falscher Begriff.*
[r] *ein schlechterdings nothwendiges Wesen* / (in the titles of the numbered sections 2 to 6 the word 'being' [in the sense of 'entity'] translates *Wesen* not *Sein*).
[s] *etwas Wirkliches.* [t] *Worterklärung.* [u] *Sacherklärung.*

right angled. This contingency only occurs when the predicates are related to their subject; and since existence is not a predicate, contingency cannot be applied at all to existence. By contrast, what is contingent in the real sense^v is that of which the non-being can be thought; that is to say, what is contingent in the real sense is that of which the cancellation is not the cancellation of all that can be thought. If, accordingly, the internal possibility of things does not presuppose a particular existence,^{w} the latter is contingent, for its opposite does not cancel possibility. Or, to express the same matter in a different way: that existence, by means of which the material element of all that can be thought is not given, and in the absence of which, therefore, there is still something left to be thought, that is to say, still something possible – the opposite of such an existence is possible in the real sense; and in that same real sense it is also contingent.

3. The necessary being is unique.^{x}

Since the necessary being contains the ultimate real ground^y of all other possibilities, it follows that every other thing is only possible in so far as it is given through the necessary being as its ground. Accordingly, every other thing can only occur as a consequence of that necessary being. Thus the possibility and the existence of all other things are dependent on it. But something, which is itself dependent, does not contain the ultimate real ground of all possibility; it is, therefore, not absolutely necessary. As a consequence, it is not possible for several things to be absolutely necessary.

2:84

Suppose that A is one necessary being and that B is another. It follows from our definition that B is only possible in so far as it is given through another ground, A, as the consequence of A. But since, *ex hypothesi,* B is itself necessary, it follows that its possibility is in it as a predicate and not as a consequence of something else; and yet, according to what has just been said, its possibility is in it only as a consequence, and that is self-contradictory.

4. The necessary being is simple.

That nothing which is compounded of many substances can be an absolutely necessary being is apparent from the following consideration. Suppose that only one of its parts is absolutely necessary; it follows that the other parts together are only possible as consequences of it; they do not belong to it as co-ordinate parts^z of it. If you were to suppose that there were several necessary parts, or that all the parts were necessary, that would contradict the previous number. There is, accordingly, only one other possibility left: each part individually must exist contingently, whereas all

---

^{v} *im Realverstande.* ^{w} *ein gewisses Dasein.* ^{x} *einig.* ^{y} *letzten Realgrund.* ^{z} *Nebentheile.*

the parts together must exist absolutely necessarily. But this is impossible, for an aggregate of substances cannot possess more necessity in existence than belongs to the parts; and since no necessity at all belongs to the parts, their existence being contingent, it follows that the existence of the whole will also be contingent. Suppose one thought that one could appeal to the definition of the necessary being,[a] so that one said that the ultimate data of some internal possibilities were given in each of the parts individually, and that all possibility was given in all the parts together. If one thought that such an appeal could be made, one would have represented something which was wholly, though covertly, incoherent. For if one were then to conceive internal possibility in such a way that some parts could be cancelled, but so cancelled that there still remained something left which could be thought and which was given through the other parts, one would have to suppose that it was in itself possible for internal possibility to be denied or cancelled. But it is entirely inconceivable and self-contradictory that something should be nothing. But this is tantamount to saying that cancelling an internal possibility is the same as eliminating all that can be thought. It is apparent from this that the data for anything which can be thought must be given in the thing of which the cancellation is also the opposite of all possibility; and that, therefore, that which contains the ultimate ground of one internal possibility also contains the ultimate ground of all possibility whatever;[b] and that, as a consequence, this ultimate ground of all possibility whatever cannot be divided among different substances.

2:85

5. The necessary being is immutable and eternal.

Since even its own possibility and every other possibility presupposes this existence,[c] it follows that no other mode of its existence[d] is possible. That is to say: the necessary being cannot exist in a variety of ways. Indeed, everything which exists is completely determinate. Now, since this being is possible simply because it exists, it follows that no possibility occurs for it, except in so far as it in fact exists. It is, therefore, not possible in any other way than as it really is. Accordingly, it cannot be otherwise determined or changed. Its non-being is absolutely impossible, and so too, therefore, are its coming-to-be and its passing-away. It is, accordingly, eternal.

6. The necessary being contains supreme reality.[e]

The data of all possibility must be found in the necessary being either as determinations of it, or as consequences which are given through the necessary being as the ultimate real ground. It is thus apparent that all

---

[a] die Erklärung des nothwendigen Wesens.
[b] ihn (i.e., den letzten Grund) auch von aller (i.e., Möglichkeit).   [c] dieses Dasein.
[d] keine andere Art der Existenz desselben.   [e] die höchste Realität.

reality is, in one way or another, embraced by the ultimate real ground.*f*
But precisely these determinations, in virtue of which this being is the
ultimate ground of all possible reality, invest that being with the highest
degree of real properties*g* which could ever inhere in a thing. Such a being
is, therefore, the most real of all possible beings, for all other beings are
only possible through it alone. But this is not to be understood to mean
that all possible reality is included among its determinations. This is a
conceptual confusion*h* which has been uncommonly prevalent until now.
All realities are attributed indiscriminately as predicates to God or to the
necessary being. That all these predicates can by no means co-exist together as determinations in a single subject is not noticed. The impenetrability of bodies, extension and such like, cannot be attributes of that which
has understanding and will. Nor does it help if one seeks to evade the
issue by maintaining that the quality in question is not regarded as true
reality. The thrust of a body or the force of cohesion are, without doubt,
2:86   something truly positive.³¹ Similarly, in the sensations of the mind, pain is
never merely a deprivation.*i*³² A confusion*j* has seemingly justified such an
idea. It is said: reality and reality never contradict each other, for both of
them are true affirmations; as a consequence, they do not conflict with
each other in the subject either. Now, although I concede that there is no
logical contradiction here, the real repugnancy is not thereby cancelled.
Such a real repugnancy*k*³³ always occurs when something, as a ground,
annihilates by means of a real opposition*l* the consequence of something
else. The motive force of a body in one direction and an equally strong
tendency in the opposite direction do not contradict each other. They are
also really possible in one body at the same time. However, one motive
force annihilates the real consequences of the other motive force; and
since the consequences of each motive force by itself would otherwise be a
real movement, the consequence of both together in one subject is
nought. That is to say, the consequence of these opposed motive forces is
rest. But rest is, indubitably, possible. From this it is also apparent that
real opposition is something quite different from logical opposition or
contradiction, for the result of the latter is absolutely impossible.³⁴ Now, in
the most real being of all there cannot be any real opposition or positive
conflict among its own determinations, for the consequence would be a
deprivation or a lack, and that would contradict its supreme reality. Since
a conflict such as this would be bound to occur if all realities existed in the
most real being as determinations, it follows that they cannot all exist in it
as determinations. Consequently, since they are all given through it, they
will either belong to its determinations or to its consequences.

---

f *durch ihn* (i.e., *durch den ersten Realgrund*) *begriffen sei* (the word *begriffen* may mean either
'understood' or 'embraced'; the opening phrase of the sentence suggests the latter).
g *den grössten Grad realer Eigenschaften.* *h* *eine Vermengung der Begriffe.* *i* *Beraubung.*
j *ein irriger Gedanke.* *k* *Realrepugnanz.* *l* *Realentgegensetzung.*

At first sight it might also seem that it follows that, since the necessary being contains the ultimate real ground of all other possibilities, it must also contain the ground of the deficiencies and the negations of the essences of things.[m] If this were admitted it would needs occasion the conclusion that the necessary being must have among its predicates negations themselves and not exclusively reality. But consider the concept of the necessary being which we have now established. Its own possibility is originally given in its existence. It is of other possibilities that the necessary being contains the real ground. It follows from this in accordance with the law of contradiction that it cannot be the real ground of the possibility of the most real being itself, nor, as a result, can it be the real ground of the possibilities which contain negations and defects.

Accordingly, the possibility of all other things, in respect of what is real in them, depends upon the necessary being as a real ground. But deficiencies, in so far as they are other things and not the original being itself, depend upon the necessary being as on a logical ground.[n] In so far as body possesses extension, force, and so on, the possibility of body is grounded in the Supreme Being. But in so far as body lacks the power of thought, this negation inheres in body itself in accordance with the law of contradiction. 2:87

Negations in themselves are not, indeed, anything, nor can they in themselves be thought. This can easily be explained in the following way. If nothing is posited apart from negations, then nothing is given at all, nor is there anything to be thought. Thus, negations can only be thought through opposite positings, or rather, there are positings possible which are not the greatest. And it is here, according to the law of identity, that negations are themselves already to be found. It is also obvious that all the negations inhering in the possibilities of other things do not presuppose a real ground (for they are not anything positive). Consequently, they merely presuppose a logical ground.

FOURTH REFLECTION: ARGUMENT IN SUPPORT OF A DEMONSTRATION OF THE EXISTENCE OF GOD

1. The necessary being is a mind.[o]

It has been proved above that the necessary being is a simple substance. It has similarly been established that not only is all other reality given through the necessary being as its ground, but also that the greatest

---

[m] der Grund der Mängel und Verneinungen der Wesen der Dinge.
[n] die Mängel aber darauf, weil es andere Dinge und nicht das Urwesen selber sind, als einem logischen Grunde.
[o] Geist.

possible reality capable of being contained in a being as a determination inheres in the necessary being. Now, there are various ways of proving that the properties of understanding and will also belong to the necessary being. For, firstly, understanding and will are, both of them, true realities,[p] and they can both co-exist together with the greatest possible reality[q] in one thing. An immediate judgement of the understanding forces one to admit the truth of this contention, even though it cannot properly speaking be given the distinctness required of a logically complete proof.

2:88 Secondly, the properties of a mind, understanding and will, are of such a kind that we cannot think of any reality which could, in their absence, serve as an adequate substitute in a being for them. Since understanding and will are properties which are capable of the highest degree of reality but, nonetheless, are to be counted only among possible properties, it would follow that understanding and will, and all reality of the nature of mind, would have to be possible in others through the necessary being as a ground, even though they would not be found as determinations in the necessary being itself. The consequent would accordingly be greater than the ground itself. For it is certain that if the Supreme Being did not itself possess understanding and will, every other being which was posited through the Supreme Being with these properties of understanding and will would, in respect of these properties of the highest kind and regardless of its dependency and its many other deficiencies of power, and so on, nonetheless have to take precedence over the Supreme Being. Now, since the consequence cannot exceed the ground, understanding and will must inhere in the necessary simple substance as properties. That is to say: the necessary simple substance is a mind.[35]

Thirdly, order, beauty and perfection in all that is possible presuppose either a being, in the properties of which these relations are grounded, or, at least, a being through which, as from a principal ground, things agreeing with these relations are possible. Now the necessary being is the sufficient real ground of everything else which is possible, apart from itself. It follows that the necessary being will possess that property, in virtue of which everything else, apart from itself, is able to become real in agreement with these relations. However, it seems that the ground of the external possibility of order, beauty and perfection, is not sufficient unless a will in agreement with the understanding is presupposed. These properties must, therefore, be ascribed to the Supreme Being.

Leaving aside all the causes which are responsible for the generation of plants and trees, everyone knows that regular flowerbeds, avenues and such like, are only possible as a result of an understanding which conceives the plan and a will which executes it. In the absence of understand-

---

[p] *beides ist wahre Realität.*   [q] *mit der grösst möglichen* (sc. *Realität*).

ing, no power or generative force,[r] nor any other data of possibility, are adequate to render the possibility of such order complete.

The proof that the necessary being must have will and understanding, and must therefore be a mind, can be derived either from one of the arguments here adduced or from all of them taken together. I shall rest contented with merely making the argument complete. It is no part of my intention to furnish a formal demonstration.

2:89

2. It is a god.

There exists something absolutely necessarily. It is one in its essence; it is simple in its substance; it is a mind according to its nature; it is eternal in its duration; it is immutable in its constitution; and it is all-sufficient in respect of all that is possible and real.[36] It is a god. I am not here offering a determinate definition[s] of the concept of God. If it were my purpose to treat the matter systematically, I should have to provide such a definition. But what I am here setting forth is intended to be an analysis which may serve as a foundation for the formal doctrine proper.[t] Meanwhile, the definition of the concept of God may be instituted in any way one deems suitable. But I am certain that the being, whose existence we have just proved, is precisely the Divine Being, whose differentiating characteristics[u] will be reduced, in one way or another, to the most concise formula.[v]

3. Remark

The third reflection establishes no more than that all reality must either be given as a determination in the necessary being, or it must be given through the necessary being as through a ground. This leaves undecided the question whether the properties of understanding and will are to be found in the Supreme Being as determinations inhering in it, or whether they are to be regarded merely as consequences produced by it in other things. If the latter alternative were the case, then it would follow that, in spite of all the excellencies manifest in the original being which issue from the sufficiency, unity and independence of its existence, as from a great ground, its nature would nonetheless be far inferior to what one must needs think when one thinks of a god. Possessing neither cognition nor choice, it would be a blindly necessary ground of other things and even of other minds, and it would differ from the eternal fate postulated by some ancient philosophers in nothing except that it had been more intelligently described. This is the reason why particular attention must be paid in

---

[r] *Hervorbringungskraft.* [s] *bestimmte Erklärung.* [t] *förmlichen Lehrverfassung.*
[u] *Unterscheidungszeichen.* [v] *in die kürzeste Benennung.*

2:90 every system to this circumstance, and this is why we have not been able to exclude it from consideration.

Nowhere in any of the arguments belonging to my proof and presented thus far has mention been made of the expression 'perfection'.ᵂ The reason for this omission is not that I thought that all reality was the same as all perfection,[37] or that perfection consisted in the highest degree of harmony in one.ˣ I have weighty reasons for strongly disagreeing with this widely held opinion. I spent a long time carefully investigating the concept of perfection, both generally and in particular. I learned that a more precise knowledge of perfection contains concealed within it a great deal which is capable of clarifying the nature of the mind, our own feeling and even the fundamental concepts of practical philosophy.

I came to notice that the expression 'perfection' in some cases deviated fairly widely from the proper senseʸ of the term because of the uncertainty which is inherent in all languages. However, in the significance of the term to which everybody pays chief regard, even in the case of the confusions just mentioned, the expression 'perfection' always presupposes relation to a being endowed with cognition and desire.ᶻ Now, it would have taken me too far afield if I had traced the argument from God and the reality inherent in Him to this relation, even though such an argument could have been constructed on that foundation. For this reason, I deemed the introduction of the concept of perfection, and the wide-ranging discussion to which it would have given rise, incompatible with the purpose of these pages.

4. Conclusion

Nobody will have any difficulty in drawing certain other obvious conclusions from the proof I have furnished. For example: I who think am not such an absolutely necessary being, for I am not the ground of all reality and I am subject to change; no other being of which the non-being is possible, that is to say, no other being of which the cancellation is not at the same time the cancellation of all possibility, is an absolutely necessary being; no thing which is subject to change or in which there exist limits, including, therefore, the world, is an absolutely necessary being; the world is not an accidentᵃ of God, for there are to be found within the world conflict, deficiency, changeability, all of which are the opposites of the

2:91 determinations to be found in a divinity; God is not the only substance which exists; all other substances only exist in dependence upon God; and so on.[38]

At this juncture I would merely add the following point. The argument

---

ᵂ *Vollkommenheit.*   ˣ *Zusammenstimmung zu Einem.*   ʸ *von dem eigenthümlichen Sinne.*
ᶻ *Erkenntniss und Begierde.*   ᵃ *Accidens.*

for the existence of God which we are presenting is based simply on the fact that something is possible. It is, accordingly, a proof which can be conducted entirely *a priori*. It presupposes neither my own existence, nor that of other minds, nor that of the physical world. It is, indeed, an argument derived from the internal characteristic mark of absolute necessity. Thus, our knowledge of the existence of this being is derived from what really constitutes the absolute necessity of that same being. This knowledge is thus acquired in a genuinely genetic fashion.[39]

None of the proofs which argue from the effects of this being to its existence as cause can ever – even granting that they are of the strictest character, which in fact they are not – render the nature of this necessity comprehensible. From the mere fact that something exists absolutely necessarily it is possible to infer that something is a first cause of something else. But from the fact that something is a first cause, that is to say, an independent cause, it only follows that, if the effects exist then the cause must also exist, not that the cause exists absolutely necessarily.[40]

Now, it is further apparent from the argument we have recommended that all the essences of other things and the real element of all possibility are grounded in this unique being;[b] in it are to be found the highest degree of understanding and will; and that is the greatest possible ground. Because of this and because everything in such a being must harmonise in the highest possible degree,[c] the following conclusion can be immediately drawn. Since a will always presupposes the internal possibility of the thing itself, it follows that the ground of possibility, that is to say, the essence of God, will be in the highest harmony with his own will. The reason for this is not that God is the ground of internal possibility in virtue of his own will. The reason is rather this: the same infinite nature is related to all the essences of things as their ground; at the same time it also has the relation of highest desire for the greatest consequences which are thereby given, and the latter can only be fruitful if the former are presupposed. Accordingly, the possibilities of things themselves, which are given through the divine nature, harmonise with his great desire. Goodness and perfection, however, consist in this harmony. And since goodness and perfection harmonise in one single principle, it follows that unity, harmony and order   2:92
are themselves to be found in the possibilities of things.

Our mature judgement of the essential properties of the things known to us through experience enables us, even in the necessary determinations of their internal possibility, to perceive unity in what is manifold and harmoniousness in what is separated.[d] It follows that the *a posteriori* mode of cognition will enable us to argue regressively to a single principle of all

---

[b] *dass alle Wesen anderer Dinge und das Reale aller Möglichkeit in diesem einigen Wesen gegründet seien.*
[c] *in der äusserst möglichen Übereinstimmung.*
[d] *eine Einheit im Mannigfaltigen und Wohlgereimtheit in dem Getrennten.*

possibility. We shall thus finally arrive at the self-same fundamental concept of absolutely necessary existence, from which the *a priori* mode of cognition initially started out. Our purpose from now on will be to see whether the internal possibility of things is itself necessarily related to order and harmony, and whether unity is to be found in this measureless manifold, so that, on this basis, we could establish whether the essences of things themselves indicate an ultimate common ground.*

*   *einen obersten gemeinschaftlichen Grund.*

Section 2. Concerning the extensive usefulness peculiar to this mode of proof in particular

---

FIRST REFLECTION: IN WHICH THE EXISTENCE OF GOD IS INFERRED A POSTERIORI FROM THE UNITY PERCEIVED IN THE ESSENCES OF THINGS

1. The unity in the manifold[f] *of the essences of things is demonstrated by appeal to the properties of space*

The necessary determinations of space afford the geometer a pleasure which is far from ordinary. They do so because of the certainty of their conviction, the exactitude of their execution, and the extensiveness of their application. The whole range of human knowledge has nothing to show which equals it, far less anything which exceeds it. But, for the present, I wish to examine this same object from an entirely different point of view. Looking at it with a philosophical eye, I come to notice that order and harmony, along with such necessary determinations, prevail throughout space, and that concord[g] and unity prevail throughout its immense manifold. Let us suppose, for example, that I wish to produce a bounded space by moving a straight line around a fixed point. I have no difficulty at all in grasping that the result is a circle, the circumference of which is at all points equidistant from the aforementioned fixed point. But 2:94 I have no reason at all to suppose that such a simple construction should conceal something highly complex which is itself subject, in virtue of that very construction, to major rules of order. And yet I discover that all the straight lines which intersect each other inside a circle at any given point, when they are extended to its circumference, are always divided in geometrical proportion.[h41] Likewise, I discover that all the straight lines which extend from a given point outside a circle so as to intersect its circumference are always divided into parts which are related to each other in

---

[f] *Mannigfaltigen* / B: multifarious / C: *molteplice* / F & Z: *diversité* / T: manifold.

[g] *Zusammenpassung.*

[h] *Indessen entdecke ich, dass alle gerade Linien, die einander aus einem beliebigen Punkt innerhalb dem Cirkel durchkreuzen, indem sie an dem Umkreis stossen, jederzeit in geometrischer Proportion geschnitten sind.*

inverse proportion to their wholes.[i42] Consider what an infinity of different positions these lines can assume in intersecting the circle as described; and consider the way in which they are nonetheless constantly subject to the same law, from which they cannot deviate. If one considers these things, one cannot but be surprised, in spite of the ease with which these truths are understood, that the description of this figure should be so straightforward, and yet that so much order and such complete unity in the manifold should issue from it.

Suppose that the following problem be propounded. Inclined surfaces of varying gradients are to be constructed, with the inclined surfaces of such a length that bodies freely rolling down them shall all take the same time to reach the bottom. Anybody with an understanding of the laws of mechanics will realise that constructing such a series of inclined planes would be a complex business. And yet this arrangement is to be found directly in the circle itself, with an infinite variety of positions, and yet in every case with the greatest precision. The reason is this: all the chords which meet the vertical diameter, regardless of whether they extend from the point at the top or the bottom, and irrespective of their angle of inclination, will all have this feature in common: free fall through these same chords takes exactly the same time in all cases.[43] I once explained this theorem, along with its proof, to an intelligent student. I recall that, once he had thoroughly understood all its details, he was as impressed by it as he would have been impressed by a miracle of nature. One is, indeed, amazed and rightly astonished to find, in such a seemingly straightforward[j] and simple thing as a circle, such wondrous unity of the manifold subject to such fruitful rules. Nor is there a miracle of nature which could, by its beauty and order, give more cause for amazement, unless it did so in virtue of its cause being less apparent, for wonder[k] is a daughter of ignorance.

2:95 The field in which I am gathering remarkable phenomena is so full of them that, without needing to take a single step, we are presented with numberless beauties at our very feet. There are solutions in geometry where what seems possible only as a result of complicated preparation presents itself without artifice,[l] as it were, in the thing itself. Everyone finds such solutions charming.[m] And the less one has to do oneself, and the more complex notwithstanding the solutions seem to be, the more charming they grow. The ring formed by two concentric circles is quite different in shape from a circular surface.[n] The task of converting the ring

---

[i] *imgleichen dass alle diejenige, die von einem Punkt ausserhalb dem Kreise diesen durchschneiden, jederzeit in solche Stücke zerlegt werden, die sich umgekehrt verhalten wie ihre Ganzen.*

[j] *schlecht* / (Kant is employing the word in the now archaic sense of 'smooth', 'simple'; cf. Grimm *schlecht* [1, 3, 4, & 7]).

[k] *Bewunderung.* [l] *ohne alle Kunst.* [m] *artig.*

[n] *der Cirkelring zwischen zwei Kreisen, die einen gemeinschaftlichen Mittelpunkt haben, hat eine von einer Cirkelfläche sehr verschiedene Gestalt.*

into such a circular surface initially strikes everyone as a difficult undertaking requiring great art for its execution. As soon, however, as I realise that the tangent which touches the circumference of the smaller circle and extends until its two ends intersect the circumference of the larger circle is the diameter of the circle whose area is equal to the area of the ring[o44] – as soon as I realise this, I cannot but be taken aback at the simplicity and ease with which the solution sought is revealed in the nature of the matter itself, requiring almost no effort on my part at all.

The purpose of our discussion has been to draw attention to the existence, in the necessary properties of space, of unity alongside the highest degree of complexity, and of the connection between things where all seem to have their own separate necessity. To achieve this objective, we have focused our attention on the figure of the circle alone, which has infinitely many properties of which only a small number is known. From this we can infer how immeasurably great is the number of the harmonious relations which inhere in the properties of space in general. Higher geometry reveals many of these relations in its account of the affinities between various species of curved line. All these relations, in addition to exercising the understanding by means of our intellectual comprehension of them,[p] also arouse the emotions,[q] and they do so in a manner similar to or even more sublime than that in which the contingent beauties of nature stir the feelings.

If, in the case of such arrangements in nature, we are justified in searching for the foundation of the extensive harmony of the manifold, are we less justified in searching for a similar foundation for the regularity[r] and unity which we perceive in the infinitely various determinations of space? Is this harmony any the less amazing for being necessary? I would maintain that its necessity makes it all the more amazing. A multiplicity, in which each individual had its own special and independent necessity, could never possess order, or harmoniousness, nor could there ever be unity in their reciprocal relationships to each other. Will this not lead one, as the harmony in the contingent provisions of nature leads one, to the supposition that there is a supreme ground of the very essences of things themselves, for unity in the ground also produces unity in the realm of all its consequences?

2:96

2. *Unity in the manifold of the essences of things proved by reference to what is necessary in the laws of motion*

If we discover an arrangement in nature, which seems to have been instituted for a special purpose, since the general properties of matter on their

---

[o] *Allein so bald ich einsehe, dass die den inwendigen Cirkel berührende Linie, so weit gezogen, bis sie zu beiden Seiten den Umkreis des grössern schneidet, der Durchmesser dieses Cirkels sei, dessen Fläche dem Inhalt des Cirkelringes gerade gleich ist.*

[p] *ausser der Übung des Verstandes durch die denkliche Einsicht derselben.*

[q] *das Gefühl.*   [r] *Ebenmasses.*

139

own could not have produced such an order, then we regard this provision as contingent and as the product of choice.^{s} Now, if new harmony, order and usefulness should make their appearance, along with mediating causes especially instituted to produce these effects, then we judge them in the same way to be contingent and the product of choice. This connection is quite alien to the nature of the things themselves. They stand in this harmonious relation^t simply because someone has chosen to connect them in this way. No general cause can be adduced to explain the sheathed character, that is to say, the retractability of the claws of the cat, the lion, and so on. The only explanation which can be given is that a Creator has ordered them in this way, with a view to protecting them from wear, for these animals must have implements suitable for seizing and retaining their prey. But suppose that matter has certain properties of a more general character, which, in addition to producing certain benefits which may be construed as their *raison d'être*, are also particularly suited to producing even more harmony, and doing so without the least provision being made to bring it about. Suppose that a simple law, which is universally agreed to be necessary for the production of a certain good, also produces fruitful effects in many other ways as well. Suppose that that simple law was the source of further usefulness and harmoniousness,^{u} not by art, but rather of necessity. And suppose, finally, that this should hold throughout the whole of material nature. If all this were supposed, then there would obviously inhere in the very essence of things themselves universal relations to unity and cohesiveness,^{v} and a universal harmony would extend throughout the realm of possibility itself. Such a state of affairs would fill us with admiration for such extensive adaptedness^w and natural harmony.^{x} Adaptedness and natu-

2:97 ral harmony such as this, although rendering punctilious^y and forced art superfluous, can nonetheless never themselves be ascribed to chance. It rather indicates that there is a unity to be found in the possibilities of things themselves; it suggests that the essences of all things are without exception dependent upon one single great ground. I shall try to explain this extremely remarkable phenomenon by means of some simple examples, carefully employing the method of slowly advancing from what is immediately certain from observation to judgements of greater generality.

Suppose that one positively insisted that there must first be some underlying purpose to explain the occurrence of a provision of nature. The necessity for an atmosphere might then be explained in terms of one of a thousand uses it might have.^{z} For the sake of argument, I shall concede

^{s} *als zufällig und als die Folge einer Wahl.* ^{t} *in dieser Harmonie.*
^{u} *Nutzen und Wohlgereimtheiten.* ^{v} *Zusammenhange.* ^{w} *Schicklichkeit.*
^{x} *Zusammenpassung.* ^{y} *peinlich.*
^{z} *Man kann einen Nutzen unter tausend wählen, weswegen man es als nöthig ansehen kann, dass ein Luftkreis sei, wenn man durchaus einen Zweck zum Grunde zu haben verlangt, wodurch eine Anstalt in der Natur zuerst veranlasst worden.*

140

the point. I propose that the untimate purpose of this provision of nature is, for example, to render possible the respiration of man and animals. Now, the air, by means of those very same attributes which are necessary to respiration, and employing no other means at all, also produces fine effects in infinite numbers; and it produces these effects of necessity, and without any special provisions having to be made. The self-same elasticity and pressure of the atmosphere makes suction possible. Young animals would have no nourishment without it; and the possibility of pumps is a necessary consequence of it. By these same means, moisture is drawn up from the earth in the form of vapours which condense into clouds, which enhance the beauty of the day and often moderate the excessive heat of the sun. In particular, these same means provide gentle moisture to the arid regions of the earth's surface by stealing from the water-courses of the low-lying areas. These very same properties of the atmosphere have other consequences, too, which are entirely natural and spontaneous. One example is the dawn, which lengthens the day and, by means of gradual intermediate degrees, renders the transition from night to day harmless to the eye. Another especially important example is the winds.

Suppose that someone were to draw up a scheme by means of which the coasts of tropical countries, which must otherwise be hotter than the regions lying further inland, might enjoy a somewhat more tolerable temperature. For this purpose, he will most naturally think of a sea-wind prevailing during the hottest hours of the day. However, since at night-time the temperature drops much more rapidly over the sea than over the land, it might not be a good thing for the same wind to blow all the time. For this reason, our planner would wish that it had occurred to Providence so to arrange things that, during the middle hours of the night, the wind should blow in the opposite direction from the land. Such an arrangement might have many other uses as well. Now, the only question would be this: by what mechanism or artificial arrangement could this alternating wind be maintained? In raising this question, one would have considerable cause for concern that, since man cannot expect that all the laws of nature should be adapted to his convenience, the mechanism for maintaining the alternating wind, while possible, might harmonise so poorly with the other necessary dispositions of nature, that the Supreme Wisdom found it good not to deploy it. But this whole worry is unnecessary. The atmosphere, operating in accordance with the general laws of motion, accomplishes on its own what an arrangement, instituted in accordance with reflective choice, would itself achieve. The self-same principle which has other extensive uses also has this use as well, without there being any need for new or special provisions. The air above the scorching ground of such a country is rarified by the heat of the day and thus necessarily yields to the denser and heavier air over the cool sea, causing the sea-wind. For this reason, it blows during the hottest hours of the day

2:98

141

until late in the evening. The sea-air, which for the same reasons was not so strongly heated during the day as the air over the land, cools more quickly during the night, contracts and causes the withdrawal of the land-air at night-time. It is common knowledge that all tropical coasts enjoy this alternating wind.[45]

I have tried to show what the relations are which the simple and very general laws of motion, in virtue of the necessity of their essence, have to order and harmoniousness. To this end, I have directed my attention to a small part of nature only, namely, to the effects produced by the atmosphere. It can easily be seen that the entire sphere of nature in all its measureless extent lies open before me ready to receive this same interpretation. It is my intention to enlarge this lovely prospect by adding some further considerations at a later stage. For the present, I should be ignoring something essential if I did not consider the important discovery made by *Maupertuis* relating to the harmony which prevails among the necessary and most general laws of motion.[46]

Our proof did, it is true, relate to laws which were both very extensive and necessary in character. But they were laws which only governed a particular kind of matter in the world. *Maupertuis*, on the other hand, proved that even the most universal laws of matter in general – whether it be at rest or in motion, whether in elastic or in non-elastic bodies, whether in the attraction of light in refraction or in its repulsion in reflection – are subject to one dominant rule, according to which the greatest possible economy of action is always observed.[47] This discovery enables us to subsume the effects produced by matter, irrespective of the great differences which these effects may have in themselves, under a universal formula which expresses a relation to appropriateness,[a] beauty and harmony. And yet the laws of motion are themselves such that matter cannot be thought independently of them. And the necessity of these laws is such that they can be derived from the universal and essential constitution of all matter without the least experiment and with the greatest distinctness. This acute and learned man immediately sensed that, in having thus introduced unity into the infinite manifold of the universe and created order in what was blindly necessary, there must be some single supreme principle to which the totality of things owed its harmony and appropriateness. He rightly believed that such a universal cohesiveness[b] in the simplest natures of things afforded a far more fitting foundation for the indubitable discovery, in some perfect and original being, of the ultimate cause of everything in the world, than any perception of various contingent and variable arrangements instituted in accordance with particular laws.[48] From that point onwards, the important question was: What employment would higher philosophy be able to make of this important

2:99

---

[a] *Anständigkeit.*   [b] *Zusammenhang.*

new insight? And I do not think that I am mistaken in my supposition when I maintain that the Royal Academy of Sciences in Berlin had this as the subject of their prize-essay question: Are the laws of motion necessary or contingent? – a question to which no adequate reply was submitted.[49]

If contingency is taken in the real sense[c] to mean the dependency of the material elements of possibility upon something else, it is manifest that the laws of motion and the universal properties of matter, subject to these laws, must depend on some one great common original being, which is the ground of order and harmoniousness. For who would wish to maintain that in an extensive manifold, in which each individual thing had its own completely independent nature, everything should nonetheless by an amazing accident be exactly so arranged that it was in harmony with everything else and that unity should manifest itself in the whole? But the following considerations make it clear that this common principle must   2:100 relate not merely to the existence of matter and the properties attributed to it, but to the very possibility and essence of matter in general.[d] The only conditions under which it is possible to conceive what is supposed to fill space and what is supposed to be capable of thrust and pressure must be the very same conditions which necessarily yield the aforementioned laws. On this basis it can be seen that these laws of the motion *of matter* are absolutely necessary. That is to say: if the possibility of matter is presupposed, it would be self-contradictory to suppose it operating in accordance with other laws. This is a logical necessity of the highest kind. It is manifest, on the same basis, that, notwithstanding, the internal possibility of matter itself, namely, the data and the real element underlying this thinkable thing, is not given independently or for itself. The internal possibility of matter is, rather, posited by some principle or other. And, in virtue of this principle, what is manifold acquires its unity, and what is diverse receives its connection.[e] And this proves the contingency of the laws of motion in the real sense of the term.

SECOND REFLECTION: DIFFERENTIATION OF THE DEPENDENCY OF ALL THINGS UPON GOD INTO MORAL AND NON-MORAL DEPENDENCY

I designate that dependency of a thing upon God *moral* when God is the ground of that thing through his will. All other dependency is *non-moral*. Accordingly, if I assert that God contains the ultimate ground even of the internal possibility of things, everyone will easily understand that this can only be a non-moral dependency, for the will makes nothing possible; it

[c] *im Realverstande.*

[d] *sondern selbst auf die Möglichkeit einer Materie überhaupt und auf das Wesen selbst.*

[e] *in welchem* (i.e., *Principium*) *das Mannigfaltige Einheit und das Verschiedene Verknüpfung bekommt.*

merely decides upon what is already presupposed as possible. In so far as God contains the ground of the existence of things, I admit that this dependency is always moral; in other words, things exist because God willed that they should exist.

The internal possibility of things, namely, furnishes Him, who has decided upon the existence of things, with the materials for it. These materials contain within them an extraordinary adaptedness*f* to harmony; the essences of these materials themselves contain within them a harmony with a whole which is orderly and beautiful in many different ways. The fact that an atmosphere exists can be attributed to God as its moral

2:101 ground because of the purpose attainable by it. But that the essence of a single ground, which is so simple, should be so fruitful, and that so much adaptedness*g* and harmony should inhere in its possibility and not require special interventions to be made in order to harmonise with the other possible things in the world, in accordance with manifold rules of order – that is certainly not to be attributed to a free choice. For every decision of a will presupposes cognition of the possibility of that which is to be decided upon.

Anything, the ground of which has to be sought in a free choice must, for that very reason, be contingent. Now, the union of numerous diverse consequences, which issue of necessity from a single ground, is not a contingent union. It cannot, therefore, be ascribed to a determination which is the product of a free will.*h* We have already seen the same thing above when we saw that the possibilities of the pump, respiration, the conversion of liquids, when present, into vapours, the winds, and so on, are inseparable from each other, for they all depend on a single ground, namely, the elasticity and pressure of the atmosphere. This harmony of the manifold in one*i* is thus in no wise contingent, and it is, therefore, not to be attributed to a moral ground.

My only concern here is the relation which holds between the essence of the atmosphere, or of any other thing at all, and the *possible* production of so many excellent consequences. That is to say: I am only considering the *adaptedness j* of their nature to so many purposes. The harmony of a single ground with so many possible consequences makes unity in such a case necessary; and to that extent the possible consequences are inseparable from each other and from the thing itself. As far as the actual production of these advantages is concerned: it is contingent either in so far as one of the things to which the thing relates may be absent, or in so far as the effect may be prevented from occurring by an outside force.

Beautiful relations inhere in the properties of space; and in the measure-

---

f Tauglichkeit.   g Schicklichkeit.   h freiwilligen Bestimmung.
i Übereinstimmung des Mannigfaltigen in Einem.   j Tauglichkeit.

less manifold of its determinations there is to be found a unity which is worthy of wonder. In so far as matter must fill space, the existence of all this harmoniousness along with all its consequences,[k] is to be attributed to the power of choice of the first cause. As for the union of so many consequences with each other, all of which stand in such great harmony with the things of the world: it would be absurd to attribute this, again, to a will. The characteristic of air, in virtue of which it offers resistance to the   2:102 material bodies moving in it, is also to be regarded as a necessary consequence of its nature. Raindrops, in falling from a great altitude, are impeded in their fall by the air, and they descend with a moderate velocity. If they were not retarded in this way they would, in falling from such an altitude, acquire a very harmful force. This advantage is not combined with the other properties of air by a special decree, for air could not exist at all without this property. The cohesiveness[l] of the parts of matter may, in the case of water, for example, be a necessary consequence of the possibility of matter in general, or it may be an arrangement which has been specially instituted. Whichever the case, the immediate effect is the spherical configuration of small quantities of water such as raindrops. The possibility of the lovely, many-hued rainbow is a product of the very general laws of motion. With a splendour and a regularity which moves the heart, it hangs suspended above the horizon when the unclouded sun shines into the shower of raindrops falling opposite. The existence of liquids and heavy bodies can only be attributed to the wish[m] of this mighty Author. But that a celestial body in its liquid state should, entirely necessarily and as a result of such universal laws, strive to assume a spherical form – a form which subsequently harmonises with the other purposes of the universe better than any other possible form, a spherical surface being capable, for example, of the most uniform dispersion of light – that is inherent in the essence of the thing itself.

The cohesiveness and resistance of matter, which the parts of matter combine with their separability, renders friction necessary. Friction is of great use, and it harmonises with the order which prevails in all the numerous changes which take place in nature; and its harmony with this order is as great as that of something which was not the consequence of such general principles but had been instituted by a special provision. If friction did not impede motions, everything would eventually be reduced to chaos: forces, once generated, would continue as a result of their being communicated to other bodies by repulsion, continuous collisions and concussions. Surfaces which support bodies would always have to be perfectly horizontal (and that is seldom possible), for otherwise the bodies

---

[k] *Das Dasein aller dieser Wohlgereimtheiten, in so fern Materie den Raum erfüllen sollte, ist mit allen ihren Folgen.*
[l] *Zusammenhang.*   [m] *Begehren.*

2:103

would always be sliding off. Spun threads only hold together as a result of friction, for the fibres, not running the whole length of the thread, would be torn apart by the least force, were they not held together by friction proportionate to the force with which the fibres are pressed against each other by being twisted together.

The reason why I have discussed such humble effects which are so little esteemed and which take their rise from the simplest and most general laws of nature, is this: I have in part been concerned to show how, from these lowly effects, one may infer the great and infinitely extended harmony of the essences of things and the important effects attributable to that harmony, even in cases where one is unable, for lack of skill, to trace many a natural order back to such simple and general grounds. But, in part, I have also been concerned to show the absurdity of attributing these same harmonies to the wisdom of God as their special ground. The fact that things, which are so beautifully related to each other, should exist at all, is to be attributed to the wise choice of Him who created them on account of that harmony. But that each of these things should, in virtue of simple grounds, contain such an extensive adaptedness to harmony of many different kinds, and that a wonderful unity in the whole should, as a result, be able to be maintained – that is inherent in the very possibility of the things in question. And since the element of contingency, presupposed by any choice, here disappears, it follows that the ground of this unity, while it may be sought in a wise being, is not to be sought in that being through the mediation of its wisdom itself.[n]

THIRD REFLECTION: CONCERNING THE DEPENDENCY OF THE THINGS OF THE WORLD UPON GOD, EITHER THROUGH THE MEDIATION OF THE ORDER OF NATURE OR INDEPENDENTLY OF THAT ORDER

1. Division of the events of the world according to whether they are subsumed under the order of nature or not so subsumed

Something is subsumed under the order of nature if its existence or its alteration is sufficiently grounded in the forces of nature. The first requirement for this is that the force of nature should be the efficient cause of the thing; the second requirement is that the manner in which the force of nature is directed to the production of this effect should itself be sufficiently grounded in a rule of the natural laws of causality. Such events are also called, quite simply, *natural* events of the world. On

2:104 the other hand, when this is not the case, that which is not subsumed

[n] *aber nicht vermittelst seiner Weisheit.*

under such a ground is something supernatural. This is either because the immediate efficient cause is external to nature, that is to say, the divine power produces it immediately; or, alternatively, it is because the manner in which the forces of nature are directed to producing the effect is not itself subject to a rule of nature. In the first case, I call the event *materially supernatural,* and in the second case *formally supernatural.* I shall adduce examples of the latter case, for it alone seems in need of some explanation, for the other is clear of itself. There are many forces in nature which have the power to destroy individuals, states, or even the entire human race. Earthquakes, hurricanes, tempests at sea, comets, and so on, are examples of such destructive forces. Furthermore, the occurrence of these events from time to time is sufficiently grounded in the constitution of nature, according to a universal law. But the vices and moral corruption of the human race are not *natural* grounds connected with the occurrence of these events, nor are they to be numbered among the laws in accordance with which they take place. The wickedness of a city has no effect upon the fires concealed within the bowels of the earth, nor was the debauchery of the first world*ᵒ* an efficient cause which could have drawn the comets out of their orbits down to earth. If such an event should occur, it is attributed to a natural cause. And that attribution implies that the event in question was a misfortune, not a punishment: man's moral conduct cannot be a cause of earthquakes according to a natural law, for there is no connection here between the cause and the effect.⁵⁰ Take for example, the destruction of the town of Port Royal in Jamaica by an earthquake.* If someone calls it a natural event he would mean that, although, according to the testimony of their preacher, the vicious deeds of the inhabitants of Port Royal would have deserved the chastisement of such a devastation, this particular event is to be regarded, nonetheless, as one of many such events which happen from time to time in accordance with a general law of nature. For earthquakes periodically convulse various regions of the earth, and it sometimes happens that there are cities located in those regions, and occasionally some of those cities are extremely wicked. On the other hand, if the earthquake is to be regarded as a punishment, then it follows that, since these forces of nature cannot, according to any natural law, have any connection with the conduct of man, they must in each individual case be especially instituted by the Supreme Being. And then the event is supernatural in the formal sense of the word, even though the intermediate cause of the event was a force of nature. And even if this event did eventually occur in the form of a punishment as a result of a protracted series of arrangements especially implanted in the causal

2:105

---

* See Raj, *Von der Welt Anfang, Veränderung und Untergang.*⁵¹

ᵒ *die Üppigkeit der ersten Welt.*

forces of the world; and even if one assumed that at the creation of the world God had already made all the provisions requisite for the later occurrence of the event at the right time as a result of the forces of nature directed to that end (as one can imagine in the case of Whiston's theory of the flood, where the flood is supposed to have been caused by a comet)[52] – even so the supernatural is in no way thereby diminished. On the contrary, the supernatural character of the event is simply shifted a long way back to the original act of creation, and, as a result, inexpressibly increased. This whole sequence of events, in so far as the manner of its ordering refers to its outcome, and in so far as the results of this sequence of events cannot be regarded as a consequence of more general laws of nature – this whole sequence of events indicates an immediate and even greater divine providential care, which is focused upon this long chain of events, with a view to avoiding the impediments which might have prevented the exact attainment of the desired effects.

On the other hand, there are punishments and rewards which are in accordance with the order of nature, because the moral behaviour of man is connected with them through the law of cause and effect. Unbridled licentiousness and immoderation lead to a debilitated and tormented life. Intrigues and deceit ultimately miscarry, and honesty is, indeed, the best policy in the end. And in all this, the effects are connected with each other according to the laws of nature. But as for those punishments, rewards and all those other events in the world in the case of which the natural forces involved would always have to be especially directed to the realisation of each individual case: even if a certain uniformity should be found among many of them, they would be subject to an immediate divine law, namely, that of the wisdom of God, but not to any natural law.

2:106

2. Division of natural events according to whether they are subsumed under the necessary or the contingent order of nature

All natural things are contingent in their existence. The combination of different kinds of thing, for example, the combination of air, earth, and water, is, without doubt, likewise contingent, and is, therefore, simply to be attributed to the power of choice of the Supreme Author.* But, although the laws of nature, like the things themselves of which they are the laws, accordingly appear to have no necessity, and although, again, the connections in which these laws can be exercised are contingent, there nonetheless remains a kind of necessity which is very remarkable. There are, namely, many laws of nature, of which the unity is necessary. Such is the case, specifically, in those instances where the principle of harmony with one law is precisely the same principle which renders other laws necessary as well. For example: the self-same elasticity and pressure of the air, which

---

* der Willkür des obersten Urhebers.

148

is the ground of the laws of respiration, is also of necessity the ground of the possibility of pumps, of the generation of clouds, of the maintenance of fire, of the winds, and so on. It is necessary that, as soon as the ground of even merely one of them be present, the ground of the others should also be present. On the other hand, if the ground of the effects of a certain kind, which are similar, according to one law, is not at the same time the ground of effects of a different kind in the same being, according to another law, then the agreement of these laws with each other is contingent, and the unity which prevails among these laws is merely contingent. What happens in the thing in accordance with these laws happens in accordance with a contingent order of nature. Human beings see, hear, smell, taste, and so on. But the properties which are the grounds of seeing are not the grounds of tasting as well. Man has to have other organs in order to hear, and likewise in order to taste. The union of such different faculties is contingent, and, because their union aims at perfection, their union is artificial in character. And then again, in the case of each organ individually, there is a unity which is artificial. In the eye, the part which permits light to enter is different from the part which refracts it, and the part which receives the image is, in its turn, different from the other parts. On the other hand, it is not one set of causes which gives the earth its spherical form, and another which prevents bodies flying off the earth as a result of the centrifugal force of its rotation,[q] and yet others again which keep the moon in its orbit. Gravity by itself[r] is a cause which is, of necessity, sufficient to produce all these effects. Now, the fact that grounds are   2:107
to be found in nature for all these effects is, without doubt, a perfection. And if the same ground which determines the one thing should also be sufficient to determine the others, then the unity which accrues to the whole is so much the greater. But this unity and, along with it, the perfection as well, are, in the present case, necessary, and they attach to the essence of the thing. And all the harmoniousness, fruitfulness and beauty, which are in so far due to that unity,[s] depend upon God either through the mediation of the essential order of nature, or through the mediation of that which is necessary in the order of nature. I hope that I shall be rightly understood. My wish is to extend this necessity, not to the existence of these things themselves, but merely to the harmony and unity which inhere in their possibility, and which constitute the necessary ground of such an extraordinary extensive adaptedness and fruitfulness. The creatures of the plant- and animal-kingdoms everywhere offer the most admirable examples of a unity which is at once contingent and yet in harmony with

---

[q] *Drehungsschwung.*   [r] *die einzige Schwere.*
[s] *Diese Einheit aber und mit ihr die Vollkommenheit ist in dem hier angeführten Falle nothwendig und klebt dem Wesen der Sache an, und alle Wohlgereimtheit, Fruchtbarkeit und Schönheit, die* (i.e., *alle Wohlgereimtheit, Fruchtbarkeit und Schönheit*) *ihr* (i.e., *der Einheit*) *in so fern zu verdanken ist.*

great wisdom. Consider the vessels which draw up sap, vessels which take in air, those which process the sap and those which exhale it, and so on. These various vessels make up a great manifold, where none is capable of producing the effects of the others, and where their combination into a unified and perfect whole is artificially devised,[t] so that the plant itself, which is related to such a diversity of purposes, constitutes a unity which is contingent in character and the product of choice.[u]

On the other hand, it is inorganic nature, in particular, which furnished numberless proofs of a necessary unity in the relation between a simple ground and a multiplicity of appropriate consequences. Indeed, the case is such that one is inclined to suppose that perhaps even when, in organic nature, many perfections may seem to be the product of provisions which have been especially made, they may, notwithstanding, be the necessary effects of a single ground, a ground which, in virtue of its essential fruitfulness, connects those perfections with many other beautiful effects. The result is that one is constrained to suppose that there may be more necessary unity even in these realms of nature than one perhaps thinks.

The forces of nature and the causal laws which govern them, contain the ground of an order of nature. This order of nature, in so far as it embraces a complex harmony in a necessary unity, has the effect of turning the combination of much perfection in *one* ground into a law. Thus, different natural effects are, in respect of their beauty and usefulness, to be regarded as 2:108 subsumed under the essential order of nature, and, by that means, as subsumed under God. By contrast, there are many perfections in a given whole, which are not possible in virtue of the fruitfulness of a single ground but require a variety of different grounds, which have been deliberately[v] combined to this end. For this reason, many arrangements which have been artificially instituted[w] will be the cause of a law. The effects which occur in accordance with that law will be subsumed under an order of nature which is contingent in character and the product of artifice;[x] and in virtue of that subsumption they will also be subsumed under God.

FOURTH REFLECTION: EMPLOYMENT
OF OUR ARGUMENT IN JUDGING THE
PERFECTION OF A WORLD ACCORDING TO THE
COURSE OF NATURE

1. What can be inferred from our argument in support of the superiority of the order of nature over the supernatural order

It is a well-known rule of philosophers, or rather of common sense in general, that nothing is to be regarded as a miracle or as a supernatural

---

[t] *künstlich.*   [u] *ein zufälliges und willkürliches Eine.*   [v] *willkürlich.*
[w] *manche künstliche Anordnung.*   [x] *der zufälligen und künstlichen Ordnung der Natur.*

event, unless there are weighty reasons for doing so. This rule implies, firstly, that miracles are rare; and secondly, that the whole perfection of the universe can, in conformity with the will of God and in accordance with the laws of nature, be attained without many supernatural influences. For everybody knows that if the world were not to achieve the purpose of its existence without the assistance of numerous miracles, then supernatural events would have to be a commonplace.*y* There are some who are of the opinion that the formal element in the natural connection of consequences with their grounds is in itself a perfection, and that this is, indeed, preferable even to a better outcome, if that can only be attained in a supernatural fashion.*z* They attach an immediate advantage to the natural as such. Everything supernatural, construed as an interruption of the order of nature, seems of itself to constitute a deformity.*a* But this difficulty is only imaginary. The good is to be found in the attainment of the end alone; and if goodness is attributed to the means, then only on account of the end. The natural order, if it does not produce perfect effects, does not contain any immediate ground of superiority in itself, for it can only be regarded as a kind of means, and a means admits no value of its own, but only a derivative value borrowed from the magnitude of the end which it realises. The sense of effort*b* which people experience in their immediate exertions has surreptitiously insinuated itself here. It is this which invests that which can be entrusted to outside forces with an advantage, even when the outcome lacks something of the usefulness intended. However, if the man who takes his wood to the saw-mill to be converted into planks could just as well effect this conversion immediately, then all the art of this machine would be but an idle plaything,*c* for its whole value consists exclusively in its being the means to this end. Thus, a thing is not good simply because it occurs in accordance with the course of nature. Rather is it the case that the course of nature is good in virtue of the fact that that which issues from it is good. God's decree included a world in which everything, for the most part, satisfied the rule of the best as a result of a natural connection. For this reason, God considered it worthy of His choice, not, indeed, because the good consisted in the world's being naturally connected, but because the world's natural connection most truly effected its perfect purposes, without the assistance of frequent miracles.

2:109

And now the following question arises. How does it come about that the universal laws of nature, in accordance with which the course of events in the world occurs, should correspond so beautifully with the will of the Supreme Being? And what reason has one for attributing to these laws the

---

y *etwas Gewöhnliches.*
z *welcher allenfalls ein besserer Erfolg, wenn er nicht anders als übernatürlicher Weise zu erhalten stände, hintangesetzt werden musste.*
a *Übelstand.*   *b* *Die Vorstellung der Mühsamkeit.*   *c* *Spielwerk.*

adaptedness of which we are speaking, so that one does not have to admit more frequently the existence of mysterious, supernatural provisions, constantly rectifying the deficiencies of those laws.* Our concept of the dependency of the very essences themselves of all things upon God here turns out to be of even greater use than expected in this question. The things of nature, even in the most necessary determinations of their internal possibilities, display the characteristic mark of dependency upon that Being, in which everything harmonises with the attributes of wisdom and goodness. One may expect to find harmony and beauty in the combination of natural things, and necessary unity in the many advantageous relations of a single ground to many appropriate laws. Where nature operates in accordance with necessary laws, there will be no need for God to correct the course of events by direct intervention; for, in virtue of the necessity of the effects which occur in accordance with the order of nature, that which is displeasing to God cannot occur, not even in accordance with the most universal laws. For how could the effects of things be contrary to the will of God, when one remembers that the contingent connection of those things depends upon the will of God, while their essential relations, as the grounds of what is necessary in the order of nature, derive from that in God which harmonises most fully with His properties in general? And so all the changes which take place in the world and which are mechanical in character and thus necessary, since they derive from the laws of motion – all such changes must always be good, for they are naturally necessary. And it is to be expected that the consequence will not be susceptible to improvement,ᵉ once their occurrence has become inevitable according to the order of nature.† I would, however, add the following remark in order to avoid any misunderstanding. The alterations which occur in the world are either necessary, and necessary in virtue of the initial order of the universe and of

2:110

---

* This question is far from being satisfactorily answered by appealing to the wisdom of God's choice, which ordered the course of nature once and for all, and ordered it so well that frequent improvements were unnecessary. For the chief difficulty is this: how could it even have been possible to unite such great perfection in a single combination of world-events according to universal laws? How, particularly considering the number of natural things and considering the immeasurable length of the series of their alterations, could a harmony have arisen, which was the product of the universal laws of the reciprocal causalityᵈ of things, but which had no need of frequent supernatural influences?

† Even if, as Newton maintained, it is naturally inevitable that a system such as the solar system will eventually run down and arrive at a state of complete stagnation and universal rest, I would not follow him in adding that it is necessary that God should restore it again by means of miraculous intervention. For, since it is an outcome to which nature is of necessity destined as a result of its essential laws, I assume from this that it is also good. This final state of the solar system ought not to strike us as a loss to be lamented, for we are ignorant of the measurelessness of nature. Ever developing in other regions of the universe, nature may, for all we know, richly compensate for this running down of the universe by great fruitfulness elsewhere.

ᵈ *gegenseitigen Wirksamkeit.*   ᵉ *unverbesserlich.*

the laws of nature, both general and particular – and everything which takes place mechanically in the corporeal world is of this character – or, alternatively, these same alterations possess, notwithstanding, an inadequately understood contingency – a case in point being the actions which issue from freedom and of which the nature is not properly understood. Changes in the world of this latter kind, in so far as they appear to have about them an indeterminacy^f in respect of determining grounds and necessary laws, harbour within themselves a possibility of deviating from the general tendency of natural things towards perfection. And, for this reason, 2:111 it can be expected that supplementary supernatural interventions may be necessary, for it is possible that the course of nature, looked at in this light, may, on occasion, run contrary to the will of God. However, even the forces of freely acting beings are not, in their connection with the rest of the universe, entirely emancipated from all laws. They are always subject, if not to necessitating grounds, yet to such grounds as render their execution certain, albeit in a different fashion and in accordance with the rules governing the power of choice. Since this is the case, it follows that the general dependency of the essences of things upon God is here, too, always a major ground for regarding the consequences as on the whole appropriate and in harmony with the rule of the best. Even in the present case, the consequences occur in accordance with the course of nature (and there is no need to be misled by apparent deviations in particular cases). Thus it is only rarely that the order of nature needs to be improved or supplemented by immediate divine intervention. Even revelation only mentions such interventions as occurring at specific times and among specific nations. Experience, too, confirms the dependency of even the freest actions upon a major natural rule. For, contingent as the decision to marry may be, it is nonetheless found that in a given country the proportion of marriages to the number of those living is fairly constant, provided that one operates with large numbers. For examples, it will be found that among one hundred and ten persons of both sexes there will be one married couple.^g The extent to which man's freedom contributes to the lengthening or shortening of life is a matter of common knowledge. Nonetheless, even these free actions must be subject to a greater order, for, on average, if one operates with large numbers, the number of mortalities stands in a very exact and constant ratio to the number of the living. These few proofs may suffice in some measure to explain the fact that even the laws of freedom do not, in respect of the rules of the general order of nature, involve any such indeterminacy.^h Such an indeterminacy would imply that the ground, which in the rest of nature establishes in the very essences of things themselves an inevitable relation

---

^f *Ungebundenheit.*
^g *und das z.E. unter 110 Menschen beiderlei Geschlechts sich ein Ehepaar findet.*
^h *Ungebundenheit.*

2:112

to perfection and harmoniousness, would not, in the natural course of free behaviour, produce at least a greater tendency to delight the Supreme Being, without the assistance of numerous miracles. However, I am more concerned about the course of natural events, in so far as they owe their necessity to laws which are implanted in them. In such an order, miracles will either not be necessary at all or only occasionally so, for it would be improper to admit that such imperfections, needing miracles to correct them, should naturally occur.

If I subscribed to the commonly held concept of natural things, according to which their internal possibility is independent and without any external ground, I should not be at all surprised if it were said that a world of unitary perfection*ⁱ* would be impossible unless there were large numbers of supernatural interventions. Indeed, I should find it strange and beyond comprehension that, in the absence of a continuous series of miracles, anything useful could be achieved as a result of a great and natural connection in such a world. For it would be an astonishing coincidence if the essences of things, each possessed of its own separate necessity, should harmonise with each other and do so in such a way that it was possible even for the Supreme Wisdom to unite them together into a great whole, irradiating a faultless harmony and beauty, in accordance with universal laws and in spite of the complexity of its relations of dependence. On the other hand, I am persuaded that it is only because there is a God that anything else is possible at all. Accordingly, I expect even the possibilities of things themselves to display a harmony which is concordant with their great principle; and I also expect these possibilities to be adapted to each other by means of universal arrangements so as to constitute a whole which properly harmonises with the wisdom of the Being, from which they derive their ground. Indeed, I should find it amazing if anything occurred or could occur in the course of nature in accordance with general laws which was displeasing to God, or in need of a miracle to improve it. And were such an event to occur, even its cause*ʲ* would be one of those things which, while happening from time to time, would be utterly incomprehensible to us.

If one has grasped the essential reason why miracles can rarely be necessary to the perfection of the world, one will have no difficulty in understanding that this also applies to what, in the previous reflection, we called supernatural events in the formal sense of the term. Such supernatural events are frequently admitted in ordinary judgements. The admission is made on the basis of a mistaken concept which leads one to

ⁱ von einiger Vollkommenheit / B: any perfection / C: *una certa perfezione* / F & Z: *tant . . . peu parfait* / T: some perfection / (Kant is using the word *einig* in the sense of 'unified', 'unitary', or 'cohesive', and thus suggesting the harmoniousness or concordant nature of the perfection. Cf. Grimm: *einig* [5]).
ʲ Veranlassung.

suppose that there is something natural in such formally supernatural events.

2. What can be inferred from our argument to the advantage of one or other of the two orders of nature

In the procedure of purified philosophy there prevails a rule which, even if it is not formally stated, is nonetheless always observed in practice. The rule maintains that in investigating the causes of certain effects one must pay careful attention to maintaining the unity of nature as far as possible. In other words, the rule maintains that one must derive a variety of effects from a single cause which is already known, and not immediately suppose the existence of new and diverse operative causes to explain different effects because of some seemingly important dissimilarity between them. Accordingly, it is presumed that there exists a great unity in nature, in respect of the adequacy of a single cause to account for many different kinds of consequences. It is thought that one is justified in regarding the union of different kinds of appearance with each other as for the most part necessary, and not as the effect of an artificial or contingent order. How many different effects derive from the single force of gravity, where it was once thought necessary to postulate different causes (as, for example, in the case of the rising of some bodies and the falling of others). Vortices for maintaining the heavenly bodies in their orbits were abandoned once that simple force of nature was recognised to be the cause of the planetary orbits.[54] It is with good reason presumed that the expansion of bodies as a result of heat, that light, electrical energy, thunderstorms, and perhaps even the force of magnetism, are many different manifestations of one and the self-same operative matter present in all of space, namely, the aether.[55] And if one finds oneself constrained to postulate a new principle to explain a type of effect, one feels a sense of thorough dissatisfaction. Even when a very precise symmetry seems to require the postulation of a spe- cially instituted and artificially devised arrangement,[k] one is still inclined to regard it as the necessary result of more general laws and to continue to observe the rule of unity, before resorting to an explanation in terms of an artificial provision. Snowflakes[l] are composed of crystals which are so regular, so delicate, so far removed from all the clumsiness[m] which blind chance would bring about, that one would be inclined to doubt the hon- esty of those who have furnished us with portrayals[n] of them, were it not for the fact that every winter affords us with numberless opportunities to verify the accuracy of these diagrams from our own experience. There are 2:114 few flowers which, to speak only of external appearance, display greater delicacy and proportion; and art has nothing at all to offer which displays

---

[k] *eine besondere künstliche Anordnung.*   [l] *Schneefiguren.*   [m] *alles Plumpe.*
[n] *Abzeichnungen.*

greater precision[o] than these products, which nature scatters with such profusion over the face of the earth. And yet it has occurred to no one to explain their origin in terms of a special snow-seed, or to imagine an artificially instituted arrangement of nature to account for them. They are rather construed as the incidental consequences of more general laws, which subsume under themselves with necessary unity the formation of this product.*

Nonetheless, nature is rich in another kind of production. And here, when philosophy reflects on the way in which this kind of product comes into existence, it finds itself constrained to abandon the path we have just described. There is manifest in this case great art and a contingent combination of factors which has been made by free choice in accordance with certain intentions.[p] Such art and free choice are the ground of a particular law of nature, which itself belongs to an artificial order of nature.[q] The structure of plants and of animals displays a constitution of this kind; and it is a constitution which cannot be explained by appeal to the universal and necessary laws of nature. Now, it would be absurd to regard the initial generation of a plant or animal as a mechanical effect incidentally arising from the universal laws of nature; nonetheless, there is a two-fold question, which has remained unanswered for the reason mentioned.[58] Is each individual member of the plant- and animal-kingdoms directly formed by God, and thus of supernatural origin, with only propagation, that is to say, only the periodic transmission for the purposes of development, being entrusted to a natural law?[r][59] Or do some individual members of the plant- and animal-kingdoms, although immediately formed by God and thus of divine origin, possess the capacity, which we cannot understand, actually to generate their own kind in accordance with a regular law of nature, and not merely to unfold them?[s][60] There are difficulties on both sides, and it is perhaps impossible to make out which difficulty is the greatest. But our concern here is merely to determine the relative weight of the various reasons, in so far as they are metaphysical in character. For example: in the light of everything we know, it is utterly unintelligible to us that a tree should be able, in virtue of an internal mechanical constitution, to form
2:115 and process its sap in such a way that there should arise in the bud or the seed something containing a tree like itself in miniature, or something

* The similarity of form which exists between mildew and plants has induced many people to count mildew among the products of the plant-kingdom.[56] However, according to other observations, it is much more likely that, in spite of its apparent regularity, it, like the Tree of Diana,[57] is an effect of the universal laws of sublimation.

[o] *Richtigkeit.* [p] *eine zufällige Vereinbarung durch freie Wahl gewissen Absichten gemäss.*
[q] *welches zur künstlichen Naturordnung gehört* / (*künstlich* has the force of 'produced by art or skill' and is to be contrasted not with 'genuine' but with 'natural').
[r] *und nur die Fortpflanzung, das ist, der Übergang von Zeit zu Zeit zur Auswicklung einem natürlichen Gesetze anvertraut sei.*
[s] *auszuwickeln.*

from which such a tree could develop. The internal forms proposed by *Buffon*,[61] and the elements of organic matter which, in the opinion of *Maupertuis*, join together as their memories dictate and in accordance with the laws of desire and aversion,[62] are either as incomprehensible as the thing itself, or they are entirely arbitrary inventions. But, leaving aside such theories, is one obliged for that reason to develop an alternative theory oneself, which is just as arbitrary, the theory, namely, that, since their natural manner of coming to be is unintelligible to us, all these individuals must be of supernatural origin? Has anyone ever offered a mechanical explanation of the capacity of yeast to generate its kind? And yet one does not appeal for that reason to a supernatural ground.

In this case, the origin of all such organic products is regarded as completely supernatural; it is, nonetheless, supposed that the natural philosophers have been left with something when they are permitted to toy with the problem of the manner of gradual propagation.[t][63] But consider: the supernatural is not thereby diminished; for whether the supernatural generation[u] occurs at the moment of creation, or whether it takes place gradually, at different times, the degree of the supernatural is no greater in the second case than it is in the first. The only difference between them relates not to the degree of the immediate divine action but merely to the *when*. As for the natural order of unfolding[v] mentioned above: it is not a rule of the fruitfulness of nature, but a futile method of evading the issue.[w] For not the least degree of an immediate divine action is thereby spared. Accordingly, the following alternatives seen unavoidable: either the formation of the fruit is to be attributed immediately to a divine action, which is performed at every mating, or, alternatively, there must be granted to the initial divine organisation of plants and animals a capacity, not merely to develop[x] their kind thereafter in accordance with a natural law, but truly to generate[y][64] their kind.

The purpose of these considerations has simply been to show that one must concede to the things of nature a possibility, greater than that which is commonly conceded, of producing their effects in accordance with universal laws.

FIFTH REFLECTION: IN WHICH THE INADEQUACY OF THE USUAL METHOD OF PHYSICO-THEOLOGY IS DEMONSTRATED

1. Of physico-theology in general

All the ways in which the existence of God can be cognised from the effects He produces can be reduced to the three following kinds. Firstly:

---

[t] *allmähligen Fortpflanzung.*   [u] *übernatürliche Erzeugung.*   [v] *Auswickelung.*
[w] *eine Methode eines unnützen Umschweifs.*   [x] *entwickeln.*   [y] *erzeugen.*

this cognition is arrived at through the perception of that which interrupts the order of nature and directly refers to the power to which nature is subject; this conviction is produced by *miracles*. Secondly: the contingent order of *nature*, which one clearly recognises as having been possible in many other ways but in which great art, power and goodness shine forth, leads to the Divine Author. Thirdly: the *necessary* unity perceived in *nature*, and the essential order of things, which is in accordance with great rules of perfection, in short, that which is necessary in the regularity of nature, leads to a supreme principle, not only of this existence, but, indeed, of all possibility.

When people have fallen into complete savagery, or when their eyes have been sealed by stiff-necked wickedness,[z] only the first method seems to have any power to persuade them of the existence of the Supreme Being. On the other hand, a well-disposed soul contemplating things in the correct fashion and seeing so much contingent beauty and purposeful combination presented by the order of nature, finds proof enough there to infer the existence of a will accompanied by great wisdom and power. This conviction, in so far as it is supposed to be sufficient to produce virtuous behaviour, that is to say, is supposed to be morally certain, can be arrived at by means of the ordinary concepts of the understanding. As for the third method of inference: its necessary precondition is philosophy, and it is a higher degree of philosophy alone which is able, with the distinctness and conviction appropriate to the magnitude of the truth concerned, to attain to the object in question.[a]

2:117   The last two methods can be called physico-theological, for they both point out the way which leads from reflections on nature to knowledge of God.

2. The advantages and defects of ordinary physico-theology

The chief characteristic of the physico-theological method, as it has been practised until now, consists in this: to start with, perfection and regularity are suitably understood in terms of their contingency. The artificial character of the order is then demonstrated by reference to all the purposeful relations it contains. The existence of a wise and benevolent will is thereupon inferred from that artificial order. The concept of the immeasurable power of the Author is then subsequently combined with the above concept of a wise and benevolent will. The combination of the two concepts is effected by means of a supplementary reflection on the magnitude of the creation.

[z] *halsstarrige Bosheit.*
[a] *Zu der dritten Art zu schliessen wird nothwendiger Weise Weltweisheit erfordert, und es ist auch einzig und allein ein höherer Grad derselben fähig, mit einer Klarheit und Überzeugung, die der Grösse der Wahrheit gemäss ist, zu dem nämlichen Gegenstand zu gelangen.*

This method is admirable. Firstly: the conviction it produces makes a strong appeal to the senses; it is, as a consequence, very vivid and persuasive. This method is, therefore, easy to grasp and intelligible even to the most ordinary understanding. Secondly: it is more natural than any other method, for, without doubt, it is with this proof that everybody initially starts. Thirdly: it furnishes a very intuitive concept[b] of the great wisdom, providence and even power of the Being who is worthy of our worship.[65] This intuitive concept takes possession of the soul, and fills it, in the most powerful fashion, with wonder, humility and reverence.* The method is also much more practical than any other, even from the point of view of the philosopher. It is true that he encounters here no determinate abstract idea of the Deity for his inquiring and brooding understanding. It is also true that the certainty of the proof is not mathematical in character, but moral. Nonetheless, so many proofs, each of such great force, take possession of the philosopher's soul; and speculation, with certain trust, follows quietly in the footsteps of the conviction which has already been established in his soul. It is unlikely that anyone would venture his whole happiness upon the pretended correctness of a metaphysical proof, especially if that proof were opposed by vivid objections which appealed to the senses. The power of the conviction produced by this method is, for the very reason that it appeals to the senses, so firm and unshakeable as to be unperturbed by any threats to it posed by syllogistic discourses[c] and distinctions, and inaccessible to the power of the objections produced by sophistry.[d] Notwithstanding, this method has its defects, and they are considerable enough, although these defects only belong, properly speaking, to the procedure of those who have employed this method.

2:118

1. Physico-theology regards all the perfection, harmony and beauty of nature as contingent and as an arrangement instituted by wisdom, whereas many of these things issue with necessary unity from the most essential rules of nature. The factor which is here most damaging to the

---

* When, among other things, I consider the microscopic observations of Dr Hill, which are to be found in the *Hamburger Magazin;*[66] when I see numerous animal species in a single drop of water, predatory kinds equipped with instruments of destruction, intent upon the pursuit of their prey, but in their turn annihilated by the still more powerful tyrants of this aquatic world; when I contemplate the intrigues, the violence, the scenes of commotion in a single particle of matter, and when from thence I direct my gaze upwards to the immeasurable spaces of the heavens teeming with worlds as with specks of dust – when I contemplate all this, no human language can express the feelings aroused by such a thought; and all subtle metaphysical analysis falls far short of the sublimity and dignity characteristic of such an intuition.

[b] *einen sehr anschauenden Begriff.*
[c] *Schlussreden* / B: syllogisms / C: *sillogismi* / F: *épilogues* / T: epilogues / Z: *arguties* / (the word *Schlussrede* may mean 'epilogue' [which would make scant sense in this context], but it also means 'syllogism').
[d] *die Macht der spitzfündiger Einwürfe.*

purpose of physico-theology is this: it regards the contingency of nature's perfection as in the highest degree necessary to the proof of the existence of a Wise Author. The consequences of this assumption is that all the necessary harmonies which exist between the things in the world come to be regarded as dangerous objections.

In order to convince oneself that this is an error, consider the following argument. Writers who adopt this method can be seen to be intent upon wresting the products of the plant- and animal-kingdoms, which are rich in numberless final intentions,^{e} not only from the power of chance, but also from the mechanical necessity of the universal laws of material nature. And in this they have not the least difficulty. The preponderance of grounds on their side is too decisive. When, however, they turn from organic to inorganic nature, they continue to employ the same method. But here they almost always find themselves enmeshed in difficulties from which they cannot extricate themselves because of the changed character of the things being examined. They continue to talk of the harmonious agreement instituted by great wisdom between the numerous useful properties of the atmosphere, the clouds, rain, winds, the dusk, and so forth. And they talk as if the property, by means of which the air is responsible for producing the winds, and that by means of which it draws up vapours, or that by means of which it becomes rarer at higher altitudes, were united together by a wise choice. And they construe this uniting together of useful properties in precisely the same way as they construe the uniting together of various characteristics in an animal, for example, in the case of the spider, the uniting together into a system of the different eyes by means of which it watches out for its prey, the wart from which the spider's thread is drawn out as through a nipple, the delicate claws and even the balls of its feet by means of which it sticks the thread together or holds on to it. In this latter case, the unity of all the combined advantages (in which perfection consists) is obviously contingent and ascribable to a wise choice, whereas in the first case it is necessary: if only one of the above capacities is attributed to the air, the others cannot possibly be separated from it. Just because no other method of judging nature's perfection is admitted except that which involves appeal to the provision made by wisdom, it follows that any widely extended unity, in so far as it is obviously recognised as necessary, constitutes a dangerous exception. We shall soon see that, according to our method, too, Divine Wisdom is inferred from such unity. That unity is not, however, inferred from the wise choice as its cause; it is rather derived from a ground in the Supreme Being which is such that it must also be a ground of great wisdom in Him. Unity is thus derived from a Wise Being, but not through His wisdom.^{f}67

2. This method is not sufficiently philosophical in character. Further-

2:119

---

^{e} *Endabsichten.* ^{f} *wohl von einem weisen Wesen, aber nicht durch seine Weisheit.*

160

more, it has often constituted a serious impediment to the dissemination of philosophical knowledge. As soon as a provision of nature is recognised as useful, there is a general tendency to explain it directly in terms of the intention of the Divine Will, or, at any rate, in terms of an order of nature which has been especially and artificially instituted. This explanation is adopted for one of two reasons: either one has got the idea fixed in one's mind that natural events could not produce such harmony merely by means of nature's most general laws alone, or, alternatively, it is felt that if one admitted that the operations of nature could produce such results, the admission would be tantamount to ascribing the perfection of the universe to blind chance, and the consequence of that would be that the Divine Author would remain unrecognised.^{g} As a consequence, limits are imposed upon natural research in such cases. Humiliated reason distances itself from any further investigation, for it regards such investigation here as prying curiosity.^{h} And the prejudice is all the more dangerous for furnishing the lazy with an advantage over the tireless enquirer; it does so under the pretext of piety and of just subjection to the great Author, in knowledge of whom all wisdom must be united.[68] The numberless uses of mountains, for example, are enumerated. As soon as a goodly number of them have been brought together, including those indispensable to the human race, one thinks that one is entitled to regard them as an arrangement directly instituted by God. For, in their view, to regard them as the effect of the universal laws of motion (and, since it is not thought that these latter are supposed to have any relation to consequences which are beautiful or useful, unless accidentally so) would be tantamount to ascribing a use which was crucial to the human race to blind chance.[69] The same thing holds true of what is said about the earth's rivers. If one listened to what the physico-theological authors have to say, one would be persuaded to imagine that the river-beds had all been hollowed out by God.[70] Nor is one proceeding in a philosophical fashion if, in regarding each individual mountain or each individual river as a special intention of God which could not have been attained by the operation of universal laws, one proceeds to imagine the means which God may have employed in order to produce these individual effects. For, according to what has been shown in the Third Reflection of this section, such a product would still be supernatural. Indeed, since it cannot be explained in terms of an order of nature (for it only arose as an individual event as a result of a special provision), it follows that such a procedure of judging is based upon a mistaken idea of the superiority of nature itself if it is construed as having to be steered by force towards an individual case. Such an approach, in our considered opinion, can only be regarded as a means of avoiding the

2:120

---

^{g} *verkannt.* ^{h} *Vorwitz.*

issue,^{i} not as a procedure of wisdom.* *Newton,* by means of incontrovertible proofs, convinced himself that the shape of the earth was such that
the direction of all the gravitational forces, modified by the centrifugal
force of rotation,^{j} remained vertical relative to the surface of the earth.
He concluded from this that the initial state of the earth had been liquid,
and that it had assumed just this form as a result of its rotation according to the laws of statics. No one knew better than he the advantages
inherent in a heavenly body's having this spherical form. He was also as
familiar as anyone with the flattening of the sphere at the poles, a
flattening which was in the highest degree necessary if the deleterious
effects of axial rotation were to be prevented. These are all of them
arrangements worthy of a wise author. Nonetheless, Newton did not
hesitate to regard them as the effects of the most necessary laws of
mechanics. Nor did he fear that in so doing he would lose sight of the
great ruler of all things.[72]

2:121

It can thus surely be supposed that Newton, in attempting to explain the
structure of the planets, their revolutions and the position of their orbits,
would not have had immediate recourse to an explanation in terms of a
divine provision, unless he had judged that a mechanical explanation was
impossible – impossible, not because it was incapable of explaining regularity and order generally (for otherwise why did this incapacity not worry
him in the previously mentioned case), but because the celestial spaces
were empty and because in such a state there could have been no causal
interaction between the planets to establish their orbits.[73] But suppose that
it had occurred to him to ask whether these spaces had always been empty,
and whether, at least in the earliest state of all when these spaces had
perhaps been filled and connected with each other, it would not have been
possible for the above mentioned effect to have been produced and thereafter maintained in existence,[74] and suppose that he had had good reason
to accept this hypothesis concerning the initial state of the universe – if
these suppositions are made, it is certain that Newton would, in a philosophically proper manner, have sought the grounds of the constitution of
the structure of the universe in the universal laws of mechanics.[75] Nor

---

* In those cases where revelation tells us that something which has happened in the world is
an extraordinary and divinely instituted event, it is to be desired that the eagerness of the
philosophers to make a public show of their physical speculations should be restrained. They
do religion no service. On the contrary, their speculations simply arouse the suspicion that
the event which they have sought to explain by natural causes may, indeed, be a natural
accident. Such is the case where the destruction of Sanherib's army is attributed to the wind
Samyel. In such instances, philosophy frequently finds itself in difficulties, as happens in
Whiston's theory, where astronomical knowledge of the comets is employed to explain the
Bible.[71]

^{i} *ein Mittel des Umschweifs.*
^{j} *alle durch den Drehungsschwung veränderte Richtungen der Schwere.*

would he, for that reason, have been concerned that this explanation would have taken the origin of the world out of the hands of the Creator and surrendered it to the power of chance.[76] Lazy self-complacency is not, therefore, entitled to employ Newton's well-known example as a pretext for treating an overhasty appeal to a divinely and directly instituted provision as if it were an explanation in the philosophical sense of the word.

There are, of course, innumerable arrangements in nature which are, from the point of view of the universal laws of nature, contingent. As such they have no other foundation than the wise intention of Him who willed that they should be connected thus and not otherwise. However, the converse conclusion may not be drawn. If a natural connection harmonises with what accords with a wise choice, it does not follow that it is also, from the point of view of the universal laws of causality, contingent, or that it has been especially instituted by an artificial provision. It can often happen with this way of thinking that mistakes are made about the imagined purposes of the law. Apart from the error itself, there is then the added disadvantage that one fails to notice the efficient causes which are at work, while adhering directly to an intention which is merely fictitious. *Süssmilch* once thought that he had discovered the reason why there is a preponderance of male births over female. He supposed that the reason lay in the providential purpose of compensating by their greater number for the loss which the male sex suffers to a higher degree than the female as a result of war and engaging in the more dangerous kinds of occupation.[77] However, later observations taught this careful and reasonable man that the surplus of boys was so diminished by death during the years of infancy that an even smaller number of males than females arrived at that age when the previously mentioned factors could begin to explain the loss.[78] There is reason to believe that this remarkable phenomenon is a case which may be subsumed under a much more general rule, namely, that the stronger part of the human species has a larger share in the activity of procreation, so that its own kind becomes predominant in the products of the two sides. On the other hand, if something has the potentiality for greater perfection, more will be required if, in the course of its development, it is to encounter all the conditions necessary to attain that perfection. For this reason, the number of those of less perfect kind who attain the degree of perfection appropriate to their kind will be greater than that of those whose perfection requires for its attainment a greater concurrence of grounds.[k] Be that as it may, it can at least be remarked that appealing to moral grounds impedes the extension of philosophical under-

2:122

[k] *dass aber dagegen, weil mehr dazu gehört, dass etwas welches die Grundlage zu grösserer Vollkommenheit hat, auch in der Ausbildung alle zu Erreichung derselben gehörige Umstände antreffe, eine grössere Zahl derer von minder vollkommener Art den Grad der Vollständigkeit erreichen werde, als derjenigen, zu deren Vollständigkeit mehr Zusammentreffung von Gründen erfordert wird.*

standing. In other words, the extension of philosophical understanding is hindered by resorting to explanations in terms of purposes, in cases where physical causes may be supposed to determine the effect as a result of their being connected with necessary and more general laws.

3. The physico-theological method can only serve to prove the existence of an Author of the connections and artificial combinations in the world; it does not prove the existence of an Author of matter itself, nor does it prove the origin of the constituent parts of the universe.[79] This considerable defect must expose all those who avail themselves of this method alone to the error known as 'refined atheism'.[/] According to this brand of atheism, God is strictly regarded as the Architect of the world, not as its Creator: He orders and forms matter, but He does not produce or create it. Since I shall be considering this inadequacy in the next reflection,[80] I shall satisfy myself with merely having noted it here.

2:123

Incidentally, the method we are considering is one of a number of methods which are most in harmony both with the dignity and with the weakness of the human understanding. There are, indeed, innumerable arrangements in nature, of which the immediate ground must be the ultimate purpose of their Author. The path which leads most easily to Him is the one which considers those provisions which are immediately subject to His wisdom. It is, therefore, right and proper that one should try to perfect the method rather than to attack it, to correct its errors rather than to despise it because of them. It is this which is the purpose of the following reflection.

SIXTH REFLECTION:
THE REVISED METHOD OF PHYSICO-THEOLOGY

1. Order and appropriateness are indications of an intelligent creator, even when they are necessary.

Nothing can be more prejudicial to the idea of a Divine Author of the universe, nor can anything be more unreasonable, than the willingness to attribute to blind chance a great and fruitful rule of appropriateness, usefulness and harmony. An example of such a theory is the swerve of the atoms in the system of *Democritus* and *Epicurus*.[81] I do not propose to linger over the absurdity and deliberate blindness of this way of thinking, for it has been made clear by others. However, I would remark that the necessity perceived in the relation of things to regular combinations, and the connection of useful laws with a necessary unity, afford proof of a Wise Author, just as well as the most accidental and artificially devised provision, although the nature of the dependency on God must be understood

---

[/] *den feineren Atheismus.*

differently in the two cases. Let me explain my meaning. The existence of order and a diverse advantageous harmony in general point to the exis- 2:124 tence of an Intelligent Author; and it does so even before one has considered whether this relation is necessary to things or contingent. According to the judgements of ordinary sound reason, the series of modifications which the world undergoes, or that connection of events which is such that an alternative connection is possible in its place, while furnishing a clear proof of contingency, has little effect in causing the understanding to suppose that there is an Author. Philosophy is required for this purpose, though, in this case, even its employment is an involved and delicate^m matter. On the other hand, great regularity and the harmoniousness of a complex harmony^n is perplexing, and even common sense itself finds it inconceivable in the absence of an Intelligent Author. Whether or not one rule of appropriateness essentially inheres in another, and whether or not their connection is the product of choice, both the chance occurrence of order and regularity, and their spontaneous emergence in a multiplicity of things, each of which has its own distinct existence, is regarded as simply impossible. The reason is that, from the point of view of its possibility, extensive harmony is never adequately given in the absence of an intelligent ground. And in this there is to be seen a direct expression of a major difference between ways of judging perfection according to its origin.

2. The necessary order of nature itself points to^o an Author of the matter which is so ordered.

The order of nature, in so far as it is regarded as contingent and arising from the power of choice of an intelligent being, is in no way proof that the things of nature, which are widely connected in such an order, also owe their existence to this Author. For it is the combination alone which presupposes an intelligent plan. It was for this reason, too, that Aristotle, along with many other philosophers of antiquity, derived, not the matter or stuff of nature, but only its form, from God.[82] It is, perhaps, only since revelation has taught us the complete dependency of the world upon God that philosophy has also made the requisite effort to regard the origin of the things themselves, which constitute the raw material of nature, as something not possible independently of an Author. I doubt whether anybody has succeeded in establishing this thesis, and I shall 2:125 produce the reasons for my view in the final section.[83] At any rate, the contingent order of the parts of the world, in so far as that order indicates that it originated from the power of choice, can contribute nothing

---

^{m} *verwickelt und schlüpferig.* ^{n} *Wohlgereimtheit in einem vielstimmichten Harmonischen.*
^{o} *bezeichnet.*

to proving it. Take the example of the structure of an animal. Its organs of sense perception are connected with the organs of voluntary movement and life, and connected in such an ingenious fashion that once one's attention has been drawn to it, one would have to be of an ill-natured disposition*p* (for no one could be so unreasonable) not to recognise the existence of a Wise Author, who had so excellently ordered the matter of which the animal was constituted. Nothing more than this can be inferred from our example. Whether this matter has existed eternally and independently in its own right, or whether it has also been generated by this same Author – these are issues which cannot be decided by reference to our example. However, one's verdict is quite different when one recognises that not all natural perfection is the work of artifice, but that the rules of great usefulness are also connected together with necessary unity, and that this agreement inheres in the possibilities of the things themselves. How is one to judge in the case of this perception of things? Is this unity, is this fruitful harmoniousness, possible independently of a Wise Author? The formal element of such great and varied regularity forbids such a conclusion. Since, however, this unity is itself, nonetheless, grounded in the possibilities of the things themselves, there must be a Wise Being, in the absence of which none of these natural things would themselves be possible, and in which, as in a great ground, the essences of such a multiplicity of natural things are united into such regular relations. But then it is clear that not only the manner of their connection, but the things themselves, are possible only in virtue of this Being. That is to say, they can only exist as the effects of this Being. It is this argument which first reveals the complete dependency of nature upon God. Now, if it be asked: 'How do these natures depend upon such a Being so that I can understand their harmony with the rules of wisdom?' – if this question be raised, I should reply: 'They depend upon something in this Being which, in virtue of its containing the ground of the possibility of things, is also the ground of that Being's own wisdom; for this wisdom presupposes the

2:126   possibility of things in general.* But granted that the ground, which underlies not only the essence of all things but also the essence of wisdom, goodness and power, is a unity, it follows that all possibility must of necessity harmonise with these properties'.

---

* Wisdom presupposes that harmony and unity are possible in the relations. That Being which is by nature completely independent can only be wise in so far as it contains the grounds of even the *possible* harmony and perfections which offer themselves for realisation by that Being. If there were no such relation to order and perfection to be found in the possibilities of things, wisdom would be a chimaera. But if this possibility were not in itself grounded in the Wise Being, then this wisdom could no longer be independent in every respect.

p boshaft.

3. Rules of the revised method of physico-theology

I shall briefly summarise the rules of the revised method of physico-theology as follows. Confidently assuming that the universal laws of nature are, in virtue of their dependency upon the Divine Being, fruitful in character, one may proceed in the following manner:

1. Even in the case of those constitutions in nature which are the most advantageous, one will always seek the cause of such advantageous dispositions among those universal laws which, in addition to producing other appropriate consequences, are also related, and related with a necessary unity, to the production of these particular effects as well.

2. One will note the element of necessity in this combination of different forms of adaptedness in a single ground. It is important to do so for two reasons. Firstly, the way in which the dependency of things upon God is inferred from this necessary combination of different forms of adaptedness in a single ground is different from the way in which that same dependency is inferred from a unity which has been artificially devised and deliberately chosen. Secondly, there is a distinction to be drawn between that which is the effect of constant and necessary laws and that which is the product of blind chance.

3. One will presume that the necessary unity to be found in nature is greater than strikes the eye. And that presumption will be made not only in the case of inorganic^q nature, but also in the case of organic^r nature as well. For even in the case of the structure of an animal, it can be assumed that there is a single disposition, which has the fruitful adaptedness to produce many different advantageous consequences.^{s} Initially, we may have supposed that a variety of special provisions must have been necessary to produce such effects. Careful attention to the necessary unity of nature is both consonant with philosophy and advantageous to the physico-theological method of inference.

4. An order which is obviously artificial will be employed to infer the wisdom of an Author, construed as the ground of that order. On the other hand, the essential and necessary unity, which is to be found in the laws of nature, will be employed to infer the existence of a Wise Being, construed as the ground of this unity. The latter inference, however, will be mediated, not by the wisdom of this Being, but by that in him which must harmonise with that wisdom.

5. From the *contingent* connections of the world one will infer the existence of a Being who has originated the manner in which the universe is assembled.^{t} From the *necessary* unity of the world, however, one will infer   2:127

---

^{q} *unorganischen.* ^{r} *organisirten.*
^{s} *dass eine einzige Anlage eine fruchtbare Tauglichkeit zu viel vortheilhaften Folgen haben werde.*
^{t} *zusammengefugt.*

167

the existence of that self-same Being, construed as the Author even of the matter and fundamental stuff of which all natural things are constituted.

6. This method will be extended by means of the universal rules which will be able to explain the grounds of the harmoniousness which exists between that which is necessary, either mechanically or geometrically, and the supreme good of the whole. And, in this connection, one will not omit to consider the properties of space itself, or to elucidate our fundamental thesis by appealing to the unity of the vast manifold of space.

4. Clarification of these rules

I should like to introduce some examples in order to render the above method more intelligible. The mountains of our planet are one of its most useful features.[84] *Burnet* regarded them as nothing more than a wild devastation inflicted upon man as a punishment for his sins, but he was obviously mistaken.[85] The usual method of physico-theology begins with an enumeration of the extensive advantages afforded by these mountainous tracts; it then proceeds to construe them as a divine provision instituted by the wisdom of God and designed to be of use in a variety of ways. This manner of arguing leads one to suppose that, in the absence of a special provision artificially devised to produce this effect, the universal laws of nature would have been incapable of giving the surface of the earth such a form. This appeal to the will of the Almighty imposes a reverential silence upon reason in its enquiries. On the other hand, according to a more enlightened way of thinking, the use and beauty of this natural provision do not constitute a reason for ignoring the universal and simple causal laws of matter, so that this arrangement can be regarded as something other than an incidental consequence of those same causal laws. The question whether the earth's spherical form does not in general produce benefits and have consequences which are even greater than those produced by the irregularities which cause its surface to deviate somewhat from a precisely spherical form – this is a question which is difficult to resolve. In spite of this, no philosopher has any reservations about regarding the earth's spherical form as the product of the most universal laws of statics, operative at the earliest period of the earth's history. Why should these unevennesses and prominences not also be the product of processes which are not artificially devised but purely natural? In the case of all large celestial bodies, it seems that the gradual transition from the liquid to the solid state is necessarily connected with the production of extensive cavities.[86] Such cavities necessarily form beneath its already solidified crust, when the lightest materials of the still molten mass within it, including air, slowly separate out and rise towards the surface. It further seems that, since the extensiveness of these cavities must be related to the size of the celestial body concerned, the collapse of these solid vaulted cavities will be correspondingly extensive.

2:128

Nor need we be taken aback or surprised by even a kind of regularity, or at least a series of unevennesses, where such productive forces are operative. For it is known that when light kinds of matter rise towards the surface at one point in a large amalgam, it has an influence upon the same movement in the adjacent region of the mixture.[u] I am not going to linger over this type of explanation, for I have no wish to express any particular attachment here to this kind of explanation. My only intention is to offer a brief explanation of the method of judging, which employs this type of argument.

The entire surface of the earth, not covered by water, is threaded in the most beneficial fashion by the courses of rivers as by furrows.[87] However, there are also so many inequalities, so many valleys and plains covering the surface of the earth that, at first sight, it looks as if the courses, in which the waters of the rivers flow, must of necessity have been especially constructed and ordered to that end.[88] Otherwise, it is argued, the waters flowing from the heights would, of necessity, have strayed far and wide in all directions, following the irregularities of the land, flooding many areas, converting valleys into lakes, and rendering the land wild and useless, rather than beautiful and well-ordered. Who can fail to notice the strong appearance of a necessary and extraordinary arrangement here? On the other hand, to assume that these things had been supernaturally instituted would be to put an end to all scientific research into the causal factors which bring rivers into existence. Not allowing myself to be misled by this kind of regularity, and not immediately assuming that the cause of such regularity must lie outside the sphere of the universal laws of mechanics, I shall, on the contrary, rely upon observation to teach me something about the way in which rivers are produced. If I adopt this procedure, I shall notice that the courses of many rivers are, even to this day, still in the process of formation, raising the height of their banks until they no longer flood the surrounding land as much as they once did. Observation convinces me that all the rivers of antiquity must really once have wandered over the sruface of the earth in the way we feared they would unless special provisions were made to prevent them from doing so. This leads me to suppose that no such extraordinary provision was ever made. The 2:129 river Amazon,[89] in one stretch of several hundred miles, shows clear signs that it once had no restricted river-bed, but that it must have flooded the land in all directions; for the land on both sides of the river is, to a great distance, as flat as the surface of a lake, and consists of river-sediment where pebbles are as rare as diamonds. Exactly the same is the case with the Mississippi.[90] And, in general, the Nile[91] and other rivers show that their channels have been greatly extended in length with the passage of time; rivers seem to have started constructing their channels and extend-

---

[u] *Denn man weiss, dass das Aufsteigen der leichten Arten in einem grossen Gemische an einem Orte einen Einfluss auf die nämliche Bewegung in dem benachbarten Theile des Gemenges habe.*

ing them from the point where they appear to have their estuaries, for near the sea, where they spread out over the flat surface of the land, rivers gradually build a channel and then flow on in an extended river-bed.[v] Experience having put me on the right scent, I think that I can now reduce the entire mechanics, governing the formation of the channels of rivers, to the following simple principles. Spring-waters and rain-waters, flowing from the heights, initially poured down in an irregular fashion, following the gradient of the ground, filling up many valleys and spreading out over many flat regions. Where the water flowed most quickly, it was not so well able, because of its speed, to deposit its sediment; instead, it deposited it far more plentifully on both sides. In this way the height of the river-banks was raised, the strongest current of water staying within its channel. With the passage of time, when the supply of water was itself diminished (something which was bound to happen for reasons which are familiar to geologists), the river no longer overflowed the banks which it had itself built up. Regularity and order emerged from wild chaos. Even today, the process can be clearly observed, particularly in river-estuaries, which are the most recently formed part of a river. The depositing of sediment must, according to this scheme, occur more frequently near those places where the river initially overflowed its new banks than further away. It will likewise be observed that where a river flows through flat country, its channel will, in many places, actually be higher than the surrounding plains.

There are certain universal laws regulating the processes of nature, which are capable of throwing some light on the relation between the laws of mechanics, on the one hand, and order and harmoniousness, on the other. One such law is: the forces of motion and resistance continue to operate on each other until they afford each other the least impediment.[92]

2:130 The reasons for this law are very easy to understand. But the relationship which the consequences of this law have to regularity and advantage is amazingly large and extensive. The epicycloid, an algebraic curve, is of the following character. To take the example of teeth and gearwheels: when they are curved epicycloidically, friction is reduced to a minimum. The celebrated Professor *Kästner*[93] somewhere mentions[94] that an experienced mining expert[95] showed him, from machines which had been in use a long while, that this epicycloidic form was indeed eventually produced by the friction arising from protracted motion. The epicycloidic curve, which is based upon a fairly complicated construction, is, with all its regularity, the effect of a common law of nature.

Let me adduce one of the effects caused by rivers as an instance of a simple[w] effect produced by nature which displays a tendency to regularity,

[v] *weil er sich zur See über den flachen Boden ausbreitete, bauet er allmählich seine Laufrinne aus und fliesst weiter in einem verlängerten Fluthbette.*
[w] *schlecht* / B: bad / C: *semplice* / F & Z: *nuissibles* / T: bad / (only C recognises that Kant is using *schlecht* in the now archaic sense of 'simple' or 'straightforward').

for it is subject to the above mentioned law. All the regions of dry-land vary greatly in gradient; it is thus to be expected that the rivers which flow over these sloping surfaces should now and again flow over precipices and cataracts.[96] And indeed precipices and cataracts really do occur, albeit only rarely. They display great irregularity and involve considerable inconvenience. But it can easily be seen that, although (as may be surmised) such waterfalls must have been frequent occurrences in the initial state of chaos, the violence with which the water plunged downwards will have eaten into and washed away the loose earth, even eroding certain types of rock which were not hard enough to resist the force of the waters. This process would have continued until the river had reduced its channel to a fairly uniform gradient. And this is why, where waterfalls are still to be found, the terrain is rocky and why the river, in very many stretches of its course, flows between sheer cliffs, into which it has probably cut its own deep channel. The fact that almost all rivers, for the greatest part of their courses, do not exceed a certain moderate velocity, and are thereby rendered navigable, has been found very useful to man. Now, to start with, the navigability of rivers was scarcely something which could have been expected to have arisen of its own accord from the extreme unevenness of the ground over which they flowed, without the intervention of art. Nonetheless, it can easily be seen that, with the passage of time, rivers would, of their own accord, reach a velocity which they could not easily exceed. Such a state would have been attained no matter how steeply the ground may have initially sloped. All that would have been important was that it was capable of erosion. For rivers will continue to wash away the ground, eating their way into the surface, lowering their courses in some places 2:131 and raising their channels in others, until what they tear away when they are swollen is more or less equal to what they deposit when they are more sluggish. Force continues to be operative until greater moderation has been attained and equilibrium established as a result of the reciprocal effects of action and reaction on each other.

Nature offers countless examples of a single thing being extremely useful in a wide variety of employments. It is a great mistake to suppose, without further ado, that these advantages are purposive or the sort of effect which involves motives, for the sake of which the divine choice ordered their causes in the world. One advantage among others, of which the moon is the cause, is this: ebb and flow set ships in motion both against and in the absence of wind by means of currents flowing throught straits and near to the mainland. Longitude at sea can be calculated by means of the moon and the satellites of Jupiter. The things produced in all the realms of nature have, each of them, great usefulness, and some of them we employ. It would be absurd to suppose, as is commonly the case, that all these benefits are motives for the divine choice. It would be ridiculous to appeal to the wisdom of the Author for having provided us with the means to calculate longitude, because of the use to which we can put the moons of Jupiter. One should take care not to incur the legitimate mockery of a Voltaire who, in a similar tone, asks: 'Why do we have noses?' and then replies: 'No doubt so that we can wear spectacles'.[97] The appeal to the divine power of choice does not adequately explain why a given means, necessary to the achievement of a single end, is advantageous in so many other respects as well. There is an admirable community to be found among the essences of all created things. This community is such that the natures of things are not alien to each other but are united in a complex harmony. They spontaneously agree with each other. Their essences contain within themselves an agreement which is extensive and necessary, and which aims at the perfection of the whole.[x] It is this which is the foundation of such a variety of benefits. If we adopt our revised method of physico-theology, these benefits can, indeed, be regarded as proofs of the existence of a supremely Wise Author. But these benefits cannot, in all cases, be regarded as provisions which have been instituted by a special wisdom, and instituted in such a way that they constitute a unity with the other provisions, made for the sake of special ancillary advantages. Without doubt, the reasons why Jupiter should have moons are complete, and they would have been complete even if the moons of Jupiter had never, as a result of the invention of the telescope, been employed for calculating longitude. Although these uses are to be construed as ancillary consequences, they are, notwithstanding, relevant to establishing the infinite greatness of the Author of all things. For they, along with millions of other things of like kind, are proofs of the great chain which links together, in the very possibilities of things, parts of the creation which seem to have no connection with each other. For the uses which emerge from the result of a freely instituted arrangement, which are known to the Author, and which are included in his decision, cannot always, on that account, be included among the motives for such a choice. They cannot be included, namely, if the motives of the choice are already, independently of the ancillary consequences, complete.[y] Certainly, water does not by nature adopt a horizontal position to enable us to see our own reflections in it. If one is to argue in a rational fashion, and if one adopts the restricted physico-theological method which we are employing here, the uses of the kind which we have observed cannot be put to the purpose envisaged. Only if that method is supplemented in the way we have specified can observations of the kind collected be effectively employed as the foundation of the important conclusion that all things are universally subject to a supremely

2:132

---

[x] *sich zu einander von selbst schicken und eine ausgebreitete nothwendige Vereinbarung zur gesammten Vollkommenheit in ihren Wesen enthalten.*
[y] *denn sonst kann man auch nicht allemal die Nutzen, die der Erfolg einer freiwilligen Anstalt nach sich zieht und die der Urheber kennt und in seinem Rathschlusse mit befasst, um deswillen zu den Bewegungsgründen solcher Wahl zählen, wenn diese nämlich auch unangesehen solcher Nebenfolgen schon vollständig wären.*

Wise Being. Extend your gaze as far as you can over the limitless uses which a created thing may, at least potentially, offer in a thousand different ways. (The palm-tree alone confers innumerable benefits on the Indians.) And then connect the most remote members of the creation with each other in relations such as these. And when you have suitably admired the products of the provisions which have been directly instituted by art, do not allow even the delightful spectacle of the fruitful relation which holds between the possibilities of created things and thoroughgoing harmony, nor the delightful spectacle of the natural[z] sequence of beauty, which is so manifold and presents itself spontaneously to our admiration – do not allow these delightful spectacles to distract you from admiring and worshipping that power, in the eternal and ultimate fountain-head of which the essences of things lie ready prepared, as it were, for use in an excellent plan.

I would remark in passing that the great reciprocal relationship which is to be found among the things in the world does not deserve to be surveyed quite so cursorily, in the light of the frequency with which those same things occasion similarities, analogies, parallels, or however else one chooses to designate them. Without pausing to consider its employment in the play of wit[a] – an employment which is often only imaginary – there is, nonetheless, it seems to me, an important topic for philosophical reflection to be found here. The question is this: how is it possible that an agreement, which is rooted in a certain common ground of uniformity and which holds between very different things, should be so great, so extensive, and yet also so precise? These analogies also constitute a very crucial means to the acquisition of cognition. Mathematics itself offers instances of such analogies. I shall, however, forbear from adducing any examples, for it is to be feared that, because of the various ways in which such similarities may be experienced, they may strike the understanding of different people in different ways. In any case, the idea which I have casually mentioned here is incomplete and not fully intelligible as it stands.

2:133

If one were to ask about the use which could be made of the great unity which prevails among the many different relations of space and which are investigated by geometry, I suspect that the universal concepts of the unity of mathematical objects might also reveal the grounds of the unity and perfection of nature. For example, of all figures, the circle is the one in which the circumference encloses the greatest possible area which can be enclosed by a line of that length. The reason, namely, is that the distance between the centre and the circumference is strictly constant throughout the figure. If a figure is to be bounded by straight lines, then the greatest possible equality in respect of the distance between the sides and the centre of the figure can only occur if the following conditions are satisfied: not only must the distances between the angles and the centre of the

---

[z] *ungekünstelt.*   [a] *Spiele des Witzes.*

173

figure be exactly equal to each other, but the perpendicular lines extended from the centre to the sides must also be exactly equal to each other. If these conditions are satisfied, a regular polygon is the product. Geometry shows that another polygon[b] with the same number of sides and the boundary of which was of the same length as its regular counterpart would always enclose a smaller space than that regular counterpart.[c] Another and, indeed, the simplest kind of equality of distance from the centre is possible: namely, when it is only the distance of the angles of the polygon from the common centre which is equal throughout. Here it appears that any irregular polygon which can be enclosed within a circle embraces the greatest space which can be encompassed by those same sides.[d98] In addition to this, consider, finally, the polygon in which the length of the sides is equal to the distance of the points of the angles from the centre, in other words, the regular hexagon. Of all figures whatever, this is the only figure which

2:134 bounds the greatest space with the shortest boundary so that if it is externally juxtaposed with other figures which are the same as itself no interstices will be left. The following observation immediately suggests itself: the reciprocal relationship between the greatest and the smallest in space depends upon equality. And since nature offers many other cases of such a necessary equality, it follows that the rules derived from the aforementioned geometrical cases relating to the universal grounds of such a reciprocal relation between the greatest and smallest, may also be applied to the necessary observance of the law of parsimony in nature.[e99] In the laws of impact, a certain equality is always necessary, for the following truths hold: in the case of rigid bodies, the velocity of the two bodies after impact is always equal; in the case of elastic bodies, they are always propelled away from each other with equal force by their elasticity, the force with which they rebound from each other being that with which the impact occurred; the centre of gravity of both rigid and elastic bodies, whether they be at rest or in motion, is in no way affected by the impact; and so on, and so forth. The variety of spatial relations is so infinite and yet it yields a cognition which is so certain and an intuition which is so clear that, just as these relations have often served admirably as symbols of cognitions of quite a different kind (for example, in the expression of probabilities), these same spatial relations can also enable us to recognise, from the simplest and most universal principles, the rules of perfection present in naturally necessary causal laws, in so far as they depend upon relations.

Before I conclude this section, I should like to enumerate all the differ-

---

[b] *ein anderes Polygon.*

[c] *und es zeigt sich durch die Geometrie, dass mit eben demselben Umkreise ein anderes Polygon von eben der Zahl Seiten jederzeit einen kleinern Raum einschliessen wurde als das reguläre.*

[d] *und da zeigt sich, dass ein jedes irreguläre Polygon welches im Cirkel stehen kann, den grössten Raum einschliesst unter allen der von eben denselben Seiten nur immer kann beschlossen werden.*

[e] *des Gesetzes der Sparsamkeit.*

ent degrees of the philosophical mode of explanation of the appearances of perfection, which occur in the world, in so far as these appearances are all regarded as being subsumed under God. I shall do so by beginning with that mode of judging where the philosophy is still concealed, and ending with that in which the philosophical effort is the greatest. I am speaking of order, beauty and appropriateness, in so far as they constitute the ground for subsuming things in the world under a Divine Author in a fashion which is appropriate to philosophy.

Firstly: An individual event in the course of nature can be regarded as something issuing immediately from a divine action. In such a case as this, the only business of philosophy is that of presenting an argument in favour of this extraordinary dependency.

Secondly: An event occurring in the world may be regarded as an individual case, the mechanism of the world having been, from the start, so 2:135 organised at creation as specifically to bring about this event. An example of such an event would be the flood, as it is construed in the systems of various modern philosophers.[100] The event, however, is not the less supernatural for having been produced by mechanical laws. Natural science is employed by the philosophers we have just mentioned. But it merely furnishes them with an opportunity to display their own dexterity, and provides them with a means for imagining a process, which could occur in accordance with the universal laws of nature, and issue in the extraordinary event envisaged beforehand. Normally, such a procedure is incompatible with the divine wisdom, which never sets out to make a parade of itself with superfluous art. Such a procedure would be criticised even in a human being. An example of such superfluous art would be the case of someone who, perfectly able to fire off a cannon directly, attached a clockwork mechanism to the firing-device so that the cannon would be discharged at a given time by means of this ingenious mechanical arrangement.

Thirdly: Certain features of nature are regarded as provisions which have existed since the creation, and which have issued immediately from the hand of the Great Architect.*ᶠ* More specifically, these features are regarded as individual provisions; they are not regarded as arrangements which have been introduced in accordance with constant law. An example of this view would be the claim that God had at the very beginning of things directly ordered the mountains,[101] the rivers, the planets and their motions.[102] In so far as it is certain that there must have been some state of nature which was the first state, where both the form and the matter of things were immediately dependent on God – to that extent there is a philosophical basis to this mode of judging. However, this method is philosophical to only a very slight degree: it is the mark of excessive haste to ascribe an arrangement immediately to the act of creation just because

ᶠ Werkmeister.

175

it is advantageous and orderly, and to do so without first examining the suitability which belongs to things in accordance with universal laws.

Fourthly: Something is attributed to an artificially devised order of nature before it has been properly established that nature is incapable of producing that phenomenon in accordance with her universal laws. For example, when something which could perhaps be accounted for in terms of ordinary mechanical forces, is explained in terms of the plant- and animal-kingdoms, simply because order and beauty are prominent there.ᵍ The philosophical character of the mode of thought which maintains that each individual animal or plant is immediately subsumed under a special act of creation is then even less than that of the view which maintains that, with the exception of a few directly created organisms, all other creatures are subsumed under them in accordance with a law which governs the ability to generate (not merely one which governs the capacity to un-

2:136   fold).ʰ¹⁰³ This latter type of theory is more philosophical because it explains a greater number of phenomena in terms of the order of nature. Its philosophical superiority could only be challenged if it could be clearly demonstrated that the order of nature was incapable of explaining the phenomenon under examination. All explanations of provisions in the world, not just those relating to the animal- and plant-kingdoms, which are presented in terms of laws which have been artificially instituted with a view to realising some specific objective – all such explanations belong to this degree of the philosophical mode of explanation.* An example of this type of explanation would be the supposition that the order of nature, which produces the phenomena of snow and the *aurora borealis,* had been introduced specifically in order to benefit the Greenlanders and the Lapps (so that they need not spend the long winter nights in darkness) – a supposition made in spite of the fact that these phenomena are probably convenient ancillary consequences arising with necessary unity from other laws. One is almost always in danger of falling into error when one alleges that certain forms of usefulness to man are the reason for some special

---

* In the second number of the third reflection of this section, I have only adduced cases from the plant- and animal-kingdoms as examples of an artificially devised order of nature. It is, however, to be remarked that any law which is instituted for the sake of some special use is artificially devised, for it is then no longer connected with the other laws of nature with necessary unity. This is evident from a number of the examples mentioned here.

ᵍ *z.B. wenn man etwas aus der Ordnung des Pflanzen- und Thierreichs erklärt, was vielleicht in gemeinen mechanischen Kräften liegt, bloss deswegen weil Ordnung und Schönheit darin gross sind /* (the crucial phrase is *aus der Ordnung;* it means not 'belonging to the order' but 'in terms of or by reference to the order').

ʰ *Das Philosophische dieser Art zu urtheilen ist alsdann noch geringer, wenn ein jedes einzelne Thier oder Pflanze unmittelbar der Schöpfung untergeordnet wird, als wenn ausser einigem unmittelbar Erschaffenen die andere Producte demselben* (i.e., *einigem unmittelbar Erschaffenen) nach einem Gesetze der Zeugungsfähigkeit (nicht bloss des Auswickelungsvermögens) untergeordnet werden.*

divine arrangement. Take, for example, the supposition that the forests and fields are for the most part green in hue because green is the one colour which has an intermediate intensity and which thus does not strain the eye. The objection may be raised that the inhabitants of the Davis Straits get almost blinded by the snow and have to resort to the use of snow-spectacles. What is objectionable is not that useful consequences are sought out and attributed to a Benevolent Author. What is objectionable is rather the fact that the order of nature which produces these useful consequences is construed as being artificially and deliberately*i* connected with other orders of nature,*j* whereas, in fact, it may perhaps be necessarily connected with them.

Fifthly: The spirit of true philosophy is most powerfully manifest in the following method of judging the perfect provisions of nature. This method is at all times ready to admit the occurrence of even supernatural events. It is likewise always ready to recognise the existence of any genuinely artificially devised order of nature. Above all, it allows neither nature's aiming at interest, nor all its harmoniousness, to hinder it from trying to discover their foundations in necessary and universal laws. And in the attempt to discover these grounds, it always pays careful attention to the preservation of unity, displaying a rational aversion to multiplying the number of natural causes in order to explain the benefits and harmony of nature. If, in addition to this, the physico-theological mode of judging also concentrates its attention on the universal rules which are capable of explaining the ground of the necessary connection, which holds between, on the one hand, that which occurs naturally without special provision, and, on the other hand, the rules relating to the advantage and convenience of rational beings, and if one then proceeds to ascend to the Divine Author – if all these conditions are satisfied, then this mode of judging will fulfil its obligations in a fitting fashion.*

2:137

SEVENTH REFLECTION: COSMOGONY[105]

A mechanical hypothesis to explain the origin of the celestial bodies and the causes of their movements, in accordance with the rules established above

The form of the celestial bodies, the mechanics in accordance with which they move and constitute the system of the universe,*k* and likewise the

---

* All that I am saying here is that this must be the path followed by human reason. For who will ever be able to save it from falling into frequent error in matters such as these? As Pope puts it:

> Go teach eternal Wisdom how to rule–
> Then drop into thyself, and be a fool![104]

i *künstlich und willkürlich.*   *j* *mit andern (sc. Ordnungen) verbunden.*   *k* *Weltsystem.*

177

numerous changes to which the positions of their orbits are subject with the passage of time – all this now forms a part of natural science and is understood with great distinctness and certainty. So great, indeed, is this distinctness and certainty that there is no other view of the matter which can be adduced to explain any natural object (which even approximates to the complexity of the present object) in such an undubitably correct fashion and with such self-evidence. If one bears this in mind, must not the idea also occur to one that the state of nature, in which this structure*l* took its rise and in which there was first impressed on that structure the movements which now continue to occur in accordance with such simple and intelligible laws – that this state of nature will be easier to understand and grasp than perhaps the majority of the things of which we also seek the origin in nature. The reasons which favour this supposition are obvious. As far as we know, all these celestial objects are spherical masses, which are neither organic in structure*m106* nor mysteriously magical in

2:138   origin. The force which moves these bodies is, in all probability, a fundamental force, which is a property of matter itself. As such, it may not and, indeed, it cannot be explained. The projectile motion*n* with which they pursue their flight, the direction of the momentum*o* imparted to them are, along with the formation of their respective masses, the chief, indeed, almost the only phenomena, for which the first natural causes are to be sought. These phenomena are all of them simple effects. They are not nearly so complex as the majority of the other phenomena of nature, in the case of which the laws governing them are not normally known with mathematical accuracy. The phenomena with which we are concerned here, in contrast, lie plainly before our eyes in a highly comprehensible scheme of things. Our enquiry, holding out such promise of success, is faced with but one impediment – the impression made upon our minds by the stirring grandeur of a natural phenomenon such as the solar system. In such a system, the natural causes are all the subject of suspicion: they seem to be too flimsy to attain their purpose, and they seem not to be compatible with the creative rights of the Supreme Author. But could not the same objection also be raised against the laws of mechanics, which enable the great system of the universe, once it has come into existence, to maintain its movements in existence? Their continuation depends upon precisely the same law which prescribes the trajectory of a stone thrown into the air. This simple law, the fruitful source of the most regular

---

l *Bau.*

m *ohne Organisation* / (the German word *Organisation* is related to the notion of a living organism, and that in a much more intimate fashion than the English word 'organisation' [See Grimm, *Organisation*]).

n *Wurfsbewegung* / B: projectile motion / C: *moto di proiezione* / F: *mouvement de progression* / T: motion / Z: *mouvement d'impulsion.*

o *Schwung.*

effects, is worthy of being entrusted with the maintenance of the entire system of the universe.

On the other hand, it will be said, one is incapable of rendering distinct the natural causes which bring the humblest plant into existence in accordance with completely comprehensible mechanical laws, and yet one dares to explain the origin of the entire system of the universe. But has any philosopher ever been able to render even the laws, which govern the growth and inner motion of an already existent plant, as clear and mathematically certain as those which regulate the motions of the celestial bodies? The nature of the objects in the two cases are completely different. In the present instance, the great and the astonishing are infinitely more accessible to the understanding than the tiny and the marvellous. The generation of a planet, together with the cause of the momentum[p] with which it is projected so as to run in a circular orbit, can, it seems, be more easily and more clearly understood than the generation of a single snow-flake. The precise proportions of a six-pointed star-shaped snow-crystal are, to all appearances, more exact then the curvature of the planetary orbits; and the axes of the snow-crystal relate to their common plane more precisely than the orbits of the celestial bodies relate to the common plane of their orbital motions.[q]

2:139

I am going to present an attempt to explain the origin of the system of the universe in terms of the general laws of mechanics. The explanation relates, not to the entire order of nature, but only to the great masses of matter and their orbits, which constitute the most primitive foundation of nature. In spite of the crudity and incompleteness of my sketch, I hope to say something which may stimulate others to make important observations of their own. Some of what I say has, in my opinion, a degree of probability which, in the case of a smaller object, would leave little room for doubt. The only possible objection which might be raised is the prejudice that the origin of the universe requires for its explanation more art than that ascribable to the universal laws of nature. It often happens that, although one does not find what one is really looking for, one stumbles in the course of one's search on other unexpected advantages. Even an unexpected advantage of this kind, if it presented itself to the reflection of someone else, would be profit enough. And even if in the process the chief purpose of the hypothesis were demolished, the benefit gained would still be profit enough. In this undertaking, I shall presuppose the universal gravitation of matter as formulated by *Newton* and his followers. If there are any who think that, by employing a definition drawn from

---

[p] *Wurfsbewegung* / B: projectile motion / C: *moto di proiezione* / F & Z: *force de projection* / T: impulse.
[q] *Kreisbewegungen.*

179

metaphysics[r] and formulated according to their own taste, they can demolish the conclusions established by men of perspicacity on the basis of
empirical observation and by means of mathematical inference – if there
are such persons, they may ignore what follows as something which has
only a remote bearing on the main purpose of this book.

1. An expanded view of the totality[s] of the universe

The six planets, together with their satellites, move in orbits which do not
markedly deviate from a common plane of reference,[t] namely, that constituted by the extended equatorial plane of the sun. The comets, on the other
hand, pursue courses which deviate very greatly from it, straying in all
directions, far from this plane of reference.[107] Now, if instead of this tiny
handful of planets and comets, there were several thousand of them belonging to the solar system, the zodiac would appear as a zone illuminated by
numberless stars, or as a band fading away into a pale glimmer. Some of the
nearer planets in the band would shine fairly brightly, whereas the more
remote planets, because of their number and faintness, would only present
a misty appearance. For with the orbital motion,[u] with which all these
planets circulated around the sun, every part of the zodiac would always be
occupied by some of them, even though others would have changed their
position. On the other hand, the comets would occupy the regions on both
sides of this bright zone in every possible dispersion.[v] Now, with our minds
prepared by this fiction (in which we have simply imagined an increase in
the number of bodies in our planetary system), let us cast our eyes on the
wider expanse of the universe. If we do so, we shall actually see a bright
zone in which the stars, though apparently at varying distances from us, are
nonetheless concentrated more densely in one particular plane than elsewhere,[w] while the celestial regions on both sides of this plane are occupied
with stars in every kind of dispersion. The Milky Way, for it is this to which I
am here referring, has precisely the orientation of a huge circle.[x][108] This
characterisation[y] is worthy of every attention: it enables us to understand
that the sun, along with our own planet, is to be found in that multitude of
stars which is most densely concentrated in a certain common plane of
reference. This analogy provides us with a strong reason for the following
suppositions: these suns, of which our own is one, constitute a universe
which is ordered on the large scale in accordance with exactly the same laws
as those in accordance with which our own solar system is ordered on the

2:140

---

[r] *eine Definition der Metaphysik* / (the German is ambiguous for it is not clear whether Kant
means a definition which is furnished by metaphysics or a definition of the notion of
metaphysics itself; the present translator inclines to the former reading).
[s] *Inbegriff.* [t] *Beziehungsplan.* [u] *Kreisbewegung.* [v] *Zerstreuung.*
[w] *dichter wie anderwärts gehäuft sind.* [x] *die Richtung eines grössten Zirkels.*
[y] *Bestimmung* / (alt: determination, characteristic).

180

small scale.[109] All these suns, together with their satellites, will share a focal point common to their orbits. The only reason why they seem not to change their position is their immeasurable distance from the earth and the slowness of their orbital motions, though a certain displacement of position[z] has actually been observed in the case of some of them. The orbits of these great celestial bodies are likewise related to a common plane, from which they do not significantly deviate, in exactly the same way as the planets of our solar system are related to a common plane. Those bodies which occupy the remaining celestial regions with much less frequency are analogous to the comets of our own planetary system.[110]

This hypothesis[a] has, in my opinion, an extremely high degree of probability. It suggests that if, in addition to the order to which our own sun belongs, and which presents to an observer located within that order the appearance of a Milky Way, there are other such higher cosmic orders,[b] then some of them will be visible as pale glimmering patches[c] in the depths of space. It can further be supposed that if the plane of reference[d] of another constellation of fixed stars should be positioned obliquely in relation to ourselves, then it would present the appearance of an elliptical figure representing, in an area which will appear small because of the vast distances involved, a system of suns similar to our Milky Way.[111] And, indeed, astronomers have long ago already actually discovered such little patches,[e] although opinions about them vary considerably, as is evident from the book by *Maupertuis* on the constellation of the stars.[112]

2:141

I hope that this reflection will be considered with some attention, and that for two reasons. Firstly: the concept of creation suggested by my hypothesis is, to an astonishing degree, a great deal more moving than the usual concept. (A numberless multitude of suns like our own make up a system, of which the members are connected by orbital motions; these systems, of which there are probably countlessly many, though we can only perceive a few of them, may themselves, in their turn, be members of a yet higher order.) Secondly: guided by an hypothesis such as the one we have proposed, even the observation of the fixed stars (or rather the slowly moving suns) near the earth can reveal a great deal which would otherwise escape notice, for lack of some plan of enquiry.[f]

2. Reasons favouring a mechanical origin of the solar system in general

All the planets without exception revolve around the sun in the same direction, deviating only slightly from the common plane of reference,

---

[z] *einige Verrückung ihrer Stellen.*　[a] *diesem Begriffe.*　[b] *mehr solche höhere Weltordnungen.*
[c] *blasse, schimmernde Plätze.*　[d] *Beziehungsplan.*　[e] *Plätzchen.*
[f] *in so fern nicht ein gewisser Plan zu untersuchen ist.*

which is the ecliptic. Their motion around the sun is just like that which solid bodies would have if they were swept along by some material substance which, occupying all the available space, executed its motion by rotating vortically on its axis.[113] The planets are all of them attracted towards the sun, and the magnitude of their centrifugal force[g] must have a high degree of accuracy, if they are to run in circular orbits.[h] But geometrical precision is not to be expected in mechanical phenomena of this kind, and it is indeed the case that all the orbits deviate, albeit only slightly, from the curvature of a circle.[i] The planets consist of materials which are, according to Newton's reckoning, the less dense the further they are from the sun. And this is exactly what one would expect if the planets had been formed from a cosmic matter[j] dispersed throughout the space in which they are now suspended.[114] For with the tendency with which everything sinks towards the sun, the materials of a denser kind must press more strongly towards the sun and be found more frequently in its proximity than materials of a lighter kind, their descent being slower on account of their lower density. However, according to the observation of *Buffon*, the matter of which the sun is composed has approximately the same density as that which the total mass of all the planets added together would have.[115] This, too, is consonant with a mechanical account of their formation, according to which the planets may have been formed at varying distances from the sun from different types of element. All the other elements, mingled together and occupying this space, may have plunged to their common focus, the sun.

2:142

If, regardless of this explanation, someone should allege that such a structure has been formed directly by the hand of God, and be unwilling to entrust anything to the law of mechanics, he will have to offer some sort of explanation as to why he finds such an account necessary here, when he would not normally be willing to admit such an account in natural sciences. He can name no purpose to explain why it should be better for the planets to move in one direction rather than in a number of different directions, nor why they should revolve around the sun in orbits approximating to a single common plane of reference rather than orbiting in all the regions of space.[116] The celestial spaces are now empty, and the planets would not, in spite of all these movements, present any impediments to each other. I readily admit that there may be concealed purposes which could not be attained by ordinary mechanical means and which no one can understand. But, be that as it may, no one is entitled to assume that such purposes exist if he wishes to base his opinion on them, unless he is able to specify what those purposes may be. Finally, if God had immediately imparted motion[k] to the planets and established their orbits, one would not expect to find the character of imperfection and deviation

---

[g] *Seitenschwung.*   [h] *Cirkelkreisen.*   [i] *Cirkelrundung.*   [j] *Weltstoff.*   [k] *Wurfskraft.*

which is to be met with in all the products of nature. If it had been a good thing for them to relate to a single plane, then one would expect that God would have fixed their orbits in that precise plane. If it had been a good thing for their orbits to approximate to circular motion, one would expect that their orbits would have been exactly circular. It is not clear why there should have been any exceptions to the strictest precision,[l] particularly in the case of things which are supposed to be the immediate product of God's own activity as an artist.[m]

Those members of the solar system which are located at the greatest distance from the sun, the comets, have very eccentric courses. If their courses were an immediate product of God's activity, they might just as well have moved in circular orbits, even though their courses deviate so much from the ecliptic. Much boldness will be deployed in thinking up 2:143 uses for such eccentric orbits. For it is easier to understand that a celestial body, no matter what region of the heavens it may occupy, should orbit around its gravitational centre at a constant distance and be ordered in accordance with this distance, than that it should, equally advantageously, be ordered to run in a very eccentric orbit.[n] As for the benefits adduced by Newton, it is obvious that they are in the highest degree improbable, unless one assumes that things have been directly arranged by God, so that the advantages alleged may serve at least as some pretence of a purpose.

The error involved in ascribing the structure of the planetary system directly to divine intentions is most clearly apparent in the invention of motives to account for the fact that the density of the planets and their distance from the sun stand in inverse proportion to each other. The effect of the sun, it is argued, decreases as its distance increases; it was proper that the density of the bodies to be heated by the sun should be adjusted proportionately. Now, it is known that the sun penetrates only a small depth beneath the surface of a celestial body. It is not, therefore, possible to infer the density of the whole mass from the sun's power to heat it. The conclusion drawn is out of all proportion to the purpose to be attained. The means employed, namely, the reduced density of the whole mass, involves a provision which is so extensive as to be, relative to the magnitude of the purpose to be attained, excessive and unnecessary.

Everything which is produced by nature, in so far as it tends towards harmoniousness, order and usefulness, agrees, it is true, with God's purposes. But it also displays the characteristic of having originated from universal laws. The effects of such universal laws extend far beyond any such individual case. Accordingly, each particular effect shows signs of an

---

[l] *von der genauesten Richtigkeit.*   [m] *eine unmittelbare göttliche Kunsthandlung.*

[n] *denn es ist eher begreiflich, dass ein Weltkörper, in einer Himmelsregion, welche es auch sei, in gleichem Abstande immer bewegt, die dieser Weite gemässe Einrichtung habe, als dass er auf die grosse Verschiedenheit der Weiten gleich vortheilhaft eingerichtet sei.*

intermingling of laws, which were not aimed exclusively at producing the individual effect alone. This is why deviations from the greatest possible exactitude in respect of a particular purpose also occur. By contrast, an immediate supernatural provision, since its execution does not at all presuppose the consequences which arise from the universal causal laws of matter, will not be marred by the interference of particular ancillary consequences arising from those laws. Such a provision will rather realise the plan with the greatest possible precision. It is in those parts of the planetary system which are closer to the common centre where a greater approximation to perfect order and strict precision are to be found. But out towards the limits of the system, and far from the plane of reference, this order and precision declines into irregularity and deviations. And this is exactly what one would expect of a constitution which was mechanical in origin. In an arrangement which is the product of an immediate divine intervention one can never encounter purposes which are only imperfectly realised: the greatest precision and accuracy will everywhere be present.[117] Such is the case, for example, in the structure of animals.

2:144

3. Brief outline of the most probable way in which a planetary system may have been mechanically formed

The arguments which have just been adduced in favour of a mechanical account of the origin of the solar system are very weighty – so weighty, indeed, that just one or two arguments on their own have long since sufficed to induce natural scientists to seek the cause of the planetary orbits among the forces of nature. They are induced to do so chiefly because the planets orbit around the sun in the same direction in which the sun itself revolves upon its axis, and because their orbits coincide so closely with the equatorial plane of the sun. *Newton* was the great destroyer of all these vortices,[118] although people continued to be attached to them, long after he had demonstrated their superfluity. The celebrated *Mairan* was a case in point.[119] The reliable and convincing proofs of the Newtonian philosophy clearly showed that there was no trace of anything in the heavens corresponding to what the vortices, which allegedly carried the planets around on their courses, were supposed to be. *Newton* demonstrated that the absence of such a current of fluidity in these spaces was so complete that even the tails of the comets continued on their way undisturbed right across all these orbits. From this it could certainly be concluded that, since the celestial spaces were now shown to be absolutely empty, or at any rate infinitely rarified, there could be no mechanical cause to impart to the planets their orbital motions.[120] However, instantly to abandon all the laws of mechanics and set up the rash hypothesis that God had directly imparted motion to the planets so that, in virtue of their gravitational attraction, they continued to move in orbit – this was a step too large to be contained within the limits of philosophy. It is immediately obvious that there remains one situation in which mechanical causes could originate the constitutions of the solar system, and it is this: if the space which is at present occupied by the planetary system and which is now empty, had previously been filled, so as to produce a community of motive forces[o] throughout all the regions of the space now affected by the sun's gravitational attraction.[121]

2:145

I can now specify the one possible condition under which alone the heavenly motions can be mechanically caused. That there is only one such possible condition is a circumstance of some considerable weight for justifying an hypothesis, and it is not one of which one can often boast. Since space is now empty, it must once have been filled, for otherwise the orbiting motive forces could never have produced their extensive effect. Accordingly, this diffused matter must subsequently have gathered itself together to form the heavenly bodies. In other words, closer examination shows that the heavenly bodies will have formed themselves from the elementary matter which was once diffused throughout the space now occupied by the solar system. The motion possessed by the particles of matter when they were dispersed, continued to be possessed by them after they had been united together to constitute distinct masses of matter.[p] Since then this space has been empty; it contains no matter which could serve to impart orbital motion to these bodies. But it has not always been empty. We perceive motions for which there cannot now be any extant natural cause; they are relics of the raw state of nature which dates from the earliest period of its history.[q][122]

I should like to take just one more step beyond this remark, with a view to drawing closer to a probable conception both of the way in which these great masses came into being and of the causes of their movements. I shall leave it to the enquiring reader himself to fill in the details of this rough outline. If the matter of which the sun and all the other heavenly bodies are constituted and which is subject to their mighty gravitational attraction were diffused throughout the whole of the space which is now occupied by the planetary system, and if there were some matter which exercised a more powerful gravitational attraction somewhere in the region of the place now occupied by the mass of the sun, then there would occur a universal falling of particles towards that spot, the gravitational attraction of the solar body increasing as its mass increased. It may easily be supposed that in the universal fall of particles, including those from even the remotest regions of the universe, the denser materials will have accumulated in the deeper regions, where everything was pressing forwards to the common centre, and they will have accumulated there with a frequency

---

[o] *eine Gemeinschaft der Bewegkräfte.*   [p] *abgesonderte Massen.*
[q] *die aber Überbleibsel des allerältersten rohen Zustandes der Natur sind.*

proportionate to their proximity to that centre, although materials of every kind of density were to be found in all the regions of space. For it would only be the heaviest particles which would have the greatest capacity to penetrate the mixture of lighter particles in this chaos, so as to get nearer

2:146 to the centre of gravity.[r] In the motions resulting from the fall of particles from differing altitudes within the sphere, the resistance offered by the colliding particles to each other can never be in exact equilibrium. As a consequence, the velocities which the colliding particles have acquired will be converted into lateral motions in one direction or another. This circumstance shows a very common rule at work relating to the effects which materials exercise on each other: they impel each other, change each other's direction, and restrict each other until they afford each other the least resistance.[123] As a result of this rule, the lateral motion of the particles must eventually unite to form a common rotation in one and the same direction. And so the particles of which the sun is constituted reached it already invested with this lateral motion; and the sun, formed from this material, must have rotated in exactly the same direction.[124]

It is, however, clear from the laws of gravitation that all the parts of this great rotating mass of cosmic matter[s] must have a tendency to traverse[t] the plane which passes through the centre of the sun in the direction of their common rotation, and which, according to our reasoning, coincides with the equatorial plane of this celestial body, unless, that is, they are already located on the plane. Thus, all these particles will be concentrated most densely and chiefly in the neighbourhood of the sun, in the region close to its elongated equatorial plane. Finally, it is also very natural that, since the particles of matter[u] must either impede or accelerate each other, in a word, must either collide with each other or drive each other on, and must continue to do so until one of them is no longer able to modify the movement of the other, it follows that in the end everything eventually ends up in a state where the only particles[v] which remain freely suspended are those which have exactly the degree of lateral swing[w] which is needed, at that distance from the sun, to balance the gravitational attraction[x] of the sun, so that all these particles rotate freely in concentric circles. This velocity is an effect of the fall; the lateral motion[y] is an effect of the colliding of the particles, and this situation continues until the resistance offered by everything in the system has been reduced to a minimum. The remaining particles,[z] which were unable to attain such exact precision, must, as their speed slowly diminished, have sunk to the focus of the general gravitational field,[a] so as to increase the mass of the sun. The

[r] *Gravitationspunkte* / B: point of gravitation / C: *centro di gravitazione* / F: *noyau central* / T: centre of gravity / Z: *point de gravitation.*
[s] *in diesem herumgeschwungenen Weltstoffe alle Theile.*   [t] *durchschneiden.*   [u] *Partikeln.*
[v] *Theilchen.*   [w] *Seitenschwung.*   [x] *Gravitation.*   [y] *die Bewegung zur Seiten.*
[z] *Theilchen.*   [a] *Mittelpunkt der allgemeinen Gravitation.*

density of this latter body will, accordingly, be more or less equal to the average density of the materials found in the space around it. However, the mass of the sun will, if the above circumstances hold, as a matter of 2:147 necessity, far exceed that of the matter which has remained suspended in the space around it.[125]

This state of affairs seems to me to be natural. Matter is diffused throughout the system. This matter is destined to form the different heavenly bodies in the narrow region immediately contiguous to the elongated plane of the solar equator; the specific gravity of this matter increases proportionately to its proximity to the centre of the system; and its momentum[b] is at all places sufficient, at this distance, to sustain an unimpeded orbital motion around the sun, sometimes at great distances from it, in accordance with the laws of gravitation.[c] In a situation such as this, if it is supposed that the planets are formed from these particles[d] of matter, then the planets cannot avoid having the centrifugal force[e] which causes them to move in almost circular orbits, though they will deviate slightly from perfect circularity since the planets themselves are constituted of particles of matter which have emanated from different altitudes. It is likewise very natural that those planets which are formed at great altitudes (where the space around them, being so much greater, causes the differences in velocity of the particles to exceed the force with which they are attracted to the centre of the planet) should have come to have even greater masses[f] than the planets in the neighbourhood of the sun.[126] I shall not mention the other ways in which my hypothesis harmonises with many other remarkable phenomena in the planetary system, for they are obvious.* Those bodies, the comets, which are formed in the most remote regions of the systems, especially when they are formed at a great distance from the plane of reference, will be incapable of this regularity. In this way, the region of space occupied by the planetary system will become empty, once everything has formed into discrete masses.[g] However, in later epochs, particles from the most extreme limits of this gravitational

---

* The above explanation applies to the formation of smaller systems which form constituent parts of the larger planetary system, as is for example the case with Jupiter and Saturn and their axial rotations, for there is an analogy between the larger and the smaller systems.[127]

[b] *Schwung* / (alt: swing, swinging motion).
[c] *nach den Centralgesetzen* / B: Central laws / C: ——— / F & Z: *lois centrales du système* / T: laws of central force / (The word *Centralgesetz* is not listed in Grimm either under Kant's spelling or under the more natural *Zentralgesetz; Centralkraft* is listed with the meaning: gravitation, attraction. This suggests that *Centralgesetz* must mean 'law of gravitation'.)
[d] *Theilchen.*
[e] *Schwungskrafte* / B: motive powers / C: *forze centrifughe* / F: *vitesses* / T: motive forces / Z: *forces motrices* / (alt: momentum).
[f] *auch grössere Klumpen.*   [g] *in abgesonderten Massen.*

187

field may still sink downwards, and they will then continue to orbit freely around the sun in the celestial spaces. These will be materials of the most extreme rarifaction, possibly the matter of which the zodiacal light is constituted.

4. Remark

2:148

The primary intention of this reflection is to give an example of the procedure which our above proofs entitle us to adopt. They remove the baseless suspicion, namely, that explaining any of the major arrangements in the world by appealing to the universal laws of nature opens a breach which enables the wicked enemies of religion to penetrate its bulwarks.[128] In my opinion, the hypothesis adduced has, to say the least, grounds enough in its favour to invite men of wide understanding to a closer examination of the scheme, a mere rough outline, presented in that hypothesis. I shall have achieved my purpose, as far as this book is concerned, if, with confidence established in the regularity and order which may issue from the universal laws of nature, the reader opens up a wider field to natural philosophy, and can be induced to recognise the possibility of an explanation such as the one offered here, or one like it, and to acknowledge the compatibility of that explanation with knowledge of a wise God.[129]

Incidentally, now that that favourite tool of so many systems, the vortex, has been banished from the sphere of nature[130] and relegated to Milton's limbo of vanity,[131] it would perhaps be worth the philosophical effort to address ourselves to the following question, and to attempt to answer it without resorting to forces which have been especially invented for the purpose. Does nature offer anything which could explain the fact that the swinging motions[h] of the planets all tend in the same direction, whereas all their other motions are explicable in terms of gravitational forces,[i] the permanent bond of nature? At least the scheme which we have outlined does not depart from the rule of unity, for even this centrifugal force[j] is derived, as a consequence of it, from gravitation; and that is appropriate to contingent motions, for they should be derived from the forces which are inherent in matter, even when it is at rest.

I would furthermore remark that, in spite of its *prima facie* similarity to the outline sketch of our system, the atomistic system of *Democritus* and *Epicurus* bears quite a different relation to the inference that the world has

---

[h] *Schwungsbewegung* / B: centrifugal motion / C: *il muoversi centrifugo* / F & Z: *mouvement tangential* / T: (orbital) motion / (Grimm lists *Schwungbewegung* with the meaning: swinging motion).
[i] *Centralkräften.*   [j] *Schwungskraft* / (alt: momentum).

a Creator to the one we have outlined.[132] In the atomistic system, movement is eternal and uncreated, while collision, the rich source of so much
order, is a contingency, an accident, for which there is no explanation at
all.[133] In the system which I have just outlined, a recognised and established law of nature leads necessarily to order, on the basis of an entirely
reasonable assumption. And since there is a cause operating here which
controls the tendency to regularity, and since there is something which
keeps nature on the course of harmoniousness and beauty, one is led to
suppose that there is a ground explaining why there is a necessary relation   2:149
to perfection.

However, let me adduce another example in order to explain how the
operation of gravity is necessarily destined to produce regularity and
beauty within the combination of diffused elements. I shall, therefore, add
an explanation of the mechanical character of the process which produces
the rings of Saturn.[134] This explanation, it seems to me, has as high a
degree of probability as can be expected of an hypothesis. All I ask is that
the following points be conceded. Let it be granted that, to begin with,
Saturn was surrounded by an atmosphere of the kind which has been
observed in the case of various comets which do not approach very close
to the sun and which lack a tail. Let it be further granted that the particles
of the vapours of this planet (to which we attribute an axial rotation) rose
upwards, and that subsequently these vapours, whether because of the
planet's cooling down or for some other reason, began to sink downwards
to the surface of the planet again. If these concessions are made, then the
rest follows with mechanical precision.[k] If these particles are to orbit
around the axis of the planet, then they must all of them have a velocity
which is equal to that of the point on the surface from which they have
risen. From this it follows that they must all tend, in virtue of this lateral
motion, to describe free orbits round Saturn, in accordance with the rules
of centripetal force.*[l] But all the particles, of which the velocity is not such
as to establish equilibrium by means of centrifugal force[m] with the gravitational attraction operating at that altitude, must of necessity collide with
and impede each other. And they will continue to do so until the only
particles left over are those which, rotating around Saturn, are able to
orbit in free circular motion, in accordance with the laws of gravitation;[n]
the other particles, however, will gradually fall back to the surface of the
planet. Now, all these circular motions must necessarily tend towards the

* Saturn rotates on its axis in accordance with our assumption. Each particle which rises
from its surface must therefore have exactly the same lateral motion as the point from which
it rose, and it must continue to have that motion at whatever altitude it reaches.

[k] *mit mechanischer Richtigkeit.*   [l] *Centralkräfte* / (alt: forces of gravity).
[m] *Centrifugalkraft.*   [n] *die in freier Cirkelbewegung nach Centralgesetzen umlaufen können.*

elongated plane of Saturn's equator. This will be familiar to anybody acquainted with the laws of gravitation. Thus, the remaining particles of Saturn's former atmosphere will eventually become concentrated in a circular plane around Saturn, a plane which occupies the extended equator of the planet.[135] The outer extremity of this plane is limited by precisely the same cause as determines the boundary of the atmosphere in the case of the comets. This belt[o] of freely moving cosmic material must inevitably become a ring; or, to express the matter more precisely, the aforementioned motion can issue in no other configuration than that of a ring. For since the particles can only derive the velocity, which enables them to orbit in circles, from the points of the surface of Saturn from which they have risen, it follows that those particles which have risen from the equator of the planet possess the greatest velocity. Now, of all the distances from the centre of the planet there is only one at which this velocity is exactly suited to generate circular motion,[p] for at smaller distances the velocity will be too weak. It follows that a circle[q] can be drawn within this belt, the centre of which coincides with the centre of Saturn itself;[r] all the particles within this circle must fall back to the surface of this planet. However, all those other particles which lie between this same circle and the circle which marks an extreme outer limit (that is to say, all the particles which are contained within a ring-like space) will henceforth continue to revolve around the planet, freely suspended in circular orbits around it.

The adoption of a solution such as this leads to consequences which can be used to calculate the period of Saturn's axial revolution.[s] And, what is more, the calculation of this period has the same degree of probability as the grounds, employed in the calculation of the period, themselves possess. For since the particles which occupy the inner edge of the ring have exactly the same velocity as that possessed by a point on Saturn's equator, and since, furthermore, this velocity, according to the laws of gravitation, has a magnitude suitable for circular motion, it follows that one can calculate the period of the orbit[t] of the particles which are located on the inner edge of the ring. The calculation is performed by using the relation between the respective distances from the centre of the planet of one of Saturn's satellites and of the inner edge of the ring; one can also use the given period of the revolution[u] of the satellite to perform the same calculation. By employing the orbital period of the particles located on the inner edge of the ring and the relation of the shortest diameter of the ring to that of the planet itself, one can establish Saturn's axial rotation. One thus finds by calculation that Saturn must revolve on its axis every five hours and roughly forty minutes.[136] And if one appeals to the analogy with

---

[o] *Limbus.*   [p] *Cirkelbewegung.*   [q] *Cirkelkreis.*
[r] *so wird ein Cirkelkreis in diesem Limbus aus dem Mittelpunkt des Saturns gezogen werden können.*
[s] *Achsendrehung.*   [t] *die Zeit des Umschwungs.*   [u] *der Zeit des Umlaufs.*

the other planets, this result seems to harmonise well with the period of their revolutions.[v]

Whether or not the assumption be conceded that Saturn may have had a comet-like atmosphere[w] to begin with, the conclusion I draw from it in order to explain my main proposition is, it seems to me, fairly certain: namely, that if such an atmosphere[x] did surround it, then the mechanical production of a floating ring must be a necessary consequence of it, and that, as a result, nature, when left to universal laws, tends to produce regularity out of chaos.

2:151

EIGHTH REFLECTION:
CONCERNING DIVINE ALL-SUFFICIENCY

The sum of all these reflections leads us to the concept of the Supreme Being. This Supreme Being embraces within itself everything which can be thought by man, when he, a creature made of dust, dares to cast a spying eye behind the curtain which veils from mortal eyes the mysteries of the inscrutable. God is all-sufficient. Whatever exists, whether it be possible or actual, is only something in so far as it is given through Him. If it be permitted to translate the communings of the Infinite with Himself into human language, we may imagine God addressing Himself in these terms: *I am from eternity to eternity: apart from me there is nothing, except it be through me.* This thought, of all thoughts the most sublime, is still widely neglected, and mostly not considered at all. That which is to be found in the possibilities of things and which is capable of realising perfection and beauty in excellent schemes has been regarded as a necessary object of Divine Wisdom but not itself as a consequence of this Incomprehensible Being. The dependency of other things has been limited to their existence alone. As a result of this limitation, a large share in the ground of so much perfection has been taken away from that Supreme Nature, and invested in I know not what eternal absurdity.[y]

The fruitfulness of a single ground in generating many consequences, the harmony and adaptedness[z] of natures to harmonise in a regular scheme of things[a] in accordance with universal laws and without frequent conflict – these are characteristics which must, in the first place, be found in the possibilities of things. It is only afterwards that wisdom can then become active in choosing them. To what limitations, emanating from a separate ground,[b] would not the Independent Being be subject, if not even these possibilities were grounded in that Being? And what incomprehensible coincidence it would be if, within the field of possibility and without supposing that there was any existent thing at all,[c] unity and fruitful har-

---

[v] *der Zeit der Umwendung.*   [w] *kometischen Atmosphäre.*   [x] *Dunstkreis.*   [y] *Undinge.*
[z] *Schicklichkeit.*   [a] *in einem regelmässigen Plane.*   [b] *fremden Gründe.*
[c] *irgend eines Existirenden.*

mony were to come into being – the unity and harmony which would enable the Supremely Wise and Powerful Being, once those external relations had been compared with his inner capacity, to bring great perfec-

2:152   tion into being. Certainly, such an account no longer places the origin of goodness undiminished in the hand of a single being. When *Hugen* invented the pendulum clock,[137] he would have found himself unable, had he considered the matter, to attribute to himself alone the regularity which constitutes the perfection of the device. The nature of the cycloid makes it possible that the time taken by free fall through the cycloidic curve is the same, whether the arc traced be long or short; this fact merely rendered *Hugen's* invention possible. The very fact that such a wide range of beautiful effects is even merely possible as a result of the simple ground of gravitation would itself, if it did not depend on the being who actually realised this whole system, obviously diminish and divide God's responsibility for the admirable*d* unity and for the great extent of so much order which is based on a single ground.

My amazement at the succession of an effect upon its cause ceases as soon as I directly and easily understand the capacity of the cause to produce its effect.*e* On this basis, amazement must cease as soon as I regard the mechanical structure of the human body, or of any other artificially devised*f* arrangement whatever, as the work of the Almighty Being, and look merely at the actuality. For, that a Being who can do anything should also be able to produce such a machine, provided that it is possible in the first place, is something which can be easily and distinctly understood. And yet, notwithstanding, some amazement is left over, no matter how we may have adduced the above consideration to render the phenomenon more comprehensible. For it is astonishing that something like an animal body should even be possible. And even if I could fully understand all its springs and pipes, all its nerve ducts and levers, its entire mechanical organisation, I should still continue to be amazed – amazed at the way so many different functions can be united in a single structure, amazed at the way in which the processes for realising one purpose can be combined so well with those by means of which some other purpose is attained, amazed at the way in which the same organisation also serves to maintain the machine and to remedy the effects of accidental injuries, amazed at the way in which it is possible for a human being to be both so delicately constituted and yet be capable of surviving for so long in spite of all the numerous causes which threaten its wellbeing. Nor, indeed, is the ground of my amazement removed once I have convinced myself that all the unity and harmony I observe around me is only possible because a Being exists which contains within it the grounds

2:153   not only of reality but also of all possibility. For although it is true that,

---

d reizenden.   *e* die Zulänglichkeit der Ursache zu ihr (i.e., der Wirkung).   *f* künstlichen.

192

employing the analogy of human behaviour, one can form some concept of how such a Being could be the cause of something real, one cannot form any concept of how that Being should contain the ground of the internal possibility of other things. It is as if this thought rises far higher than mortal creatures can reach.

Even in judging the constitution of possible things, when we lack immediate grounds for decision, this high concept of the Divine Nature, understood in terms of its all-sufficiency, can serve as a means for inferring possibility which is distinct from but construed as a consequence arising from the Divine Nature as from a ground.*g* The following question may be raised: among all possible worlds, is there not to be found an endless gradation of degrees of perfection, since no natural order is possible, beyond which there cannot be thought an order which is still more excellent. Furthermore, even if I were to admit the existence of a highest order, there would still be another question which could be raised, namely: whether the different worlds themselves which were unsurpassed by any others would be exactly equal to each other in respect of their perfection.[138] With questions like these it is difficult, perhaps impossible, to arrive at an answer simply by considering possible things. But when I consider the two questions in relation to the Divine Being and realise that if one world is chosen in preference to another without there being any preference in the *judgement* of the Being responsible for the choice, or, indeed, chosen in a manner incompatible with the judgement, such a choice would indicate that the various active powers of this Being were not in perfect agreement with each other, that differing modes of action did not correspond to a difference of motive, would, in short, indicate that there was a defect in the Most Perfect Being*h* – when I realise all this, then I conclude with strong conviction that the two cases proposed for consideration above must be fictitious and impossible. On the basis of all the preparations we have made above, I can understand why, of the following two arguments, the second will have a great deal more to recommend it than the first. The first argument infers from certain presupposed possibilities which cannot be adequately verified that the Most Perfect Being must of necessity behave in a certain way (this Being is so constituted that the concept of the supreme harmony to be found in it is seemingly weak-

---

g *Dieser hoher Begriff der göttlichen Natur, wenn wir sie nach ihrer Allgenugsamkeit gedenken, kann selbst in dem Urtheil über die Beschaffenheit möglicher Dinge, wo uns unmittelbar Gründe der Entscheidung fehlen, zu einem Hülfsmittel dienen, aus ihr als einem Grunde auf fremde Möglichkeit als eine Folge zu schliessen.*

h *und erkenne, dass der Vorzug der Wahl, der einer Welt vor der andern zu Theil wird, ohne den Vorzug in dem Urtheile eben desselben Wesens, welches wählt, oder gar wider dieses Urtheil einen Mangel in der Übereinstimmung seiner verschiedenen thätigen Kräfte und eine verschiedene Beziehung seiner Wirksamkeit ohne eine proportionirte Verschiedenheit in den Gründen, mithin einen Übelstand in dem vollkommensten Wesen lasse.*

ened). The second argument deduces the possibility of that which is recognised to be most appropriate to this Being from the harmony which is acknowledged to exist and which the possibility of things must have with the Divine Nature.[i] I shall, therefore, suppose that, in the possibilities of all worlds, there cannot be any relations which are such as must be a source of embarrassment to the rational choice of the Supreme Being. For it is precisely this Supreme Being which contains within it the ultimate ground of all this possibility. This possibility cannot, therefore, contain anything which does not harmonise with its source.

2:154

The concept of divine *all-sufficiency*, expanded to include all that is possible or real, is a far more appropriate expression for designating the supreme perfection of the Divine Being than the concept of the *infinite*, which is commonly employed. For no matter how this latter concept be interpreted, its fundamental meaning is manifestly mathematical. It signifies the relation of one magnitude to another, which is taken as a measure; this relation is greater than any number. Hence, divine cognition would be called infinite, in the strict sense of the term, if, compared with some other alleged type of cognition, it has a relation to it which surpasses every possible number. Now, such a comparison as this brings the divine determinations into an improper relationship of homogeneity[j] with those of created things. Furthermore, the comparison fails to convey with precision what one is hoping to establish, namely, the undiminished possession of all perfection. The expression 'all-sufficiency', on the other hand, designates everything which can be conceived under the notion of perfection. However, the designation 'infinity' is beautiful and genuinely aesthetic.[k] Extension beyond all numerical concepts stirs the emotions, and, in virtue of a certain embarrassment which it causes, it fills the soul with astonishment. The expression we are commending, on the other hand, is one which satisfies the demands of logical rigour to a greater degree.

---

[i] *als aus der erkannten Harmonie, die die Möglichkeiten der Dinge mit der göttlichen Natur haben müssen, von demjenigen, was diesem Wesen am anständigsten zu sein erkannt wird, auf die Möglichkeit zu schliessen.*
[j] *Gleichartigkeit.*   [k] *schön und eigentlich ästhetisch.*

Section 3. In which it is shown that there is no other possible argument in support of a demonstration of the existence of God save that which has been adduced

1. Classification of all possible arguments in support of a demonstration of the existence of God

The conviction of the great truth, *There is a God*, if it is to have the highest degree of mathematical certainty, has this peculiarity: it can only be reached by a single path.[1] It confers on this reflection an advantage: once one is convinced that there is no choice possible among a variety of arguments, philosophical efforts will have to be united in a single argument. These endeavours will aim to correct mistakes which may have crept into the argument in the course of its elaboration, not to reject it.

With a view to showing this, I would begin by reminding the reader that he must not lose sight of the requirement which must actually be satisfied. What has to be proved, namely, is the existence, not merely of a very great and very perfect first cause, but of the Supreme Being who is above all beings. Furthermore, what has to be proved is the existence, not of one or more such beings, but of one unique such Being. And, finally, these things must be proved with mathematical certainty and not by appealing to grounds which are merely probable.

All arguments for the existence of God must derive from one or other of two sources: either from the concepts of the understanding of the merely *possible*, or from the empirical concept of the *existent*. In the first case, the argument may proceed either from the possible as a *ground* to the existence of God as a *consequence*, or from the possible as a *consequence* to the divine existence as a *ground*. In the second case, the argument may proceed from that, the existence of which we experience, to the existence merely of a first and *independent cause*, and then, by subjecting that concept to analysis, proceed to the derivation of its divine characteristics; alterna-

---

[1] *Die Überzeugung von der grossen Wahrheit: es ist ein Gott, wenn sie den höchsten Grad mathematischer Gewissheit haben soll, hat dieses Eigne: dass sie nur durch einen einzigen Weg kann erlangt werden.*

tively, the argument may proceed directly from that which experience teaches us to both the existence and the properties of the Divine Being.

2. *Examination of the arguments of the first kind*

If the argument is to proceed from the concept of the merely *possible* as a ground to existence as a consequence, then that same existence must be discoverable in the concept by means of analysis, for the only way in which it is possible to derive a consequence from a concept of the possible is by logical analysis. But then existence would have to be contained in the possible as a predicate. But, since according to the First Reflection of the First Section of this book this is never the case, it is obvious that a proof of the truth we are examining is not possible in this manner.

There is, however, a famous proof constructed on this foundation, the so-called Cartesian proof.[139] In it one begins by thinking the concept of a possible thing, in which one imagines that all true perfection is united. It is now assumed that existence is also a perfection of things. The existence of a Most Perfect Being is thus inferred from the possibility of such a Being. One could draw the same inference from the concept of anything which was merely imagined to be the most perfect thing of its kind. One could, for example, infer the existence of a most perfect world from the mere fact that such a world can be thought. Without entering into an elaborate refutation of this proof, which is to be found in other philosophers,[140] I would merely refer the reader to the explanation given at the beginning of this work, namely, that existence is not a predicate at all, and therefore not a predicate of perfection either. Hence, it is in no wise possible to infer from a definition,[m] which contains an arbitrary combination of various predicates[n] used to constitute the concept of some possible thing, the existence of this thing, nor, consequently, the existence of God either.

On the other hand, the inference from the possibilities of things as consequences to the existence of God as ground is an argument of quite a different kind. What is under investigation here is whether the fact that something is possible does not presuppose something existent, and whether that existence, without which not even internal possibility can occur, does not contain such properties as we combine together in the concept of God. To begin with, it is clear in this case that I cannot infer an existence from conditioned possibility, unless I presuppose the existence of that which is possible only under certain circumstances. For conditioned possibility merely signifies that something can exist only in certain connections; the existence of the cause is only demonstrated in so far as the consequence exists. But here the cause is not to be inferred from the

2:157

---

[m] *Erklärung.*   [n] *eine willkürliche Vereinbarung verschiedener Prädikate.*

existence of the consequence.[o] Hence, such a proof can only be conducted from internal possibility, if it is to occur at all. It will further be noticed that it must spring from the absolute possibility of all things in general.[p] For it is only internal possibility itself by reference to which we are supposed to come to know[q] that it presupposes some existence, and not from the particular predicates, in virtue of which one possible thing differs from another. For a difference of predicates occurs even in the case of what is merely possible, and never designates anything existent. Accordingly, a divine existence would have to be inferred in the manner mentioned from the internal possibility of everything which can be thought. The whole of the First Section of this work demonstrated the possibility of this happening.

3. Examination of the arguments of the second kind

The proof employing the rules of causal inference[r] proceeds from the empirical concepts of that which exists to the existence of a first and independent cause, and then, by subjecting that concept to logical analysis,[s] it proceeds to the properties of that cause which designate divinity. This is a famous proof, and it enjoys considerable prestige as a result of the work of the philosophers of the school of *Wolff* in particular.[141] Nonetheless, the proof is wholly impossible. I admit that the argument is valid as far as the proposition: *If something exists, then something else also exists*   2:158 *which does not itself depend on any other thing.* I thus admit that the existence of some one or several things, which are not themselves the effects of something else, is well established. Now, the second step of the argument which proceeds as far as the proposition that this independent thing is *absolutely necessary*, is far less reliable, for the argument has to employ the principle of sufficient reason which is still contested.[142] Nonetheless, I am ready to subscribe to everything, even up to this point. Accordingly, there exists something necessarily. The qualities of supreme perfection and unity must now be derived from this concept of the absolutely necessary Being. But the concept of absolute necessity, which is the foundation of the argument, can be taken in two ways, as has been shown in the first section of this work. According to the first way, which we called logical necessity, it must be shown that the opposite of that thing, in which all perfection or reality is to be found, contradicts itself, and that therefore that being whose predicates are all truly affirmative is, alone and uniquely, absolutely necessary in existence. And since, from the self-same thorough-

---

[o] *und das Dasein der Ursache wird nur in so fern dargethan, als die Folge existirt, hier aber soll sie* (i.e., *die Ursache) nicht aus dem Dasein derselben* (i.e., *der Folge) geschlossen werden.*

[p] *aus der absoluten Möglichkeit aller Dinge überhaupt.*

[q] *von der (sc. Möglichkeit) erkannt werden.*   [r] *nach den Regeln der Causalschlüsse.*

[s] *logische Zergliederung.*

going union of all reality' in one Being, it must be established that it is a unique Being, it is clear that the analysis of the concepts of that which is necessary will be based on such grounds as must enable me to draw the converse conclusion: that that in which all reality is, exists necessarily. Now, according to the previous number, this inference is impossible. But not only that; it is in particular remarkable that in this kind of proof the empirical concept, which is presupposed but not actually employed, is not the foundation upon which the argument is based at all. This proof, like the Cartesian proof, is based exclusively on concepts, in which the existence of a Being is supposed to be found in the identity or conflict of its predicates.*

2:159 It is not my intention to analyse the proofs themselves, which a number of philosophers employ in accordance with this method. It is easy to uncover their fallacies, and, indeed, this has already, in part, been done by others. But it may, nonetheless, be hoped that the errors of these proofs can be remedied by making a number of corrections. Our reflection, however, makes it plain that, no matter how they be revised, these proofs can never be anything but arguments from concepts of possible things, not inferences from experience. At best, therefore, they are to be counted among the proofs of the first kind.¹⁴³

Now, as for the second proof of this kind, where the existence of God, together with His properties, is inferred from the empirical concepts of existent things, the situation is quite different. This proof is not only possible, it also wholly deserves to be brought to proper perfection by the concerted efforts of philosophers. The things of the world, which reveal themselves to our senses, display distinct characteristic marks of their contingency. Not only this, they also, by means of the magnitude, order and purposeful provisions, which are everywhere to be encountered, afford proofs of the existence of a rational Author endowed with great wisdom, power and goodness. The great unity of such an extensive whole permits one to conclude that all these things have been brought into existence by one single Author. And even if these inferences lack geometrical rigour,ᵘ their force is nonetheless indisputably such that no rational creature, employing the rules of natural common sense,ᵛ will be left for one moment in any doubt about these matters.

* This is the most important of the conclusions I wish to establish. If I equate the necessity of a concept with the fact that the opposite is self-contradictory, and if I then assert that such is the constitution of the infinite, then to presuppose the existence of a necessary Being would be completely superfluous for it already follows from the concept of the infinite. Indeed, that premised existence is completely superfluous in the proof itself, for, in the course of its presentation, the concepts of necessity and infinity are regarded as interchangeable notions. It follows that infinity is actually derived from the existence of what is necessary, for the infinite (and, indeed, the infinite alone) exists necessarily.

ᵗ *Vereinbarung aller Realität.*   ᵘ *geometrische Strenge.*   ᵛ *natürliche gesunde Verstand.*

4. *There are only two possible proofs of the existence of God*

From all these judgements it is evident that, if one wishes to argue from the concepts of possible things, the only possible argument for the existence of God is that in which the internal possibility of all things is itself regarded as something which presupposes some existence or other. This has been shown in the first section of this work. It is likewise evident that, if the argument, which takes as its starting point what experience of existing things teaches us, is to ascend to the very same truth, then the proof can only establish the existence and constitution of the supreme cause if it starts out from the properties which things within the world are perceived to possess, and from the accidental arrangement of the universe as a whole. Permit me to call the first of these two proofs the ontological and the second the cosmological proof. 2:160

The cosmological proof is, it seems to me, as old as human reason itself. It is so natural, so persuasive, and extends its reflections so far, as it keeps pace with the progress of our understanding, that it must endure as long as rational beings wish to engage in that noble contemplation, the aim of which is to come to know God from his works. The efforts of *Derham*,[144] *Nieuwentyt*[145] and many others, have conferred honour on human reason in this respect. Nonetheless, a great deal of vanity has sometimes crept in: under the catchword of religious enthusiasm,[w] an appearance of respectability has been conferred on all kinds of natural cognition and even on pure figments of the imagination.[x] But, in spite of all its excellence, this mode of proof will never be capable of mathematical certainty or precision. It will never establish more than the existence of some incomprehensibly great Author of the totality which presents itself to our senses. It will never be able to establish the existence of the most perfect of all possible beings. That there is only one first Author, may be the most probable thing in the world; but the conviction it produces will never attain the completeness necessary to challenge the most insolent scepticism.[y] This means that we cannot infer the existence of properties in the cause which are more in number or greater in quantity than is necessary to understand the degree and the nature of the effects arising from that cause – assuming, that is, that the only reason we have for supposing that this cause exists is that afforded us by the effects. Now, we recognise the existence of much perfection, greatness[z] and order in the world. But the only conclusion we can draw from this with logical rigour[a] is that the cause of these things must possess a high degree of understanding, power and goodness; we are not, however, entitled to conclude that this same cause is omniscient, or omnipotent, and so on. The whole, in which we

---

[w] *durch die Lösung des Religionseifers.*
[x] *allerlei physischen Einsichten oder auch Hirngespinsten.*   [y] *der frechsten Zweifelsucht.*
[z] *Grösse.*   [a] *mit logischer Schärfe.*

descry unity and thoroughgoing connectedness,[b] is immeasurable. We can with good reason conclude from this that a single Author was responsible for the whole. We must, however, acknowledge that we are not acquainted with the whole of creation. We must judge accordingly and say that that part of creation with which we are familiar entitles us to infer the existence 2:161 of but one Author, and that this encourages us to suppose that that part of creation with which we are not acquainted will be similarly constituted. And although it is highly reasonable to think in this fashion, it is not strict inference.

On the other hand, and without flattering ourselves too much, our outline of the ontological proof seems to be capable of the rigour required of a demonstration. However, if the question were raised, which of the two proofs was the superior, our reply would be this: if it is logical exactitude and completeness which is at issue, then the ontological proof is superior. If, however, one is looking for accessibility to sound common sense,[c] vividness of impression, beauty and persuasiveness in relation to man's moral motives, then the advantage must be conceded to the cosmological proof. It is doubtless more important, while also convincing sound understanding, to inspire man with noble feelings, which are richly productive of noble actions, than to instruct him with carefully weighed syllogisms, so that the demands of a subtler speculation are satisfied. If one is going to proceed with fairness, then the advantage of general utility cannot be denied to the well-known cosmological proof.

It is, accordingly, not a flattering strategy which is eager for the applause of others, but honesty, when I willingly concede superiority in respect of usefulness to an exposition of the important knowledge of God and his qualities, such as *Reimarus* offers in his book on natural religion[146] – an advantage which it enjoys over every other proof, including my own, in which greater attention is paid to logical rigour. I shall not consider the value of this or the other writings of *Reimarus*, which chiefly consists in an unaffected employment of a sound and admirable common sense. It must, however, be said that such reasons do have great demonstrative power[d] and stimulate more intuition than do logically abstract concepts, though such concepts do explain the object with greater precision.

An enquiring understanding, once it is engaged on the track of an investigation, will not rest satisfied until everything around it has become clear, until, if I may so express myself, the circle which circumscribes his question closes completely. For this reason, no one will dismiss an endeavour such as this present one, addressing itself as it does to logical exacti-
2:162 tude in a cognition which is as important as this, as futile or unnecessary – particularly since there are many cases where, without such care, the application of concepts would remain uncertain and doubtful.

[b] *durchgängige Verknüpfung.*   [c] *Fasslichkeit für den gemeinen richtigen Begriff.*
[d] *Beweiskraft.*

5. There is not more than a single demonstration of the existence of God possible; the argument which serves as its foundation has been given above.

There are four possible arguments for the existence of God, and we have reduced them to two main types. It is evident from what we have said so far that both the Cartesian proof and the proof which proceeds from the empirical concept of existence, and involves the analysis of the concept of an independent thing, are both false and utterly impossible. And by this I do not mean that they are proofs which simply lack proper rigour; I mean that they prove nothing at all.*e* It has further been shown that the proof which derives the existence of God and the properties of the Divine Being from the properties of the things to be found in the world contains an argument which is at once powerful and very beautiful; unfortunately, it is incapable of the rigour required of a demonstration. Now, there is only one alternative left: either no strict proof of the existence of God is possible at all, or the proof must be based upon the argument we have adduced above. Since we are speaking simply of the possibility of a proof, no one will maintain the former, and the outcome of the matter harmonises with what we have shown. There is only one God, and there is only one argument which enables us to apprehend*f* His existence and to apprehend it with the perception of the necessity which absolutely destroys everything which opposes it – a judgement to which the very nature of the object of our enquiry could immediately lead us. All other things which exist could also not exist. The experience of contingent things cannot, therefore, furnish us with an effective argument by means of which we can apprehend the existence of that Being, of which it is impossible that it should not be. The difference between the existence of God and that of other things is to be found simply in the fact that the denial of the divine existence is absolutely nothing. The inner possibility, the essence of things, is that of which the cancellation eliminates all that can be thought. In this, therefore, consists the distinctive characteristic mark of the existence of the essence of all beings.*g* It is in this that the proof of God's existence ought to be sought. And should you come to think that the proof is not to be found here after all, then abandon this unbeaten path and follow the broad highway of human reason. It is absolutely necessary that one should convince oneself that God exists; that His existence should be demonstrated, however, is not so necessary.

2:163

e *sondern gar nicht beweisen.*   *f* *einsehen.*

g *das eigene Merkmal von dem Dasein des Wesens aller Wesen* / (the word *Wesen* may mean either 'essence' or 'being' [in the sense of 'entity']; the final phrase may thus be translated 'the essence of all essences').

Attempt to introduce the concept of negative magnitudes into philosophy
by M. Immanuel Kant (1763)

Versuch den Begriff der negativen Grössen in die Weltweisheit einzuführen von M. Immanuel Kant (1763)

Versuch

den Begriff

der negativen Größen

in die Weltweisheit einzuführen

von

M. Immanuel Kant.

Attempt to introduce the concept of negative
magnitudes into philosophy

by
M. Immanuel Kant

The use to which mathematics can be put in philosophy consists either in the imitation of its method or in the genuine application of its propositions to the objects of philosophy. With respect to the first of these two uses: it has not been noticed that it has had only one benefit,[a] in spite of the great advantage expected of it to start with. Furthermore, the high-sounding titles, with which philosophers, jealous of geometry, were induced to decorate the propositions of philosophy, have now been gradually abandoned. The impropriety of provocative gestures made in lowly circumstances, and the stubborn refusal of the importunate *non liquet*[1] to yield to all this pomp, have come to be modestly recognised.

By contrast, the second use to which mathematics has been put in philosophy has been all the more beneficial to the parts of philosophy affected. These parts of philosophy, by turning the doctrines of mathematics to their own advantage, have attained to heights, to which they would not otherwise have been able to aspire.[2] But the parts of philosophy to which I am referring are only the insights of physics – unless, that is, one is obliged to include in philosophy the logic of probability.[b] As for metaphysics, this science, instead of turning certain of the concepts or doctrines of mathematics to its own advantage, has, on the contrary, frequently armed itself against them. And where it might, perhaps, have been able to gain secure foundations on which to base its reflections, it is to be seen trying to turn mathematical concepts into subtle fictions, which have little truth to them outside the field of mathematics. It is not difficult to guess which side will have the advantage if two sciences enter into a dispute with each other, where the one excels all others in certainty and distinctness, while the other has only just started out on the path to these objectives.   2:168

Take an example. Metaphysics seeks to discover the nature of space and establish the ultimate principles, in terms of which its possibility can be understood.[3] Now, nothing could be of more use in such an undertaking

---

[a] *von einigem Nutzen* / Carabellese (Assunto) (hereafter C): *di una qualche utilità* / Ferrari (hereafter F) & Kempf (hereafter K): *de quelque utilité* / (Kant is employing the word *einiger* in the now archaic sense of 'one single', 'only one'; the modern sense would, in the present context, yield an incoherency).
[b] *die Logik der Erwartungen in Glücksfällen.*

than the capacity to acquire reliably established data from some source or other, with a view to using them as the foundation of one's reflection. Geometry furnishes a number of such data relating to the most universal properties of space, for example, that space does not consist of simple parts.[4] And yet these data are ignored and one relies simply on one's ambiguous consciousness of the concept, which is thought in an entirely abstract fashion. If it should then happen that speculation, conducted in accordance with this procedure, should fail to agree with the propositions of mathematics, then an attempt is made to save the artificially contrived[c] concept by raising a specious objection against this science, and claiming that its fundamental concepts have not been derived from the true nature of space at all, but arbitrarily invented.[d] The mathematical observation of motion, combined with cognition of space, likewise furnishes many data, which are capable of keeping the reflections of metaphysics concerning time on the path of truth. The celebrated *Euler*, among others, has provided a stimulus to reflections such as these.* But it seems easier to linger among obscure abstractions which are difficult to test, than to enter into relations with a science which only admits intelligible and obvious insights.

The concept of the infinitely small, in which mathematics so frequently issues, is rejected with presumptuous audacity as a figment of the imagination[e] by people who ought rather to consider the possibility that they do not understand the matter well enough to pass judgement on it. Notwithstanding, nature herself seems to yield proofs of no little distinctness showing that this concept is very true. For if there are forces which operate continuously for a given time so as to produce movements – and gravity, to all appearances, is such a force – then the force which gravity exercises at the very beginning or in a state of rest must be infinitely small in comparison with that which it communicates over a period of time.[f] It is difficult, I admit, to penetrate the nature of these concepts. But this difficulty can, at best, only justify the cautiousness with which hesitant conjectures are made; it cannot justify the dogmatic declarations of impossibility.

2:169

My present intention is to consider a concept which is familiar enough in mathematics but which is still very unfamiliar in philosophy; and I wish to consider this concept in relation to philosophy itself. The considerations which I am about to offer only constitute modest beginnings, which is what generally happens when an attempt is made to open up new perspectives. But perhaps they may give rise to some important consequences. The neglect from which the concept of negative magnitudes has

---

* *Histoire de l'académie royale des sciences et belles lettres: l'année 1748.*[5]

[c] *erkünstelten.*   [d] *willkürlich ersonnen* / (*willkürlich* in the sense of: 'as a result of choice').
[e] *als erdichtet.*
[f] *so muss die Kraft, die sie im Anfangsaugenblick oder in Ruhe ausübt, gegen die, welche sie in einer Zeit mittheilt, unendlich klein sein.*

suffered has given rise in philosophy to a number of errors. It has also occasioned some misinterpretations of the views of others. For example, if the celebrated *Dr Crusius*[6] had chosen to acquaint himself with what the mathematicians think when they employ this concept, he would not have thought that the following comparison made by *Newton* was false, and indeed, false to the point of being astonishing.* Newton, namely, compares[8] the attractive force which, at an increased distance though still in close proximity to the bodies, gradually turns into a repulsive force,[g] with those series in which the cessation of positive magnitudes marks the start of negative magnitudes. For negative magnitudes[h] are not negations of magnitudes,[i] as the similarity of the expressions has suggested, but something truly positive in itself, albeit something opposed to the positive magnitude. And thus negative attraction is not rest, as *Crusius* supposed, but genuine repulsion.[9]

But let me proceed to the treatise itself, in order to show what application this concept may have in philosophy generally.

---

* Crusius, *Naturlehre*, Part II, §295.[7]

[g] *welche in vermehrter Weite, doch nahe bei den Körpern, nach und nach in eine zurückstossende ausartet.*

[h] *die negative Grössen.*   [i] *Negationen von Grössen.*

2:170   The concept of negative magnitudes has long been employed in mathematics,[10] and it has also been of the utmost consequence there. Nonetheless, the representation which most people have formed of the concept of negative magnitudes, and the elucidation[j] which they have given of it, have been strange and inconsistent. This has not, however, resulted in any errors of application, for the particular rules governing its employment took the place of the definition and guaranteed its correct use. And whatever error there may have been in the judgement about the nature of this abstract concept it remained fruitless and without effect. No one, perhaps, has indicated with greater distinctness and precision[k] what is to be understood by negative magnitudes than the celebrated *Kästner** in whose hands everything becomes exact, intelligible and agreeable.[12] In connection with his discussion of negative qualities, he criticises the mania for division and subdivision, characteristic of one highly abstract philosopher.[13] The force of the criticism is much more general than is actually expressed there. It may be regarded as a challenge to establish exactly how powerful the pretended perspicacity of many thinkers actually is, by testing it against a true and useful concept, with a view to fixing its nature philosophically, the correctness of the concept having already been secured by mathematics. And this is the sort of situation which spurious metaphysics is eager to avoid, for learned nonsense cannot create the illusion of thoroughness[l] here as easily as it can elsewhere. My purpose is to secure for philosophy the benefit of a concept which has hitherto not been used but which is nonetheless of the utmost importance. Since this is my purpose, I wish for no other judges than those who, endowed with general understanding,[m] are similar to the author whose writings have stimulated me to undertake this task. As for the metaphysical intelligentsia[n] who are in possession of a perfect understanding of things, one would have to be very inexperienced to imagine that their wisdom could be increased by any addition, or their madness diminished by any subtraction.

* *Anfangsgründe der Arithmetik*, pp. 59–62.[11]

[j] *Erläuterung.*   [k] *deutlicher und bestimmter.*   [l] *das Blendwerk der Gründlichkeit.*
[m] *von allgemeiner Einsicht.*   [n] *die metaphysische Intelligenzen.*

Section 1. Elucidation of the concept of negative magnitudes in general 2:171

Two things are opposed to each other if one thing cancels[o] that which is posited[p] by the other. This opposition is two-fold: it is either *logical* through contradiction, or it is *real*, that is to say, without contradiction.

The first opposition, namely logical opposition, is that upon which attention has been exclusively and uniquely concentrated until now. The opposition consists in the fact that something is simultaneously affirmed and denied of the very same thing. The consequence of the logical conjunction is *nothing at all* (*nihil negativum irrepraesentabile*),[14] as the law of contradiction asserts. A body which is in motion is something; a body which is not in motion is also something (*cogitabile*);[15] but a body which is both in motion and also, in the very same sense, not in motion, is nothing at all.

The second opposition, namely real opposition, is that where two predicates of a thing are opposed to each other, but not through the law of contradiction. Here, too, one thing cancels that which is posited by the other; but the consequence is *something* (*cogitabile*).[16] The motive force of a body in one direction and an equal tendency of the same body in the opposite direction do not contradict each other; as predicates, they are simultaneously possible in one body. The consequence of such an opposition is rest, which is something (*repraesentabile*).[17] It is, nonetheless, a true opposition. For that which is posited by the one tendency, construed as existing on its own, is cancelled by the other tendency, and the two tendencies are true predicates of one and the self-same thing, and they belong to it 2:172
simultaneously. The consequence of the opposition is also nothing, but nothing in another sense to that in which it occurs in a contradiction (*nihil privativum, repraesentabile*).[18] We shall, in future, call this nothing: zero = 0. Its meaning is the same as that of negation (*negatio*), lack, absence – notions which are in general use among philosophers – albeit with a more precise determination which will be specified later on.

In the case of logical repugnancy,[q] attention is concentrated exclusively on that relation in virtue of which the predicates of a thing cancel each other and their respective consequences through contradiction. And in

[o] *aufhebt.* [p] *gesetzt.* [q] *Bei der logischen Repugnanz.*

the case of such logical repugnancy, no attention is paid to which of the two predicates is truly affirmative (*realitas*)[19] and which truly negative (*negatio*).[20] For example: being dark and not dark at the same time and in the same sense is a contradiction in the same subject. The first predicate is logically affirmative, the other logically negative, although, in the metaphysical sense, the former is a negation. Real repugnancy[r] is also based upon the relation of the two predicates of the same thing to each other; but this relation is quite different from that which is present in logical repugnancy. That which is affirmed by the one is not negated by the other, for that is impossible. It is rather the case that both predicates, A and B, are affirmative. However, since the consequences of the two, each construed as existing on its own, would be *a* and *b*, it follows that, if the two are construed as existing together, neither consequence *a* nor consequence *b* is to be found in the subject; the consequence of the two predicates A and B, construed as existing together, is therefore zero. Suppose that someone has an active debt[s] A = 100 thalers with regard to another person; that active debt is the ground of a correspondingly large income.[t] But suppose that this same person also has a passive debt[u] B = 100 thalers; then that passive debt is the ground of a correspondingly large expenditure.[v] The two debts together are the ground of zero, that is to say, the ground for neither giving nor receiving money. It is easy to see that this zero is a relative nothing,[w] for it is only a certain consequence which does not exist. In the present case, it is a certain capital which does not exist, and, in the case mentioned above, it was a certain motion which did not exist. On the other hand, in the case of cancellation through contradiction it is absolutely nothing[x] which exists. Accordingly, the *nihil negativum*[21] cannot be expressed by zero = 0, for this involves no contradiction. It is possible to think that a certain motion should not be; but that a certain motion should both be and not be cannot be thought at all.

Mathematicians make use of the concepts of this real opposition in the case of mathematical magnitudes. In order to indicate them, the mathematicians designate them by means of the signs '+' and '−'.[22] Since every such opposition is reciprocal, it can easily be seen that one magnitude cancels the other, either complete or in part, without, for that reason, any distinction being made between those magnitudes which are preceded by '+' and those which are preceded by '−'. Suppose that a ship sails from Portugal to Brazil. Let all the distances which it covers with the east wind be designated by '+', while those which it covers with the west wind are designated by '−'. The numbers themselves signify miles. The week's journey is +12 +7 −3 −5 + 8 = 19 miles; this is the distance the ship

2:173

---

[r] *Realrepugnanz.*   [s] *Activschuld.*   [t] *ein Grund einer eben so grossen Einnahme.*   [u] *Passivschuld.*
[v] *so ist dieses ein Grund, so viel wegzugeben.*   [w] *ein verhältnissmässiges Nichts.*
[x] *schlechthin Nichts.*

has sailed westwards. The magnitudes preceded by '−' have this sign in front of them simply to signify opposition, for they are to be combined with those magnitudes which are preceded by '+'. But if they are combined with magnitudes which are preceded by '−', then there is no longer any opposition, for opposition is a reciprocal relation[y] which only holds between '+' and '−'. And since subtraction is a cancelling which occurs when opposed magnitudes are taken together, it is evident that the '−' cannot really be a sign of subtraction, as is commonly supposed; it is only the combination of '+' and '−' together which signifies subtraction. Hence the proposition '−4 −5 = −9' is not a subtraction at all, but a genuine increase and addition[z] of magnitudes of the same kind. On the other hand, the proposition '+9 −5 = 4' does signify a subtraction, for the signs of opposition indicate that the one cancels as much in the other as is equal to itself. Likewise, the sign '+' on its own does not really signify addition itself. The sign '+' only signifies addition in so far as the magnitude which it precedes is supposed to be combined with another magnitude which is also preceded by '+', or is thought of as preceded by '+'. If, however, it is to be combined with a magnitude preceded by '−', this can only occur by means of opposition, and then both the sign '+' and the sign '−' signify a subtraction, one magnitude cancelling as much in the second magnitude as is equal, namely, to the first, as for example '−9 +4 = −5'. For this reason, the sign '−', as it occurs in the example '−9 −4 = −13', does not signify a subtraction but an addition, in exactly the same way as the sign '+', as it occurs in the example '+9 +4 = +13', signifies addition. For, in general, if the signs are the same, then the signified things must be simply added together, but if the signs are different they can only be combined through opposition, that is to say, by means of subtraction. Accordingly, in mathematics these two signs only serve to distinguish magnitudes which are opposed to each other, in other words, those magnitudes which, when combined, cancel each other either wholly or in part. The two signs have the following functions: firstly, they enable one to recognise the reciprocal relationship holding between magnitudes; secondly, they enable one to establish to which of the two types of magnitude the balance belongs, after one magnitude has been subtracted from the other. Thus, in the case above, one would arrive at the same result if the ship's course with the east wind had been indicated by '−' and its course with the west wind by '+'. The only difference would be that the final balance[a] would have been designated by '−'.

2:174

This is the origin of the mathematical concept of **negative magnitudes**. A magnitude is, relative to another magnitude, negative, in so far as it can only be combined with it by means of opposition; in other words, it can only be combined with it so that the one magnitude cancels as much in the other as is equal to itself. Now this, of course, is a reciprocal relation, and magnitudes which are opposed to each other in this way reciprocally cancel an equal amount in each other. It follows that, strictly speaking, no magnitude can be called absolutely negative: '+a' and '−a' must each be called the negative magnitude of the other. However, since this can always be added in thought,[b] the mathematicians have in the past adopted the practise of calling the magnitudes preceded by '−' 'negative magnitudes'. But, in adopting this practise, one must not lose sight of the fact that the above designation does not signify a special kind of thing, which is distinctive in virtue of its inner constitution; it rather signifies the following reciprocal relation: magnitudes preceded by '−' are to be taken together in an opposition with certain other things which are designated by '+'.

In order to extract what is philosophically significant from this concept and to do so without particularly looking at magnitude, we shall begin by offering the following remark. The mathematical concept of negative magnitudes involves the opposition which we have above called 'real opposition'. Suppose that there are +8 units of capital[c] and −8 units of passive debt; no contradiction is involved in attributing them to the same person. However, one of these magnitudes cancels an amount which is equal to that which is posited by the other, and the consequence is zero. I shall, accordingly, call the debts 'negative units of capital'.[d] But in doing so I do not mean that they are negations or mere denials[e] of units of capital, for if they were they would themselves be designated by zero, and then the capital, combined with the debts, would yield as the value of the property '8 +0 = 8', which is false. What I mean when I call debts 'negative units of capital' is this: debts are the positive grounds of the diminishment of the units of capital.[f] Now, this whole nomenclature only ever signifies the relation of certain things to each other, and without this relation the concept would instantly cease to exist. It follows that it would be absurd to

2:175 think of a special sort of thing and to call such things negative things, for even the mathematical term 'negative magnitudes' is not sufficiently exact. For negative things would in general signify negations (*negationes*), but that is not at all the concept we wish to establish. On the contrary, it is sufficient that we have now defined[g] the reciprocal relations which constitute the whole concept and which consist in real opposition. However, we should like to make it immediately clear from the expressions themselves which we are employing that the one member of the opposition is not the contradictory opposite of the other member, and that, if the second member of the opposition is something positive, the first member is not a mere

[b] *im Sinne.*   [c] *+8 Capitalien.*   [d] *negative Capitalien.*
[e] *Negationen oder blosse Verneinungen* / (elsewhere, both *Negation* and *Verneinung* are translated by 'negation').
[f] *positive Gründe der Verminderung der Capitalien.*   [g] *erklärt.*

negation of the second, but, as we shall be seeing in a moment, something affirmative which is opposed to it. In order to make this clear, we shall adopt the method of the mathematicians and call descent 'negative ascent'; falling 'negative rising'; retreat 'negative advance'. In this way, it is instantly apparent from the expression itself that, for example, falling is not to be distinguished from rising merely in the way in which 'not a' is distinguished from 'a'. It is rather the case that falling is just as positive as rising. It is only when the former is combined with the latter that it contains the ground of a negation. It is, of course, obvious that, since everything depends here on the reciprocal relation, I can just as well call descent 'negative rising', as I can call rising 'negative descent'. Similarly, units of capital are just as much negative debts, as the latter are negative units of capital. But it is rather more appropriate to apply the name *'negative'* to that on which the intention is primarily focused in a given case, if one wishes to designate its real opposite.[h] For example, it is rather more appropriate to call debts negative 'negative units of capital' than to call units of capital 'negative debts', although there is no difference to be found in the reciprocal relation itself; the difference is to be found, rather, in the connection which the result of this reciprocal relation has to the rest of the intention. There is only one other thing which I wish to do and that is to remind the reader that I shall, on occasion, make use of the expression, 'one thing is the *negative* (thing) of the other'.[i] Take the following example: 'The negative of rising is setting'. What I intend to convey by this expression is not that the one thing is the negation of the other, but rather that there is something which stands in a relation of real opposition to something else.

In the case of such real opposition, notice should be taken of the following principle, which is to be regarded as a **fundamental rule**. A real repugnancy only occurs where there are two things, as *positive grounds*, and where one of them cancels the consequence of the other. Suppose that motive force is a positive ground: a real conflict[j] can only occur in so far as there is a second motive force[k] connected with it, and in so far as each reciprocally cancels the effect of the other. The following consideration may serve as a general proof. *Firstly:* the determinations which conflict with each other must exist in the same subject. For suppose that there is one determination in one thing and another determination, no matter what, in a second thing: no actual opposition[l] arises in such a situation.* *Secondly:* one of the opposed determinations in a real opposition[n] cannot be the contradictory opposite[o] of the other; for if it were, the

2:176

---

* We shall discuss *potential* opposition[m] at a later stage.[23]

[h] *sein reales Gegentheil.*   [i] *dass ein Ding die Negative (Sache) von dem andern sei.*
[j] *realer Widerstreit.*   [k] *Bewegkraft.*   [l] *keine wirkliche Entgegensetzung* (alt: no real opposition).
[m] *potentialen Entgegensetzung.*   [n] *Realentgegensetzung.*   [o] *das contradictorische Gegentheil.*

conflict would be logical and, as we proved above, impossible. *Thirdly:* a determination cannot negate anything other than what is posited by the other determination, for otherwise there would be no opposition at all. *Fourthly:* in so far as they conflict with each other, the two determinations cannot both be negative, for if they were neither of them would posit anything to be cancelled by the other. Accordingly, in every real opposition the two predicates must both of them be positive, but positive in such a way that, when they are combined, there is a reciprocal cancellation of the consequences in the same subject. In this way, if two things, of which one is regarded as the negative of the other, are viewed in themselves, they are both positive; but if they are combined in one subject, the consequence of the combination is zero. The passage of the ship westwards is just as much a positive motion as its passage eastwards; but if we are dealing with one and the same ship, the distances thus covered cancel each other out, either completely or in part.

Now, in saying this I do not wish to be taken to mean that these things, which are really opposed to each other, do not contain within themselves many negations as well. A ship which is sailing westwards is, in virtue of that very fact, not sailing eastwards, or in a southerly direction, *etc, etc;* nor is it in all places at the same time – all of these determinations being just so many negations which all attach to the ship's motion. But that which, in spite of all these negations, is positive, both in the easterly and in the westerly motion, is the only thing which can be involved in a real conflict, of which the consequence is zero.

It is precisely this which can be explained by means of general signs.[p] All true negations which are hence possible (for the negation of what is being simultaneously posited in the subject is impossible), can be expressed by zero = o; the affirmation can be expressed by any positive sign.
2:177 Their combination, however, in one and the same subject can be expressed by '+' and '−'. Here it can be seen that 'A + o = A', 'A − o = A', 'o + o = o', 'o − o = o'* are none of them oppositions; in no case is something cancelled which had been posited. Likewise, A + A is not a cancellation. The only other case left is this: 'A − A = o'; this formula expresses the following idea: there are two things, of which one is the

* It might be thought that 'o − A' constituted another case, and one which has been omitted here. Philosophically speaking, however, this case is impossible, for something positive can never be subtracted from nothing. If this expression has a valid use in mathematics, it is because zero does not in the least degree modify either the increase or the decrease which is produced by other magnitudes.[q] A + o − A is still A − A; the zero is accordingly completely superfluous. The idea, deriving from this, that negative magnitudes are *less than nothing,* is accordingly empty and absurd.[24]

[p] *durch allgemeine Zeichen.*

[q] *so kommt es daher, weil das Zero weder die Vermehrung noch Verminderung durch andre Grössen im geringsten etwas ändert.*

negative of the other; both are A and both are therefore truly positive; but they are positive in such a way that one of them cancels that which is posited by the other; the cancellation is signified by means of the sign '−'.

The **second rule**, which is really the reverse of the first, runs as follows: wherever there is a positive ground and the consequence is nonetheless zero then there is a real opposition. In other words: this ground is connected with another positive ground, which is the negative of the first ground. If a ship on the open sea is actually being driven by an easterly wind, but it still fails to move from the spot, or at any rate does not move as much as the force of the wind would lead one to expect, then there must be a current in the sea which is flowing in the opposite direction. Generally speaking this means: the cancellation of the consequence of a positive ground always demands a positive ground as well. Suppose that there is some ground or other for a consequence b; it follows that the consequence can never be 0, unless there exists a ground for −b, in other words, a ground for something truly positive which is opposed to the first ground: b − b = 0. If the estate left by someone at his death amounts to a capital of 10,000 thalers, then it follows that the whole inheritance cannot amount to a mere 6000 thalers, except in so far as 10,000 − 4000 = 6000, that is to say, in so far as the inheritance is combined with a debt or some other expense which amounts to 4000 thalers. What I shall be saying later will contribute substantially to the elucidation of these laws.

The following remark is offered by way of conclusion to the present section. A negation, in so far as it is the consequence of a real opposition, will be designated a *deprivation*[r] (*privatio*). But any negation, in so far as it does not arise from this type of repugnancy, will be called a *lack*[s] (*defectus*, 2:178 *absentia*).[25] The latter does not require a positive ground, but merely the lack of such a ground. But the former involves a true ground of the positing and another ground which is opposed to it and which is of the same magnitude. In a body, rest is either merely a lack, that is to say, a negation of motion, in so far as no motive force is present, or alternatively, such rest is a deprivation, in so far as there is, indeed, a motive force present, though its consequence, namely the motion, is cancelled by an opposed force.

[r] *Beraubung.*   [s] *Mangel.*

Section 2. *In which philosophical examples embodying the concept of negative magnitudes are adduced*

1. A body, in virtue of its impenetrability, resists the motive force of another body attempting to penetrate the space which it occupies.[t] In spite of the motive force of the second body, the impenetrability of the first body is nonetheless a ground of that second body's rest. It follows from what has already been said that impenetrability just as much presupposes a true force in the parts of the body, in virtue of which they collectively occupy a space, as does the force in virtue of which another body strives to enter this space.[26]

By way of elucidation, imagine two springs which are opposed to each other. Without any doubt they maintain each other in a state of rest by means of forces which are equal to each other. Place between the two a spring of the same elasticity; this spring, by its effort, will produce the same effect, and, in accordance with the rule of the equality of action and reaction,[u] it will maintain the two springs in a state of rest. On the other hand, if this spring is replaced by a solid body which is put between the other two springs, the same effect will be produced: the impenetrability of the solid body will maintain the aforementioned springs in a state of rest. The cause of impenetrability is thus a true force, for it produces the same effect as a true force.[v] Now, if you call *attraction* a cause, of any kind you please,[w] in virtue of which one body constrains other bodies to press upon the space which it itself occupies or to set it in motion (though here it is sufficient simply to think of this attraction), then impenetrability is a *negative attrac-*
2:180 *tion.* This serves to show that impenetrability is as much a positive ground as any other motive force in nature. And since negative attraction is really true repulsion, it follows that the forces with which the elements are invested and in virtue of which these latter occupy a space, albeit in such a way that they impose limitations even on space itself by means of the conflict of the

---

[t] *einnimmt.* [u] *Wirkung und Gegenwirkung.* [v] *denn sie thut dasselbe, was eine wahre Kraft thut.*
[w] *welche es auch sein mag* / (The *es* ought strictly to be *sie* in order to agree with the feminine *Kraft.* The sentence may be ambiguous and could be read to mean: 'which it may well be').

two forces which are opposed to each other – it follows, I say, that these forces will give rise to the elucidation of many phenomena.ˣ And in this matter, I think that I have arrived at knowledge which is distinct and reliable, and which I propose to make known in another treatise.²⁷

2. Let us take an example from psychology. Consider the following question: Is displeasureʸ simply the lack of pleasure? Or is displeasure a ground of the deprivation of pleasure? And in this case, displeasure, while being indeed something positive in itself and not merely the contradictory opposite of pleasure, is opposed to pleasure in the real sense of the term. The question thus amounts to this: can displeasure be called *negative pleasure?* Now, right from the beginning, inner feelingᶻ tells us that displeasure is more than a mere negation. For no matter what pleasure one may have, there will always, as long as we remain finite beings, be lacking some other possible pleasure. If someone takes a medicine which tastes like pure water, he may perhaps take pleasure inᵃ the expectation of health; on the other hand, he experiences no pleasure in the taste; but this lack is not yet displeasure. Now administer to him a medicine which consists of wormwood. The sensation which wormwood produces is very positive. What we have here is not a mere lack of pleasure, but something which is a true ground of the feeling which we call displeasure.

But our elucidation can, at best, only establish that displeasure is not merely a lack, but a positive sensation. That it is also something positive, as well as something which is really opposed to pleasure, can be rendered most clearly apparent by the following consideration. Suppose that the news is brought to a Spartan mother that her son has fought heroically for his native country in battle. An agreeable feeling of pleasure takes possession of her soul. She is thereupon told that her son has died a glorious death in battle. This news diminishes her pleasure a great deal, and reduces it to a lower degree. Let us say that the number of degrees of pleasure which are produced by the first announcement on its own are 4a. And let the displeasure merely be a negation = o. It follows that, when these two are combined, the value of the pleasure is 4a + o = 4a; and in that case the pleasure produced by the first announcement would thus not be diminished by the news of her son's death, and that is wrong. Let the pleasure which is produced by the news of his attested valour accordingly

2:181

ˣ *und da die negative Anziehung eigentlich eine wahre Zurückstossung ist, so wird in den Kräften der Elemente, vermöge deren sie einen Raum einnehmen, oder aber so, dass sie diesem selbst Schranken setzen, durch den Conflictus zweier Kräfte, die einander entgegengesetzt sind, Anlass zu vielen Erläuterungen gegeben.*

ʸ *Unlust /* (Kant's argument depends on the explicit contrast between *Lust* and the negative *Unlust*. In order to preserve this contrast *Unlust* has been translated by 'displeasure' in the now archaic and obsolete sense signifying the opposite of 'pleasure' [not in its modern sense signifying 'annoyance at' or 'anger with']).

ᶻ *die innere Empfindung.*   ᵃ *hat vielleicht eine Lust über.*

219

be = 4a; and let the pleasure which remains, once the displeasure produced by the announcement of his death has taken effect, be = 3a; it follows that the displeasure is = a, and it is the negative of pleasure, namely −a, and hence the value of the resulting balance of pleasure is 4a − a = 3a.

The calculation^b of the total value of the complete pleasure in a mixed state would also be highly absurd if displeasure were a mere negation and equal to zero. Suppose that someone has purchased an estate, and that the annual yield of that estate amounted to 2000 thalers. Let the degree of pleasure arising from this income, in so far as the pleasure is pure, be expressed as 2000. However, everything which the owner has to spend from this income and of which he has to forego the enjoyment, is a ground of displeasure: ground rent: 200 thalers; servants' wages: 100 thalers; renovations: 150 thalers annually. If displeasure were a mere negation = 0, then it would follow that, all in all, the pleasure which he would derive from his purchase would be 2000 + 0 + 0 + 0 = 2000. In other words, his pleasure would be as great as it would have been if he had been able to enjoy the income from the estate without any outgoings at all. But it is obvious that the degree of the pleasure he takes in these incomes is determined by what he has left after his expenditures have been deducted; and thus the degree of his pleasure is 2000 −200 −100 −150 = 1550. Displeasure is accordingly not simply a lack of pleasure. It is a positive ground which, wholly or partly, cancels the pleasure which arises from another ground. For this reason, I call it a *negative pleasure.* The lack of both pleasure and displeasure, in so far as it arises from the absence of their respective grounds, is called *indifference^c* (*indifferentia*). The lack of both pleasure and displeasure, in so far as it is a consequence of the real opposition of equal grounds, is called *equilibrium^d* (*aequilibrium*). Both indifference and equilibrium are zero, though the former is a negation absolutely,^{e} whereas the latter is a deprivation. The state of mind, in which pleasure and displeasure are equally opposed so that there is something which is left over from one of these two feelings, is the *preponderance^f* of pleasure or displeasure (*suprapondium voluptatis vel taedii*). *Maupertuis,* employing concepts such as these, attempts in his essay on moral philosophy, to calculate the sum of human happiness.[28] And, indeed, his would be the only way in which it could be calculated; but, unfortunately, the calculation is not humanly possible, for it is only feelings of the same kind^g which can feature in such calculations. But the feelings which we experience in the highly complex circumstances of life appear to vary a great deal, according to the variety of ways in which our emotions are affected.

2:182

---

^{b} *Schätzung /* (alt: estimation). ^{c} *Gleichgültigkeit.* ^{d} *Gleichgewicht.*
^{e} *eine Verneinung schlechthin.* ^{f} *Übergewicht.* ^{g} *gleichartige Empfindungen.*

The calculation performed by this learned man yielded a negative balance, a result with which, however, I do not concur.

For these reasons, *aversion* can be called a *negative desire, hate* a *negative love, ugliness* a *negative beauty, blame* a *negative praise.* It might, perhaps, be thought that all this is nothing but juggling with words.[h] But the only people who will judge in this way will be those who do not realise what advantage is to be derived from an expression's directly indicating a relation to concepts which are already familiar – an advantage of which the slightest experience of mathematics will easily convince everyone. The error into which many philosophers have fallen as a result of neglecting this truth is obvious. One finds that they generally treat evils[i] as if they were mere negations, even though it is obvious from our explanations that there are evils of lack (*mala defectus*) and evils of deprivation (*mala privationis*). Evils of lack are negations: there is no ground for the positing of what is opposed to them.[j] Evils of deprivation presuppose that there are positive grounds which cancel the good for which there really exists another ground. Such evils of deprivation are *negative* goods. These latter evils are greater than the former. Not giving is, relatively to someone in need, an evil; but taking from, extorting from, stealing from are, relatively to someone in need, far greater evils. *Taking from* is a *negative giving* to. A similar thing can be seen in the case of logical relations. *Errors* are *negative truths* (and negative truths are not to be confused with the truth of negative propositions); a *refutation* is a *negative proof.* But I fear I am spending too much time on this matter. My only purpose is to give currency[k] to these concepts. Their usefulness will become apparent when they are employed, and I shall try to say something about this in the Third Section.

3. The concepts of real opposition also have a useful application in moral philosophy. *Vice*[l] (*demeritum*) is not merely a negation; it is a *negative virtue*[m] (*meritum negativum*). For vice can only occur in so far as a being has within him an inner law (either simply conscience[n] or consciousness of a positive law as well), which is contravened by this actions. This inner law is a positive reason for a good action, and the consequence can only be zero if the consequence which would result from consciousness of the law on its own is cancelled. What we have here is, accordingly, a deprivation, a real opposition, and not merely a lack. Let it not be supposed that what I have just said relates only to *errors of commission*[o] (*demerita commissionis*) but not to *errors of omission*[p] (*demerita omissionis*) as well. An animal lacking reason does not practise any virtue. But this omission is not a vice (*demeritum*), for the animal has not contravened any inner law. It was not driven by inner moral feeling[q] to a good action. And the zero, the omission

2:183

---

[h] *Krämerei mit Worten.*   [i] *die Übel.*   [j] *zu deren entgegengesetzter Position kein Grund ist.*
[k] *in den Gang zu bringen.*   [l] *Untugend.*   [m] *negative Tugend.*   [n] *bloss das Gewissen.*
[o] *Begehungsfehler.*   [p] *Unterlassungsfehler.*   [q] *inneres moralisches Gefühl.*

construed as a consequence, was not the product of its resisting that inner moral feeling, nor was it the result of the operation of a counteracting force.[r] The omission under consideration here is a negation absolutely, arising from the lack of a positive ground; it is not a deprivation. By contrast, imagine a human being who fails to help someone whom he sees in distress and whom he could easily help. There is a positive law to be found in the heart of every human being, and it is a law which is present in this man's heart as well; it commands that we love our neighbour. In the present example, the law must be outweighed. For this omission to be possible, it is necessary that there should be actual inner action arising from motives.[s] This zero is the consequence of a real opposition. And it really does initially cost some people a noticeable effort to omit performing some good, to the performance of which they detect within themselves positive impulses. Habit facilitates everything, and this action is in the end scarcely noticed any longer. Accordingly, sins of commission and sins of omission do not differ *morally* from each other in kind, but only in *magnitude.*[t] *Physically*, that is to say, from the point of view of their external consequences, they may also well differ from each other in kind. The person who receives nothing suffers an evil of lack, and the person from whom something has been taken suffers an evil of deprivation. But, as far as the moral state of the person responsible for the sin of omission is concerned: all that is needed for the sin of commission is a greater degree of action. The situation is like that of a counterweight at the end of a lever: it exercises a genuine force merely to maintain the burden in a state of equilibrium; there only needs to be a slight increase of force in order actually to shift the burden on the other side. In exactly the same way, someone who fails to honour his debts will, in certain circumstances, cheat in order to make a profit. And the person who fails to help another person when it is in his power to do so will, as soon as the motives are stronger,[u] harm that person. Love and lovelessness[v] are the contradictory opposites of each other. *Lovelessness* is a true negation. But in respect of the person, towards whom one is conscious of an obligation to love, this negation is only possible through a real opposition, and consequently only

2:184   as a deprivation. And, in such a case, *not to love* and *to hate* differ only in degree. All omissions, while being instances of a lack of greater moral perfection, though not *sins* of omission, are, on the other hand, nothing but negations absolutely of a certain virtue, not deprivations or vice. The instances of lack in the case of saints[w] and the errors of noble souls[x] are of

---

[r] *vermittelst eines Gegengewichtes.*   [s] *eine wirkliche innere Handlung aus Bewegungsursachen.*

[t] *der Grösse nach.*   [u] *so bald sich die Bewegungsursachen vergrössern.*

[v] *Liebe und Nicht-Liebe* / (both *Unlust* and *Untugend* are common words; *Nicht-Liebe*, although not a neologism, is very uncommon; *Unliebe*, although common, would not suit Kant's purposes, for it signifies the mere *absence* of love).

[w] *die Mängel der Heiligen.*   [x] *die Fehler edler Seelen.*

this kind. What is missing is a certain more powerful ground of perfection. It is not on account of the operation of a countervailing cause that the lack obtains.[y]

One could extend the application of the above concepts to the objects of moral philosophy a great deal further. *Prohibitions* are *negative commands*, *punishments* are *negative rewards*, and so on. But if I have explained the use of this idea in general then my purpose has been, for the moment, attained. I realise, of course, that readers of an enlightened understanding will have found the above explanation unnecessarily long. But I shall be pardoned for my discursiveness if they remember that, apart from themselves, there is a breed of people who are not very amenable to teaching, and who, having spent their whole lives poring over a single book, understand nothing which is not contained therein; in their case even the most extreme discursiveness would not be superfluous.

4. Let us now take an example from natural science. In nature there are many deprivations which result from the conflict of two operative causes,[z] of which the one cancels the effect of the other through real opposition. It is, however, often uncertain whether it is not perhaps merely the negation of lack, due to the absence of a positive case, or whether it is not the effect of the opposition of genuine forces, just as rest may be attributed either to the absence of a cause of motion or to the conflict of two motive forces impeding each other. There is, for example, the well-known question whether coolness requires a positive cause, or whether as a lack it is to be attributed simply to the absence of the cause of heat.[29] I should like to consider this matter a little, at least as far as it is relevant to my purposes. Doubtless, coldness itself is simply the negation of warmth, and it can easily be seen that it is possible in itself, even in the absence of any positive cause. But it can with equal ease be seen that it can also be the effect of a positive cause, and that it does actually on occasion arise from such a cause – and all this can be understood independently of what opinion one may entertain concerning the origin of warmth. Absolute coldness is unknown in nature, and if it is discussed, then it is understood only in a comparative sense.[a] Now, experience and rational argument[b] agree in con-   2:185
firming the thought of the celebrated *van Muschenbroek*[30] that increase in temperature consists not in internal concussion,[c] but rather in the real passage of the elemental fire[d] from one material to the other,[31] though this passage is probably accompanied by an inner concussion, the concussion thus excited also serving to facilitate the exit of the elemental fire from the bodies. On this basis, if the element of fire is in a state of equilibrium among the bodies in a certain space they are, relative to each other,

---

[y] *und der Mangel äussert sich nicht um der Entgegenwirkung willen.*
[z] *zweier wirkenden Ursachen.*   [a] *vergleichungsweise.*   [b] *Vernunftgründe.*
[c] *in der innern Erschütterung.*   [d] *des Elementarfeuers.*

neither hot nor cold. If this equilibrium is removed, then the material into which the elemental fire passes is, relatively to the body which is thus deprived of the elemental fire, *cold*, whereas the latter body, in so far as it yields this heat to that material, is called, relatively to the material receiving the elemental fire, *warm*. The state which prevails during this change is called, in the former case, 'growing warm'[e] and in the latter case 'growing cold';[f] this process of change continues until everything reaches the state of equilibrium again.

Now, there is probably nothing which can be more easily imagined than that the attractive forces of matter should continue to set this subtle and elastic fluid[g] in motion and to fill the mass of bodies with it, until it has everywhere reached a state of equilibrium.[32] That state of equilibrium is reached, namely, when the spaces are filled with that subtle and elastic fluid proportionately to the attractive forces operating there. And here it is obvious that a material which cools another material when it is in contact with it steals the elemental fire, with which the mass of the second body is filled, by means of a true force (attraction). It is also clear that the coldness of the first body can be called a *negative warmth*, for the negation, resulting from it in the warmer body, is a deprivation. But the introduction of this designation here serves no useful purpose; it is scarcely better than juggling with words.[h] In my discussion of this matter, my attention is focused exclusively on what follows.

It has long been known that magnetic bodies have two extremities which are opposed to each other and which are called 'poles'. Of these two poles, the one repels the like-named pole in another such body, and attracts the other. However, the celebrated Professor *Aepinus* showed in his treatise on the similarity between electrical and magnetic energy[33] that electrified bodies, when treated in a certain way, likewise display two poles, of which he called the one the *positive* pole and the other the

2:186 *negative*. This phenomenon can be perceived most clearly when a tube is brought sufficiently close to an electrified body, but in such a way that it draws no spark from it. Now, my contention is this: whenever the temperature is raised or lowered, in other words, whenever the degree of heat or coldness is changed, and in particular changed rapidly, and whenever that change occurs at one end of a continuous intervening space, or at one end of an elongated body[i] what happens is this. There are always two poles, so to speak, of warmth to be found: one of them is positive, that is to say, its temperature is higher than the previous temperature of the body in question, while the other pole is negative, its temperature, namely, being lower than the previous temperature of the body, in other words, it is cold. It is

---

[e] *Erwärmung.*   [f] *Erkältung.*   [g] *dieses subtile und elastische Flüssige.*   [h] *Wortspiel.*
[i] *in einem zusammenhängenden Mittelraum oder in die Länge ausgebreiteten Körper an einem Ende / C: in una zone centrale unica oppure ad una estremità di un corpo esteso in lunghezza / F: dans un milieu continu ou dans un corps allongé / K: dans un milieu continu.*

known that there are various underground caverns within which frost prevails with an intensity which is proportionate to the intensity with which the sun heats the air and the ground above the cavern. *Mathias Bel*,[34] who describes such underground caverns in the Carpathian Mountains, adds that it is a custom of the peasants in Transylvania to cool their drink by burying it in the ground and making a fast burning fire above the spot. It seems that, during this process,[j] the layer of earth cannot grow positively warm on the upper surface without the negative of it being produced at a somewhat greater depth. *Boerhave* also mentions[35] the fact that the fire of the blacksmith's forge causes coldness at a certain distance. This opposition also seems to prevail in the open air above the surface of the earth as well, particularly when rapid changes of temperature are taking place. *Jacobi* somewhere in the *Hamburger Magazin* mentions[36] the fact that, when intensely cold weather occurs, which frequently affects countries extending over a considerable area, then it commonly happens that there is an extensive stretch of territory in the interior of which there are substantial areas where the weather is temperate and mild. Similarly, *Aepinus*[37] found in the case of the tube, of which I made mention above, that, from the positive pole at one end to the negative pole at the other extremity, the positively electric and the negatively electric areas alternated with each other at certain intervals. It seems that a rise in temperature cannot occur in one region of the atmosphere without producing the effect, so to speak, of a negative pole in some other region, that is to say, coldness. On the same basis, the converse happens as well: a sudden drop in temperature in one place leads to an increase in temperature somewhere else. A similar phenomenon can be observed in the following case: if a metal rod is heated at one end, and if the rod is suddenly cooled by being plunged into water, the temperature at the other end increases.* 2:187
The difference between the temperature poles accordingly vanishes once

---

* The experiments needed to verify the existence of opposed temperature poles could, it seems to me, be easily carried out. Take an horizontal lead tube about a foot long; bend an inch or two of each end into a vertical position; fill the tube with alcohol and then, having inserted a thermometer at one end, ignite the alcohol at the other extremity. My surmise is that the negative opposition would quickly show itself. Similarly, in order to perceive the effect produced by cooling one end of the tube, one could employ salinated water, and insert crushed ice at one end. I shall take this opportunity to make a further comment on the sort of observation I should like to see made which would, in all probability, do much to explain the coldness and heat which is artificially generated when certain compound substances are dissolved. I am persuaded, namely, that the difference between these phenomena is primarily related to whether or not the compound liquids, once they have been thoroughly mixed, occupy a greater or a smaller volume than that occupied by the constituents combined before they were mixed together. I maintain that in the former case the thermometer will register an increase in temperature, while in the latter case it will indicate a drop in temperature. For when the constituents produce a medium of greater density after they have been mixed

[j] *in dieser Zeit.*

the transmission[l] of heat or the deprivation of heat has had time enough to be diffused uniformly throughout the whole material, just as Professor *Aepinus's*[38] tube is uniformly electrified once it has drawn the spark. It is perhaps also the case that the extreme coldness of the upper regions of the atmosphere is not to be attributed simply to the absence of any means of heating them. Perhaps it is rather to be attributed to a positive ground: in respect of temperature, the upper regions of the atmosphere become negative in proportion to the degree in which the lower regions of the atmosphere and the ground are positive. In general, the force of magnetism, electricity and heat seem to occur in virtue of the self-same mediating matter.[m][39] All these phenomena can be produced by friction, and I suspect that the difference of the poles and the opposition of the positive and negative causality[n] may, if the matter is handled skillfully, be detected in the phenomena of heat as well. *Galileo's* inclined surface,[40] *Huygen's* pendulum clock,[41] *Torricelli's* column of mercury,[42] *Otto Guerick's* atmospheric pump,[43] and *Newton's* glass prism[44] have furnished us with the key to some of the great mysteries of nature. The negative and positive causality of different forms of matter, particularly in the case of electricity, seems to conceal important truths. It is to be hoped that a more fortunate posterity, on whose happy existence we direct our gaze, will one day discover the universal laws which govern these phenomena, which for the moment only appear to us under the form of a still ambiguous harmony.[o]

2:188

together there is more matter exercising attractive force to draw the element of the nearby fire into itself than there was beforehand in the same volume of space. But not only that, it is also to be surmised that the power of attraction will itself increase as the density increases. It is furthermore to be surmised that the power of expansion inherent in the condensed aether only increases, perhaps, in proportion to its density, just as is the case with air. For according to *Newton,* the forces of attraction operating between bodies which are very close to each other stand in a proportion which is much greater than the inverse proportion of the distances.[k] Thus, if the mixture has a density which is greater than the density of the two mixable constituents taken in conjunction before they have been mixed together, it will, relatively to nearby bodies, exercise a greater attraction on the elemental fire; by robbing the thermometer of that elemental fire it will thus cause coldness to make its appearance. But everything will take place in the reverse fashion if the compound yields a medium of less density. For, in so far as it surrenders a quantity of elemental fire, nearby materials will draw it to themselves and display the phenomenon of heat. Not all the experiments yield results which correspond to one's surmises. But if experiments are to be more than a matter of mere accident, they must be instituted by and conducted in accordance with a surmise.

[k] *weil nach dem Newton die Anziehung in grosser Naheit in viel grösserer Proportion stehen als der umgekehrten der Entfernungen.*
[l] *Mittheilung.* [m] *durch einerlei Mittelmaterie.*
[n] *die Entgegensetzung der positiven und negativen Wirksamkeit.*
[o] *zweideutigen Zusammenstimmung.*

Section 3. Containing some reflections which may serve to prepare the application of the above concept to the objects of philosophy

What I have said so far merely amounts to a preliminary examination of an object[p] which is as important as it is difficult. In advancing to general principles from the examples which have been introduced and which are easy enough to understand, there are good grounds for extreme concern: in pursuing this untrodden path mistakes may be made which only come to be noticed as one advances. Accordingly, what I have yet to say on the matter is to be regarded as an experiment[q] which is very imperfect. And yet it is my expectation that any attention, which may be paid to it, will be beneficial in a variety of different ways. I am fully aware that an admission of this kind is a very poor sort of recommendation to those who demand an assertive and dogmatic tone, if they are to permit themselves to be steered in the desired direction. I do not feel the least regret at losing this kind of acclaim. It seems to me, however, that, in a branch of knowledge as difficult to handle[r] as metaphysics, it is much more appropriate that one's thought should first of all be presented to public examination in the guise of tentative experiments[s] than that they should be announced from the beginning with all the adornments of pretended thoroughness[t] and complete conviction. It commonly happens with that latter course that all improvement is rejected out of hand, and any weakness which may be found in what one has to say becomes incurable.

1. Anybody can easily understand why something does not exist, when 2:190 the positive ground for its existence is lacking. But how that which exists should cease to be – that is not so easy to understand. There exists at this moment in my soul, for example, the representation of the sun, and it exists in virtue of the power of my imagination. The next moment, I cease to think of this object. The representation which was, ceases to be in me, and the next state is the zero of the preceding one. Supposing that I wanted to offer the following as an explanation of this ceasing to be: the thought ceased to be because I stopped producing the representation the

---

[p] *die erste Blicke, die ich auf einen Gegenstand . . . werfe.*   [q] *Versuch.*
[r] *einer so schlupfrigen Erkenntnis.*   [s] *unsicherer Versuche.*   [t] *angemasster Gründlichkeit.*

227

moment afterwards. If that were my explanation, the answer would not differ from the question at all, for what is at issue here is precisely how an action, which really occurs, can stop, that is to say, how it can cease to be.

I accordingly maintain that *every passing-away is a negative coming-to-be.*[u] In other words, for something positive which exists to be cancelled, it is just as necessary that there should be a true real ground as it is necessary that a true real ground should exist in order to bring it into existence when it does not already exist. The reason for this is to be found in what has been said above. Suppose that *a* is posited, then only $a - a = 0$. In other words, only in so far as an equal but opposed real ground is combined with the ground of *a* is it possible for *a* to be cancelled. Physical nature everywhere offers examples of this principle. A movement never stops, either completely or in part, unless a motive force which is equal to the force which would have been able to generate the lost movement is combined with it in a relation of opposition.[v] But also our inner experience of the cancellation of representations and desires which have become real in virtue of the activity of the soul completely agrees with this. In order to banish and eliminate a sorrowful thought a genuine effort, and commonly a large one, is required. And that this is so is something which we experience very distinctly within ourselves. It costs a real effort to eradicate an amusing representation which incites us to laughter, if we wish to concentrate our minds on something serious. Every abstraction is simply the cancelling of certain clear representations; the purpose of the cancellation is normally to ensure that what remains is that much more clearly represented. But everybody knows how much effort is needed to attain this purpose. *Abstraction*[w] can therefore be called *negative attention.* In other words, abstraction can be called a genuine doing and acting[x] which is opposed to the action[y] by means of which the representation is rendered clear; the combination of the two yields zero, or the lack of a clear 2:191 representation. For otherwise, if it were a negation and a lack absolutely, it would not require any more expenditure of energy than is required not to know something, for not knowing something never needs a ground.

Exactly the same necessity for a positive ground for cancelling an inner accident[z] of the soul is manifested in overcoming the appetites. And here one can make use of the examples introduced above. In general, however, even leaving aside the cases adduced above where one is actually conscious of this opposed activity, there is no good reason for doubting the occurrence of this activity, even if we do not clearly notice it within us. I am now thinking, for example, of a tiger. This thought disappears, and in its stead the thought of a jackal occurs to me. It is, of course, true that, in the succession of representations, one cannot detect within oneself any

---

[u] *ein jedes Vergehen ist ein negatives Entstehen.* [v] *in der Entgegensetzung.* [w] *Abstraction.*
[x] *Thun und Handeln.* [y] *Handlung.* [z] *Accidens.*

special effort of the soul operating[a] to cancel one of the representations mentioned above. But what an admirably busy activity[b] is concealed within the depths of our minds which goes unnoticed even while it is being exercised. And it goes unnoticed because the actions in question are very numerous and because each of them is represented only very obscurely. Everybody is familiar with the facts which prove that this is the case. One need only consider, for example, the actions which take place unnoticed within us when we *read*. The phenomenon cannot fail to fill us with astonishment. For discussions of this matter, reference can be made, for instance, to the logic of *Reimarus*,[45] which considers the phenomenon. We must therefore conclude that the play of our representations and, in general, of all the activities of our soul, in so far as the consequences which they produce are actual and then cease to exist, presuppose the occurrence of opposed actions of which one is the negative of the other. The conclusion follows from the certain grounds which we have adduced above, even though inner experience cannot always inform us of such opposed activities.

If one considers the grounds which form the foundation of the rule which we have here introduced, the following point will be instantly noticed: in what concerns the *cancellation* of an existing *something*, there can be no difference between the accidents of mental natures[c] and the effects of operative forces[d] in the physical world. These latter effects, namely, are never cancelled except by means of a true, opposed motive force *of something else*. And an inner accident, a thought of the soul, cannot cease to be without a truly active power of exactly *the self-same* thinking subject. The difference here only relates to the different laws governing the two types of being; for the state of matter can only ever be changed by means of an *external* cause, whereas the state of the mind can also be changed by means of an *internal* cause. The necessity of the real opposition, however, always remains the same, in spite of the above difference. 2:192

I would repeat what I have already said: the supposition that one has understood the cancellation of the positive effects of the activity of our souls by calling them *omissions* involves the use of a deceptive concept.[e] It is a very remarkable fact that the more one subjects one's most common and most reliable judgements to scrutiny, the more one discovers such delusions,[f] for we rest satisfied with words, but fail to understand the things themselves. The fact that I do not now have a certain thought, assuming that I did not have that thought before, can, of course, be understood well enough if I say that I am omitting to think the thought in question; for, in this case, the expression signifies the absence of the

---

[a] *die da wirkte.*   [b] *bewunderungswürdige Geschäftigkeit.*
[c] *unter den Accidenzien der geistigen Naturen.*   [d] *wirksamer Kräfte.*   [e] *ein betrügerischer Begriff.*
[f] *Blendwerke.*

ground; and it is by reference to that absence that the absence of the consequence is understood. But if the question is: why does the thought which existed in me a little while ago no longer exist in me? then the answer given above is utterly inadequate. For this non-existence is now a deprivation, and the omission^g here has quite a different sense,* namely, the cancellation of an activity which existed a little while ago. But it is the question which I am raising, and in raising it I shall not so easily allow myself to be fobbed off^h with a word. In applying the above-mentioned rule to all kinds of natural phenomena, great care is necessary, if one is to avoid confusing something negative with something positive – a confusion which can easily occur. For the sense of the proposition which I have here introduced relates to the coming-into-being and passing-away of something which, in this case, is positive. For example: the ceasing to exist of a flame because the fuel which nourishes it has been exhausted is not a negative coming-to-be; that is to say, it is not based upon a true motive force which is opposed to that which brings the flame into being. For the continued existence of a flame is not the continuation of a motion, which already exists, but rather the constant generation of new motions of other combustible particles of vapour.†^{i} The flame's ceasing to exist is, accordingly, not the cancellation of an actual motion, but the lack of new motions and the absence of several separations,^{j} for their cause is missing, namely, the continued feeding of the fire. And in that case, this must be regarded, not as the cancellation of an existing thing, but rather as the lack of the ground of a possible positing (of further separation).^{k} But enough of this problem. My purpose in writing this is to provide those experienced in this type of knowledge with an occasion for further reflection. Needless to say, those who are not experienced in this type of knowledge would, of course, be entitled to demand a fuller explanation.

2:193

2. The propositions, which I intend to present under this number, seem to me to be extremely important. Before presenting them, however, I must add a further determination to the general concept of negative magnitudes. It is a determination which I have hitherto deliberately ignored, so as not unnecessarily to increase the number of the objects requiring careful attention. So far I have merely considered the grounds of real opposition, in so far as they *actually* posit in one and the same thing determinations, of which one is the opposite of the other. A case in point

---

* This sense itself does not even really belong to the word.

† All bodies, the parts of which are suddenly transformed into vapour and thus exercise repulsion, which is opposed to cohesion, emit fire and burn. The reason for this is that the elementary fire, which previously existed in a state of compression, is suddenly released and expands.[46]

^{g} *das Unterlassen.* ^{h} *abspeisen.* ^{i} *brennbare Dunsttheilchen.* ^{j} *mehrerer Trennungen.*
^{k} *der weiteren Absonderung.*

would be the motive forces of one and the same body which tend in exactly the opposite direction; and here the grounds cancel their reciprocal consequences, namely the motions. For this reason, I shall, for the time being, call this opposition *actual opposition* (*oppositio actualis*). On the other hand, to take predicates of the following kind: although they belong to different things and although the one predicate does not immediately cancel the consequence of the other predicate, nonetheless, they may each legitimately be called the negative of the other; and they may be legitimately so called in virtue of the fact that each is so constituted that it is either capable of cancelling the consequence of the other, or it is capable of cancelling something which is determined like that consequence and which is equal to it.[1] This opposition may be called *possible opposition* (*oppositio potentialis*). Both oppositions are real; that is to say, they are both different from logical opposition; both of them are constantly being employed in mathematics, and they both deserve to be employed in philosophy as well. Take the case of two bodies which are moving towards each other along precisely the same straight line, each with the same force as the other. These forces are communicated to each other when the two bodies collide. For this reason, one of them can be called the negative of the other, and that in the first sense of the word, namely through actual opposition. In the case of two bodies which are moving away from each other in opposite directions along the same straight line, each with the same force as the other, one is the negative of the other. But, in this case, they do not communicate their forces to each other. For this reason, they only stand in potential opposition to each other, for each body would, if it were to collide with a body moving in the same direction as the other, cancel as much force in it as exists in that other body. And that is also how, in what is about to follow, I shall understand all the grounds of real opposition in the world, not merely those which belong to motive forces. However, in order to give an example of the other cases, one could say that the pleasure which one person has, and the displeasure*m* which another person has, stand in potential opposition to each other, for it sometimes happens that the one really does cancel the consequences of the other, for when there is such real conflict, one person often destroys what the other person has taken pleasure in creating. Since I am taking the grounds, which are really opposed to each

2:194

---

[1] *Dagegen nennt man mit Recht solche Prädikate, die zwar verschiedenen Dingen zukommen und eins die Folgen des andern unmittelbar nicht aufheben, dennoch eins die Negative des andern, in so fern ein jedes so beschaffen ist, dass es doch entweder die Folge des andern, oder wenigstens etwas, was eben so bestimmt ist wie diese Folge und ihr gleich ist, aufheben könnte* (Only C has recognised the structure of this complex sentence [*Dagegen nennt man . . . solche Prädikate . . . eins die Negative des andern* ('on the other hand, one calls . . . such predicates . . . one the negative of the other')]).

m *Unlust* / (See note *y*, page 219).

other in both senses of the word, in an entirely general sense, I hope that no one will insist on my always making these concepts clear by means of examples *in concreto*. Just as everything which appertains to motions can be rendered clear and intelligible to intuition, so, by contrast, the real grounds within us, which are not mechanical in character, reveal themselves to be difficult and indistinct,[n] if any attempt is made to explain the relationship between them and their consequences, whether in opposition or in harmony. Accordingly, I shall rest content with explaining the following propositions in their general sense.

The first proposition is this: *In all the natural changes which occur in the world, the sum of that which is positive is neither increased nor diminished, provided that the sum is calculated by adding together positings which agree with each other[o] (not opposed to each other) and subtracting from each other positings which are really opposed to each other.*

All change consists in this: either something positive, which was not, is posited; or something positive, which was, is cancelled. The change is natural if its cause, like its effect, belongs to the world. In the first case, accordingly, where a positing, which was not, is posited,[p] the change is a *coming-to-be.* The state of the world prior to this change is, in respect of this positing, equal to zero = o, and the real effect = A exists in virtue of this coming-to-be.[q] I maintain, however, that if A arises,[r] then, in a natural change occurring in the world, −A must also arise. In other words, no natural ground of a real consequence can exist without its being at the same time the ground of another consequence, which is the negative of the first.* For since the consequence is nothing = o, unless the ground is posited, the sum of the positing contains no more in the consequence than was contained in the state of the world, in so far as it contained the ground of that consequence. But this state contained the zero of that positing, which is to be found in the consequences. That is to say, the positing, which is to be found in the consequence, did not exist in the previous state. It follows that the change which issues from it can only ever be equal to zero in the totality of the world, viewed from the perspective of its real or potential consequence.[s] Now, on the one hand, the consequence is

2:195

---

* Such is the case, for example, when one body collides with another: the production of a new motion occurs simultaneously with the cancellation of another motion which is equal to it and which precedes it. Similarly, too, it is not possible for someone in a boat to push a floating object away from him in a given direction without himself being propelled in the opposite direction.

[n] *schwer und undeutlich.*   [o] *einstimmig.*   [p] *eine Position, die nicht war, gesetzt wird.*
[q] *ein Enstehen.*   [r] *entspringt.*
[s] *Es enthielt aber dieser Zustand von derjenigen Position, die in der Folge ist, das Zero, das heisst, in dem vorigen Zustand war die Position nicht, die in der Folge anzutreffen ist, folglich kann die Veränderung, die daraus fliesst, im Ganzen der Welt nach ihren wirklichen oder potentialen Folgen auch nicht anders als dem Zero gleich sein.*

positive and $= A$; on the other hand, however, the whole state of the universe is, as before in respect of the change A, supposed to be zero $= 0$; but this is impossible, unless $A - A$ is to be taken together. It follows from these considerations that a positive change only ever occurs naturally in the world, if its consequence consists, as a whole, in a real or potential opposition, which cancels itself. But this sum total yields zero $= 0$; prior to the change it was also $= 0$; it follows that it is neither increased nor diminished by the change.

In the second case, where the change consists in the cancellation of something positive, the consequence $= 0$. But, according to what was said before, the state of the entire ground was not merely $= A$, but $A - A = 0$. Thus, according to the mode of calculation which I am here presupposing, positing^t in the world is neither increased nor diminished.

I should like to attempt to clarify this principle, which seems to me to be important. In the changes which occur in the physical world, the following mechanical rule is firmly established and has long since proved to be true. The rule is expressed as follows: *Quantitas motus, summando vires corporum in easdem partes et subtrahendo eas quae vergunt in contrarias, per mutuam illorum actionem (conflictum, pressionem, attractionem) non mutatur.*[47] Although, in pure mechanics, this rule is not derived immediately from the metaphysical ground, from which we have derived the general proposition, its validity does indeed, as a matter of fact, depend on this foundation. For the law of inertia, which is the foundation of the usual proof, derives its truth simply from the argument^u adduced, as I could easily show, if I could go into the matter in detail.^{v}

The elucidation of the rule, with which we are concerned, is by nature $2:196$ difficult in those cases of change which are not mechanical, such as those occurring in our soul, or which depend in any way on the soul. In general, it is not possible to offer an account of these effects or their causes which is nearly as intelligible or as intuitively distinct^w as can be offered of those which occur in the physical world. Notwithstanding, I should like to try to cast some light on the matter, as far as it seems possible to me to do so.

Aversion^x is just as much something positive as desire. The former is a consequence of a positive displeasure,^{y} just as desire is the positive consequence of a pleasure. Only in so far as we simultaneously experience pleasure and displeasure in relation to one and the same object do feelings of desire and aversion stand in actual opposition to each other. But in so far as the same ground which occasions pleasure in an object is at the same time the ground of a true displeasure relative to *another* object, the grounds of the desires are at the same time the grounds of the feelings of aversion; and the ground of a desire is at the same time the ground of something

---

^{t} *die Position.* ^{u} *Beweisgrund.* ^{v} *wenn ich weitläufig sein dürfte.*
^{w} *fasslich und anschauend deutlich.* ^{x} *Verabscheuung.* ^{y} *Unlust.*

which stands in a real, albeit only potential, opposition to it. The situation is the same as that of the movements of bodies which are moving away from each other along the same straight line in opposite directions: even though neither strives to cancel the movement of the other, the one may still be regarded as the negative of the other, for they are posited as being potentially opposed to each other. In the same way, a degree of desire for fame arises in someone, and the same degree of revulsion[z] arises in that same person at the same time in relation to the opposite of fame. The revulsion is, it is true, only potential, as long as circumstances do not yet stand in actual opposition to the desire for fame. Nonetheless, what firmly establishes in the soul a positive ground of the same degree of displeasure is exactly the same as the cause of the desire for fame, for the circumstances in the world may turn out to be opposed to what favours the desire for fame.* In a little while we shall see that such is not the case with the Most Perfect Being. We shall, indeed, see that the ground of His supreme pleasure[c] actually excludes all possibility of displeasure.

2:197 In the case of the actions of the understanding we even find that the clearer or the distincter a certain idea is made, the more the remaining ideas are obscured and the more their clarity is diminished, so that that which is positive and becomes actual in the case of such a change, is combined with a real and actual opposition. If one takes everything together, following the method of calculation mentioned above, then the degree of what is positive is neither increased nor diminished by the opposition as a result of the change.

The second proposition is as follows: *All the real grounds of the universe, if one adds those together which agree with each other and subtracts from one another those which are opposed to each other, yields a result[d] which is equal to zero.* The totality of the world is in itself nothing, except in so far as it is something in virtue of the will of another.[e] Accordingly, the sum of all existing reality, in so far as it is grounded in the world, is equal to zero = 0, if it is regarded in itself. Now, although all possible reality in relation to the divine will yield a result[f] which is positive, the essence[g] of a world is nonetheless not thereby cancelled. But the being of the world necessarily implies that the existence of that which is grounded in the world, is, in and

---

* It is for this reason that the Stoic wise man has to eradicate all those drives which involve feelings of great sensual desire; for those feelings also lay the foundations of deep dissatisfaction and discontent,[a] which may, according to the vicissitudes of fortune,[b] cancel out the entire value of those sensual pleasures.

[z] *Abscheu.*   [a] *Unzufriedenheit und Missvergnugens.*
[b] *nach dem abwechselnden Spiel des Weltlaufs.*   [c] *Lust.*   [d] *Fazit.*
[e] *Das Ganze der Welt ist an sich selbst Nichts, ausser in so fern es durch den Willen eines andern Etwas ist /* (the sentence is ambiguous: the second clause could be translated 'except in so far as it is [exists] in virtue of the will of another Something').
[f] *Fazit.*   [g] *Wesen* (alt. being).

for itself alone, equal to zero. Thus, the sum of that which exists in the world is, in relation to the ground which exists externally to it, positive. But, the sum of that which exists in the world is, in relation to the real grounds within the world relatively to each other, equal to zero. Now, since in the first relation there can never occur an opposition between the real grounds of the world and the divine will, it follows that, from this point of view, there is no cancellation, and the sum is positive. But since, in the second relation, the result is zero, it follows that the positive grounds must stand in an opposition, and that when they are regarded as standing in this opposition and when they are added together they must then yield zero.[48]

NOTE TO THE SECOND NUMBER

I have discussed these two propositions with a view to inviting the reader to reflect on the matter. I also admit that even for me they are not sufficiently clear, and I concede that they cannot be understood with enough clarity[h] in terms of their grounds. However, I am deeply convinced that incomplete experiments, presented in the form of abstract cognition in a problematic fashion,[i] can contribute a great deal to the growth of higher philosophy, for it is often the case that, in the examination of a very deep and obscure question,[j] a second person arrives at enlightenment more easily than the person who raised the question in the first place and whose efforts had perhaps been able to resolve only half the difficulties. The content of these propositions seems to me to have a certain dignity about it, which may well encourage a precise examination of them – provided, of course, that a thorough understanding of their sense has been attained, and that is not so easy in cognition of this kind.

2:198

I shall, however, attempt to anticipate a number of misinterpretations. I would have been completely misunderstood, if I had been taken to be using the first principle to mean that the sum of reality, in general, is neither increased nor diminished by changes in the world. This is so remote from my meaning that even the mechanical rule, which was introduced as an example, establishes exactly the opposite. For the collision of bodies with each other sometimes increases and sometimes diminishes the sum of the movements, considered in themselves; what remains the same, however, is the result,[k] *when it is calculated in the manner which has been specified.*[l] For in many cases the oppositions are merely potential; and then the motive forces do not actually cancel each other, and an increase therefore occurs. However, if one performs the calculation in accordance

---

[h] *Augenscheinlichkeit.*   [i] *im abstracten Erkenntnisse problematisch vorgetragen.*
[j] *in einer tief verborgenen Frage.*   [k] *das Fazit.*   [l] *nach der zugleich beigefügten Art geschätzt.*

with the method specified as a guide,^{m} then these forces must also be subtracted from each other.

One must judge in exactly the same way when this principle is applied to changes of a non-mechanical character. One would be guilty of the same misunderstanding if one were to suppose, on the basis of that same principle, that the perfection of the world could in no wise increase. For that principle does not, of course, at all deny that the sum of reality in general could increase by natural means. Furthermore, the perfection of the world in general very much consists in this conflict of real opposed grounds, just as the material part of the world is, in the most obvious fashion, maintained in a regular course simply by means of the conflict of forces, and it is always a serious mistake to conflate the sum of reality with the magnitude of perfection.^{n}[49] We have seen above that displeasure is just as positive as pleasure, but who would call it a perfection?

3. We have already remarked that it is often difficult to decide whether certain negations of nature are merely lacks arising from the absence of a ground, or deprivations resulting from the real opposition of two positive grounds. Examples of this are common in the material world. The parts of any body which cohere together press against each other with true forces

2:199 (of *attraction*) and the effect of these strivings would be a reduction in spatial volume, were it not for the fact that equally true activities operated in the same degree against them^o as a result of the repulsion of the elements, the operation of the repulsion being the ground of impenetrability.[50] Rest occurs in this case, not because there is any lack of motive forces, but because there are motive forces acting against each other. It is in exactly this fashion that the weights on the arms of scales are at rest, if the weights are placed in the scale-pans in accordance with the laws of equilibrium. This concept can be extended far beyond the limits of the material world. In exactly the same way, there is no reason to suppose that, when we seem to be in a state of complete mental inactivity, the sum of the real grounds of thought and desire is smaller than it is in the state when some degrees of this activity^p reveal themselves to consciousness. If you ask a man of even the greatest learning at a moment when he is relaxing and at rest to recount something to you or to share part of his knowledge of things with you, you will find that he knows nothing in this state, that he is empty and that he has no definite thoughts or judgements. But stimulate him by asking him a question or by expressing a view of your own, and his learning will reveal itself in a series of activities. And the tendency^q of that succession of activities will be to make both him and you aware of his understanding of things.^{r} Without any doubt, the real grounds of this

^{m} *nach der einmal zur Richtschnur angenommenen Schätzung.*
^{n} *die Summe der Realität mit der Grösse der Vollkommenheit.*
^{o} *inhen im gleichen Grade entgegenwirkten.* ^{p} *Wirksamkeit.* ^{q} *Richtung* (lit: direction).
^{r} *Einsicht.*

occurrence had long been present in him, but since the consequence, as far as consciousness was concerned, was zero, those real grounds must have been opposed to each other. Thus it is with the thunder which, invented by art for our destruction and carefully preserved in the arsenal of a prince ready for a future war, lies in menacing silence until, touched by a treacherous spark, it explodes in lightning and lays waste to everything around it. Tensions, constantly ready to explode, lay dormant within it, the prisoners of powerful forces of attraction, waiting for the stimulus of a spark of fire, to be released.[51] There is something imposing and, it seems to me, profoundly true in this thought of *Leibniz:* the soul embraces the whole universe with its faculty of representation, though only an infinitesimally tiny part of these representations is clear.[52] It is, indeed, the case that concepts of every kind must have as the foundation on which alone they are based the inner activity of our minds.[s] External things may well contain the condition under which concepts present themselves[t] in one way or another; but external things do not have the power actually to produce those concepts. The power of thought possessed by the soul[u] must contain the real grounds of all concepts, in so far as they are supposed to arise in a natural fashion within the soul. The phenomena of the coming-to-be and passing-away of cognitions are to be attributed, it would seem, simply to the agreement or opposition of all this activity. The views expressed here may be regarded as elucidations of the first proposition of the previous number.[53]

2:200

In moral matters, likewise, zero is not always to be regarded as a negation due to lack; nor is a positive consequence of greater magnitude always to be regarded as proof of greater activity having been employed to bring about this consequence. Suppose that someone has ten degrees of passion – miserliness,[v] say – and that this is sufficient, under certain circumstances, to conflict with the rules of duty. Let him apply twelve degrees of effort, and let them be exercised in accordance with the principles of benevolence.[w] The result will be two degrees, and that will be the extent to which he will be benevolent and beneficent.[x] Imagine another person who has three degrees of miserliness and seven degrees of capacity to act in accordance with the principles of obligation. The action will be four degrees in magnitude, and that will be the extent to which he will benefit another person after the conflict of his desires. But what is indisputable is this: in so far as the passion in question can be regarded as natural and involuntary,[y] the moral value of the action performed by the first person will be greater than that performed by the second, even though, if one were to assess the actions by reference to the *living* force,

---

[s] *auf der inneren Thätigkeit des Geistes.*   [t] *sie sich . . . hervorthun.*
[u] *Die Denkungskraft der Seele.*   [v] *Geldgeiz.*
[w] *nach Grundsätzen der Nächstenliebe* (alt: principles of charity).   [x] *wohlthätig und hulfreich.*
[y] *unwillkürlich.*

the consequence of the latter case exceeds that of the former. For this reason, it is impossible for us, with certainty, to infer from another person's actions the degree of that person's virtuous disposition.*z* He who sees into the inmost chambers of the heart*a* has reserved for Himself alone the right to pass judgement on others.

4. If one wished to venture the application of these concepts to the cognition which men may have of the Infinite Divinity – a cognition which is so fragile – with what difficulties are our greatest efforts not then surrounded? The foundation of these concepts can only be found within ourselves.*b* It is therefore in most cases unclear whether this idea is to be applied by us to this incomprehensible object in a literal fashion or only by means of a certain analogy.*c* Even today, *Simonides* is still regarded as a man of wisdom; after a great deal of hesitation and delay he gave the following answer to his prince: the more I reflect on God, the less able I am to understand Him.54 That answer is not the language of the learned rabble:*d* it knows nothing and understands nothing, but it talks about everything; and what it says – on that it stubbornly insists.*e* In the Supreme Being there can be neither grounds of deprivation nor of real opposition. For since everything is given in and through Him, it follows that, in virtue of His possessing all determinations*f* in His own existence, no inner cancellation is possible. For this reason, the feeling of displeasure*g* is not a predicate which can be appropriately applied to the Divinity. No one ever desires an object without positively feeling aversion for its opposite. In other words, if someone desires something, that person's will relates not only to the contradictory opposite of his desire; it also relates to that which is really opposed to his desire (aversion), namely, a consequence which arises from positive displeasure.*h* To every desire, which a conscientious teacher has to educate his pupil well, there is positively opposed any outcome which is not in agreement with his desire, such an outcome being a ground for displeasure. The relations of objects to the Divine Will are of quite a different nature. Strictly speaking, in that Being, no external object is a ground of either pleasure or displeasure; for He does not in the least depend on anything distinct from Himself. The reason why this pure pleasure does not inhere in the Being, who is the ground of His own blessedness, is not because the good exists externally to Him. On the contrary, the reason is this: the good exists because the eternal representation of its possibility, and the pleasure connected with it, is the ground of the desire being satisfied.*i* If this is compared with the

z den Grad der tugendhaften Gesinnung.   *a das Innerste der Herzen.*
b nur von uns selbst hernehmen können.   *c vermittelst einiger Analogie.*   *d des gelehrten Pöbels.*
e darauf pocht er.   *f den Allbesitz der Bestimmungen.*   *g Unlust.*
h d.i. nicht allein so, dass die Beziehung seines Willens das contradictorische Gegentheil der Begierde, sondern ihr Realentgegengesetztes (Abscheu), nämlich eine Folge aus positiver Unlust, ist.
i der vollzogenen Begierde.

concrete representation of the nature of the desire of all creatures, it will be noticed that the will of the Uncreated Being can have very little in common[j] with that of created beings. And even when one considers the other determinations as well, what we have just said will come as no surprise if the following fact is properly understood. The difference in quality must be immeasurably great when a comparison is made between things, on the one hand, which are nothing in themselves, and that Being, on the other, in virtue of which alone everything is.

GENERAL REMARK

The self-styled 'thorough' philosophers increase daily in number. They look so deeply into everything that nothing remains hidden from them which they cannot explain or understand. I can thus already anticipate that the concept of real opposition, which I laid down as a foundation at the beginning of this treatise, will strike them as very shallow. And the concept of negative magnitudes, which is based on the concept of real opposition, will seem to them not to be thorough enough. I make no secret of the frailty of my understanding.[k] This frailty is the explanation of my understanding least what everybody else seems to understand with ease. I flatter myself that my incapacity entitles me to the support of these great minds, so that their high wisdom may bridge the gaps which my imperfect under-   2:202
standing found itself unable to fill.

I fully understand how a consequence is posited by a ground in accordance with the rule of identity: analysis of the concepts shows that the consequence is contained in the ground. It is in this way that necessity is a ground of immutability; that composition is a ground of divisibility; that infinity is a ground of omniscience, *etc., etc.* And I can clearly understand the connection of the ground with the consequence, for the consequence is really identical with part of the concept of the ground. And, in virtue of the fact that the consequence is already contained in the ground, it is posited by the ground, in accordance with the rule of agreement.[l] But what I should dearly like to have distinctly explained to me, however, is how one thing issues from another thing, though not by means of the law of identity. The first kind of ground I call the logical ground, for the relation of the ground to its consequence can be understood logically. In other words, it can be clearly understood by appeal to the law of identity. The second kind of ground, however, I call the real ground, for this relation belongs, presumably, to my true concepts, but the manner of the relating can in no wise be judged.

As for this real ground and its relation to its consequence my question presents itself in the following simple form: How am I to understand **the fact that, because something is, something else is?** A logical conse-

---

[j] *wenig Ähnliches.*   [k] *aus der Schwäche meiner Einsicht.*   [l] *nach der Regel der Einstimmung.*

quence is only really posited because it is identical with the ground. Human beings are capable of error: the ground of this fallibility is to be found in the finitude of man's nature, for if I analyse the concept of a finite mind, I see that fallibility is to be found in it. In other words, I recognise that fallibility is identical with what is contained in the concept of a mind.[m] But the will of God contains the real ground of the existence of the world. The will of God is something. The world which exists is *something completely different.* Nonetheless, the one is posited by the other. The state of mind in which I hear the name *Stagirite* is something, and it is in virtue of that something that something else, namely my thought of a philosopher, is posited. A body A is in motion; another body B, lying in the direct path of A, is at rest. The motion of A is something; the motion of B is something else; and yet the one is posited by the other. Now, you may subject the concept of divine willing to as much analysis as you please: you will never encounter in that concept an existent world as something which is contained within the concept of God's willing, or as something posited by that concept through identity. Likewise in the other cases. Nor am I willing to be fobbed off[n] by the words 'cause' and 'effect', 'force' and 'action'. For if I already regard something as a cause of something else, or if I attach the concept of force to it, then I am already thinking of the cause as containing the relation of the real ground to its consequence, and then it is easy to understand that the consequence is posited in accordance with the rule of identity. For example, the existence of the world can be understood with complete distinctness in terms of the omnipotent will of God. But here 'power' signifies something in God, in virtue of which other things are posited. But this word already designates the relation of a real ground to its consequence; but it is this relation which I wish to have explained. I would take this opportunity merely to remark that the distinction made by *Crusius*[55] between the ideal and the real ground[o] is completely different from my own distinction. *Crusius*'s ideal ground is identical with the ground of cognition;[p] and in that case it is easy to understand that if I already regard something as a ground, I can infer from it the consequence. Hence, according to his principles, the west wind is a real ground of rain clouds; but it is also an ideal ground, for I am able to recognise[q] and protect the latter by appeal to the former. But according to our concepts, the real ground is never a logical ground, and the rain is not posited by the wind in virtue of the rule of identity. The distinction between logical opposition and real opposition, which we drew above, is parallel to the distinction between the logical ground and the real ground, which is under discussion here.

2:203

[m] *Geistes* / (strictly speaking: *finite mind;* cf. Lasswitz, AK 2:480).
[n] *Ich lasse mich auch . . . nicht abspeisen.*   [o] *Ideal- und Realgrund.*   [p] *Erkenntnissgrund.*
[q] *erkennen.*

The former distinction, that between logical and real opposition, is clearly understood by means of the law of contradiction. And I understand how, if I posit the infinity of God, the predicate of mortality is cancelled by it, and it is cancelled because mortality contradicts infinity. But how the motion of one body is cancelled by the motion of another body – that is another question, for the motion of the second body does not stand in contradiction[r] to the motion of the first body. If I presuppose impenetrability, which stands in real opposition[s] to any force which strives to penetrate the space occupied by a given body, I can already understand why the motions are cancelled. But in making that presupposition, I have reduced one real opposition to another. Now, let the attempt be made to see whether real opposition in general can be explained. Let us see whether we can offer a distinct explanation of how it is that, *because something is, something else is cancelled,* and whether we can say anything more than I have already said on the matter, namely that it simply does not take place in virtue of the law of contradiction. I have reflected upon the nature of our cognition with respect to our judgement concerning grounds and consequences, and one day I shall present a detailed account of the fruits of my reflections.[56] One of my conclusions is this:[t] the relation of a real ground to something, which is either posited or cancelled by it, cannot be expressed by a judgement; it can only be expressed by a concept. That concept can probably be reduced by means of analysis[u] to simple concepts of real grounds, albeit in such a fashion that in the end all our cognitions of this relation reduce to simple, unanalysable concepts of real grounds, the relation of which to their consequences cannot be rendered distinct at all. In the meantime, those philosophers who lay claim to the possession of an understanding which knows no limitations[v] will test the methods of their philosophy to see how far they can advance in a question such as this present one.

2:204

---

[r] *im Widerspruch steht.* [s] *im realer Entgegensetzung steht.* [t] *Aus demselben findet sich.*
[u] *durch Auflösung.* [v] *Schranken.*

Inquiry concerning the distinctness of the principles of natural theology and morality, being an answer to the question proposed for consideration by the Berlin Royal Academy of Sciences for the year 1763 (1764)

Untersuchung über die Deutlichkeit der Grundsätze der natürlichen Theologie und der Moral. Zur Beantwortung der Frage, welche die Königl. Akademie der Wissenschaften zu Berlin auf das Jahr 1763 aufgegeben hat (1764)

Untersuchung

über die

Deutlichkeit der Grundsätze

der

natürlichen Theologie und der Moral.

Zur
Beantwortung der Frage,
welche die
Königl. Akademie der Wissenschaften zu Berlin
auf das Jahr 1763
aufgegeben hat.

Verum animo satis haec vestigia parva sagaci
Sunt, per quae possis cognoscere caetera tute.

Inquiry concerning the distinctness of the principles of natural theology and morality

*Being an answer to the question
proposed for consideration by the
Berlin Royal Academy of Sciences
for the year 1763*

Verum animo satis haec vestigia parva sagaci
Sunt, per quae possis cognoscere caetera tute.[1]

The question proposed for consideration is such that, if it is appropriately answered, higher philosophy must as a result acquire a determinate form. If the method for attaining the highest possible degree of certainty in this type of cognition has been established, and if the nature of this kind of conviction[a] has been properly understood, then the following effect will be produced: the endless instability of opinions and scholarly sects[b] will be replaced by an immutable rule which will govern didactic method[c] and unite reflective minds in a single effort. It was in this way that, in natural science, *Newton's* method transformed the chaos of physical hypotheses into a secure procedure based on experience and geometry.[2] But what method is this treatise itself to adopt, granted that it is a treatise in which metaphysics is to be shown the true degree of certainty to which it may aspire, as well as the path by which the certainty may be attained? If what is presented in this treatise is itself metaphysics, then the judgement of the treatise will be no more certain than has been that science which hopes to benefit from our inquiry by acquiring some permanence and stability;[d] and then all our efforts will have been in vain. I shall, therefore, ensure that my treatise contains nothing but empirical propositions which are certain,[e] and the inferences which are drawn immediately from them. I shall rely neither on the doctrines of the philosophers, the uncertainty of which is the very occasion of this present inquiry, nor on definitions,[f] which so often lead to error.[g] The method I shall employ will be simple and cautious. Some of the things I shall have to say may be found to be lacking in certainty; but such things will only have an elucidatory function and will not be employed for purposes of proof.

[a] *Überzeugung.*   [b] *Schulsecten.*
[c] *Lehrart* / Beck (1949) (hereafter B): method of instruction / Carabellese (Assunto) (hereafter C): *norma dottrinaria* / Ferrari (hereafter Fe): *méthode d'enseignement* / Fichant (hereafter Fi): *mode de connaissance* (*Lehrart*).
[d] *einigen Bestand und Festigkeit.*   [e] *sichere Erfahrungssätze.*   [f] *Definitionen.*   [g] *trügen.*

First reflection: General comparison of the manner in which certainty is attained in mathematical cognition with the manner in which certainty is attained in philosophical cognition

§1. MATHEMATICS ARRIVES AT ALL ITS DEFINITIONS[h] SYNTHETICALLY, WHEREAS PHILOSOPHY ARRIVES AT ITS DEFINITIONS ANALYTICALLY[3]

There are two ways in which one can arrive at a general concept: either by the *arbitrary combination*[i] of concepts, or by *separating out*[j] that cognition which has been rendered distinct by means of analysis.[k4] Mathematics only ever draws up its definitions in the first way. For example, think arbitrarily[l] of four straight lines bounding a plane surface so that the opposite sides are not parallel to each other. Let this figure be called a *trapezium*. The concept which I am defining[m] is not given prior to the definition[n] itself; on the contrary, it only comes into existence as a result of that definition. Whatever the concept of a cone may ordinarily signify, in mathematics the concept is the product of the arbitrary representation[o] of a right-angled triangle which is rotated on one of its sides. In this and in all other cases the definition[p] obviously comes into being as a result of *synthesis*.[q5]

The situation is entirely different in the case of philosophical definitions. In philosophy, the concept of a thing is always given, albeit confusedly or in an insufficiently determinate fashion. The concept has to be

---

[h] *Definitionen.* [i] *willkürliche Verbindung.*

[j] *Absonderung von* / B: setting apart / C: *isolando* / Fe & Fi: *abstraction à partir de* / Walford (hereafter W): *separation* from.

[k] *durch Absonderung von demjenigen* / (the sentence is ambiguous because of the ambiguity of the *von* [either 'from' or 'of']).

[l] *willkürlich.* [m] *erkläre.* [n] *Definition.* [o] *aus der willkürlichen Vorstellung.*

[p] *Erklärung* / B: definition / C: *spiegazione* / Fe & Fi: *définition* / W: explanation.

[q] *durch die Synthesin.*

analysed;[r] the characteristic marks which have been separated out[s] and the concept which has been given have to be compared with each other in all kinds of contexts; and this abstract thought[t] must be rendered complete[u][6] and determinate. For example, everyone has a concept of time. But suppose that that concept has to be defined.[v] The idea of time has to be examined in all kinds of relation if its characteristic marks are to be discovered by means of analysis:[w] different characteristic marks which have been abstracted have to be combined together to see whether they yield an adequate concept;[x][7] they have to be collated with each other[y] to see whether one characteristic mark does not partly include another within itself. If, in this case, I had tried to arrive at a definition of time synthetically, it would have had to have been a happy coincidence indeed if the concept, thus reached synthetically, had been exactly the same as that which completely expresses the idea[z] of time which is given to us.[8]

2:277

Nonetheless, it will be said, philosophers sometimes offer synthetic definitions as well, and mathematicians on occasion offer definitions which are analytic. A case in point would be that of a philosopher arbitrarily[a] thinking of a substance endowed with the faculty of reason and calling it a spirit.[b][9] My reply, however, is this: such determinations of the meaning of a word are never philosophical definitions. If they are to be called definitions[c] at all, then they are merely grammatical definitions. For no philosophy is needed to say what name is to be attached to an arbitrary concept.[d] *Leibniz* imagined a simple substance which had nothing but obscure representations,[e] and he called it a *slumbering monad.*[10] But, in doing so, he did not define[f] the monad. He merely invented[g] it, for the concept of a monad was not given to him but created by him. Mathematicians, on the other hand, it must be admitted, sometimes have offered analytic definitions.[h] But it must also be said that for them to do so is always a mistake. It was in this way that *Wolff* considered similarity in geometry: he looked at it with a philosophical eye, with a view to subsuming the geometrical concept of similarity under the general concept.[11] But he could have spared himself the trouble. If I think of figures, in which the angles enclosed by the lines of the perimeter are equal to each other, and in which the sides enclosing those angles stand in identical relations to each other[i] – such a figure could always be regarded as the definition of similarity between figures, and likewise with the other similarities between spaces. The general definition of similarity is of no concern whatever to the geometer.[12] It is fortunate for mathematics that, even though the

[r] *zergliedern.*   [s] *die abgesonderte Merkmale.*   [t] *abstracten Gedanken.*   [u] *ausführlich.*

[v] *erklärt.*   [w] *Zergliederung.*   [x] *einen zureichenden Begriff.*   [y] *unter einander zusammengehalten.*

[z] *Idee.*   [a] *willkürlicher Weise.*   [b] *Geist.*   [c] *Erklärungen.*   [d] *einem willkürlichen Begriff.*

[e] *dunkle Vorstellungen.*   [f] *erklärt.*   [g] *erdacht.*   [h] *analytisch erklärt.*

[i] *denn wenn ich mir Figuren denke, in welchen die Winkel, die die Linien des Umkreises einschliessen, gegenseitig gleich sind, und die Seiten, die sie einschliessen einerlei Verhältniss haben.*

geometer from time to time gets involved in the business of furnishing analytic definitions[j] as a result of a false conception of his task, in the end nothing is actually inferred from such definitions, or, at any rate, the immediate inferences which he draws ultimately constitute the mathematical definition itself. Otherwise this science would be liable to exactly the same wretched discord as philosophy itself.

2:278　　The mathematician deals with concepts which can often be given a philosophical definition[k] as well. An example is the concept of space in general. But he accepts such a concept *given* in accordance with his clear and ordinary representation. It sometimes happens that philosophical definitions[l] are given to him from other sciences; this happens especially in applied mathematics. The definition[m] of fluidity is a case in point. But, in a case like that, the definition does not arise within mathematics itself; it is merely employed there. It is the business of philosophy to analyse concepts which are given in a confused fashion,[n] and to render them complete and determinate.[o] The business of mathematics, however, is that of combining and comparing given concepts of magnitudes, which are clear and certain,[p] with a view to establishing what can be inferred from them.

§2. MATHEMATICS, IN ITS ANALYSES,[q] PROOFS AND INFERENCES EXAMINES THE UNIVERSAL UNDER SIGNS IN CONCRETO; PHILOSOPHY EXAMINES THE UNIVERSAL BY MEANS OF SIGNS IN ABSTRACTO

Since we are here treating our propositions only as conclusions derived immediately from our experiences, I *first of all* appeal, with regard to the present matter, to arithmetic, both the general arithmetic of indeterminate magnitudes, and the arithmetic of numbers, where the relation of magnitude to unity is determinate.[13] In both kinds of arithmetic, there are posited first of all not things themselves but their signs, together with the special designations of their increase or decrease, their relations *etc.* Thereafter, one operates with these signs according to easy and certain rules, by means of substitution, combination,[r] subtraction and many kinds of transformation,[s] so that the things signified are themselves completely forgotten in the process, until eventually, when the conclusion is drawn, the meaning of the symbolic conclusion is deciphered.[t] *Secondly*, I would draw attention to the fact that in geometry, in order, for example, to

---

[j] *Erklärungen.*　[k] *Erklärungen.*　[l] *Erklärungen.*　[m] *Erklärung.*
[n] *die als verworren gegeben sind.*　[o] *ausführlich und bestimmt zu machen.*　[p] *klar und sicher.*
[q] *Auflösungen.*　[r] *Verknüpfung.*　[s] *Veränderung.*　[t] *entziffert wird.*

discover the properties of all circles, one circle is drawn; and in this one circle, instead of drawing all the possible lines which could intersect each other within it, two lines only are drawn. The relations which hold between these two lines are proved; and the universal rule, which governs the relations holding between intersecting lines in all circles whatever, is considered in these two lines *in concreto*.[14]

If the procedure of philosophy is compared with that of geometry it becomes apparent that they are completely different. The signs employed in philosophical reflection are never anything other than words. And words can neither show in their composition the constituent concepts of which the whole idea, indicated by the word, consists; nor are they capable of indicating in their combinations the relations of the philosophical thoughts to each other.[15] Hence, in reflection in this kind of cognition, one has to focus one's attention on the thing itself:[u] one is constrained to represent the universal *in abstracto* without being able to avail oneself of that important device which facilitates thought and which consists in handling individual signs rather than the universal concepts of the things themselves. Suppose, for example, that the geometer wishes to demonstrate that space is infinitely divisible. He will take, for example, a straight line standing vertically between two parallel lines; from a point on one of these parallel lines he will draw lines to intersect the other two lines.[16] By means of this symbol[v] he recognises with the greatest certainty that the division can be carried on *ad infinitum*. By contrast, if the philosopher wishes to demonstrate, say, that all bodies consist of simple substances, he will first of all assure himself that bodies in general are wholes composed of substances, and that, as far as these substances are concerned, composition is an accidental state, without which they could exist just as well;[w] he will then infer, therefore, that all composition in a body could be suspended in imagination, but in such a way that the substances, of which the body consists, would continue to exist; and since that which remains of a compound when all composition whatever has been cancelled is simple, he will conclude that bodies must consist of simple substances.[17] In this case, neither figures nor visible signs are capable of expressing either the thoughts or the relations which hold between them. Nor can abstract reflection be replaced by the transposition of signs in accordance with rules, the representation of the things themselves being replaced in this procedure by the clearer and the easier representation of the signs.[18] The universal must rather be considered *in abstracto*.[19]

2:279

---

[u] *die Sache selbst vor Augen haben muss.*   [v] *Symbolo.*
[w] *gleichwohl* / B: still / C: ——— / Fe: *pourtant* / Fi: *aussi bien* / (*gleichwohl* cannot, in this context, have its usual adversative sense of 'although' but its original sense [cf. Grimm, *gleichwohl* (1)]).

§3. IN MATHEMATICS, UNANALYSABLE CONCEPTS AND INDEMONSTRABLE PROPOSITIONS ARE FEW IN NUMBER, WHEREAS IN PHILOSOPHY THEY ARE INNUMERABLE

The concepts of magnitude[x] in general, of unity, of plurality,[y] of space, and so on, are, at least in mathematics, unanalysable.[z] That is to say, their analysis[a] and definition[b] do not belong to this science at all. I am well aware of the fact that geometers often confuse the boundaries between the different sciences, and on occasion wish to engage in philosophical speculation in mathematics. Thus, they seek to define[c] concepts such as those just mentioned, although the definition in such a case has no mathematical consequences at all. But this much is certain: any concept is unanalysable with respect to a given discipline if, irrespective of whether or not it be definable[d] elsewhere, it need not be defined, not, at any rate, in this discipline. And I have said that concepts are rare in mathematics. I shall go still further and deny that, strictly speaking, any such concepts at all can occur in mathematics; by which I mean that their definition by means of conceptual analysis[e] does not belong to mathematical cognition – assuming, that is, that it is actually possible elsewhere. For mathematics never defines[f] a given concept by means of analysis; it rather defines an object by means of arbitrary combination;[g] and the thought of that object first becomes possible in virtue of that arbitrary combination.

2:280

If one compares philosophy with this, what a difference becomes apparent. In all its disciplines, and particularly in metaphysics, every analysis which can occur is actually necessary, for both the distinctness of the cognition and the possibility of valid inferences[h] depend upon such analysis. But it is obvious from the start that the analysis will inevitably lead to concepts which are unanalysable.[20] These unalaysable concepts will be unanalysable either in and for themselves or relatively to us. It is further evident that there will be uncommonly many such unanalysable concepts, for it is impossible that universal cognition of such great complexity should be constructed from only a few fundamental concepts. For this reason, there are many concepts which are scarcely capable of analysis at all,[i] for example, the concept of a *representation*, the concepts of *being next to each other* and *being after each other*. Other concepts can only be partially analysed, for example, the concepts of *space, time* and the many different *feelings* of the human soul, such as the feeling of the *sublime*, the *beautiful*, the *disgusting*,[j] and so forth. Without exact knowledge[k] and analysis of

---

[x] *Grösse.*   [y] *Menge* / B & W: quantity / C: *quantità* / Fe & Fi: *multiplicitée.*   [z] *unauflöslich.*
[a] *Zergliederung.*   [b] *Erklärung.*   [c] *erklären.*   [d] *können erklärt werden.*
[e] *ihre Erklärung durch Zergliederung der Begriffe.*   [f] *erklärt.*   [g] *durch willkürliche Verbindung.*
[h] *sowohl die Deutlichkeit der Erkenntniss als die Möglichkeit sicherer Folgerungen.*
[i] *beinahe gar nicht aufgelöset werden können.*   [j] *des Ekelhaften.*   [k] *Kenntniss.*

these concepts, the springs of our nature will not be sufficiently understood; and yet, in the case of these concepts, a careful observer will notice that the analyses are far from satisfactory. I admit that the definitions[l] of *pleasure* and *displeasure*,[m] of *desire* and *aversion*, and of numberless other such concepts, have never been furnished by means of adequate analyses. Nor am I surprised by this unanalysability. For concepts which are as diverse in character as this must presumably be based upon different elementary concepts. The error, committed by some, of treating all such cognitions as if they could be completely analysed into a few simple concepts is like the error into which the early physicists fell. They were guilty, namely, of the mistake of supposing that all the matter of which nature is constituted consists of the so-called four elements – a view which has been discredited by more careful observation.

Furthermore, there are only a few fundamental *indemonstrable propositions* in mathematics. And even if they admit of proof elsewhere, they are nonetheless regarded as immediately certain in this science. Examples of such propositions are: *the whole is equal to all its parts taken together; there can only be one straight line between two points*, and so forth. Mathematicians are accustomed to setting up such principles at the beginning of their inquiries[n] so that it is clear that these are the only obvious propositions which are immediately presupposed as true, and that all other propositions are subject to strict proof.

2:281

If a comparison were to be made between this and philosophy, and, in particular between this and metaphysics, I should like to see drawn up a table of the indemonstrable propositions which lie at the foundation of these sciences throughout their whole extent.[o] Such a table would constitute a scheme of immeasurable scope.[p] But the most important business of higher philosophy consists in seeking out these indemonstrable fundamental truths; and the discovery of such truths will never cease as long as cognition of such a kind as this continues to grow. For, no matter what the object may be, those characteristic marks, which the understanding initially and immediately perceives in the object, constitute the *data* for exactly the same number of indemonstrable propositions, which then form the foundation on the basis of which definitions can then be drawn up.[q] Before I set about the task of defining[r] what space is,[21] I clearly see

---

[l] *Erklärungen.* [m] *Unlust.* [n] *Disciplinen.* [o] *durch ihre ganze Strecke zum Grunde liegen.*

[p] *einen Plan ausmachen, der unermesslich wäre.*

[q] *woraus die Definitionen können erfunden werden* / B: on which definitions can be established / C: *che costituiscono anche la base dalla quale si possono ricavare le definizioni* / Fe & Fi: *à partir desquels les définitions peuvent être trouvées* / W: the foundation from which definitions can be drawn up / (grammatically, *woraus* should relate to *Grundlage* ['foundation'], but that would make little sense logically; perhaps it should be construed as referring to the indemonstrable propositions).

[r] *erklären.*

that, since this concept is given to me, I must first of all, by analysing it, seek out those characteristic marks which are initially and immediately thought in that concept. Adopting this approach, I notice that there is a manifold in space of which the parts are external to each other;^{s} I notice that this manifold^t is not constituted by substances, for the cognition I wish to acquire relates not to things in space but to space itself;^{22} and I notice that space can only have three dimensions *etc.* Propositions such as these can well be explained if they are examined *in concreto* so that they come to be cognised intuitively; but they can never be proved. For on what basis could such a proof be constructed, granted that these propositions constitute the first and the simplest thoughts I can have of my object, when I first call it^u to mind? In mathematics, the definitions are the first thought which I can entertain of the thing defined,^{v} for my concept of the object only comes into existence as a result of the definition.^{w} It is, therefore, absolutely absurd to regard the definitions as capable of proof. In philosophy, where the concept of the thing to be defined^x is given to me,

2:282 that which is initially and immediately perceived in it must serve as an indemonstrable fundamental judgement.^{y} For since I do not yet possess a complete and distinct concept of the thing, but am only now beginning to look for such a concept, it follows that the fundamental judgement cannot be proved by reference to this concept. On the contrary, such a judgement serves to generate this distinct cognition and to produce the definition sought.^{z} Thus, I shall have to be in possession of these primary fundamental judgements prior to any philosophical definition of the things under examination. And here the only error which can occur beforehand is that of mistaking a derivative characteristic mark for one which is primary and fundamental.^{a} The following reflection will contain some considerations which will put this claim beyond doubt.

---

^{s} *dass darin vieles ausserhalb einander sei.* ^{t} *dieses Viele.*

^{u} *ihn* (must refer to *der Raum* ['space'] and not to *meinem Objecte* ['my object'] because it is neuter).

^{v} *von dem erklärten Dinge.* ^{w} *durch die Erklärung.* ^{x} *die ich erklären soll.* ^{y} *Grundurtheile.*

^{z} *In der Weltweisheit, wo mir der Begriff der Sache, die ich erklären soll, gegeben ist, muss dasjenige, was unmittelbar und zuerst in ihm wahrgenommen wird, zu einem unerweislichen Grundurtheil dienen. Denn da ich den ganzen deutlichen Begriff der Sache noch nicht habe, sondern allererst suche, so kann er aus diesem Begriffe so gar nicht bewiesen werden, dass er vielmehr dazu dient, diese deutliche Erkenntniss und Definition dadurch zu erzeugen.* (It is not clear to what the *er* [in the third clause of the second sentence] refers. The only masculine antecedent is *Begriff* ['concept'], but that would yield no sense. The only possible candidate would seem to be *Grundurtheil*: admittedly *Urtheil* is neuter, but Kant may have mistakenly supposed that because *Teil* may be either masculine or neuter, the compound word could be either, as well. This reading, although not grammatically justified, does yield philosophical sense. Fe and Fi adopt this reading, but without comment.)

^{a} *ein Uranfängliches Merkmal.*

254

§4. THE OBJECT OF MATHEMATICS IS EASY AND SIMPLE, WHEREAS THAT OF PHILOSOPHY IS DIFFICULT AND INVOLVED²³

The object of mathematics is magnitude.*²⁴ And, in considering magnitude, mathematics is only concerned with how many times something is posited.ᶜ This being the case, it is obvious that this science must be based upon a few, very clear fundamental principles of the general theory of magnitudesᵈ (which, strictly speaking, is general arithmetic). There, too, one sees the increase and decrease of magnitudes, their reduction to equal factors in the theory of roots – all of them originating from a few simple fundamental concepts. And a few fundamental concepts of space effect the application of this general cognition of magnitudes to geometry. In order to convince oneself of the truth of what I am saying here all one needs to do is contrast, for example, the ease one has in understanding an arithmetical object which contains an immense multiplicity, with the much greater difficulty one experiences in attempting to grasp a philosophical idea, in which one is trying to understand only a little. The relation of a *trillion* to unity is understood with complete distinctness, whereas even today the philosophers have not yet succeeded in explaining the concept of freedom in terms of its elements,ᵉ that is to say, in terms of the simple and familiar concepts of which it is composed.²⁵ In other words, there are infinitely many qualities which constitute the real object of philosophy, and distinguishing them from each other is an extremely strenuous business. Likewise, it is far more difficult to disentangleᶠ complex and involved cognitions by means of analysis than it is to combine simple given cognitions by means of synthesis and thus to establish conclusions. I know that there are many people who find philosophy a great deal easier than higher mathematics.ᵍ But what such people understand by philosophy is simply what they find in books which bear that title. The outcome of the two inquiries shows the difference between them. Claims to philosophical cognition generally enjoy the fate of opinions and are like the meteors, the brilliance of which is no guarantee of their endurance. Claims to philosophical cognition vanish, but mathematics endures. Metaphysics is without doubt the most difficult of all the things into which man has insight.ʰ But so far no metaphysics has ever been written. The question posed for consideration by the Royal Academy of Sciences in Berlin shows that there is good reason to ask about the path in which one proposes to search for metaphysical understanding in the first place.²⁶

2:283

ᵇ *Grösse.*   ᶜ *wie vielmal etwas gesetzt sei.*   ᵈ *Grundlehren der allgemeinen Grössenlehre.*
ᵉ *aus ihren Einheiten.*   ᶠ *aufzulösen.*   ᵍ *höhern Mathesis.*
ʰ *die schwerste unter allen menschlichen Einsichten.*

Second reflection: The only method for attaining the highest possible degree of certainty in metaphysics

Metaphysics is nothing other than the philosophy of the fundamental principles of our cognition. Accordingly, what was established in the preceding reflection about mathematical cognition in comparison with philosophy will also apply to metaphysics. We have seen that the differences which are to be found between cognition in mathematics and cognition in philosophy are substantial and essential.[i] And in this connection, one can say with Bishop *Warburton* that nothing has been more damaging to philosophy than mathematics, and in particular the *imitation* of its method in contexts where it cannot possibly be employed.[27] The *application* of the mathematical method in those parts of philosophy involving cognition of magnitudes is something quite different, and its utility is immeasurable.[28]

In mathematics I begin with the definition[j] of my object, for example, of a triangle, or a circle, or whatever. In metaphysics I may never begin with a definition. Far from being the first thing I know about the object, the definition is nearly always the last thing I come to know. In mathematics, namely, I have no concept of my object at all until it is furnished by the definition. In metaphysics I have a concept which is already given to me, although it is a confused one. My task is to search for the distinct, complete[k] and determinate concept. How then am I to begin? *Augustine* said: 'I know perfectly well what time is, but if someone asks me what it is I do not know.'[29] In such a case as this, many operations have to be performed in unfolding obscure ideas, in comparing them with each other, in subordinating them to each other and in limiting them by each other.[l] And I would go as far as to say that, although much that is true and much that is penetrating has been said about time, nonetheless no real definition[m][30] has ever been given of time. For, as far as the nominal definition[n][31] is concerned, it is of little or no use to us, for even without the nominal definition the word is understood well enough not to be misused. If we had as

2:284

[i] *namhafte und wesentliche.* [j] *Erklärung.* [k] *ausführlichen.*
[l] *viel Handlungen der Entwickelung dunkler Ideen, der Vergleichung, Unterordnung und Einschränkung.*
[m] *Realerklärung.* [n] *Namenerklärung.*

many correct definitions of time as there are definitions to be found in the books devoted to the subject, with what certainty could inferences be made and conclusions drawn. But experience teaches us the opposite.

In philosophy and in particular in metaphysics, one can often come to know a great deal about an object with distinctness and certainty, and even establish reliable conclusions on that basis prior to having a definition of that object, and even, indeed, when one had no intention of furnishing one. In the case of any particular thing, I can be immediately certain about a number of different predicates, even though I am not acquainted with a sufficiently large number of them to be able to furnish a completely determinate *concept of the thing,* in other words, a definition. Even if I had never defined[o] what an *appetite* was, I should still be able to say with certainty that every appetite presupposed the representation of the object of the appetite; that this representation was an anticipation[p] of what was to come in the future; that the feeling of pleasure was connected with it; and so forth. Everyone is constantly aware of all this in the immediate consciousness of appetite. One might perhaps eventually be able to arrive at a definition of appetite on the basis of such remarks as these, once they had been compared with each other. But as long as it is possible to establish what one is seeking by inference from a few immediately certain characteristic marks of the thing in question, and to do so without a definition, there is no need to venture on an undertaking which is so precarious.[q] In mathematics, as is known, the situation is completely different.

In mathematics, the significance of the signs[r] employed is certain, for it is not difficult to know what the significance was which one wished to attribute to those signs. In philosophy generally and in metaphysics in particular, words acquire their meaning as a result of linguistic usage,[s] unless, that is, the meaning has been more precisely determined by means of logical limitation.[t] But it frequently happens that the same words are employed for concepts which, while very similar, nonetheless conceal within themselves considerable differences. For this reason, whenever such a concept is applied, even though one's terminology may seem to be fully sanctioned by linguistic usage,[u] one must still pay careful attention to   2:285
whether it is really the same concept which is connected here with the same sign. We say that a person *distinguishes*[v] gold from brass if, for example, he recognises[w] that the density to be found in the one metal is not to be found in the other. We also say that an animal distinguishes[x] one kind of provender from another if it eats the one and leaves the other untouched. Here, the word 'distinguishes' is being used in both cases

---

[o] *erklärt.*   [p] *Vorhersehung.*   [q] *schlüpfrig.*   [r] *die Bedeutung der Zeichen.*   [s] *Redegebrauch.*
[t] *durch logische Einschränkung.*
[u] *wenn gleich die Benennung desselben nach dem Redegebrauch sich genau zu schicken scheint.*
[v] *unterscheidet.*   [w] *erkennt* (alt: 'knows' or 'cognises').   [x] *unterscheidet.*

even though, in the first case, it means 'recognise the difference',^{y} which is something which can never occur without *judging*,^{z} whereas in the second case it merely signifies that *different actions are performed*^{a} when different representations are present, and in this case it is not necessary that a judgement should occur. All that we perceive in the case of the animal is that it is impelled to perform different actions by different sensations; and that is something which is perfectly possible without its in the least needing to make a judgement about similarity^b or difference.^{32}

From all this there flow quite naturally the rules which govern the method by which alone the highest possible degree of metaphysical certainty can be attained. These rules are quite different from those which have hitherto been followed. They promise, if they are adopted, to produce a happier outcome than could ever have been expected on a different path. The *first* and the most important *rule* is this: one ought not to start with definitions,^{c} unless that is, one is merely seeking a nominal definition,^{d33} such as, for example, the definition: that of which the opposite is impossible is necessary. But even then there are only a few cases where one can confidently establish a distinctly determinate concept right at the very beginning. One ought, rather, to begin by carefully searching out what is immediately certain in one's object, even before one has its definition. Having established what is immediately certain in the object of one's inquiry, one then proceeds to draw conclusions from it. One's chief concern will be to arrive only at judgements about the object which are true and completely certain. And in doing this, one will not make an elaborate parade^e of one's hope of arriving at a definition.^{f} Indeed, one will never venture to offer such a definition, until one has to concede the definition, once it has presented itself on the basis of the most certain of judgements.^{g} The *second rule* is this: one ought particularly to distinguish^h those judgements which have been immediately made about the object and relate to what one initially encountered in that object with certainty. Having established for certain that none of these judgements is contained in another, these judgements are to be placed at the beginning of one's inquiry, as the foundation of all one's inferences, like the axioms of geometry. It follows from this that, when one is engaged in metaphysical reflection, one ought

2:286 always particularly to distinguish^i what is known for certain, even if that knowledge does not amount to a great deal. Nonetheless, one may experiment with cognitions which are not certain^j to see whether they may not

---

^{y} *den Unterschied erkennen.* ^{z} *ohen zu Urtheilen.* ^{a} *unterschiedlich gehandelt wird.*
^{b} *Übereinstimmung.* ^{c} *Erklärungen.* ^{d} *Worterklärung.* ^{e} *Staat zu machen.* ^{f} *Erklärung.*
^{g} *welche man niemals wagen, sondern dann, wenn sie sich aus den augenscheinlichsten Urtheilen deutlich darbietet, allererst einräumen muss.*
^{h} *besonders auszeichnet.* ^{i} *auszeichne.*
^{j} *obgleich man auch Versuche von ungewissen Erkenntnissen machen kann.*

put us on the track of certain cognition; but care must be taken to ensure that the two sorts of cognition are not confused. I shall not mention the other rules of procedure which this method has in common with every other rational method. I shall merely proceed to render these rules distinct by means of examples.

The true method of metaphysics is basically the same as that introduced by *Newton* into natural science and which has been of such benefit to it. *Newton's* method maintains that one ought, on the basis of certain experience and, if need be,[k] with the help of geometry, to seek out the rules in accordance with which certain phenomena of nature occur. Even if one does not discover the fundamental principle of these occurrences in the bodies themselves,[l] it is nonetheless certain that they operate in accordance with this law. Complex natural events are explained once it has been clearly shown how they are governed by these well-established rules.[34] Likewise in metaphysics: by means of certain inner experience, that is to say, by means of an immediate and self-evident inner consciousness,[m][35] seek out those characteristic marks which are certainly to be found in the concept of any general property.[n] And even if you are not acquainted with the complete essence of the thing, you can still safely employ those characteristic marks to infer a great deal from them about the thing in question.

EXAMPLE OF THE ONLY CERTAIN[o] METHOD FOR METAPHYSICS ILLUSTRATED BY REFERENCE TO OUR COGNITION OF THE NATURE OF BODIES

For the sake of brevity, I refer the reader to the proof which is briefly given at the end of Section 2 of the First Reflection.[36] I do so with a view to first establishing here as my foundation the proposition: all bodies must consist of simple substances. Without determining what a body is, I nonetheless know for certain that it consists of parts which would exist even if they were not combined together. And if the concept of a substance is an abstracted[p][37] concept, it is without doubt one which has been arrived at by a process of abstraction from the corporeal things which exist in the world. But it is not even necessary to call them substances. It is enough that one can, with the greatest certainty, infer from them that bodies consist of simple parts. The self-evident analysis[q] of this proposition could easily be offered, but it would be too lengthy to present here.[38] Now, employing infallible proofs of geometry, I can demonstrate that space does not consist of simple parts; the arguments involved are sufficiently well

2:287

---

[k] *allenfalls.* [l] *Wenn man gleich den ersten Grund davon in den Körpern nicht einsieht.*
[m] *durch sichere innere Erfahrung, d.i. ein unmittelbares augenscheinliches Bewusstsein.*
[n] *irgend einer allgemeinen Beschaffenheit.* [o] *sicher* (alt: 'sure' or 'certain').
[p] *abstrahirter Begriff.* [q] *die augenscheinliche Zergliederung.*

known.[39] It follows that there is a determinate number of parts in each body, and that they are all simple, and that there is an equal number of parts of space occupied by the body,[r] and they are all compound. It follows from this that each simple part of the body (each element) occupies a space.[s][40] Suppose that I now ask: What does 'occupying a space' mean? Without troubling myself about the essence of space, I realise that, if space can be penetrated[t] by anything without there being anything there to offer resistance, then one may, if need be, say that there was something in this space but never that the space was being occupied by it.[u][41] By this means I cognise that a space is occupied by something if there is something there which offers resistance to a moving body attempting to penetrate that same space. But this resistance is impenetrability.[v][42] Accordingly, bodies occupy space by means of impenetrability. But impenetrability is a *force*, for it expresses a resistance, that is to say, it expresses an action which is opposed to an external force.[w] And the force which belongs to a body must also belong to the simple parts of which it is constituted. Accordingly, the elements of every body fill their space by means of the force of impenetrability.[43] However, I proceed to ask whether the primary elements are not themselves extended since each element in the body fills a space?[44] At this juncture, I can for once introduce a definition[x] which is immediately certain. It is the definition, namely, that a thing is *extended*[y] if, when it is posited in itself (*absolute*),[z] it fills a space, just as each individual body, even if I imagine that nothing existed apart from it, would fill a space. However, if I consider an absolutely[a] simple element, then, if it is posited on its own (with no connection with anything else), it is impossible that there should exist within it a multiplicity of parts existing externally to each other,[b] and impossible that it should occupy a space *absolute*.[c] It cannot, therefore, be extended. However, the cause of the element occupying a space is the force of impenetrability which it directs against numerous external things. I therefore realise that whereas the multiplicity of its external action flows from that fact, multiplicity in respect of inner parts does not.[d] Hence, the fact that it occupies a space in the body (*in nexu aliis*)[45] is not the reason for its being extended.[e][46]

I shall just add a few words in order to reveal the shallowness[f] of the

---

[r] *den* (i.e., *Raum*) *er* (i.e., *Körper*) *einnimmt.*   [s] *einen Raum einnehmen.*
[t] *durchdrungen werden.*
[u] *es wäre etwas in diesem Raume, niemals aber, dieser Raum werde davon eingenommen.*
[v] *Undurchdringlichkeit.*   [w] *eine einer äussern Kraft entgegengesetzte Handlung.*   [x] *Erklärung.*
[y] *ausgedehnt.*   [z] *absolute* (Kant employs the Latin term *absolute* ['absolutely']).
[a] *schlechterdings.*   [b] *dass in ihm vieles sich ausserhalb einander befände.*   [c] *absolute.*
[d] *so sehe ich, dass daraus wohl eine Vielhelt in seiner äussern Handlung, aber keine Vielheit in Ansehung innerer Theile.*
[e] *mithin es darum nicht ausgedehnt sei, weil es in dem Körper (in nexu cum aliis) einen Raum einnimmt.*
[f] *seicht.*

proofs offered by the metaphysicians when, in accordance with their cus- 2:288
tom, they confidently establish their conclusions on the basis of defini-
tionsᵍ which have been laid down once and for all as the foundation of
their argument. The conclusions instantly collapse if the definitions are
defective. It is well-known that most *Newtonians* go further than *Newton*
himself and maintain that bodies, even at a distance, attract each other
immediately (or, as they put it, through empty space).⁴⁷ I do not propose to
challenge the correctness of this proposition, which certainly has much to
be said for it. What, however, I do wish to say is that metaphysics has not
in the least refuted it. First of all, bodies are *at a distance* from each otherʰ
if they *are not touching* each other.ⁱ That is the exact meaning of the
expression. Now, suppose that I ask what I mean by 'touching'. Without
troubling about the definition, I realise that whenever I judge that I am
touching a body I do so by reference to the resistance which the impenetrability of that body offers. For I find that this concept originates ultimately
from the senseʲ of touch. The judgement of the eye only produces the
surmise that one body will touch another; it is only when one notices the
resistance offered by impenetrability that the surmise is converted into
certain knowledge. Thus, if I say that one body acts upon another immediately *at a distance*ᵏ then this means that it acts on it immediately, but not by
means of impenetrability. But it is by no means clear here why this should
be impossible, unless, that is, someone shows either that impenetrability is
the only force possessed by a body, or at least that a body cannot act on
any other body immediately, without at the same time doing so by means
of impenetrability. But this has never yet been proved, nor does it seem
very likely that it ever will be. Accordingly, metaphysics, at least, has no
sound reason to object to the idea of immediate attraction at a distance.
However, let the arguments of the metaphysicians make their appearance.
To start with, there appears the definition: The immediate and reciprocal
presenceˡ of two bodies is touch. From this it follows that if two bodies act
upon each other immediately, then they are touching each other. Things
which are touching each other are not at a distance from each other.
Therefore, two bodies never act immediately upon each other at a distance *etc.* The definition is surreptitious.ᵐ Not every immediate presence
is a touching, but only the immediate presence which is mediated by
impenetrability. The rest is without foundation.ⁿ

I shall now proceed with my treatise. It is clear from the example I have
adduced that both in metaphysics and in other sciences there is a great 2:289
deal which can be said about an object with certainty, before it has been

---

ᵍ *Erklärung* (even in the German, the plural would have been grammatically more natural;
the sense is in no way affected by this change).
ʰ *voneinander entfernt.*   ⁱ *einander nicht berühren.*   ʲ *Gefühl.*
ᵏ *ein Körper wirkt in einen entfernten unmittelbar.*   ˡ *Die unmittelbare gegenseitige Gegenwart.*
ᵐ *erschlichen.*   ⁿ *und alles übrige ist in den Wind gebauet.*

defined.[o] In the present case, neither body nor space has been defined,[p] and yet there are things which can be reliably said of both. What I am chiefly concerned to establish is this: in metaphysics one must proceed analytically throughout, for the business of metaphysics is actually the analysis of confused cognitions.[q] If this procedure is compared with the procedure which is adopted by philosophers and which is currently in vogue in all schools of philosophy, one will be struck by how mistaken the practice of philosophers is. With them, the most abstracted concepts,[r48] at which the understanding naturally arrives last of all, constitute their starting point, and the reason is that the method[s] of the mathematicians, which they wish to imitate throughout, is firmly fixed in their minds. This is why there is a strange[t] difference to be found between metaphysics and all other sciences. In geometry and in the other branches of mathematics,[u] one starts with what is easier and then one slowly advances to the more difficult operations.[v] In metaphysics, one starts with what is the most difficult: one starts with possibility, with existence in general, with necessity and contingency, and so on – all of them concepts which demand great abstraction and close attention. And the reason for this is to be sought chiefly in the fact that the signs for these concepts undergo numerous and imperceptible modifications[w] in use; and the differences between them must not be overlooked. One is told that one ought to proceed synthetically throughout.[x] Definitions are thus set up[y] right at the beginning, and conclusions are confidently drawn from them. Those who practise philosophy in this vein congratulate each other for having learnt the secret of thorough thought from the geometers.[z] What they do not notice at all is the fact that geometers acquire their concepts by means of *synthesis*,[a] whereas philosophers can only acquire their concepts by means of *analysis*[b] – and that completely changes the method of thought.

If philosophers, having entered the natural path of sound reason, first seek out what they know for certain about the abstracted concept[c49] of an object (for example, space or time); and if they refrain from claiming to offer definitions;[d] and if they base their conclusions on these certain *data* alone, making sure that, even though the sign for the concept in question has remained unchanged, the concept itself has not undergone modification whenever its application has changed – if philosophers adopt this approach then, although they may not, perhaps, have quite so many opinions to *hawk* around,[e] the views they do have to offer will be of sound

---

[o] *ohne ihn erklärt zu haben.*   [p] *erklärt worden.*   [q] *verworrene Erkenntnisse aufzulösen.*
[r] *Die allerabgezogenste Begriffe.*   [s] *Plan.*   [t] *sonderbare.*
[u] *in der Geometrie und andern Erkenntnissen der Grössenlehre.*   [v] *schwereren Ausübungen.*
[w] *viele unmerkliche Abartungen.*   [x] *Es soll durchaus synthetisch verfahren werden.*
[y] *Man erklärt daher.*   [z] *Messkünstler.*   [a] *durchs Zusammensetzen.*   [b] *durch Auflösen.*
[c] *abgezogen.*   [d] *Erklärungen.*   [e] *feil zu bieten.*

value. I should like to adduce one more example of this latter procedure.[f]
Most philosophers adduce as examples of obscure concepts[g][50] those which
we have in deep sleep. *Obscure* representations are representations of   2:290
which we are not conscious. Now, some experiences show that we also
have representations in deep sleep, and since we are not conscious of
them it follows that they were obscure. In the case before us here, the
term '*consciousness*' is ambiguous. Either one is not conscious that one has
a representation, or one is not conscious that one has had a representation.[h] The former signifies the obscurity[i] of the representation as it occurs
in the soul, while the latter signifies nothing more than that one does not
remember the representation. Now, all that the example adduced shows is
that there can be representations which one does not remember when one
is awake; but from this it by no means follows that they may not have been
clearly present in consciousness while one was sleeping.[51] A case in point
would be the example, adduced by *Sauvage*,[52] of the person suffering from
catalepsy, or the ordinary actions of sleep-walkers. People have a tendency
to jump too readily to conclusions, without paying attention to differing
cases and investing the relevant concept with a significance appropriate to
each respective instance. This may explain why, in the present case, no
attention has been paid to what is probably a great mystery of nature: the
fact, namely, that it is perhaps during sleep that the soul exercises its
greatest facility in rational thought.[j] The only objection which could be
raised against this supposition is the fact that we have no recollection of
such rational activity when we have woken up; but that proves nothing.

Metaphysics has a long way to go yet before it can proceed synthetically.
It will only be when analysis has helped us towards concepts which are
understood distinctly and in detail[k] that it will be possible for synthesis to
subsume compound cognitions under the simplest cognition,[l] as happens
in mathematics.

[f] *von dem letzteren* / B: of the latter mistake / C: *di quanto ho detto* / Fe & Fi: *de la dernière de
ces règles* / (the reference of this phrase must be to the two procedures he has described; he
makes no mention of two mistakes [B] nor of two rules [Fe & Fi]).
[g] *ein Exempel dunkler Begriffe.*   [h] *dass man sie habe, oder, dass man sie gehabt habe.*
[i] *Dunkelheit.*   [j] *die grösste Fertigkeit der Seele im vernünftigen Denken.*
[k] *deutlich und ausführlich.*
[l] *wird die Synthesis den einfachsten Erkenntnissen die zusammengesetzte ... unterordnen können.*

Third reflection: On the nature of metaphysical certainty

§1. PHILOSOPHICAL CERTAINTY IS ALTOGETHER DIFFERENT IN NATURE FROM MATHEMATICAL CERTAINTY

One is certain if one knows that it is impossible that a cognition should be false.[53] The degree of this certainty, taken objectively, depends upon the sufficiency in the characteristic marks of the necessity of a truth.[m] But taken subjectively, the degree of certainty increases with the degree of intuition to be found in the cognition of this necessity.[n] In both respects,[54] mathematical certainty is of a different kind to philosophical certainty. I shall demonstrate this with the greatest possible clarity.[o]

The human understanding, like any other force of nature, is governed by certain rules. Mistakes are made, not because the understanding combines concepts without rule,[p] but because the characteristic mark which is not perceived in a thing is actually denied of it. One judges that that of which one *is not conscious* in a thing *does not exist.* Now, *firstly,* mathematics arrives at its concepts synthetically; it can say with certainty that what it did not intend to represent in the object by means of the definition is not contained in that object. For the concept of what has been defined[q] only comes into existence by means of the definition;[r] the concept has no other significance at all apart from that which is given to it by the definition.[55] Compared with this, philosophy and particularly metaphysics are a great deal more uncertain in their definitions,[s] should they venture to offer any. For the concept of that which is to be defined[t] is given. Now, if one should fail to notice some characteristic mark or other, which nonetheless belongs to the adequate distinguishing of the concept in question,[u] and if one judges that no such characteristic mark belongs to the complete[v]

---

[m] *das Zureichende in den Merkmalen von der Nothwendigkeit einer Wahrheit.*
[n] *so ist er in so fern grösser, als die Erkenntniss dieser Nothwendigkeit mehr Anschauung hat.*
[o] *auf das Augenscheinlichste.*   [p] *regellos.*   [q] *der Begriff des Erklärten.*   [r] *Erklärung.*
[s] *Erklärungen.*   [t] *der Begriff des zu Erklärenden.*
[u] *das gleichwohl zu seiner* (i.e., *der Begriff des zu Erklärenden*) *hinreichender Unterscheidung gehört.*
[v] *ausführlichen.*

concept, then the definition will be wrong and misleading. Numberless examples of such errors could be adduced, and for that very reason I refer only to the above example of touching.[56] *Secondly*, mathematics, in its inferences and proofs, regards its universal knowledge under signs *in concreto*, whereas philosophy always regards its universal knowledge *in abstracto*, as existing alongside[w] signs. And this constitutes a substantial difference in the way in which the two inquiries attain to certainty. For since signs in mathematics are sensible means to cognition,[x] it follows that one can know that no concept has been overlooked, and that each particular comparison has been drawn in accordance with easily observed rules *etc.* And these things can be known with the degree of assurance characteristic of seeing something with one's own eyes. And in this, the attention is considerably facilitated by the fact that it does not have to think things in their universal representation;[y] it has rather to think the signs as they occur in their particular cognition[z] which, in this case, is sensible in character. By contrast, the only help which words, construed as the signs of philosophical cognition, afford is that of reminding us of the universal concepts which they signify. It is at all times necessary to be immediately aware of their significance. The pure understanding must be maintained in a state of constant attention;[a] how easy it is for the characteristic mark of an abstracted concept to escape our attention without our noticing, for there is nothing sensible which can reveal to us the fact that the characteristic mark has been overlooked.[b] And when that happens, different things are taken to be the same thing, and the result is error.

2:292

What we have established here is this: the grounds for supposing that one could not have erred in a philosophical cognition which was certain can never be as strong as those which present themselves in mathematics. But apart from this, the intuition involved in this cognition[c] is, as far as its exactitude[d] is concerned, greater in mathematics than it is in philosophy. And the reason for this is the fact that, in mathematics, the object is considered under sensible signs *in concreto*,[e] whereas in philosophy the object is only ever considered in universal abstracted concepts;[f] and the clarity of the impression made by such abstracted concepts can never be as great as that made by signs which are sensible in character. Furthermore, in geometry the signs are similar to the things signified, so that the certainty of geometry is even greater, though the certainty of algebra[g] is no less reliable.

---

[w] *neben.*   [x] *sinnliche Erkenntnissmittel.*   [y] *in ihrer allgemeinen Vorstellung.*
[z] *in ihrer einzelnen Erkenntniss.*   [a] *Der reine Verstand muss in der Anstrengung erhalten werden.*
[b] *da nichts Sinnliches uns dessen Verabsäumung offenbaren kann.*
[c] *die Anschauung dieser Erkenntniss.*   [d] *Richtigkeit.*   [e] *in sinnlichen Zeichen in concreto.*
[f] *in allgemeinen abgezogenen Begriffen.*   [g] *Buchstabenrechnung.*

§2. METAPHYSICS IS CAPABLE OF A CERTAINTY WHICH IS SUFFICIENT TO PRODUCE CONVICTION

Certainty in metaphysics is of exactly the same kind as that in any other philosophical cognition, for the latter can only be certain if it is in accordance with the universal principles furnished by the former. We know from experience that, even outside mathematics, there are many cases where, in virtue of rational principles, we can be completely certain, and certain to the degree of conviction. Metaphysics is nothing but philosophy applied to insights of reason which are more general, and it cannot possibly differ from philosophy in this respect.[h]

Errors do not arise simply because we do not know certain things. We make mistakes because we venture to make judgements, even though we do not know everything which is necessary for doing so. A large number of errors, indeed almost all of them, are due to this latter kind of overhastiness.[i] You have certain knowledge of some of the predicates of a thing. Very well! Base your conclusions on this certain knowledge and you will not go wrong. But you insist on having a definition at all costs. And yet you are not sure that you know everything which is necessary to drawing up such a definition; nonetheless, you venture on such an undertaking and thus you fall into error. It is therefore possible to avoid errors, provided that one seeks out cognitions which are certain and distinct, and provided that one does not so lightly lay claim to be able to furnish definitions. Furthermore, you could also establish a substantial part of an indubitable conclusion,[j] and do so with certainty; but do not, on any account, permit yourself to draw the whole conclusion,[k] no matter how slight the difference may appear to be. I admit that the proof we have in our possession for establishing that the soul is not matter[l] is a good one.[57] But take care that you do not infer from this that the soul is not of a material nature.[m] For this latter claim is universally taken to mean not merely that the soul is not matter, but also that it is not a simple substance of the kind which could be an element of matter.[n] But this

2:293

---

[h] *Die Metaphysik ist nur eine auf allgemeinere Vernunfteinsichten angewandte Philosophie, und es kann mit ihr unmöglich anders bewandt sein.*

[i] *Vorwitz.* [j] *auf einen betrachtlichen Theil einer gewissen Folge schliessen.*

[k] *Erlaubt euch ja nicht, den Schluss auf die ganze Folge zu ziehen.*

[l] *dass die Seele nicht Materie sei.* [m] *dass die Seele nicht von materialer Natur sei.*

[n] *Denn hierunter versteht jedermann nicht allein, dass die Seele keine Materie sei, sondern auch nicht eine solche einfache Substanz, die ein Element der Materie sein könne.* / (The final clause is ambiguous, for it is grammatically unclear whether *die* is subject or predicate. B assumes the latter: 'that it is not a simple substance such as an element of matter could be'; C adopts the former: '*tale poter essere un elemento di materia*'; so do Fe & Fi: '*qu'elle n'est pas un substance simple qui puisse être un élément de la matière*'. Since Kant's concern here is not whether the soul is a simple substance but whether the soul is material, the reading of C, Fe, and Fi seems the more likely.)

requires a separate proof – the proof, namely, that this thinking being does not exist in space in the way in which a corporeal element exists in space, that is to say, in virtue of impenetrability; it also requires proof that this thinking being could not, when combined with other thinking beings, constitute something extended, a conglomerate.[o] But no proof has actually been given yet of these things. Such a proof, were it to be discovered, would indicate the incomprehensibility of the way in which a spirit is present in space.[58]

§3. THE CERTAINTY OF THE FIRST FUNDAMENTAL TRUTHS OF METAPHYSICS IS NOT OF A KIND DIFFERENT FROM THAT OF ANY OTHER RATIONAL COGNITION,[p] APART FROM MATHEMATICS

The philosophy of *Crusius** has recently claimed to give metaphysical cognition quite a different form.[59] It has done so by refusing to concede to the law of contradiction the pre-eminent right to be regarded as the supreme and universal principle of all cognition. *Crusius* introduced a large number of other principles which were immediately certain and indemonstrable, and he maintained that the correctness of these principles could be established by appeal to the nature of our understanding, 2:294
employing the rule that what I cannot think as other than true is true. Such principles include: what I cannot think as existing has never existed; all things must be somewhere and somewhen, *etc.*[q60] I shall briefly indicate the true character of the first fundamental truths of metaphysics; at the same time, I shall offer a brief account of the true content of *Crusius*'s method, which is not as different from that of the philosophy contained in this treatise as may, perhaps, be thought. On this basis, it will also be possible to establish in general the degree of possible certainty to which metaphysics can aspire.

All true propositions must be either affirmative or negative. The *form* of every *affirmation* consists in something being represented as a characteristic mark of a thing, that is to say, as identical with the characteristic mark

* I have deemed it necessary here to mention the method of this new philosophy. It quickly became so famous and it has been so widely admitted to have been instrumental in clarifying many of the things we know that it would have been a major omission not to have mentioned it in a work which is concerned with metaphysics in general. What I am touching upon here is merely the method which is peculiar to it; for the differences which exist between particular individual propositions is not of itself sufficient to distinguish one philosophical system from another in any essential respect.

[o] *Klumpen.* [p] *vernünftigen Erkenntniss.*

[q] *was ich nicht existirend denken kann, das ist einmal nicht gewesen; ein jedes Ding muss irgendwo und irgendwenn sein u.d.g.*

of a thing. Thus, every affirmative judgement is true if the predicate is *identical* with the subject. And since the *form* of every *negation* consists in something being represented as in conflict[r] with a thing, it follows that a negative judgement is true if the predicate *contradicts* the subject. The proposition, therefore, which expresses the essence of every affirmation and which accordingly contains the supreme formula of all affirmative judgements, runs as follows: to every subject there belongs a predicate which is identical with it. This is the *law of identity*. The proposition which expresses the essence of all negation is this: to no subject does there belong a predicate which contradicts it. This proposition is the *law of contradiction*, which is thus the fundamental formula of all negative judgements. These two principles together constitute the supreme universal principles, in the formal sense of the term, of human reason in its entirety.[61] Most people have made the mistake of supposing that the law of contradiction is the principle of all truths whatever, whereas in fact it is only the principle of negative truths. Any proposition, however, is indemonstrable if it is immediately thought under one of these two supreme principles and if it cannot be thought in any other way. In other words, any proposition is indemonstrable if either the identity or the contradiction is to be found immediately in the concepts, and if the identity and the contradiction cannot or may not be understood through analysis by means of intermediate characteristic marks.[s] All other propositions are capable of proof. The proposition, a body is divisible, is demonstrable, for the identity of the predicate and the subject can be shown by analysis and therefore indirectly: a body is *compound*, but what is compound is *divisible*, so a *body* is divisible. The intermediate characteristic mark here is *being compound*. Now, in philosophy there are, as we have said above, many indemonstrable propositions. All these indemonstrable propositions are subsumed under the formal first principles, albeit immediately. However, insofar as they also contain the grounds of other cognitions, they are also the first material principles of human reason. For example: *a body is compound* is an indemonstrable proposition, for the predicate can only be thought as an immediate and primary characteristic mark in the concept of a body.[62] Such material principles constitute, as *Crusius* rightly says, the foundation of human reason and the guarantor of its stability.[t] For, as we have mentioned above, they provide the stuff of definitions[u] and, even when one is not in possession of a definition,[v] the *data* from which conclusions can be reliably drawn.

And *Crusius* is also right to criticise other schools of philosophy for ignoring these material principles and adhering merely to formal principles. For on their basis alone it really is not possible to prove anything at

2:295

---

[r] *widerstreitend.*   [s] *vermittelst eines Zwischenmerkmals.*
[t] *die Grundlage und Festigkeit der menschlichen Vernunft.*   [u] *Erklärungen.*   [v] *Erklärung.*

all. Propositions are needed which contain the intermediate concept by means of which the logical relation of the other concepts to each other can be known in a syllogism. And among these propositions there must be some which are the first. But it is not possible to invest some propositions with the status*ʷ* of supreme material principles unless they are obvious*ˣ* to every human understanding. It is my conviction, however, that a number of the principles adduced by *Crusius* are open to doubt, and, indeed, to serious doubt.

This celebrated man proposes setting up a supreme rule to govern all cognition and therefore metaphysical cognition as well. The supreme rule is this: *what cannot be thought as other than true is true, etc.* However, it can easily be seen that this proposition can never be a ground of the truth of any cognition. For, if one concedes that there is no other ground of truth which can be given, apart from the impossibility of thinking it other than true, then one is in effect saying that it is impossible to give any further ground of truth, and that this cognition is indemonstrable. Now, of course, there are many indemonstrable cognitions. But the feeling of conviction which we have with respect to these cognitions is merely an avowal,*ʸ* not an argument establishing*ᶻ* that they are true.⁶³

Accordingly, metaphysics has no formal or material grounds of certainty which are different in kind from those of geometry.*ᵃ* In both meta-   2:296
physics and geometry, the formal element of the judgements exists in virtue of the laws of agreement and contradiction.*ᵇ* In both sciences, indemonstrable propositions constitute the foundation on the basis of which conclusions are drawn. But whereas in mathematics the definitions are the first indemonstrable concepts of the things defined,*ᶜ* in metaphysics, the place of these definitions is taken by a number of indemonstrable propositions which provide the primary data. Their certainty may be just as great as that of the definitions of geometry. They are responsible for furnishing either the stuff, from which the definitions*ᵈ* are formed, or the foundation, on the basis of which reliable conclusions are drawn. Metaphysics is as much capable of the certainty which is necessary to produce conviction*ᵉ* as mathematics. The only difference is that mathematics is easier and more intuitive in character.*ᶠ*

ʷ den Werth.   *ˣ augenscheinlich.*   *ʸ Geständnis.*   *ᶻ Beweisgrund.*   *ᵃ der Messkunst.*
ᵇ In beiden geschieht das Formale der Urtheile nach den Sätzen der Einstimmung und des Widerspruchs.
ᶜ der erklärten Sachen.   *ᵈ Erklärungen.*   *ᵉ eine zur Überzeugung nöthige Gewissheit.*
ᶠ einer grössern Anschauung theilhaftig.

Fourth reflection: Concerning the distinctness and certainty of which the fundamental principles of natural theology and morality are capable

§ I. THE FUNDAMENTAL PRINCIPLES OF NATURAL THEOLOGY ARE CAPABLE OF THE GREATEST PHILOSOPHICAL CERTAINTY[64]

Firstly, distinguishing one thing from another is easiest and most distinct if the thing in question is the only possible thing of its kind. The object of natural religion is the unique first cause; its determinations are such that they cannot easily be confused with those of other things. But the greatest conviction is possible when it is absolutely necessary that these and no other predicates belong to a thing. For in the case of contingent determinations it is generally difficult to discover the variable conditions of its predicates. Hence, the absolutely necessary being is an object such that, as soon as one is on the right track of its concept, it seems to promise even more certainty than most other philosophical cognition. In this part of my undertaking, all that I can do is consider the possible philosophical cognition of God in general; for if we were to examine the philosophical theories relating to this object which are actually current, we should be taken too far afield. The chief concept which here offers itself to the metaphysician is

2:297   that of the absolutely necessary existence of a being.[g] In order to arrive at this concept, the metaphysician could first of all ask the question: *is it possible that absolutely nothing at all should exist?* Now, if he realises that, were absolutely nothing at all to exist, then no *existence* would be given and there would be *nothing to think* and there would be no *possibility*[h] – once that is realised, all that needs to be investigated is the concept of the existence of that which must constitute the ground of all possibility. He will develop this idea and establish the determinate concept of the absolutely necessary being.[65] I do not wish to become involved in a detailed investigation of this

---

[g] *die schlechterdings nothwendige Existenz eines Wesens.*
[h] *dass alsdann gar kein Dasein gegeben ist, auch nichts zu denken, und keine Möglichkeit statt finde.*

project,[i] but I shall say this much: as soon as the existence of the unique,[j] most perfect and necessary Being is established, then the concepts of that Being's other determinations will be established with much greater precision, for these determinations will always be the greatest and most perfect of their kind; they will also be established with much greater certainty, for the only determinations which will be admitted will be those which are necessary.[66] Suppose, for example, that I am to determine the concept of the divine *omnipresence*. I have no difficulty in recognising the following fact. The being, upon which everything else depends – for it is itself independent – determines through its presence the *place*[k] of everything else in the world; it does not, however, determine *for itself* a place among those things, for if it did it would belong to the world as well. Therefore, strictly speaking, God does not exist in any *place*,[l] although He is present to all things in all the *places in which things exist.*[m][67] Likewise, I realise that, whereas the things in the world which follow upon one another are in His power, nonetheless He does not in virtue of that fact determine for Himself a moment of time in this series; as a consequence, nothing is past or future in relation to God. If, therefore, I say that God foresees the future, this does not mean that God sees that which *relative to Him is future.* It rather means that God sees that which, relative to certain things in the world, is future, that is to say, that which follows upon a state of those certain things in the world. From this it can be seen that cognitions of the future, the past and the present are not, relative to the action of the divine understanding, different from each other;[n] God rather cognises them all as actual things in the universe. This foreknowledge[o] can be imagined much more determinately and with much greater distinctness in God than in a thing which belongs to the totality of the world.

Metaphysical cognition of God is thus capable of a high degree of certainty in all those areas where no analogon[p] of contingency is to be encountered. But when it comes to forming a judgement about His free actions, about providence,[q] or about the way in which He exercises justice and goodness, there can only be, in this science, an approximation to certainty, or a certainty which is moral. For there is still a great deal of obscurity[r] surrounding the concepts which we have of these determinations, even when they occur in ourselves.

[i] *diesen Plan.*   [j] *einigen.*   [k] *den Ort.*   [l] *an keinem Ort.*
[m] *aber er ist allen Dingen gegenwärtig in allen Orten wo die Dinge sind.*   [n] *verschieden.*
[o] *dieses Vorhersehen.*   [p] *Analogon.*   [q] *Vorsehung.*   [r] *noch viel Unentwickeltes.*

2:298

§2. THE FUNDAMENTAL PRINCIPLES OF
MORALITY IN THEIR PRESENT STATE[s] ARE NOT
CAPABLE OF ALL THE CERTAINTY NECESSARY
TO PRODUCE CONVICTION

In order to make this claim clear I shall merely show how little even the fundamental concept of *obligation*[t] is yet known, and how far practical philosophy must still be from furnishing the distinctness and the certainty of the fundamental concepts and the fundamental principles which are necessary for certainty in these matters. The formula by means of which every obligation is expressed is this: one *ought* to do this or that and abstain from doing the other. Now, every *ought* expresses a necessity of the action and is capable of two meanings. To be specific: either I ought to do something (as a *means*) if I want something else (as an *end*),[u] or I *ought immediately* to do something else (as an *end*) and make it actual. The former may be called the necessity of the means (*necessitas problematica*),[68] and the latter the necessity of the ends (*necessitas legalis*).[69] The first kind of necessity does not indicate any obligation at all. It merely specifies a prescription as the solution to the problem concerning the means I must employ if I am to attain a certain end.[v] If one person tells another what actions he must perform or what actions he must abstain from performing if he wishes to advance his happiness, he might perhaps be able, I suppose, to subsume all the teachings of morality[w] under his prescription. They are not, however, obligations any longer except in the sense, say, in which it would be my obligation to draw two intersecting arcs if I wanted to bisect a straight line into two equal parts. In other words, they would not be obligations at all; they would simply be recommendations to adopt a suitable procedure,[x] if one wished to attain a given end.[70] Now since no other necessity attaches to the employment of means than that which belongs to the end, all the actions which are prescribed by morality under the condition of certain ends are contingent. They cannot be called obligations as long as they are not subordinated to an end which is necessary in itself. Take the following examples: I ought to advance the total greatest perfection;[y] or: I ought to act in accordance with the will of God. To whichever of these two principles the whole practical philosophy[z] is to be subordinated, the principle chosen must, if it is to be a rule and ground of obligation,[a] command the action as being immediately necessary and not

2:299 conditional upon some end. And here we find that such an immediate

---

[s] *nach ihrer gegenwärtigen Beschaffenheit.*   [t] *Verbindlichkeit.*   [u] *Zweck.*

[v] *sondern nur die Vorschrift als die Auflösung in einem Problem, welche Mittel diejenige sind, deren ich mich bedienen müsse, wie ich einen gewissen Zweck erreichen will.*

[w] *Lehren der Moral.*   [x] *Anweisungen eines geschickten Verhaltens.*

[y] *ich soll . . . die gesammte grösste Vollkommenheit befördern.*   [z] *die ganze praktische Weltweisheit.*

[a] *eine Regel und Grund der Verbindlichkeit.*

supreme rule of all obligation must be absolutely indemonstrable. For it is impossible, by contemplating a thing or a concept of any kind whatever, to recognise[b] or infer what one ought to do, if that which is presupposed is not an end, and if the action is a means. But this cannot be the case;[c] if it were, our principle would not be a formula of obligation; it would be a formula of problematic skill.[d]

Having convinced myself after long reflection on this matter, I can now briefly show the following. The rule: perform the most perfect action in your power, is the first *formal ground* of all obligation *to act*.[e] Likewise, the proposition: abstain from doing that which will hinder the realisation of the greatest possible perfection, is the first *formal ground* of the duty to *abstain from acting*.[f]¹ And just as, in the absence of any material first principles, nothing flowed from the first formal principles of our judgements of the truth, so here no specifically determinate obligation[g] flows from these two rules of the good, unless they are combined with indemonstrable material principles of practical cognition.

It is only recently, namely, that people have come to realise that the faculty of representing the *true* is *cognition*,[h] while the faculty of experiencing the *good* is *feeling*,[i] and that the two faculties are, on no account, to be confused with each other. Now, just as there are unanalysable concepts of the true, that is to say, unanalysable concepts of that which is encountered in the objects of cognition, regarded in itself,[j] so too there is an unanalysable feeling of the good[k] (which is never encountered in a thing absolutely but only relatively to a being endowed with sensibility).[l] One of the tasks of the understanding is to analyse and render distinct the compound and confused concept of the good by showing how it arises from simpler feelings of the good. But if the good is simple,[m] then the judgement: 'This is good', will be completely indemonstrable.[n] This judgement will be an immediate effect of the consciousness of the feeling of pleasure combined with the representation of the object.[o] And since there are quite certainly many simple feelings of the good to be found in us, it follows that there are many such unanalysable representations. Accordingly, if an action is

---

[b] *erkennen.*   [c] *Dieses aber muss es nicht sein.*   [d] *problematischen Geschicklichkeit.*

[e] *Verbindlichkeit zu Handeln.*   [f] *Pflicht zu Unterlassen.*

[g] *keine besonders bestimmte Verbindlichkeit.*   [h] *die Erkenntniss.*   [i] *das Gefühl.*

[j] *d.i. desjenigen, was in den Gegenständen der Erkenntniss, für sich betrachtet angetroffen wird.*

[k] *ein unauflösliches Gefühl des Guten.*   [l] *ein empfindendes Wesen.*

[m] *Allein ist dieses einmal einfach* / (The translators are in disagreement about the reference of the *dieses:* because it is neuter it cannot be *Empfindungen* [the view of B & Fe] nor *Begriff* [the view of Fi]. There are only two possibilities: *das Gefühl des Guten* [which is too far back] and *das Gute* [at the end of the preceding clause], which is the view of C and the present translator.)

[n] *völlig unerweislich.*

[o] *eine unmittelbare Wirkung von dem Bewusstsein des Gefühls der Lust mit der Vorstellung des Gegenstandes.*

immediately represented as good, and if it does not contain concealed within itself a certain other good, which could be discovered by analysis and on account of which it is called perfect, then the necessity of this action is an indemonstrable material principle of obligation. Take for example the principle: love him who loves you. This is a practical principle which is, it is true, subsumed, albeit immediately, under the supreme formal and affirmative rule of obligation. For since it cannot be further shown by analysis why a special perfection is to be found in mutual love,[p] it follows that this rule has not been proved practically. In other words, the rule has not been proved by tracing it back to the necessity of another perfect action. It is rather subsumed immediately under the universal rule of good actions. It is perhaps possible that the example I have adduced does not present the matter with sufficient distinctness and persuasiveness.[q] However, the limits of a treatise such as the present one – limits which, perhaps, I have already overstepped – do not permit me the completeness I would wish. An immediate ugliness[r] is to be found in the action, which conflicts with the will of Him, from Whom all goodness comes and to Whom we owe our existence. This ugliness is clearly apparent,[s] provided[t] that we do not straightaway focus our attention on the disadvantages, which may, as consequences, accompany such behaviour. Hence, the proposition: do what is in accordance with the will of God, is a material principle of morality. Nonetheless, it is formally though immediately subsumed under the supreme universal formula, of which mention has already been made. In both practical and in theoretical philosophy one must avoid lightly taking for indemonstrable that which in fact is capable of proof. Notwithstanding, those principles, which as postulates contain the foundations of all the other practical principles, are indispensable. *Hutcheson*[72] and others have, under the name of moral feeling,[u] provided us with a starting point from which to develop some excellent observations.[v]

It is clear from what has been said that, although it must be possible to attain the highest degree of philosophical certainty in the fundamental principles of morality, nonetheless the ultimate fundamental concepts of obligation need first of all to be determined more reliably.[w] And in this respect, practical philosophy is even more defective than speculative philosophy, for it has yet to be determined whether it is merely the faculty of

2:300

---

[p] *Gegenliebe.*   [q] *nicht deutlich und überzeugend genug.*   [r] *eine unmittelbare Hässlichkeit.*
[s] *klar.*
[t] *wenn gleich* / B: even if / C: *anche quando* / Fe: *même si* / Fi: *quoiqu'on* / (the words *wenn gleich* cannot have their usual adversative force without committing Kant to a view which is the very opposite of the position he is maintaining: Kant's point is that if we *do* look at the disadvantages which arise from the action, the intrinsic and immediate ugliness of the action will be obscured and not apparent at all).
[u] *des moralischen Gefühls.*   [v] *einen Anfang zu schönen Bemerkungen geliefert.*
[w] *sicherer bestimmt.*

cognition,[x] or whether it is feeling (the first inner ground of the faculty of desire)[y] which decides its first principles.

Postscript

Such are the thoughts I surrender to the judgement of the Royal Academy of Sciences. I venture to hope that the reasons presented here will be of some value in clarifying the subject, which was what was requested. In what concerns the care, precision and elegance[z] of the execution: I have preferred to leave something to be desired in that respect, rather than to allow such matters to prevent my presenting this inquiry for examination at the proper time, particularly since this defect is one which could easily be remedied should my inquiry meet with a favourable reception.[a]

[x] *Erkenntnissvermögen.*   [y] *Begehrungsvermögen.*   [z] *Sorgfalt, Abgemessenheit und Zierlichkeit.*
[a] *auf den Fall der günstigen Aufnahme.*

Appendix: Abridgement of Moses Mendelssohn's prize-winning essay on the distinctness of the principles of metaphysics and natural theology read at the public meeting of the Prussian Royal Academy of Sciences on 2 June 1763 by M. Merian

[Mendelssohn's prize-winning essay was originally published under the title *Über die Evidenz in den metaphysischen Wissenschaften* in the collection published by the Prussian Royal Academy of Sciences in Berlin in 1764 under the title *Dissertation qui a remporté le prix proposé par l'Académie des sciences et belles-lettres de prusse sur la nature, les espèces et les degrés de l'évidence. Avec les pièces qui ont concouru.* The official abridgement composed in French (the official language of the Academy) is also to be found in the same collection. The present translation is based on the French text of the abridgement found in Fichant (1973), pp. 105–17, which is, in turn, based on *Moses Mendelssohn: Schriften zur Philosophie, Aesthetik und Apologetik* (edited by Moritz Brasch), Vol. I, pp. 45 ff.]

The abstract which I am going to read has been drawn up in order to give an idea of this dissertation of those of our colleagues who are unable to read it in the original German. The abstract will display the author's arguments and the chief characteristics of his work, drawn up with all the exactitude of which I am capable.

INTRODUCTION

If we compare the fate of literature and the fine arts with that of philosophy, we shall see, on the one hand, lasting monuments which the passage of time cannot erode, and, on the other, a perpetual flux of sentiments, a vast ruin of systems destroyed by systems. The ancients have left us immortal writings, architectural remains and pieces of sculpture which we still regard as masterpieces. Our poets, our artists, our orators limit their ambition to copying them, and they have rather failed to match them than surpassed them. The glory of Homer has survived for so many centuries, while that of Aristotle, who was for so long the God of the Schoolmen, has almost been eclipsed. Would it not seem that the principles of taste are more sure and less subject to change than those of reason?

However, the changes themselves which philosophy has undergone, do honour to the spirit of man; these changes are so many advances towards perfection, so many new regions discovered in the empire of truth. The natural sciences, which shared in a weaker beginning, have progressed still further: the physics of antiquity has become more useless to us than their metaphysics.

Such is not the case with mathematics. The fate of this science has something about it which is completely specific to it. Although the point at which it has arrived is infinitely far removed from its origin, its principles have undergone no revolution. The first principles of ancient geometry are those of modern geometry. In enlarging its sphere, it has lost nothing of that which it once embraced within a space which, while admittedly more constricted, was even then all radiant with the light of self-evidence.

The attempt has been made in our century to give that same self-evidence to speculative philosophy, but the outcome of the effort has not matched the hopes which had been entertained for this famous undertaking. Those metaphysicians who are the most convinced of the soundness of their doctrine have been constrained to agree that it lacks that triumphant self-evidence which has subjugated the understanding, and the numerous contradictions from which it has suffered constitute an objection to which there is no reply.

These reflections lead our author to the problem proposed by the Academy. This is how he thinks it can be resolved:

The certainty of a proposition is not sufficient to render it self-evident. More is needed if it is to be capable of being grasped in such a way as to produce complete agreement and more is needed if our mind is to be incapable of resisting the arguments which demonstrate it. The fundamental concepts of the differential calculus are as certain as the rest of geometry, but they are not as luminous. Exactly the same is the case with metaphysics. The fundamental truths of this science, which are capable of the greatest certainty, can, by means of a sequence of connected arguments, be reduced to principles which are as incontrovertible as the principles of mathematics; but they lack the second characteristic of self-evidence. They lack that character of light which penetrates the understanding and which leaves no shadow in the mind. It is this which the author undertakes to prove in the following four sections.

SECTION I. ON THE SELF-EVIDENCE OF THE PRINCIPLES OF MATHEMATICS

The certainty of mathematics is based on the principle of contradiction. It is by means of this principle that all the truths of mathematics are derived from the notion of quantity, which is the general object of mathematics. The truths of mathematics are all contained in this primordial notion. It would be impossible to derive them from it if they did not already exist within it in the first place, though they exist in it only obscurely. Analysis, which causes them to emerge, is for the mind what the microscope is for the eye: it introduces nothing new. Analysis merely gives to our notions a more extended field, in which we can discern an infinity of things which had hitherto escaped our eyes. It is thus that Socrates acted as mid-wife to the mind. But that which the Greek philosopher took for an act of recollection is attributed by the philosophy, to the maxims of which our author subscribes, to the developing of our obscure ideas. On this subject he offers some very ingenious remarks. We shall not follow him in this incidental section in order not to wander too far from our subject.

The force of mathematical certainty is thus the product of the intimate and necessary connection of the ideas, all of which reduce to the general notion of quantity. Geometry, in the strict sense of the term, has as its object, continuous quantity; arithmetic has for its object discontinuous quantity; finally, successive quantity furnishes the measure of time, though this can be expressed only by simultaneous quantities, either arithmetical or geometrical.

The various branches of mathematics, regarded from this point of view, offer us an inexhaustible supply of discoveries. It is above all important to notice that there remains a kind of quantity which the geometers have not yet started to examine, or of which at any rate they have hitherto only furnished very superficial sketches: I mean the non-extended quantities of which the parts, being neither successive nor simultaneous, merge into each other. To this class or quantity belong degrees, intensities, both in physics and in morals. If one has measured motive force, velocity, temperature, then it has only been done by reducing them to lines and geometrical figures. But so far there is no measure for calculating the intrinsic value of things, their possibility, reality, beauty, perfection, clarity, certainty, and so forth.

One cannot, however, deny that this theory is possible in itself. Every day we make comparisons and rough estimates of the degrees of things. This natural geometry presupposes the possibility of an artificial and more exact geometry. After all, degrees are quantities; they accordingly fall under the general object of mathematics and become susceptible to the same analysis.

But the chief difficulty consists in tracing the limits of such quantities. In ordinary geometry, these limits are easily distinguished by the senses; they are surfaces, lines, points. But here, in the case of degrees, the limits escape observation, they merge and get lost in the recesses of the subject. Besides, all degrees relate to the qualities which serve as their foundation, of which the distinctive characteristic marks have to be abstracted before their precise quantity can be fixed, a task which is equally difficult. Our philosopher illustrates this by means of an essay of the moral kind; he then shows that the appreciation of qualities, in general, and of sensible qualities, in particular, suffers from difficulties which are far greater.

Another privilege of ordinary mathematics consists in the employment of signs which always correspond exactly to the nature, or at least, to the order of our thoughts. In geometry, they are the very picture of the object signified. They are synthesised and analysed with our notions. In arithmetic and algebra, the only signs there are are those which are simplest; their number is very small and they are arbitrary; but they cease to be arbitrary as soon as they enter into combination. In formulae and equations, everything is determined in a manner proportionate to the advance of our understanding. By contrast, the signs which one is obliged to employ for non-extended quantities always remain arbitrary and they cannot be subsumed under a general rule. It is this which forces mathematicians, when they are obliged to treat such subjects, to resort to the use of the characters of geometry and algebra. This can be seen in dynamics and the sciences related to it.

A distinction must be made between pure mathematics and applied or mixed mathematics. The former is restricted to the world of the understanding and the realm of possibilities. Here, the highest degree of certainty is to be found, for all that one needs to do is to compare ideas, and to demonstrate that the derived notions are identical with the primitive notion. But when this science is transposed to the real world, it needs sensory experience; without it, all its operations are suspended. Before being able, for example, to apply the theorems which are based on the properties of rectilinear figures, it is necessary for the senses to have revealed to the geometer such really existent figures; for so far his operations have been limited to simple possibility.

It is not that mixed geometry loses its self-evidence. If one were to concede to the idealists that the external world was nothing, and that bodies were only phenomena or appearances, geometry would not be any the less infallible. As soon as there are constants and regular phenomena which always present the same aspect under the same circumstances, the geometer can apply his compass and calculus; and it matters very little to him whether these phenomena are substances or modes, or whether they exist outside or inside him.

SECTION 2. ON THE SELF-EVIDENCE OF
METAPHYSICAL PRINCIPLES

Mathematics is the science of quantities; metaphysics is the science of *qualities;* and by this one is to understand the internal characteristic marks which distinguish each thing from that which it is not. Now, there is no quantity without quality, nor, reciprocally, any quality without quantity; for, on the one hand, when I say *more* or *less*, I necessarily understand something of which this *more* or *less* can be affirmed; on the other hand, all quality is enclosed within limits, and it is in virtue of this that it is more or less what it is. It is apparent from this that these two sciences reflect each other's light. Above all, it is apparent that the geometry of non-extended quantities cannot dispense with metaphysics.

Just as there is a pure geometry, so there is a pure metaphysics. Pure metaphysics is exclusively concerned with abstractions: it presupposes no reality and is concentrated within the ideal world. It is metaphysics which discloses all the notions which are contained in the prolific notion of quality. Thus, the procedure of the metaphysician is here the same as that of the geometer; his advance is quite as regular, his principles are quite as sure, his deductions are quite as unshakeable.

However, the same self-evidence is not to be found there, for this metaphysical certainty cannot be rendered as sensible to the mind. The privilege which mathematics enjoys in this respect does not, as is believed, derive from the fact that geometrical figures are the pictures of objects. Arithmetic and algebra do not draw such pictures, but they are not, on that account, any the less self-evident. The source of this defect in metaphysics must, therefore, be sought elsewhere.

Firstly, it speaks a language which is entirely arbitrary, in which neither the nature nor the connection of the signs have anything in common with the connection of the things signified. As a result, definitions increase in number and multiply to infinity. The greatest mental concentration is necessary if one is continuously to combine expression and thought; and as soon as concentration is relaxed, the risk arises that one will lose oneself in fruitless verbiage.

Secondly, the nature itself of *quality*, which is the object of this science, gives birth to difficulties which are still more alarming. The internal characteristic marks of things are closely linked and, so to speak, interwoven with each other; and if one does not know them all, one does not know any of them with self-evidence. It is this which obliges the philosopher, with each step he takes, to look back, to return to the first principles, to trace all the scattered rays of light which the different notions reflect from each other. This is why the philosopher constantly needs to revise his position, and it is to these revisions alone that we owe the happy revolutions which have taken place in metaphysics.

Let us suppose, finally, that he has overcome all these difficulties and it remains for him to realise the object of his contemplations; it is only after he has shown that it exists in the universe that he is permitted to infer from it the reality of the conclusions he has drawn from it. And here his task is arduous in a way different from that in which the task of the mathematician is arduous. The mathematician appeals to the evidence of the senses, but he is not concerned about the truth or falsity of the evidence. By contrast, the philosopher must summon the senses themselves, even the inner sense, before the court of reason; he must distinguish the true from the false, the certain from the uncertain, and extricate himself from all the deceptions and all the illusions which cloud the understanding. It is apparent enough how much that must impede conviction and weaken the self-evidence.

Speculative philosophy has only two sure paths by which it can pass from the world of possibles to the world of realities. The first starts from the inner sense. By its means I am assured that I think, and from it I conclude that my own existence is certain. The second is an immediate passage from possibility to being, which only occurs in a single case, of which I shall say more below. Descartes was the first to open these two paths. Prior to him, metaphysics was built on sensible experience – a defective method, according to our author, which exposes metaphysics to the attacks of Pyrrhonism.

These are the difficulties which the metaphysician finds in the subject itself of his speculations. But they are not the only ones. More substantial difficulties arise from the weakness and failings of the human heart.

The geometer is always indifferent and impartial in his researches. Whether the tangent does or does not form a right-angle with the diameter is a matter of complete indifference to us; we have no other interest than that of truth. Ignorance is the only enemy which mathematics has to combat. Philosophy, by contrast, still struggles against prejudice. Since its doctrines have an influence on our opinions, on our conduct, on our happiness, we have almost all of us decided the issue before examining it. And when reason comes to reduce our chimerical systems to smoke, our hearts are too hardened and our minds too stubborn to listen to its lessons. Few people have courage enough to perform a generous execution on themselves or to sacrifice their prejudices.

Everybody, having decided the issue in advance, thinks that he has the right to judge. Philosophical terms often occur in ordinary life, and one only needs to hear or utter them a certain number of times to think that one has been initiated into the mysteries of philosophy. In what concerns geometry, the ignorant hold their tongues and await the decision of the experts. In the subject of metaphysics, by contrast, namely in morality and politics, each acts the expert, settling and deciding issues without rhyme or reason. This drawback is unavoidable unless we wish to limit the freedom of conscience and introduce despotism into the republic of letters – a cure which would be worse than the malady itself.

SECTION 3. ON THE SELF-EVIDENCE OF THE PRINCIPLES OF NATURAL THEOLOGY

Even if one only considers by abstraction the totality of the characteristics which constitute the divine essence, one can see that all these attributes are interdependent on each other in such a way that if only one of them is given there is not one which cannot be deduced from it with complete certainty and with a self-evidence which is close to that of geometry.

But, considered under this aspect, natural theology is still only an ideal science. The atheist who denies the existence of these attributes and the existence of the being who possesses them is in the same situation as the idealist who denies the external reality of the objects of geometry. For, in respect of the connection of ideas which represent these things, neither the atheist nor the idealist can gainsay it. The geometer asks no more. But the speculative thinker must go further. The most important thing which remains for him to do is to demonstrate the actual existence of the Supreme Being, the idea of which only contains possible existence. This is the point at which metaphysics parts company from geometry and launches into a flight which is more sublime.

The preceding section showed the two paths which lead from abstraction to reality. Both of them lead us to the existence of God, the one by the *a priori* proof, the other by the *a posteriori* proof.

The first of these proofs is the well-known proof offered by Descartes and restated by Leibniz. And it is here, according to our author, that one can infer existence from simple possibility. He offers two different versions of this argument; we shall content ourselves with adducing the first version.

If something does not exist, one must concede one of two things: either it is impossible for it to exist, in which case the properties which are supposed to constitute its nature conflict with and reciprocally destroy each other; or, alternatively, it is merely possible for it to exist but it lacks the determination of a cause which is capable of realising it, in which case its reality is not involved in its nature: it is contingent and dependent. The completely perfect being cannot exist in this latter manner because, if it were dependent, it would not be completely perfect. It must, therefore, of necessity be the case either that it really exists, or that the notion of its nature itself involves a manifest contradiction. But, for this contradiction to occur, it is necessary that some of the properties which determine its essence should destroy each other, that is to say, it is necessary that that which is denied by the one is affirmed by the other. But all negation presupposes a lack, a limitation, the absence of some reality. But the idea of the completely perfect being includes within it all realities, prescribes all limits, excludes all defects. It is therefore contradictory that this idea could involve a contradiction. The completely perfect being thus exists in virtue of its possibility alone.

The reflections which follow depend upon the principle of sufficient reason which the author attempts first to explain, and then to establish and secure from the objection of fatalism. We shall pass over these details in order to arrive at the second proof of the existence of God, which has been derived from this same principle.

This proof has for its foundation an experience which cannot deceive and which is secure from scepticism. I exist. I do not exist through myself. My existence is contingent. It is thus necessary to seek the reason of my existence outside myself, and outside all contingent beings; in other words, the reason of my existence can only be found in the existence of a necessary being.

The experience which forms the foundation of this demonstration teaches us at the same time which of the properties belonging to the things which exist in the world are to be attributed to the Divine Nature and which are to be excluded from it. Since this experience relates to a reality, to our own being, it authorises us to introduce into the essence of God only real properties, banishing from this essence all privations. We can thus conclude that the Supreme Being possesses all the positive qualities which we feel within ourselves; for the same reason, we must separate from Him all sensible and corporeal qualities. Extension, movement, colour, sound, our bodies themselves, are nothing real; these things are only appearance. These appearances are, it is true, based on the real existence of the simple beings which constitute the totality of the universe; but the limits of our mind only permit us to acquire confused representations and illusory images.

This section ends with an examination of those proofs of the existence of God which are less strict. These proofs derive both from the order and beauty which we observe, both on the large and on the small scale, in the system of the visible world, from the laws of movement, and from final causes. These proofs are not demonstrative; although they have a very high degree of probability, it is not possible to guarantee that probability from doubt and contradiction. However, if these proofs are not convincing to all minds, they are of great use to minds which are already convinced. They make strong impressions on the heart; they arouse the love, and excite the admiration and the respect which we owe to the Author of all things.

But care must be taken not to deprive them of their energy by employing them in an ill-considered fashion or by giving them a false application, for then they are reduced to nothing more than proofs of our own ignorance. It was in this manner that the pagan religion, which filled all the spaces of the world with divinities, exposed itself to the mockery of the Epicureans by immediately resorting to the direct action of a superior and invisible power in the breath of Zephyrus, in the murmur of nature, in the least accidents of human nature.

Quorum operum causas nulla ratione videre possunt, haec fieri divino numine rentur.

['Unable in any way to see the causes of these things, they declare that they come to be in virtue of the divine presence.']

SECTION 4. ON THE SELF-EVIDENCE OF THE PRINCIPLES OF MORALS

There is a speculative and a practical morality. The former examines the general rules which govern our duties; the latter applies these rules to particular circumstances.

If there is, for all human beings, a common reason which takes cognisance of their actions, then there are common duties; and the maxims which set out these duties are the *laws of nature*.

In order to discover the most universal principle of these laws, one needs only to establish the focal point to which all our actions, all our inclinations and all our desires tend. That focal point is indisputably the happiness or perfection of our being. It is to this point also that both crime and virtue equally tend; the lowest of criminals no less than the most honourable of men has this end in view. The only difference is in the outcome, which depends on the choice of means. If the former is mistaken and is lost, it is because he takes the false good for the true good, and the appearance of perfection for perfection itself.

Give to yourself and to other human beings all the perfection which it is in your power to confer. That perfection is the first of the laws, the fundamental maxim of the law of Nature; and from it derive all our duties towards God, towards our neighbour and towards ourselves.

It can also be proved by the nature of human freedom. A free being can only determine itself on the basis of motives; and these motives are always a perfection which the agent sees or which he thinks he sees in the object which he chooses. Obligation is simply the moral necessity to act in accordance with the best motives. Thus every free being is obliged to direct his conduct to the greatest perfection of the universe; and this motive is, of all motives, the noblest and the most excellent.

Finally, this law accords with the Divine Will and with the end of creation. The Supreme Intelligence does only what is best; it always sets before itself as the end of its action the greatest perfection of its handiwork. This clearly proves that it wishes that created intelligences should conform to his views and co-operate in the execution of this project which is so magnificent. This obligation is all the more binding for not being founded on arbitrary power, nor on the right alone of property, but on a wisdom which never departs from the eternal laws of perfection and which, without binding us by a physical constraint, only wishes to oblige in a manner which is consonant with our nature. For punishments themselves and rewards, the sanction of natural law, are only motives.

Having, by this same principle, developed the fundamental concepts of *natural law* and the duties of distributive justice, our author concludes that the theory of morality is rigorously and mathematically demonstrable. But he refuses to credit it with geometrical self-evidence, firstly, because no branch of philosophy can aspire to such self-evidence, and, secondly, because morality, being built on metaphysics, cannot be more self-evident than the science which serves as its foundation; on the contrary, the light which it borrows must of necessity grow weaker with its passage.

In so far as the universal precepts of practical morality are limited to regulating our feelings and affections, these precepts possess the most complete and the most convincing certainty. These maxims are maxims such as: love virtue; submit your passions to the control of reason; and others which are similar to them.

The same does not hold of particular precepts, which presuppose a given case and which relate to the various circumstances in which we find ourselves, circumstances which are often very complex and which the slightest accident may change. Here the certainty decreases; and, as the circumstances are divided and subdivided, the certainty passes down through the entire scale of probabilities.

In such situations, one can regulate one's conduct by an infallible principle. One rarely has the power and still less the leisure to enter into long discussions, and to go back to the fundamental sources of our duties. To reason and to demonstrate when it was necessary to act would be to neglect our duties themselves.

What, then, is our guide here? It is conscience, that inner sense, that spiritual taste which gives us an immediate view of the moral truth, which instantly brings us to the conclusion, at which reason only arrives by slow gradations. In this consists the approbation of the heart, just as conviction is the approbation of the mind. Nor may one suppose that it is vague and indeterminate. It operates in accordance with immutable principles which use has rendered familiar to us, and which have been converted, so to speak, into our substance. Without this approbation, the science of morals is nothing but a dead science, a sterile theory. It is this approbation which causes the seeds of virtue to germinate and bear fruit; it is from this living source that all beautiful and all great actions are seen to issue.

Morality furnishes us with a means of maintaining a happy agreement between the inner sense and reason, and of submitting the inner faculties to them. These faculties consist in gathering together in our mind all the motives which can carry us towards virtue, in meditating thoroughly on them, in investing them with a pleasing sentiment by embellishing them with the charm of the fine arts, and in setting before ourselves for imitation the best examples and the most perfect models.

These are the kinds of help which human weakness seems to need. If there is some genius favoured by heaven, of which the intellectual view should be sufficiently extended and sufficiently penetrating to embrace in a single glance and to grasp the entire system of morals, even down to its last springs, it alone could dispense with such help. It alone could feel the pure enthusiasm of reason. But that is a phoenix which only makes a rare appearance and which perhaps has never been seen in the fields of philosophy.

Such are the ideas of our author on the problem posed by the Academy. With respect to the application to metaphysics of the method employed by geometers, our author's initial intention had been to devote a separate section to it; but he believes that his opinions on this subject emerge sufficiently clearly in the course of the work. Geometry does not owe its triumphs to this method; and metaphysicians, by abusing it, have only succeeded in making themselves ridiculous.

I think that I have faithfully acquitted myself of the task of abridging the dissertation and that I have given an exact idea of its contents. I have not, however, managed to convey an impression of the elegancy of the style in which it is written and which reveals one of the finest writers in Germany.

M. Immanuel Kant's announcement of the programme of his lectures for the winter semester 1765–1766 (1765)

M. Immanuel Kants Nachricht von der Einrichtung seiner Vorlesungen in dem Winterhalbenjahre von 1765–1766 (1765)

M. Immanuel Kants

Nachricht

von der

Einrichtung seiner Vorlesungen

in dem Winterhalbenjahre

von 1765—1766.

M. Immanuel Kant's announcement of the programme of his lectures for the winter semester 1765–1766

2:303

There is always a certain difficulty involved in the instruction[a] of young 2:305 people, and it is this: the knowledge one imparts to them is such that one finds oneself constrained to outstrip their years.[b] Without waiting for their understanding to mature, one is obliged to impart knowledge to them, which, in the natural order of things, can only be understood by minds which are more practised and experienced.[c] It is this which is the source of the endless prejudices of the schools – prejudices which are more intractable and frequently more absurd than ordinary prejudices. And it is this, too, which is the source of that precocious prating[d] of young thinkers, which is blinder than any other self-conceit and more incurable than ignorance. This difficulty, however, is one which cannot be entirely avoided, and the reason is this. In an epoch which is characterised by an elaborately complex social organisation,[e] a knowledge of higher things[f] is regarded as a means to advancement and comes to be thought of as a necessity of life. Such knowledge ought by nature, however, really to be regarded merely as one of life's adornments – one of life's inessential beauties, so to speak. Nonetheless, even in this branch of instruction, it is possible to make public education[g] more adapted to nature, even though it will not be possible to bring it into perfect harmony with it. The natural progress of human knowledge is as follows: first of all, the understanding develops by using experience to arrive at intuitive judgements,[h] and by their means to attain to concepts. After that, and employing reason, these concepts come to be known in relation to their grounds and consequences. Finally, by means of science,[i] these concepts come to be known as parts of a well-ordered whole. This being the case, teaching must follow exactly the same path. The teacher is, therefore, expected to develop in his pupil firstly the man of *understanding,* then the man of *reason,* and finally the man of *learning.*[j] Such a procedure has this advantage: even if, as usually happens, the pupil should never reach the final phase, he will 2:306 still have benefitted from his instruction. He will have grown more experienced and become more clever,[k] if not for school then at least for life.

If this method is reversed, then the pupil picks up a kind of reason, even before his understanding has developed. His science is a borrowed science which he wears, not as something which has, so to speak, grown within him, but as something which has been hung upon him.[l] Intellectual aptitude[m] is as unfruitful as it ever was. But at the same time it has been

---

[a] *Unterweisung.* [b] *dass man genöthigt ist, mit der Einsicht den Jahren vorzueilen.*
[c] *von einer geübteren und versuchten Vernunft.* [d] *die frühkluge Geschwätzigkeit.*
[e] *in dem Zeitalter einer sehr ausgeschmuckten bürgerlichen Verfassung.* [f] *die feinere Einsichten.*
[g] *den öffentlichen Unterricht.* [h] *anschauenden Urtheilen.* [i] *ermittelst der Wissenschaft.*
[j] *den Verständigen, dann den Vernünftigen Mann und endlich den Gerlehrten.*
[k] *geübter und kluger.*
[l] *und trägt erborgte Wissenschaft, die an ihm gleichsam nur geklebt und nicht gewachsen ist.*
[m] *Gemüthsfähigkeit.*

corrupted to a much greater degree by the delusion of wisdom." It is for this reason that one not infrequently comes across men of learning (strictly speaking, people who have pursued courses of study)° who display little understanding. It is for this reason, too, that the academies send more people out into the world with their heads full of inanities*P* than any other public institution.*q*

The rule for proceeding is, therefore, as follows. Firstly, the understanding must be brought to maturity and its growth expedited by exercising it in empirical judgements and focusing its attention on what it can learn by comparing the impressions which are furnished by the senses. It ought not to venture any bold ascent from these judgements and concepts to higher and more remote judgements and concepts. It ought rather to make its way towards them by means of the natural and well-trodden pathway of the lower concepts, for this path will gradually take it further than any bold ascents ever could. But all this should be done, not in accordance with that capacity for understanding which the teacher perceives, or thinks he perceives in himself, and which he mistakenly presupposes in his pupils, but rather in accordance with that capacity for understanding which must of necessity be generated in that faculty by the practice which has just been described. In short, it is not *thoughts* but *thinking*'' which the understanding ought to learn. It ought to be *led*, if you wish, but not *carried*, so that in the future it will be capable of *walking* on its own, and doing so without stumbling.

The peculiar nature of philosophy itself demands such a method of teaching.*s* But since philosophy is strictly speaking an occupation only for those who have attained the age of maturity, it is no wonder that difficulties arise when the attempt is made to adapt it to the less practised capacity of youth. The youth who has completed his school instruction has been accustomed *to learn*. He now thinks that he is going *to learn philosophy*.*t* But that is impossible, for he ought now *to learn to philosophise.*u1 Let me explain myself more distinctly. All the sciences which can be learned in the strict sense of the term can be reduced to two kinds: the *historical* and the *mathematical*. To the first there belong, in addition to history proper, natural history, philology, positive law, *etc.* In everything historical, it is one's own experience or the testimony of other people which constitute what is actually given and which is therefore available for use, and which may, so to speak, simply be
2:307   assimilated. In everything mathematical, on the other hand, these things are

---

" *durch den Wahn der Weisheit.*   ° *Gelehrte (eigentlich Studirte).*   *P abgeschmackte Köpfe.*
q Stand des gemeinen Wesens.   ' *nicht Gedanken, sondern denken.*
s Eine solche Lehrart erfordert die der Weltweisheit eigene Natur / (It is not grammatically clear whether *Eine solche Lehrart* ['such a method of teaching'] or *die der Weltweisheit eigene Natur* ['the peculiar nature of philosophy itself'] is the subject. The context seems to require the latter; Ferrari [hereafter Fe] and Fichant [hereafter Fi] are also of this view.)
t Philosophie lernen.   *u philosophiren lernen.*

constituted by the self-evidence of the concepts and the infallibility of the demonstration.[v] It is thus possible in both types of knowledge to learn. That is to say, it is possible to impress either on the memory or on the understanding that which can be presented to us as an already complete discipline. In order, therefore, to be able to learn philosophy as well there must already be a philosophy which actually exists in the first place. It must be possible to produce a book and say: 'Look, here is wisdom, here is knowledge on which you can rely.[w] If you learn to understand and grasp it, if you take it as your foundation and build on it from now on, you will be philosophers'. Until I am shown such a book of philosophy, a book to which I can appeal, say, as I can appeal to *Polybius* in order to elucidate some circumstance of history, or to *Euclid* in order to explain a proposition of mathematics – until I am shown such a book, I shall allow myself to make the following remark. One would be betraying the trust placed in one by the public[x] if, instead of extending the capacity for understanding of the young people entrusted to one's care and educating them to the point where they will be able in the future to acquire a more mature insight *of their own[y]* – one would be betraying the trust placed in one by the public, if, instead of that, one were to deceive them with a philosophy which was alleged to be already complete and to have been excogitated by others for their benefit.[z] Such a claim would create the illusion of science. That illusion is only accepted as legal tender in certain places and among certain people. Everywhere else, however, it is rejected as counterfeit currency.[a] The method of instruction, peculiar to philosophy, is *zetetic,* as some of the philosophers of antiquity expressed it (from ζητεῖν). In other words, the method of philosophy is the method of *enquiry.[b]* It is only when reason has already grown more practised and only in certain areas, that this method becomes *dogmatic,* that is to say, *decisive.[c]* The philosophical writer, for example, upon whom one bases one's instruction, is not to be regarded as the paradigm of judgement. He ought rather to be taken as the occasion for forming one's own judgement about him, and even, indeed, for passing judgement against him. What the pupil is really looking for is proficiency in the method of reflecting and drawing inferences *for himself.* And it is that proficiency alone which can be of use to him. As for the positive knowledge which he may also perhaps come to acquire at the same time – that must be regarded as an incidental consequence. To reap a superabundant harvest of such knowledge, he needs only to plant within himself the fruitful roots of this method.

If one compares the above method with the procedure which is commonly adopted and which differs so much from it, one will understand a

[v] *die Augenscheinlichkeit der Begriffe und die Unfehlbarkeit der Demonstration.*
[w] *zuverlässige Einsicht.*   [x] *des Zutrauens des gemeinen Wesens.*   [y] *reifern eigenen Einsicht.*
[z] *sie mit einer dem Vorgeben nach schon fertigen Weltweisheit hintergeht, die ihnen zu gute von andern ausgedacht wäre.*
[a] *verrufen.*   [b] *forschend.*   [c] *entschieden.*

number of things which would otherwise strike one as surprising. For example: why is there no other kind of specialised knowledge[d] which exemplifies so many *masters* as does philosophy? Many of those who have learned history, jurisprudence, mathematics and so forth, nonetheless modestly disclaim that they have learned enough to be able to teach the subject themselves. But why, on the other hand, is it rare to find someone who does not in all seriousness imagine that, in addition to his usual occupation, he is perfectly able to lecture on, say, logic, and moral philosophy, and other subjects of the kind, should he wish to dabble in such trivial matters?[e] The reason for this divergence is the fact that, whereas in the former science there is a common standard,[f] in the latter science each person has his own standard. It will likewise be clearly seen that it is contrary to the nature of philosophy to be practised as a means to earning one's daily bread[g] – the essential nature of philosophy is such that it cannot consistently accommodate itself to the craze of demand or adapt itself to the law of fashion[h] – and that it is only pressing need, which still exercises its power over philosophy, which can constrain it to assume a form which wins it public applause.

In the course of the present semester which has just begun, I propose to hold private lectures[2] on the following science, which I intend to handle in an exhaustive fashion.

1. *Metaphysics.* I have sought to show in a short and hastily composed work* that this science has, in spite of the great efforts of scholars, remained imperfect and uncertain because the method peculiar to it has been misunderstood. Its method is not *synthetic*, as is that of mathematics, but *analytic*.[4] As a result, that which is simple and the most universal in mathematics[i] is also what is easiest, whereas in the queen of the sciences[j] it is what is most difficult. In mathematics, what is simple and universal must in the nature of things come first, while in metaphysics it must come at the end. In mathematics one begins the doctrine with the definitions; in metaphysics one ends the doctrine with them; and so on in other respects.[k] For some considerable time now I have worked in accordance with this scheme. Every step which I have taken along this path has revealed to me both the source of the errors which have been committed, and the criterion of judgement by reference to which alone those errors can be avoided, if they can be avoided at all. For this reason, I hope that I

---

* The second of the treatises published by the *Berlin Royal Academy of Sciences* on the occasion of the award of the prize for the year 1763.[3]

[d] *keine Art Gelehrsamkeit vom Handwerke.*
[e] *wenn er sich mit solchen Kleinigkeiten bemengen wollte.* [f] *gemeinschaftlicher Massstab.*
[g] *eine Brodkunst zu sein.*
[h] *indem es ihrer wesentlichen Beschaffenheit widerstreitet sich dem Wahne der Nachfrage und dem Gesetze der Mode zu bequemen.*
[i] *Grössenlehre.* [j] *Hauptwissenschaft.* [k] *und so in andern Stücken mehr.*

shall be able in the near future to present a complete account of what may serve as the foundation of my lectures in the aforementioned science.[5] Until that time, however, I can easily, by applying gentle pressure, induce A. G. Baumgarten, the author of the text book on which this course will be based[6] – and that book has been chosen chiefly for the richness of its contents and the precision of its method – to follow the same path. Ac- 2:309 cordingly, after a brief introduction, I shall begin with *empirical psychology*, which is really the metaphysical science of *man* based on experience.[l] For in what concerns the term 'soul', it is not yet permitted in this section to assert that man has a soul. The second part of the course will discuss *corporeal nature* in general. This part is drawn from the chapters of the *Cosmology*[7] which treat of *matter* and which I shall supplement with a number of written additions in order to complete the treatment. In the first of these sciences (to which, on account of the analogy,[m] there is added empirical zoology, that is to say, the consideration of animals) we shall examine all the organic phenomena[n] which present themselves to our senses. In the second of these sciences we shall consider everything which is *inorganic*[o] in general. Since everything in the world can be subsumed under these two classes, I shall then proceed to ontology, the science, namely, which is concerned with the more general properties of all things. The conclusion of this enquiry will contain the distinction between *mental* and *material* beings,[p] as also the connection or separation of the two, and therefore *rational psychology*. The advantage of this procedure is this: it is the already experienced student who is introduced to the most difficult of all philosophical investigations. But there is another advantage as well: in every reflection, the abstract is considered in the form of a concrete instance, furnished by the preceding disciplines, so that everything is presented with the greatest distinctness. I shall not have to anticipate my own argument; in other words, I shall not have to introduce anything by way of elucidation which ought only to be adduced at a later stage – an error which is both common and unavoidable in the synthetic method of presenting things. At the end there will be a reflection on the cause of all things, in other words the science which is concerned with God and the world. There is one other advantage which I cannot but mention. Al- though it is a product of accidental causes, it is not, however, to be lightly esteemed. It is an advantage which I hope will accrue from the employ- ment of this method. Everyone knows with what eagerness the spirited and volatile youth attend the start of a course, and how subsequently the

---

[l] *die metaphysische Erfahrungswissenschaft vom Menschen.*
[m] *um der Analogie willen* / (alt: for the sake of the analogy).   [n] *alles Leben.*   [o] *alles Leblose.*
[p] *geistigen und materiellen Wesen* / (in *Dreams* [1766] *geistige Wesen* has been translated 'spirit-beings', and that is a possible translation here; the context, however, suggests that 'mental beings' is more appropriate).

lecture theatres grow gradually increasingly empty. Now, I am assuming that what ought not to happen will, in spite of all reminders, continue to happen in the future. Nonetheless, the aforementioned method of teaching has a utility of its own. The student, whose enthusiasm has already evaporated even before he has got to the end of empirical psychology (though this is scarcely to be expected if such a procedure as the one I have described is adopted) will, nonetheless, have benefitted this much: he will have heard something which he can understand, on account of its
2:310 easiness;[q] he will have heard something which he can enjoy, in virtue of its interest;[r] and he will have heard something which he can use, because of the frequency with which it can be given an application in life.[s] On the other hand, if he should be deterred from proceeding further by ontology, which is difficult to understand, that which he might perhaps have grasped if he had continued could not have been of any further use to him at all.

2. *Logic.* Of this science there are really two kinds.[8] The first kind is a critique and canon of *sound understanding.*[t] In one direction, it borders on crude concepts and ignorance,[u] and, in the other, it borders on science and learning.[v] It is with this type of logic that all philosophy, at the start of academic instruction, ought to be prefaced. It is, so to speak, a quarantine (if the expression be permitted) which must be observed by the apprentice who wishes to migrate from the land of prejudice and error, and enter the realm of a more enlightened reason and the sciences.[w] The second kind of logic is the critique and canon of *real learning.*[x] The only way in which it can be treated is from the point of view of the sciences of which it is supposed to be the organon. The purpose of such a treatment is to make the procedure employed by the science concerned more consonant with the rules, and to render the nature of the discipline itself, as well as the means for improving it, accessible to the understanding. In this way, I shall add at the end of the metaphysics a reflection on the method which is peculiar to it, and which can serve as an organon of this science.[9] This reflection would have been out of place at the beginning, for it is impossible to make the rules clear, unless there are some examples to hand by means of which the rules can be elucidated *in concreto.* The teacher must, of course, be in possession of the organon, before he presents his account of the science in question, so that he can be guided by it; but he must never present the organon to his audience except at the end of his presen-

[q] *fasslich durch seine Leichtigkeit.* [r] *annehmlich durch das Interessante.*
[s] *durch die häufige Fälle der Anwendung im Leben.*
[t] *eine Kritik und Vorschrift des gesunden Verstandes.* [u] *an die grobe Begriffe und Unwissenheit.*
[v] *an die Wissenschaft und Gelehrsamkeit.*
[w] *aus dem Lande des Vorurtheils und des Irrthums in das Gebiet der aufgeklärteren Vernunft und der Wissenschaften.*
[x] *eigentlichen Gelehrsamkeit.*

tation. The critique and the canon of the whole of philosophy in its entirety, this complete logic,ʸ can therefore only have its place in instruction at the end of the whole of philosophy. The reason is this. It is the knowledge of philosophy, which we have come to acquire,ᶻ and the history of man's opinions which alone make it possible for us to reflect on the origin both of its insights and of its errors. And it is this alone which enables us to draw up a precise ground-plan, on the basis of which an edifice of reason, which is permanent in duration and regular in structure, can be erected.[10]

I shall be lecturing on logic of the first type. To be more specific, I shall base my lectures on *Meier's* handbook,[11] for he has, I think, kept his eye focused on the limits of the intentions which we have just now mentioned. And he also stimulates us to an understanding, not only of the cultivation of reason in its more refined and learned form,ᵃ but also of the development of the ordinary understanding, which is nonetheless active and sound. The former serves the life of contemplation, while the latter serves the life of action and society.ᵇ And in this, the very close relationship of the materials under examination leads us at the same time, in the *critique of reason*, to pay some attention to the *critique of taste*, that is to say, *aesthetics*. The rules of the one at all times serve to elucidate the rules of the other. Defining the limits of the two is a means to a better understanding of them both.

2:311

3. *Ethics.* Moral philosophyᶜ has this special fate: that it takes on the semblance of being a science and enjoys some reputation for being thoroughly grounded, and it does so with even greater ease than metaphysics, and that in spite of the fact that it is neither a science nor thoroughly grounded. The reason why it presents this appearance and enjoys this reputation is as follows. The distinction between good and evil in actions, and the judgement of moral rightness,ᵈ can be known, easily and accurately, by the human heart through what is called sentiment,ᵉ and that without the elaborate necessity of proofs.ᶠ In ethics, a question is often settled in advance of any reasons which have been adduced – and that is something which does not happen in metaphysics. It will not, therefore, come as a surprise that no one raises any special difficulties about admitting grounds, which only have some semblance of validity.ᵍ For this reason, there is nothing more common than the title of a moral philosopher, and nothing more rare than the entitlement to such a name.

ʸ *die Kritik und Vorschrift der gesammten Weltweisheit als eines Ganzen, diese vollständige Logik.*
ᶻ *die schon erworbene Kenntnisse derselben.*
ᵃ *neben der Cultur der feineren und gelehrten Vernunft.*
ᵇ *jene für das betrachtende, diese für das thätige und bürgerliche Leben.*
ᶜ *Die moralische Weltweisheit.* ᵈ *die sittliche Rechtmässigkeit.* ᵉ *Sentiment.*
ᶠ *ohne den Umschweif der Beweise.*
ᵍ *Gründe, die nur einigen Schein der Tüchtigkeit haben als tauglich.*

For the time being, I shall lecture on *universal practical philosophy*[h] and the *doctrine of virtue*,[i] basing both of them on *Baumgarten*.[12] The attempts of *Shaftesbury*,[13] *Hutcheson*[14] and *Hume*,[15] although incomplete and defective, have nonetheless penetrated furthest in the search for the fundamental principles of all morality. Their efforts will be given the precision and the completeness which they lack. In the doctrine of virtue I shall always begin by considering historically and philosophically what *happens* before specifying what *ought to happen*. In so doing, I shall make clear what method ought to be adopted in the study of *man*. And by *man* here I do not only mean *man* as he is distorted by the mutable form which is conferred upon him by the contingencies of his condition,[j] and who, as such, has nearly always been misunderstood even by philosophers. I rather mean the unchanging *nature* of man, and his distinctive position within the creation. My purpose will be to establish which perfection is appropriate to him in the state of *primitive* innocence and which perfection is appropriate to him in the state of *wise* innocence.[k][16] It is also my purpose to establish what, by contrast, the rule of man's behaviour is when, transcending the two types of limit,[l] he strives to attain the highest level of physical or moral excellence, though falling short of that attainment to a greater or lesser degree. This method of moral enquiry is an admirable discovery of our times, which, when viewed in the full extent of its programme, was entirely unknown to the ancients.[17]

2:312

4. *Physical geography*.[18] Right at the beginning of my academic career, I realised that students were being seriously neglected, particularly in this respect: early on they learned the art of subtle argumentation[m] but they lacked any adequate knowledge of historical matters which could make good their lack of *experience*. Accordingly, I conceived the project of making the history of the present state of the earth, in other words, geography in the widest sense of the term, into an entertaining and easy compendium of the things which might prepare them and serve them for the exercise of practical reason, and which might arouse within them the desire to extend even further the knowledge which they had begun to acquire in their study of the subject. The name which I gave to the discipline, constituted by that part of the subject on which my chief attention was at the time focused, was that of *physical geography*. Since then I have gradually extended the scheme, and I now propose, by condensing that part of the subject which is concerned with the physical features of the earth, to gain the time necessary for extending my course of lectures to include the other parts of the subject, which are of even greater general utility. This

---

[h] *allgemeine praktische Weltweisheit.*   [i] *Tugendlehre.*

[j] *durch die veränderliche Gestalt, welche ihm sein zufälliger Zustand eindrückt.*

[k] *welche Volkommenheit ihm im Stande der rohen und welche im Stande der weisen Einfalt angemessen sei.*

[l] *indem er aus beiderlei Grenzen herausgeht.*   [m] *vernünfteln.*

discipline will therefore be a *physical, moral* and *political* geography.[19] It will contain, *first of all*, a specification of the remarkable features of *nature* in its three realms. The specification will, however, be limited to those features, among the numberlessly many which could be chosen, which particularly satisfy the general desire for knowledge, either because of the fascination which they exercise in virtue of their rarity, or because of the effect which they can exercise on states by means of trade and industry. This part of the subject, which also contains a treatment of the natural relationship which holds between all the countries and seas in the world, and the reason for their connection,[n] is the real foundation of all history. Without this foundation, history is scarcely distinguishable from fairy-stories. The *second* part of the subject considers *man*, throughout the world, from the point of view of the variety of his natural properties and the differences in that feature of man which is moral in character.[o] The consideration of these things is at once very important and also highly stimulating as well. Unless these matters are considered, general judgements about man would scarcely be possible. The comparison of human beings with each other, and the comparison of man today with the moral state of man in earlier times, furnishes us with a comprehensive map of the human species. *Finally*, there will be a consideration of what can be regarded as a product of the reciprocal interaction of the two previously mentioned forces, namely, the condition of the *states* and nations throughout the world. The subject will not be considered so much from the point of view of the way in which the condition of states depends on accidental causes, such as the deeds and fates of individuals, for example, the sequence of governments, conquests, and intrigues between states. The condition of states will rather be considered in relation to what is more constant and which contains the more remote ground of those accidental causes, namely, the situation of their countries, the nature of their products, customs, industry, trade and population.[20] Even the reduction, if I may use the term, of a science of such extensive prospects to a smaller scale has its great utility.[p] For it is only by this means that it is possible to attain that unity without which all our knowledge is nothing but a fragmentary patchwork.[q] In a sociable century, such as our own, am I not to be permitted to regard the stock which a multiplicity of entertaining, instructive and easily understood knowledge offers for the maintenance of social intercourse[r] as one of the benefits which it is not demeaning for science

2:313

---

[n] *das natürliche Verhältniss aller Länder und Meere und den Grund ihrer Verknüpfung.*

[o] *und dem Unterschiede desjenigen, was an ihm moralisch ist.*

[p] *Selbst die Verjüngung, wenn ich es so nennen soll, einer Wissenschaft von so weitläufigen Aussichten nach einem kleineren Massstabe hat ihren grossen Nutzen* / (the phrase *die Verjüngung . . . nach einem kleineren Massstab* ['the reduction . . . to a smaller scale'] is a technical term borrowed from the field of cartography).

[q] *Stückwerk.*   [r] *zum Unterhalt des Umganges.*

to have before its eyes? At least it cannot be pleasant for a man of learning frequently to find himself in the embarrassing situation in which *Isocrates*, the orator, found himself: urged on one occasion when he was in company to say something, he was obliged to reply: *What I know is not suitable to the occasion; and that which is suitable to the occasion I do not know.*[5]

This is a brief indication of the subjects on which I shall be lecturing in the university[1] in the course of the coming semester which has just started. I thought it necessary to say something in this connection in order to explain my method, where I have now found it opportune to make some alterations. *Mihi sic est usus: Tibi ut opus facto est, face. (Terence).*[21]

---

[5] *Was ich weiss, schickt sich nicht und was sich schickt, weiss ich nicht.*   [1] *der Akademie.*

300

Dreams of a spirit-seer elucidated by dreams of metaphysics (1766)

*Träume eines Geistersehers, erläutert durch Träume
der Metaphysik* (1766)

Träume eines Geistersehers,

erläutert

durch

Träume der Metaphysik.

velut aegri somnia, vanae
Finguntur species.

HOR.

Dreams of a spirit-seer elucidated by dreams of metaphysics

> *Velut aegri somnia, vanae*
> *Finguntur species*
> Horace[1]

Preamble, which promises very little for the execution of the project

The realm of shades[a] is the paradise of fantastical visionaries. Here they find a country without frontiers which they can cultivate at their pleasure. Hypochondriacal exhalations, old wives' tales and monastery miracles do not leave them short of building materials. Philosophers prepare the ground plan which they then proceed to modify or reject, as is their wont. Holy *Rome* alone possesses lucrative provinces in that realm: the two tiaras of the invisible realm support the third fragile diadem of its terrestrial power. And the keys which unlock the two gates to the other world simultaneously and sympathetically unlock the coffers of this world. Such exploitation-rights to that spirit-realm, having been legitimised by considerations of state-interest, place themselves far beyond the reach of all the futile objections raised by pedantic scholars.[b] The use or misuse of these rights has become a practice so venerable that it no longer needs to subject itself to the humiliation of such a demanding cross-examination. But why is it that the popular tales which find such widespread acceptance, or which are, at least, so weakly challenged, circulate with such futility and impunity,[c] insinuating themselves even into scholarly theories, and that, in spite of the fact that they do not even enjoy the support of that most persuasive of proofs, the proof from advantage (*argumentum ab utili*)? What philosopher, torn between the assurances of a rational and firmly convinced eyewitness, on the one hand, and the inner resistance of an insuperable scepticism, on the other hand, has not, on some occasion or other, created the impression of the utmost imaginable foolishness? Is he completely to deny the truth of all such apparitions?[d] What reasons can he adduce to refute them?

Is he to admit the probability of even only one of these stories? How   2:318 important such an admission would be! And what astonishing implications would open up before one, if even only *one* such occurrence could be supposed to be proven! There is, I suppose, a third possibility left, namely,

---

[a] *Schattenreich* / (both the German *Schatten* and the English word 'shade' may mean both 'shadow' and 'ghost').

[b] *Schulweisen.*   [c] *so ungenützt oder ungeahndet.*

[d] *Geistererscheinungen* / (see Glossary for *Erscheinung*).

305

not to meddle with such prying or *idle* questions, but to concern oneself only with what is *useful*. But this suggestion, being reasonable, has always been rejected by the majority of thorough scholars.

To believe *none* of the many things which are recounted with some semblance of truth, and to do so without any reason, is as much a foolish prejudice as to believe *anything* which is spread by popular rumour, and to do so without examination. For this reason, the author of this essay, in attempting to avoid the former prejudice, allowed himself to be in part carried away by the latter. He confesses, with a certain humiliation, to having been naive enough to investigate the truth of some of the stories of the kind mentioned. He found what one usually finds when one has no business searching at all, exactly nothing!*e* Now, I suppose that this in itself is already a sufficient reason for writing a book. But there was also another factor, which has already on a number of occasions forced books out of modest authors: the insistent importunity of friends, both known and unknown. Not only that, but the author went to the expense of purchasing a lengthy work,[2] and, what was worse, he put himself to the trouble of reading it, as well! Such effort was not to be wasted. Such are the origins of the present treatise. Given its subject-matter, it ought, so the author fondly hopes, to leave the reader completely satisfied: for the bulk of it he will not understand, parts of it he will not believe, and as for the rest – he will dismiss it with scornful laughter.

e *wo man nichts zu suchen hat* / (Kant is exploiting the literal sense ['where one has nothing to seek'] of a colloquial phrase ['where one has no business to be']).

FIRST CHAPTER: A TANGLED METAPHYSICAL KNOT, WHICH CAN BE EITHER UNTIED OR CUT AS ONE PLEASES

If one were to draw up a compendium of everything concerning spirits which is recited by schoolboys, related by the common people and demonstrated by philosophers, it would, it seems, constitute no small part of our knowledge. Notwithstanding, I would venture the following opinion. If it were to occur to someone to linger for a while over the question: What exactly is this thing which, under the name of *spirit,*[f] people claim to understand so well, all the know-alls[g] would be put in a very embarrassing position. The methodical gossip of the universities[h] is frequently nothing but an agreement to exploit the instability of the meaning of words[i] with a view to evading questions which are difficult to answer. And the reason for this evasiveness is the fact that the easy and generally reasonable answer 'I do not know' is frowned upon in the academies. Certain modern philosophers, as they like to be called, have no difficulty in disposing of this question. Their answer runs: A spirit is a being endowed with reason. No miraculous powers[j] are needed, therefore, to see spirits; for, whoever sees human beings sees beings endowed with reason. But, the argument continues, this being, which in man is endowed with reason,[k] is only a part of man, and this part of man, the part which animates him, is a spirit. Very well, then, before you go on to prove that only a spirit-being can be endowed with reason, please make sure that I have first of all understood what sort of concept I am to form for myself of a spirit-being. The self-deception in this case, though plain enough to be seen with half-opened eyes, nonetheless has an origin which can easily be understood. For that about which one knows a great deal early on in life as a child – of that, one can be sure, one will certainly know nothing later on in life when one has reached maturity. And the man of thoroughness will in the end at best be the sophist of his youthful delusions.

2:320

I do not, therefore, know whether spirits exist or not. And, what is more, I do not even know what the word *'spirit'* means. However, since I

---

[f] *unter dem Namen eines Geistes* (see Glossary for *Geist*).　　[g] *alle diese Vielwisser.*
[h] *Das methodische Geschwätz der hohen Schulen.*　　[i] *durch veränderliche Wortbedeutungen.*
[j] *Wundergabe.*　　[k] *dieses Wesen, was im Menschen Vernunft hat.*

have frequently used the word or heard others use it, it follows that something or other must be understood by the term, irrespective of whether this something be a figment of the imagination or something real. In order to disentangle this hidden meaning,^{l} I shall compare my ill-understood concept with all its different applications.^{m} By noticing with which cases my concept is compatible and with which it is inconsistent, I hope to unfold the concealed sense of the concept.^{n*}

Take, for example, a cubic foot of space and suppose that there is something which fills this space, that is to say, that there is something which resists the attempt by any other thing to penetrate this space. No one would call the being which existed in space in this fashion a spirit-being. Such a being would obviously be called *material,* for it is extended, impenetrable and, like everything corporeal, capable of division and subject to the laws governing impact.³ Thus far we still find ourselves on the well-trodden path followed by other philosophers. But imagine a simple being and at the same time endow it with reason. Would that then fully correspond to the meaning of the word *spirit?* In order to discover the

2:321   answer to this question, what I propose to do is this: while allowing that

* If the concept of a spirit had been derived by abstraction^o from our own empirical concepts, the procedure for rendering the concept distinct would be easy: one would simply have to indicate the characteristic marks which are revealed by the senses as belonging to this type of being, and by means of which we distinguish such beings from material beings. However, people talk of spirits even when there is some doubt as to whether such beings exist at all. It follows that the concept of the spirit-nature cannot be treated as if it were a concept derived by abstraction^p from experience. But if you ask: How then has one arrived at this concept in the first place, granted that it has not been by a process of abstraction?^{q} my reply to this question is as follows: There are many concepts which are the product of covert and obscure inferences made in the course of experience; these concepts then proceed to propagate themselves by attaching themselves to other concepts, without there being any awareness of the experience itself on which they were originally based or of the inference which formed the concept on the basis of that experience.^{r} Such concepts may be called *surreptitious^s concepts.* There is a great number of such concepts; some of them are nothing but delusions of the imagination,^{t} whereas others are true, for even obscure^u inferences are not always erroneous. Linguistic usage and the association of an expression with various stories which always contain the same essential characteristic,^{v} furnish that expression with a determinate meaning. This meaning can subsequently be unfolded only if the hidden sense is drawn out of its obscurity by comparing it with all the different kinds of cases in which the expression is employed and which either agree with or contradict that meaning.^{w}

^{l} *Um diese versteckte Bedeutung auszuwickeln.*
^{m} *so halte ich meinen schlecht verstandenen Begriff an allerlei Fälle der Anwendung.*
^{n} *dessen verborgenen Sinn zu entfalten.* ^{o} *abgesondert.* ^{p} *abstrahirter.* ^{q} *durch Abstraktion.*
^{r} *Viele Begriffe entspringen durch gemeine und dunkele Schlüsse bei Gelegenheit der Erfahrungen und pflanzen sich nacher auf andere fort ohne Bewusstsein der Erfahrung selbst oder des Schlusses, welcher den Begriff über dieselbe errichtet hat.*
^{s} *erschlichene.* ^{t} *ein Wahn der Einbildung.* ^{u} *dunkele.* ^{v} *einerlei Hauptmerkmal.*
^{w} *welche* (i.e., *eine bestimmte Bedeutung) folglich nur dadurch kann entfaltet werden, dass man diesen versteckten Sinn durch eine Vergleichung mit allerlei Fällen der Anwendung, die mit ihm einstimmig sind, oder ihm widerstreiten, aus seiner Dunkelheit hervorzieht.*

the aforementioned simple being possesses reason as an *internal* quality, I shall for the moment only regard it in its *external* relations. I now proceed to raise the following question: suppose that I wished to place this simple substance in that cubic foot of space which is full of matter: would it be necessary for a simple element of that matter to vacate its place so that the spirit could occupy it? Do you think that the question must be answered affirmatively? Very well! In that case, the space in question, if it were to admit a second spirit, would have to lose a second elementary particle. And if one were to continue with this process, the cubic foot of space would eventually be filled with spirits. And this cluster^x of spirits would offer resistance by means of impenetrability in exactly the same fashion as if the cubic foot of space were full of matter. And this cluster of spirits would be subject to the laws of impact just as much as matter itself. Now, although such substances were in themselves endowed with the power of reason, externally they would nonetheless be indistinguishable from the elements of matter, in the case of which one is also only acquainted^y with the powers of their external presence; as for what may belong to their inner properties – of that one has no knowledge whatever. There cannot, therefore, be any doubt that simple substances, which are such that they could be compounded together to form a cluster, would not be called spirit-beings. You will, therefore, only be able to retain the concept of a spirit if you imagine beings which could be present in a space which was already occupied by matter;* beings, therefore, which lack the quality of impenetrability, will never constitute a solid whole, no matter how many of them are united together. Simple beings of this kind are called immaterial beings, and if they are possessed of reason, they are called spirits. But simple substances, which yield an impenetrable and extended whole when they are compounded together, are called material entities, while the totality of such simple substances is called matter. Either the word 'spirit' is empty of all sense, or its meaning is the meaning we have specified.

To advance from the definition which explains what the concept of a spirit involves to the proposition that such natures are real, or, indeed, even merely possible, involves an unusually large step. The writings of philosophers[4] contain some very sound and reliable proofs, establishing,

2:322

* It can easily be seen here that I am speaking only of spirits which belong to the universe as constituents of it;^{z} I am not speaking of the Infinite Spirit, who is its Creator and Sustainer. For the concept of the spirit-nature of the latter is easy, for it is merely negative and consists in denying that the properties of matter belong to it, for they are incompatible with an infinite and absolutely necessary substance. On the other hand, in the case of a spirit-substance, such as the human soul, which is supposed to exist in union with matter, the following difficulty arises: on the one hand, I am supposed to think such substances as existing in a reciprocal relation with physical beings so that they constitute wholes, while on the other hand I am supposed to think of the only kind of combination we know – that which occurs among material beings – as being cancelled.

^{x} *Klumpe.* ^{y} *kennt.* ^{z} *die als Theile zum Weltganzen gehören.*

for example, that everything which thinks must be simple, that every substance which thinks rationally is an entity of this kind,[a] and that the indivisible 'I' cannot be distributed throughout a whole constituted by many things which are combined together. My soul will, therefore, be a simple substance. But this proof still leaves the question unresolved whether the soul is one of those substances which, when they are united together in space, form an extended and impenetrable whole, and is thus material, or whether it is immaterial and therefore a spirit, or, indeed, whether a being of the type which is called a *spirit-being* is even possible.

And in this connection, I find myself constrained to warn against precipitate judgements, which are the judgements which most easily insinuate themselves into the deepest and darkest questions. It is commonly the case, namely, that that which belongs to ordinary empirical concepts is usually regarded as if its possibility were also understood. On the other hand, it is, of course, impossible to form any concept of that which deviates from common empirical concepts and which no experience can explain, even analogically. And for that reason one tends to dismiss it at once as impossible. All matter offers a resistance in the space which it occupies; it is, for that reason, called impenetrable.[5] That this occurs is something which experience teaches us; and it is by abstraction from this experience that the general concept of matter is generated within us. But, although the resistance which something exercises in the space which it occupies is thus *recognised*,[b] to be sure, it is not for that reason *understood*.[c] For, like everything else which operates in opposition to an activity, this resistance is a true force.[6] The direction of that force is opposed to the direction indicated by the extended lines of the *approach*.[d] For this reason, this force is a force of *repulsion*, and it must be attributed to matter, and therefore to the elements of matter, as well. Now, every rational being will readily admit that the human understanding has reached its limit here.[e] It is experience alone which enables us to perceive that those things which exist in the world, and which we call *material*, possess such a force; but experience does not ever enable us to understand the possibility of such a force. Now, suppose that I posited the existence of substances which were of a different kind: they are present in space but they possess forces which differ from the *motive force*[f] of which the effect is impenetrability. If I supposed that such substances existed, it would

2:323

---

[a] *eine Einheit der Natur* / Carabellese (hereafter C) & Salmona (hereafter S): *un unità di natura* / Courtès (hereafter Co) & Lortholary (hereafter L): *une unité naturelle* / Goerwitz (hereafter G): unit of nature / Manolesco (hereafter M): a natural unity / Venturini (hereafter V): *un unità della natura* / (See note *v*, p. 326, for an account of the use of *der Natur* to mean 'of the kind'. Grimm cites this phrase to illustrate the use of the word *Einheit* to mean 'monad'.)
[b] *erkannt.* [c] *begriffen.*
[d] *und da ihre Richtung derjenigen entgegen steht, wornach die fortgezogene Linien der Annäherung zielen.*
[e] *dass hier die menschliche Einsicht zu Ende sei.*
[f] *die mit andern Kräften im Raume gegenwärtig sind, als mit jener treibenden Kraft.*

310

be altogether impossible for me to think of them *in concreto* as displaying activity, unless it bore analogy with my empirical representations. And, in so far as I have denied them the property of *filling* the space in which they operate,[7] I would have deprived myself of a concept by means of which the things which present themselves to my senses are otherwise thinkable for me; and the inevitable result must, therefore, be a kind of unthinkability. But this cannot be regarded as a known impossibility[g] for the simple reason that the opposite will, in respect of its possibility, likewise remain incomprehensible, even though its actuality presents itself to the senses.

We may, accordingly, accept the possibility of immaterial beings without any fear that we shall be refuted, though there is no hope either of our ever being able to establish their possibility by means of rational argument.[h] Such spirit-natures would be present in space, but present in space in such a way that they could always be penetrated by corporeal beings; for the presence of such spirit-natures would involve *being active in* but not *filling* space,[i] in other words, the presence in space of such spirit-natures would not involve resistance, the ground of solidity. Now, if we accepted the existence of such a *simple* spirit-substance, then, in spite of its indivisibility, one would be able to say that the place of its immediate presence was not a point, but itself a space. For, to appeal to analogy for help: even the simple elements of bodies must of necessity each of them fill a little space in the body, which is a proportionate part of that body's whole extension, for points are not parts of space at all but limits of space. Since this filling of space occurs by means of an active force (of repulsion) and therefore only indicates a sphere[j] of greater activity but not a multiplicity of the constituent parts of the operative subject,[k] the filling of space does not contradict the simple nature of such a subject.[8] Admittedly, this possibility cannot be rendered more distinct, but then that is never possible with the fundamental relations of causes and effects. In exactly the same way, there is at any rate no demonstrable contradiction confronting me, even though the thing itself remains unintelligible, if I assert that a spirit-substance, though simple, nonetheless *occupies*[l] a space (that is to say, is capable of being immediately active in it) without *filling*[m] it (that is to say, without offering any resistance in that space to material substances).[9] Nor would such an immaterial substance have to be called extended, any more than the units[n] of matter,[10] for only that which occupies a space when it is separated from everything and exists *for itself* on its own *is extended*. But those substances which are elements of matter can only occupy a space in virtue of the *external* effect they produce on other substances. But when these substances exist separately for themselves, and

2:324

[g] *eine erkannte Unmöglichkeit.* [h] *Vernunftgründe.*
[i] *eine Wirksamkeit im Raume, aber nicht dessen Erfüllung.* [j] *Umfang.*
[k] *des wirksamen Subjects.* [l] *einnehme.* [m] *erfüllen.*
[n] *Einheiten* / C, S, & V: *unità* / Co & L: *unités* / G & M: units / (see note *a* on p. 310 for this use of the word *Einheit*).

when no other things are thought of as existing in connection with them, and when there are not even to be found in them things which exist externally to each other, these substances contain no space. This applies to corporeal elements. It would also apply to spirit-natures. The limits of extension determine shape. Spirit-beings cannot, therefore, be thought of as having a shape. These are the reasons, which are difficult to understand, for the conjectured possibility of immaterial beings in the universe. If there is anyone who knows of an easier method for arriving at this knowledge,[o] let him not refuse to enlighten one who is eager to learn, and who, in the course of his investigations, has often found himself confronted with Alpine peaks, where others only see before them an easy and comfortable pathway, along which they advance, or think they do.

Now, suppose that it has been proved that the human soul was a spirit (though it is apparent from what has been said above that no such thing has as yet been proved), the next question to which we might then proceed would perhaps be the following: where is the place[p] of this human soul in the world of bodies? My answer would run like this: The body, the alterations of which are *my* alterations – this body is *my* body; and the place of that body is at the same time *my place.* If one pursued the question further and asked: Where then is *your* place (that of the soul) in this body? then I should suspect there was a catch in the question. For it is easy to see that the question already presupposes something with which we are not acquainted through experience, though it may perhaps be based on imaginary inferences. The question presupposes, namely, that my thinking 'I' is in a place which is distinct from the places of the other parts of that body which belongs to my self. But no one is immediately conscious of a particular place in his body; one is only immediately conscious of the space which one occupies relatively to the world around. I would therefore rely on ordinary experience and say, for the time being: Where I feel, it is there that *I am.* I am as immediately in my finger-tip as I am in my head. It is I myself whose heel hurts, and whose heart beats with emotion. And when my corn aches, I do not feel the painful impression in some nerve located in my brain; I feel it at the end of my toe. No experience teaches me to regard some parts of my sensation of myself as remote from me.[q] Nor does any experience teach me to imprison my indivisible 'I' in a
2:325 microscopically tiny region of the brain, either so as to operate from there the levers governing my body-machine,[r] or so as myself to be affected in that region by the workings of that machinery.[s] For that reason, I would insist on its strict refutation before I could be persuaded to dismiss as

[o] *Einsicht.* [p] *Ort.*

[q] *einige Theile meiner Empfindung von mir für entfernt* / (none of the translators has recognised that *von mir* belongs not to *entfernt* but to *Empfindung*).

[r] *und von da aus den Hebezeug meiner Körpermaschine in Bewegung zu setzen.*

[s] *oder dadurch selbst getroffen zu werden.*

absurd what used to be said in the schools:[¹] *My soul is wholly in my whole body, and wholly in each of its parts.*[¹¹] Sound common sense often apprehends a truth before it understands the reasons by means of which it can prove or explain that truth. Nor would I be entirely disconcerted by the objection which maintained that I was, in this way, thinking of the soul as extended and as diffused throughout the whole body, roughly in the way in which it is pictured for children in the *orbis pictus*.[¹²] The reason why I should not be disconcerted is this: I would dispose of the objection with the following remark: immediate presence in the totality of a space only proves a sphere of external activity; it does not prove a multiplicity of internal parts, nor, therefore, any extension or shape. They only occur when a space is to be found in a being which is posited *for itself on its own*, that is to say, when there are parts existing externally to each other. Finally, either I should know this little concerning the spirit-property of my soul, or, if this were disallowed, I should be content to know nothing at all of the matter.

If the objection were raised that these ideas are incomprehensible, or – and this is taken to be the same thing by most people – that they are impossible, that would not disturb me either. I would take my place at the feet of these wise men in order to hear them speaking thus: The human soul has its seat in the brain, and its abode is an indescribably tiny place in it.* It is here that the soul, like the spider sitting at the   2:326

---

* Examples of injuries have been adduced where a substantial part of the brain has been lost without the injured person losing his life or suffering any impairment to the power of thought.[ᵘ] According to the idea which is commonly entertained and which I am reporting here, the removal or displacement of a single atom of the brain would suffice instantly to deprive a person of his soul. The current opinion of the soul which assigns it to a place in the brain, would seem to have originated chiefly from the fact that, when one engages in deep thought, one has the distinct feeling that the nerves of the brain are being strained. But if this conclusion were correct, it would also prove that the soul was situated in other places as well. For example, in anxiety or joy, the sensation seems to have its seat in the heart. Many emotions, indeed the majority of them, manifest their chief force in the diaphragm. Pity moves the intestines, and other instincts express their origin and their sensibility in other organs. The reason which has persuaded people to think that they feel the *reflective* soul particularly in the brain is, perhaps, this: all reflection requires the mediation of *signs* for the ideas which are to be awakened, if the ideas, accompanied and supported by the signs, are to attain the required degree of clarity. The signs of our representations, however, are primarily those which are received either through hearing or through sight: these two senses are activated by impressions in the brain, the organs of these senses being also closest to that part of the body. Now, if the excitation of these signs, which Descartes calls *ideas materiales*,[¹³] is really a stimulation of the nerves producing a motion which is similar to the motion produced by sensation, then it follows that in reflection the tissue of the brain will, in particular, be forced to vibrate in harmony with the earlier impression, and, as a result, to grow fatigued. For if thought is accompanied by emotion[ᵛ] as well, one feels not only the exertions of the brain but also the assaults being

---

[¹] *was die Schullehrer sagten.*   [ᵘ] *ohne dass es dem Menschen . . . die Gedanken gekostet hat.*
[ᵛ] *affectvoll.*

centre of its web, receives sensations. The nerves of the brain strike or agitate the soul. The effect of this, however, is that a representation is formed, not indeed of this immediate impression, but of the impression made on quite remote parts of the body, albeit as an object existing outside the brain. From this seat in the brain, the soul also operates the ropes and levers of the whole machine, causing voluntary*ʷ* motions as it pleases. Propositions such as these admit only of a very superficial proof, or of no proof at all. And ultimately, since we are only inadequately acquainted with the nature of the soul, such propositions can only be refuted in a correspondingly weak fashion. I am not willing, therefore, to become involved in one of those scholarly wrangles in which it is commonly the case that both sides have the most to say precisely when their ignorance of the subject is the most complete. What I do wish to do is simply to examine the conclusions to which a theory of this kind may lead me. Since, therefore, according to the propositions recommended to me, my soul, in its manner of being present in space, would not differ from any element of matter, and since the power of the understanding is an inner property which I cannot perceive in these elements of matter, even if that same property were present in all of them, it follows that no valid reason can be adduced for supposing that my soul is not one of the substances which constitute matter, or for supposing that its particular manifestations should not originate exclusively from the place which it occupies in such an ingenious*ˣ* machine as the body of an animal, and in which the confluence of the nerves*ʸ* assures the inner capacity of thought and the power of will. But in that case one would no longer be able to recognise with certainty any distinctive characteristic mark*ᶻ* of the soul, which distin-

2:327 guished it from the raw elementary matter of corporeal natures. And then the idea jokingly proposed by Leibniz that in drinking our coffee we may perhaps be swallowing atoms destined to become human souls would no longer be a laughing matter.[14] But, in such a case, would not this thinking 'I' be subject to the common fate of material natures? Just as it had by chance been drawn from the chaos of all the elements in order to animate an animal machine, why should it not at some time in the future, when the contingent combination has been dissolved, return once more to that chaos of elements? It is sometimes necessary to alarm the thinker who has gone astray by drawing his attention to the consequences of his error, so that he pays more careful attention to the principles by means of which he has allowed himself to be led on, as in a dream.

I must confess that I am very much inclined to assert the existence of immaterial natures in the world, and to place my own soul in the class of

made by the sensitive parts of the body, which normally stand in a relation of sympathy with the representations of the soul when it is stirred by passion.

ʷ willkürlich.   *ˣ künstlich.*   *ʸ Nervenvereinigung.*   *ᶻ kein eigenthümliches Merkmal.*

these beings.* But in that case, how mysterious is the community^c which exists between a spirit and a body: and yet at the same time, how natural is that incomprehensibility, granted that the concepts we have of external actions are derived from the concepts we have of matter, and granted also that they are always connected with the conditions of exerting pressure or striking a blow^f – conditions which are not fulfilled here? For how, after all, should an immaterial substance obstruct matter,^g so that matter in its motion should collide with a spirit? And how could corporeal things produce effects on another being, which differed from them, and which offered no opposition to them by means of impenetrability, or in any way prevented them from also occupying the space in which it was present? It seems that a spirit-being is present in the matter, with which it is combined, in the most intimate fashion; and it seems not to act on those forces which inhere in the elements and in virtue of which they are related to each other; it seems rather to operate on the inner principles of their state.^h For every substance, including even a simple element of matter, must after all have some kind of inner activity as the ground of its producing an external effect, and that in spite of the fact that I cannot specify in what that inner activity consists.† On

2:328

---

* The reason which inclines me to this view is very obscure even to myself, and it will probably remain so, as well. It is a reason which applies at the same time to the sentient being of animals. The principle *of life* is to be found in something in the world which seems to be of an immaterial nature. For all *life* is based upon the inner capacity to determine itself *voluntarily*.^a On the other hand, the essential characteristic mark of matter consists in the filling of space in virtue of a necessary force which is limited by an external force operating against it. It follows from this, therefore, that the state of all that which is material is *dependent* and *constrained*,^b whereas those natures which are supposed to be *spontaneously active*^c and to contain within themselves the ground of life in virtue of their inner force – in short, those natures whose own power of will is capable of spontaneously determining and modifying itself – such natures can scarcely be of material nature. One cannot reasonably demand that such an unfamiliar type of being, which is known in most cases only hypothetically, should be understood conceptually in the divisions of its various species. At any rate, those immaterial beings which contain the ground of animal life are different from those which comprise reason in their spontaneous activity^d and are called spirits.

† Leibniz said that this inner ground of all its external relations and their changes was a *power of representation*.[115] This thought, which was not developed by Leibniz, was greeted with laughter by later philosophers. They would, however, have been better advised to have first considered the question whether a substance, such as a simple part of matter, would be possible in the complete absence of any inner state. And, if they had, perhaps, been unwilling to rule out such an inner state, then it would have been incumbent on them to invent some other possible inner state as an alternative to that of representations and the activities dependent on representations. Anybody can see for himself that if a faculty of obscure representations is attributed even to the simple, elementary particles of matter, it does not follow that matter itself has a faculty of representation, for many substances of this kind, connected together into a whole, can after all never constitute a unified thinking entity.

---

^a *nach Willkür.*   ^b *abhängend und gezwungen.*   ^c *selbst thätig.*   ^d *Selbstthätigkeit.*
^e *die Gemeinschaft.*   ^f *mit den Bedingungen des Druckes oder Stosses.*
^g *der Materie im Wege liegen.*   ^h *auf das innere Principium ihres Zustandes.*
^i *eine Vorstellungskraft.*

the other hand, if one were to accept such principles, the soul would, even in these inner determinations, construed as effects, intuitively cognise the state of the universe, the cause of those determinations. But which necessity it is which causes a spirit and a body together to form a single being, and what grounds they are which, in the case of certain forms of destruction, then cancel this unity again – these questions, along with various others, far transcend my powers of understanding. I am not normally particularly bold in measuring the capacity of my understanding against the mysteries of nature. Nonetheless, I am sufficiently sure of myself not to fear any opponent, no matter how dreadful his weapons may be (assuming always, that is, that I also had some inclination to the dispute) so that I can in this case test argument against argument in *refutation,* for among men of learning such testing is really the art of demonstrating each other's ignorance.[j]

2:329

SECOND CHAPTER: A FRAGMENT OF OCCULT PHILOSOPHY, THE PURPOSE OF WHICH IS TO REVEAL OUR COMMUNITY WITH THE SPIRIT-WORLD

The initiate has already accustomed the untutored understanding, which clings to the outer senses, to higher concepts of an abstract character. He is now able to see spirit-forms, stripped of their corporeal shell, in the half-light with which the dim torch of metaphysics reveals the realm of shades. Let us now, therefore, having completed our difficult preparation, embark on our perilous journey.

> *Ibant obscuri sola sub nocte per umbras,*
> *Perque domos Ditis vacuas et inania regna.*
> Virgil[16]

When it is in a state of inertia and rest,[k] *dead* matter, which fills the universe, is, according to its own proper nature, in a single self-same condition: it has solidity, extension and shape. Its manifestations,[l] which are based upon all these grounds, permit a *physical* explanation which is also mathematical; this explanation, when the physical and the mathematical are combined, is called *mechanical.* On the other hand, there is a type of being which contains the ground of *life* in the universe. Such beings are, therefore, not of the kind which enlarge the mass of lifeless matter as constituents, or increase its extension. Nor are they affected by lifeless matter acting in accordance with the laws of contact and impact.[m] They rather, by means of their inner activity, animate both themselves and also the dead stuff of nature. If one turns one's attention to this type of being, one will find oneself persuaded, if not with the distinctness of a demonstration, then at

---

[j] *um in diesem Falle mit ihm den Versuch der Gegengründe im Widerlegen zu machen, der bei den Gelehrten eigentlich die Geschicklichkeit ist, einander das Nichtwissen zu demonstrieren.*
[k] *Trägheit und Beharrlichkeit.* [l] *Erscheinungen.* [m] *Berührung und des Stosses.*

least with the anticipation of a not untutored understanding,[n] of the existence of immaterial beings. The particular causal laws in accordance with which they operate are called *pneumatic*,[o] and, in so far as corporeal beings are the mediating causes[p] of their effects in the material world, they are called *organic*. Since these immaterial beings are spontaneously active principles,[q] and thus substances and natures existing in their own right, it follows that the conclusion which first suggests itself is this: these immaterial beings, if they are directly united may perhaps together constitute a great whole, which could be called the immaterial world (*mundus intelligibilis*).[17] For on what basis of probability could one wish to assert that such beings, which are similar to each other in nature, could stand in community[r] with each other only as a result of the mediation of other beings (corporeal things) of a different constitution,[s] for this latter claim is even more mysterious than the former.

2:330

This *immaterial world* may therefore be regarded as a whole existing in its own right; the parts of that immaterial world stand in a relation of reciprocal connection and community[t] with each other, even without the mediation of corporeal things; it follows that this latter relation is contingent and only belongs to some of the parts. Indeed, even in those cases where the relation is mediated by corporeal things, there is nothing to prevent those very same immaterial beings, which act on each other through the mediation of matter, from also standing in a special and thorough-going connection which is independent of the mediation of matter; they would at all times reciprocally affect each other as immaterial beings, so that their relation to each other through the mediation of matter would only be contingent and would be based upon a special divine provision, whereas their relation to each other independently of matter would be natural and indissoluble.

If, in this way, we combine all the principles of life in the whole of nature, construing them as so many incorporeal substances standing in community with each other, while also construing them as in part united with matter, we shall thereby imagine a great totality of the immaterial world, an immeasurable but unknown hierarchy of beings and active natures, in virtue of which alone the dead stuff of the corporeal world is animated. It will, perhaps, forever be impossible to determine with certainty how far and to which members of nature life extends, or what those degrees of life, which border on the very edge of complete lifelessness, may be.[u] *Hylozoism*[18] invests everything with life, while *materialism*, when

---

[n] *mit der Vorempfindung eines nicht ungeübten Verstandes.*   [o] *pneumatisch.*   [p] *Mittelursachen.*
[q] *selbstthätige Principien.*   [r] *Gemeinschaft.*   [s] *von fremder Beschaffenheit.*
[t] *in wechselseitiger Verknüpfung und Gemeinschaft.*
[u] *Bis auf welche Glieder aber der Natur Leben ausgebreitet sei, und welche diejenigen Grade desselben seien, die zunächst an die völlige Leblosigkeit grenzen, ist vielleicht unmöglich jemals mit Sicherheit auszumachen.*

317

carefully considered, deprives everything of life. Maupertuis ascribed the lowest degree of life to the organic particles of nourishment consumed by animals; other philosophers regard such particles as nothing but dead masses,[v] merely serving to magnify the power of the levers of animal machines. The undisputed characteristic mark of life, belonging to that which we perceive by means of our outer senses is, doubtless, free movement, which shows us that it has originated from the power of the will.[w] However, the conclusion that, when this characteristic mark is not encountered, then every degree of life is also lacking, is not certain. Boerhaave says somewhere:[19] *The animal is a plant which has its root in its stomach* (inside itself). Someone else might, with equal propriety, play with these concepts and say: *the plant is an animal which has its stomach in its root*

2:331 (outside itself). It is, therefore, possible for plants to lack the organs of voluntary motion and, in lacking them, to lack the external characteristic marks of life, which are certainly necessary to animals, for a being which has the instruments of its nourishment within itself must be able to move itself according to need. A being, on the other hand, which has the instruments of its nourishment outside itself and sunk in the element which supports it, is already adequately provided for by forces external to itself. Even though such a being contains within itself a principle of inner life, namely, vegetation, it does not need an organic arrangement[x] to be made for external voluntary activity.[y] None of this is necessary for my argument,[z] for, apart from the fact that I should have very little to say in favour of such conjectures, these conjectures, which are regarded as dusty and outmoded whims, are also exposed to fashionable mockery. The ancients, namely, thought that three different types of life could be assumed to exist: *vegetative, animal,* and *rational.*[a] When the ancients combined the three immaterial principles of these three different types of life in man, they may well have erred. But when they distributed these immaterial principles among the three different classes of creature which grow and reproduce their kind, they were saying something which, although, of course, probably not capable of proof, was not for that reason absurd. This is particularly true in the case of the judgement of a person who wished to consider the separate life of the amputated parts of some animals, that quality of irritability[b] which has been so well attested but which is also at the same time such an inexplicable property of the filaments of animal bodies and of some plants, and finally the close kinship between the polyps and other zoophytes with plants. Moreover, the appeal to immaterial principles is the resort of lazy philosophy. For that reason, explanation of this sort is to be avoided at all costs, if the causes of

---

[v] *todte Klumpen.* [w] *aus Willkür.* [x] *keine organische Einrichtung.* [y] *willkürlichen Thätigkeit.*
[z] *Ich verlange nichts von allem diesem auf Beweisgründen.*
[a] *das Pflanzenartige, das Thierische, und das Vernünftige.* [b] *Irritabilität.*

phenomena in the world, which are based upon the laws of the motion of mere matter and which are uniquely and alone capable of intelligibility, are to be known in their full extent. Nonetheless, I am convinced that *Stahl*,[20] who is disposed to explain animal processes in organic terms, was frequently closer to the truth than *Hofmann*[21] or *Boerhaave*,[22] to name but a few.[23] These latter, ignoring immaterial forces, adhere to mechanical causes, and in so doing adopt a more philosophical method. This method, while sometimes failing of its mark, is generally successful. It is also this method alone which is of use in science. But as for the influence of incorporeal beings: it can at best be acknowledged to exist; the nature of its operation and the extent of its effects, however, will never be explained.

The immaterial world would thus, then, include, firstly, all created 2:332 intelligences, some of them being united with matter so as to form a person, others not; the immaterial world would, in addition, include the sensible subjects[c] in all animal species; finally it would include all the other principles of life wherever they may exist in nature, even though this life does not manifest itself by any of the external characteristic marks of voluntary motion. All these immaterial natures, whether they exercise an influence on the corporeal world or not, and all rational beings, of which the animal nature is an accidental state of their being, whether they exist here on earth or on other heavenly bodies, and whether they are now animating the raw stuff of matter, or will do so in the future, or have done so in the past – all these beings, I say, would, according to this account, stand in a community consonant with their nature. This community would not be based on the conditions which limit the relationship of bodies. It would be a community in which distance in space and separation in time, which constitute the great chasm in the visible world which cancels all community, would vanish. The human soul, already in this present life, would therefore have to be regarded as being simultaneously linked to two worlds. The human soul, in so far as it is connected with a body so as to constitute a personal unity, clearly senses only the material world. On the other hand, as a member of the spirit-world, the human soul would both receive and impart the pure influences of immaterial natures, so that, as soon as its connection with the material world had been dissolved, the community in which it at all times stands with spirit-natures would continue to exist on its own; and that community would perforce reveal itself to the consciousness of the human soul in the form of a clear intuition.[d]*

---

* When heaven is spoken of as the seat of the blessed, ordinary people tend to represent it as existing above, high up in the measureless spaces of the universe. What is forgotten, however, is the fact that our own earth, if viewed from those regions, would also appear to be one of the stars in the heavens, and that the inhabitants of other worlds could point to us with

[c] *die empfindende Subjecte.*   [d] *sich ihrem Bewusstsein zum klaren Anschauen eröffnen müsste.*

2:333 The constant use of the careful language of reason is now actually becoming tiresome. Why should I not be permitted, as well, to speak in the academical tone? It is more decisive and it dispenses both the author and the reader from the duty of thinking, which must sooner or later lead both of them to a state of tiresome indecision. Accordingly, it is as good as proved, or it could easily be proved, if one were willing to take the time and trouble to go into the matter, or, better still, it will one day, I know not when or where, be proved that the human soul, even in this life, stands in an indissoluble communion^e with all the immaterial natures of the spirit-world; that, standing in a reciprocal relation with these natures, it both has an effect upon them and receives impressions from them, though the human soul *qua* human being is not conscious of them, provided that everything is in good order. On the other hand, it is also likely that spirit-natures cannot immediately receive any conscious sensible impression of the corporeal world,^{f} for they are not linked with any portion of matter so as to constitute a person, so that, by that means, they could become conscious of their place in the material universe. Nor, lacking ingenious^g organs, could they become conscious of the relation of extended beings either to themselves or to each other. It is, however, likely that they are able to exercise an influence^h on the souls of human beings, for the latter are beings of the same nature as themselves. And it is also likely that they do, at all times, stand in reciprocal communion with human beings. But if they do so, it is in such a fashion that, in the communication of representations, those representations which the soul contains within itself as a being which is dependent on the corporeal world, cannot be communicated to other spirit-beings. And, again, the concepts which these latter spirit-beings entertain cannot, in so far as they are intuitive representations of immaterial things, be communicated to the clear consciousness of human beings, not, at any rate, in the specific form which is characteristic of

---

as much justification and say: Behold! The dwelling place of eternal bliss, a heavenly home which has been prepared for our eventual reception there. A curious illusion has the effect, namely, that the high flight taken by hope is always connected with the concept of ascent: what is forgotten is the fact that, no matter how high one's ascent, one must sink back down again, if at any rate, one is to gain a secure foothold in another world. But, according to the ideas which we have introduced here, heaven would in fact be the spirit-world, or, if you like, the blessed part of that world. And this world would have to be sought neither above nor below oneself, for such an immaterial whole would have to be represented, not in terms of remoteness from or nearness to corporeal things, but in terms of the spiritual connections of its *parts* to each other. In any case, the members of that world are aware of themselves only in terms of such relations.

^{e} *in einer unauflöslich verknüpften Gemeinschaft.*
^{f} *keine sinnliche Empfindung von der Körperwelt mit Bewusstsein.* ^{g} *künstliche.*
^{h} *einfliessen können.*

them,[i] for the materials of which the two types of ideas are constituted are different in kind.

It would be a fine thing if the systematic constitution of the spirit-world which we have presented here could be inferred, or even supposed as simply probable, not merely from the concept of the spirit-nature as such, which is far too hypothetical in character, but from some real generally accepted observation. Accordingly, if the reader will bear with me, I shall venture such an attempt here. It will, admittedly, take me some distance from my path; it will also be far enough removed from self-evidence. But, 2:334 in spite of this, it seems to give rise to conjectures of a kind which are not disagreeable.

Among the forces which move the human heart, some of the most powerful seem to lie outside the heart. In other words, there are forces which do not seem to relate as mere means, for example, to the advancement of self-interest[j] or the satisfaction of private need, as to an objective which lies *within* the person himself; they rather cause the tendencies of our impulses to shift the focal point of their union *outside ourselves* and to locate it in other rational beings.[k] From this there arises a conflict between two forces, namely, the force of egoism,[l] which relates everything to itself, and the force of altruism,[m] by means of which the heart is driven or drawn out of itself towards others. I am not going to linger over the drive, which makes us so heavily and so universally dependent on the judgement of others, and causes us to regard the approval or applause of others as so necessary to perfecting our own good opinion of ourselves,[n] though this tendency sometimes gives rise to a wrong-headed and misguided conception of honour.[o] In spite of this, however, there may exist even in the least selfish and most sincere of temperaments a hidden tendency to compare that which one knows for oneself to be *good* or *true*[p] with the judgement of others, with a view to bringing such opinions into harmony. Nonetheless, there may also exist a tendency to halt, so to speak, any human soul on the path of knowledge, if it appears to be pursuing a path different from the one we have chosen ourselves. All of this perhaps reveals that, when it

---

[i] *in ihrer eigentlichen Beschaffenheit.* [j] *auf die Eigennützlichkeit.*

[k] *dass die Tendenz unserer Regungen den Brennpunkt ihrer Vereinigung ausser uns in andere vernünftige Wesen versetzen.*

[l] *Eigenheit.* [m] *der Gemeinnützigkeit.*

[n] *zur Vollendung des unsrigen (scil. Urtheils) von uns selbst.*

[o] *ein übelverstandener Ehrenwahn* / (the word *übelverstanden* is to be understood in the sense of 'wrongheaded'; under *Ehrenwahn* Grimm offers *notio falsa honoris* ['false conception of honour']).

[p] *dasjenige, was man für sich selbst als gut oder wahr erkennt* / (the phrase is ambiguous: it is not grammatically clear whether *für sich selbst* attaches to *erkennt* [the view of C, G, and V] or to *gut oder wahr* [the view of Co and L]; the context rather supports the former view).

comes to our own judgements, we sense our dependency on the *universal human understanding,* this phenomenon being a means of conferring a kind of unity of reason on the totality of thinking beings.

I shall, however, pass over this otherwise not insubstantial observation, and concentrate for the time being on another which is more illuminating and more important for our purpose. When we relate external things to our need, we cannot do so without at the same time feeling ourselves bound and limited by a certain sensation; this sensation draws our attention to the fact that an alien will,[q] so to speak, is operative within ourselves, and that our own inclination needs external assent as its condition. A secret power forces us to direct our will towards the well-being of others or regulate it in accordance with the will of another,[r] although this often happens contrary to our will[s] and in strong opposition to our selfish inclination. The focal point at which the lines which indicate the direction of our drives converge,[t] is therefore not merely to be found within us; there are, in addition, other forces which move us and which are to be found in the will of others[u] outside ourselves. This is the source from which the moral impulses take their rise. These impulses often incline us to act against the dictates of self-interest.[v] I refer to the strong law of obligation and the weaker law of benevolence.[w] Each of these laws extort from us many a sacrifice, and although self-interested inclinations from time to time overrule them both, these two laws, nonetheless, never fail to assert their reality in human nature. As a result, we recognise that, in our most secret motives, we are dependent upon the *rule of the general will.*[x] It is this rule which confers upon the world of all thinking beings its *moral unity* and invests it with a systematic constitution, drawn up in accordance with purely spiritual laws. We sense within ourselves a constraining[y] of our will to harmonise with the general will. To call this sensed constraining '*moral feeling*', is to speak of it merely as a manifestation[z] of that which takes place within us, without establishing its causes. Thus it was that *Newton* called the certain law governing the tendencies inherent in all particles of matter to draw closer to each other the *gravitation* of matter, not wishing to entangle his mathematical demonstrations in possible vexatious philosophical disputes concerning the cause of those tendencies. Nonetheless, he did not hesitate to treat gravitation as a genuine effect produced by the universal activity of matter operating on itself;[a] for this reason he also gave it the name '*attraction*'. Are we, then, to suppose that it would not in the same way be possible to represent the phenomenon of the moral impulses in thinking natures, who are reciprocally related to

2:335

[q] *ein fremder Wille.*   [r] *nach fremder Willkür.*   [s] *ungern.*
[t] *der Punkt, wohin die Richtungslinien unserer Triebe zusammenlaufen.*   [u] *in dem Wollen anderer.*
[v] *wider den Dank des Eigennutzes.*   [w] *Gütigkeit.*
[x] *abhängig von der Regel des allgemeinen Willens.*   [y] *Nöthigung.*   [z] *Erscheinung.*
[a] *als eine wahre Wirkung einer allgemeinen Thätigkeit der Materie ineinander.*

each other, as the effect of a genuinely active force, in virtue of which spirit-natures exercise an influence on each other? If the phenomenon of the moral impulses were represented in this way, the moral feeling would be this *sensed dependency* of the private will on the general will: it would be an effect produced by a natural and universal reciprocal interaction. And it would be in virtue of this reciprocity that the immaterial world would attain its moral unity, and that as a result of having formed itself into a system of spiritual perfection, in accordance with the laws governing the cohesive unity peculiar to it. If one concedes to these thoughts enough plausibility to justify the effort of measuring them against their conse-quences,[b] one may perhaps find oneself, because of their charm, being imperceptibly prejudiced in their favour. For in this case, the anomalies[c] seem to vanish which are normally so embarrassingly conspicuous in the contradiction between the moral and the physical circumstances of man here on earth. All the morality of actions, while never having its full effect in the corporeal life of man according to the order of nature, may well do so in the spirit-world, according to pneumatic laws. True intentions, the clandestine motives of numerous endeavours which have been frustrated by powerlessness,[d] self-conquest, even sometimes the covert malice of seemingly good actions – all these, in respect of physical success in the corporeal world, are for the most part lost.[e] In the immaterial world, however, these same things would have to be regarded as fruitful grounds. And, in respect of the immaterial world, in accordance with pneumatic laws, and in virtue of the connection between the private and the general will, in other words, in virtue of the connection between the unity and the whole of the spirit-world, these same things will either exercise an effect which is consonant with the moral quality of the free will,[f] or themselves also be reciprocally affected by such an effect. For since the moral char-acter of the deed[g] concerns the inner state of the spirit, it follows that it can only naturally produce an effect, which is consonant with the whole of morality, in the immediate community of spirits.[h] As a result, it would now happen that man's soul would already in this life and according to its moral state have to occupy its place among the spirit-substances of the universe, just as, in accordance with the laws of motion, the various types of matter in space[i] adopt an order, consonant with their corporeal powers,

2:336

---

[b] *wenn man diesen Gedanken so viel Scheinbarkeit zugesteht als erforderlich ist, um die Mühe zu verdienen sie an ihren Folgen zu messen.*
[c] *Unregelmässigkeiten.*   [d] *aus Ohnmacht fruchtlosen Bestrebungen.*
[e] *sind mehrentheils für den physischen Erfolg in dem körperlichen Zustande verloren.*
[f] *eine der sittlichen Beschaffenheit der freien Willkür angemessene Wirkung.*
[g] *das Sittliche der That.*
[h] *so kann es auch natürliche Weise nur in der unmittelbaren Gemeinschaften der Geister die der ganzen Moralität adäquate Wirkung nach sich ziehen.*
[i] *die Materien des Weltraums.*

relatively to each other.* If, then, the community of the soul with the corporeal world is eventually dissolved by death, life in the other world would simply be a natural continuation of the connection in which the soul had already existed during this present life. And all the consequences of the morality practised here would re-appear there in the effects, which a being, standing in an indissoluble community with the entire spirit-world, would already have exercised earlier in that world in accordance with pneumatic laws. The present and the future would, therefore, be of one piece, so to speak, and constitute a continuous whole,*j* even according

2:337 to the *order of nature*. This latter circumstance is of particular importance. For, in a speculation which is based simply on principles of reason, the necessity of having to resort to an extraordinary Divine Will in order to resolve a difficulty arising from the imperfect harmony between morality and its consequences in the world, amounts to a serious difficulty. And the reason is this: no matter how probable our judgement, based on our concepts of the Divine Wisdom, concerning that will may be, a strong suspicion will always remain that the feeble concepts of our understanding may perhaps have been applied to the Supreme Being in a fashion which is very much mistaken. For man's obligation is simply to judge the Divine Will by appeal either to the harmoniousness which he really perceives in the world, or to the harmoniousness which, using the rule of analogy, he may suppose the world to have. He is not, however, entitled to imagine new and arbitrary arrangements in the present or the future world, employing some scheme originated by his own wisdom, which he then promptly converts into a rule for the Divine Will.

We shall now steer our reflection back on to the path we were following before, and proceed on our way towards the objective which we have set ourselves. If the spirit-world and the participation of our souls in it is as our outline account has represented it, then scarcely anything appears more strange than the fact that the community with spirits*k* is not a wholly universal and commonplace phenomenon. The rarity of the phenomena is almost more extraordinary than their possibility. However, this difficulty

---

* The reciprocal effects which take their origin from the ground of morality and which human beings and the members of the spirit-world exercise upon each other in accordance with the laws of pneumatic influence – these reciprocal effects might be construed in the following terms: there naturally arises from these reciprocal effects a closer community between a good or a bad soul, on the one hand, and a good or a bad spirit, respectively, on the other; as a result, the former associate themselves with that part of the spirit-republic which is consonant with their moral constitution, participating in all the effects which may, in accordance with the order of nature, arise therefrom.

j *ein stetiges Ganzes.*

k *Geistergemeinschaft* / C: *comunione degli spiriti* / Co & L: *commerce avec les esprits* / G: communion with spirits / S & V: *commercio con gli spiriti.*

can fairly easily be remedied; and, indeed, it has already been in part overcome. For the representation which the human soul, using an immaterial intuition,[l] has of itself as a spirit, in so far as it regards itself as standing in relation to beings of a similar nature, is quite different from the representations it has when the soul's consciousness represents itself as a *human being* by means of an image drawn from the impression made on the organs of the body[m] and which can only be represented in relation to material things. Accordingly, while it is true that there is one single subject which is simultaneously a member of the visible and the invisible world, it is nonetheless not one and the same person, for the representations of the one world are not, on account of their different constitution, the accompanying ideas of the representations belonging to the other world. And hence what I think as spirit is not remembered by me as   2:338 human being; and, conversely, my state as a human being does not enter at all into the representation of myself as a spirit. Furthermore, no matter how clear and intuitive the representations of the spirit-world may be* this would still not suffice to make me as a human being conscious of them; for in so far as even the representation of *oneself* (that is to say, of the soul) as a spirit has been acquired by means of inferences, it is not in the case of any human being an intuitive empirical concept.

---

* This may be explained by means of a certain dual personality which belongs to the soul even with respect to this life. Certain philosophers,[24] with not the slightest qualm that anyone might object, think that they can appeal to the state of deep sleep to prove the reality of obscure representations,[n] when in fact all that can be said with certainty in this matter is that we do not, when we are awake, remember any of the representations which we may perhaps have had in deep sleep. And all that follows from this is that these representations are not clearly represented when we wake up; what does not follow is that these representations at the time when we were sleeping were obscure.[25] I suspect on the contrary, that these representations may be clearer and more extensive than even the clearest of the representations we have when we are awake. For that is what is to be expected of a being, as active as the soul, when the external senses are in a state of perfect rest. But since the body of the person is not sensed at the time, the accompanying idea of the body is lacking on awakening; and it is this idea which can assist in bringing to consciousness the fact that the previous state of the thoughts belongs to one and the same person. The actions of some sleep-walkers, who on occasion display greater understanding in this state than usual while remembering nothing about it when they wake, nonetheless confirm the possibility of what I suspect is the case with deep sleep. Dreams, on the other hand, that is to say, the representations which the sleeper has and which he remembers when he wakes, are not relevant here. For when a person dreams, he is not completely asleep; to a certain degree he has clear sensations, and weaves the actions of his spirit[o] into the impressions of the external senses. Hence it is that he subsequently remembers them in part; and hence it is that he also finds in them nothing but wild and extravagant chimaeras,[p] as must happen, since the ideas of the imagination[q] and those of external sensation have been jumbled together with each other.

[l] *durch ein immaterielles Anschauen.*   [m] *aus dem Eindrucke körperlicher Organen.*
[n] *dunkeler Vorstellungen.*   [o] *Geisteshandlung.*   [p] *wilde abgeschmackte Chimären.*
[q] *Ideen der Phantasie.*

2:339

This heterogeneity[r] between spirit-representations and those which belong to the bodily life of man need not, however, be regarded as an impediment serious enough to prevent all possibility of our becoming aware, from time to time, even during this present life, of the influences which emanate from the spirit-world. For these influences can enter the personal consciousness of man, not, it is true, directly, but, nonetheless, in such a fashion that they, in accordance with the law of association of ideas,[s] excite those images which are related to them, and awaken representations which bear an analogy with our senses.[t] They are not, it is true, the spirit-concept[u] itself, but they are symbols of it. For after all, it is always exactly the same substance which belongs to and is a member of both this world and the other world. The two kinds of representation belong to the same subject and they are linked with each other. The possibility of this being the case can, to a certain extent, be rendered intelligible if we consider the way in which the higher concepts of reason, which are fairly close to the spirit-concepts, normally assume, so to speak, a corporeal cloak in order to present themselves in a clear light. It is for this reason that the moral characteristics of the Divinity are represented under the representations of anger, jealousy, compassion, revenge, and so forth. It is for this reason, too, that poets personify the virtues, vices and other qualities of the kind,[v] albeit in such a fashion that the true idea of the understanding shines through. Thus, the geometer represents time by a line, although space and time only agree in their relations;[w] they thus, presumably, only agree with each other analogically, never qualitatively. Hence, even with philosophers, the representation of the divine eternity takes on the semblance of an infinite time, in spite of the care which is taken not to conflate the two notions. One of the chief reasons why mathematicians are commonly disinclined to admit the existence of Leibnizian monads is probably because they cannot avoid representing them as tiny little lumps.[x] It is thus not improbable that spirit-sensations may enter consciousness, if they arouse images in our imagination[y] which are akin to

---

[r] *Ungleichartigkeit.*   [s] *nach dem Gesetz der vergesellschafteten Begriffe.*
[t] *analogische Vorstellungen unserer Sinne* / C & V: *rappresentazioni analoghe* (V: *analogiche*) *dei nostri sensi* / Co & L: *des représentations analogiques de nos sens* / G: analogous ideas of our senses / M: analogous representations of our senses / S: *nei nostri rappresentazioni analoghe.*
[u] *geistiger Begriff.*
[v] *oder andere Eigenschaften der Natur* / C & V: *o altre proprietà della natura* / Co & L: *ou autres qualités naturelles* / G: and other qualities of human nature / M: and other natural properties / S: *o altre qualità naturali* / (None of the translators has recognised that the phrase *der Natur* is being used in a colloquial sense and has the force of *dieser Natur* [often employed, as here, to complete a list] and ought thus to be translated by 'of the kind' or 'such as have just been mentioned'. Serious philosophical problems would be raised by attributing to Kant the view that virtue and vice were *natural* qualities. G alone *senses* the difficulty, for he translates *der Natur* by 'of human nature'.)
[w] *nur eine Übereinkunft in Verhältnissen haben.*   [x] *kleine Klümpchen.*   [y] *Phantasien.*

them. In this way, ideas which are communicated by means of spirit-influence would clothe themselves in the signs of that *language,* which the human being normally uses: the sensed presence of a spirit would be clothed in the image of a *human figure;* the order and beauty of the immaterial world would be clothed in the images of our imagination^z which normally delight our senses in life, and so forth.

Phenomena^a of this type cannot, however, be something common and usual; they can only occur with persons whose organs* are endowed with an exceptionally high degree of sensitivity for intensifying the images of the imagination,^b according to the inner state of the soul, and by means of harmonious movement, and do so to a greater degree than usually happens, or, indeed, ought to happen with people of sound constitution. Such out of the ordinary persons would, at certain moments, be assailed by the vision^c of certain objects as external to them, which they would take for the presence of spirit-natures presenting themselves to their corporeal senses, though the occurrence is in such a case only an illusion of the imagination, but of such a kind that the cause of the illusion is a genuine spirit-influence. That spirit-influence cannot be felt immediately; it can only reveal itself to consciousness by means of the images of the imagination^d which are akin to it, and which assume the semblance of sensations.^e

The concepts which we have acquired by learning,^f and many erroneous opinions, indeed, which have insinuated themselves into the mind in some other way,^g will have played a role in a case such as this, where delusion and truth are mingled together, and where a real spirit-sensation, although providing the basis of the experience, has nonetheless been transformed into a phantom^h of sensible things. But it will also be admitted that the capacity thus to develop the impressions emanating from the spirit-world so that they can be clearly intuited in this life can scarcely be of much use, for, in a case like this, the spirit-impression is of necessity so intimately interwoven with the illusion of the imagination,ⁱ that it cannot be possible to distinguish the element of truth in such an experience from the crude illusions^j which surround it. Moreover, such a state would indicate a genuine malady, for it presupposes a modification in the balance of the nerves which are set in unnatural motion even by the merely

2:340

---

* By this I do not mean the organs of outer sensation but rather the sensorium of the soul,[26] as it is called; that is to say, that part of the brain, of which the movement usually accompanies the many different images and representations of the thinking soul, as the philosophers maintain.

^z *Phantasien.*   ^a *Erscheinungen.*   ^b *Bilder der Phantasie.*
^c *Apparenz /* (*Apparenz* is not listed in Grimm; it would seem to be a Latin-based neologism invented by Kant, presumably as a synonym for *Erscheinung.*)
^d *Bilder der Phantasie.*   ^e *Schein der Empfindung.*   ^f *Erziehungsbegriffe.*
^g *oder auch mancherlei sonst eingeschlichene Wahn.*   ^h *Schattenbilder.*
ⁱ *Hirngespinst der Einbildung.*   ^j *groben Blendwerk.*

spiritually sensing soul.[k] Finally, it would not be at all surprising if the spirit-seer were at the same time a fantastical visionary, at least in respect of the images accompanying these apparitions of his. It would not be surprising, for representations well up and burst forth which are by nature alien and incompatible with the representations which human beings have in the bodily state; they introduce ill-assorted images into outer sensation, so that wild chimaeras and wondrous caricatures[l] are hatched out, and, passing before the mind in a long train, they dupe the deluded senses, even though the original representation may have been based upon a true spirit-influence.

We need no longer be at a loss to furnish seeming explanations[m] of the ghost stories which philosophers so often encounter, or of all the different kinds of spirit-influences which are periodically the subject of discussion.

2:341 Departed souls and pure spirits can never, it is true, be present to our outer senses, nor can they in any fashion whatever stand in community with matter, though they may indeed act upon the spirit of man, who belongs, with them, to one great republic. And they can exercise this influence in such a way that the representations, which they awaken in him, clothe themselves, according to the law of his imagination, in images which are akin to them, and create the vision[n] of objects corresponding to them, so that they present the appearance of existing externally to him. This deception can affect any of the senses. And no matter how much the deception is intermingled with absurd figments of the imagination, one need not let this prevent one from supposing that there are underlying spirit-influences at work here. I should be insulting the reader's perspicacity, if I were to devote further time to discussing the application of this type of explanation. For metaphysical hypotheses have about them such an uncommon degree of flexibility that one would have to be very clumsy not to be able to adapt this present hypothesis to any story whatever, and to do so even before investigating its veracity – something which is in many cases impossible and in many more highly discourteous.

However, if one draws up a balance of the advantages and disadvantages which could accrue to someone who was to a certain extent organised not only for the visible world but also for the invisible (assuming that there ever was such a person), such a balance would seem to be a gift like that with which Juno honoured Tiresias:[27] she first made him blind, so that she could grant him the gift of prophecy. For to judge from the above propositions, intuitive knowledge[o] of the *other* world can only ever be attained here by forfeiting something of that understanding which one needs for this *present* world. Nor do I know whether certain philosophers, even, who with such application and absorption train their metaphysical

---

[k] *bloss geistig empfindenden Seele.*   [l] *wunderliche Fratzen.*   [m] *scheinbare Vernunftgründe.*
[n] *Apparenz.*   [o] *die anschauende Kenntnis.*

telescopes on those remote regions and find themselves able to report wonders from those distant places, ought to be wholly released from this hard condition. At least I do not begrudge them any of their discoveries. My only concern is that someone of sound understanding but little tact may give them to understand what *Tycho de Brahe's* coachman said in reply to him when the former claimed to be able to travel the shortest route at night-time by means of the stars: *My dear master, you may have a thorough understanding of the heavens, but here on earth you are a fool.*[28]

THIRD CHAPTER: ANTI-CABBALA[29] — A FRAGMENT OF ORDINARY PHILOSOPHY, THE PURPOSE OF WHICH IS TO CANCEL COMMUNITY WITH THE SPIRIT-WORLD

Aristotle somewhere says: *When we are awake we share a common world, but when we dream each has a world of his own.*[30] It seems to me that one ought, perhaps, to reverse the final clause and be able to say: if different people have each of them their own world, then we may suppose that they are dreaming. On this basis, if we consider *those who build castles in the sky* in their various imaginary worlds,[p] each happily inhabiting his own world to the exclusion of the others – if we consider, for example, the person who dwells in the world known as *The Order of Things,* a world tinkered to-gether[q] by *Wolff* from a small quantity of building-material derived from experience and a larger quantity of surreptitious concepts,[31] or the person who inhabits the world which was conjured out of nothing by *Crusius* employing the magical power of a few formulae concerning *what can* and *what cannot be thought*[32] – if we consider these people, we shall be patient with their contradictory visions, until these gentlemen have finished dreaming their dreams. For if they should eventually, God willing, awake completely, that is to say, if they should eventually open their eyes to a view which does not exclude agreement with the understanding of other human beings, then none of them would see anything which did not, in the light of their proofs, appear obvious and certain to everybody else as well. And the philosophers will all inhabit a common world together at the same time, such as the mathematicians have long possessed. And this important event must now be imminent, if we are able to believe certain signs and portents which made their appearance some while ago above the horizon of the sciences.

There is a certain affinity between the *dreamers of reason* and the dream-ers of *sense.*[r] The latter commonly include those who from time to time have dealings with spirits. And the reason for including the latter is exactly

---

[p] *die Luftbaumeister der mancherlei Gedankenwelten.*   [q] *gezimmert.*
[r] *In gewisser Verwandtschaft mit den Träumern der Vernunft stehen die Träumer der Empfindung.*

the same as that for including the former: they see something which no other normal person sees; they have their own community with beings which reveal themselves to no one else, no matter how good his senses may be. Assuming that the apparitions^s are nothing but figments of the imagination, the designation 'reveries'^{t} is appropriate in so far as both types of image are, in spite of the fact that they delude the senses by presenting themselves as genuine objects, hatched out by the dreamer himself. However, if one were to imagine that the two deceptions were sufficiently similar in the manner of their origin to justify our regarding the source of the one as sufficient to explain the other, one would be seriously mistaken. If someone, while fully awake, should be so absorbed by the fictions and chimaeras hatched out by his ever fertile imagination as to take little notice of the sense-impressions which were of the greatest importance to him at the time, we should be justified in calling him a *waking dreamer.* For the impressions of the senses only need to lose a little more of their strength and our waking dreamer will sleep, and what were chimaeras before will be genuine dreams. The reason why those chimaeras were not already dreams during wakefulness is this: he represents them at the time as being *in himself,* whereas other objects, which he senses, he represents as *outside* himself. As a consequence, he counts the former as the products of his own activity, while he regards the latter as something which he receives from outside and by which he is affected. For in this case, everything depends on the relation in which the objects are thought as standing relatively to himself as a human being, and, thus, relatively to his body. Hence, the images in question may very well occupy him greatly while he is awake, but, no matter how clear the images may be, they will not deceive him. For although, in this case, he also has a representation of himself and of his body in his brain, and although he relates his fantastical images to that representation, nonetheless, the real sensation of his body creates, by means of the outer senses, a contrast or distinction with respect to those chimaeras. As a result, he is able to regard his fantastical images as hatched out by himself and the real sensation as an impression of the senses.^{u} If now he should fall asleep, the representation which the senses give him of his body is extinguished, and all that remains are the representations he has created himself. In contrast to these representations, the other chimaeras are thought of as standing in an external relationship. And furthermore, as long as sleep continues, these representations must deceive the dreamer, for there is no sensation which allows him, by comparing the two, to distinguish the original image^v from the phantom, in other words, the outer from the inner.

Spirit-seers, therefore, differ entirely from waking-dreamers, and they differ not merely in degree but in kind. For spirit-seers, when they are

---

^{s} *Erscheinungen.* ^{t} *Träumereien.* ^{u} *empfunden.* ^{v} *Urbild.*

fully awake and often when their other sensations possess the highest degree of vividness, refer certain objects to external positions among the other things which they really perceive around them. And the question here is simply how it happens that they transpose the illusion of their imagination[w] and locate it outside themselves, and do so in relation to their body, of which also they are aware by means of the outer senses. It cannot be the great distinctness of these figments of their imagination which is the cause of this phenomenon, for what counts here is the place to which the figment of the imagination is transposed as an object. Hence, the question which I wish to have answered is this: How does the soul transpose such an image, which it ought, after all, to represent as contained within itself, into quite a different relation, locating it, namely, in a place *external* to itself among the objects which present themselves to the sensation which the soul has. Nor shall I allow myself to be fobbed off with an answer which adduces other cases which have some kind of similarity with this kind of deception, and which occur, for example, in the state of fever. For whether the victim of the delusion[x] be in a state of health or illness, what one wishes to know is not whether such deceptions also occur in other circumstances, but rather how the deception is possible.

2:344

However, in using our outer senses, what we find is that, in addition to the clarity with which the objects are represented, we include the place of these objects in our sensations. This may not always, perhaps, occur with the same exactitude[y] in all cases; nonetheless, it constitutes a necessary condition of the sensation, and if it were not satisfied it would be impossible to represent things as external to themselves. This being the case, it is highly probable that our soul, in its representation, transposes the object of sensation, locating it at the point at which the various lines, which are caused by the object and which indicate the direction of the impression, converge, when they are extended.[z] Hence, if one takes the lines, which indicate the direction in which the light-rays enter the eye, and extend them backwards, the point at which they intersect is seen as a radiant point.[a] This point, which is called the optical point[b], is, it is true, in respect to the effects produced, the *point of divergence.* In respect of the representation entertained, however, it is the *point of convergence* of the lines indicating the direction in which the sensation is transmitted when it makes an

---

[w] *Blendwerk ihrer Einbildung.*   [x] *des Betrogenen.*   [y] *Richtigkeit.*

[z] *Hierbei wird es sehr wahrscheinlich, dass unsere Seele das empfundene Object dahin in ihrer Vorstellung versetze, wo die verschiedene Richtungslinien des Eindrucks, die* (i.e., *die verschiedene Richtungslinien*) *dasselbe* (i.e., *das empfundene Object*) *gemacht hat, wenn sie* (i.e., *die verschiedene Richtungslinien*) *fortgezogen werden, zusammenstossen.*

[a] *Daher sieht man einen strahlenden Punkt an demjenigen Orte, wo die von dem Auge in der Richtung des Einfalls der Lichtstrahlen zurückgezogene Linien sich schneiden.*

[b] *Sehpunkt /* (Grimm defines *Sehpunkt* as 'the point at which one looks, at which one directs one's attention'. Grimm quotes the present sentence from Kant and seems to suggest that Kant's usage [based as it is on a geometrical definition] is very slightly deviant.)

impression (*focus imaginarius*).ᶜ³³ It is in this way that the place of a visible object, even when it is seen with one eye only, is determined. This happens, in particular, when the reflection of a body in a concave mirror is seen as a spectreᵈ in mid-air, precisely at the point at which the rays emanating from a point of the object intersect each other prior to their entering the eye.*

2:345 Perhaps one can make the same assumption in the case of the impressions made by sounds, for their impulses also travel in straight lines, so that the sensation one has of a sound is at the same time accompanied by the representation of a *focus imaginarius*.³⁴ This focus is located at the point at which the straight lines, emanating from the system of nerves which has been set vibrating in the brain, converge, when they are extended outwards. For, to a certain extent, one notices both the directionᵍ and the distance of an object which we hear making a sound, even if the sound is a quiet one and comes from behind us, and in spite of the fact that the straight lines which can be drawn from it do not meet the opening of the ear but fall upon other parts of the head; one is accordingly forced to believe that the lines indicating the direction of the vibration are extended outwardly in the representation of the soul, the object making the sound being located at the point at which those lines converge. Exactly the same thing can, it seems to me, also be said of the other three senses, which differ from sight and hearing in so far as the object of sensation is in immediate contact with the organs of sensation, so that the lines indicating the direction of the sensible stimulusʰ have their focal point in the organs themselves.

In order to apply this to the images of the imagination, permit me to establish as my foundation the assumption made by *Descartes*³⁵ and accepted by most philosophers since. I refer, namely, to the view that all the representations of the faculty of imagination are simultaneously accompanied by certain movements in the nerve-tissueⁱ or nerve-spiritʲ of the brain. These movements are called *ideas materiales*.³⁶ I am referring, in

---

* It is in this fashion that the judgement, which we make concerning the apparent place of nearby objects, is commonly represented in optics.ᵉ And it also harmonises very well with our experience. However, these very same rays of light, which emanate from a point, do not, because of the refraction which takes place in the optic fluid,ᶠ diverge when they meet the optic nerves, but converge there in a point. Hence, if the sensation merely occurred in this nerve, the *focus imaginarius* would have to be located, not outside the body, but at the back of the eye itself. This raises a difficulty which I cannot, for the moment, solve, and which seems to be incompatible both with the claims made above and with experience itself.

ᶜ aber in der Vorstellung der Sammlungspunkt der Directionslinien nach welchen die Empfindung eingedrückt wird (focus imaginarius).
ᵈ Spectrum. ᵉ Sehekunst. ᶠ Augenfeuchtigkeiten. ᵍ Gegend.
ʰ die Richtungslinien des sinnlichen Reizes. ⁱ Nervengewebe. ʲ Nervengeiste.

other words, to the view that all the representations of the faculty of imagination are, perhaps, accompanied by the concussion or vibration[k] of the subtle element, which is secreted by the nerve-tissue or nerve-spirit. This concussion or vibration is similar to the movement which the sensible impression may make and of which it is the copy.[l] The concession I ask is this: that the chief difference between the motion of the nerves in the images of the imagination and the motion of the nerves in the sensation consists in the fact that the lines indicating the direction of the motion[m] intersect in the former case inside the brain, whereas in the latter case they intersect outside it. In the case of the clear sensations of waking life, the *focus imaginarius*, at which the object is represented, is placed outside me, whereas, in the case of the images of imagination, which I may entertain at the same time as the clear sensations of my waking life, the *focus imaginarius* is located within me. For this reason, I cannot, as long as I am awake, fail to distinguish my imaginings, as the figments of my own imagination, from the impression of the senses.

If this is admitted, I think I can offer a reasonable explanation of that   2:346
type of mental disturbance[n] which is called madness,[o] and which, if it is more serious, is called derangement.[p37] The distinctive feature of this malady consists in this: the victim of the confusion[q] places mere objects of his own imagination outside himself, taking them to be things which are actually present before him. Now, I have said that, in the usual order of things, the lines indicating the direction of the motions[r] which accompany the image of the imagination in the brain as their material auxiliary,[s] must intersect inside the brain, and that consequently the place, at which the image, consciously entertained by the ordinary waking person, is apprehended, is thought of as lying inside himself.[t] If, therefore, I suppose that, as a result of some accident or malady, certain organs of the brain are so distorted and their natural balance so disturbed that the motion of the nerves, which harmoniously vibrate with certain images of the imagination, moves along the lines indicating the direction which, if extended, would intersect outside the brain – if all this is supposed, then the *focus*

---

[k] *Erschütterung oder Bebung.*
[l] *vielleicht mit der Erschütterung oder Bebung des feinen Elements, welches von ihnen abgesondert wird, und die derjenigen Bewegung ähnlich ist, welche der sinnliche Eindruck machen könne, wovon er die Copie ist.*
[m] *die Richtungslinien der Bewegung.* [n] *Störung des Gemuths.*
[o] *Wahnsinn* / C: *mania* / Co: *fausse perception* / G: insanity / L: *égarement* / M: neurosis / S & V: *vaneggiamento.*
[p] *Verrückung* / C & S: *pazzia* / Co: *hallucination* / G: trance / L: *folie* / M: madness / V: *follia.*
[q] *der verworrene Mensch.* [r] *die Directionslinien der Bewegung.* [s] *materielle Hülfsmittel.*
[t] *und mithin der Ort, darin er sich seines Bildes bewusst ist, zur Zeit des Wachens in ihm selbst gedacht werde.*

imaginarius is located outside the thinking subject,* and the image which is the product of the mere imagination, is represented as an object present to the outer senses. The dismay which is felt at the supposed appearance of something which, according to the natural order of things, ought not to be present, will, even if such a phantom of the imagination were only weak to begin with, soon excite the attention, and confer upon the apparent sensation^v a vividness so great as not to permit the deluded person any doubt as to the veracity of his experience. This deception can affect any outer sense, for each of them yields copied images in the imagination, and the displacement of the nerve-tissue^w can cause the *focus imaginarius* to be displaced and located at the point from which the sensible impression produced by a corporeal body, which was actually present, would come. It will not, therefore, be surprising if the fantastical visionary should think he very distinctly sees or hears many things which no one else perceives. And likewise it would not be surprising if these figments of his imagination should appear to him and suddenly disappear: nor would it be surprising if they were to deceive one sense, for example, the sense of sight, and yet be imperceptible to all the other senses, for example, the sense of touch, and thus appear to lack solidity. Ordinary ghost stories tend so markedly to display such characteristics^x as strongly to warrant the suspicion that they may well have arisen from a source such as I have described. And thus, even the popular concept of *spirit-beings,* which we extracted above from ordinary linguistic usage, is very much in accordance with this type of delusion. Nor is this concept untrue to its origin, for the essential characteristic mark of this concept is supposed to be constituted by the property of being present in space but not impenetrable.

2:347

---

* One might adduce as an example displaying a remote similarity to the case under consideration, the state of someone drunk who, in his drunken condition, sees double with both eyes. The cause of the double vision is the fact that the dilation of the blood vessels creates an impediment to directing the axes of the eyes in such a way that their lines, when extended, intersect at the point at which the object is to be found. In exactly the same way, the distortion of the vascular tissue of the brain, which may perhaps be merely temporary, and which may, as long as it lasts, only affect some of the nerves, may have the effect, even when we are awake, of making certain images of the imagination appear outside ourselves even when we are awake. This deception may be compared with an experience which is very common. When one is emerging from sleep and one finds oneself in a state of relaxation which is not far removed from slumber itself, and if, with drowsy half-opened eyes, one looks at the various threads of the bedcover or of the curtains surrounding the bed, or at the tiny marks on the wall close-by, it is easy to turn them into the forms of human faces, and such like. The deception^u ceases once we exert our will and concentrate our attention. In this case, the displacement of the *focus imaginarius* of the images of the imagination is to a certain extent subject to the power of the will, whereas in the case of derangement it cannot be prevented by any power of the will.

^u *Das Blendwerk.*   ^v *Scheinempfindung.*   ^w *Verrückung des Nervengewebes.*
^x *Die gemeine Geistererzählungen laufen so sehr auf dergleichen Bestimmungen hinaus.*

It is also highly probable that the concepts of spirit-forms, inculcated into us by education,[y] provide the sick mind with materials for its delusive imaginings, and that a brain which was free from all such prejudices, even if it were affected by some disturbance,[z] would not so easily hatch out such images. Furthermore, it can also be seen from this that, since the malady of the fantastical visionary does not really affect the understanding but rather involves the deception of the senses, the wretched victim cannot banish his illusions by means of subtle reasoning. He cannot do so because, true or illusory, the impression of the senses itself precedes all judgement of the understanding and possesses an immediate certainty,[a] which is far stronger than all other persuasion.

The result of these observations involves the following embarrassing difficulty:[b] the deep speculations of the previous chapter are rendered wholly superfluous, and the reader, no matter how ready he may be to give some support to the plans which exist only in idea,[c] will nonetheless prefer the concept which enables him to resolve the difficulties with greater ease and speed, and which can expect more general support. For, apart from the fact that it seems more consonant with a rational mode of thought to draw the grounds of one's explanation from the material with which experience furnishes us rather than to lose oneself in the dizzy concepts[d] of a reason which is half-engaged in creating fictions and half-engaged in drawing inferences,[e] this approach also furnishes some occasion for mockery, as well; and mockery, whether it be justified or not, is a more powerful instrument than any other for checking futile enquiries. For to wish to offer, in a serious fashion, interpretations of the figments of the imagination of fantastical visionaries instantly arouses grave doubts; and philosophy, which allows itself to be caught in such low company, falls under suspicion. It is true that I have not, in what I have said above, disputed the madness of such apparitions.[f] On the contrary, although I have not made madness the cause of the imagined spirit-community, I have connected the two by supposing madness to be a natural effect of such a community. But what foolishness is there, after all, which could not be made to harmonise with a fathomless philosophy? I do not, therefore, blame the reader at all if, instead of regarding the spirit-seers as semi-citizens of the other world, he simply dismisses them without further ado as candidates for the asylum, thus saving himself the trouble of any further enquiry. But if this is the footing on which everything is to be taken, then the method of treating such adepts of the spirit-realm will also have to be very different from that suggested by the ideas elaborated above. And whereas it was once found necessary in the past on occasion to *burn* some of them, it will

2:348

---

[y] *die Erziehungsbegriffe von Geistergestalten.*   [z] *Verkehrtheit.*   [a] *Evidenz.*   [b] *dieses Ungelegene.*
[c] *den idealischen Entwurfen.*   [d] *in schwindlichten Begriffen.*
[e] *einer halb dichtenden, halb schliessenden Vernunft.*   [f] *Erscheinungen.*

now suffice simply to *purge* them. Nor would it be necessary, if this was how things stood, to range so far afield, and, with the help of metaphysics, to seek out mysteries in the fevered brains of deluded enthusiasts. The sharp-sighted *Hudibras* would have been able to solve the riddle on his own, for his opinion was: *if a hypochondriacal wind should rage in the guts, what matters is the direction it takes: if downwards, then the result is a f——; if upwards, an apparition or an heavenly inspiration.*[g][838]

FOURTH CHAPTER: THEORETICAL CONCLUSION ESTABLISHED ON THE BASIS OF ALL THE OBSERVATIONS CONTAINED IN THE FIRST PART

2:349

Scales, intended by civil law to be a standard of measure in trade, may be shown to be inaccurate if the wares and the weights are made to change pans. The bias[h] of the scales of understanding is revealed by exactly the same stratagem,[i] and in philosophical judgements, too, it would not be possible, unless one adopted this stratagem, to arrive at a unanimous result[j] by comparing the different weighings. I have purified my soul of prejudices; I have eradicated every blind attachment which may have insinuated itself into my soul in a surreptitious manner with a view to securing an entry for a great deal of bogus knowledge. Now, whether or not it confirms or cancels my previous judgements, whether it determines me or leaves me undecided, nothing is important or venerable for me except that which, having followed the path of honesty, occupies its place in a tranquil mind open to any argument. Whenever I encounter something which instructs me, I appropriate it. The judgement of the opponent who refutes my arguments becomes my own judgement, once I have put it on the scales and weighed it first of all *against* the scale of self-love, and then, having transferred it to that scale, against my own alleged reasons, and found it to be of superior quality.[k] I formerly used to regard the human understanding in general merely from the point of view of my own understanding. Now I put myself in the position of someone else's reason, which is independent of myself and external to me,[l] and regard my judgements, along with their most secret causes, from the point of view of other people. The comparison of the two observations yields, it is true, pronounced parallaxes, but it is also the only method for preventing optical deception, and the only means of placing the concepts in the true positions which they occupy relatively to the cognitive faculty of human nature. It will be objected that this is very solemn language for a subject as

---

[g] *eine Erscheinung oder eine heilige Eingebung.*   [h] *Parteilichkeit.*   [i] *Kunstgriff.*
[j] *einstimmiges Fazit.*
[k] *gegen die Schale der Selbstliebe und nachher in derselben gegen meine vermeintliche Gründe abgewogen und in ihm einen grösseren Gehalt gefunden habe.*
[l] *in die Stelle einer fremden und äusseren Vernunft.*

indifferent as the one we are discussing and which deserves to be called more an idle distraction*m* than a serious occupation. Nor is such a judgement mistaken. And although one does not need to make massive preparations in what concerns a trifle, one may, nonetheless, indeed make such preparations if such a trifle presents itself. A care greater than necessary*n* in small matters may serve as an example in great matters. With one exception, I do not find that there are any attachments in my mind, nor do I find that any unexamined inclination has insinuated itself into my mind, which had deprived it of its readiness to be guided by any kind of reason, whether for or against. But the scales of the understanding are not, after all, wholly impartial. One of the arms, which bears the inscription: *Hope for the future*, has a mechanical advantage; and that advantage has the effect that even weak reasons, when placed on the appropriate side of the scales, cause speculations, which are in themselves of greater weight, to rise on the other side. This is the only defect,*o* and it is one which I cannot easily eliminate. Indeed, it is a defect which I cannot even wish to eliminate. Now, I admit that all the stories concerning the apparition of departed souls or about the influences exercised by spirits, and all the theories relating to the supposed nature of spirit-beings and of their connection with us, only have a significant weight when placed in the scale-pan of hope; on the other hand, when placed in the scale-pan of speculation, such things seem to weigh no more than empty air. If the answer to the question we are considering did not harmonise with an inclination which was already pronounced, what rational being, do you suppose, would remain undecided as to which of the following possibilities was the greater: that a type of being exists which has nothing in common with anything which the senses teach him, or that certain experiences, not uncommon in a number of cases, are to be attributed to self-deception and one's own invention?

2:350

Indeed, it is this which seems in general to be the chief cause for the belief in the ghost-stories, which meet with such universal acceptance. And even the initial delusions, produced by the alleged apparitions of those who have died, are probably the result of the fond hope*p* that one will oneself somehow survive death. For often, in the shades of the night, the senses have been deceived by illusions,*q* and ambiguous forms have been converted into phantoms*r* harmonising with the opinions one held beforehand. And on this foundation, philosophers finally formed the rational idea*s* of spirits, which they then incorporated into the body of their teaching. On examination, my own pretentious theory of the community of spirits will be found to follow exactly the same direction as that adopted by popular inclination. For the propositions concur only in yielding a

m Spielwerk.   *n entbehrliche Behutsamkeit.*   *o Unrichtigkeit.*   *p schmeichelhaften Hoffnung.*
q der Wahn der Sinne betrog.   *r aus zweideutigen Gestalten Blendwerke schuff.*   *s Vernunftidee.*

concept which explains how the human spirit *leaves* this world;* in other words, our state after death. But I make no mention of how it *comes into* the world, that is to say, no mention of generation and reproduction. Indeed, I make no mention even of how it is *present* in the world, that is to say, how an immaterial nature can exist in a body and how it can exercise an influence by means of the body. And there is a very good reason for all this, and it is as follows: I am completely ignorant about all these matters. And as a consequence, I might, I suppose, have been content to remain just as ignorant about the future state, as well, but for the fact that the bias of a favourite opinion served to recommend the reasons which presented themselves, feeble as they are.

2:351

It is exactly the same ignorance which prevents my venturing wholly to deny all truth to the many different ghost-stories which are recounted, albeit with a reservation which is at once commonplace but also strange: I am sceptical about each one of them individually, but I ascribe some credence to all of them taken together. The reader is free to judge for himself. But for my part, the arguments adduced in the second chapter are sufficiently powerful to inspire me with seriousness and indecision when I listen to the many strange*u* tales of this type. However, since there is never any lack of justifying reasons, if one's mind is already made up beforehand, I do not propose to incommode the reader by further extending my defence of this way of thinking.

Since I now find myself at the conclusion of the theory of spirits, I venture to add one more remark: this reflection, if properly used by the reader, will bring the whole of our philosophical understanding of such beings to completion.*v* From now on it will be possible, perhaps, *to have all sorts of opinions* about but no longer *knowledge* of such beings.*w* This claim may sound somewhat immodest. For certainly there is in nature no object known to the senses of which it can be said that one has ever *exhausted* it either by observation or by reason, not even if it were a droplet of water, or a grain of sand, or something even simpler – so measureless is the com-

---

* Among the ancient Egyptians the symbol of the soul was the butterfly; the Greek word for the soul had exactly the same meaning.³⁹ It is easy to see that the hope, which makes of death nothing but a transformation, has generated this idea and its symbols. But this does nothing to destroy our confidence that the concepts which have sprung from this source are correct. Our inner sentiment and the judgements which are made by *what is analogous to reason*, and which are based on that inner sentiment,*t* lead, provided they are neither of them corrupted, precisely where reason would lead, if it were more enlightened and more extensive.

t Unsere innere Empfindung und die darauf gegründete Urtheile des Vernunftähnlichen / (the clause is obscure and ambiguous: it is unclear whether *des Vernunftähnlichen* is to be construed as an instrumental genitive [the view of C, V, and the present translator] or as an objective genitive [the view of Co, L, and S]).

u befremdlichen.   *v alle philosophische Einsicht von dergleichen Wesen vollende.*

w und dass man davon vielleicht künftighin noch allerei meinen, niemals aber mehr wissen könne.

plexity^x of that which nature, in the least of its parts, presents for analysis to an understanding as limited as that of man. But the situation is quite different when it comes to the philosophical theory^y of spirit-beings. The theory can be completed, albeit in the *negative* sense of the term, by securely establishing the limits of our understanding^z and by convincing us that the various different appearances of *life* in nature, and the laws governing them, constitute the whole of that which it is granted us to know. But the principle of this life, in other words, the spirit-nature which we do not know but only suppose, can never be positively thought, for, in the entire range of our sensations, there are no *data* for such positive thought. One has to make do with negations if one is to think something which differs so much from anything of a sensible character. But even the possibility of such negations is based neither on experience, nor on inferences, but on a fiction, in which reason, stripped of all assistance whatever, seeks its refuge. On this basis, the pneumatology of man can be called a theory of his necessary ignorance in respect of a type of being which is supposed to exist; as such it is quite adequate to its task.

2:352

I shall now put to one side, as something settled and completed, the whole matter of spirits, an extensive branch of metaphysics. It will from now on be of no concern to me. In thus reducing the scope of my enquiry and ridding myself of a number of completely futile investigations, I hope to be able to invest the modest^a abilities of my understanding in a more profitable fashion in the objects which are left. The wish to extend the tiny measure of one's energy to cover all kinds of windy projects is in most cases a futile wish. In this, as in other cases, prudence demands that one cut the coat of one's projects to the cloth of one's powers.^{b} If great things are beyond one's power, one must rest satisfied with what is moderate.^{c}

---

^{x} *Mannigfaltigkeit.* ^{y} *philosophischen Lehrbegriff.* ^{z} *die Grenzen unserer Einsicht.* ^{a} *geringe.*
^{b} *den Zuschnitt der Entwürfe den Kräften angemessen zu machen.* ^{c} *das Mittelmässige.*

FIRST CHAPTER: A STORY, THE TRUTH OF
WHICH IS RECOMMENDED TO THE READER'S
OWN FREE EXAMINATION[d]

Sit mihi fas audita loqui – Virgil[40]

The arrogance of philosophy causes it to be exposed to all kinds of futile question. And philosophy often finds itself seriously embarrassed when it is confronted by certain stories: it is unable either *to doubt* some of them with impunity or *to believe* others without being mocked. In the case of the stories which circulate concerning spirits,[e] the two problems to a certain extent arise together, the former in listening to someone solemnly recount such stories, the latter in recounting them to others. And it is, indeed, the case that there is no reproach more bitter to the philosopher than that of credulity and being duped by popular error. Those who know how to create the impression of cleverness at no great expense pour their scornful laughter on anything which, because it is unintelligible both to the ignorant and to the wise, reduces them both to more or less the same level. It is, therefore, not surprising that phenomena of this kind, which are so frequently alleged to occur, should find wide acceptance, though publicly they are either denied or, indeed, hushed up. One can be sure, therefore, that no academy of sciences will ever make this material the subject of a prize question, not because the members of such academies are wholly free from the tendency to subscribe to the opinion in question, but because the rule of prudence rightly excludes[f] the questions which are indiscriminately thrown up both by prying inquisitiveness and by idle curiosity. And thus it is that stories of this kind are probably only ever believed secretly, whereas publicly they are dismissed with contempt by the incredulity which is currently in fashion.[g]

2:354 However, it seems to me that this whole question is neither sufficiently important nor sufficiently prepared for us to be able to arrive at any decision in the matter. For this reason, I have no hesitation in introducing at this juncture a report of the kind mentioned and presenting it in a

---

[d] *beliebigen Erkundigung.* [e] *Geistergeschichten.* [f] *Schranken setzt.*
[g] *durch die herrschende Mode des Unglaubens.*

completely impartial spirit to the reader's judgement, whether favourable or unfavourable.

In Stockholm there dwells a certain Schwedenberg,[41] a gentleman of comfortable means and independent position. For the last twenty years or more he has, as he himself tells us, devoted himself exclusively to cultivating the closest contact with spirits and with the souls of the dead, to obtaining information from them about the other world, and, in exchange, to giving them information about this present world, to composing hefty volumes devoted to his discoveries, and periodically travelling to London in order to supervise their publication.[42] He is not exactly reticent about his secrets, speaking freely with everyone about them: he seems to be completely convinced of the truth of his claims, giving no impression of deliberate fraud or charlatanry.[43] If one is to believe the man himself, he is the arch-spirit-seer of all spirit-seers, just as he is the arch-visionary of all visionaries, whether one relies on the descriptions furnished by his acquaintances or on his own writings. Nonetheless, this circumstance cannot deter those who are otherwise favourably disposed towards spirit-influences from supposing that there is still something true behind such fantasies. However, the credentials of all plenipotentiaries from the other world consist in the proofs of their extraordinary calling, which they furnish by means of certain specimens in the present world. That being the case, I must, selecting from what is circulated as an attestation of the extraordinary power of the man in question, at least mention that which finds some credence with the majority of people.

Towards the end of the year 1761,[44] Schwedenberg received a summons from a certain princess. Her great understanding and insight ought to have made it almost impossible that she should have been deceived in such a case. The occasion of the summons was the rumour, which was in general circulation, concerning the alleged visions of this man. After asking him a number of questions, more with a view to mocking his imaginings than to obtaining genuine news of the other world, the princess, in dismissing Schwedenberg, entrusted him with a secret mission, which had a bearing on his community with spirits.[h] Some days later Schwedenberg appeared with the answer, which was such as to fill the princess, on her own admission, with the greatest astonishment, for she declared the answer to be true, even though it was not one which could have been imparted to him by any living person. This story is taken from the report made by an ambassador to the court there, who was present at the time, and sent to another foreign ambassador in Copenhagen. The story coincides exactly with what a special enquiry was able to establish concerning the matter.[45]

2:355

[h] der in seine Geistergemeinschaft einschlug.

The following stories have no other guarantee than that of common hearsay; the proof provided by such a source is very dubious.[46] Madame *Marteville,* the widow of a Dutch envoy to the Swedish court, received instructions from the relatives of a goldsmith demanding that she settle an outstanding account relating to a silver tea-service which had been made for her. The lady, who was familiar with her late husband's punctiliousness in financial matters, was convinced that the debt must already have been settled during his life-time; but she found no proof of such a settlement among his posthumous papers. Women are particularly prone to lend credence to stories of prophecy, interpretations of dreams, and all kinds of other wondrous things. She accordingly revealed her affair to Schwedenberg, with the request that – assuming that what was said of him was true and that he was in contact with the spirits of the dead – he obtain information from her late husband in the other world concerning the circumstances surrounding the above-mentioned request for payment. Schwedenberg promised to do so. A few days later, he visited the lady's home again, informing her that he had obtained the information she wanted; he informed her that the missing receipts were to be found in a secret compartment in a cabinet, which he pointed out to her and which she thought had been completely emptied. On the basis of this description, a search was instantly undertaken, and, in addition to finding her late husband's secret Dutch correspondence, they also discovered the missing receipts. In this way, all the claims which had been raised against her were rendered completely void.[47]

The third story is such that it must be possible to furnish a complete proof of its truth or falsity. It was, if I am rightly informed, towards the end of the year 1759, when Schwedenberg, returning from England, disembarked one afternoon at *Gothenburg.* That same evening he joined a company of people at the invitation of a local merchant. After he had spent

2:356 some while there, he reported to the company, with every sign of consternation, that at that very moment a dreadful conflagration was raging in Stockholm in the *Südermalm.* After a few hours had passed, in the course of which he periodically withdrew to be on his own, he informed the assembled company that the fire had been brought under control, at the same time describing the extent to which the fire had spread. That very same evening, this wondrous news[48] was noised abroad and by the next morning it had spread to every part of the town. But it was only after the lapse of two days that the report of the fire eventually reached Gothenburg from Stockholm – a report which coincided completely, it was said, with Schwedenberg's visions.[49]

The reader will probably ask what on earth could have induced me to engage in such a despicable business as that of spreading fairy-tales abroad, which every rational being would hesitate to listen to with patience – and, indeed, not merely disseminating them but actually making them the subject of philosophical investigations. However, since the philosophy, with which we have prefaced the work, was no less a fairy-story from the *cloud-cuckoo-land* of metaphysics,[i] I can see nothing improper about having them make their appearance on the stage together. And, anyway, why should it be more respectable to allow oneself to be misled by credulous trust in the sophistries of reason[j] than to allow onself to be deceived by an incautious belief in delusory stories?

The frontiers between folly and understanding are so poorly marked that one can scarcely proceed for long in the one region without occasionally making a little sally into the other. As for the ingenuousness which sometimes allows itself, notwithstanding the opposition of the understanding, to be persuaded into making some concessions to many assertions which are solemnly made with self-assurance, such ingenuousness seems to be a remnant of the ancient ancestral loyalty,[k] which is, it must be conceded, no longer really appropriate to our present state, and which therefore often turns into folly. But for that very reason, it is not to be regarded as a natural legacy of stupidity.[l] Hence, in the case of the strange story with which I have concerned myself, I leave it to the reader to analyze that dubious mixture of reason and credulity into its elements, and to establish the proportion in which the two ingredients are present in my own mode of thought. For in the case of such a criticism, all that matters is that the criticism should observe the proprieties.[m] I am thus sufficiently protected from mockery by the fact that, in committing this folly, if that is what you would wish to call it, I nonetheless find myself in a learned and numerous company. And that, so *Fontenelle* thought, is already a sufficient guarantee against the accusation of imprudence.[50] For it has always been the case and will, I suppose, continue to be so in the future, that certain 2:357 absurdities have found acceptance even among rational people, and that for no other reason than that they are the object of general discussion. Among such absurdities are to be found, to name but a few, faith-healing,[n] water-divining, premonitions, the operation of the imagination of pregnant women, the influence exercised by the phases of the moon on animals and plants. Was it not, indeed, recently that common country folk thoroughly avenged themselves on the learned for the mockery with which the latter tended to treat them for their credulity? For by a great deal of hearsay children and women eventually induced a substantial number of intelligent men to take a common wolf for a hyaena, and that in spite of the fact that any sensible person could see that there are not likely to be any African predators prowling around the forests of France.[51] The infirmity of the human understanding combined with man's curiosity is respon-

---

[i] *ein Märchen . . . aus dem Schlarafenlande der Metaphysik.*   [j] *Scheingründe der Vernunft.*
[k] *ein Rest der alten Stammehrlichkeit.*   [l] *ein natürliches Erbstück der Dummheit.*
[m] *Anständigkeit.*   [n] *Sympathie.*

sible for his initially snatching up truth and delusion indiscriminately. But gradually he refines his concepts; a few of them survive the process, and the rest are thrown away as rubbish.

If there is anyone to whom these tales about spirits should appear to be a matter of importance, that person can always – assuming, that is, that he has the money to do so and nothing better to do – venture on a journey of enquiry, to investigate these stories more closely, just as *Artemidorus*[52] travelled around Asia Minor, benefitting oneiromancy[o] in the process. Furthermore, posterity, with a similar turn of thought, will be full of gratitude to him for having prevented the eventual emergence of a second *Philostratus*,[53] who, after the lapse of many years, would have turned our Schwedenberg into a new *Apollonius of Tyana*,[54] when after such a lapse of time, hearsay would have ripened into formal proof, and the interrogation of eyewitnesses – a troublesome business, which is, however, extremely necessary – would then have become an impossibility.

SECOND CHAPTER: ECSTATIC JOURNEY OF AN ENTHUSIAST[p] THROUGH THE SPIRIT-WORLD

Somnia, terrores magicos, miracula, sagas,
Nocturnos lemures, portentaque Thessala – Horace[55]

2:358

I cannot blame the cautious reader at all, if, in the course of this book, he has begun to feel reservations about the method which the author has thought proper to follow. For by placing the dogmatic part of the work before the historical part, and thus reasons[q] before experience, I must have created the suspicion that I was proceeding in a cunning fashion. For, although I might perhaps already have had the story in my mind, I nonetheless proceeded as if I knew nothing apart from the pure, abstract observations, my purpose being to end by surprising the completely unsuspecting reader with a welcome confirmation derived from experience. And, indeed, this is a stratagem[r] which philosophers have very successfully deployed on a number of occasions. For it is not to be forgotten, that all knowledge has two ends by which it can be caught; an *a priori* end, and one which is *a posteriori*. Various modern students of nature, it is true, have declared that one must start with the *a posteriori* end; they think that the eel of science can be caught by the tail, their view being that, if enough empirical cognitions[s] are acquired, they can then gradually ascend to higher general concepts. Whether or not this is a prudent procedure, it is far from being sufficiently learned or philosophical, for this manner of proceeding soon leads to a *Why?* to which no answer can be given. And

[o] *zum Besten der Traumdeutung.*   [p] *Schwärmers.*   [q] *Vernunftgründe.*   [r] *Kunstgriff.*
[s] *Erfahrungskenntnisse.*

this is about as creditable to a philosopher as it would be to a merchant who, when requested by a client to settle a bill of exchange, politely requested the creditor to call again some other time. Thus, to avoid this difficulty, men of penetrating understanding have started from the opposite extremity, namely, from the pinnacle of metaphysics. But this approach involves a new difficulty: one starts, I know not whence, and arrives, I know not where; the advance of the arguments refuses to correspond to experience.[t] Indeed, it looks as if the atoms of *Epicurus*, having spent an eternity in a state of continuous fall, are more likely to form a world as a result of their accidental collision with each other[56] than the most general and most abstract concepts are to explain it. The philosopher, therefore, clearly recognised that his rational arguments,[u] on the one hand, and experience or factual description,[v] on the other hand, would probably, like two parallel lines, continue to run side by side to the unthinkable,[w] without ever meeting. Our philosopher thus reached an agreement with his fellow philosophers, as if they had come to a formal understanding with each other on the matter. Their agreement was this: each would adopt his own starting point in his own fashion; after that, rather than follow the straight line of reasoning,[x] they would rather impart to their arguments an imperceptible clinamen[y][57] by stealthily squinting at the target of certain experiences or testimonies;[z] they would thus steer reason in such a fashion that it would be bound to arrive at precisely that point which would surprise the unsuspecting student; they would prove, namely, what they all along knew was going to be proved. Our philosophers then proceeded to call this path the *a priori* path, even though that path had already been covertly laid down by means of markers planted in the direction of the *a posteriori* point.[a] The adept who knew what was going on, would naturally be obliged not to betray his master. Adopting this ingenious method,[b] various men of merit have even suddenly come upon mysteries of religion on the bare path of reason. Their procedure is exactly like that of the romantic author: he makes his heroine flee to distant countries so that, by means of an happy adventure, she may acci-

2:359

---

[t] *der Fortgang der Gründe nicht auf die Erfahrung treffen will.*   [u] *Vernunftgründe.*

[v] *Erzählung* / (*Erzählung:* not in the sense of a fictional story but in the sense of a factual report).

[w] *ins Undenkliche* / C: *all'infinito* / Co & L: *indéfiniment* / G: into infinity / M: right into the realm of the unthinkable / S & V: *indefinitamente* / (C, Co, L, G, V, & S, following Hartenstein, all suppose that *Undenkliche* is a slip of the pen for *Unendliche;* the mocking, sarcastic, and playful tone of this work makes it quite possible that Kant actually intended to surprise the reader with *Undenkliche* in a context where *Unendliche* would have been expected).

[x] *in der geraden Linie der Schlussfolge.*   [y] *mit einem unmerklichen Clinamen der Beweisgründe.*

[z] *dadurch dass sie nach dem Ziele gewisser Erfahrungen oder Zeugnisse verstohlen hinschielten.*

[a] *ob er wohl unvermerkt durch ausgesteckte Stäbe nach dem Punkte a posteriori gezogen war.*

[b] *sinnreichen Lehrart.*

dentally meet her admirer: *et fugit ad salices et se cupit ante videri* (Virgil).[58] With such illustrious predecessors, therefore, I should not have had any reason to be ashamed if I had also employed the same stratagems[c] to help my enquiry on its way to the desired conclusion. But I would earnestly implore the reader not to believe any such thing of me. And, anyway, of what use would this method be to me now, since it is impossible for me to deceive anyone now that I have let the secret out of the bag? Not only that, but I find myself in the following unfortunate predicament: the testimony, upon which I have stumbled, and which bears such an uncommon likeness to the philosophical figment of my imagination,[d] looks so desperately deformed and foolish, that I must suppose that the reader will be much more likely to regard my arguments as preposterous because of their affinity with such testimonies than he will be to regard these testimonies as reasonable because of my arguments.[e] I accordingly declare, without beating about the bush, that, as far as such seductive comparisons are concerned, I have no sense of humour. I declare, without further ado, either that one must suppose that there is more cleverness and truth in Schwedenberg's writings than first appearances would suggest, or that, if there is any agreement between him and my system, it is a matter of pure chance. It would be as it sometimes is with frenzied poets when, so it is believed or so at least they claim, they predict the future: their prophecies now and again correspond to what actually happens.

I now arrive at the purpose of this work, namely, the writings of my hero. If many writers, who are now forgotten or whose name will one day fall into oblivion, have the substantial merit of not having been miserly in the expenditure of their understanding in the composition of their hefty works, then Schwedenberg doubtless deserves the greatest honour of all. For certainly, his flask in the lunar world is full to the brim; it is surpassed by none of the moon-flasks which *Ariosto* saw there and which were filled with the reason which was lacking down here, and which their possessors would one day have to seek out again.[59] For Schwedenberg's lengthy work is completely empty and contains not a single drop of reason. Nonetheless, there prevails in that work such a wondrous harmony with what the most subtle ruminations of reason[f] can produce on a like topic, that the reader will pardon me if I should find here the same curious phenomenon[g] in the play of the imagination which so many other collectors have found in the play of nature. I am thinking, for example, of the way in which they discover the Holy Family in the irregular patterns of marble, or monks, baptismal fonts and organs in stalactites and stalagmites, or even the discovery by the mocking *Liscow*[60] on a frozen window-pane of the triple crown and the number of the beast –

2:360

---

[c] *Kunststück.*   [d] *und was meiner philosophischen Hirngeburt so ungemein ähnlich ist.*
[e] *Vernunftgründe.*   [f] *feinste Ergrübelung der Vernunft.*   [g] *diejenige Seltenheit.*

none of them things which anyone else would see unless their heads were already filled with them beforehand.

The great work of our Author consists of eight quarto volumes stuffed full of nonsense. He presents it to the world as a new revelation under the title *Arcana coelestia*.[61] In it his visions[h] are employed to discover the secret meaning of the first two books of Moses; and a similar method of exegesis[i] is applied to the whole of the Scriptures. None of these visionary interpretations[j] are of any concern to me here. For those interested, however, accounts of them are to be found in the first volume of Dr Ernesti's *Theologische Bibliothek*.[62] It is only the *audita et visa*,[63] in other words, only what his own eyes are supposed to have seen and his own ears to have heard, which we are chiefly concerned to extract from the appendices attached to the chapters of his book. For it is these which constitute the foundation of all the other daydreams,[k] and which have also pretty well started the adventure on which we have embarked above in the airship of metaphysics.[l] The style of the author is dull. The stories he tells and the arrangement they receive seem, in truth, to have arisen from *fanatical intuition.* There is little reason to suspect that the speculative fantasies of a perversely ruminative reason may have induced him to invent these stories or to use them for purposes of deception. To that extent, therefore, they have some importance and really do deserve to be presented in a small anthology, and possibly more so than many of the playthings invented by the empty-headed sophists who swell our journals, for the systematic delusion of the senses in general is a much more remarkable phenomenon than the deception of reason, the causes of which are well enough known. The deception of reason could to a large extent be prevented by subjecting the powers of the mind to control by the will,[m] and by exercising rather more restraint over an idle inquisitiveness. The deception of the senses, 2:361 on the other hand, concerns the ultimate foundation of all our judgements, and if that foundation were defective, there is little that the rules of logic could do to remedy the situation! In the case of the author we are discussing, I accordingly separate *sensory delusion* from *the delusions of his reason*.[n] I shall ignore the misguided sophistries which result from his going beyond his *visions,* just as, in other connections, one often has to separate a philosopher's *observations*[o] from his *sophistries.*[p] Even *illusory experiences*[q] are generally more instructive than the *illusory arguments* of reason.[r] Thus, while depriving the reader of some of the moments which he would perhaps otherwise have devoted, with not much greater benefit,

---

[h] *Erscheinungen.*   [i] *Erklärungsart.*   [j] *schwärmende Auslegungen.*   [k] *Träumereien.*
[l] *auf dem Luftschiffe der Metaphysik.*   [m] *durch willkürliche Richtung der Gemüthskräfte.*
[n] *Ich sondere also bei unserm Verfasser den Wahnsinn vom Wahnwitz ab /* (Kant distinguishes two forms of madness, the one affecting the senses [*Wahnsinn*], the other the mind [*Wahnwitz*]).
[o] *was er beobachtet.*   [p] *Was er vernünftelt.*   [q] *Scheinerfahrungen.*
[r] *Scheingründe aus der Vernunft.*

to the reading of *thorough* books devoted to this subject, I have at the same time taken account of the delicacy of his taste, for, by omitting many wild chimaeras, I have distilled the quintessence of the book into a few drops. And in doing this, I promise myself as much gratitude from the reader as a certain patient thought he owed his physicians for only having made him eat the bark of the quinquina, when they could have easily made him eat the whole tree.

Schwedenberg divides his visions*[s]* into three types. The *first* type involved being liberated from the body. This state is an intermediate state between sleeping and waking; in this state he saw, heard and, indeed, felt spirits. This only happened to him three or four times. The *second* type of vision involved being carried off by the spirit. In this state he was, let us say, walking along a road without losing his way; at the same time, he was in entirely different places in the spirit, clearly seeing dwelling places, people, forests, and so forth, and doing so for a period of several hours, until he suddenly became conscious of himself again in his real place. This happened to him two or three times. The *third* type of vision is the usual one and one which he experienced daily in a state of complete wakefulness. It is from this type of vision that the stories he recounts are chiefly taken.

According to Schwedenberg, everybody stands in an equally intimate relation with the spirit-world, though they have no awareness of doing so. The difference between himself and other people consists simply in *the fact that his inmost being was opened up,*[t] a gift of which he always speaks with veneration (*Datum mihi est ex divina Domini misericordia*).[64] It is clear from the context that this gift is supposed to consist in becoming conscious of the obscure representations*[u]* which the soul receives in virtue of its constant connection with the spirit-world. Hence it is that he distinguishes between the outer and inner memory in man. A person has outer memory as someone belonging to the visible world, whereas a person has inner memory in virtue of the connection with the spirit-world. This is also the foundation of the distinction between the outer and the inner man. Schwedenberg's own superiority consists in the fact that, already in this life, he sees himself as a person who belongs to the community of spirits and that he is recognised by them as someone belonging to that community. It is also in this inner memory that everything, which has vanished from outer memory, is conserved, none of a person's representations ever getting lost. After death, the memory of everything which had ever entered his soul and which had so far remained concealed from him, goes to make up the complete book of his life.

The presence of spirits affects only a person's inner sense, it is true. But this causes them to appear to him as existing outside himself, and,

2:362

---

[s] *Erscheinungen.*   *[t]* *dass sein Innerstes aufgethan ist.*   *[u]* *dunkelen Vorstellungen.*

indeed, as existing in human form. The spirit-language is an immediate communication of ideas, but that language is at all times combined with the appearance of the language which the person concerned normally speaks, and it is represented as being external to him. One spirit reads the representations which are to be found clearly contained in the memory of another spirit. In this way, the spirits see in Schwedenberg the representations which he has of this world, and they do so with such clear intuition that they are themselves deceived, frequently imagining that they are seeing these things immediately, though, in fact, that is impossible, for no pure spirit has the least sensation[v] of the corporeal world. But neither can they have any representation of the corporeal world simply in virtue of their community with the souls of other living people, for the inmost being of such people[w] is not opened up; in other words, their inner sense contains nothing but obscure representations. Hence, Schwedenberg is the very oracle of the spirits, who are as curious to contemplate the present state of the world in him, as he is to contemplate the wonders of the spirit-world in their memory, as in a mirror. Although these spirits, likewise, stand in the closest connection with all the other souls of living people and act upon them or are themselves acted upon by them, they nonetheless have as little knowledge of this as do human beings, for their inner sense,[x] which belongs to their spirit-personality, is completely obscure.[y] The spirits, therefore, suppose that the effect produced in them, as a result of the influence of human souls, is something which is thought by them alone, just as human beings, in this life, also suppose that all their thoughts and all the operations of their willing[z] arise only from within themselves, even though, as a matter of fact, they are often transmitted to them from the invisible world. Nonetheless, each human soul, already in this life, has its place in the spirit-world, and belongs to a certain society which is at all times consonant with the soul's inner state of truth and goodness, that is to say, consonant with the inner state of its understanding and will. However, the positions[a] of the spirits, relative to each other, have nothing in common with the space of the corporeal world. Hence, in what concerns their spirit-positions,[b] the soul of someone in India may often be the closest neighbour of the soul of someone in Europe. On the other hand, those who, from the corporeal point of view, live in the same house, may, from the point of view of their spirit-relations referred to above, exist at quite some distance from each other. If a person should die, the soul of that person does not change its position; it becomes aware of itself[c] as occupying the position it already occupied relative to other spirits in this life. Furthermore, although the relation of spirits to each other does not constitute a true space, nonetheless, that relation does

2:363

---

[v] *mindeste Empfindung.*   [w] *ihr Innerstes.*   [x] *innerer Sinn.*   [y] *ganz dunkel.*
[z] *Willensregungen.*   [a] *Stellen.*   [b] *geistige Lagen.*   [c] *empfindet sich.*

present the appearance of true space^d to them. Their connections with each other are represented under the concomitant condition of nearness,^{e} while their differences are represented as distances,^{f} just as the spirits themselves are not really extended, though they do present the appearance^g of human forms to each other. In this imagined space there is to be found a thorough-going community of spirit-natures. Schwedenberg converses with the souls of the departed whenever he pleases, and he reads in their memory (in their faculty of representation)^h the state in which they contemplate themselves, seeing it as clearly as if he were looking at it with bodily eyes. Furthermore, the enormous distance between the rational inhabitants of the world is to be regarded, from the point of view of the spirit-universe, as nothing: it is as easy for him to converse with an inhabitant of the planet Saturn, as it is with the soul of a human being who has died. Everything depends on the relation of their inner state and on the connection which they have with each other, according to their agreement in the *true* and the *good*. More distant spirits can, however, easily enter into communion^i with each other through the mediation of other spirits. For this reason, too, a human being does not need to have actually lived on the other heavenly bodies to be able one day to know them with all their wonders. His soul reads in the memory of other citizens of the universe after they have died the representations which they have of their life and their dwelling place, and he sees the objects contained therein as clearly as if he saw them by means of an immediate intuition.^{j}

2:364   A central concept in Schwedenberg's fantasies is this: corporeal beings have no substance of their own; they only exist in virtue of the spirit-world, though each body subsists not in virtue of one spirit alone but in virtue of all spirits together. For this reason, cognition of material things has a double significance: it has an external sense which consists in the relation of matter to itself; and it has an internal sense, in so far as material things, construed as effects, designate the forces of the spirit-world, which are the causes of those material things.^{k} Thus the human body involves the parts being related to each other in accordance with the laws which govern matter. But in so far as the human body is maintained by the spirit which dwells within it, its various members and their functions have a value which is indicative of the powers of the soul; and it is in virtue of the operation of these powers that the various members come to acquire their form, activity and permanency. This inner sense is unknown to man, and it is this inner sense which Schwedenberg, whose inmost being was

---

^{d} *Apparenz desselben.* ^{e} *unter der begleitenden Bedingung der Naheiten.* ^{f} *als Weiten.*

^{g} *die Apparenz.* ^{h} *(Vorstellungskraft).* ^{i} *in Gemeinschaft kommen.*

^{j} *durch ein unmittelbares Anschauen.*

^{k} *Daher hat die Erkenntniss der materiellen Dinge zweierlei Bedeutung: einen äusserlichen Sinn in Verhältniss der Materie aufeinander und einen inneren, in so fern sie als Wirkungen die Kräfte der Geisterwelt bezeichnet, die ihre Ursachen sind.*

opened up, wished to make known to man. The same thing holds of all the other things in the visible world; they have, as we have said, one significance when they are construed as things, and that significance is of minor importance; they have another significance when they are construed as signs, and that significance is of greater importance. This is also the origin of the new interpretations which he has wished to make of the Scriptures. For the inner sense, namely, the symbolic reference[l] of all the things recounted in the Scriptures to the spirit-world is, as he enthusiastically fancies,[m] the kernel of their value, the rest being but the husk. But, then again, the important thing in this symbolic connection of corporeal things, as images, with the inner spirit-state, is the fact that all spirits at all times present themselves to each other under the semblance[n] of extended forms, and the influences which these spirit-beings exercise upon each other, also arouse within them the appearance[o] of yet other extended beings, and, as it were, the appearance of a material world, the images of which are, indeed, merely symbols of their inner state. Nonetheless, they produce a deception of the senses of such clarity and permanency[p] as to equal the actual sensation of such objects. (A future interpreter will conclude from this that Schwedenberg is an idealist, since he denies of the matter of this world that it subsists in its own right, and may, for that reason, regard it simply as a coherent appearance[q] arising from the connections holding in the spirit-world.) He speaks, therefore, of the gardens, the extensive regions, the dwelling-places, the galleries and arcades of the spirits, which he saw with his own eyes in the brightest light. He assures us that, having on many occasions spoken with all his friends after they had died, he almost always found that those who had died only recently could scarcely be persuaded that they had died, for they saw themselves surrounded by a world similar to the one in which they had lived. Moreover, he assures us that societies of spirits[r] sharing one and the same inner state found that the region in which they were living and the things contained therein also presented to them one and the same appearance.[s] An alteration in their state, however, was connected with the appearance[t] of an alteration of place. Now, whenever spirits communicate their thoughts to human souls, those thoughts are always connected with the appearance[u] of material things; they only present themselves to the person receiving them in virtue, ultimately, of their relation to the spirit-sense, albeit with every appearance of reality.[v] It is this which explains the origin of that supply of wild and inexpressibly ridiculous forms, which our enthusiast thinks he sees in all clarity in his daily dealings with the spirits.

I have already indicated that, according to our author, the various

2:365

---

[l] *die symbolische Beziehung.*   [m] *wie er schwärmt.*   [n] *unter dem Anschein.*   [o] *Apparenz.*
[p] *eine so klare und dauerhafte Täuschung des Sinnes.*   [q] *eine zusammenhängende Erscheinung.*
[r] *Geistergesellschaften.*   [s] *Apparenz.*   [t] *Schein.*   [u] *Apparenz.*
[v] *mit allem Schein der Wirklichkeit.*

different powers and properties of the soul stand in sympathy with the organs of the body, over which they exercise control. The whole of the outer person corresponds, therefore, to the whole of the inner person. Thus, if a noticeable spirit-influence, emanating from the invisible world, should particularly affect one or other of that person's powers of the soul, the person concerned will be harmoniously aware of the apparent[w] presence of that influence in the members of his outer person, which correspond to the powers of the soul. He now refers a great variety of bodily sensations[x] to that source, those sensations being at all times linked with the spirit-contemplation. The absurdity of that contemplation is, however, too great for me to venture mentioning even a single one of them.

On this basis, it is possible, if one thinks it worth the effort, to form a concept of an imagination, than which none is more quixotic or bizarre,[y] and in which all his daydreams are united. Just as various powers and abilities constitute that unity which is the soul or the inner person, so the different spirits (the chief characteristics of which are related to each other in the same way in which the various different capacities of a spirit are related to each other) constitute a society. This society of spirits presents the appearance of a Great Man.[z] In this phantom, each spirit sees itself as located in the place and in those seeming organs which suit its own particular organisation within such a spirit-body. But all spirit-societies together, and the whole world of all these invisible beings in their turn, present themselves under the appearance of the *Greatest Man.*[a] This enormous and gigantic fantasy – the product, perhaps, of a representation dating from earliest childhood, such as is employed, for example, in our schools, when an entire region of the world is presented to the children, by way of mnemonic, under the image of a seated maiden, and the like – this fantasy contains a thorough-going community of the most intimate kind between one spirit and all, and between all spirits and one. And no matter what the position of the living beings in this world relative to each other may be, or how they have an entirely different position in the Greatest Man, that position they never alter; it only appears to be a place situated in a measureless space, whereas in fact it is a specific mode of the relations in which they stand and of the influences which they exercise.[b]

I am tired of reproducing the wild figments of the imagination of this worst of all enthusiasts, or of pursuing his fantasies further so as to include his descriptions of the state after death. I also have other reservations as well. For, although the naturalist displays in his show-cabinet, among those items of animal generation which he has collected and pre-

2:366

---

[w] *apparente.*

[x] *Dahin bezieht er nun eine grosse Mannigfaltigkeit von Empfindungen an seinem Körper.*

[y] *abenteuerlichsten und seltsamsten.*   [z] *die Apparenz eines grossen Menschen.*

[a] *in der Apparenz des grössten Menschen.*

[b] *in der That aber eine bestimmte Art ihrer Verhältnisse und Einflüsse.*

served in chemical preparations, not only natural formations, but also monsters, he must, nonetheless, be careful not to allow them to be seen by just anyone, or to be seen too clearly. For among the curious there may easily be pregnant women, on whom they could make a bad impression. And since my readers may include some who may likewise be in respect of ideal conception,^c in the family way,^d I should very much regret it if they were, for example, to take fright at what they read. However, since I have warned them from the very start, I disclaim all responsibility, and I hope that the mooncalves, to which their fertile imagination may give birth as a result of this circumstance, will not be laid on my doorstep.

Incidentally, I have not surreptitiously added to the daydreams of our author by including any of my own. I have made a faithful selection, offering it to the reader who is careful of his comfort and his purse (he may not be *that* ready to satisfy his passing curiosity by sacrificing £7 sterling). Admittedly, I have omitted most of the immediate intuitions, for such wild figments of the imagination could only disturb the reader's sleep of a night. It is also true that I have, now and again, employed a rather more familiar language^e to clothe the confused sense of his revelations. But this has not at all detracted from the accuracy of the chief features of my outline. Notwithstanding, it would be futile to wish to conceal, since it is obvious to everybody, that the result of all this labour is, in the last analysis, nothing. Since the personal visions, alleged in this book, cannot serve as proofs of themselves, it follows that the only motive   2:367 for dealing with them is to be found in the supposition that the author, in order to attest their truth, would, perhaps, appeal to occurrences of the kind mentioned above, such as could be confirmed by living witnesses. But no such instance is anywhere to be found. Thus it is that we withdraw from a foolish undertaking – and not without some abashment. We would merely add the following reasonable, albeit somewhat belated, remark: to think sensibly^f is generally an easy enough matter, but only, unfortunately, after one has allowed oneself to be deceived for a while.

In examining this subject, I have devoted myself to a thankless task, which the enquiries and insistent demands of inquisitive and idle friends have imposed upon me. In putting my efforts at the service of this frivolity I have not only deceived their expectations,^g I have also, at the same time, failed to contribute anything towards satisfying either the curious, by providing them with information, or the studious, by offering them reasons. If this was the only purpose of this effort, then I have been wasting my time. I have lost the confidence of the reader, for, by following a

---

^c *in Ansehung der idealen Empfängnis.*   ^d *in anderen Umständen.*   ^e *gangbare Sprache.*
^f *das Klugdenken.*
^g *dessen Erwartung* / (*dessen* must be a slip of Kant's pen for the plural *deren*).

tiresome detour, I have conducted him in his enquiry and in his thirst for knowledge to precisely the point of ignorance from which he set out in the first place. But, in fact, I did have a purpose in mind, and one which is, it seems to me, more important than the purpose I claimed to have. And in my opinion that purpose has been achieved. Metaphysics, with which, as fate would have it, I have fallen in love but from which I can boast of only a few favours, offers two kinds of advantage. The first is this: it can solve the problems thrown up by the enquiring mind, when it uses reason to spy after the more hidden properties of things. But hope is here all too often disappointed by the outcome. And, on this occasion, too, satisfaction has escaped our eager grasp.

> *Ter frustra comprensa manus effugit imago*
> *Par levibus ventis volucrique simillima somno.*
> Virgil[65]

The second advantage of metaphysics is more consonant with the nature of the human understanding. It consists both in knowing whether the task has been determined by reference to what one can know, and in knowing what relation the question has to the empirical concepts, upon 2:368 which all our judgements must at all times be based. To that extent metaphysics is a science of the *limits of human reason*.[h] A small country always has a long frontier;[i] it is hence, in general, more important for it to be thoroughly acquainted with its possessions, and to secure its power over them, than blindly to launch on campaigns of conquest. Thus, the second advantage of metaphysics is at once the least known and the most important, although it is also an advantage which is only attained at a fairly late stage and after long experience. Although I have not precisely determined this limit,[j] I have nonetheless indicated it sufficiently to enable the reader, once he has reflected on the matter further, to establish that he can spare himself the trouble of all futile research into a question, the answering of which demands *data* which are to be found in a world other than the one in which he exists as a conscious being. Thus, I have wasted my time in order to save it. I have deceived my reader in order to benefit him. And although I have not furnished him with any new insights, I have, nonetheless, eliminated the illusion and the vain knowledge which inflates the understanding and fills up the narrow space which could otherwise be occupied by the teachings of wisdom and of useful instruction.

The impatience of the reader, who has been tired without being instructed by my reflections so far, may be appeased by what *Diogenes*,[66] it is said, promised to his yawning audience, when he came to the final page of a boring book: *Courage, gentlemen, land is in sight!* So far we have been

---

[h] *Grenzen der menschlichen Vernunft.*
[i] *und da ein kleines Land jederzeit viel Grenze hat* / (it is not at all clear why Kant specifies *klein*).
[j] *diese Grenze.*

wandering, like *Democritus*, in empty space,[67] whither the *butterfly-wings* of metaphysics have raised us, conversing there with spirit-forms. Now, when the *styptic*[k] power of self-knowledge has folded those silken wings, we find ourselves back on the humble[l] ground of experience and common sense, happy if we regard it as the place to which we have been assigned: the place from which we may never depart with impunity, the place which also contains everything which can satisfy us, as long as we devote ourselves to what is useful.

THIRD CHAPTER: PRACTICAL CONCLUSION DRAWN FROM THE TREATISE AS A WHOLE

To pursue every curiosity and to allow no limits to the thirst for knowledge apart from that of impotence – such zealousness does not ill-become *learning*.[m] But, from among the innumerable tasks which spontaneously offer themselves, to choose that task, the solution of which is of importance to man – such choice is the merit of *wisdom*. When science has run its course, it naturally arrives at the point of modest mistrust and says, dissatisfied with itself: *How many are the things which I do not understand!* But reason, matured by experience into wisdom, serenely speaks through the mouth of *Socrates*, who, surrounded by the wares of a market-fair, remarked: *How many are the things of which I have no need.*[68] In this way, two very dissimilar aspirations eventually flow together, even though to begin with they started out in very different directions, the one being vain and dissatisfied, the other composed and contented. For, in order to choose rationally one must already have knowledge of what is superfluous, indeed, impossible. But, eventually science arrives at the determination of the limits[n] imposed upon it by the nature of human reason. All the fathomless projects, however, which may not in themselves, perhaps, be unworthy, except that they lie outside the sphere of man, fly to the *limbo* of vanity.[69] It is then that even metaphysics becomes that which it is far from being at the moment, and which one would least expect it to be, namely, the *companion of wisdom*. For, as long as the opinion survives that it is possible to attain to an understanding of such remote things, *wise simplicity* will call in vain that such great aspirations are superfluous. The feeling of satisfaction which accompanies the extension of knowledge will very easily assume the appearance of dutifulness and convert that deliberate and reflective contentment into the *foolish simplicity*, which wishes to oppose

2:369

---

[k] *die stiptische Kraft.*   [l] *niedrigen.*

[m] *Einem jeden Vorwitz nachzuhängen und der Erkenntnissucht keine andere Grenze zu verstatten als das Unvermögen, ist ein Eifer, welche der* Gelehrsamkeit *nicht übel ansteht.*

[n] *aber endlich gelangt die Wissenschaft zu der Bestimmung der . . . Grenzen /* (a certain ambiguity attaches to this sentence: it is not clear whether *gelangt . . . zu der Bestimmung* means 'arrives at the task of determining' or 'succeeds in determining').

the ennoblement of our nature. Questions concerning the spirit-nature, freedom, predestination, the future state, and such like, initially activate all the powers of the understanding; and those questions, in virtue of their elevated character, draw a person into a speculation which is eager to triumph; that eagerness is indiscriminate in its constructing of sophistries and drawing of conclusions,[o] in its teachings and refutations – as always happens with specious understanding.[p] But if this enquiry should turn into philosophy, and if this philosophy should subject its own procedure to judgement, and if it should have knowledge not only of the objects themselves but also of their relation to the human understanding, its frontiers will contract in size and its boundary-stones will be securely fixed. And those boundary-stones will never again permit enquiry to leave the realm which is its home,[q] and cross the boundary to range abroad. We found that some philosophy was necessary if we were to know the difficulties surrounding a concept which is commonly treated as very ordinary and very easy to handle.[70] Somewhat more philosophy removes this phantom of knowledge[r] still further away, convincing us that it lies wholly beyond the horizon of man. For in the relations of cause and effect, substance and action, philosophy, to start with, serves to unravel the complex phenomena and reduce them to simpler representations. But if one eventually arrives at relations which are fundamental, then the business of philosophy is at an end. It is impossible for reason ever to understand how something can be a cause, or have a force; such relations can only be derived from experience. For our rule of reason only governs the drawing of comparisons in respect of *identity* and *contradiction*.[s] If something is a cause, then *something* is posited by something *else;* there is not, however, any connection between the two things here which is based on agreement. Similarly, if I refuse to regard that same something as a cause, no contradiction will ever arise, for there is no contradiction in supposing that, if something is posited, something else is cancelled. It follows from this that if the fundamental concepts of things as causes, of powers and of actions are not derived from experience, then they are wholly arbitrary,[t] and they admit of neither proof nor refutation. I know, of course, that thinking and willing move my body, but I can never reduce this phenomenon, as a simple experience, to another phenomenon[u] by means of analysis; hence, I can recognise the phenomenon[v] but I cannot understand it. That my will moves my arm is no more intelligible to me than someone's claiming that my will could halt the moon in its orbit. The only difference between the two cases is this: I

2:370

---

[o] *welche ohne Unterschied klügelt und entscheidet.* [p] *Scheineinsicht.*
[q] *eigenthümlichen Bezirk* / (lit: own proper region). [r] *dieses Schattenbild der Einsicht.*
[s] *die Vergleichung nach der Identität und dem Widerspruche.* [t] *gänzlich willkürlich.*
[u] *auf eine andere* / (the word *andere* may grammatically refer to either *Erscheinung* or to *eine einfache Erfahrung;* philosophically, the former seems more plausible).
[v] *sie* / (the word *sie* is ambiguous in the same way as *andere* [see the preceding note]).

experience the former, whereas my senses have never encountered the latter. I am acquainted with the alterations which take place within me as within a living subject; in other words, I am acquainted with my thoughts, with my power of will, and so forth. And since these determinations are different in kind from everything which, taken together, constitutes my concept of body, I naturally think of myself as an incorporeal and permanent being. Whether this incorporeal and permanent being will also think independently of the body can never be established by appealing to the nature of that being, which is known from experience. I am connected with beings of my own kind through the mediation of corporeal laws, but I can in no wise establish from what is given to me whether, in addition, I am not also connected, or could not ever be connected, with such beings, in accordance with other laws, which I shall call pneumatic laws, and be so independently of the mediation of matter. All judgements, such as those concerning the way in which my soul moves my body, or the way in which it is now or may in the future be related to other beings like itself, can never be anything more than fictions^w – fictions which are, indeed, far from having even the value of those which feature in natural science and which are called hypotheses. In the case of such hypotheses one does not invent fundamental forces;^{x} one rather connects the forces, which one already knows through experience, in a manner which is appropriate to the phenomena; their possibility must, therefore, at all times be capable of proof. By contrast, in the former case, one actually assumes the existence of new fundamental relations of cause and effect, where it is impossible ever to have the least concept of their possibility, and where one is therefore inventing these relations in a creative or chimaeric fashion,^{y} call it what you will. The fact that various true or alleged phenomena are rendered intelligible by means of such assumed fundamental ideas establishes nothing in favour of these ideas. For it is easy to specify the ground of anything, if one is entitled to invent activities and causal laws as one feels inclined. We must therefore wait until we may, perhaps, be instructed in a future world, by means of new experiences and new concepts of forces within our thinking self, which are as yet concealed from us. It was thus that later observations, after they had been analysed by mathematics, revealed to us the force of attraction in matter. And of the possibility of this force one will never be able to form a more complete concept (for it seems to be a fundamental force). If anyone had wished to invent such a property beforehand, without having any proof from experience at his disposal, he would have justly deserved to have been treated as a fool and made the object of mockery. Now, since the considerations adduced by reason do not, in such a case, have the least force either to invent or to

2:371

---

^{w} *Erdichtungen.* ^{x} *Grundkräfte.* ^{y} *schöpferisch oder chimärisch.*

confirm² such a possibility or impossibility, it follows that all one can do is to concede to experience the right to decide the issue. In exactly the same way, I leave it to time, which brings experience, to establish something definite concerning the much lauded curative powers of the magnet in dental maladies. And that confirmation will be furnished if we are able to show that there are as many observations of magnetic rods exercising an influence on flesh and bone as there are of their exercising an influence on iron and steel. If, however, certain alleged experiences cannot be brought under any law of sensation, which is unanimously accepted by the majority of people,ᵃ and if, therefore, these alleged experiences establish no more than an irregularity in the testimony of the senses (as is, in fact, the case with the ghost-stories which circulate), it is advisable to break off the enquiry without further ado, and that for the following reason. The lack of agreement and uniformity in this case deprives our historical knowledge of all power to prove anything, and renders it incapable of serving as a foundation to any law of experience, concerning which the understanding could judge.

2:372

Just as, on the one hand, a somewhat deeper enquiry serves to teach us that the convincing and philosophical insight in the case under discussion is *impossible*, so, on the other hand, one will have to admit, if one considers the matter quietly and impartially, that it is superfluous and *unnecessary*. Science in its vanity,ᵇ readily excuses its activity on the grounds of its importance. And here too the claim is likewise commonly made that a rational understandingᶜ of the spirit-nature of the soul is very necessary to the conviction that there is life after death, and that this conviction, in its turn, is necessary if one is to have a motive for leading a virtuous life. But idle curiosity adds that the genuineness of the apparitions of the souls of the dead can furnish a proof of all this from experience. But true wisdom is the companion of simplicity, and since, in the case of the latter,ᵈ the heart commands the understanding, it normally makes the elaborate apparatus of learningᵉ superfluous, its purpose needing only the means which lie within the reach of everyone. What, is it only good to be virtuous because there is another world? Or is it not rather the case that actions will one day be rewarded because they are good and virtuous in themselves? Does not the heart of man contain within itself immediate moral prescriptions? Is it really necessary, in order to induce man to act in accordance with his destiny here on earth, to set the machinery moving in another

---

ᶻ *weder zur Erfindung noch zur Bestätigung.*

ᵃ *in kein unter den meisten Menschen einstimmiges Gesetz der Empfindung.*

ᵇ *Die Eitelkeit der Wissenschaft.* ᶜ *Vernunfteinsicht.*

ᵈ *bei ihr* / (the phrase *bei ihr* may grammatically refer to either *Weisheit* or to *Einfalt*: philosophically, the latter seems more plausible).

ᵉ *die grosse Zurüstungen der Gelehrsamkeit.*

world?*f* Can that person really be called honest, can he really be called virtuous, who would readily abandon himself to his favourite vices, were it not for the deterrence of future punishment? Would one not rather have to say that, although he fears to practise wickedness, he nourishes within his soul a vicious character, that he loves the advantage of actions which present the appearance of virtue,*g* while hating virtue itself? And, indeed, experience teaches that there are many people who, instructed and convinced of the existence of a future world, nonetheless abandon themselves to vice and baseness, thinking only of the means by which they can cunningly evade the future consequences which threaten them. But there has never existed, I suppose, an upright soul which was capable of supporting the thought that with death everything was at an end, and whose noble disposition has not aspired to the hope that there would be a future. For this reason, it seems more consonant with human nature and moral purity*h* to base the expectation of a future world on the sentiments of a nobly constituted soul than, conversely, to base its noble conduct on the hope of another world. Such is also the character of the *moral faith:*i* its simplicity is able to dispense with many of the subtleties of sophistry; it alone and uniquely is fitting to man in whatever situation he finds himself, for it leads him directly to his true purposes. Let us, therefore, leave all these clamourous theories*j* about such remote objects to the speculation and care of idle minds. These theories are, indeed, a matter of indifference to us. And although the fleeting illusion*k* of reasons for or against may perhaps win the applause of the schools, it will scarcely decide anything relating to the future fate of people of honest character. Nor has human reason been endowed with the wings which would enable it to fly so high as to cleave the clouds which veil from our eyes the mysteries of the other world. And to those who are eager for knowledge of such things and who attempt to inform themselves with such importunity about mysteries of this kind, one can give this simple but very natural advice: that it would probably be best *if they had the good grace to wait with patience until they arrived there.* But since our fate in that future world will probably very much depend on how we have comported ourselves at our posts in this world, I will conclude with the advice which *Voltaire* gave to his honest *Candide* after so many futile scholastic disputes: *Let us attend to our happiness, and go into the garden and work!*71

2:373

---

f durchaus die Maschinen an eine andere Welt ansetzen.

g der tugendähnlichen Handlungen / C & S: *azioni conformi a virtù* / Co: *actions qui ressemblent à la vertu* / G: actions similar to virtue / L: *actions d'apparence vertueuse* / V: *azioni che hanno l'apparenza della virtù.*

h der Reinigkeit der Sitten.   *i der moralische Glaube.*   *j alle lärmende Lehrverfassungen.*

k der augenblickliche Schein.

Concerning the ultimate ground of the differentiation of directions in space (1768)

Von dem ersten Grunde des Unterschiedes
der Gegenden im Raume (1768)

Von dem erſten Grunde

des Unterſchiedes der Gegenden im Raume.

Concerning the ultimate ground of the differentiation of directions[1] in space

The celebrated *Leibniz* possessed many genuine insights, and by their   2:377
means he enriched the sciences. But he also entertained projects which
were of still greater importance. The world, however, was to wait in vain
for their realisation. It is not my purpose here to decide what the reason
for this failure may have been.[2] *Leibniz* may have regarded his efforts as
too imperfect – a reservation which is typical of men of great merit, and
one which has constantly deprived learning of many valuable fragments.
Or it may have been with him, as *Boerhaave* supposed that it was with great
chemists: they often claimed to possess the ability to perform certain feats[a]
as if they had already executed them, whereas in fact they merely possessed the conviction and the assurance that they could do so,[b] and that
they could not fail in the undertaking if only they set their minds to the
performance.[3] At any rate, it looks as if a certain mathematical discipline,
which *Leibniz* called *analysis situs*,[4] and the loss of which was lamented by
Buffon among others when he was considering the foldings together of
nature in the seeds[c5] – it looks as if this discipline was never more than a
thought in *Leibniz's* mind.[d] I do not know exactly to what extent the object
which I propose examining here is related to what the great *Leibniz* had in
mind.[6] But to judge by the meaning of the term, what I am seeking to
determine philosophically here is the ultimate ground of the possibility of
that of which *Leibniz* was intending to determine the magnitudes mathematically.[e7] For the positions of the parts of space in reference to each
other presuppose the direction[8] in which they are ordered in such a
relation.[f] In the most abstract sense of the term, direction does not consist
in the reference of one thing in space to another – that is really the
concept of position – but in the relation of the system of these positions to
the absolute space of the universe.[g] In the case of any extended thing, the
position of its parts relative to each other can be adequately known by
reference to the thing itself.[h] The direction, however, in which this order
of parts is orientated, refers to[i] the space outside the thing. To be specific: 2:378
it refers not to places in the space[j] – for that would be the same thing as
regarding the position of the parts of the thing in question in an external
relation – but rather to universal space as a unity, of which every extension

[a] *Kunststücke.*
[b] *da sie eigentlich nur in der Überredung und dem Zutrauen zu ihrer Geschicklichkeit standen.*
[c] *Zusammenfaltungen der Natur in den Keimen.*
[d] *Gerdankending /* (alt: figment of [Leibniz's] imagination).
[e] *wovon er die Grössen mathematisch zu bestimmen vorhabens war.*
[f] *Denn die Lagen der Theile des Raums in Beziehung auf aufeinander setzen die Gegend voraus,
nach welcher sie in solchem Verhältniss geordnet sind.*
[g] *sondern in dem Verhältnisse des Systems dieser Lagen zu dem absoluten Weltraum.*
[h] *Bei allem Ausgedehnten ist die Lage seiner Theile gegen einander aus ihm selbst hinreichend zu
erkennen.*
[i] *die Gegend aber, wohin diese Ordnung der Theile gerichtet ist, bezieht sich auf.*
[j] *nicht auf dessen Örter.*

must be regarded as a part. It will not be surprising if the reader should find these concepts still very obscure. I shall be explaining them in due course. I shall not, therefore, add anything further for the moment, apart from the following remark. My purpose in this treatise is to see whether there is not to be found in the intuitive judgements about extension,[k] such as are to be found in geometry, clear proof that: *Absolute space, independently of the existence of all matter and as itself the ultimate foundation of the possibility of the compound character of matter, has a reality of its own.*[l] Everybody knows how unsuccessful the philosophers have been in their efforts to place this point once and for all beyond dispute, by employing the most abstract judgements of metaphysics. Nor am I familiar with any attempt to attain this end so as to speak *a posteriori* (in other words, by employing other indisputable propositions which, while lying outside the realm of metaphysics, are nonetheless capable of furnishing a touchstone of their correctness through their application *in concreto*) apart, that is, from the treatise of the illustrious *Euler* the Elder, which is to be found in the *Proceedings of the Berlin Royal Academy of Sciences* for the year 1748.[9] This treatise, however, does not quite achieve its purpose. It only shows the difficulties involved in giving a determinate meaning to the universal laws of motion if one operates with no other concept of space than that which arises from abstraction from the relation between actual things.[m] It does not, however, consider the no less serious difficulties which arise if, in applying the laws just mentioned, one attempts to represent them *in concreto,* employing the concept of absolute space.[n] The proof, which I am seeking here, is intended to furnish, not engineers, as was *Euler's* purpose, but geometers themselves with a convincing argument which they could use to maintain, with the certainty to which they are accustomed, the actuality of their absolute space.[o] The following considerations are offered by way of preparation.

Because of its three dimensions, physical space can be thought of as having three planes, which all intersect each other at right angles. Concerning the things which exist outside ourselves: it is only in so far as they stand in relation to ourselves that we have any cognition of them by means of the senses at all. It is, therefore, not surprising that the ultimate ground, on the basis of which we form our concept of directions in space, derives 2:379 from the relation of these intersecting planes to our bodies. The plane upon which the length of our body stands vertically is called, with respect to ourselves, horizontal. This horizontal plane gives rise to the difference

---

[k] *in den anschauenden Urtheilen der Ausdehnung.*

[l] *dass der absolute Raum unabhängig von dem Dasein aller Materie und selbst als der erste Grund der Möglichkeit ihrer Zusammensetzung eine eigne Realität habe.*

[m] *der aus der Abstraktion von dem Verhältniss wirklicher Dinge entspringt.*

[n] *nach dem Begriffe des absoluten Raumes.*   [o] *die Wirklichkeit ihres absoluten Raumes.*

between the directions[p] which we designate by the terms *above* and *below*. On this plane it is possible for two other planes to stand vertically and also to intersect each other at right angles, so that the length of the human body is thought of as lying along the axis of the intersection.[q] One of these two vertical planes divides the body into two externally similar halves, and furnishes the ground of the difference between the *right* and the *left* side. The other vertical plane, which also stands perpendicularly on the horizontal plane,[r] makes possible the concept of the side *in front* and the side *behind*. For example, in the case of a page of writing, we first distinguish the top from the bottom, we notice the difference between the front and the back, and then we look at the position of the letters from left to right, or from right to left. In this example, no matter how the page be turned, the position of the parts arranged on the surface of the page and taken in relation to each other is exactly the same, and the pattern which the arrangement of the parts presents is in all respects identical.[s] But as we have presented the matter[t] the difference of the directions is so important and so closely connected with the impression made by the visual object that the self-same writing, when viewed with everything transposed from right to left, ceases to be recognisable.

Even our judgements relating to the cardinal points of the compass[u] are, in so far as they are determined in relation to the sides of our body, subject to the concept which we have of directions in general.[v] Independently of this fundamental concept, all that we know of relations in heaven or on earth is simply the positions of objects relative to each other. No matter how well I may know the order of the compass points,[w] I can only determine directions by reference to them if I know whether this order runs from right to left, or from left to right.[x] Similarly, the most precise map of the heavens, if it did not, in addition to specifying the position of the stars relative to each other, also specify the direction by reference to the position of the chart relative to my hands,[y] would not enable me, no matter how precisely I had it in mind, to infer from a known direction, for example, the north, on which side of the horizon I ought to expect the sun to rise.[10] The same thing holds of geographical and, indeed, of our most

[p] *diese Horizontalfläche giebt Anlass zu dem Unterschiede der Gegenden.*

[q] *in der Linie des Durchschnitts.*   [r] *die andere, welche auf ihr perpendicular steht.*

[s] *und in allen Stücken einerlei Figur* / Carabellese (hereafter C): *è identica in tutti i pezzi* / Handyside (hereafter H): always the same outlines /Irvine (hereafter I): the form remains in all particulars the same / Walford (hereafter W): and the figure is, in all parts, one and the same /Zac (hereafter Z): *et dans chaque unité la figure est la même.*

[t] *bei dieser Vorstellung.*

[u] *Weltgegenden* / C: *regioni cosmiche* / H: cosmic regions / Z: *regions de l'espace.*

[v] *Gegenden überhaupt.*   [w] *die Ordnung der Abtheilungen des Horizonts.*

[x] *nach welcher Hand diese Ordnung fortlaufe.*

[y] *wenn . . . nicht noch durch die Stellung des Abrisses gegen meine Hände die Gegend determinirt würde.*

2:380

ordinary knowledge of the position of places. Such knowledge would be of no use to us unless we could also orientate[z] the things thus ordered, along with the entire system of their reciprocal positions, by referring them to the sides of our body.[a] Indeed, there is a well-known characteristic distinctive of certain natural phenomena, which is sometimes employed to distinguish one species from another. The distinctive characteristic in question consists in the particular direction in which the order of the parts is turned.[b] In virtue of this distinctive characteristic, two creatures may be distinguished from each other, even though they may be exactly the same in respect of size, proportion and even the relative position of their parts.[c] In the case of human beings, the hair on the crown of the head grows in a spiral from the left to the right. All hops wind around their poles from left to right, whereas beans wind in the opposite direction.[d] Almost all snails, with the exception of perhaps, only three species, have shells which, when viewed from above, that is to say, when their curvature[e] is traced from the apex to the embouchure, coil from left to right.[f][11] This determinate property is invariably to be found in the members of a given species, and it is to be found in them quite independently of the hemisphere of the earth in which they occur, and quite independently of the direction[g] of the daily movements of the sun and moon – with us it is from left to right, while in the antipodes it is from right to left – for the cause of the curvature[h] in the case of the natural phenomena just mentioned is to be found in the seeds themselves. On the other hand, where a given rotation[i] can be attributed to the course of those two celestial bodies – *Mariotte*[12] claims to have observed such a law operating in the case of the winds: he maintains that from new to full moon[j] the winds tend to change their direction clockwise through all the points of the compass[k] – then this circular movement must rotate in the opposite direction in the other hemisphere. And this is something which *Don Ulloa*[13] claims to have found actually confirmed by his observations in the south seas.

---

[z] *nach den Gegenden stellen können.*

[a] *die (i.e., unsere gemeinste Kenntniss der Lage der Örter) uns zu nichts hilft, wenn wir die so geordnete Dinge und das ganze System der wechselseitigen Lagen nicht durch die Beziehung auf die Seiten unseres Körpers nach den Gegenden stellen können.*

[b] *in der bestimmten Gegend, wornach die Ordnung ihrer Theile gekehrt ist.*

[c] *und selbst die Lage der Theile unter einander.*   [d] *nehmen eine entgegengesetzte Wendung.*

[e] *Drehung.*

[f] *haben ihre Drehung wenn man von oben herab, d.i. von der Spitze zur Mundung, geht, von der Linken gegen die Rechte.*

[g] *Richtung* / (*Richtung* always signifies the direction of a *motion*, whereas *Gegend* signifies the direction of an *orientation*).

[h] *Windung* / (lit: winding, twisting, turning).   [i] *Drehung.*

[j] *vom neuen zum vollem Lichte* / C: *dal principiare del giorno fino a giorno chiaro* / H & I: from new to full moon / Z: *de la nouvelle à la pleine lune.*

[k] *gerne von der linken zur Rechten den ganzen Compass durchlaufen.*

Since the distinct feeling[l] of the right and the left side is of such great necessity for judging directions, nature has established an immediate connection between this feeling and the mechanical organisation of the human body. In virtue of this organisation, one side of the body, the right side, namely, enjoys an indisputable advantage over the other in respect of skill and perhaps of strength, too. Hence, all the peoples of the world are right-handed (apart from a few exceptions which, like that of squinting, do not upset the universality of the regular natural order). When mounting a horse or stepping over a ditch, it is easier to move one's body from right to left than in the opposite direction. It is everywhere the right hand which is used in writing. It is with the right hand that one does everything   2:381
requiring skill or strength. But just as the right side of the the body seems to enjoy the advantage of *power*, so does the left side of the body have the advantage over the right in respect of sensitivity, if one is to believe certain scientists, such as *Borelli*[14] and *Bonnet*.[15] The former asserts of the left eye, the latter of the left ear, that the sense in them is stronger than that in their respective counterparts on the right side. And thus it is that the two sides of the body are, in spite of their great external similarity, sufficiently distinguished from each other by a clear feeling. And they are distinguished from each other in this way even if one ignores the different positions of the internal organs and the perceptible beating of the heart – whenever it contracts, the tip of the heart touches the left side of the chest with an oblique movement.[m]

What we are trying to demonstrate, then, is the following claim. The ground of the complete determination of a corporeal form[n] does not depend simply on the relation and position of its parts to each other; it also depends on the reference of that physical form to universal absolute space, as it is conceived by the geometers. This relation to absolute space, however, cannot itself be immediately perceived, though the differences, which exist between bodies and which depend exclusively on this ground alone, can be immediately perceived. If two figures drawn on a plane surface are equal and similar,[o][16] then they will coincide with each other. But the situation is often entirely different when one is dealing with corporeal extension, or even with lines and surfaces, not lying on a plane surface.[p] They can be exactly equal and similar, and yet still be so different in themselves that the limits of the one cannot also be the limits of the other. The thread of a screw which winds round its pin from left to right will never fit a nut of which the thread runs from right to left. Even if the size of the screw is the same as the size of the nut, and even if the number of times which the thread winds round the pin of the screw is the same as

[l] *das verschiedene Gefühl.*   [m] *mit seiner Spitze in schiefer Bewegung an die Linke Seite der Brust.*
[n] *der vollständige Bestimmungsgrund einer körperlichen Gestalt.*   [o] *einander gleich und ähnlich.*
[p] *in einer Ebene.*

the number of times which the thread winds round the inside of the nut, the nut and the screw will never match each other. A spherical triangle can be exactly equal and similar to another such triangle, and yet still not coincide with it.*q* But the most common and clearest example is furnished by the limbs of the human body, which are symmetrically arranged relative to the vertical plane of the body.*r* The right hand is similar and equal to the left hand. And if one looks at one of them on its own, examining the proportion and the position of its parts to each other, and scrutinising the magnitude of the whole, then a complete description of the one must apply in all respects to the other, as well.

2:382 I shall call a body which is exactly equal and similar to another, but which cannot be enclosed in the same limits as that other, its *incongruent counterpart.*[517] Now, in order to demonstrate the possibility of such a thing, let a body be taken consisting, not of two halves which are symmetrically arranged relatively to a single intersecting plane, but rather, say, a *human hand.* From all the points on its surface let perpendicular lines be extended to a plane surface*t* set up opposite to it; and let these lines be extended the same distance behind the plane surface, as the points on the surface of the hand are in front of it; the ends of the lines, thus extended, constitute, when connected together, the surface of a corporeal form. That form is the incongruent counterpart of the first. In other words, if the hand in question is a right hand, then its counterpart is a left hand. The reflection of an object in a mirror rests upon exactly the same principles. For the object always appears as far behind the mirror as it is in front of it.*u* Hence, the image of a right hand in a mirror is always a left hand. If the object itself consists of two incongruent counterparts, as the human body does if it is divided by means of a vertical intersection running from front to back, then its image is congruent with that object. That this is the case can easily be recognised if one imagines the body making half a rotation; for the counterpart of the counterpart of an object is necessarily congruent with that object.*v*

Let that suffice to explain the possibility of spaces which are perfectly similar and equal and yet incongruent. Let us now proceed to the philosophical application of these concepts. It is apparent from the ordinary example of the two hands that the shape of the one body may be perfectly similar to the shape of the other, and the magnitudes of their extensions*w* may be exactly equal, and yet there may remain an inner difference*x*

q *ohne ihn doch zu decken.*   *r* *welche gegen die Vertikalfläche desselben symmetrisch geordnet sind.*
s *sein incongruentes Gegenstück.*   *t* *Tafel.*
u *Denn es* (i.e., *das Object*) *erscheint jederzeit eben so weit hinter demselben* (i.e., *dem Spiegel*), *als es* (i.e., *das Object*) *vor seiner Fläche steht.*
v *denn das Gegenstück vom Gegenstück eines Objects ist diesem nothwendig Congruent.*
w *die Grösse der Ausdehnung.*   *x* *ein innerer Unterschied.*

between the two, this difference consisting in the fact, namely, that the surface which encloses the one cannot possibly enclose the other. Since the surface which limits the physical space of the one body cannot serve as a boundary to limit the other, no matter how that surface be twisted and turned, it follows that the difference must be one which rests upon an inner ground.[y] This inner ground cannot, however, depend on the difference of the manner in which the parts of the body are combined with each other.[z] For, as we have seen from our example, everything may in this respect be exactly the same. Nonetheless, imagine that the first created thing was a human hand. That human would have to be either a right hand or a left hand. The action of the creative cause in producing the one would have of necessity to be different from the action of the creative cause producing the counterpart.[a]

2:383

Suppose that one were to adopt the concept entertained by many modern philosophers, especially German philosophers, according to which space simply consists in the external relation of the parts of matter which exist alongside each other.[b] It would follow, in the example we have adduced, that all actual space[c] would simply be *the space occupied by this hand*. However, there is no difference in the relation of the parts of the hand to each other, and that is so whether it be a right hand or a left hand; it would therefore follow that the hand would be completely indeterminate in respect of such a property. In other words, the hand would fit equally well on either side of the human body; but that is impossible.

Our considerations make it plain that the determinations of space are not consequences of the positions of the parts of matter relative to each other.[d] On the contrary, the latter are the consequences of the former. Our considerations, therefore, make it clear that differences, and true differences at that, can be found in the constitution of bodies; these differences relate exclusively to *absolute* and *original space*,[e] for it is only in virtue of absolute and original space that the relation of physical things to each other is possible. Finally, our considerations make the following point clear: absolute space is not an object of outer sensation; it is rather a fundamental concept[f] which first of all makes possible all such outer sensation. For this reason, there is only one way in which we can perceive

---

[y] *so muss diese Verschiedenheit eine solche sein, die auf einem inneren Grunde beruht.*

[z] *die unterschiedliche Art der Verbindung der Theile des Körpers unter einander.*

[a] *und um die eine hervorzubringen, war eine andere Handlung der schaffenden Ursache nöthig, als die wodurch ihr Gegenstück gemacht werden konnte.*

[b] *dass der Raum nur in dem äusseren Verhältnisse der neben einander befindlichen Theile der Materie.*

[c] *aller wirkliche Raum.*

[d] *die Bestimmungen des Raumes Folgen von den Lagen der Theile der Materie gegen einander.*

[e] *auf den absoluten und ursprünglichen Raum.*   [f] *Grundbegriff.*

that which, in the form of a body, exclusively involves reference to pure space,[g] and that is by holding one body against other bodies.[h]

A reflective reader will not, therefore, dismiss the concept of space, as it is construed by geometers and as it has also been incorporated into the system of natural science by penetrating philosophers, as a mere figment of the imagination, though the concept is not without its difficulties. Such difficulties reveal themselves when the attempt is made, employing the ideas of reason,[i] to understand the reality of space, which is intuitive enough for inner sense.[j] But this difficulty always presents itself when one attempts to philosophise about the ultimate data of our cognition.[k] That difficulty, however, is never so decisive as the difficulty which arises when an accepted concept has implications which contradict our most obvious experience.

[g] was in der Gestalt eines Körpers lediglich die Beziehung auf den reinen Raum angeht.
[h] durch die Gegenhaltung mit andern Körpern.   [i] durch Vernunftideen.
[j] welche dem innern Sinne anschauend gnug ist.   [k] über die ersten data unserer Erkenntniss.

*On the form and principles of the sensible
and the intelligible world*
[Inaugural dissertation] (1770)

De mundi sensibilis atque intelligibilis forma et principiis
(MDCCLXX)

DE
MUNDI SENSIBILIS
ATQUE
INTELLIGIBILIS
FORMA ET PRINCIPIIS.

DISSERTATIO PRO LOCO

PROFESSIONIS LOG. ET METAPH. ORDINARIAE RITE SIBI VINDICANDO,

QUAM

EXIGENTIBUS STATUTIS ACADEMICIS

PUBLICE TUEBITUR

IMMANUEL KANT.

RESPONDENTIS MUNERE FUNGETUR

MARCUS HERTZ,

BEROLINENSIS, GENTE IUDAEUS, MEDICINAE ET PHILOSOPHIAE CULTOR,

CONTRA OPPONENTES

GEORGIUM WILHELMUM SCHREIBER,
REG. BOR. ART. STUD.

IOHANNEM AUGUSTUM STEIN,
REG. BOR. I. U. C.

ET

GEORGIUM DANIELEM SCHROETER,
ELBING. S. S. THEOL. C.

IN AUDITORIO MAXIMO

HORIS MATUTINIS ET POMERIDIANIS CONSUETIS

D. XXI. AUG. A. MDCCLXX.

On the form and principles of the sensible and the intelligible world

A dissertation for the proper obtainment
of the post of ordinary professor of logic and metaphysics which,
according to the requirement of the statutes of the university,
will be publicly defended
by
Immanuel Kant.
The function of respondent will be undertaken by
Marcus Herz
of Berlin, of Jewish descent,
a student of medicine and philosophy,
against opponents:
Georg Wilhelm Schreiber
of Königsberg in Prussia,
student in the Faculty of Philosophy;
Johann August Stein
of Königsberg in Prussia,
candidate in both laws;
and
Georg Daniel Schröter
of Elbing,
candidate in sacred theology,
in the large lecture theatre.
At the usual morning and afternoon hours
on 21 August of the year 1770.

To the Most August
Serene and Mighty
Prince and Master,

The Lord Frederick,

King of the Prussians,
Margrave of Brandenburg,
Arch-Chamberlain and Elector
of
The Holy Roman Empire,
Sovereign Duke of Silesia,
etc. etc. etc.

To the Most Clement
Father of His Country,
To His Most Indulgent King and Master,

these first fruits
of the office entrusted to him
are offered
in devotion

by

His Most Humble

Immanuel Kant

Section 1. On the concept^a of a world^b in general

§ 1

In the case of a substantial compound, just as analysis does not come to an end until a part is reached which is not a whole, that is to say a SIMPLE, so likewise synthesis does not come to an end until we reach a whole which is not a part, that is to say a WORLD.[1]

In this exposition of the underlying concept, I have, in addition to the characteristic marks^c which belong to the distinct cognition of an object, also paid some little attention to the *two-fold genesis* of the concept out of the nature of the mind. For since this genesis,^d by serving as an example, can help us to secure a deeper insight into the method of metaphysics, it seems to me that it should not be underestimated. Thus, it is one thing, given the parts, to conceive for oneself the *composition* of the whole, using an abstract concept of the understanding,^e and it is another thing to *follow up* this general *concept*, as one might do with some problem of reason, by the sensitive^f faculty of cognition, that is to say, to represent the same concept to oneself in the concrete by a distinct intuition.[2] The former is done by means of the concept of *composition* in general, in so far as a number of things are contained under it (in reciprocal relations to each other), and thus by means of ideas of the understanding which are univer-

---

^a *notio* / Alquié (hereafter A): *notion* / Beck (1986) (hereafter B), Handyside (hereafter Ha), & Kerferd (hereafter K): notion / Carabellese (hereafter C): *nozione* / Eckhof (hereafter E): idea / Hinske (hereafter H): *Begriff* / (Kant employs *notio* and *conceptus* as synonyms and both words have been translated by the single English equivalent 'concept'. See Glossary: note 4).
^b MUNDO / A: *le* MONDE / B, Ha, & K: a WORLD / C: *nel* MONDO / H: *eine* WELT / (Latin lacks both the definite and the indefinite article. Generally this creates no problems, but occasionally, as here, the translator is confronted with a necessary choice. Beck (1986) expresses the matter succinctly: 'Since Kant admits other possible and the possibility of other actual worlds, it is important here to read the definition as entirely general: *any* whole which is not a part of another whole is a world'.)
^c *notas* / A: *caractères* / B: characteristics / C: *note* / E, Ha, & K: marks / H: *Merkmalen.*
^d *quae* / (*quae* may grammatically refer either to *exposito* [the reading of B & Ha] or to *genesis* [the reading of A, C, & K]).
^e *intellectus* / (see Glossary: note 16).
^f *sensitivam* / A: *sensitive* / B & Ha: sensitive / C: *sensitiva* / E: sensuous / H: *sinnlich* (see Glossary: note 12).

sal. The latter case rests upon the *conditions* of time, in so far as it is possible, by the successive addition of part to part, to arrive genetically, that is to say, by SYNTHESIS,[3] at the concept of a compound; this case falls under the laws of *intuition*. In a similar way, when a substantial compound has been given, we arrive without difficulty at the idea of things which are simple by taking away generally the concept of *composition*, which derives from the understanding. For the things which remain when every element of conjunction has been removed are *simple* things. However, under the laws of cognitive intuition, this only happens, that is to say, all composition is only cancelled, by means of a regress from the given whole to all its 2:388 *possible parts whatsoever*, that is to say, by means of analysis,* which in its turn rests upon the condition of time. But for a compound there must be a *multiplicity[j]* of parts, and for a whole there must be a *totality[k]* of parts. The analysis and the synthesis will only be completed, the concept of a *simple* will only emerge by means of analysis, and the concept of a *whole* will only emerge by means of synthesis, if the respective processes can be carried out in a finite and specifiable period of time.

But, in the case of a *continuous magnitude,[l]* the *regression* from the whole to the parts, which are able to be given, and in the case of an *infinite* magnitude, the *progression* from the parts to the given whole, have in each case *no limit.[m]* Hence it follows that, in the one case, complete analysis, and, in the other case, complete synthesis, will be impossible. Thus, in the first case, the whole cannot, according to the laws of intuition, be thought completely as regards *composition* and, in the second case, the compound cannot be thought completely as regards *totality*. From this it is clear how, since *unrepresentable* and *impossible* are commonly treated as having the same meaning, the concepts both of the *continuous* and of the *infinite* are frequently rejected. For, indeed, *according to the laws of intuitive cognition, any representation of these concepts is absolutely impossible.*[4] Now, al-

---

* A double meaning is commonly assigned to the words 'analysis' and 'synthesis'. Thus, synthesis is either *qualitative*, in which case it is a progression through a series of *things which are subordinate to each other,[g]* the progression advancing from the ground to that which is grounded,[h] or the synthesis is *quantitative*, in which case it is a progression within a series of *things which are co-ordinate with each other,[i]* the progression advancing from a given part, through parts complementary to it, to the whole. In the same way, analysis, taken in its first sense, is a regression from *that which is grounded to the ground*, whereas, in its second sense, it is a regression from a *whole to its possible or mediate parts*, that is to say, to parts of parts; thus, it is not a division but a *subdivision* of a given compound. Here we use both 'synthesis' and 'analysis' only in their second sense.

[g] *subordinatorum.*　　[h] *a ratione ad rationatum.*　　[i] *coordinatorum.*
[j] *multitudo* / A: *multitude* / B & Ha: *aggregate* / C: *moltitudine* / E: *multiplicity* / H: *Vielheit* / K: *manifold.*
[k] *omnitudo.*　　[l] *quanto continuo.*　　[m] *termino.*

though I am not here pleading a case for these concepts* – concepts which have been expelled in disgrace from not a few schools, especially the concept of the continuous – nonetheless it will be of the greatest importance to have given a warning that the people who use such a $\quad$ 2:389 perverse method of arguing are guilty of the gravest errors. For whatever *conflicts with* the laws of the understanding and the laws of reason is undoubtedly impossible. But that which, being an object of pure reason, simply *does not come under* the laws of intuitive cognition, is not in the same position. For this lack of accord between the *sensitive* faculty and the faculty of the *understanding* – the nature of these faculties I shall explain later – points only to the fact that *the abstract ideas which the mind entertains when they have been received from the understanding very often cannot be followed up in the concrete and converted into intuitions.* But this *subjective* resistance often creates the false impression of an *objective* inconsistency. And the incautious are easily misled by this false impression into taking the limits, by which the human mind is circumscribed, for the limits within which the very essence of things is contained.[6]

Moreover, in the case of substantial compounds, whether they be given by the testimony of the senses or in some other way, it can easily be shown by an argument, which is based on reasons deriving from the understanding, that both simples and a world are given. But, in framing my definition, I have also pointed out the causes, which are to be found in the character of the subject, so that the notion of a world may not appear purely arbitrary and, as happens in mathematics, constructed only for the purposes of deducing the consequences which follow from it. For the

---

* Those who reject the actual mathematical infinite[5] do not exactly make the task difficult for themselves. They construct, namely, a definition of the infinite which is such that they are able to extract a contradiction from it. For them, the *infinite* is *that magnitude than which a greater magnitude is impossible;* and the mathematical infinite is for them that multiplicity[n] (of a unit which can be given) than which a larger multiplicity is impossible. They then substitute *largest* for *infinite,* and, since a largest multiplicity is impossible, they readily conclude against an infinite, which they themselves have constructed. Alternatively, they call an infinite multiplicity an *infinite number,* and declare that an infinite number is absurd, which it obviously is. But they are fighting with figments of their own imagination.[o] But suppose they conceive of the mathematical infinite as a magnitude which, when related to a measure treated as a unit, constitutes a *multiplicity larger than any number;* and suppose, further, that they had noticed that *measurability* here only denotes relation to the unit adopted by the human understanding as a standard of measurement, and by means of which it is only possible to reach *the definite concept of a multiplicity* by successively adding one to one, and the *complete* concept, which is called a *number,* only by carrying out this progression in a finite time, then they would have seen very clearly that things which do not accord with a fixed[p] law of a certain subject do not, for that reason, pass beyond all understanding. For there could be an understanding, though certainly not a human understanding, which might distinctly apprehend a multiplicity at a single glance, without the successive application of a measure.

n   multitudo.   o   cum umbris ingenii.   p   certa.

mind which is focused upon the concept of a compound, whether it be engaged in analysing it or synthesising[q] it, demands and adopts for itself limits,[r] within which it may rest, whether it be proceeding *a priori* or *a posteriori*.

§2

In the definition of a world the following are the factors which require attention:

I. MATTER (in the transcendental sense), that is the *parts*, which are here taken to be *substances*.[7] We were able to remain wholly unconcerned about the agreement of our definition with the ordinary meaning of the word, for the only question which our definition raises concerns a problem which arises in accordance with reason, namely, how it is possible for several substances to coalesce into one thing, and upon what conditions it depends that this one thing is not a part of something else. But, indeed, the force of the word 'world', as it is found in common use, springs to the mind of its own accord. For no one assigns *accidents* to a *world* as its parts, but only to its *state* as *determinations*. Hence, the so-called *egoistic* world,[8] which is completely constituted by a unique simple substance together with its accidents, is not properly called a world, unless, perhaps, it is called an *imaginary* world. For the same reason, it is wrong to attribute to the world as a whole the series of successive things (namely, successive states) as part of it. For modifications are *not parts* of a subject; they are what are determined by a ground.[s] Finally, I have not here raised the question of the nature of the substances which constitute the world, 2:390 whether, namely, they are *contingent* or necessary. Nor do I gratuitously store away the determination of this question in my definition, intending subsequently, as often happens, to extract therefrom this very same determination by some specious method of argument. But I shall later show[9] that the contingency of the substances which constitute the world can be fully established by appeal to the conditions here posited.

II. FORM, which consists in the *co-ordination*, not in the subordination, of substances. For *co-ordinates* are related to one another as complements to a whole, while *subordinates* are related to one another as caused and cause, or, generally, as principle and that which is governed by principle.[t] The former relationship is reciprocal and *homonymous*, so that any correlate is related to the other as both determining it and being determined by it. The latter relationship is *heteronymous*, for on the one side it is a relation of dependence only, and on the other it is a relation of causality. This co-ordination is conceived of as *real* and objective, not as ideal and depending upon the subject's power of choice, by means of which any multiplicity

---

[q] *tam resolvendo quam componendo.*   [r] *terminos.*   [s] *rationata.*   [t] *principium et principiatum.*

whatsoever may be fashioned into a whole by a process of adding together at will. For by taking several things together, you achieve without difficulty a *whole of representation* but you do not, in virtue of that, arrive at the *representation* of a *whole*. Accordingly, if there happened to be certain wholes consisting of substances, and if these wholes were not bound to one another by any connection, the bringing of these wholes together, a process by means of which the mind forces the multiplicity into an ideal unity, would signify nothing more than a plurality of worlds held together in a single thought. But the connection, which constitutes the *essential* form of a world, is seen as the principle of the *possible influences* of the substances which constitute the world. For actual influences do not belong to the essence but to the state, and the transeunt forces themselves, which are the causes of the influences, suppose some principle by which it may be possible that the states of the several things, the subsistence of each of which is nonetheless independent of that of the others, should be mutually related to one another as states determined by a ground.[u] If you abandon this principle, you are debarred from positing as possible a transeunt force in the world. And, indeed, this *form*, which is *essential* to a world, is for that reason *immutable* and not subject to any change. And this is the case, first of all, on account of a *logical ground*. For any change presupposes the identity of the subject, whereas determinations succeed one another. Hence, the world, remaining the same throughout all its successive states, preserves the same fundamental form. For the identity of the *parts* is not sufficient for the identity of the whole; the identity of the whole requires an identity of characteristic *composition*. But, above all, the same result follows because of a *real ground*.[v] For the nature of a world, being the first internal principle of each and every one of the variable determinations which belong to its state, cannot be opposed to itself; consequently, it is naturally, that is to say, in virtue of itself,[w] immutable. Accordingly, in any world there is a certain constant and invariable form, which, as the perennial principle of each contingent and transitory form belonging to the state of that world, must be regarded as belonging to its nature. Those who consider this investigation to be superfluous are baffled by the concepts of *space* and *time*. They treat them as primitive conditions which are already given in themselves, and, in virtue of which to be sure, and independently of any other principle, it would be not only possible but also necessary that a number of actual things should be mutually related to one another as joint parts[x] and should constitute a whole. I shall, however, shortly explain that these notions are not *rational* at all, and that they are not *objective* ideas of any connection, but that they are appearances, and that, while they do, indeed, bear witness to some common principle constituting a universal connection, they do not expose it to view.

2:391

---

[u] *rationata.* [v] *e ratione reali.* [w] *a se ipsa.* [x] *compartes.*

III. ENTIRETY,[y] which is the *absolute* totality[z] of its component parts. For when we consider some *given* compound, although that compound were still to be a part of another compound, there is always present a certain *comparative* totality, namely, the totality of the parts which belong to that magnitude itself. But, in this present case, whatever things are related to one another as joint parts with respect to any whole *whatsoever*, are understood as posited together. This absolute *totality*[a] may present the aspect[b] of an everyday and readily accessible concept, especially when it is stated negatively, as is the case in our definition.[10] Yet, when we reflect upon it more deeply, it is seen to present the philosopher with a very serious problem. For it is hardly possible to conceive how the *never to be completed series* of the states of the universe, which succeed one another to *eternity*, can be reduced to a whole, which comprehends absolutely all its changes. Indeed, it necessarily follows from its very infinity that the series has no *limit.*[c] Accordingly, there is no series of successive things except one which is part of another series. It follows that, for this same reason, comprehensive completeness or *absolute totality* seems to have been banished altogether here. For, although the notion of a part could be taken universally, and although all the things which are contained under this notion might constitute a single thing if they were regarded as posited in the same series, yet it seems to be required by the concept of *a whole* that all these things should *be taken simultaneously*. And, in the case given, this is impossible. For since nothing succeeds the whole series, and since, if we posit a series of things in succession, there is nothing which is not followed by something else, except when it is last in the series, there will be something which is last for eternity, and that is absurd. It may, perhaps, be thought that the difficulty which confronts the totality of a successive infinite does not apply in the case of a *simultaneous infinite,* because *simultaneity* seems expressly to declare that there is combination *of all things at the same time.* But if a simultaneous infinite were admitted, one would also have to concede the totality of a successive infinite – for if the latter is denied, the former is also cancelled. For a simultaneous infinite provides eternity with inexhaustible matter for progressing successively through its innumerable parts to infinity. Yet this series, when completed with all its numbers, would be actually given in a simultaneous infinite, and, thus, a series which could never be completed by successive addition could nevertheless be given *as a whole.* Let him who is to extricate himself from this thorny question note that neither the successive nor the simultaneous co-ordination of several things (since both co-ordinations depend on concepts of time) belongs to a concept of a whole which derives from the

2:392

[y] UNIVERSITAS / A: L'ENSEMBLE / B: wholeness / C: UNIVERSITÀ / H: *Die* GESAMMTHEIT.
[z] *omnitudo* / A: *groupe complet* / B: totality / C: *omnitudine* / H: *Allheit* / K: allness.
[a] *totalitas.* [b] *speciem.* [c] *ut careat termino.*

understanding[d] but only to the conditions of *sensitive intuition.*[e] Accordingly, even if these co-ordinations could not be sensitively conceived, they would not, for that reason, cease to belong to the understanding. It is sufficient for this concept that co-ordinates should be given in some way or other, and that they should all be thought as constituting a unity.[f]

[d] *ad conceptum intellectualem totius.*   [e] *ad condiciones intuitus sensitivi.*
[f] *tanquam pertinentia ad unum.*

Section 2. On the distinction between sensible things and intelligible things in general

§3

Sensibility[g] is the *receptivity* of a subject in virtue of which it is possible for the subject's own representative state to be affected in a definite way by the presence of some object.[11] *Intelligence*[h] (rationality) is the *faculty* of a subject in virtue of which it has the power to represent things which cannot by their own quality come before the senses of that subject. The object of sensibility is the sensible; that which contains nothing but what is to be cognised through the intelligence is intelligible. In the schools of the ancients, the former was called a *phenomenon* and the latter a *noumenon*. Cognition, in so far as it is subject to the laws of sensibility, is *sensitive*, and, in so far as it is subject to the laws of intelligence, it is *intellectual* or rational.[12]

§4

In this way, whatever in cognition is sensitive is dependent upon the special character of the subject in so far as the subject is capable of this or that modification by the presence of objects: these modifications may differ in different cases, according to the variations in the subjects. But whatever cognition is exempt from such subjective conditions relates only to the object. It is thus clear that things which are thought sensitively are representations of things *as they appear*, while things which are intellectual are representations of things *as they are*. In a representation of sense there is, first of all, something which you might call the *matter*, namely, the *sensation*, and there is also something which may be called the *form*, the *aspect*[i] namely of sensible things which arises according as the various things which affect the senses are co-ordinated by a certain natural law of the mind.[13] Moreover, just as the sensation which constitutes the *matter* of a sensible representation is, indeed, evidence for the presence of some-

2:393

[g] *Sensualitas* / A: *Sensibilité* / B: Sensibility / C: *Sensorialità* / H: *Sinnlichkeit* / K: *Sensuality*.
[h] *intelligentia* / (alt: power of the understanding).
[i] *species* / A: *configuration* / B: general configuration / C: *specie* / E: appearance / H: *Gestalt* / Ha: general characteristic / K: specificity.

384

thing sensible, though in respect of its quality it is dependent upon the nature of the subject in so far as the latter is capable of modification by the object in question, so also the *form* of the same representation is undoubtedly evidence of a certain reference or relation in what is sensed, though properly speaking it is not an outline or any kind of schema*ʲ* of the object, but only a certain law, which is inherent in the mind and by means of which it co-ordinates for itself that which is sensed*ᵏ* from the presence of the object. For objects do not strike the senses in virtue of their form or aspect. Accordingly, if the various factors in an object which affect the sense are to coalesce into some representational whole there is needed an internal principle in the mind, in virtue of which those various factors may be clothed with a certain *aspect*, in accordance with stable and innate laws.

§5

There thus belong to sensory cognition*ˡ* both matter, which is sensation and in virtue of which cognitions are called *sensory*,*ᵐ* and form, in virtue of which, even if it were to be found free from all sensation, representations are called *sensitive*.*ⁿ* On the other hand, in so far as that which belongs to the understanding*ᵒ* is concerned, it must above all be carefully noted that the use of the understanding, or the superior faculty of the soul, is twofold. By the first of these uses, the concepts themselves, whether of things or relations, *are given*, and this is the REAL USE. By the second use, the concepts, no matter whence they are given, are merely subordinated to each other, the lower, namely, to the higher (common characteristic marks), and compared with one another in accordance with the principle of contradiction, and this use is called the LOGICAL USE.[14] Now, the logical use of the understanding is common to all the sciences, but not so the real use. For when a cognition has been given, no matter how, it is regarded either as contained under or as opposed to a characteristic mark common to several cognitions, and that either immediately and directly, as is the case in *judgements*, which lead to a distinct cognition,[15] or mediately, as is the case in *ratiocinations*, which lead to a complete*ᵖ* cognition.[16] If, therefore, sensitive cognitions are given, sensitive cognitions are subordinated by the logical use of the understanding to other sensitive cognitions, as to common concepts, and phenomena are subordinated to more general laws of phenomena. But it is of the greatest importance here to have noticed that cognitions must always be treated as sensitive cognitions, no matter how extensive the logical use of the understanding may have been in relation to them. For they are called sensitive *on account of their genesis* and not on account of their *comparison* in respect of identity or opposition.

ʲ adumbratio aut schema. *ᵏ sensa.* *ˡ sensualem . . . cognitionem.* *ᵐ sensuales.* *ⁿ sensitivae.*
ᵒ intellectualia. *ᵖ adaequatam.*

Hence, even the most general empirical laws are nonetheless sensory; and the principles of sensitive form which are found in geometry (determinate relations in space), no matter how much the understanding may operate upon them by reasoning according to the rules of logic from what is sensitively given (by pure intuition), nonetheless do not cease to belong to the class of what is sensitive. But in the case of sensible*q* things and phenomena, that which precedes the logical use of the understanding is called *appearance,**r*** while the reflective cognition,[17] which arises when several appearances are compared by the understanding, is called *experience.* Thus, there is no way from appearance to experience except by reflection in accordance with the logical use of the understanding. The common concepts of experience are called *empirical,* and the objects of experience are called *phenomena,* while the laws both of experience and generally of all sensitive cognition are called the laws of phenomena. Thus empirical concepts do not, in virtue of being raised to greater universality, become intellectual in the *real sense,* nor do they pass beyond the species of sensitive cognition; no matter how high they ascend by abstracting, they always remain sensitive.

2:394

§6

As for that which belongs strictly to the understanding,*s* and in the case of which the *use of the understanding is real:* such concepts, whether of objects or of relations, are given by the very nature of the understanding: they contain no form of sensitive cognition and they have been abstracted*t* from no use of the senses. It is, however, necessary to notice here the extreme ambiguity of the word '*abstract*',*u* and I think that it would be better to eliminate this ambiguity beforehand lest it spoil our investigation into that which belongs to the understanding.*v* Properly speaking, we ought, namely, to say: *to abstract from some things,* but not: *to abstract something.*[18] The former expression indicates that in a certain concept we should not attend to the other things which are connected with it in some way or other, while the latter expression indicates that it would be given only concretely, and only in such a way that it is separated from the things which are joined to it. Hence, a concept of the understanding *abstracts* from everything sensitive, but it is *not abstracted* from what is sensitive. Perhaps a concept of the understanding would more rightly be called *abstracting**w*** rather than *abstracted.**x*** For this reason, it is more advisable to

---

q in sensualibus / A: *les données propres à la connaissance sensible* / B: in things of sense / C: *Nei fatti sensoriali* / E: sense-percepts / H: *Bei den Sinneserkenntnissen* / Ha: in things sensual / K: in sensual things.

r apparentia. *s intellectualia stricte talia.* *t abstracti.* *u abstracti.* *v de intellectualibus.*
w abstrahens. *x abstractus* (alt: abstracted).

call concepts of the understanding '*pure ideas*', and concepts which are only given empirically '*abstract*[y] concepts'.

§7

From this one can see that the sensitive is poorly defined as that which is *more confusedly* cognised, and that which belongs to the understanding as that of which there is a *distinct* cognition. For these are only logical distinctions which *do not touch* at all the things *given*, which underlie every logical comparison. Thus, sensitive representations[z] can be very distinct and representations which belong to the understanding[a] can be extremely confused.[19] We notice the first case in that paradigm of sensitive cognition, *geometry,* and the second case in the organon of everything which belongs to the understanding, *metaphysics.* And it is obvious how much effort is devoted by metaphysics to dispelling the clouds of confusion which darken the common understanding, although it is not always so happily successful as geometry is. Nonetheless, each and every one of these cognitions preserves the sign of its ancestry, so that those belonging to the first group, however distinct they be, are called sensitive because of their origin, while those belonging to the second group continue to belong to the understanding, even though they are confused. Such, for example, is the case with *moral* concepts, which are cognised not by experiencing them but by the pure understanding itself. But I am afraid it may be that the illustrious WOLFF has, by this distinction between what is sensitive and what belongs to the understanding, a distinction which for him is only logical, completely abolished, to the great detriment of philosophy, the noblest of the enterprises of antiquity, the discussion of the *character of phenomena and noumena,* and has turned men's minds away from that enquiry to things which are often only logical minutiae.[20]

2:395

§8

Now, the philosophy which contains the *first principles* of the use of the *pure understanding* is METAPHYSICS. But its propaedeutic science is that science which teaches the distinction between sensitive cognition and the cognition which derives from the understanding; it is of this science that I am offering a specimen in my present dissertation. Since, then, empirical principles are not found in metaphysics, the concepts met with in metaphysics are not to be sought in the senses but in the very nature of the pure understanding, and that not as *innate* concepts but as concepts abstracted from the laws inherent in the mind (by attending to its actions on

---

^y *abstractos* (alt: abstracted).   ^z *sensitiva.*   ^a *intellectualia.*

the occasion of an experience), and therefore as *acquired* concepts. To this genus belong possibility, existence, necessity, substance, cause *etc.*, together with their opposites or correlates. Such concepts never enter into any sensory representations as parts, and thus they could not be abstracted from such a representation in any way at all.

§9

The concepts of the understanding[b] have, in particular, two ends. The first is *elenctic,* in virtue of which they have a negative use, where, namely, they keep what is sensitively conceived distinct from noumena, and, although they do not advance science by the breadth of a fingernail, they nonetheless preserve it from the contagion of errors. The second end is *dogmatic,* and in accordance with it the general principles of the pure understanding, such as are displayed in ontology or in rational psychology, lead to some paradigm,[c] which can only be conceived by the pure understanding and which is a common measure for all other things in so far as they are realities. This paradigm is NOUMENAL PERFECTION. This, however, is perfection either in the theoretical sense* or in the practical sense. In the former sense, it is the Supreme Being, GOD; in the latter sense, it is MORAL PERFECTION. *Moral philosophy,* therefore, in so far as it furnishes the first *principles of judgement,*[d] is only cognised by the pure understanding and itself belongs to pure philosophy. Epicurus, who reduced its criteria to the sense of pleasure or pain,[21] is very rightly blamed, together with certain moderns, who have followed him to a certain extent from afar, such as Shaftesbury[22] and his supporters. In any genus of things, the quantity of which is variable, the *maximum* is the common measure and principle of cognising. The *maximum of perfection* is nowadays called the ideal, while for Plato it was called the idea (as in the case of his idea of the state). It is the principle of all things which are contained under the general concept of some perfection, in as much as the lesser degree, it is held, can only be determined by limiting the maximum. But, although God, as the ideal of perfection, is the principle of cognising, He is also, at the same time, in so far as He really exists, the principle of the coming into being of all perfection whatsoever.

2:396

---

* We consider something theoretically in so far as we attend only to those things which belong to being, whereas we consider it practically if we look at those things which ought to be in it in virtue of freedom.

[b] *intellectualium* / A: *Les notions intellectuelles* / B & E: intellectual concepts / C: *concetti intellectualium* / H: *die Verstandeserkenntnisse* / Ha: concepts of the understanding / K: Things intellectual.
[c] *exemplar.* [d] *diiudicandi.*

§10

There is (for man) no *intuition* of what belongs to the understanding,^e but only a *symbolic cognition;* and thinking^f is only possible for us by means of universal concepts in the abstract, not by means of a singular concept in the concrete. For all our intuition is bound to a certain principle of form, and it is only under this form that anything can be *apprehended* by the mind immediately or as *singular,* and not merely conceived discursively by means of general concepts.[23] But this formal principle of our intuition (space and time) is the condition under which something can be the object of our senses.[24] Accordingly, this formal principle, as the condition of sensitive cognition, is not a means to intellectual intuition. Moreover, since it is only through the senses that all the matter of our cognition is given, the noumenon as such cannot be conceived by means of representations drawn from sensations. Thus, the concept of the intelligible as such is devoid of all that is *given* in human intuition. The *intuition,* namely, of our mind is always *passive.* It is, accordingly, only possible in so far as it is 2:397 possible for something to affect our sense. Divine intuition, however, which is the principle of objects, and not something governed by a principle, since it is independent, is an archetype and for that reason perfectly intellectual.

§11

Now, although phenomena, properly speaking, are aspects^g of things and not ideas, and although they do not express the internal and absolute quality of objects, nonetheless cognition of them is in the highest degree true. For, first of all, in so far as they are sensory concepts or apprehensions, they are, as things caused, witnesses to the presence of an object, and this is opposed to idealism.[25] Consider, however, judgements about things which are sensitively cognised. Truth in judging consists in the agreement of a predicate with a given subject. But the concept of a subject, in so far as it is a phenomenon, would only be given through its relation to the sensitive faculty of cognising, and it is in accordance with the same relation that predicates would be given which were sensitively observable. It is, accordingly, clear that representations of a subject and a predicate arise according to common laws; and they thus furnish a foothold^h for cognition which is in the highest degree true.

^e *intellectualium.*   ^f *intellectio.*
^g *species* / A: *apparences* / B: semblances / C: *apparenze* / H: *Abbilder* / K: species.
^h *anseam praedere* / (lit.: provide a handle).

§ 12

Whatever, as object, relates to our senses is a phenomenon. But things which, since they do not touch the senses, contain only the singular form of sensibility, belong to pure intuition (that is to say, an intuition devoid of sensation but not for that reason deriving from the understanding). Phenomena are reviewed and set out, *first*, in the case of the phenomena of external sense, in PHYSICS, and *secondly*, in the case of the phenomena of inner sense, in empirical PSYCHOLOGY. But pure (human) intuition is not a universal or logical concept *under which*, but a singular concept *in which*, all sensible things whatever are thought, and thus it contains the concepts of space and time. These concepts, since they determine nothing as to the *quality* of sensible things, are not objects of science, except in respect of *quantity*. Hence, PURE MATHEMATICS deals with *space* in GEOMETRY, and *time* in pure MECHANICS. In addition to these concepts, there is a certain concept which in itself, indeed, belongs to the understanding but of which the actualisation[i] in the concrete requires the auxiliary notions of time and space (by successively adding a number of things and setting them simultaneously side by side). This is the concept of *number*, which is the concept treated in ARITHMETIC. Thus, pure mathematics, which explains the form of all our sensitive cognition, is the organon of each and every intuitive and distinct cognition. And since its objects themselves are not only the formal principles of every intuition, but are *originary intuitions*, it provides us with a cognition which is in the highest degree true, and, at the same time, it provides us with a paradigm of the highest kind of evidence[j] in other cases. *Thus there is a science of sensory things,*[k] although, since they are phenomena, the use of the understanding is not real but only logical. It is, hence, clear in what sense we are to suppose that science was denied in the case of phenomena by those who drew their inspiration from the Eleatic School.[26]

2:398

[i] *actuatio.*   [j] *summae evidentiae.*   [k] *sensualium.*

Section 3. On the principles of the form of the sensible world

§13

The principle of the form of the universe is that which contains the ground of the universal connection,*l* in virtue of which all substances and their states belong to the same whole which is called *a world*. The principle of the form of the *sensible world* is that which contains the ground of the *universal connection* of all things, in so far as they are *phenomena*. The form of the *intelligible* world recognises an objective principle, that is to say, some cause in virtue of which there is a combining together*m* of the things which exist in themselves. But the world, in so far as it is regarded as phenomenon, that is to say, the world in relation to the sensibility of the human mind, does not recognise any other principle of form than a subjective one, that is to say, a fixed*n* law of the mind, in virtue of which it is necessary that all the things which can be objects of the senses (through the qualities of those objects) are seen as *necessarily* belonging to the same whole. Accordingly, whatever the principle of the form of the sensible world may, in the end, be, its embrace is limited to *actual things*, in so far as they are thought capable of *falling under the senses*. Accordingly, it embraces neither immaterial substances, which are already as such, by definition, excluded from the outer senses, nor the cause of the world, for, since it is in virtue of that cause that mind itself exists and is active through all its senses, that cause cannot be an object of the senses. These formal principles of the *phenomenal universe* are absolutely primary and universal; they are, so to speak, the schemata and conditions of everything sensitive in human cognition. I shall now show that there are two such principles, namely, space and time.

§14

On time[27]

1. *The idea of time does not arise from but is presupposed by the senses.* For it is only through the idea of time that it is possible for the things which come

l *rationem nexus universalis.* *m* *colligatio.* *n* *certam.*

391

2:399 before the senses to be represented as simultaneous or successive. Nor does succession generate the concept of time; it makes appeal to it. And thus the concept of time, regarded as if it had been acquired through experience, is very badly defined, if it is defined in terms of the series of actual things which exist one *after* the other. For I only understand the meaning of the little word *after* by means of the antecedent concept of time. For those things come *after* one another which exist at *different times,* just as those things are *simultaneous which exist at the same time.*

2. *The idea of time is singular* and not general. For no time is thought of except as a part of the same one boundless time. If you think of two years, you can only represent them to yourself as being in a determinate position in relation to each other; and if they should not immediately succeed each other, you can only represent them to yourself as joined to one another by some intermediate time. But among different times, the time which is *earlier* and the time which is *later* cannot be defined in any way by any characteristic marks which can be conceived by the understanding, unless you are willing to involve yourself in a vicious circle. The mind only discerns the distinction between them by a singular intuition. Moreover, you conceive all actual things as situated *in* time, and not as contained *under* the general concept of time, as under a common characteristic mark.

3. Therefore, *the idea of time is an intuition.* And since, in so far as it is the condition of the relations to be found in sensible things, it is conceived prior to any sensation; it is not a sensory but a *pure intuition.*

4. *Time is a continuous magnitude,* and it is the principle of the laws of what is continuous[o] in the changes of the universe. For the continuous is a magnitude[p] which is not composed of simples. But by means of time it is nothing but relations which are thought, granted that there are no beings which stand in relation to each other. Thus, in time as a magnitude there is composition; and should this composition be conceived as wholly cancelled, it would leave nothing at all behind it. But if nothing at all is left of a compound when all composition has been cancelled, then this compound is not composed of simple parts. Therefore, *etc.* Accordingly, any part whatever of time is itself a time. And the things which are in time, simple things, namely *moments,* are not parts of time, but *limits*[q] with time between them.[28] For if two moments are given, time is only given if actual things succeed one another in those moments. Therefore, in addition to a given moment, there must be a time, in the later part of which there is another moment.

Now, the metaphysical law of *continuity* is as follows: *All changes are continuous* or flow: that is to say, opposed states only succeed one another through an intermediate series of different states. For two opposed states

[o] *continui.* [p] *quantum.* [q] *termini.*

are in different moments of time. But between two moments there will always be an intervening time, and, in the infinite series of the moments of that time, the substance is not in one of the given states, nor in the other, and yet it is not in no state either. It will be in different states, and so on to infinity.

2:400

The celebrated Kästner,[29] with a view to subjecting this law of Leibniz[30] to examination, challenges its defenders* to show that *the continuous movement of a point along all the sides of a triangle is impossible.* For, if the law of continuity were granted, such continuous motion would unquestionably require proof. Here, then, is the demonstration asked for. Let the letters *abc* denote the three angle-points of a rectilinear triangle. If something moveable passes in continuous motion along the lines *ab, bc,* and *ca,* that is to say, along the whole perimeter of the figure, it necessarily follows that it moves through point *b* in the direction *ab* and also through the same point *b* in the direction *bc.* But since these movements are diverse they cannot exist *simultaneously.* Therefore, the moment of the presence of the moveable point at the vertex *b,* in so far as it is moving in the direction *ab,* is different from the moment of the presence of the moveable point at the same vertex *b,* in so far as it is moving in the direction *bc.* But between the two moments there is a time. Therefore, the moveable point is present at the same point through some time, that is to say, *it is at rest,* and therefore it does not proceed in a continuous motion. And this is contrary to the hypothesis. The same demonstration is valid for motion along any specifiable straight lines which form an angle. Therefore, according to the doctrines of Leibniz, a body does not change its direction in a motion which is continuous, except along a line no part of which is straight, in other words, along a line which is a curve.

5. *Time is not something objective and real,*[31] nor is it a substance, nor an accident, nor a relation. Time is rather the subjective condition which is necessary, in virtue of the nature of the human mind, for the co-ordinating of all sensible things in accordance with a fixed law. It is a *pure intuition.* For it is only through the concept of time that we co-ordinate both substances and accidents, according to both simultaneity and succession. And, thus, the concept of time, as the principle of form, is prior to[r] the concepts of substance and accident. But as for relations or connections[s] of any kind: in so far as they confront the senses they contain nothing which tells us whether they are simultaneous with or successive to each other, apart from their positions in time, and those positions have to be determined as being either at the same or at different points of time.

***

* *Höhere Mechanik,* p. 354.

[r] *antiquior.*
[s] *relationes . . . s. respectus / (relatio* and *respectus* are synonyms; elsewhere they have both been translated by 'relation').

Those who assert the objective reality of time either conceive of time as some continuous flux within existence,[1] and yet independently of any existent thing (a most absurd fabrication) – this is a view maintained, in particular, by the English philosophers[32] – or else they conceive of it as something real which has been abstracted from the succession of internal states – the view maintained by Leibniz[33] and his followers. Now, the falsity of the latter opinion clearly betrays itself by the vicious circle in the commonly accepted definition of time. Moreover, it completely neglects *simultaneity*,* the most important corollary[v] of time. It, thus, throws into confusion all use of sound reason, for, rather than requiring that the laws of motion should be determined by reference to the measure of time, it demands that time itself should be determined, in respect of its own nature, by reference to things which are observed to be in motion or in any series of internal changes. In this way, all the certainty of our rules is completely destroyed. That we are only able to calculate the *quantity* of time in the concrete, namely, either by *motion* or by *a series of thoughts*, is due to the fact that the concept of time rests exclusively on an internal law of the mind, and is not some kind of innate intuition.[w] Accordingly, the action of the mind in co-ordinating what it senses[x] would not be elicited without the help of the senses. Indeed, far from its being the case that anyone has ever yet deduced the concept of time from some other source, or explained it with the help of reason, the very principle of contradiction itself presupposes the concept of time and bases itself on it as its condition. For *A* and *not-A* are not *inconsistent* unless they are thought *simultaneously* (that is to say, at the same time), about the *same thing*, for they *can belong* to the same thing *after one another* (that is to say, at different times). Hence, it is only in time that the possibility of changes can be thought, whereas time cannot be thought by means of change, only *vice versa*.

2:401

---

* Simultaneous things are not simultaneous because they do not succeed one another. For if succession is removed, then some conjunction, which existed in virtue of the series of time, is, indeed, abolished; but *another* true relationship, such as the conjunction of all things, does not instantly spring into existence as a result. For simultaneous things are joined together at the same moment of time, just as successive things are joined together by different moments. Accordingly, though time has only one dimension, yet the *ubiquity* of time (to speak with Newton),[34] in virtue of which *all* the things which can be thought sensitively are at *some time*, adds a further dimension to the magnitude[u] of actual things, in so far as they hang, so to speak, from the same point of time. For, if you were to represent time by a straight line extended to infinity, and simultaneous things at any point of time by lines drawn perpendicular to it, the surface thus generated would represent the *phenomenal world* in respect both of substance and of accidents.

[1] *in exsistendo* / A: *d'existence* / B & Ha: – / C: *nella sua existenza* / E: in what exists / K: in existence.
[u] *quanto.* [v] *consectarium.* [w] *intuitus quidam connatus.* [x] *sua sensa.*

6. Now, although *time*, posited in itself and absolutely, would be an imaginary being, yet, in so far as it belongs to the immutable law of sensible things[y] as such, it is in the highest degree true. And it is a condition, extending to infinity, of intuitive representation[z] for all possible objects of the senses. For since simultaneous things as such cannot come before the senses except with the help of time, and since changes can only be thought by means of time, it is clear that this concept contains the universal form of phenomena. Hence, it is clear that all observable events in the world, all motions and all internal changes necessarily accord with the axioms which can be known about time and which, in part, I have already expounded. For *it is only under these conditions that they can be objects of the senses and can be co-ordinated with each other*. It is, therefore, contradictory to wish to arm reason against the first postulates of pure time, for example, continuity, *etc.*, for they are the consequences of laws which are more primary and more fundamental than anything else.[a] And reason itself, in using the principle of contradiction, cannot dispense with this concept. To that extent, therefore, the concept of time is fundamental and originary.[b]

2:402

7. Time, therefore, is an absolutely first *formal principle of the sensible world*. For all things which are in any way sensible can only be thought as either simultaneous or as placed after each other, and, thus, as enfolded, as it were, by a period of one single time, and as related to one another by a determinate position in that time. Thus, there of necessity arises as a result of this concept, which is primary in respect of everything sensitive, a formal whole which is not a part of another whole; that is to say, there arises the *phenomenal world*.

§ 15

On space[35]

A. *The concept of space is not abstracted from outer sensations.* For I may only conceive of something as placed outside me by representing it as in a place which is different from the place in which I am myself; and I may only conceive of things outside one another by locating them in different places in space. The possibility, therefore, of outer perceptions as such *presupposes* the concept of space; it does not *create* it. Likewise, too, things which are in space affect the senses, but space itself cannot be derived from the senses.

---

[y] *sensibilium.*   [z] *in infinitum patens intuitivae representationis.*
[a] *quibus nihil prius, nihil antiquius reperitur.*   [b] *primitivus et originarius.*

B. *The concept of space is a singular representation* embracing all things *within itself;* it is not an abstract common concept containing them *under itself.* For what you speak of as *several places* are only parts of the same boundless space related to one another by a fixed position. And you can only conceive to yourself a cubic foot if it be bounded in all directions by the space which surrounds it.

C. *The concept of space is thus a pure intuition,* for it is a singular concept, not one which has been compounded from sensations, although it is the fundamental form of all outer sensation. Indeed, this pure intuition can easily be seen in the axioms of geometry, and in any mental construction of postulates, even of problems. That space does not have more than three dimensions, that between two points there is only one straight line, that from a given point on a plane surface a circle can be described with a given straight line, *etc.* – none of these things can be derived from some

2:403 universal concept of space; they can only be *apprehended* concretely, so to speak, in space itself. Which things in a given space lie in one direction[c] and which things incline in the opposite direction cannot be described discursively nor reduced to characteristic marks of the understanding[d] by any astuteness of the mind. Thus, between solid bodies which are perfectly similar and equal[e] but incongruent,[f] such as the left and right hands (in so far as they are conceived only according to their extension), or spherical triangles from two opposite hemispheres, there is a difference, in virtue of which it is impossible that the limits of their extension should coincide – and that, in spite of the fact that, in respect of everything which may be expressed by means of characteristic marks intelligible to the mind through speech,[g] they could be substituted for one another. It is, therefore, clear that in these cases the difference, namely, the incongruity, can only be apprehended by a certain pure intuition.[36] Hence, geometry employs principles which are not only indubitable and discursive, but which also fall under the gaze of the mind.[h] And the *evidence* in demonstrations (evidence being the clarity of certain cognition, in so far as it is likened to sensory cognition) is not only greatest in geometry; it is the only evidence there is in the pure sciences, and it is the *paradigm* and the means of all *evidence* in the other sciences. For, since geometry contemplates *relations of space* and since the concept of space contains within itself the very form of all sensory intuition, nothing can be clear and distinct[i] in things perceived by outer sense unless it be by the mediation of the same intuition, the contemplation of which is the function of the science of geometry. But geometry does not demonstrate its own universal propositions by thinking an object through a universal concept, as happens in the case of what is

[c] *plaga.* [d] *notas intellectuales.* [e] *similibus atque aequalibus.* [f] *discongruentibus.*
[g] *quanquam per omnia, quae notis menti per sermonem intelligibilis effere licet.*
[h] *sub obtutum mentis cadentibus.* [i] *perspicuum.*

rational; it does so, rather, by placing it before the eyes by means of a singular intuition, as happens in the case of what is sensitive.*

D. *Space is not something objective and real,*[39] nor is it a substance, nor an accident, nor a relation; it is, rather, subjective and ideal; it issues from the nature of the mind in accordance with a stable law as a scheme, so to speak, for co-ordinating everything which is sensed externally.*[n]* Those who defend the reality of space either conceive of it as an *absolute* and boundless *receptacle* of possible things – an opinion which finds favour with most geometers, following the English[40] – or they contend that it is the relation *itself* which obtains between existing things, and which vanishes entirely when the things are taken away, and which can only be thought as being between actual things*[o]* – an opinion which most of our own people, following Leibniz,[41] maintain. As for the first empty fabrication of reason: since it invents an infinite number of true relations without there being any beings which are related to one another, it belongs to the world of fable. But the error into which those who adopt the second opinion fall is much more serious. To be specific, the proponents of the first view only put a slight impediment in the way of certain concepts of reason, or concepts relating to noumena, and which are in any case particularly inaccessible to the understanding, as for example questions about the spiritual world, about omnipresence, *etc.* The proponents of the second view, however, are in headlong conflict with the phenomena themselves, and with the most faithful interpreter of all phenomena, geometry. For, without mentioning the obvious circle in the definition of space in which they are necessarily entangled, they cast geometry down from the summit of certainty, and thrust it back into the rank of those sciences of which the principles are empirical. For if all the properties of space are merely borrowed by experience from outer relations, then there would only be a comparative universality to be found in the axioms of geometry, a universality such as is obtained by induction, that is to say, such as extends no further than observation. Nor would the axioms of geometry possess any necessity apart from that which was in accordance with the estab-

2:404

---

* It is easy to demonstrate that space must necessarily be conceived of as a continuous magnitude, and I shall pass over it here.[37] But the result of this is that the simple in space is not a part but a limit.*[j]* Now, a limit*[k]* in general is that which, in a continuous magnitude, contains the ground of its boundaries.*[l]* A space, which is not the limit of another space, is *complete (solid).*[38] The limit of a solid is a *surface;* the limit of a surface is a *line;* the limit of a line is a *point.* There are, therefore, three sorts of limits in space, just as there are three dimensions. Of these limits, two (surface and line) are themselves spaces. The concept of *a limit* does not enter*[m]* any other magnitude apart from space and time.

[j] terminus.   *[k]* Terminus.
[l] limitum / (Terminus and limes are synonyms and have elsewhere both been translated by 'limit').
[m] ingreditur.   *[n]* omnia omnino externe sensa.   *[o]* nonnisi in actualibus cogitabilem.

lished laws of nature, nor any precision apart from that which was arbitrarily constructed.[p] And we might hope, as happens in empirical matters, one day to discover a space endowed with different fundamental properties, perhaps even a rectilinear figure bounded by two straight lines.

E. Although the *concept of space* as some objective and real being or property be imaginary, nonetheless, *relatively to all sensible things whatsoever*, it is not only a concept which is in the highest degree true, it is also the foundation of all truth in outer sensibility. For things cannot appear to the senses under any aspect[q] at all except by the mediation of the power of the mind which co-ordinates all sensations according to a law which is stable and which is inherent in the nature of the mind. Since, then, nothing at all can be given to the senses unless it conforms with the fundamental axioms of space and its corollaries[r] (as geometry teaches), whatever can be given to the senses will necessarily accord with these axioms even though their principle is only subjective. For it will only accord with itself, and the laws of sensibility will only be the laws of nature, *in so far as nature can come before the senses.*[s] Accordingly, nature is completely subject to the prescriptions of geometry, in respect of all the properties[t] of space which are demonstrated in geometry. And this is so, not on the basis of an invented hypothesis but on the basis of one which has been intuitively given, as the subjective condition of all phenomena, in virtue of which condition alone nature can be revealed to the senses. Assuredly, had not the concept of space been given originally by the nature of the mind (and so given that anyone trying to imagine any relations other than those prescribed by this concept would be striving in vain, for such a person would have been forced to employ this self-same concept to support his own fiction), then the use of geometry in natural philosophy would be far from safe. For one might then doubt whether this very concept of space, which had been derived from experience, would agree sufficiently with nature, since the determinations from which it had been abstracted might perhaps be denied. And, indeed, a suspicion of this kind has even entered the minds of some.[42] Accordingly, *space is* an absolutely first *formal principle of the sensible world,* not only because it is only in virtue of this concept that the objects of the universe can be phenomena but above all for this reason, that by its essence space is nothing if not unique, embracing absolutely all things which are externally sensible;[u] it thus constitutes a principle of *entirety,*[v] that is to say, a principle of a whole which cannot be a part of another whole.

2:405

---

[p] *arbitrario conficta.*   [q] *specie* / A: aspect / B: manner / C: *forma* / H: *Gestalt* / K: species.
[r] *consectariis.*
[s] *quanquam horum principium non sit nisi subiectivum, tamen necessario hisce consentiet, quia eatenus sibimet ipsi consentit, et leges sensualitatis erunt leges naturae, quatenus in sensu cadere potest.*
[t] *affectiones.*   [u] *omnia omnino externe sensibilia.*   [v] *universitatis.*

COROLLARY

These, then, are the two principles of sensitive cognition. They are not, as is the case with the representations of the understanding,[w] general concepts but singular intuitions which are nonetheless pure. In these intuitions, the parts and, in particular, the simple parts do not, as the laws of reason prescribe, contain the ground of the possibility of a compound. But, following the paradigm of sensitive intuition, it is rather the case that *the infinite contains the ground* of each *part* which can be thought, and, ultimately, the ground of the simple, or, rather, of the *limit.*[x] For it is only when both infinite space and infinite time are given that any definite space and time can be specified by *limiting.*[y][43] Neither a point nor a moment can be thought in themselves unless they are conceived of as being in an already given space and time as the limits of that same space and time. Therefore, all the fundamental properties[z] of these concepts lie beyond the limits[a] of reason, and, thus, they cannot in any way be explained by the understanding.[b] Nonetheless, these concepts constitute *the underlying foundations upon which the understanding rests,*[c] when, in accordance with the laws of logic and with the greatest possible certainty, it draws conclusions from the primary data of intuition. Indeed, of these concepts *the one* properly concerns the intuition of an *object,* while the other concerns its *state,* especially its *representative* state. Thus, space is also applied as an image[d] to the concept of *time* itself, representing it by a *line* and its limits[e] (moments) by points.[44] Time, on the other hand, more nearly *approaches* a *universal* and *rational concept,* for it embraces in its relations absolutely all things,[f] namely, space itself and, in addition, the accidents which are not included in the relations of space, such as the thoughts of the mind. Furthermore, whereas time does not dictate laws to reason, it does, nonetheless, *constitute* the main *condition in virtue of which the mind is able to*   2:406 *compare its notions, in accordance with the laws of reason.* Thus, I can only judge what is impossible if I predicate both *A* and *not-A* of the same subject *at the same time.* Above all, if we focus[g] the understanding on experience, we shall see that the relation of cause and caused, at least in the case of external objects, requires relations of space.[45] In the case of all objects, however, whether they be external or internal, it is only with the assistance of the relation of time that the mind can be instructed as to what is earlier and what is later, that is to say, as to what is cause and what is caused.[46] And we can only render the *quantity* of space itself intelligible

---

[w] *intellectualibus.*   [x] *termini.*   [y] *limitando.*   [z] *affectiones primitivae.*

[a] *extra cancellos* / (*cancellus:* lit.: lattice; grille in the law courts; fig: limit, barrier).

[b] *intellectualiter.*   [c] *sunt substrata intellectus.*

[d] *typus* / A: image / B: image / C: *tipo* / H: *Bild* / K: diagram / (*typus:* lit.: bas-relief; surveyor's ground-plan).

[e] *terminos.*   [f] *complectando omnia omnino suis respectibus.*   [g] *advertimus.*

399

by expressing it numerically, having related it to a measure taken as a unity.[47] This number itself is nothing but a multiplicity which is distinctly known by counting, that is to say, by successively adding one to one in a given time.

Finally, the question arises for everyone, as though of its own accord, whether each of the two *concepts* is *innate*[h] or *acquired.* The latter view, indeed, already seems to have been refuted by what has been demonstrated. The former view, however, ought not to be that rashly admitted, for it paves the way for a philosophy of the lazy, a philosophy which, by appealing to a first cause, declares any further enquiry futile. But *each of the concepts has,* without any doubt, *been acquired,* not, indeed, by abstraction from the sensing of objects[i] (for sensation gives the matter and not the form of human cognition), but from the very action of the mind, which coordinates what is sensed by it,[j] doing so in accordance with permanent laws. Each of the concepts is like an immutable image,[k] and, thus, each is to be cognised intuitively. For sensations, while exciting this action of the mind, do not enter into and become part of[l] the intuition. Nor is there anything innate here except the law of the mind, according to which it joins together in a fixed manner the sense-impressions made by the presence of an object.[48]

[h] *connatus.*   [i] *a sensu . . . objectorum . . . abstrahens.*   [j] *sensa sua.*
[k] *typus* / A: *des sortes de types* / B: type / C: *tipi immutabili* / H: *Bild* / K: diagram.   [l] *influunt.*

Section 4. On the principle of the form of the intelligible world

§16

Those who take space and time for some real and absolutely necessary bond,[m] as it were, linking all possible substances and states, do not think that anything further is required in order to understand how a certain originary relation, as the fundamental condition of possible influences and the principle of the essential form of the universe, should belong to a plurality of existing things. For, since whatever things exist are, in their opinion, necessarily somewhere, it appears superfluous to them to enquire why these same things are present to each other in a fixed manner.[n] For this, it seems to them, would be determined in itself by the entirety of space,[o] which includes all things. But, apart from the fact that this concept, as has already been demonstrated, rather concerns the sensitive laws of the subject than the conditions of the objects themselves, even if you were to grant to this concept the greatest possible reality, it would still only signify the intuitively given possibility of universal co-ordination. Accordingly, the following question, which can only be solved by the understanding, remains untouched, namely: *what is the principle upon which this relation of all substances itself rests, and which, when seen intuitively, is called space?* The hinge, then, upon which the question about the principle of the form of the intelligible world turns is this: to explain how it is possible *that a plurality of substances should be in mutual interaction with each other,[p]* and in this way belong to the same whole, which is called a world. We are not here contemplating the world in respect of its matter, that is to say, in respect of the natures of the substances of which it consists, whether they are material or immaterial. We are contemplating the world in respect of its form, that is to say, in respect of how, in general, a connection between a plurality of substances comes to be, and how a totality between them is brought about.[q]

2:407

---

[m] *vinculo.*   [n] *cur sibi certa ratione praesto sint.*   [o] *ex spatii . . . universitate.*   [p] *commercio.*
[q] *quipote generatim inter plures locum habeat nexus et inter omnes totalitatis.*

§17

If a plurality of substances is given, *the principle* of a possible *interaction* between them *does not consist in their existence alone,*[50] but something else is required in addition, by means of which their reciprocal relations may be understood. For they do not necessarily relate to anything else simply in virtue of their subsistence, unless, perhaps, they relate to their cause. But the relation of caused to cause is not interaction but dependence. Therefore, if any interaction should occur between them and outer things, a special ground, which determines this interaction precisely, will be needed.

And it is in this, indeed, that the πρῶτον Ψεῦδος[51] of the theory of physical influence, in the vulgar sense of that term, consists. It rashly assumes, namely, that there is an interaction of substances and transeunt forces, which can be cognised by means of their existence alone. Accordingly, it is not so much a system as indifference to all philosophical system, as to something which is superfluous to the argument. If we free this concept from that blemish, we have a kind of interaction, which is the only one which deserves to be called real, and, in virtue of which, the whole, constituted by the world,[r] deserves to be called real, rather than ideal or imaginary.

§18

A whole consisting of necessary substances[s] is impossible. For the existence of each such substance is fully established without appealing to any dependence on anything else whatsoever, for such dependence does not belong to necessary things at all. And, thus, it is clear that not only does the interaction of substances (that is to say, the reciprocal dependence of their states) not follow from their existence, it cannot belong to them as necessary substances at all.

2:408

§19

Accordingly, a whole consisting of substances[t] is a whole which consists of contingent beings,[u] and the *world, in its own essence, is composed of mere contingent beings.* Furthermore, no necessary substance is connected[v] with the world unless it is connected with it in the way in which a cause is connected with what is caused. It is, accordingly, not connected with the world in the way in which a part is connected with its complementary parts to form a whole[w] (for the connection of constituent parts is one of recipro-

---

[r] *mundi totum.*   [s] *totum e substantiis necessariis.*   [t] *Totum . . . substantiarum.*
[u] *totum contingentium.*   [v] *in nexu.*   [w] *ut pars cum complementis suis ad totum.*

cal dependence, and such dependence does not belong to a necessary being). Therefore, the cause of the world is a being which exists outside the world,^{x} and thus it is not the soul of the world; its presence in the world is not local but virtual.[52]

§20

The substances which constitute the world are beings which derive from another being,^{y} though not from a number of different beings; *they all derive from one being.* For suppose that they are caused by a number of necessary beings; the effects, of which the causes are free from any reciprocal relation, would not be in interaction. Therefore, the UNITY *in the conjunction of substances in the universe is a corollary of the dependence of all substances on one being.*^{z} Hence, the form of the universe is testimony to the cause of its matter, and only *the unique cause of all things taken together*^{a} *is the cause of its entirety,*^{b} and there is no *architect* of the world who is not also, at the same time, its *Creator.*[53]

§21

If there were a number of necessary first causes existing along with the things caused by them, their products^c would be *worlds,* not *a world,* for they would not in any way be connected to the same whole. And, conversely, if there were to be a number of actual worlds existing outside one another, then there would be a number of necessary first causes. But if such were the case, then there would be no interaction between one world and another, nor would there be any interaction between the cause of one world and a world which was caused by another cause.

Thus, a number of actual worlds existing outside one another *is not impossible simply in virtue of the concept itself* (as Wolff wrongly concluded from the notion of a complex or multiplicity, a notion which he thought sufficient for a whole as such).[54] It is impossible in virtue of this condition alone: *that only one necessary cause of all things should exist.* If, indeed, a number of necessary causes were to be admitted, then *it would be possible for there to be a number of worlds,* in the strictest metaphysical sense, *existing outside each other.*[55]

§22

2:409

Granted that the inference from a given world to the unique cause of all its parts is valid, then, if, conversely, the argument proceeded in the same

---

^{x} *extramundanum.* ^{y} *substantiae mundanae sunt entia ab alio.* ^{z} *ab Uno.* ^{a} *universorum.*
^{b} *universitatis.* ^{c} *opificia.*

way from a given cause, which was common to all the parts, to the connection between them and, thus, to the form of the world (although I confess that this conclusion does not seem as clear to me), then the fundamental connection of substances would not be contingent but necessary, for all the substances are *sustained by a common principle.* The harmony arising from their very subsistence, a subsistence founded on their common cause, would accordingly arise in accordance with common rules. Now, I call a harmony of this kind a *generally established* harmony, whereas the harmony which only occurs in virtue of the fact that each individual state of a substance is adapted to the state of another substance would be an *individually^d established harmony.* And the interaction arising from the former harmony would be real and *physical,* whereas that arising from the latter would be ideal and *sympathetic.* Thus all interaction of the substances in the universe is *externally established* (by means of the common cause of them all). And it is either established generally by means of physical influence (in its more correct form) or it is obtained individually^e for the states of each substance. But, in this latter case, interaction between substances is either founded *originarily^f* through the primary constitution of each substance, or it is imposed^g *on the occasion^h* of some change. Of these in turn, the former is called *pre-established harmony*[56] and the latter *occasionalism.*[57] Thus, if as a result of all substances being sustained by one being, the *conjunction of all substances,* in virtue of which they form a unity, were *necessary,* then there would be a universal interaction of substances by means of *physical influence,* and the world would be a real whole. But if not, the interaction would be sympathetic (that is to say, harmony without true interaction), and the world would only be an ideal whole. For myself, indeed, although the former of these alternatives has not been demonstrated, it has nonetheless been rendered fully acceptable for other reasons.

SCHOLIUM

If even a small step beyond the limits of the apodeictic certainty which befits metaphysics were permitted, it would seem worthwhile to investigate certain matters concerning not merely the laws but also the causes of sensitive intuition, which may be known through the *understanding* alone. For, indeed, the human mind is only affected by external things, and the world is only exposed to its view, lying open before it to infinity, in so far^i as the mind itself, together with all other things, is sustained by the same infinite force of one being. Hence, the mind only senses external things in 2:410 virtue of the presence of the same common sustaining cause. Accordingly,

^d *singulariter.* ^e *individualiter.* ^f *originarie.* ^g *impressum.* ^h *occasione.*
^i *mundusque ipsius adspectus non patet in infinitum, nisi.*

space, which is the sensitively cognised universal and necessary condition of the co-presence of all things, can be called PHENOMENAL OMNIPRES-ENCE.*j* (For the cause of the universe is not present to each and every thing simply in virtue of the fact that that cause is in the places in which they are. It is rather the case that places exist, that is to say, that relations of substances are possible, because the cause of the universe is inwardly present to all things.) Furthermore, the possibility of all changes and successions, of which possibility the principle, in so far as it is sensitively cognised, is to be found in the concept of time, presupposes the continued duration*k* of a subject,[58] the opposed states of which follow in succession. But that, of which the states flow, only endures if it is sustained by something else. And, thus, the concept of time, as the concept of some-thing unique, infinite and immutable,* in which all things are and in which all things endure, is the *phenomenal eternity* of the general *cause.l* However, it seems more advisable to keep close to the shore of the cogni-tions granted to us by the modest*m* character of our understanding, rather than put out into the deep sea of such mystical investigations as Malebranche did. His view, the view *namely that we intuit all things in God,* is very close indeed to the one which is expounded here.[59]

---

* It is not moments of time which appear to succeed one another, for, if this were the case, another time would have to be presupposed for the succession of the moments. It is rather the case that actual things seem, as a result of sensitive intuition, to descend, so to speak, through a continuous series of moments.

j OMNIPRAESENTIA PHAENOMENON.   *k* *perduribilitatem.*
l *est causae generalis aeternitas phaenomenon.*   *m* *mediocritatem.*

Section 5. On method in metaphysics concerning what is sensitive[n] and what belongs to the understanding[o]

§23

In all the sciences of which the principles are given intuitively, whether it be by sensory intuition (experience) or by sensitive but pure intuition (the concepts of space, time and number), that is to say, in natural science and mathematics, *use gives the method.* After a science has attained a certain fullness and orderliness,[p] trial and error show what path and what procedure must be pursued if it is to be brought to completion, and made to shine the more purely, once the blemishes both of mistakes and of confused thoughts have been eliminated. It was in exactly this way that grammar, after a richer use of speech had been established, and style, after elegant examples of poetry and oratory had been furnished, provided a foothold[q] for rules and method.[r] But the *use* of the *understanding* in sciences of this kind, the fundamental concepts and axioms of which are given by sensitive intuition, is only the *logical* use of the understanding. That is to say, it is the use by which we simply subordinate cognitions to one another, according to their universality and in conformity with the principle of contradiction, and by which we subordinate phenomena to more general phenomena, and the corollaries of pure intuition to intuitive axioms. But in pure philosophy, such as metaphysics, the *use of the understanding* in dealing with principles is *real;*[60] that is to say, the fundamental concepts of things and of relations, and the axioms themselves, are given in a fundamental fashion by the pure understanding itself; and, since they are not intuitions, they are not immune to error. Here, in pure philosophy, *method precedes all science.* And everything which is attempted before the rules[s] of this method have been properly hammered out and firmly established will appear to have been rashly conceived and to deserve to be relegated to the vain playthings of the mind. For, since it is the right use of reason which here sets up[t] the very principles themselves, and since it is in

2:411

---

[n] *sensitiva.*   [o] *intellectualia.*   [p] *amplitudinem aliquam et concinnitatem.*
[q] *ansam* / (lit: handle).   [r] *disciplinae.*   [s] *praecepta.*   [t] *constituat.*

virtue of the natural character of reason alone*u* that objects and also the axioms, which are to be thought with respect to objects, first become known, the exposition of the laws of pure reason is the very genesis of science; and the distinguishing*v* of these laws from supposititious laws is the criterion of truth. Hence, since the method of this science may not be well known at the present time, apart, that is, from the kind which logic teaches generally to all the sciences, and since the method which is suited to the particular character of metaphysics*w* may be wholly unknown, it is no wonder that those who have devoted themselves to this enquiry, seem, hitherto, to have accomplished scarcely anything at all with their endless rolling of their Sisyphean stones. However, although I have neither the intention nor the opportunity of discoursing here on such a distinguished and extensive theme, I shall, nonetheless, briefly outline the things which constitute no despicable part of this method, namely, *the infection of sensitive cognition by cognition deriving from the understanding,*x* not only in so far as it misleads the unwary in the application of principles, but also in so far as it invents spurious principles themselves in the guise*y* of axioms.

§24

Every method employed by metaphysics, in dealing with what is sensitive and what belongs to the understanding, amounts, in particular, to this prescription: great care must be taken *lest the principles which are native*z* to sensitive cognition transgress their limits, and affect what belongs to the understanding.* For the *predicate* in any judgement which is asserted by the understanding,*a* is the condition, in the absence of which, it is maintained, the subject cannot be thought; the predicate is, thus, a principle of cognising. If the predicate is a sensitive concept it will only be the condition of a possible sensitive cognition; and thus it will, in particular, harmonise with the subject of a judgement, the concept of which is likewise sensitive. But if the predicate were to be applied to a concept of the understanding, such a judgement would only be valid from the point of view of subjective laws. Hence, the predicate may not be predicated and stated objectively of a concept itself of the understanding; it may be predicated *only as the condition, in the absence of which the sensitive cognition of the given concept cannot occur.** But since the illusions*b* of the understanding, produced by the covert

2:412

---

* In distinguishing principles which only assert laws of sensitive cognition from those which also say something about the objects themselves, the use of this criterion is fruitful and easy. For, should the predicate be a concept of the understanding, its relation to the subject of the judgement, however much the subject be sensitively thought, always denotes a characteristic

u *per ipsius indolem solam.*   *v* *distinctio.*   *w* *singulari metaphysicae ingenio.*
x *nempe sensitivae congnitionis cum intellectuali contagium* / (Kant must mean: *nempe intellectualis cognitionis cum sensitiva contagium*).
y *sub specie.*   *z* *domesticos.*   *a* *intellectualiter enuntiato.*   *b* *praestigiae.*

misuse^c of a sensitive concept, which is employed as if it were a characteristic mark deriving from the understanding, can be called (by analogy with the accepted meaning of the term) *a fallacy of subreption*, the confusion of what belongs to the understanding with what is sensitive will be the *metaphysical fallacy of subreption* (an *intellectuated^d phenomenon*, if the barbarous expression may be pardoned). Accordingly, I shall call such a *hybrid* axiom, which tries to pass off^e what is sensitive as if it necessarily belonged to a concept of the understanding, *a subreptic axiom*. And from these spurious axioms, indeed, there have arisen principles which deceive the understanding and which have disastrously permeated the whole of metaphysics. I am, however, of the opinion that this is a question into which we must go more deeply if we are to have a readily available and clearly cognisable criterion for these judgements, a touchstone, so to speak, by which we may distinguish them from genuine judgements. At the same time, should they perchance seem to be firmly rooted in the understanding, we shall also require a certain art of assaying,^f by means of which we shall be able fairly to calculate how much may belong to what is sensitive, and how much to what belongs to the understanding.

§25

The PRINCIPLE OF REDUCTION for any subreptic axiom is, therefore, this: *If of any concept of the understanding whatsoever there is predicated generally anything which belongs to the relations of* SPACE AND TIME, *it must not be asserted objectively; it only denotes the condition, in the absence of which a given* 2:413 *concept would not be sensitively cognisable.* That an axiom of this kind would be spurious and, if not actually false, at least rashly and hazardously asserted, is clear from the fact that, since the subject of the judgement is conceived by the understanding it belongs to the object, whereas the predicate, since it contains determinations of space and time, belongs only to the conditions of sensitive human cognition. This cognition, since it does not necessarily attach to every cognition of the same object, cannot be asserted universally of a given concept of the understanding. But that

mark which applies to the object itself. But *should the predicate be a sensitive concept*, since the laws of sensitive cognition are not conditions of the possibility of things themselves, it will not be valid of the *subject, which is thought by the understanding*, of a judgement, and thus it will not be possible to assert it objectively. Thus, in the case of the well-known popular axiom: *Whatever exists, is somewhere*, since the predicate contains the conditions of sensitive cognition, it will not be possible to assert it generally of the subject of the judgement, namely, of anything whatsoever which *exists*. Accordingly, this formula, if it prescribes objectively, is false. But should the proposition be converted so that the predicate becomes a concept of the understanding, it will turn out to be in the highest degree true, namely: *whatever is somewhere, exists*.

^c *per subornationem.*　　^d *intellectuato.*　　^e *venditat.*　　^f *artem quandam docimasticam.*

the understanding should fall so easily into this fallacy of subreption results from the fact that it is deluded by the authority of a certain other rule which is in the highest degree true. For we rightly assume that *whatever cannot be cognised by any intuition at all is simply not thinkable,* and is, thus, impossible. But since we cannot, by any effort of the mind, nor even by invention, attain any other intuition than that which occurs in accordance with the form of space and time, it comes about that we treat as impossible every intuition whatsoever which is not bound by these laws (leaving aside a pure intuition of the understanding which is exempt from the laws of the senses, such as that which is divine and which Plato calls an idea).⁶¹ And thus it is that we subject all things which are possible to the sensitive axioms of space and time.

§26

But all the illusions of sensitive cognitions, which masquerade under the guise*g* of cognitions of the understanding and from which subreptic axioms arise, can be reduced to three species, of which the following may be taken to be the general formulae:

1. The same sensitive condition, under which alone the *intuition* of an object is possible, is a condition of the *possibility* itself of the *object.*

2. The same sensitive condition, under which alone *it is possible to compare*h *what is given so as to form a concept of the understanding of the object,* is also a condition of the possibility itself of the object.

3. The same sensitive condition, under which alone some *object* met with can be *subsumed under a given concept of the understanding,* is also the condition of the possibility itself of the object.

§27

The subreptic axiom of the FIRST class is: *Whatever is, is somewhere and somewhen.**⁶² But by this spurious principle all beings, even if they were to be cognised by the understanding, are bound in their existence by the

2:414

---

* Space and time are conceived as though they contained *within themselves* all the things which in any way present themselves to the senses. Thus, according to the laws of the human mind, an intuition of an entity is only ever given if that being is contained *in space and time.* This prejudice may be compared with another prejudice which is not strictly speaking a subreptic axiom but rather an imposture of the imagination and which may be expressed in the following general formula: Whatever exists, *space and time are in it;* that is to say, every substance is *extended* and continuously *changed.* For although people whose concepts are rather crude are firmly bound by this law of the imagination they nonetheless have no difficulty in recognising that it only applies to the imagination in its efforts to adumbrate for itself the aspect*i* of things, and that it does not apply to the conditions of existence.

g sub specie. *h conferri.* *i species.*

conditions of space and time. It is on this basis that there come to be bandied about those idle questions about the places in the corporeal universe of immaterial substances (though, just because they are immaterial, there is no sensitive intuition of them, nor any representation of them under such a form), about the seat of the soul, and about other questions of the kind. And since what is sensitive and what derives from the understanding are improperly mixed together, like squares and circles, it often happens that one of the parties to the dispute presents the appearance of someone milking a billy-goat, and the other of someone holding a sieve underneath.[63] But the presence of immaterial things in the corporeal world is a virtual not a local presence (though the latter is improperly but repeatedly asserted to be the case).[64] But space contains the conditions of possible reciprocal actions only in respect of matter. But as to what constitutes the external relations of force in the case of immaterial substances, whether those relations be between the immaterial substances themselves or between immaterial substances and bodies: that is quite beyond the human understanding, as the extremely perspicacious Euler, for the rest a great investigator and judge of phenomena, penetratingly noted (in letters sent to a certain princess of Germany).[65] When one arrives at the concept of a Supreme Being existing outside the world, it is impossible to express the extent of the delusion created by[j] these shadows which flit before the understanding. The *presence* of God is imagined to be *local*, and God is enfolded in the world as if He were contained all at once in infinite space, the intention being to compensate for this limitation, it would seem, by means of this local presence conceived *absolutely*,[k] so to speak, that is to say, conceived as infinite.[66] But it is absolutely impossible to be in several places at the same time, for different places are outside one another. It follows that what is in several places is outside itself and present to itself externally, and that is a contradiction. As for time: having not only exempted it from the laws of sensitive cognition but also transferred it beyond the limits of the world to the being itself which exists outside the world, considering time to be a condition of the existence of this being, they find themselves caught in a labyrinth from which there is no escape. Hence, the absurd questions with which they torment their spirits, for example, why did not God establish the world many centuries earlier?[67] They persuade themselves that it can, indeed, easily be conceived how God sees things which are present, that is to say, actual *at the time at which He is*. But they think it is difficult to understand how He sees in advance things which are to be, that is to say, actual *at a time at which He* 2:415   *is not yet* (as if the existence of a necessary being were to descend

---

[j] *ludificentur*.
[k] *per eminentiam* / A: *eminente* / B: *per eminentiam* / C: *per eminenza* / H: *Vorzugsweise* / K: *eminently*.

successively down through all the moments of imaginary time, and, when a part of His own duration had already been exhausted, He were to see in advance the eternity through which He was still to live, together with the simultaneous events of the world). All these problems vanish like smoke, once the concept of time has been rightly understood.

§28

Prejudices of the SECOND kind conceal themselves to a still greater extent. For they impose on the understanding through the sensitive conditions which constrain the mind if, in certain cases, it wishes to arrive at a concept of the understanding. Of these prejudices, the one affects the cognition of quantity, the other affects the cognition of qualities in general. The first is: *every actual multiplicity can be given numerically*, and thus every magnitude is finite. The second is: *whatever is impossible, contradicts itself.* In each case, although the concept of time does not enter into the concept itself of the predicate, and although it is not considered to be a characteristic mark of the subject, it nonetheless serves as a means for giving form to the concept of the predicate. Thus, as a condition, it affects the concept formed by the understanding[l] of the subject, for it is only with its help that we reach the latter concept.

Accordingly, to take the case of the first prejudice: since every magnitude and every series whatsoever is only cognised distinctly as a result of successive co-ordination, the concept formed by the understanding[m] of a magnitude and a multiplicity arises only with the help of this concept of time, and it never reaches completion unless the synthesis can be achieved in a finite time. Hence it is that an *infinite series* of co-ordinates cannot be comprehended distinctly because of the limits of our understanding. Thus, by the fallacy of subreption, such a series would appear impossible. According to the laws of the pure understanding, namely, any series of caused things has its own *principle;* that is to say, in a series of caused things there is no regress which is without a limit. According to sensible laws, however, any series of co-ordinates has its own specifiable *beginning.* These propositions, of which the latter involves the *measurability* of the series and the former the *dependence* of the whole, are mistakenly supposed to be identical. In the same way, *the argument of the understanding,* which proves that, if there is a substantial compound, then there are principles of composition, that is to say, simples, has added to it something *supposititious.* This addition, which has been covertly drawn[n] from sensitive cognition, maintains, namely, that in such a compound there is no regress in the composition of the parts to infinity; that is to say, that there is a definite number of parts in any compound. And the sense of this latter proposition

---

[l] *conceptum intellectualem.*   [m] *conceptus intellectualis.*   [n] *sobornatum.*

2:416   is certainly not the twin of the former, and it is thus rash to substitute it for the former. Accordingly, that the magnitude of the world is limited (not a maximum), that it acknowledges a principle of itself, that bodies consist of simples – these things can, indeed, be known under the certain sign of reason.*o* But that the universe, in respect of its mass, is mathematically finite, that its past duration*p* can be given according to a measure, that there is a definite number of simples constituting any body whatsoever – these are propositions which openly proclaim their origin in the nature of sensitive cognition. And, however much they may be treated as true in other respects, they suffer nonetheless from the undoubted blemish of their origin.[68]

But as for what concerns the *second subreptic axiom:* it arises from the rash conversion of the principle of contradiction. But the concept of time attaches to this fundamental judgement to the extent that, when contradictory opposites are given *at the same time* about the same thing, there would clearly emerge an impossibility which is asserted as follows: *whatever simultaneously is and is not, is impossible.* Here, since something is predicated by the understanding in a case which has been given in accordance with sensitive laws, the judgement is completely true and in the highest degree self-evident. On the other hand, however, if you were to convert the same axiom so that you were to say: *everything impossible simultaneously is and is not,* or involves a contradiction, you are predicating something generally by means of sensitive cognition about an object of reason. You are thus subjecting a concept of the understanding, which relates to the possible or the impossible, to the conditions of sensitive cognition, namely, to the relations of time. This, indeed, is in the highest degree true for the laws, by which the human understanding is constrained and limited; it cannot, however, in any way be conceded objectively and generally. For understanding *only notices an impossibility* if it is able to notice the simultaneous assertion of opposites about the same thing, that is to say, only when a contradiction occurs. Thus, wherever such a condition is not satisfied, no judgement of impossibility is open to the human understanding. But, by treating the subjective conditions of judging as objective, the conclusion is rashly drawn that, in such a case, no judgement of impossibility is open to any understanding at all, and, accordingly, that *whatever does not involve a contradiction is, therefore, possible.* This is why so many vain fabrications of I know not what *forces* are invented at pleasure. Freed from the obstacle of inconsistency,*q* they burst forth in a horde from any architectonic mind,*r* or, if you prefer, from any mind which inclines to chimaeras. For since a *force* is nothing else but the *relation* of a substance *A* to *something else B* (an accident), as of a ground to that which is grounded, it follows that the possibility of each force *does not rest upon the identity* of

---

o *sub rationis signo . . . certo.*   *p* *aetas ipsius transacta.*   *q* *repugnantia.*   *r* *ingenio architectonico.*

cause and caused, or of substance and accident. And thus it also follows that the impossibility of falsely fabricated forces *does not depend upon contradiction alone.* One may not, therefore, accept any *originary force*[s] as possible unless *it has been given by experience;* nor can its possibility be conceived *a priori* by any perspicacity of the understanding.

2:417

§29

The subreptic axioms of the THIRD species issue from the conditions which are peculiar to the *subject.* From these conditions they are rashly transferred to *objects.* These axioms do not proliferate in virtue of the fact that (as is the case with the axioms of the second class) it is *through what is sensitively given* that the sole way lies open to the concepts of the understanding. They proliferate because[t] it is only with their help that a concept of the understanding can *be applied to a case given* by experience. That is to say, it is only with their help that it is possible to cognise whether something is contained under a fixed concept of the understanding or not. Of this kind is the well-worn maxim, which is maintained in certain schools: *whatever exists contingently, at some time did not exist.*[69] This supposititious principle arises from the proverty of the understanding, which generally clearly sees the *nominal* characteristic marks of contingency or necessity, but rarely the *real* characteristic marks. Hence, whether the opposite of some substance is possible will only be known if *it be established that at some time the substance was not in existence,* for it can scarcely be learned by means of characteristic marks obtained *a priori.* And changes are more reliable witnesses of contingency than contingency is of changeability, so much so that, if we encountered nothing flowing or transitory in the world, it would be with difficulty that any concept of contingency would arise for us. Accordingly, whereas the direct proposition: *whatever at some time was not, is contingent,* is in the highest degree true, the converse of that proposition only indicates the conditions under which it is alone possible for us to determine whether something exists necessarily or contingently. And, thus, if it is to be asserted as a subjective law (which it really is), it ought to be expressed as follows: *if it is not established that there was a time when a certain thing did not exist, the sufficient characteristic mark of its contingency will not be given by a common concept of the understanding.* Finally, this subjective law is tacitly converted into an objective condition, as if there could be no contingency at all without this addition. There then arises a counterfeit and erroneous axiom. For, although this world exists contin-

---

[s] *vim originariam.*

[t] *non ita pullulant, ut . . . sed quia /* (The present translator has accepted the argument of A [*Pléiade I*, p. 1954] who points out that the syntax of this clause ['do not proliferate in such a way that . . . but because . . .'] is out of joint. The first part of the above phrase has accordingly been translated: 'do not proliferate in virtue of the fact that . . .'.)

gently, *it is everlasting,* that is to say, it is simultaneous with every time, so that it would, therefore, be wrong to assert that there had been a time at which it did not exist.

§30

In addition to the subreptic principles, there are also certain other principles, which are closely related to them. They do not, it is true, communicate to a given concept of the understanding any taint of sensible cognition. But the understanding, however, is nonetheless so deluded by them

2:418 that it takes them for arguments which derive from the object, although they only commend themselves to us *in virtue of their harmonising*[u] with the free and extensive use of the understanding, as is appropriate to its particular nature. And thus, like the principles which have been enumerated by us above, they rest on *subjective* grounds, not, it is true, on the laws of sensitive cognition, but on the laws of the cognition which belongs to the understanding itself. In other words, they rest on the conditions under which it seems to the understanding itself easy and practical to deploy its own perspicacity. Let me here insert some mention of these principles by way of a conclusion. As far as I know, they have not yet been distinctly expounded elsewhere. Now, I call *principles of harmony*[v] those rules of judging to which we gladly submit ourselves and to which we cling as to axioms, doing so for the simple reason that *if we abandoned them, our understanding would scarcely be able to make any judgements about a given object at all.* To this group belong the following principles. The FIRST is that in virtue of which we suppose that *all things in the universe take place in accordance with the order of nature.*[70] Epicurus, indeed, professes this principle without any restriction;[71] but all philosophers unanimously profess this principle, admitting but the rarest exceptions, and that only under extreme necessity. We judge in this way, not because we possess such a comprehensive knowledge of the events which take place in the world[w] in accordance with the common laws of nature, nor because we perceive the impossibility or the very slight hypothetical possibility of supernatural events, but rather because, if we abandoned the order of nature,[x] the understanding would have no use at all, and because the hasty appeal to supernatural events is the cushion of a lazy understanding. For this same reason, *comparative miracles,*[y] such as the influence of spirits, are carefully excluded from the explanation of phenomena. For, since their nature is unknown to us, the understanding, to its own detriment, would be turned away from the light of experience, by which alone it has the means to furnish itself with the laws of judging, towards the shadows of species and

---

[u] *per convenientiam.*   [v] *principia convenientiae.*   [w] *mundanorum.*
[x] *si ab ordine naturae discesseris.*   [y] *miracula comparativa.*

414

causes[z] which are unknown to us. The SECOND principle is the well-known *predilection[a] for unity*, which is characteristic of the philosophical mind and from which has issued that widely accepted canon: *principles are not to be multiplied beyond what is absolutely necessary.*[72] We support this principle, not because we clearly see, either by reason or by experience, a causal unity in the world; we are rather driven to search for it by an impulsion of our understanding, which only deems itself to have been successful in the explanation of phenomena if it finds itself able to descend from a single principle to a number of things determined by that ground.[b] The THIRD principle of this kind is: *Nothing material at all comes into being or passes away,*[73] and all the changes which take place in the world concern its form alone. This postulate is, at the urging of the common understanding, spread abroad through all the schools of the philosophers, not because it has been taken as discovered or demonstrated by *a priori* arguments. It is spread because, if you concede that matter itself is in flux   2:419 and transitory, there would be nothing left at all which was stable and enduring, which would further advance the explanation of phenomena in accordance with universal and constant laws, and which would, therefore, further advance the use of the understanding.

Thus much on method, especially as it relates to the distinction between sensitive cognition and that deriving from the understanding. If some day this method is given an exact expression by a more careful investigation, it will serve as a propaedeutic science, and it will be of immense service to all who intend to penetrate the very recesses of metaphysics.

NOTE. Since, in this last section, it is the search for a method which occupies every page, and since the rules, which teach us the true form of arguing about sensitive things, shine with their own light, and do not borrow it from the examples which have been adduced for the sake of illustration, I have only mentioned these examples in passing, so to speak. It is not strange, therefore, that to the majority of people some things there will seem to have been asserted with more temerity than truth, and when some day a more extended treatment will be allowed, they will indubitably demand greater strength of argument.[c] Thus, what I have adduced in §27 on the locality of immaterial things needs explanation, which the reader may, if he please, find in Euler, l.c., vol. II, pp. 49–52.[74] For the soul is not in interaction with the body because it is detained in a certain place in the body; a determinate place in the universe is rather attributed to the soul because it is in reciprocal interaction with a certain body; and when this interaction is interrupted any position[d] it has in space is destroyed. And, thus, its *locality* is *derivative* and is bestowed upon it contingently; it is *not a fundamental* and necessary condition attaching to its existence. For all the things which in themselves cannot be the objects

[z] *ad umbras . . . specierum et causarum.*   [a] *favor.*   [b] *ab eodem principio ad plurima rationata.*
[c] *maius argumentorum robus.*   [d] *positus.*

of the outer senses (such as man possesses), that is to say, *immaterial things,* are altogether exempt from the universal condition of *externally, namely spatially, sensible things.* Hence, the absolute and immediate locality of the soul can be denied, though a hypothetical and mediate locality may be assigned to it.

Factual notes

NEW ELUCIDATION

The editor wishes to acknowledge his indebtedness to J. A. Reuscher for the material which has been derived from his notes to his translation of Kant's *Nova Dilucidatio* (Beck, 1986, pp. 106–9) and incorporated in the following notes: 2, 6, 8, 9, 10, 11, 12, 13, 14, 15, 19, 23, 24, 25, 26, 27, 31, 33, 35, 36, 37, 38, 40, 41, 42, 49, 52, 53, 56, 60, 66. This material has been reprinted by permission of the publisher from Lewis White Beck et al., *Kant's Latin Writings: Translations, Commentaries and Notes* (New York: Peter Lang Publishing, 1986. All rights reserved.), pp. 106–9.

1 The dissertation was defended for Kant by a certain Christoph Abraham Borchard, who composed the dedication, which was printed on the back of the title page of the first edition (published by J. H. Hartung of Königsberg in 1755) of this work, and which has not been included in the text itself in the Academy edition (although it is cited by Lasswitz in his introduction to the work [AK 1:565]). The dedication ran: 'To the Most Illustrious, Most Noble and Most Excellent Lord, Lord Johann von Lehwald, Field Marshall to the August King of the Prussians, Supreme Commander of the Fortresses of Pillau and Memel, Most Worthy Knight of the Celebrated Order of the Black Eagle, Most Vigilant General of the Infantry. To the Incomparable Hero, to his Lord and Most Gracious Patron, are dedicated, with the sentiment of deepest obligation, these pages as proof of his gratitude and loyalty for the many favours received by your most humble servant Christoph Abraham Borchard.'

2 Cf. *Inquiry* (1764), Third Reflection, §§2 & 3 (AK 2:292–6).

3 Cf. *False Subtlety* (1762), §1 (AK 2:47), where Kant distinguishes between affirmation and negation as two fundamental logical forms of judgement. In §2 of that treatise (AK 2:49), he goes on to speak of two basic rules of syllogistic reasoning, one for affirming, and one for negating, syllogisms. Neither of the two basic rules admits of noncircular proof.

4 Throughout his life Leibniz entertained the project of the *ars characteristica*, the art of representing ideas, both simple and complex, so as to display both the internal constitution and structure of ideas and their relationship to each other by means of signs or conventional symbols (Leibniz sometimes employing an arithmetical and sometimes an algebraic notation). A fully developed *ars characteristica* would constitute a perfect logical language transcending all natural languages and embodying a complete system of algorithmic logic. Leibniz envisaged the *ars characteristica* as an organon, analogous to geometry, for facilitating the discovery and extension of material truth. Leibniz's *ars*

417

characteristica influenced, among others, Lambert in his *Neues Organon* (1764) and anticipated Frege's *Begriffschrift* ('Conceptual Notation' [Halle: 1879]). Leibniz's *ars characteristica* was never fully developed; his thoughts on the matter are contained in a variety of papers and essays, of which the most important are: *Dissertation on the Art of Combinations* (1666) (Loemker, pp. 73–84); *On the General Characteristic* (ca.1679) (Loemker, pp. 221–8); *On Universal Synthesis and Analysis, or the Art of Discovery and Judgement* (1679?) (Loemker, pp. 229–34) and *Two Studies in the Logical Calculus* (1679) (Loemker, pp. 235–47). For a later statement of Kant's critical estimate of Leibniz's project, see *Inquiry* (1764), First Reflection, §§2 & 3 (AK 2:278–82).

5   Cf. Aesop, *Fabulae ad litteram digestae*, LXIII; see also La Fontaine, *Fables choisies mises en vers* (1668) (*Livre* V, Fable IX: *Le labourieur et ses enfants*). The final words of the *Fable* sum up its sense: *Mais le père fut sage / De leur montrer avant sa mort / Que le travail est un trésor.*

6   Cf. Boerhaave, *Elementa chimiae* (1724) (Vol. I, p. 119).

7   Kant cites this view of Boerhaave's in *Directions in Space* (1768) (AK 2:377).

8   Cf. Daries, *Introductio in artem inveniendi* (1742). The symbolic equation is also found in Baumgarten, *Metaphysica* (1739), §9 (7th edition: 1779).

9   Cf. *Inaugural Dissertation* (1770), §27 (AK 2:413–15), where Kant maintains that real possibility cannot be inferred from the logical modalities. See also §14 (AK 2:398–402) and §28 (AK 2:415–17). See also *Negative Magnitudes* (1763) (AK 2:165–204).

10 Excluding Wolff, however. Cf. Wolff, *Philosophia prima* (1729), §8.

11 Cf. Descartes, *Principia philosophiae* (1644), (III, §§63–4 and IV, §28). Kant's account of Descartes's views is not entirely accurate.

12 Cf. Wolff, *Philosophia prima* (1729), §56.

13 Cf. Crusius, *Dissertatio de usu et limitibus* (1743), §§II & III et passim.

14 Cf. Wolff, *Philosophia prima* (1729), §309; also *Theologia naturalis* (1736–7), §28; see also Baumgarten, *Metaphysica* (1739), §820 (in the 7th edition: 1779).

15 Kant's critique of the Cartesian ontological proof is restated at greater length in *The Only Possible Argument* (1763) (AK 2:78–9) and more briefly in the *Inquiry* (1764) (AK 2:297).

16 Cf. Wolff, *Philosophia prima* (1729), §303.

17 Kant's proof of the existence of God from the possibility of things is restated at greater length in *The Only Possible Argument* (1763) (AK 2:77–87; see especially AK 2:83) and more briefly in the *Inquiry* (1764) (AK 2:296–7).

18 Cf. *The Only Possible Argument* (1763) (AK 2:83–4) for another statement of the view that there can be only one absolutely necessary being. The same view is also stated in the *Inaugural Dissertation* (1770), §18 (AK 2:407–8).

19 Cf. Wolff, *Philosophia prima* (1729), §303.

20 Kant uses the same example – that of a triangle having three sides – as illustration of the principle of identity in Proposition IV of this section (AK 1:392 footnote).

21 Cf. Descartes, *Meditationes* (1641), *Meditatio* V.

22 See Proposition VI, Scholium (AK 1:394).

23 Cf. Crusius, *Entwurf* (1745), §31.

24 Cf. Crusius, *Entwurf* (1745), §§83 & 380.

25 Cf. Wolff, *Philosophia prima* (1729), §70.

26 Cf. Baumgarten, *Metaphysica* (1739), §20 et passim (7th edition: 1779).

27 Cf. Daries, *Elementa metaphysica* (1743), *Praecognitio*, §6.

28 Cf. Crusius, *Dissertatio de usu et limitibus* (1743); also *Anweisung vernünftig zu leben* (1744), §164; *Weg zur Gewissheit* (1747), §154.

29 Cf. note 27 above.

30 Cf. note 28 above.

31 Cf. Crusius, *Entwurf* (1745), §126 (2nd edition: 1753).

32 The Stoics, while maintaining the freedom and autonomy of the soul, also developed a doctrine of strict determinism or fatalism. Derived from the pre-Socratic philosophers (especially Heraclitus, Democritus, and Leucippus), the doctrine of fate is found in the teachings of the earliest Stoics. The classic statement of Stoic fatalism is found in Chrysippus. To him Gellius attributed the following statement: 'Fate is a certain eternal and inflexible sequence and concatenation of things which snakes its way along and weaves its path through the eternal series of consequences from which it is fashioned and out of which it is constituted' (*Noctes Atticae* ['Attic Nights'], VII, 2). This passage is quoted by Kant later in this discussion (cf. note 35). For further statements of the Stoic view of fate, see Seneca, *De Providentia* (V, viii) and Cicero, *De Fato*, XVII.

33 Kant may have in mind here the fact that Crusius's charge that determinism impairs freedom and morality is a repetition of that against Wolff, which had led to the latter's dismissal from the University of Halle in 1723.

34 Chrysippus of Soli or Tarsus (ca. 280–206 B.C.): Stoic logician who laid the foundations of propositional logic. Cf. *Diogenes Laertius*, VII, 7.

35 This passage is a paraphrase of a passage which is cited by Crusius in his *Dissertatio de usu et limitibus* (1743), and which contains the definition of fate ascribed by Gellius to Chrysippus in the *Noctes Atticae* ('Attic Nights') VII, 2. A translation of the passage is to be found in note 32 above.

36 Cf. Crusius, *Entwurf* (1745), §§125–6 (2nd edition: 1753).

37 Cf. Leibniz, *Théodicée* (1710), §132; cf. Wolff, *Vernünftige Gedancken von Gott, der Welt and der Seele des Menschen* (1719), §575; cf. Baumgarten, *Metaphysica* (1739), §707 (in the 7th edition: 1779).

38 Cf. Crusius, *Entwurf* (1745), §126.

39 Cf. 'Refutation of the Arguments' of the present work (AK 1:406). See also *Dreams* (1766) (AK 2:333 footnote); *Critique of Pure Reason* (1781/1787) A320 / B376 (AK 4:203–4 / AK 3:249–50); also *Anthropology* (1798) (AK 7:135–7) and the *Logic* (1800), Introduction (AK 9:33).

40 Cf. Wolff, *Psychologica empirica* (1732), §933; cf. Baumgarten, *Metaphysica* (1739), §704 (7th edition: 1779). The theory of freedom expounded here by Kant is in part a repetition of and in part an improvement on Wolff's theory in *Vernünftige Gedancken von Gott, der Welt und der Seele des Menschen* (1719), §§511,521, and §970. Kant, in the *Critique of Practical Reason* (1788) (AK 5:95–101) rejects this theory as a 'wretched subterfuge' as sustaining a freedom 'no better than that of a turnspit, which when once wound up also carries out its motions of itself'.

41 Cf. Crusius, *Entwurf* (1745), §269 and §§271–3 (in the 2nd edition: 1753).

42 This is the first of Kant's attempts to demonstrate the general conservation

principle. Later proofs are found in the *Inaugural Dissertation* (1770), §30 (AK 2:417–19) and the *Critique of Pure Reason* (1781/1787) A182–9 / B225–32 (AK 4:124–8 / AK 3:162–6).

43 The smaller elastic body is repelled by the larger while imparting its force to the latter. If one were to add up the absolute quantity of motion, regardless of its direction, of the repelled smaller body and of the moving larger body, a sum would result which exceeds the quantity of the original motion. But the correct calculation involves subtracting the quantities of motion in different directions. The best way of understanding this is to consider the motion of the centre of gravity of the system consisting of both bodies: the quantity of motion of that centre will then be found to obey the conservation principle here formulated by Kant.

44 In the case of an object which is inducing motion in another object which is at rest relative to the first, the second object in turn will be returned to a state of rest by the resistance due to yet another object (or objects), where this resistance equals the original force exerted by the first object.

45 Cf. *On Fire* (1755) (AK 1:383–4).

46 Cf. Hales, *Vegetable Staticks* (1727), Chapter VI of which contains a number of references to experiments with gunpowder. Kant's library contained a German translation of this work. See also Hales, *Attempt to Analyse the Air* (1727).

47 Kant's mention both of the elastic matter of air and igneous matter refers to a view which treats phenomena such as fire or heat and magnetic and electric charges as 'subtle matters' or as substances, a view which he holds himself and discusses in *On Fire* (1755), Propositions I–V (AK 1:371–5) and Proposition VIII (AK 1:376–8). See also *Physical Monadology* (1756) with its discussion of an elastic medium in Proposition XIII (AK 1:486).

48 Cf. Leibniz, *Monadologie* (1714), §56, where the case is maintained that, as a result of the connection between all created or finite substances, every single such substance stands in relations which express all others. Therefore, Leibniz maintains, every particular created substance is a perpetual living mirror of the universe. In §57 he observes that each created substance is but a perspective of a single universe, varied according to its point of view which differs for each such substance. In this context, the metaphor of a stronger light stands for the notion of degree of apperception; differences in perspective are, it turns out, differences in degrees of apperception.

49 Baumgarten enunciated the principle of consequence in his *Metaphysica* (1739), §23 (in the 7th edition: 1779).

50 Cf. Proposition XII (AK 1:410–11).

51 Leibniz originated the principle of the identity of indiscernibles. Formulations of the principle are found in *First Truths* (ca. 1680–4), *Discours de la métaphysique* (1686), Chapter IX; and in the *Monadologie* (1714), §9 (cf. Loemker, pp. 267–71, 303–30, and 643–53 respectively).

52 Cf. *Critique of Pure Reason* (1781/1787) A263–6 / B319–22 (AK 4:171–2 / AK 3:216–18); see also A280–2 / B336–8 (AK 4:180–1 / AK 3:226–7).

53 Cf. *A Collection of Papers* (1717). See in particular Leibniz's Paper IV, §3 and Paper V, §21 (Loemker, pp. 687–91 and 696–717 respectively).

54 Cf. notes 51 and 52 above.

55 This principle can be viewed as foreshadowing the Second and Third Analogy of the *Critique of Pure Reason* (1781/1787) A189–215 / B232–62 (AK 3:166–83 / AK 4:128–43).

56 Cf. Wolff, *Philosophia prima* (1729), §§721–2; Baumgarten, *Metaphysica* (1739), §704 (7th edition: 1779).

57 This is the earliest of Kant's many refutations of material idealism. Entirely different arguments are employed in the *Inaugural Dissertation* (1770), §11 (AK 2:397) and the *Critique of Pure Reason* (1787) A366–80 (AK 4:230–8).

58 Cf. Leibniz, *Monadologie* (1714), §78; see also Leibniz's letter to des Bosses of 16 June 1712 (Gerhardt [P], II, 450–2). See also *Inaugural Dissertation*, §22 (AK 2:409).

59 Cf. Crusius, *Weg zur Gewissheit* (1747), §§79–81.

60 Cf. *Inaugural Dissertation* (1770), §§16–22 (AK 2:406–10) for a fuller version of the thesis of Proposition XIII.

61 A similar statement of this Leibnizian view of space is found in *Living Forces* (1747) (AK 1: 23–4) and in *Physical Monadology* (1756), Proposition V, Scholium (AK 1:480), Proposition VI (AK 1:481), and Proposition VII (AK 1:481).

62 On other actual and possible worlds, see *Inaugural Dissertation* (1770), Section IV (AK 2:406–10).

63 Cf. *The Only Possible Argument* (1763) (AK 2:124–7) for a fuller statement of this proof of the existence of God. See also the earlier argument in this dissertation in Proposition VII (AK 1:395–6).

64 The Manichaeans, named after the Persian Mani or Manichaeus (216–276 B.C.), maintained that there were two independent principles, one of good (light) and one of evil (darkness), which were personified by Ormuzd and Ahriman respectively.

65 In his later *Motion and Rest* (1758), Kant accepts the Leibnizian conception of space as constituted by relations between finite substances (AK 2:16). In *Physical Monadology* (1756), Kant defends the view that both the spatial extent and the mass of physical monads in space are functions of forces of repulsion and attraction, with space itself not a substance but an appearance of the external relations of substances. Cf. *Physical Monadology*, especially Proposition VII (AK 1:481–2).

66 Cf. Wolff, *Philosophia rationalis* (1728), especially §558, where physical influence is defined as the transfer of some reality from one substance to another. A theory of physical influence had also been defended by Kant's teacher Martin Knutzen, in his *Commentatio philosophica de commercio mentis et corporis per influxum physicum explicando* ('Philosophical Treatise concerning the Interaction between Mind and Body explained by means of Physical Influence') (1735). See also *Inaugural Dissertation* (1770), §§16–22 (AK 2:406–10).

67 Cf. note 58 above.

68 Cf. Malebranche, *De la recherche de la vérité* (1674–5), (2 vols.), Book VI, Part II, Chapter 3. (Cf. *Oeuvres de Malebranche*, edited by G. Rodis-Lewis [Paris: 1979], Vol. 1, 643–53.)

PHYSICAL MONADOLOGY

The editor wishes to acknowledge his indebtedness to L. W. Beck for the material which has been derived from his notes to his translation of Kant's *Monadologia physica* (Beck, 1986, pp. 133-4) and incorporated in the following notes: 3, 5, 6, 7, 9, 10, 13, 15, 16, 19, 24, 26, 29, 30. This material has been reprinted by permission of the publisher from Lewis White Beck et al., *Kant's Latin Writings: Translations, Commentaries and Notes* (New York: Peter Lang Publishing, 1986. All rights reserved.), pp. 133-4.

1   A good example of the mediation of geometry is provided in Kant's summary found in the preface to the *Universal Natural History* (1755) of the Newtonian world picture, as it applies to the solar system (AK 1:243-6). At one point (AK 1:243), Kant characterises the sun's gravitational influence on the planets as in a manner 'established . . . by geometry'.

2   Cf. Virgil, *Ecloga*, VIII, 26-8: *quid non speremus amantes? / iungetur iam gryphes equis, aeveoque sequenti / cum canibus timidi venient ad pocula damnae* ['for what may we lovers not hope? / Griffins may now with mares mate, and in the age to come / timid deer with hounds shall drink'].

3   For Kant's use of these terms as synonyms, cf. Wolff, *Cosmologia generalis* (1731), §§183-6.

4   Cf. Leibniz, *Monadologie* (1714), §36.

5   The most important philosopher not to accept the principle of sufficient reason was Crusius. Cf. Crusius, *Dissertatio de usu et limitibus* (1743).

6   The proof of this theorem is based on that of Jacques Rohault found in his *Traité de physique* ('Treatise on Physics') (Paris: 1671). The same proof is found in Keill, *Introductio ad veram physicam* (1702), pp. 22-3. Rohault uses his proof to demonstrate the infinite divisibility of *matter*.

7   According to Crusius, physical lines consist of a series of smallest substances; mathematical lines consist of simple points which are, however, purely imaginary, abstract, and physically unreal. Cf. Crusius, *Entwurf* (1745), §§50, 105, and §§115-19.

8   See note 6 above.

9   Cf. Second Antinomy in the *Critique of Pure Reason* (1781/1787) A524 / B551-2 (AK 3:357-8), where Kant distinguishes between 'matter is infinitely divisible' and 'matter consists of an infinite number of parts'. The former is opposed to the teaching of the present work, but it is the latter which he calls the 'dialectical principle of monadology', maintaining that it would be true if appearances were things in themselves. Cf. *Critique of Pure Reason* (1781/1787) A442 / B469-70 (AK 3:306). See also *Metaphysical First Principles* (1786) (AK 4:504-5).

10 This repeats Euler's criticism of monads considered as infinitely small parts of bodies: If monads are extended, however small they may be, they are divisible; but if they are infinitely divisible (i.e., without magnitude), then no composition of them can be extended. Cf. Euler, *Gedancken von den Elementen der Körper* (1746).

11 Rohault used the sort of proof which Kant gives for Proposition III in order to show that bodies, located in space, are infinitely divisible. See note 6 above.

12   Leibniz held that space and time are not substances. In *First Truths* (ca. 1680–4) (Loemker, pp. 267–71) he writes: 'Space, time, extension and motion are not things but well-founded modes of our consideration. Extension, motion, and bodies themselves, in so far as they consist in extension and motion alone, are not substances but true phenomena, like rainbows and parhelia' (Loemker, p. 270).

13   On the internal determination of substance, see the Third Amphiboly of the Concepts of Reflection: The Inner and The Outer: *Critique of Pure Reason* (1781/1787) A265–6 / B321–2 (AK 4:172 / AK 3:217–18). Concerning space and inner determination, see also *New Elucidation* (1755), Proposition XIII, Application (AK 1:415).

14   Cf. *Dreams* (1766) (AK 2:320–1), where Kant distinguishes between 'being in space' and 'filling or occupying space'.

15   Cf. Baumgarten, *Metaphysica* (1739), §223.

16   Cf. Keill, *Introductio ad veram physicam* (1702), p. 4; see also *Epistola in qua leges attractionis aliaque physices principia traduntur* (1708) (in *The Philosophical Transactions of the Royal Society*, XXVI, 97–110).

17   Kant ought to have said, 'why, at *some* given distance'. What he actually says is, mathematically and physically, incorrect.

18   If repulsive force did not decrease over distance, physical monads would permanently and with constant force repel each other at all distances. Repulsive force originates from individual physical monads and spreads outwards. Such force will also at some particular distance be balanced by an attractive force and, in this sense, cease at that distance. If none of this were so, Kant goes on to explain, bodies would not have any 'cohesive structure'. Cf. the Scholium appended to the present discussion.

19   Cf. *Metaphysical First Principles* (1786) (AK 4:517–23), where Kant asserts that proof of the inverse-distance laws of forces is a 'purely mathematical problem with which metaphysics is no longer concerned'.

20   See note 16 above.

21   The volume of a sphere is equal to $4\pi r^3/3$ with r being the radius of the sphere. Hence, given the relation between force and volume which Kant has just been talking about, this particular inverse-ratio law follows.

22   Kant ought to say: 'it will be the spherical surface towards which the attraction is exercised at a given distance'. What he actually says makes no sense, either mathematically or physically.

23   This is the well-known Newtonian inverse-square law of attraction.

24   In the *Critique of Pure Reason* (1781/1787) A173–4 / B215–16 (AK 3:156–7 / AK 4:119–20), Kant discusses differences in degree of forces between qualitatively different bodies of the same extensive magnitude. In the present discussion, he simply assumes that the ratios of the attractive and the repulsive forces are always identical for all qualitatively different kinds of fundamental, simple bodies.

25   See note 24 above.

26   Cf. Newton, *Principia mathematica* (1687), Book III, Proposition VI, especially Corollaries 3 & 4.

27   Cf. Keill, *Introductio ad veram physicam* (1702).

28 Cf. Leibniz, *Hypothesis physica nova* ('A New Physical Hypothesis') (1671) (Gerhardt [P], IV, 177–219).

29 Cf. Descartes, *Principia philosophiae* (1644), Part III, §§90–3.

30 Kant, in arguing against Descartes, is adapting to his own purposes the latter's account of the origin of subtle matters through the attrition and friction of grosser matters. Cf. Descartes, *Principia philosophiae* (1644), Part III, §§46–50.

31 Cf. Kant's account of fire or heat and of magnetic and electric fluids, an account which treats such phenomena as 'subtle matters' or as substances, in *On Fire* (1755), Propositions I–IV (AK 1:371–4) and Propositions VII–VIII (AK 1:376–8).

32 Cf. Proposition X, Scholium (AK 1:485) above.

33 Kant is once more alluding to the doctrine of subtle matters, the *materia medians*. See note 31.

OPTIMISM

The editor wishes to acknowledge his indebtedness to Menzer (AK 2:462) especially for material in notes 11 and 12, and to Tonelli (1959), pp. 198–204 for material in notes 9, 10, 11, and 12.

1 Leibniz developed this doctrine in his *Théodicée* (1710).

2 For the origins of the dispute to which Kant here alludes see the introduction to this translation, pp. lv–lvi.

3 Cf. *The Only Possible Argument* (1763) (AK 2:153).

4 Kant's definition of relative perfection is the same as Wolff's definition of perfection in general. Cf. Wolff, *Philosophia prima* (1730), §503; see also Meier, *Metaphysik* (1755–9), §94.

5 Cf. *The Only Possible Argument* (AK 2:90).

6 Kant's definition of absolute perfection is the same as that offered by Crusius. Cf. Crusius, *Entwurf* (1745), §180; see also Reinhard, *Vergleichung* (1757), pp. 45 & 46.

7 Cf. *Negative Magnitudes* (1763) (AK 2:176).

8 Reinhard's prize-winning essay was published by the Prussian Royal Academy in 1755. Reinhard translated and published his essay at Leipzig in 1757 under the title *Vergleichung*. Kant's library contained a copy of this translation.

9 The view here attacked by Kant is to be found in Reinhard, *Vergleichung* (1757), pp. 62 and 63. Kant's reference to a 'further elucidation' reserved for 'another occasion' is probably an allusion to the development of the idea of negative and positive qualities, which was to appear in *Negative Magnitudes* (1763).

10 The opponents of optimism included Bayle, Le Clerc, Wolff, Daries, and Crusius.

11 The analogy between the concepts of the most perfect world and the greatest number was maintained in Crusius, *Entwurf* (1745), §386, and Reinhard, *Vergleichung* (1757), p. 68.

12 For a statement of precisely this view, cf. Crusius, *Entwurf* (1745), §388, and

Reinhard, *Vergleichung* (1757), p. 83. Kant returns to this issue in *The Only Possible Argument* (AK 2:153).

13   Cf. *The Only Possible Argument* (AK 2:153).

14   Cf. *The Only Possible Argument* (AK 2:153).

15   Kant employed Meier's *Auszug* (1752) as the basis for his lectures on logic. It is this work to which Kant is here alluding.

16   Kant is alluding to Baumgarten's *Metaphysica* (1739). Baumgarten's *Initia* (1760), his chief work on ethics, did not appear until a year after the publication of Kant's *Optimism* (1759).

17   Kant first lectured on physical geography in 1756. The programme of his lectures is found in *West Winds* (1757) (AK 2:1–12). Since no suitable textbook existed on the subject, Kant employed his own notes. Kant's lectures on physical geography were eventually published, with Kant's approval, by Rink in 1802 (AK 9:151–436).

18   Kant probably based his lectures on mathematics and mechanics on two of Wolff's works, both of which were in Kant's library: *Auszug* (1713–15) and *Auszug aus den Anfangs-Gründen* (1749).

FALSE SUBTLETY

The editor wishes to acknowledge his indebtedness to Lasswitz (AK 2:466–7) and Tonelli (1957) for some of the information in the Introduction, and to Ferrari (Alquié, Vol. I, pp. 1495–9) especially for material in notes 1, 22, 25, 30, 32, 34, 35, and 36; to Lasswitz (AK 2:467), especially for material in notes 17 and 41; to Tonelli (1959), pp. 204–9, especially for material in notes 3, 20, 36, and 37; and to Zac, pp. 125–9, especially for material in notes 11, 12, and 13.

1   *Vernunftschluss:* cf. *Logic* (1800), §§56–8 (AK 9:120–1), §§59–80 (AK 9:121–31), and §§85–93 (AK 9:133–6). Kant distinguishes *Vernunftschlüsse* (lit: 'inference of reason') from *Schlüsse der Urtheilskraft* (lit: 'inferences of judgement'); for the latter, cf. *Logic* (1800), §§81–4 (AK 9:131–3).

2   *Merkmal:* cf. *Logic* (1800), Introduction VIII (AK 9:58–61). Kant offers the following definition: 'A characteristic mark is that in a thing which constitutes a part of the knowledge of that thing. . . . Accordingly, all our concepts are characteristic marks, and all thinking is simply representing by means of characteristic marks' (AK 9:58).

3   Cf. Meier, *Auszug* (1752), §§292–3; see also A. F. Hoffmann, *Vernunftlehre* ('Theory of Reason') (Leipzig: 1737), pp. 3 and 4.

4   *Realerklärung:* cf. *Logic* (1800), §106 (AK 9:143). Kant offers the following definition: 'Real definitions [*Sach-Erklärungen oder Real-Definitionen*] are . . . definitions which, in so far as they present the possibility of the object in terms of its internal characteristic marks, are such as to be sufficient for knowledge of the object in respect of its internal determination'. Kant maintains that real definitions of empirical objects are impossible.

5   Cf. J. G. Sulzer, *Analyse de la raison* in *Histoire de l'Académie royale des sciences et belles lettres de Prusse* (Berlin: 1758), p. 438.

6   'The characteristic mark of a characteristic mark is also the characteristic mark of the thing itself.' Cf. *Logic* (1800), §63 (AK 9:123).

7   'That which conflicts with a characteristic mark conflicts with the thing itself.' Cf. *Logic* (1800), §63 (AK 9:123).

8   The full statement of the rule runs: *dictum de omni et nullo* ('that which is said of all and of none'). Cf. *Logic* (1800), §63 (AK 9:123), where Kant offers the following formulation: 'That which belongs to or contradicts the species or kind also belongs to or contradicts all the objects which are contained under that species or kind'. This principle derives from the principle of categorical syllogisms: *nota notae est nota rei ipsius; repugnans notae, repugnat rei ipsius* (cf. notes 6 and 7 above).

9   'That which is said of all'. Cf. note 8 above.

10 'That which is said of none'. Cf. note 8 above.

11 *Unmittelbare Schlüsse:* conversion, subalternation, and contraposition.

12 *logische Umkehrung:* cf. *Logic* (1800), §51 (AK 9:118).

13 *Contraposition:* cf. *Logic* (1800), §54 (AK 9:119).

14 Cf. *Logic* (1800), §65 (AK 9:125).

15 Cf. *Logic* (1800), §65 (AK 9:125).

16 'Mixed syllogism'.

17 As Lasswitz suggests (AK 2:488), the sense of the sentence requires the addition of the clause *wohl jedoch einen vermengten* ('though he would presumably have a mixed syllogism'). Cf. Wille, *Kant-Studien*, VIII, 336.

18 The words 'this syllogism' refer to the syllogism 'Nothing which is perishable . . .' cited above.

19 Cf. *Logic* (1800), §65 (AK 9:125).

20 This view is also stated by C. Thomasius, *Introductio ad philosophiam aulicam* ('Introduction to Court-Philosophy') (Leipzig: 1688), pp. 163, 167–8, and 171, and by Crusius, *Weg zur Gewissheit* (1747), §§330–5.

21 Cf. *Logic* (1800), §69 (AK 9:129), where Kant says: 'The rule of the first figure is that the *major premise* should be a *universal* proposition, and that the *minor premise* should be an *affirmative* proposition.'

22 The syllogism is in BARBARA; the first figure has three other modes: CELARENT, DARII, and FERIO.

23 Cf. *Logic* (1800), §71 (AK 9:127), where Kant says: 'In the second figure the minor premise stands correctly; the major premise must therefore be converted and converted in such a way that it remains universal. This is only possible if it is universally negative. If, however, it is affirmative it must be counterposed. In both cases the conclusion is negative.'

24 'Mixed syllogism'.

25 The syllogism is in CESARE. The method employed by Kant will not work for the only other valid mode of the second figure, namely BAROCO, for the conversion of the major premise yields a particular affirmative proposition and no conclusion can be drawn from two particular premises.

26 Cf. *Logic* (1800), §72 (AK 9:127), where Kant says: 'In the third figure the *major premise* stands correctly: the *minor premise* must, therefore, be converted but converted in such a way that an affirmative proposition results. But this is only possible if the affirmative proposition is *particular;* it follows that the *conclusion* is *particular*'.

27 'By logical conversion'.

28 Kant's syllogism is in the mode of DARAPTI, which is converted into DARII. The method will not work for DISAMIS.

29 Cf. *Logic* (1800), §65 (AK 9:125).

30 This method will not work for BOKARDO: the major premise cannot be converted; the conversion of the minor premise yields a particular proposition and thus no conclusion can be drawn.

31 Cf. *Logic* (1800), §72 (AK 9:128), where Kant says: 'In the fourth figure, if the *major premise* is universal and negative it can be converted simply, and likewise the *minor premise,* if it is particular; the conclusion is therefore negative. If, on the other hand, the *major premise* is universal and affirmative, it can either be converted only *per accidens* or counterposed; the conclusion is, therefore, either particular or negative'.

32 Kant thus admits only syllogisms in the negative modes of the fourth figure, namely, CAMENES, FESAPO, and FRESISON. The positive modes, BRAMANTIP and DIMARIS, are rejected as invalid. Kant's syllogism is in FRESISON.

33 By 'syllogism of the second kind' Kant means an affirmative syllogism.

34 Kant's syllogism is in BRAMANTIP.

35 Kant is alluding to Crusius, *Weg zur Gewissheit* (1747).

36 This view was already stated in C. Thomasius, *Introductio ad philosophiam aulicam* ('Introduction to Court-Philosophy') (Leipzig: 1688), pp. 163, 167-8, and 171, and in Crusius, *Weg zur Gewissheit* (1747), §§330-5.

37 Kant's claim that the doctrine of the four figures of the syllogism was uncritically accepted by everyone is simply not true. Even Aristotle recognised the superiority and primacy of the first figure.

38 Cf. *Logic* (1800), Introduction V and VIII (AK 9:35 and 61-4). The same account of clarity and distinctness is found in Meier, *Auszug* (1752), §§143 and 147.

39 *den ersten Parag:* Kant means §1.

40 Cf. *Logic* (1800), §§88 and 89 (AK 9:134).

41 Kant is referring to Meier, *Versuch* (1749), and stating views similar to those in Reimarus's *Allgemeine Betrachtungen* (1762), §22.

42 'To any subject whatever there belongs a predicate which is identical to the subject itself.'

43 'To no subject whatever does there belong a predicate which contradicts the subject itself.'

44 'The characteristic mark of a characteristic mark is the characteristic mark of the thing itself.' Cf. *Logic* (1800), §63 (AK 9:123).

45 'The opposite of a characteristic mark is opposed to the thing itself.' A slightly different formulation of this principle is presented at the beginning of §2 of this present work (AK 2:49). See also *Logic* (1800), §63 (AK 9:123).

46 Cf. *Inquiry* (1764), Third Reflection, §3 (AK 2:295).

47 Kant is alluding to Leibniz and Wolff who claim that all truths derive from the single principle of contradiction. Kant attacks this view in the *New Elucidation* (1755), Proposition I (AK 1:388 & 389) and in the *Inquiry* (1764), Third Reflection, §3 (AK 2:294).

48 Kant is probably alluding to Crusius. For a brief critique of Crusius's views

on indemonstrable propositions cf. *Inquiry* (1764), Third Reflection, §3 (AK 2:295).

THE ONLY POSSIBLE ARGUMENT

The editor wishes to acknowledge his indebtedness to Menzer (AK 2:470) for some of the information in the Introduction, and to the *Encyclopaedia Britannica*, especially for material in notes 134, 135, and 136; to the *Encyclopaedia Filosofica* for material in note 37; to Menzer (AK 2:471–3), especially for material in notes 18, 19, 20, 46, 49, 52, 53, 56, 57, 66, 77, 78, 85, 94, 95, 100, 119, 131, 140, 141, 146, and to Zac (Alquié, 1986, Vol. I, pp. 1508–29), especially for material in notes 1, 9, 14, 15, 20, 22, 23, 31, 32, 38, 39, 46, 48, 56, 58, 59, 60, and 63.

1   'Do not contemptuously dismiss these gifts of mine, prepared by me for you with faithful care, until you have understood them.' (Lucretius, *De rerum natura*, I, 52 & 53). It has been pointed out that Kant fails to 'complete' the quotation with the two lines which immediately follow: *Nam tibi de summa caeli ratione deumque / Disserere incipiam et rerum primordia pandam . . .'* ('for I am about to expound to you the ultimate nature of the heavens and of the gods, and to lay before your eyes the principles of things').

2   *Demonstration:* cf. *Logic* (1800), Introduction, IX (AK 9: 71), where Kant says: 'A proof which is the ground of mathematical certainty is called a demonstration . . .' The essential elements of any proof whatever are its *matter* and *form*, or the argument (*Beweisgrund*) and its consistency (*Consequenz*). The difference between a demonstration and an argument is thus one of form, and corresponds to the distinction between *Definition* and *Erklärung* (cf. note 4 below). Kant defines the notion of a demonstration in the *Critique of Pure Reason* (1781/1787), A734 / B762 (AK 3:481): 'Only an apodeictic proof, in so far as it is intuitive, can be called a demonstration'. Kant there goes on to maintain that only mathematics can contain proofs which are at once intuitive and apodeictic and thus demonstrations in the strict sense of the term.

3   *Beweisgrund:* the entry in Grimm simply lists the single Latin equivalent, *argumentum,* and cites the title of this present work of Kant as a paradigm of its use. Lewis and Short contrast *argumentum* (which appeals to *facts*) and *ratio* (which appeals to *reasons*). See note 2 above for the distinction between *Beweisgrund* and *Demonstration*.

4   *Definition:* Kant employs the terms *Definition* and *Erklärung* as synonyms in this work. Both terms have been translated by 'definition'. In the *Critique of Pure Reason* (1781/1787) A729 & 730 / B757 & 758 (AK 4:478 & 479), Kant distinguishes the two: only *Definitionen* are strict definitions, for they alone are capable of distinctness and completeness; this latter characteristic they owe to their being the product of synthesis and are thus arbitrary or stipulative (*willkürlich:* 'the product of will and deliberate choice'). Only mathematical concepts are capable of definition in this strict sense. *Erklärungen*, which are the product of analysis, do not admit of this degree of distinctness and completeness. The justification for translating both *Definition* and *Erklärung* by the single English equivalent, in spite of Kant's distinc-

tion, is to be found in the following fact, to which Kant himself draws attention towards the end of the above passage (A730 / B758) (AK 4:479): there is only one native German word (*Erklärung*) for *Exposition, Explikation, Deklaration,* and *Definition,* and hence, says Kant, 'we may relax the strictness of the requirement that philosophical *Erklärungen* be denied the honorific title of *Definitionen*'.

5   The work appeared anonymously in March 1755; it was reviewed that same year and by 1756 Kant's authorship had become publicly known. Very few copies of the book reached the public, however, because the publishers went bankrupt and the entire stock of the firm was seized by the courts. Kant did not prepare a second edition of the work, though he did commission Gensichen to prepare an abbreviated edition of the book. These extracts appeared, with Kant's approval, in April 1791. The Seventh Reflection of the Second Section of the present work (AK 2:137–51) also contains a brief outline of the contents of the work.

6   The full title of the work by Lambert referred to by Kant was: *Kosmologische Briefe über die Einrichtung des Weltbaues;* it was published at Augsburg in 1761, six years after Kant's own work. The same year saw the publication of a second work by Lambert on astronomy: *Insigniores orbitae cometarum proprietates* (Augsburg: 1761). In a letter to Kant, dated 13 November 1765 (AK 10:53), Lambert assures Kant that he had arrived at one of the central ideas of the thesis of the *Universal Natural History* (1755), the wheel-like form of the Milky Way, as early as 1749. This letter also contains an allusion to Wright of Durham.

7   The pagination relates to the original 1763 edition. Kant is referring to the Seventh Reflection of the Second Section (AK 2:137–51).

8   Kant is again referring to the original edition. The errors, and thus the list to which Kant here alludes, were eliminated from later editions.

9   Leibniz, of whom Kant is possibly thinking, held the opposite view. Cf. Leibniz, *Méditations sur la connaissance, la verité et les idées* (1784).

10   Kant makes the same point in his *Inquiry* (1764), First Reflection, §3 and Second Reflection (AK 2:280 & 283). As instances of wholly unanalysable concepts Kant there lists: representation, being next to, being after. As instances of only partially analysable concepts he lists: space, time, the feeling of the sublime, of beauty, of the repulsive, pleasure, displeasure, desire, and revulsion.

11   Cf. *Negative Magnitudes* (1763), Preface (AK 2:167 & 168) and *Inquiry* (1764), First Reflection (AK 2:276–83).

12   'Logical relation'.

13   *Merkmal:* cf. *Logic* (1800), Introduction, VIII (AK 9:58–61) and Note 2 to *False Subtlety* (1762).

14   Cf. *Critique of Pure Reason* (1781/1787) A592–602 / B620–30 (AK 3:397–403) for a discussion of the distinction between the logical and the existential senses of the term 'being'.

15   Cf. *Inquiry* (1764), First Reflection, §3 and Second Reflection (AK 2:280 & 283) and note 10 above.

16   It has been suggested that Kant's account of Spinoza derives from the

misleading article on Spinoza in Bayle's *Dictionnaire historique et critique* (Rotterdam: 1702).

17 For a later and lengthier statement of the thesis that existence is not a real or determining predicate cf. *Critique of Pure Reason* (1781/1787) A592–602 / B620–30 (AK 3:397–403).

18 Cf. Wolff, *Philosophia prima* (1730), §174; also *Vernünftige Gedanken von der Welt* (1720), §14.

19 Cf. Baumgarten, *Metaphysica* (1739), §55 (3rd edition: 1750).

20 Cf. Crusius, *Entwurf* (1745), §§46–8 (2nd edition: 1753).

21 The eternal Jew, *Ahasuerus:* a legendary figure doomed to live until the end of the world for having taunted Jesus on his way to the cross. According to the mediaeval chronicler, Roger of Wendover (in his *Fiores historiarum*), the wandering Jew had been the doorkeeper of Pontius Pilate; he had struck Jesus on his way to crucifixion and urged him to go faster; Jesus had replied: 'I go and you will wait until I return'.

22 Cf. Crusius, *Entwurf* (1745), §§44–8 (2nd edition: 1753).

23 Cf. Leibniz, *Monadologie*, §44.

24 In the *Critique of Pure Reason*, this was to become the transcendental ideal (cf. B385–6 [AK 3:398–9]).

25 Cf. *Inquiry* (1764), First Reflection, §3 (AK 2:280).

26 *Nominal-Erklärung:* cf. *Logic* (1800), §106 (AK 9:143). Kant there employs two terms as synonyms: *Namen-Erklärung* and *Nominal-Erklärung;* elsewhere he also uses a third term: *Worterklärung.* Kant defines nominal definitions as definitions 'which contain the meaning which is arbitrarily [*willkürlich:* 'the product of a deliberate and voluntary choice'] attributed to a certain term [*Namen:* 'name'], and which therefore designate only the logical essence of their object, or which serve merely to distinguish it from other objects'. Kant later adds, in Note 2 (AK 9: 144), that 'empirical objects admit only nominal definitions'.

27 *Realerklärung:* cf. *Logic* (1800), §106 (AK 9:143). Kant there employs two terms as synonyms: *Sach-Erklärung* and *Real-Definition.* Kant defines real definitions as definitions 'which, by displaying the possibility of the object in terms of its inner characteristic marks, are sufficient for knowledge of the object from the point of view of its inner determinations'. Kant later adds, in Note 2 (AK 9: 144), that real definitions 'derive from the essence of the thing, the first ground of its possibility. [They] thus contain that which at all times belongs to the thing – the real essence [*Realwesen*] of the thing. . . . Real definitions must always be sought in the things of morality. . . . There are real definitions in mathematics, for the definition of an arbitrary [*willkürlichen:* 'the product of a deliberate and voluntary choice'] concept is always *real.*'

28 It is not entirely clear to which passage Kant is referring by the words 'the final reflection of this work'. He probably means the Third Section (AK 2:155–63 and especially 156 & 157).

29 Cf. *Logic* (1800), §106 (AK 9:143) and note 26 above.

30 Cf. *Logic* (1800), §106 (AK 9:143–4) and note 27 above.

31 Cf. *Motion and Rest* (1758) (AK 2:23–4), *Physical Monadology* (1756) (AK 1:480–3), and *Negative Magnitudes* (1763) (AK 2:179–80 and 193–5).

32 Cf. *Negative Magnitudes* (1763) (AK 2:282–302).
33 Cf. *Negative Magnitudes* (1763) (AK 2:171–2; 175–6).
34 Cf. *Negative Magnitudes* (1763) (AK 2:171–2; 179–80).
35 Cf. Kant's later critique of the cosmological argument in the *Critique of Pure Reason* (1781/1787) A603–14 / B631–42 (AK 3:403–10).
36 Cf. Kant's discussion of the concept of all-sufficiency at the end of the Eighth Reflection of the Second Section (AK 2:154).
37 The identity of reality and perfection had been maintained by Spinoza (*Ethica* [1677], Book II, Definition 6, and Book IV, Preface), Leibniz (*Quod ens perfectissimum exsistit*), and Wolff (*Theologia naturalis* [1736–7], Volume II, §5).
38 This amounts to a critique of Spinoza's pantheism. See note 16 above.
39 Cf. Wolff, *Philosophia rationalis* (1728), §195.
40 Cf. Kant's later critique of the physico-theological argument in the *Critique of Pure Reason* (1781/1787) A620–30 / B648–58 (AK 3:413–19).
41 Cf. Euclid, *Elements,* Book III, Theorem XXXV: 'If in a circle two straight lines cut one another, the rectangle contained by the segments of the one is equal to the rectangle contained by the segment of the other.'
42 Cf. Euclid, *Elements,* Book III, Theorem XXXVI: 'If a point be taken outside a circle and from it there fall on the circle two straight lines, and if one of them cut the circle and the other touch it, the rectangle contained by the whole of the straight line which cuts the circle and the straight line intercepted on it outside the point and the convex circumference will be equal to the square on the tangent.'
43 Proof that a series of particles sliding down a series of chords from the highest point of a fixed vertical circle will, assuming the absence of friction, all take the same time.

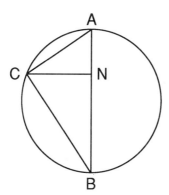

Let ABC be the circle; let AC be one of the chords; let CN be horizontal. Let $AC = s$ and let $ACN = a$. The interval occupied in sliding down AC is

$$\sqrt{\frac{2s}{g \sin a}} \quad \text{seconds}$$

But $AC = AB \sin a$; that is, $s/\sin a = AB = 2r$, the length of the radius being r. Hence, the interval in question is

$$2 \sqrt{\frac{r}{g}}$$ seconds, which is the same for each chord

44 The proof of this claim is as follows: Let A and B be two concentric circles, and let X be the ring formed by A and B. Let r be the radius of the smaller circle, s the radius of the larger circle, and t the tangent which touches B and cuts the circumference of A at its two extremities:

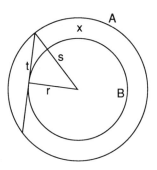

$t^2 + r^2 = s^2$

$t^2 = s^2 - r^2$

Area of inner circle $= \pi r^2$

Area of outer circle $= \pi r^2$

Area of ring $= \pi (s^2 - r^2)$

45 Cf. Kant's *Theory of the Winds* (AK 1:492–4) and the *Physical Geography*, §68 (AK 9:290).

46 Cf. Maupertuis, *Essais de cosmologie* (Leyden: 1751), where what is called the *principe de la moindre quantité d'action* is formulated in the following terms: *dans le choc des corps le mouvement se distribue de manière, que la quantité d'action, que suppose le changement arrive, est la plus petite qu'il soit possible. Dans le repos les corps, qui se tiennent en équilibre, doivent être tellement situés, que s'il leur arrivait quelque petit mouvement, la quantité d'action serait la moindre.* For an account of the universalisation of this principle, see also: *Accord des différentes lois de la nature* (1744). See also *Les lois du mouvement et du repos* (1746).

47 See note 46 above.

48 Maupertuis in his *Essais de Cosmologie* (1751) rejects both the metaphysical proof of God's existence (as lying beyond his competence) and the teleological proof (as involving an illegitimate use of an otherwise sound principle). He bases his proof on the ultimate unity of the laws of nature and, in particular, on his own principle of the least quantity of action. Maupertuis's

proof is strongly reminiscent of some of Kant's own arguments in *The Only Possible Argument* (1763).

49 The precise wording of the title was as follows: *Si la verité des principes de la statique et de la mécanique est nécessaire ou contingent.* The problem was set in 1756 for the 1758 prize, but the lack of suitable submissions led to the prize not being awarded. The problem was set a second time in 1758 for the 1760 prize, but again no satisfactory entries were received, and the prize was never awarded.

50 Kant had already elaborated this thesis in his three essays on earthquakes, composed on the occasion of the 1755 Lisbon earthquake. Cf. *Terrestrial Convulsions* (1756) (AK 1:417–27); *Earthquake* (1756) (AK 1:429–61); *Further Reflection* (1756) (AK 1:463–72); see also *Physical Geography* (1802), Part I, Section 2, §§49 & 51 (AK 9:260–3 & 268–70).

51 Kant is referring to John Ray's *Miscellaneous Discourses* (1692), of which the second edition appeared under the title *Three Physical-Theological Discourses* (1693).

52 Kant is alluding to Whiston's *A New Theory of the Earth* (1696), of which a German translation appeared in 1713.

53 Kant's meaning is not immediately clear. Indeed, Hartenstein, Rosenkranz, and Schiele assume that '110' must be a misprint for '10'. This revision is adopted without comment or explanation by Festugière and Zac. Menzer rightly rejects the emendation (AK 2:475). Kant is not saying, as the emendators must assume, that for every married couple there are 108 people who are unmarried. What he must be saying is that in a random sample of 110 adults there will be two who are married *to each other*. Cf. Johann Peter Süssmilch, *Die göttliche Ordnung* (2nd edition: 1761–2), p. 118 et passim. Menzer informs us (AK 2:472) that Kant has adopted the figure '110' on the basis of Süssmilch's assertion: 'If, however, one is willing to take agricultural villages, such as those in Brandenburg and Finland, the ratio of 1 to 108 up to 115 may be employed.' On p. 121 the figure for Berlin is given as 110, with the comment: 'This agrees almost completely with the villages of Brandenburg.'

54 The Cartesian theory of vortices to account for the orbits of the planets was abandoned as a result of the criticisms made of the theory by Newton who argued in the *Principia mathematica* that the theory was incompatible with the empirical facts. For example, the tails of comets were unaffected by the vortices; vortices would in any case be superfluous if the theory of universal gravitation were true.

55 Cf. *On Fire* (1755) (AK 1:369–84 and especially 376–84). It is Kant's conviction that the *medians materia elastica* fills all space, including the spaces between the atoms, and accounts for the phenomena of heat, electricity, magnetism, and the tensile qualities of metals. See also *Physical Monadology* (1756), Proposition XIII (AK 1:486).

56 Kant is probably alluding to *Des Herrn Joseph Monti Abhandlung vom Schimmel* ('Herr Joseph Monti's Treatise on Mildew') in the *Hamburger Magazin*, vol. XIX (1757), pp. 563–87.

57 Cf. Maupertuis, *Conjectures sur la formation du foetas* published in *Mémoires de*

l'académie royale des sciences (Paris: 1744): *Lorsqu'on mêle de l'argent et de l'esprit de nitre avec du mercure et de l'eau, les parties de ces matières peuvent elles-mêmes s'organiser pour former une végétation si semblable à un arbre qu'on n'a pas pu lui refuser le nom d'Arbre de Diane . . . Depuis la découverte de cette admirable végétation, l'on en a trouvé plusieurs autres; l'une, dont le fer est la base, imite si bien un arbre qu'on y voit non seulement un tronc, des branches et des racines, mais jusqu'à des feuilles et des fruits.*

58 Cf. *Critique of Judgement* (1790), §81 (AK 5:421–4).

59 Cf. *Critique of Judgement* (1790), §81 (AK 5:422), where Kant calls this theory *Occasionalism;* he rejects it as unphilosophical, for each organic being is construed as the product of a miracle.

60 Cf. Buffon, *Histoire naturelle* (1740–1804), Vol. II, pt.ii, p. 71. Buffon offers an account of the formation of the foetus in terms of *moules intérieurs* ('internal moulds or matrices'): the organic molecules contained in the seeds of the two sexes are, once the fluids are mixed, arranged and united by attraction in moulds or matrices; from this the foetus develops. See also Kant's *Critique of Judgement* (1790), §81 (AK 5:422–3). Kant calls this theory *Praestabilism* ('prestabilism') of which he distinguishes two versions: (1) *Evolutionstheorie* ('theory of unfolding'): the theory of individual preformation; (2) *Involutionstheorie* ('theory of enfolding'): better known as the theory of epigenesis: the theory of generic preformation. Each organic being is regarded according to the former theory as the *educt* of its begetter, according to the latter as the *product.*

61 Cf. Buffon, *Histoire naturelle* (1740–1804), Vol. II, pt.ii: *De la reproduction en général,* p. 71.

62 Cf. Maupertuis, *Conjectures sur la formation du foetus* (1744), see note 57 above.

63 Cf. *Critique of Judgement* (1790), §81 (AK 5:421–4).

64 Kant is alluding to the theory of epigenesis according to which the germ or embryo is created entirely new by the procreative power; the theory is opposed to individual preformationism. Cf. *Critique of Judgement* (1790), §81 (AK 5:421–4).

65 Cf. *Critique of Pure Reason* (1781/1787), A623 / B651 (AK 3:415–16).

66 Kant is alluding to John Hill, the author of the celebrated *A General Natural History* (1748–52), who communicated many of his experiments to the *Hamburger Magazin* during the period 1753 to 1758.

67 Kant is reiterating the point made at the end of the Second Reflection of the Second Section (AK 2:103).

68 Kant discusses the same issue at greater length in the preface to the *Universal Natural History* (1755) (AK 1:221–31).

69 Cf. *Physical Geography* (1802), Part I, Section 2, §§42–6 (AK 9:241–56).

70 Cf. *Physical Geography* (1802), Part I, Section 2, §59 (AK 9:276–9).

71 Kant is alluding to Whiston's *A New Theory of the Earth* (1696).

72 Kant's view of Newton is, in this connection, something of an oversimplification. Newton in fact attached considerable theological importance to the necessity for divine intervention (in initiating the order and motions of the planets of the solar system, and preventing, by periodic corrections, its decline into disorder and chaos). Such was also the view of Clarke.

73   Cf. *Universal Natural History* (1755) (AK 1:338).

74   Cf. *Universal Natural History* (1755) (AK 1:261-9).

75   Kant is here stating the central thesis of the *Universal Natural History;* it is restated in the Seventh Reflection of the Second Section of the present work.

76   Cf. *Universal Natural History* (1755), Preface (AK 1:221-8).

77   Cf. Süssmilch, *Die göttliche Ordnung* (1741); in particular, see Chapter V: *Von der Fortpflanzung und Verhältniss des männlichen und weiblichen Geschlechtes* ('Concerning the Propagation of the Male and Female Sex and Their Relation'), §61.

78   Süssmilch, in the second edition of *Die göttliche Ordnung* (1761-2) demolishes his own earlier opinion in the manner indicated by Kant (cf. §§423 and 424) and attempts a new explanation of the phenomenon (cf. §430).

79   Cf. *Critique of Pure Reason* (1781/1787) for a later statement of the same objection to the physico-theological argument: A627-8 / B655-6 (AK 3:416-17).

80   Cf. in particular Kant's proof that 'the necessary order of nature itself points to a Creator of the matter which is so ordered' (AK 2:124-6).

81   The classic statement of the Epicurean doctrine of the *clinamen* or swerve of the atoms is to be found in Lucretius, *De rerum natura*, II, 216-50. Kant reverts to the topic of the difference between his own views and those of Epicurus a little later in the present work (AK 2:147-51). The same topic is also discussed in the preface to the *Universal Natural History* (1755) (AK 1:226-8). The doctrine of the *clinamen* was an invention of Epicurus and is not, as Kant seems to suggest, to be found in Democritus.

82   Aristotle maintained that matter was ungenerated and thus eternal; he rejected the idea that the world was created. Cf. Aristotle, *De caelo*, 279b, 12-280a, 31 and 301b, 31.

83   Kant must be referring to the Eighth Reflection of the Second Section of the present work (AK 2:151-4).

84   Cf. *Physical Geography* (1802), Part I, Section 2, §§42-6 (AK 9:241-8).

85   Kant is alluding to Burnet's *Telluris theoria sacra* (1681-9). The third edition (1702) contains the theory of the origin of mountains. Kant misrepresents Burnet, who explicitly denies that the flood was instituted as a punishment, though he does maintain that God 'adjusts and accommodates the natural world to morality' so that 'the order and arrangement of the former always corresponds to the nature of the latter'. Cf. also Burnet, *The Sacred Theory of the Earth* (1730), Vol. I, Bk. I, Chap. 3, pp. 188-205.

86   Cf. *Physical Geography* (1802), Part I, Section 2, §§47-8 (AK 9:256-60).

87   Cf. *Physical Geography* (1802), Part I, Section 2, §§55-9 (AK 9:276-8).

88   Cf. *Physical Geography* (1802), Part I, Section 2, §59 (AK 9:278-9).

89   Cf. *Physical Geography* (1802), Part I, Section 2, §§58-9 and §74 (AK 9:278 and 297).

90   Cf. *Physical Geography* (1802), Part I, Section 2, §74 (AK 9:297).

91   Cf. *Physical Geography* (1802), Part I, Section 2, §§61 & 74 (AK 9:280 and 296).

92   Maupertuis discovered the *principe de la moindre quantité* and announced its discovery in an important *mémoire* which he read to the Prussian Royal

Academy of Sciences on 15 April 1744. Cf. Maupertuis, *Les lois du mouvement* (1746) and the *Essais de cosmologie* (1751). For a formulation of the law of least action see note 46 above.

93 Kästner, the celebrated mathematician and astronomer who did much to popularise his subjects, was also the author of the *Anfangsgründe der höhern Mechanik* ('First Principles of Advanced Mechanics') (Göttingen: 1758). Kant admired Kästner, and his library contained three of his works.

94 The source of the reference cannot be established.

95 Kant is probably alluding to Borlach of Kosen, author of *Anfangsgründe der angewandten Mathematik* ('First Principles of Applied Mathematics').

96 Cf. *Physical Geography* (1802), Part I, Section 2, §60 (AK 9:279–80).

97 Kant is alluding to a passage in Chapter 1 of Voltaire's *Candide, ou l'optimisme* (1759) where the Leibnizian Pangloss is made to say: *Il est démontré . . . que les choses ne peuvent être autrement: car, tout étant fait pour une fin tout est nécessairement pour la meilleure fin. Remarquez bien que les nez ont été faits pour porter des lunettes, aussi avons-nous des lunettes.* Voltaire discusses teleology in the article *Fin, causes finales* in his *Dictionnaire philosophique* (1764); but Kant cannot be alluding to that, because it was not published until a year after the present work. Kant may, however, have been familiar with Voltaire's article, for it had also appeared in Bayle's *Dictionnaire historique et critique* (Rotterdam: 1695–7).

98 Treash substitutes 'regular' for 'irregular'. This 'revision' is based on a misunderstanding. Kant, having established the thesis that completely regular polygons embrace a greater area than their irregular counterparts, proceeds to maintain an analogous thesis with respect to *irregular* polygons: those which contain an element of regularity embrace a larger area than those which are completely irregular; the greater the regularity, the greater the area embraced.

99 Kant is alluding to Maupertuis's law of least action. Cf. note 46 above.

100 Kant is probably alluding to Ray's *The Wisdom of God* (1691) and Burnet's *Telluris theoria sacra* (1681–9).

101 As had been maintained by Burnet (see note 85 above).

102 As had been maintained by Newton, who had been unable to explain the origin of the constitution and motions of the solar system in purely mechanical terms.

103 Kant is alluding to the theories of epigenesis and unfolding. Cf. *Critique of Judgement* (1790), §81 (AK 5:421–4); see also note 60 above.

104 Kant is quoting from Pope's *Essay on Man* (1733–4), Epistle II, 29–30. The translator has quoted directly from Pope rather than translating Kant's quotation from the German translation of B. H. Brokes (*Versuch vom Menschen*) which appeared in 1740. The German reads: *Geh, schreibe Gottes weiser Ordnung des Regimentes Regeln vor, / Dann kehre wieder in dich selber zuletzt zurück und sei ein Thor* ('Go, prescribe to God's wise order the rules of governance, / then return again in the end into yourself and be a fool').

105 The Seventh Reflection contains, in abbreviated form, the cosmological theory which Kant had developed in his *Universal Natural History* (1755).

106 Kant may possibly be alluding to the star-gods theory of the celestial bodies

which is found in Plato's *Timaeus*, which construes the stars as organic beings. Cf. *Critique of Judgement* (1790), §65 (AK 5:375), where Kant comments on the word *Organisation* in a footnote.

107   Cf. *Universal Natural History* (1755) (AK 1:243 & 247).

108   Cf. *Universal Natural History* (1755) (AK 1:251). This idea was first suggested to Kant by Wright's *An Original Theory* (1750). Kant's acquaintance with this work may have been mediated by the accounts of it which appeared in 1751 in the *Hamburger freyen Urtheilen und Nachrichten*. Lambert, as is apparent from his letter to Kant, dated 13 November 1765 (AK 10:53), was also familiar with the work of Wright of Durham.

109   Cf. *Universal Natural History* (1755) (AK 1:247).

110   Cf. *Universal Natural History* (1755) (AK 1:247-50).

111   Cf. *Universal Natural History* (1755) (AK 1:251).

112   Kant is alluding to Maupertuis, *Discours* (1732). See also *Universal Natural History* (1755) (AK 1:254), where Kant refers to the above work of Maupertuis and to the view there expressed that these 'patches' were 'enormously large heavenly bodies which, because of their flattening out as a result of rotation about their axes, present an elliptical appearance if they are viewed from the side'.

113   Kant is alluding to the Cartesian theory of vortices.

114   Cf. *Universal Natural History* (1755) (AK 1:259-77).

115   Kant is referring to Volume I of Buffon's *Histoire naturelle* (1740-88).

116   Kant is attacking the Newtonian assumption that the present structure of the universe is to be regarded as an ultimate datum directly dependent on the will of God. Cf. Newton, *Opticks* (1704), Query XXXI.

117   Cf. *Critique of Judgement* (1790), §67 (AK 5:377-81).

118   Newton rejected the Cartesian theory of vortices because of its incompatibility with Kepler's laws of planetary motion.

119   Kant is probably alluding to arguments presented by Mairan in his *Dissertation* (1741) and in his *Lettre à Madame du Chatelet* (1741), works to which Kant also refers in his *Living Forces* (1747), §33 (AK 1:45).

120   Cf. *Universal Natural History* (1755) (AK 1:262).

121   Cf. *Universal Natural History* (1755) (AK 1:262-3).

122   Cf. *Universal Natural History* (1755) (AK 1:263).

123   Cf. note 46 above.

124   Cf. *Universal Natural History* (1755) (AK 1:264-5).

125   Cf. *Universal Natural History* (1755) (AK 1:265-7).

126   Cf. *Universal Natural History* (1755) (AK 1:267-9).

127   Cf. *Universal Natural History* (1755) (AK 1:290-304).

128   Cf. *Universal Natural History* (1755) (AK 1:221-8).

129   Cf. *Universal Natural History* (1755) (AK 1:221-8).

130   Cf. note 118 above.

131   Milton describes Limbo as the 'paradise of fools' in *Paradise Lost* (1667), III, 495. Kant has conflated the two ideas in his phrase *Limbus der Eitelkeit*.

132   Cf. *Universal Natural History* (1755) (AK 1:225); also note 35 above.

133   The doctrine of the *clinamen* or spontaneous swerve of the atoms was maintained by Epicurus to account both for the existence of compound

bodies and the possibility of human freedom. Cf. Lucretius, *De rerum natura* II, 216-50.

134 Cf. *Universal Natural History* (1755) (AK 1:290-304). It was Huygens who, in 1655, established the existence of the rings of Saturn (which had been taken earlier for tiny satellites or protuberances ['handles'] attached to the planet). The discovery had been made possible by the superior telescope which he had invented shortly before. Wishing to secure his claim to have been the first to make the discovery of the rings, but to secure further time to verify his hypothesis, he initially published his conclusion in the following enigmatic sequence of letters: *aaaaaaa ccccc d eeeee g h iiiiiii llll mm nnnnnnnnn oooo pp q rr s ttttt uuuuu*, the cryptogram for *Annulo cingitur, tenui, plano, nusquam cohaerente, ad eclipticam inclinato*. ('It is girdled by a thin flat ring, nowhere touching, inclined to the ecliptic.')

135 In fact the rings of Saturn do not occupy the elongated equator of the planet. The plane of the ring is inclined about 27° to the planet's orbit and about 28° to the ecliptic.

136 Kant's estimate is wildly inaccurate. The first determination of the rotation of Saturn was made in 1794 by Herschel, who calculated the period as 10 hours and 16 minutes. The period was correctly calculated in 1876 by Asaph Hall as 10 hours, 14 minutes, and 24 seconds.

137 In 1656, Huygens invented the pendulum clock, employing the principle established by Galileo that the period of swing of a pendulum is independent of the length of the pendulum and is constant. Huygens published the details of his important invention in his *Brevis institutio* (1658) and in the celebrated *Horologium oscillatorium* (1673).

138 Cf. *Optimism* (1759) (AK 2:30-3).

139 Cf. Descartes, *Meditationes* (1641), Meditationes III and IV.

140 Cf. Baumeister, *Institutiones metaphysicae* (1738); also Crusius, *Entwurf* (1745), §235 (2nd edition: 1753).

141 Cf. Daries, *Elementa metaphysica* (1754), §44 (of the part entitled *Elementa theologiae naturalis*); also Baumgarten, *Metaphysica* (1739), §§308-10 and §851 (3rd edition: 1750); also Baumeister, *Institutiones metaphysicae* (1738), §78 et passim.

142 Cf. Crusius, *Dissertatio* (1743).

143 Cf. *Critique of Pure Reason* (1781/1787) A608-9 / B636-7 (AK 3:406-7).

144 Kant is probably alluding to Derham's *Astro-Theology* (1715).

145 Kant is alluding to Nieuwentijdt's *Het regt Gebruik* (1715).

146 Cf. Reimarus, *Die vornehmsten Wahrheiten* (1754).

NEGATIVE MAGNITUDES

The editor wishes to acknowledge his indebtedness to Lasswitz (AK 2:478) for some of the information in the Introduction, and to the *Encyclopaedia Filosofica*, especially for material in note 49; to Ferrari (Alquié, Vol. I, pp. 1503-8), especially for material in notes 1, 6, 7, 29, and 52; to Lasswitz (AK 2:478-9), especially for material in notes 5, 6, 7, 13, 35, 36, and 55 and to D. E. Smith, *History of Mathematics* (Toronto: 1925) for the information contained in notes 10 and 24.

1   *Non liquet:* legal formula expressing the idea 'there is a doubt' or 'the matter is not clear'. Kant, in one of his lectures on logic, alludes to Pyrron's frequent use of this challenge against the dogmatism of the Sophists (AK 24:36).

2   Cf. *Inquiry* (1764) (AK 2:276–83).

3   Cf. *Inquiry* (1764) (AK 2:281).

4   Cf. *Physical Monadology* (1756), Proposition III (AK 1:478–9); also *Inquiry* (1764) (AK 2:287).

5   Kant is alluding to Euler's *Reflexions sur l'espace et le temps* (1748).

6   Kant is alluding to Crusius's *Anleitung* (1749).

7   Crusius wrote no work entitled *Naturlehre* ('Theory of Nature'); Kant is alluding to his *Anleitung* (1749).

8   Newton is discussing the attraction and repulsion of fundamental particles of matter, not of large bodies. Cf. Newton, *Opticks* (1704), Book III, Query XXXI.

9   Cf. Newton, *Opticks* (1704), Book III, Part 1, Query XXXI, where Newton writes: 'And as in algebra, where affirmative quantities vanish and cease, there negative ones begin; so in mechanics, where attraction ceases, there a repulsive virtue ought to succeed'.

10 Negative numbers were first employed by the Hindus to represent debts. Brahmagupta (ca. 628 A.D.) was the first mathematician to employ negative numbers. The Arabs borrowed the concept from the Hindus. The first European mathematician to employ negative numbers was the German mathematician Michael Stifel (ca. 1487–1567), the author of the celebrated *Arithmetica integra* who was responsible for popularising the 'German' symbols ('+' and '−') at the expense of the 'Italian' ('p' and 'm'). Stifel did not regard negative numbers as numbers in the full sense, calling them *numeri absurdi*. This was also the view of Pascal, Cardano, Newton, Arnauld and, to a certain extent, Leibniz, too. The problem of the sense in which negative numbers were numbers at all preoccupied mathematicians throughout the sixteenth and seventeenth centuries.

11 Cf. Kästner: *Anfangsgründe der Arithmetik* (1758), where the relativity of the negative is emphasised in the following definition: 'Opposed magnitudes are magnitudes which are such that, when considered under such conditions, the one diminishes the other'.

12 Kant is probably alluding to Kästner's *Anfangsgründe der Arithmetik* (1758), the first volume of his great four-volume *Anfangsgründe der Mathematik* (1758–69).

13 Kant may be referring to Crusius's *Weg zur Gewissheit* (1747), §7.

14 'A negative nothing which is incapable of being represented'.

15 'Capable of being thought'.

16 'Capable of being thought'.

17 'Capable of being represented'.

18 'A negative nothing which is capable of being represented'.

19 'Reality'.

20 'Negation'.

21 'A negative nothing'.

439

22 The '+' and '−' symbolism was introduced by the German mathematician Michael Stifel; it replaced the 'Italian' 'p' and 'm' symbolism. Cf. note 10 above.

23 Kant discusses *potential opposition* in the Third Section of the present work (AK 2:193–4).

24 Descartes, although in part accepting negative numbers, regarded negative roots of equations as false on the grounds that they represent numbers less than nothing. Presumably, mathematicians who denied that negative numbers were real or true numbers (Stifel, Cardano, Vieta), or that subtracting from 0 was an absurdity (Pascal), or that negative numbers were fictions or mere symbols (Leibniz), did so because negative numbers and negative magnitudes were taken to be less than nothing and thus themselves nothing at all. It is worth pointing out that Wallis (1616–1703) maintained in his *Arithmetica infinitorum* (1655) that negative numbers were *larger* than infinity, arguing that, because the ratio a/0 (where 'a' is positive) is infinite, it follows that if 'a' is replaced by a negative number, the ratio must be greater than infinity. Wallis was therefore committed to the view that negative numbers were not less than 0. This was also the view of Euler.

25 '(Defect, absence)'.

26 Cf. *Physical Monadology* (1756), Proposition VIII (AK 1:482–3).

27 Cf. Kant's discussions of impenetrability in *Physical Monadology* (1756), Propositions VIII and IX (AK 1:482–3); *Inquiry* (1764) (AK 2:286–8); *Metaphysical First Principles* (1786) (AK 4:500–2). It is not *clear* whether Kant's words 'in another treatise' refer to a work which was never published or, which seems unlikely, to the *Inquiry* (1764).

28 Kant is referring to Maupertuis's *Essai de philosophie morale* (1749). In the second chapter, entitled *Que dans la vie ordinaire la somme des maux surpasse celle des biens*, Maupertuis attempts to quantify pleasure and pain, and to construct a hedonistic calculus.

29 Cf. Descartes, *Meditationes* (1641), Meditation III: '*les idées que j'ai du froid et de la chaleur sont si peu claires et si peu distinctes, que par leur moyen je ne puis pas discerner si le froid est seulement une privation de la chaleur, ou le chaleur une privation du froid*'.

30 Kant is referring to van Musschenbroek's *Epitome* (1726); cf. in particular Chapter XXVI, *De Igne*, §§788–93.

31 Cf. *On Fire* (1755), Propositions VII and VIII (AK 1:376–8).

32 Cf. *On Fire* (1755), Propositions I–IV (AK 1:371–4) and Propositions VII and VIII (AK 1:376–7); also *Physical Monadology* (1756), Proposition XIII (AK 1:486). Kant maintained that the *medians materia elastica* filled all space, including the spaces between the atoms; it was regarded by Kant as explaining the phenomena of heat, electricity, magnetism, and the tensile properties of metals.

33 Kant is alluding to two works by Aepinus: *Sermo academicus* (1759) and the important *Tentamen* (1759). The latter is generally regarded as being one of the most important contributions to the development of the theory of electricity.

34 Kant is referring to Bel's monumental *Notitia Hungariae* (1735–42).

35 Cf. Boerhaave, *De mercurio experimenta* in *Philosophical Transactions of the Royal Society*, Nos. 430, 443, and 444, (London: 1733 and 1736).

36 Cf. Jacobi, *Sammlung einiger Erfahrungen* in *Hamburger Magazin*, vol. XXI, 1758.

37 Cf. note 32 above.

38 Cf. note 32 above.

39 *Mittelmaterie:* the German synonym for *materia medians*. Cf. note 31 above.

40 Kant is alluding to the fact that Galileo, in about 1604, engaged in research which established the principle that falling bodies obey the law of uniformly accelerated motion.

41 Huygens, as a result of his astronomical researches culminating in the discovery of the rings of Saturn, had come to recognise the need for a more accurate method of measuring time. Employing the principle established by Galileo (that the period of oscillation of a pendulum is independent of its length and is constant), Huygens invented the pendulum clock in 1656. The principles of this important invention are contained in his *Brevis institutio* (1658) and in his celebrated *Horologium oscillatorium* (1673).

42 On the death of Galileo (for whom he had acted as amanuensis) Toricelli was appointed Galileo's successor at the Florentine Academy. A year later, in 1643, Toricelli discovered the principle of the barometer (which was known as the Toricellean Tube) and thus the possibility of a vacuum in nature.

43 The German physicist and engineer, Guericke, invented the air pump in 1650 (the result of his attempts to create a vacuum). Its efficacy in creating a vacuum was spectacularly demonstrated before the Emperor Ferdinand at Regensburg in 1654: teams of horses were unable to drag apart the two halves of a sphere (the so-called Magdeburg hemispheres) from which the air had been extracted. Guericke published his findings in his *Experimenta nova* (1672).

44 In addition to his two monumental achievements in the fields of mathematics and the theory of gravitation, Newton's third great achievement was in the field of optics. Newton demonstrated that white light was a mixture of lights of different colours and that the prism was able to separate them because each colour had its own degree of refraction. Newton described this discovery, which he made in 1667, as 'in my judgement the oddest, if not the most considerable detection, which has been made in the operations of nature'. Newton's theory of light is contained in his *Opticks* (1704).

45 Kant is referring to Reimarus, *Vernunftlehre* (1756), §35.

46 Cf. *On Fire* (1755), Proposition XI (AK 1:383–4).

47 'If one adds together those forces or bodies which tend in the same direction and subtracts those which tend in the opposite direction, the quantity of motion is not changed by their reciprocal action (collision, pressure, attraction).'

48 The thesis of this paragraph is developed in detail by Kant in his *Living Forces* (1747) (AK 1:1–181). Kant there attempts to mediate in a dispute which had arisen between Descartes and Leibniz concerning the calculation of force. Neither Descartes, nor Leibniz, nor Kant arrived at the correct solution. The correct account of the matter had in principle been established

by Boscovich in 1745, and the correct mathematical formula was to be published by D'Alembert in the 1758 edition of his *Traité de dynamique*.

49 The identity of reality and perfection had been maintained by Spinoza in his *Ethica* (1677), Book II, Definition 6, and Book IV, Preface; by Leibniz in his *Quod ens perfectissimum exsistit* and by Wolff in his *Theologia naturalis* (1736–7), Vol. II, §5.

50 Cf. *Physical Monadology* (1756), Propositions VI–VIII (AK 1:481–3).

51 Cf. *On Fire* (1755), Proposition XII (AK 1:383–4); also *New Elucidation* (1755), Proposition X: Elucidation (AK 1 407–8).

52 Cf. Leibniz, *Monadologie*, §60.

53 Kant is referring to the passage which is numbered '2' (AK 2:193); the proposition to which Kant is alluding is the italicised paragraph (AK 2:194).

54 Kant is alluding to the story that Simonides, having been asked by King Hieron for his opinion of God, postponed giving his answer, first by one day, then two, and then by four, and so on. Hieron, surprised by the ever lengthening delays, asked Simonides for an explanation. His reply was supposed to have been: 'The more I meditate on the matter, the more difficult and obscure it becomes'.

55 Cf. Crusius, *Entwurf* (1745), §34 et seq. (2nd edition: 1753); also *Weg zur Gewissheit* (1747), §140 et seq.

56 The 'one day' turned out to be far in the future with the eventual appearance in 1781 of the *Critique of Pure Reason*.

INQUIRY

The editor wishes to acknowledge his indebtedness to Menzer (AK 2:492–4) for information in the Introduction, and to Ferrari (Alquié, Vol. I, pp. 1499–1503) for information in note 10; to Fichant, pp. 77–9, especially for information in notes 10, 11, 16, 23, 24, 25, 32, 34, 58, 63, and 71; and to Lasswitz (AK 2:494–5), especially for information in notes 11, 27, and 51.

1 'But to a wise spirit these small clues will be sufficient: by their means you can safely come to know the rest.' Lucretius, *De rerum natura*, I, 402–3. The regulations governing the prize-essay competition required that all entries be submitted anonymously and identified only by a motto. Each entry was to be accompanied by a sealed envelope bearing on the outside the motto and containing within the name of the competitor. Kant's motto was the above quotation from Lucretius.

2 Cf. *On Fire* (1755) (AK 1:371), where Kant speaks of 'the thread of experience and geometry, without which the way out of the labyrinth of nature can hardly be found'. Kant's *Universal Natural History* (1755) is a spectacular instance of the application of this double method.

3 Throughout the *Inquiry* (1764) Kant employs the terms *Definition* and *Erklärung* as synonyms, and both words have been translated by the single English equivalent 'definition'. For a justification of this translation the reader is referred to note 6 to the Glossary and to note 4 to *The Only Possible Argument* (1763) above. All occurrences of *Erklärung* are registered by a linguistic note. For a systematic account of Kant's theory of definition cf.

Logic (1800), §§99–109 (AK 9:140–5); see also *Critique of Pure Reason* (1781/1787) A729–30 / B757–8 (AK 3:477–80).

4 Throughout Kant's discussion it is important to bear the following distinctions in mind: (1) obscure representations (*dunkle Vorstellungen*): representations of which we are not conscious (cf. *Logic* [1800], Introduction V [AK 9:33] and *Dreams* (1766) [AK 2:33]); (2) clear representations (*klare Vorstellungen*): representations of which we are conscious and which we can distinguish from other representations (cf. *Logic* [1800], Introduction V and VIII [AK 9:33 and 61–2] and *Critique of Pure Reason* [1781/1787] B414 [AK 3:27]); (3) distinct representations (*deutliche Vorstellungen*): representations in the case of which the characteristic marks (*Merkmale*) and their relations are clearly apprehended (cf. *Logic* [1800], Introduction V and VIII [AK 9:34–5 and 61–4]; *False Subtlety* [1762], §6 [AK 2:58–9] and *Anthropology* [1798], I, §6 [AK 7:137–8]); (4) complete representations (*ausführliche Vorstellungen*): representations in the case of which *all* their characteristic marks and all the details of their relations are clearly and distinctly apprehended (cf. *Logic* [1800], Introduction VIII [AK 9:62] and *Critique of Pure Reason* [1781/ 1787], B755 [AK 3:477]). Kant claims that rendering *objects* distinct is the function of synthesis, whereas rendering *concepts* distinct is the task of analysis. Likewise, synthesis *creates* a distinct concept, whereas analysis *renders* a concept *distinct* (cf. *Logic* [1800], Introduction VIII [AK 9:64]).

5 For an account of Kant's conception of synthetic definition cf. *Logic* (1800), §102 (AK 9:141).

6 Cf. *Logic* (1800), Introduction VIII (AK 9:62); also *Critique of Pure Reason* (1781/1787) B755 (AK 3:477).

7 Cf. *Logic* (1800), Introduction VIII (AK 9:60).

8 For an account of Kant's conception of analytic definition cf. *Logic* (1800), §104 (AK 3:142).

9 Cf. Baumgarten, *Metaphysica* (1739), §402; also Wolff, *Vernünftige Gedanken von Gott* (1719), §896; also *Dreams* (1766) (AK 2:320).

10 Cf. Leibniz, *Principes de la nature et de la grace;* also *Monadologie*, §§20 and 24; also Baumgarten, *Metaphysica* (1739), §401.

11 Cf. Wolff, *Elementa matheseos universae* (1717): see in particular the following passage from the preface to Volume I (p. 96): 'Hence, I shall define things which are not normally defined, and I shall everywhere demonstrate things which are presupposed by others without proof . . . Euclid and all those who have hitherto followed his example have demonstrated everything by means of the principle of congruency alone. Since, however, the most learned Leibniz imparted the concept of similarity to me and showed me that it has an extensive application in geometry, and since I have meditated upon it and come to recognise its importance, I have not hesitated at all to introduce the principle of similarity into geometry. You will, therefore, understand many things which are demonstrated with the greatest ease by means of that principle which are not normally demonstrated, except indirectly, in a different fashion by means of the principle of congruency.'

12 For an entirely opposed view, cf. Leibniz's *On Analysis Situs* (Loemker, p. 255), where the importance is emphasised of a distinct definition of *similarity*

(and thus of *form* or *quality* as distinct from *quantity*) for the practice of geometry. Leibniz's definition amounts to this: 'we call two presented figures similar if nothing can be observed in the one, viewed by itself, which cannot be equally observed in the other'.

13 Kant is distinguishing between algebra (the general arithmetic of *indeterminate* magnitudes) and arithmetic proper (the arithmetic of numbers, where the relation of magnitude to unity is *determinate*). In the *Critique of Pure Reason* (1781/1787) A717 / B745 (AK 3:453–4) algebra and arithmetic are presented in terms of the distinction between *Grössen* or *quanta* ('magnitudes') and *blosse Grösse* or *quantitas* ('mere magnitude'). Cf. *Critique of Judgement* (1790), §§25–7 (AK 5:248–60).

14 Cf. *Logic* (1800), §16 (AK 9:99).

15 This is a partial description of and a trenchant attack on the Leibnizian *ars characteristica*. Cf. Kant's sceptical estimate of the Leibnizian project in the *New Elucidation* (1755), Proposition II, Scholium (AK 1:389–90).

16 Kant has borrowed this example from J. Keil's *Introductio ad veram physicam* (1702); see in particular *Lectio III*. Kant employs the same example and develops it in greater detail in the *Physical Monadology* (1756), Proposition III (AK 1:478). Keil's proof is itself based on that of Jacques Rohault, *Traité de physique* (Paris: 1671). It is there employed, however, to prove the infinite divisibility of *matter*.

17 Cf. *Physical Monadology* (1756), Proposition II (AK 1:477).

18 Kant seems to be suggesting that the Leibnizian *ars characteristica* would be incapable of handling a case such as that described. Cf. note 15 above.

19 Cf. *Logic* (1800), §16 (AK 9:99).

20 Kant insists on the same point in *The Only Possible Argument* (1763) (AK 2:70 and 73–4).

21 Kant addresses himself to the same problem in the preface to *Negative Magnitudes* (AK 2:168).

22 Cf. *Physical Monadology* (1756), Proposition IV, Scholium (AK 1:479), Proposition V, Scholium (AK 1:480), and Proposition VII (AK 1:481). See also *Dreams* (1766) (AK 2:323–4).

23 Kant's view of the relation between philosophy and mathematics is, in respect of this *fourth* contrast, modified in the *Critique of Pure Reason* (1781/1787) B742–3 (AK 3:469–70).

24 In the *Critique of Pure Reason* (1781/1787) B 742–3 (AK 3:469–70) Kant draws attention to the fact that mathematics may also be concerned with qualities (for example, the topological qualities of lines and surfaces) and philosophy with quantities (for example, totality and infinity). The crucial difference between the two disciplines is primarily one of method.

25 Leibniz expressed exactly the opposite view in the Preface to the *Essais de théodicée* (1710) and also in the *Nouveaux essais* (1765), Book IV, Chapter 3, §19, where Leibniz writes: *Les figures géometriques paraissent plus simples que les choses morales; mais elles ne le sont pas parce que le continu enveloppe l'infini.*

26 The theme of this First Reflection is discussed in almost the same terms in the *Critique of Pure Reason* (1781/1787) B740–60 (AK 3:468–80).

27 Kant is alluding to a passage in the Introduction to Warburton's *Julian* (1750).

28 Kant briefly discusses this same theme in the preface to *Negative Magnitudes* (AK 2:167–9).

29 Saint Augustine, *Confessions*, XI, 14: *Quid est ergo tempus? Si nemo ex me quaerat, scio; si quaerenti explicare velim, nescio* ('What, therefore, is time? If no one asks me what it is, I know; if I wish to explain what it is to someone who has asked me about it, I do not know what it is').

30 Cf. *Logic* (1800), §106 (AK 9:143–4).

31 Cf. *Logic* (1800), §106 (AK 9:143–4).

32 Kant employs exactly the same argument with exactly the same examples in the *False Subtlety* (1763) (AK 2:59–60). Kant's argument is directed against the thesis maintained by Meier in his *Versuch eines Lehrgebäudes* (1749) (see in particular §23 et seq. and §40 et seq.).

33 Cf. note 31 above.

34 Cf. Newton, *Principia mathematica* (1687), Book III, (*Regulae philosophandi:* especially *regulae* III and IV, and the final Scholium); also *Opticks* (1704), Query XXXI. See also Keil, *Introductio ad veram physicam (1702), (Lectio I: De methodo philosophandi)*.

35 Cf. *False Subtlety* (1762) (AK 2:60).

36 The passage referred to is to be found at AK 1:279.

37 Cf. *Logic* (1800), §6 (AK 9:94–5).

38 A fuller proof is found in *Physical Monadology* (1756), Propositions I and II (AK 1:477). Later, Kant was to argue the infinite divisibility of matter *qua* phenomenon: cf. *Metaphysical First Principles* (1786), Chapter 2, Theorem 4 and Note 1 (AK 4:503–5).

39 Cf. *Physical Monadology* (1756), Proposition III (AK 1:478–9).

40 Cf. *Physical Monadology* (1756), Proposition V (AK 1:480).

41 A more detailed and systematic account of the distinction between *im Raum sein* ('being in space') and *einen Raum einnehmen* ('occupying a space') and their respective relations to *das Durchdringen* ('penetrate'), *das Widerstehen* ('resist'), *Widerstand* ('resistance'), and *Undurchdringlichkeit* ('impenetrability') is found in *Physical Monadology* (1756), Proposition V (AK 1:480). A related distinction, that between *Wirksamkeit im Raum* ('exercising an effect in space' – something which does not necessarily involve the presence of a corporeal body) and *Erfüllung des Raumes* ('filling of space' – something which is only possible in virtue of resistance and impenetrability) is drawn in *Dreams* (1766) (AK 2:323–4). The distinction between *einnehmen* ('occupy') and *erfüllen* ('fill') is later taken up by Kant in the *Metaphysical First Principles* (1786), Chapter 2, Definition I and Note (AK 4:496–7); see also Theorem 1, Proof and Note (AK 4:497–8).

42 Cf. *Physical Monadology* (1756), Proposition VIII (AK 1:482–3); also *Metaphysical First Principles* (1786), Chapter 2, Theorem 2, Proof and Definition 4 (AK 4:499 and 501–2).

43 Cf. *Physical Monadology* (1756), Proposition VIII (AK 1:482); also *Negative Magnitudes* (AK 2:179–80).

44 Cf. *Physical Monadology* (1756), Proposition V (AK 1:480).

45 '(In connection with other bodies)'.

46 Cf. *Physical Monadology* (1756), Propositions VI and VII (AK 1:480–2).

47 Cf. *Physical Monadology* (1756), Proposition IX, Scholium (AK 1:483); also

Metaphysical First Principles (1786), Chapter 2, Proposition VII (AK 4:512–15). See also A. Koyré, *Newtonian Studies* (London: 1965) and especially 'Appendix C: Gravity an Essential Property of Matter,' where Koyré points out that Newton himself did not regard gravity as an 'innate, essential and inherent property of matter', quoting Newton's request (expressed in a letter to Bentley in 1692) not to ascribe to him the Epicurean notion of 'attraction as action at a distance through a vacuum without mediation', a notion Newton describes as an 'utter absurdity'. Koyré also points out that Newton's views are not so explicitly stated in the *Principia mathematica* (1687). Newton's followers had fewer scruples about adopting the notion of action at a distance through a vacuum without mediation.

48 Cf. *Logic* (1800), §6 (AK 9:94–5).

49 Cf. *Logic* (1800), §6 (AK 9:94–5).

50 Cf. *Logic* (1800), Introduction V (AK 9:33); *Dreams* (1766) (AK 2:338 footnote).

51 Kant employs exactly the same argument in the *Dreams* (1766) (AK 2:338 footnote).

52 Kant is alluding to an observation published by Sauvages (a disciple of the vitalist, Stahl) in the *Mémoires de l'Académie des sciences de Paris* for the year 1742: a German translation appeared in the *Hamburger Magazin* (Vol. VII, pp. 489–512) in 1745 under the title: *Betrachtungen über die Seele in der Erstarrung und Schlafwanderung* ('Observations on the Soul in Catalepsy and Sleepwalking').

53 Kant discusses certainty in the *Logic* (1800), Introduction IX (AK 9:70–1).

54 In other words, from both the objective and subjective points of view.

55 Cf. *Critique of Pure Reason* (1781/1787) B759 (AK 3:479).

56 Kant is alluding to the discussion of touching in the section which bears the title *Example* (AK 2:288).

57 The proof is presented in syllogistic form in the *False Subtlety* (1762) (AK 2:52).

58 Kant discusses this problem at greater length in the *Dreams* (1766) (AK 2:319–28).

59 Kant is alluding to Crusius, *Weg zur Gewissheit* (1747).

60 Cf. Crusius, *Weg zur Gewissheit* (1747), §§258–61.

61 Kant denies that there can be one single principle of all truths whatever: affirmative and negative truths require distinct principles. This thesis is argued in the *New Elucidation* (1755), Propositions I–III (AK 1:387–91).

62 For another discussion of such indemonstrable propositions cf. *False Subtlety* (AK 2:60–1).

63 Cf. Crusius, *Dissertatio* (1743), §27; also *Entwurf* (1745), §15; also *Weg zur Gewissheit* (1747), §§258–61. See also Kant's own discussion of this theme in *Logic* (1800), Introduction II (AK 9:16–21) and *Dreams* (1766) (AK 2:342).

64 Cf. *The Only Possible Argument* (1763) (AK 2:155–63).

65 Kant employs this proof on two other occasions: *New Elucidation* (1755), Proposition VII (AK 1:395–6) and *The Only Possible Argument* (AK 2:78–9).

66 Cf. *The Only Possible Argument* (AK 2:87–92).

67 For other statements of the same position cf. *Physical Monadology* (1756), Propositions VI and VII (AK 1:480–2) and Proposition IX, Scholium (AK 1:483).

68 (Problematic necessity): Kant seems to be identifying problematic and hypothetical necessity. Later, Kant distinguishes between two types of hypothetical necessity: problematic and assertoric. Cf. *Groundwork* (1785) (AK 4:414–6) and *Critique of Practical Reason* (1788) (AK 5:21–3 footnote).

69 (Legal necessity): This notion seems to correspond to what Kant was later to call the categorical imperative.

70 What Kant here calls *Anweisungen eines geschickten Verhaltens* ('recommendations to adopt a prudent procedure') he later distinguishes into *Regeln der Geschicklichkeit* ('rules of skill') and *Rathschläge der Klugheit* ('counsels of prudence'). Cf. *Groundwork* (1785) (AK 4:413–17).

71 In *Optimism* (1759) Kant had accepted the Wolffian identity of reality and perfection (AK 2:30–1); in *The Only Possible Argument* (1763) Kant distances himself from this position (AK 2:89–90). It is to this latter passage that Kant is alluding at the beginning of the present paragraph. For Wolff's identification of reality and perfection cf. *Vernünftige Gedanken von der Menschen Tun und Lassen* (1720), §8.

72 Kant's library contained two of Hutcheson's works in German translation. The two translations had appeared shortly before the composition of the present work. The two works in question were Hutcheson's *Inquiry* (1725) of which the German translation appeared in 1762, and the *Essay* (1728) of which the German translation appeared in 1760.

ANNOUNCEMENT

The editor wishes to acknowledge his indebtedness to Ferrari (Alquié, Vol. I, pp. 1532–4), especially for material in note 17; to Fichant, pp. 100–3, especially for material in notes 10, 16, and 19; and to Lasswitz (AK 2:497) for material in note 21.

1 Kant discusses this distinction at greater length in *Logic* (1800), Introduction III (AK 9:25–6).

2 It was not until 1770 (at the age of forty-six) that Kant was appointed *Professor ordinarius* with a regular salary from the university. Until then Kant was merely a *Privatdozent* holding free courses and remunerated directly by the students themselves. It was in this sense that Kant's classes prior to 1770 were *Privatvorlesungen*.

3 Kant is referring to the *Inquiry* (1764), and in particular to Reflection III, §1 (AK 2:290–2).

4 Cf. *Inquiry* (1764), Reflection I (AK 2:276–83).

5 Kant mentions the project of a work devoted to the method of metaphysics in his letters to Lambert on 31 December 1765 (AK 10:52–3) and Mendelssohn on 8 April 1766 (AK 10:67–8). See also Kant's letters to Herz on 7 June 1771 (AK 10:117) and on 21 February 1772 (AK 10:124). The pursuit of this project culminated in the *Critique of Pure Reason* (1781).

6 Kant is referring to Baumgarten's *Metaphysica* (1739). He had adopted this

text as the manual for commentary in his lectures. At the end of his *Theory of Winds* (1756) (AK 1:503), Kant refers to this book as 'the most useful and the most profound of all the works of its kind'.

7　Baumgarten wrote no work with this title; Kant is referring to the *Metaphysica* (1739).

8　Cf. *Logic* (1800), Introduction I (AK 9:11–16).

9　Cf. *Inquiry* (1764), Reflection II (AK 2:283–90).

10　Kant expresses a different view in the *Inaugural Dissertation* (1770), §23 (AK 2:411): 'But in pure philosophy *method precedes all science*'.

11　Kant is referring to Meier's *Auszug* (1752), of which the full text with Kant's annotations is in AK 16.

12　Kant is referring to Baumgarten's *Initia* (1760). The full text with Kant's annotations is in AK 19.

13　Kant is probably alluding to Shaftesbury's *Inquiry* (1699), of which a German translation had appeared in 1747, and possibly to *The Moralists* (1709), of which a German translation appeared in 1745.

14　Kant is probably referring to Hutcheson's *Inquiry* (1725), of which Kant's library contained the 1762 German translation, and the *Essay* (1728), of which Kant's library also contained the 1760 German translation.

15　Kant is probably referring to Hume's *Treatise* (1739–40) and the *Enquiry* (1751). Kant's library contained a German edition of Hume in four volumes, *Vermischte Schriften* (1754–6), of which the fourth volume contained Hume's ethical and religious writings.

16　Cf. *Dreams* (1766) (AK 2:369).

17　Kant is alluding throughout this paragraph to Rousseau, whose influence on Kant was particularly strong at this period. It is especially evident in *Observations* (1764). In his *Remarks on Observations of the Feeling of the Beautiful and the Sublime*, Kant, comparing Newton and Rousseau, says of the latter that he 'was the first to discover beneath the multiplicity of the forms assumed by man his deeply concealed nature and the hidden in virtue of which Providence is . . . justified' (AK 20:59).

18　Kant held lectures on physical geography for forty years from 1756 to 1796. The programme of his lecture course was first published in the *West Winds* (1757) (AK 2:1–12). Kant attached considerable importance to this course of lectures which was published, with Kant's approval, by Rink in 1802 (AK 9:151–436).

19　The division of the subject in the *Physical Geography* (AK 9:151–436) contains a somewhat different classification: *mathematical, moral, political, commercial*, and *theological* geography (AK 9:164–5).

20　Such a view of history was to be developed by Herder in his *Ideen zur Philosophie der Geschichte der Menschheit* ('Ideas towards a Philosophy of the History of Humankind') (Riga: 1784–91). Herder enrolled as a medical student at the University of Königsberg in 1762, but he switched to theology and became acquainted with Kant, who admitted the young Herder to his classes free of charge. Kant also introduced Herder to the writings of Montesquieu, Hume, and Rousseau. Kant's review of Herder's *Ideen: Recensionen von J. G. Herders Ideen zur Philosophie der Geschichte der Menschheit* (1785) (AK 8:43–66) is not very complimentary.

21 'For my part, such is my practice; you, for your part, do what you deem fitting.' Terence. *Heautontimoroumenos* ('The Self-Tormentor'), line 80.

DREAMS

The editor wishes to acknowledge his indebtedness to Menzer (AK 2:499–500) for information in the Introduction, and to Lortholary (Alquié, Vol. I, pp. 1534–8), especially for material in notes 1, 55, and 71; and to Menzer (AK 2:501–2), especially for material in notes 4, 11, 13, 14, 19, 20, 21, 25, 26, and 30.

1 'Like the dreams of a sick man, empty semblances are fashioned.' Horace: *Ars poetica* 7–8. Kant has substituted *finguntur* for *fingentur*, although this does not affect the meaning.

2 Kant is referring to Swedenborg's *Arcana coelestia* (1749–56).

3 Cf. *Physical Monadology* (1756), Propositions VII and VIII (AK 1:481–3).

4 Cf. Daries, *Elementa metaphysica* (1743), especially *Psychologia metaphysica*, §4; also Baumgarten, *Metaphysica* (1739), §742.

5 Cf. *Physical Monadology* (1756), Proposition VIII (AK 1:482–3); *Negative Magnitudes* (1763) (AK 2:178–9) and *Metaphysical First Principles* (1786) (AK 4:501).

6 Cf. *Negative Magnitudes* (1763) (AK 2:178–9).

7 Cf. *Physical Monadology* (1756), Propositions V and VI (AK 1:480–1).

8 Cf. *Physical Monadology* (1756), Propositions V–VII (AK 1:480–2).

9 Cf. *Physical Monadology* (1756), Proposition V (AK 1:480); *Metaphysical First Principles* (1786) (AK 4:496–8); *Inquiry* (1764) (AK 2:286–8).

10 Kant seems to be using the term *Einheit* as a synonym for *monas;* etymologically, the words have the same meaning. This surmise is supported by Grimm. The view Kant states here is that of Leibniz.

11 Cf. Daries, *Elementa metaphysica* (1743), especially *Psychologia rationalis*, §103 and Corollary 1, which contains the passage quoted by Kant: *totam animam in toto corpore omnibusque partibus corporis organicis praesentam esse* ('that the whole soul is present in the whole body and in all the organic parts of the body').

12 Kant is alluding to the famous illustrated encyclopaedic reader which was published by the Dutchman J. A. Comenius (1592–1670) at Nuremberg in 1658 under the title *Orbis sensualium pictus, hoc est omnium fundamentalium in mundo rerum et in vita actionum pictura et nomenclatura* ('The Painted World of the Things we Perceive, Being the Pictures and Names of All the Fundamentals both in the World of Things and in the Life of Actions'). This celebrated educational work was popular throughout the eighteenth century, especially among the Pietists.

13 Cf. Wolff, *Philosophia rationalis* (1728), §102 et passim. Also Baumeister, *Philosophia definitiva* (1735), p. 181. See also Descartes, *Traité* (1649), Articles XXIII, XXXV, and XLII.

14 Cf. Michael Gottlob Hansche, *Godefridi Guilelmi Leibnitii Principia philosophia more geometrico demonstrata* ('Gottfried Wilhelm Leibniz's Principles of Philosophy Demonstrated in Geometrical Fashion'), (Frankfurt and Leipzig: 1728), p. 135.

15 Cf. *Negative Magnitudes* (1763) (AK 2:199–200).

16 'Like shadowy forms they wander through the lonely night among the ghosts, traversing the desolate abodes and the empty realms of Pluto.' Virgil, *Aeneid*, VI, 268–9.

17 '(The intelligible world)'.

18 *Hylozoismus:* the doctrine that matter and life are inseparable; related to the doctrine of panpsychism, the doctrine that all reality, including all matter, is invested with or is an expression of life. Leibniz's doctrine of the monads is closely related to these doctrines.

19 Cf. Boerhaave, *Elementa chimiae* (1724) and in particular p. 64 of Volume I, where the passage cited by Kant is to be found: *alimenta plantarum radicibus externis, animalium internis, hauriuntur* ('the nutriments of plants are absorbed by means of external roots, that of animals by internal roots').

20 Cf. Stahl, *Theoria medica vera* (1707), especially Section I: *Physiologia membrum* ('Physiology of the Organs') 1. *De scopo seu fine corporis* ('Concerning the Purpose or End of the Body'); see also *De vera diversitate corporis mixti et vivi . . . demonstratio* ('Demonstration relating to the True Diversity of the Compound and Living Body . . .').

21 Cf. Hofmann, *Opera omnia medico-physica* (1740–53) and especially Vol. 1, Chap. 1 (i–iii).

22 Cf. Boerhaave, *De usu ratiocinii mechanici in medicina* (1705); also *Institutiones medicae* (1708).

23 Cf. Kant's fragment *On Philosophers' Medicine of the Body* (AK 15:939–53), which defends the vitalist position of Stahl against the mechanistic outlook of Hofmann and Boerhaave. See Beck (1986), pp. 217–43.

24 Cf. Daries, *Elementa metaphysica* (1743–4) and especially *Psychologia empirica*, §26.

25 Cf. *Inquiry* (1764) (AK 2:289–90); also *Logic* (1800), Introduction V (AK 9:33).

26 Cf. Wolff, *Philosophia rationalis* (1728), §102 et passim. See also Baumeister, *Philosophia definitiva* (1735), p. 181. See also Descartes, *Traité* (1649), Articles XXIII, XXX–XXXV and XLII; also Newton, *Opticks* (1704), Book III, Part 1, Queries 23 and 24.

27 Cf. Ovid, *Metamorphoseon*, III, 316–38. Ovid derives his material from Apollodorus, III, vi §7, who offers two divergent accounts of the blindness and prophetic powers of Tiresias.

28 Kant is the only source for this story about Tycho de Brahe. The same story is related by Plato of Thales (*Theaetetus*, 174a) and it is repeated by Diogenes Laertius (*Vitae philosophorum*, I, xxxiv). The story is also reminiscent of La Fontaine's fable *L'astrologue qui se laisse tomber dans un puits* (*Fables*, II, xiii), which derives from Aesop (Fable XL) and Babrius (Fable XX).

29 *Anti-Cabbala:* Kant is alluding to the system of occult theosophy maintained by Jewish rabbis and certain mediaeval Christians. The Cabbalists maintained that God is the origin of all being; that creation is a process of emanation; that man is a microcosm of the universe; that evil will be conquered by the triumph of goodness; that writing was revealed to man as a means of penetrating the divine mysteries. The Cabbalists assumed, in particular, that every word, letter, number, and accent in scripture contained a

hidden sense, so that biblical interpretation was for them a matter of discovering occult meanings. The word 'cabbala' came to signify any hermetic or esoteric doctrine or science, and hence occultism in general.

30   Kant's attribution of this dictum to Aristotle is erroneous: it is in fact a fragment of Heraclitus (Fragment LXXXIX), which reads: 'The waking have a single and a common world; but in sleep each turns away from this common world to his own world'. Cf. H. Diels and W. Kranz, *Die Fragmente der Vorsocratiker* (Dublin: 1903; 6th edition: 1972), p. 171.

31   Cf. Wolff, *Vernünftige Gedanken von Gott* (1719).

32   Cf. Crusius, *Entwurf* (1745).

33   'Imaginary focus'; cf. Newton, *Opticks* (1704), Book I. Part 1, Axiom viii.

34   'Imaginary focus'; see note 33 above.

35   Cf. Descartes, *Traité* (1649), Articles XXIII, XXXV, and XLII.

36   'Material ideas'; see note 13 above.

37   Kant distinguishes three fundamental types of mental illness in his *Maladies of the Mind* (AK 2:257-71), which was published two years before the present work. They are: (1) *Verrückung:* derangement. It is defined as a disturbance (*Verkehrtheit*) of the concepts of experience (AK 2:264-5); (2) *Wahnsinn:* madness. It is defined as disorder of the judgement (AK 2:265-8); (3) *Wahnwitz:* insanity. It is defined as a disorder of reason in respect of more general judgements (AK 2:268-9). See also *Anthropology* (1798), §§45 and 52 (AK 7:202-4 & 214-17).

38   Kant quotes from the German translation of Butler's *Hudibras* (1663-78) which appeared in Hamburg and Leipzig in 1765. The original passage reads as follows: 'As wind i' th' Hypocondres pent,/ Is but a Blast if downward sent; / But if it upward chance to fly,/ Becomes new Light and Prophecy' (*Hudibras*, II, iii, 773-6). (Goerwitz declined to translate this passage because of its impropriety.)

39   Kant is right: *psyche* may indeed mean 'butterfly'. Cf. Aristotle, *Historia animalium* (551a, 14); Theophrastos, *Historia plantarum* (II, iv, 4); Plutarch, *Moralia* (2.636c). (Cf. Liddell and Scott, ψυχη VI.)

40   'May I be permitted to say what I have heard' (Virgil, *Aeneid*, VI, 266).

41   Kant's idiosyncratic spelling of Swedenborg's name has been retained. Kant spells it correctly in his letter to Charlotte von Knobloch of 10 August 1763 (AK 10:43-8), so we may assume that the form 'Schwedenberg' was deliberate. Swedenborg's family name was Svedborg; his ennoblement after the Battle of Frederikshall for engineering services to the crown led to the change of form (the 'en' having the same significance as the German 'von') in 1719.

42   By 1766, Swedenborg had, apart from his numerous scientific works, published: (1) *Arcana coelestia* (1749-56); (2) *De coelo* (1758); (3) *Sapientia angelica de divino amore* (1763) and (4) *Sapientia angelica de divina providentia* (1764).

43   Kant, in his letter to Charlotte von Knobloch of 10 August 1763 (AK 10:43-8), reports the impression made by Swedenborg on an English acquaintance who had been engaged by Kant to make enquiries in Stockholm. The initially sceptical Englishman found his suspicions undermined by the personal

451

charm of Swedenborg. Kant writes: 'According to his first report, the story which I have already mentioned [concerning the Queen of Sweden herself and reported to Kant by a Danish officer (cf. note 45)] was, according to the most respected people in Stockholm, exactly as I have already recounted it to you. At that time, he had not yet spoken to Swedenborg, though he was hoping to do so; he had difficulty, however, in persuading himself of the truth of all the stories which were recounted by the most reasonable people of the town about Swedenborg's mysterious dealings with the invisible spirit-world'. Kant then adds: 'However, the letters which my friend subsequently sent were of an entirely different character. Not only had he spoken to Swedenborg, he had also visited him in his house; and he now felt utterly astonished about the whole strange affair. Swedenborg was reasonable, agreeable, open-hearted, and a scholar' (AK 10:45).

44 Kant's explicit mention of the date 1761 clearly demonstrates the falsity of Borowski's dating of Kant's letter to Charlotte von Knobloch, which also contains this report.

45 The account of this episode in Kant's letter to Charlotte von Knobloch (AK 10:44–5) contains more detail and runs as follows: 'I received the following report from a Danish officer who was a friend and had been a student of mine. It had been at the table of the Austrian Ambassador to Copenhagen, Dietrichsen, that he, along with other guests, had personally read the letter which Dietrichsen had at that time received from Baron von Lützow, the Mecklenburg Ambassador to Stockholm. In this letter, Lützow, whom I have just mentioned, informed Dietrichsen that he, Lützow, along with the Dutch Ambassador, and as a guest of the Queen of Sweden, had been personally present at the strange incident involving Swedenborg, which will already be familiar to you, gracious lady. The reliability of such a report puzzled me. For it can scarcely be supposed that one ambassador would convey in writing to another a piece of information *intended for public use* announcing something untrue concerning the Queen, the head of the very court to which he was accredited, particularly since he claims to have been present, along with a sizeable company, when the incident occurred. Now, so as to avoid blindly rejecting the prejudice against apparitions and visions by adopting a new prejudice, I thought that it would be sensible to investigate the story more closely. I wrote to the officer, whom I mentioned above, asking him to undertake all sorts of enquiry for me. He replied that he had spoken about the matter a second time to Count Dietrichsen, that the incident really had occurred as reported, and that Professor Schlegel had assured him that the matter was beyond all doubt. Since he was then leaving town to join the army which was under the command of General St. Germain, he advised me to write to Swedenborg myself, in order to ascertain the more particular circumstances of the incident. I accordingly wrote to this strange man, and my letter was personally delivered to him by an English merchant in Stockholm. I was informed that the letter had been favorably received by Swedenborg, and that he had promised to reply to it. The reply, however, never materialised. In the meantime, I had made the acquaintance of a gentleman of refinement, an Englishman, who spent last summer here in Königsberg. On the basis of

the friendship which we had both forged, I charged him with the task, in the course of the visit he was about to make to Stockholm, of gathering more precise information about Swedenborg's amazing gift. According to his first report, the story which I have already mentioned was, according to the most respected people in Stockholm, exactly as I have already recounted it to you.'

It is worth noting that the allusion in the above passage from Kant's letter to Charlotte von Knobloch to the fact that the Danish officer, from whom Kant had initially received this report, 'was then leaving town to join the army which was under the command of General St. Germain' helps to date this important letter. St. Germain took command of an army of Danish troops against Russia in 1762; that army was in Mecklenburg in the spring of 1762 (cf. I. F. Tafel, *Supplement zu Kants Biographie und zu den Gesamtaus-gaben seiner Werke* [Stuttgart: 1845], pp. 25–7; see also Manolesco, p. 178). The letter must have been written not earlier than the spring of 1762, and not later than 1763, for it was in that year that Dietrichsen left his ambassadorial post.

46 Kant's estimate of the reliability of these reports is much higher in his letter to Charlotte von Knobloch. He writes: 'I trust that you will be so kind as to read my account of the following two events. They were witnessed by people who are still all of them alive; and the person who informed me of them was able to investigate them on the very spot and at the very time of their occurrence' (AK 10:45). Later, speaking of the report of Swedenborg's vision of the Stockholm fire, Kant remarks: 'It is, however, the following event in particular which seems to me to have the greatest evidential force; it really does deprive every doubt of any justification' (AK 10:46). He adds at the end of the report: 'What doubt could be cast on the credibility of this event? The friend who wrote to me describing the episode, personally investigated not only everything which happened in Stockholm; he also, two months ago, investigated everything which happened in Gothenburg as well. He is well acquainted with the leading families of the place, and he was able to inform himself thoroughly by questioning the inhabitants of the whole town, where most of the eye-witnesses still live, for 1756 is not so long ago' (AK 10:47). It is not at all clear what can have induced Kant so radically to have revised his estimate of the reliability of the reports he cites in both the letter and in the *Dreams* (1766).

47 Kant's report of this episode in his letter to Charlotte von Knobloch (AK 10:45–6) runs as follows: 'Some time after the death of her husband, Madamme Harteville [*sic*], widow of the Dutch Ambassador to Stockholm, received a reminder from the goldsmith, Croon, that a bill for a silver service, which her husband had commissioned from him, had not yet been settled. The widow, though convinced that her late husband was far too meticulous and punctilious in his affairs not to have settled this debt, was unable to produce a receipt. Distressed as she was in this way, and the sum involved being considerable, she asked Swedenborg to call on her. After apologising several times for troubling him she asked him whether, assuming that he had the extraordinary gift of conversing with the souls of the departed, he would have the goodness to enquire of her husband about the

situation with respect to the demand for payment for the silver service. Swedenborg readily complied with the lady's request. Three days later the lady in question was entertaining a group of friends to coffee. Swedenborg called on her, and informed her with characteristic matter-of-factness that he had spoken to her husband. The debt had been settled seven months prior to his death, and the receipt was to be found in a cabinet in the upstairs room. The lady reported that this cabinet had been thoroughly cleared out and that the receipt had not been found among any of the papers. Swedenborg said that her husband had described to him how, if a drawer on the left hand side of the cabinet were pulled out a board would be revealed which should be pushed aside, whereupon a concealed drawer would be discovered in which he had kept his secret Dutch diplomatic correspondence and in which the receipt was also to be found. Thus informed, the lady betook herself, along with all her visitors, to the upper room. The cabinet was opened, the instructions were punctiliously observed, and the drawer, of which she had known nothing, was discovered, and, to the utter astonishment of everybody present, the papers described were found in it'.

Again, the report of this episode contains allusions to certain datable events which are relevant to deciding the date of Kant's important letter to Charlotte von Knobloch: Madame Marteville's husband died in 1760 (and thus the letter could not have been written in 1758 as Borowski claims). According to Tafel, *Supplement zu Kant's Biographie* (Stuttgart: 1845), p. 275, the event Kant reported occurred in 1761. Tafel based his claims on information provided by the second husband of Madame Marteville.

48 The news not of the fire itself but of Swedenborg's vision.

49 The report of this episode as it is presented in Kant's letter to Charlotte von Knobloch (AK 10:46–7) runs as follows: 'It is, however, the following event in particular which seems to me to have the greatest evidential force; it really does deprive every doubt of any justification. It was in the year 1756; Swedenborg, returning from a journey to England, disembarked at Gothenburg at 4 o'clock in the afternoon of a Saturday towards the end of the month of September. Mr. William Castel invited him to his house, together with a company of fifteen persons. At about six o'clock in the evening Swedenborg absented himself and then returned a little later, pale and aghast. He said that there was at that very moment a dangerous conflagration raging in Stockholm on the Südermalm (Gothenburg is more than fifty miles from Stockholm), and that it was rapidly spreading. He was restless and went out frequently. He said that the house of one of his friends, whom he named, had already been reduced to ashes, and that his own house was threatened. At eight o'clock after he had gone out again, he joyfully exclaimed: "Praise be to God, the fire has been extinguished, and that three doors from my own house!" This news caused a great deal of excitement throughout the whole town [Gothenburg] and particularly among the company to which Swedenborg belonged. That same evening the Governor [of the town of Gothenburg] was informed, and on Sunday morning Swedenborg was summoned before him and interrogated by him about the matter. Swedenborg described the fire precisely, how it had started, how it had been extinguished and how long it had lasted. That same

day the news spread throughout the entire city, where it caused even more excitement on account of the fact that the Governor had taken an interest in it, for there were many people who were concerned either for their friends or for their possessions. On Monday evening a mounted messenger, despatched by the merchants of Stockholm at the time of the fire, arrived in Gothenburg. The fire was described in the letters he brought exactly as had been recounted by Swedenborg himself. On Tuesday a royal courier arrived at the Governor's with news of the fire, the damage it had caused, and the houses it had affected; this report differed not at all from the account furnished by Swedenborg at the time of the fire, which had been extinguished at eight o'clock. What doubt could be cast on the credibility of this event? The friend who wrote to me describing the episode, personally investigated not only everything which happened in Stockholm; he also, two months ago, investigated everything which happened in Gothenburg as well. He is well acquainted with the leading families of the place, and he was able to inform himself thoroughly by questioning the inhabitants of the whole town, where most of the eye-witnesses still live, for 1756 is not so long ago.'

The fire in Stockholm did occur in 1756 but not, as Kant claims, 'towards the end of the year' but on 19 July (cf. Tafel, *Supplement to Kants Biographie*, [Stuttgart: 1845], pp. 21–3).

50   Kant is alluding to Bernhard le Bovier de Fontenelle (1657–1757), the author of the celebrated *Entretiens sur la pluralité des mondes* (Paris: 1686).

51   Kant is alluding to an episode which aroused widespread public interest (and still does in France) and which occurred a year or so prior to the publication of Kant's *Dreams* (1766), and which was known as the case of the Beast of Gevaudan (1765).

52   Artemidorus of Ephesus (second century A.D.) was the author of a celebrated work on dreams, the *Oneirokritikos* ('Critique of Dreams').

53   Flavius Philostratus (ca. 170–250 A.D.) was the author of the *Life of Apollonius of Tyana*, a romantic and sensational biography of the neo-Pythagorean sage. (See note 54 below.)

54   Apollonius of Tyana (1st century A.D.) was a neo-Pythagorean sage and teacher who was converted into a religious cult-figure by the biography written by Philostratus. (See note 53 above.)

55   'Dreams, magical terrors, wonders, witches, ghosts of the night, Thessalonian portents' (Horace, *Epistolae*, II, ii, 208–9).

56   An allusion to the Epicurean doctrine of the clinamen (or swerve) of the atoms. Cf. Lucretius, *De rerum natura*, II, 216–93.

57   See note 56 above.

58   'and flees towards the willow trees, hoping to be seen before she disappears' (Virgil, *Bucolica*, III, 63).

59   Cf. Ariosto, *Orlando furioso* (1532), XXXIV, 67–87. Astolfo is taken to the moon by Saint John, where he finds everything which has been lost on earth, including, contained in a flask, the reason which Orlando had lost and which Astolfo brings back for him to earth. It seems most unlikely that Kant would have read Ariosto; his knowledge of the above episode probably derives from Fontenelle, whom Kant read and admired and who gives a lengthy account

of precisely the moon-flask passage above in his *Entretiens sur la pluralité des mondes* (1686) (see *Second soir: Que la lune est une terre habitée*) (cf. note 50 above).

60   Cf. Liscow, *Sammlung* (1739) and in particular, No. 2 *Vitrea fracta*.

61   See Biographical-Bibliographical Sketches for full details of this work.

62   See Biographical-Bibliographical Sketches for full details of this work.

63   'Things heard and seen'.

64   'Given to me out of the divine mercy of the Lord'.

65   'Thrice did the image escape my vain embrace, like to the light breezes and a fleeting dream' (Virgil, *Aeneid*, II, 793–4 and also, a second time, VI, 701–2).

66   Kant is referring to Diogenes the Cynic. The anecdote is in Diogenes Laertius, *Vitae philosophorum*, VI, xxxviii.

67   Kant is referring to Democritus of Abdera (ca. 460 – ca. 371 B.C.), the founder, along with his teacher Leucippus, of the atomistic theory, according to which all phenomena whatever are simply functions of the motions of atoms in an absolute void. It is specifically to this idea that Kant is here alluding.

68   The source of this anecdote about Socrates is Diogenes Laertius, *Vitae philosophorum*, II, xxv.

69   Kant is alluding to a phrase in Milton's *Paradise Lost* (1667), III, 495; the same allusion occurs in *The Only Possible Argument* (AK 2:148).

70   The concept to which Kant is referring is that of a spirit.

71   Kant has amalgamated into a single phrase the sentiments of the Turk and of the philosopher *Martin*, adapting the famous final sentence of Voltaire's *Candide* (1759): *Cela est bien dit, repondit Candide, mais il faut cultiver notre jardin.*

DIRECTIONS IN SPACE

The editor wishes to acknowledge his indebtedness to the *Encyclopaedia Britannica* for material in note 4; to Lasswitz (AK 2:507–8), especially for material in notes 3 and 12; to Loemker, especially for material in note 4; and to Zac, pp. 131–6, for material in note 5.

1   Contrary to the practice of all other translators (with the single exception of Rabel) *Gegend* has been translated not by 'region' but by 'direction'. Three considerations have led to this decision: (1) the coherency of Kant's argument requires that a clear distinction be drawn between *Lage* ('position'), *Ort* ('place'), and *Gegend*. To translate this term by 'region' would be to erode the distinction between *Ort* and *Gegend*. (2) If *Gegend* had the meaning traditionally attributed to it in this work then there would clearly be no limit to the number of *Gegenden* which could be distinguished in space. But Kant maintains that ultimately there are only six: right and left, above and below, in front of and behind. These Kant explicitly describes as *Unterschiede der Gegenden* ('differences of directions'). All places (or regions – a region is a more or less precisely delimited area of space, in other words, a place) are ultimately discriminated by reference to the six directions just mentioned. (3) Kant makes a number of specific claims which can only be rendered intelligible in terms of directionality: (a) the definition of *Gegend* and the denial that

Gegend can be understood in terms of the parts of a thing relative to each other or of places in space relatively to each other (AK 2:377–8); (b) the account of the difficulty in recognising or reading the mirror-image of a sheet of handwriting (AK 2:379); (c) the claim that maps and charts can only be interpreted if direction is established by reference to the right and left hands (AK 2:379); (d) the claim that directionality plays a crucial role in the description and discrimination of species of plant (beans and hops) and animal (snails) (AK 2:380); (e) the explanation of the phenomenon of incongruent counterparts (AK 2:381–3); (f) the attempt to explain the possibility of our apprehending the relation of spatial particulars to absolute space in general, alleged by Kant to be necessary to the full description of the spatial qualities of a thing. This issue underlies Kant's implicit criticism of Leibniz's *analysis situs* and, indeed, the whole discussion (AK 2:381). Only one other question remains: (4) Does the word *Gegend* actually have the meaning attributed to it here? The answer must, of course, be affirmative. Although it is most commonly used to signify 'region', 'area', 'locality', 'place', 'neighbourhood', it may also mean 'direction'. Langenscheidt distinguishes seven senses of the word; the third sense distinguished is: '(*Richtung*) direction'. Grimm lists three groups of meanings, of which only the first is relevant; within this first group five uses are distinguished. It is the fifth which is pertinent to the present problem. Grimm asserts of this fifth sense that it is 'sharply to be distinguished from the concept of area before or around', adding that it is the concept of 'a direction determined by reference to the speaker'. This sense is illustrated by ordinary questions such as: *In welcher Gegend liegt der und der Ort?* ('In which direction does such and such a place lie?'); *Aus welcher Gegend kommt der Wind?* ('From which direction is the wind blowing?'). Kirchmann in his *Erläuterungen zu Immanuel Kant's kleinern Schriften über Logik und Metaphysik* (Berlin: 1873) says (p. 116): 'The essay will be better understood if the word *Gegenden* is replaced by the word *Richtungen* ['directions']; this indicates Kant's meaning more clearly, Kant himself designating *Gegend* as that whither something is directed'. Kirchmann fails to recognise that, as Grimm indicates, *Gegend* may, in any case, mean 'direction'. He also fails to recognise that Kant reserves the word *Richtung* to signify the direction of a *motion*. The word *Gegend* is reserved by Kant to signify the direction of an *orientation*. Kant employs the word *Gegend* in the sense of 'direction' elsewhere as well (for example: *Dreams* [AK 2:345], where he sharply distinguishes 'the direction and the distance of an object').

2   Although Leibniz published major works on law, history, and theology, nearly all his work in the fields of logic, mathematics, epistemology, and metaphysics either remained unpublished or else appeared in the form of short essays and papers (mostly published in learned journals such as the *Acta Eruditorum*, the *Journal des Scavans*, and *L'Europe Savante*). Apart from the *Théodicée* (1710) Leibniz published no systematic account of his philosophy (his greatest philosophical work, the *Nouveaux essais*, was only published posthumously in 1765). More specifically, Leibniz's ideas on the *ars characteristica* and the *analysis situs* only exist in fragmentary and undeveloped form.

3   Kant is referring to Boerhaave, *Elementa chimiae* (1724), Vol. I, p. 2. Kant

refers to this same surmise of Boerhaave in the *New Elucidation* (1755) (AK 1:390).

4   *Analysis situs* ('analysis of situation'): The Leibnizian project grew out of his dissatisfaction with the Cartesian reduction of geometry to algebra. Algebra, Leibniz insisted, was the characteristic for indeterminate numbers or magnitudes only and could not directly express situation, angles, or motion; it was also compelled to presuppose the elements of geometry, so that the analyses it offered were incomplete and insufficiently radical. The *analysis situs*, a specific application of the *ars characteristica*, was intended to be a genuinely geometrical form of analysis directly expressing situation, angles, and motion. Leibniz sharply distinguishes *analysis situs* from *mathematical analysis* (the analysis of magnitudes, whether determinate, as in arithmetic, or indeterminate, as in algebra). The fundamental conception of the new analysis was not that of *equality* (defined in terms of sameness of *magnitude*) – and thus its fundamental operation was not the equation, as in the Cartesian reduction of geometry to algebra – but that of *congruence* (cf. Loemker, pp. 254–8; Gerhardt [M], II, 20–7), which was defined in terms of being able to occupy the same space. Later, the concept of congruence was to give way to the concept of *similarity* (defined in terms of sameness of *form* or *quality*). Leibniz writes: 'Things are similar which cannot be distinguished when observed in isolation from each other' (Loemker, p. 255; cf. Loemker, pp. 254–8; Gerhardt [M], V, 178–83). The two relations of *congruence* and *similarity* were both regarded by Leibniz as particular derivatives of the logical principle of identity or equivalence. Leibniz was confident that the *analysis situs*, if fully developed (and Leibniz, as Kant rightly points out, only sketched the outlines of such an enquiry) would be capable not only of *describing* the spatial characteristics of figures, machines, plants, animals, and all motions whatever, and even, indeed, the ultimate constitution of matter itself, it would also be able to offer complete solutions, constructions, and demonstrations of all such spatial properties: all configurations would be reduced to their elements and ultimate principles. Most important, Leibniz envisaged the *analysis situs* as an organon for the *enlargement* of knowledge which would facilitate, for example, the invention of new machines. The *analysis situs* was thus envisaged as fulfilling a three-fold function: description, explanation, and organon. Although Leibniz recognised the vast importance of the *analysis situs*, he never advanced beyond the outline sketches which merely adumbrate and illustrate the idea. Nonetheless, it may be regarded as a precursor of modern twentieth-century topology (originated in the nineteenth century by the work of Riemann, Cantor, and Poincaré), which is concerned, not with the shape or magnitude of configurations, but with their fundamental spatial qualities (their 'connectivity'). The fundamental conception of topology, as in the *analysis situs*, is not equality (sameness of magnitude or quantity) but congruence (sameness of form or quality: topological equivalence or homomorphicism). The relation of the Leibnizian *analysis situs* to geometry is roughly analogous to the relation of algebra to arithmetic. (It is not without interest to note that Leibniz, in a discussion of congruence [Loemker, pp. 240–51], claims of two triangles which are actually *incongruent* 'that one can

be applied to or placed on the other without changing anything in the two figures except their place'. In fact, one of them must be turned through the third dimension.)

5   Kant is alluding to Buffon's celebrated theory of the generation of organic forms. Buffon rejected epigenesis, which maintained that procreation actually created *de novo* the germ or embryo. The theory championed by Buffon, known as the theory of individual preformation, maintained that every germ cell contained the organism of its kind fully formed and complete in all its parts, and that the development consisted merely in increase in size from microscopic proportions to those of the adult. The act of procreation thus simply involves the unfolding of the forms and structures which already exist enveloped together in the seed itself. Kant characterises Buffon's theory as a form of 'prestabilism' in the *Critique of Judgement*, §81 (AK 5:421–31). Kant is probably thinking of the following passage from Buffon: '*Tout ce qui a immédiatement rapport à la position manque absolument à nos sciences mathématiques. Cet art que Leibnitz appelait Analysis situs n'est pas encore né et cependant cet art qui nous ferait connaître les rapports de position entre les choses serait aussi utile et peut être plus nécessaire aux sciences naturelles que l'art qui n'a que la grandeur des choses pour object; car on a plus souvent besoin de connaître la forme que la matière. Nous ne pouvons donc pas, lorsqu'on nous présente une forme developpée, reconnaître ce qu'elle était avant son developpement; et de même lorsqu'on nous fait voir une forme enveloppée, c'est-à-dire une forme dont les parties sont repliées les unes sur les autres, nous ne pouvons juger ce qu'elle doit produire par tel ou tel développement. N'est-il pas évident que nous ne pouvons juger en aucune facon de la position relative de ces parties repliées qui sont comprises dans un tout qui doit changer de figure en se développant?*' (Buffon, *Histoire naturelle* [1749–88], IV, ix, 73).

6   Both Kant and Leibniz are concerned with the qualitative properties of space, the former dealing with them philosophically, the latter attempting to do so mathematically. It might be argued that one of the implications of Kant's discussion (and perhaps its chief motive) is the demonstration of the impossibility of the Leibnizian *analysis situs*.

7   This must be a slip of Kant's pen, for the *analysis situs* was not concerned with quantities or magnitudes at all, but only with the fundamental qualities or *formal* properties of space. See note 4 above.

8   See note 1 on *Gegend* above.

9   Kant is alluding to Euler's *Reflexions sur l'espace et le temps* (1748). See also Euler, *Theoria motus* (1765); also *Negative Magnitudes* (1763) (AK 2:168).

10   Kant makes exactly the same point in *Orientation in Thought* (1786) (AK 8:134–5).

11   Cf. *Metaphysical First Principles* (1786) (AK 4:483–4).

12   Cf. Mariotte, *De la nature de l'air* in *Oeuvres de Mariotte* (1717), Vol. I, pp. 160–1; see also Francis Bacon, *Historia naturalis et experimentalis de ventis* ('A Natural and Experimental Account of the Winds') (Leyden: 1628). See also Kant's own *Theory of the Winds* (1756) (AK 1:502).

13   Cf. de Ulloa, *Redacion del viage* (1748).

14 Cf. Borelli, *Bemerkungen* (1759).

15 Kant may be alluding to one of two works by Bonnet: *Essai de psychologie* (1754) or *Essai analytique* (1760).

16 *einander gleich und ähnlich* ('equal and similar to each other'): this phrase appears in a variety of forms throughout the essay. The term *gleich* ('equal') is a *quantitative* notion signifying 'equal in magnitude' (where magnitude may relate to the length of a line, the size of an angle, the area of a figure, and so forth). The term *ähnlich* ('similar') is a *qualitative* notion signifying 'similarity in form, shape and structure'. Kant says: 'It is apparent from the ordinary example of the two hands that the figure (*Figur:* 'form', 'shape' or 'structure') of one body may be perfectly similar [*völlig ähnlich*] to the figure of the other, and the magnitudes of their extensions [*die Grösse der Ausdehnung*] may be exactly equal [*ganz gleich*]' (AK 2:382). These two technical concepts are defined by Leibniz as follows: 'Besides quantity, figure in general includes also quality or form. And as those figures are *equal* whose magnitude is the same, so those are *similar* whose form is the same. The theory of similarities or of forms lies beyond mathematics and must be sought in metaphysics. Yet it has many uses in mathematics also, being of use even in the algebraic calculus itself. But *similarity* is seen best of all in the *situations* or figures of geometry. Thus true geometric analysis ought not only consider equalities and proportions which are truly reducible to equalities but also similarities and, arising from the combination of equality and similarity, congruences'. Leibniz, *On analysis situs*, in Loemker, pp. 254–5; Gerhardt (M), V, 178–83.

17 Kant discusses the problem of incongruent counterparts on three other occasions: (1) *Inaugural Dissertation* (1770), §15 (AK 2:403); (2) *Prolegomena* (1783), §13 (AK 4:285–6); (3) *Metaphysical First Principles* (1786) (AK 4:483–4).

INAUGURAL DISSERTATION

The editor wishes to acknowledge his indebtedness to L. W. Beck for the material which has been derived from his notes to his revision of Handyside's translation of Kant's *Inaugural Dissertation* (Beck, 1986, pp. 188–92) and incorporated in the following notes: 8, 20, 34, 36, 42, 50, 52, 54, 58, 59, 66, 67. This material has been reprinted by permission of the publisher from Lewis White Beck et al., *Kant's Latin Writings: Translations, Commentaries and Notes* (New York: Peter Lang Publishing, 1986. All rights reserved.), pp. 188–92.

1   Kant, in Section IV, §21 of the present work (AK 2:408) maintains that the possibility of a number of actual worlds is not ruled out by the concept of a world. It is, furthermore, a thesis of the *Inaugural Dissertation* (1770) that there is a sensible and an intelligible world, and that it is at least possible that they are not numerically identical. Kant, in short, entertains the possibility of there actually being more than one world. In the *New Elucidation* (1755), Proposition XIII, Application (AK 1:414), Kant asserts that 'the possibility that there might be, had it so pleased God, a number of worlds, even in the metaphysical sense, is not absurd'. It may also be worth noting that Kant in the *Living Forces* (1747) had asserted that the three-dimensionality of space was a function of

Newton's inverse-square law governing forces between bodies and suggested, by implication, that a world (constituted of a different kind of matter) with a different geometry was therefore possible. (AK 1:24–5).

2   In a letter to Kant, dated 13 November 1765 (AK 10:51–4), Lambert argues that among the simples of cognition are axioms derived from the matter of cognition (as opposed to its form), and in a letter of 3 February 1766 (AK 10:62–7), he added to this the claim that simple concepts are individual or singular and that objective (i.e., material or nonformal) individual concepts are to be 'found' by means of directly intuiting them. He also maintained that form determines the order or the arrangement of matter.

3   In the *Critique of Pure Reason* (1781/1787) A77 / B103 (AK 3:91 / AK 4:64), Kant characterises synthesis more generically as that which collects and unifies elements to form a particular content. In the footnote appended to the present discussion, he acknowledges that the notions of synthesis and analysis are being employed in a more restricted sense.

4   The claim that intuition does not afford us any representation of the infinitely small or the infinitely large is still made and defended by Kant in the *Critique of Pure Reason* (1781/1787), A169–70 / B211–12 (AK 3:154–5 / AK 4:117–18); also the first two Antinomies A426–33 / B454–71 (AK 3:294–307).

5   Cf. Aristotle, *Physica*, III, 5; Hume, *A Treatise of Human Nature* (1739), Book I, Part II, Sections 1 and 2; Leibniz, *Nouveaux essais* (1765), Book II, xvii. Descartes, by contrast, maintained the possibility of a real infinite in *Meditationes de prima philosophia* (1641), Meditation III; and also in *Principia philosophiae* (1744), Part II, Principles XX and XXI.

6   Mendelssohn, in a letter of 25 December 1770 (AK 10:113–16), pointed out to Kant that he had independently expressed 'similar thoughts concerning the infinite in extension'.

7   Compare Kant's discussion first of matter and then of form with the two letters from Lambert of 13 November 1765 and 3 February 1766 (AK 10:51–4 & 62–7).

8   Cf. Baumgarten, *Metaphysica* (1739), §438 (7th edition: 1779). According to Leibniz in the *Nouveaux essais* (1765), each soul is a little world (cf. Book II, Chapter 1, §1).

9   In §§18 and 19 (AK 2:407–9).

10   Kant is referring to his definition of a world in the first paragraph of the present treatise, which defines a world to be a whole which is *not* a part.

11   This should be compared with the *Critique of Pure Reason* (1781/1787) B1 (AK 3:27), where Kant holds that some representations are brought about by means of objects affecting the senses. See also A19 / B33 (AK 3:49 & 4:29), where sensibility is defined as receptivity or the capacity to be affected by objects.

12   Once, in §1 (AK 2:389), Kant mentions both understanding and reason, but in the *Inaugural Dissertation* (1770) he on the whole identifies the two faculties. For the later distinction between the two faculties, see the *Critique of Pure Reason* (1781/1787) A643 / B671 (AK 3:427). As far as the distinction between phenomena and noumena is concerned, Lambert, in his letter to

Kant of 13 October 1770 (AK 10:103–11), refers to the sharp distinction which Kant is drawing here and then demands proof that the two 'nowhere come together', thereby preparing the ground for his subsequent criticism of Kant's doctrine of the subjectivity of the forms of intuition.

13   Cf. Lambert's letters to Kant of 13 November 1765 (AK 10:51–4) and 3 February 1766 (AK 10:62–7). Cf. note 2 above.

14   For Kant's views on subordination, see *Logic* (1800), §§9–15 (AK 9:96–9).

15   For Kant's views on distinct concepts, see *Logic* (1800), Introduction V and VIII (AK 9:34–5 and 61–4); *False Subtlety* (1762), §6 (AK 2:58–9); and *Anthropology* (1798), I, §6 (AK 7:137–8).

16   For Kant's views on complete concepts, see *Logic* (1800), Introduction VIII (AK 9:62); *False Subtlety* (1762), §6 (AK 2:58–9); *Critique of Pure Reason* (1781/1787) B755 Footnote (AK 3:477).

17   Cf. *Logic* (1800), §6 (AK 9:94–5).

18   Cf. *Logic* (1800), §6 (AK 9:94–5).

19   Kant is here criticising Leibniz. Cf. *Critique of Pure Reason* (1781/1787) A264 / B320 (AK 3:217 / AK 4:171), where Kant discusses the Leibnizian view that perceptions are always confused representations.

20   Cf. Wolff, *Psychologia empirica* (1743), §§54–5.

21   Cf. Epicurus, *Letter to Menoeceus*, cxxix.

22   Kant is probably alluding to Lord Shaftesbury's *Inquiry* (1699), of which a German translation appeared in 1747, and possibly *The Moralist* (1709), of which a German translation appeared in 1745. Mendelssohn, in a letter to Kant of 25 December 1770 (AK 10:113–16), objected to Kant's characterisation of Shaftesbury as a distant follower of Epicurus, on the grounds that, whereas Epicurus maintained that pleasure was the highest good, Shaftesbury construed pleasure only as the criterion of the good.

23   Cf. Kant's views on singularity in the *Logic* (1800), §§1 and 15 (AK 9:91 and 99).

24   Cf. *Critique of Pure Reason* (1781/1787) A19–21 / B33–5 (AK 3:49–50 / AK 4:29–31).

25   This anticipates part of the argument of the later Refutation of Material Idealism. Cf. *Critique of Pure Reason* (1781/1787) B276–7 (AK 3:191–2).

26   The Eleatic School, founded by Xenophanes, included among its members Parmenides and Zeno. It maintained that the empirical world of motion, change, and multiplicity was absolutely unreal and, indeed, impossible, for the phenomena of motion, change and multiplicity could not be given an analysis which was free from contradiction. It followed that knowledge of phenomena, and thus scientific knowledge of nature, was impossible. Only metaphysical knowledge of Being was possible. In the *Critique of Pure Reason* (1781/1787) A502 / B530 (AK 3:345) Kant refers to Zeno as 'a subtle dialectician' and defends him against the charges of inconsistency levelled at him by Plato. For example, Kant defends Zeno's view that God (or the world) is neither in motion nor at rest, for motion and rest both presuppose place, and the concept of 'place' only has meaning within the world.

27   Compare the seven points which Kant is about to make with the Metaphysical Exposition of the Concept of Time in the *Critique of Pure Reason* (1781/1787) A30–2 / B46–8 (AK 3:57–9 / AK 4:35–7).

28 Cf. *Critique of Pure Reason* (1781/1787) A169–70 / B211–12 (AK 3:154–5 / AK 4:117–18).

29 Cf. Kästner, *Anfangsgründe der höheren Mechanik* (1758), Part III, §188.

30 Leibniz argues for the continuity of changes on the ground that God realises the maximal number of compossibilities. Cf. *Discours de la métaphysique* (1686), §§14 & 15.

31 Lambert and Mendelssohn, in letters to Kant, and Schultz, in his 1771 review of the *Inaugural Dissertation,* all object to Kant's fundamental claim. After complimenting Kant on his treatment of continuity in the immediately preceding discussion, Lambert in his letter of 13 October 1770 (AK 10:103–11) agreed with Kant that time is a necessary condition of any representation of objects of the senses. He, furthermore, went on to agree with Kant's immediately following claim that time is a pure intuition and not a substance or a mere relation. But, he argued, because change among our representations is real, so must be the time in which such changes take place. Similarly, Mendelssohn, in a letter of 25 December 1770 (AK 10:113–16), argued in the same way as Lambert and then added the observation that because subjects, undergoing changes in their representations, are also objects of representations, there are also changes among objects of representations. Hence, once again, time must be real. In his well-known letter to Herz of 21 February 1772 (AK 10:129–35), Kant referred to these views of Lambert and Mendelssohn, as well as to those of Schultz, who had reviewed the present dissertation in the *Königsbergischen gelehrten und politischen Zeitungen* (for 22 and 25 November 1771). Kant replied to the argument from the reality of changes among representations by arguing that such reality only means that there is something real corresponding to that which undergoes the changes, with the world in itself being neither changeable nor unchangeable, as had already been maintained by Baumgarten in his *Metaphysica* (1739), §18. (In this connection, cf. Kant's approving mention of Zeno, referred to in note 26.) Schultz had, in addition, argued that space may be an intellectual intuition, and hence objective. (A comparable claim could, presumably, be made for time. In this debate between Lambert, Mendelssohn, Schultz and Kant, time and space can, for the most part, be treated in identical fashion.) Kant gave the 'clear answer' that space is not objective because in its representation no representation of substance or of any real connections is to be met with.

32 Cf. Newton, *Principia mathematica* (1687), Book I, Scholium.

33 Cf. Leibniz, *First Truths* (ca. 1680) (Loemker, p. 269), where Leibniz declares that time is not a thing. Cf. also Leibniz's *Monadologie* (1714), §14, where sense perceptions are treated as the passing states of simple substances.

34 Cf. Newton, *Principia mathematica* (1687), General Scholium (fourth paragraph) in the second edition (1713). The passage in question did not occur in the first edition, of 1687.

35 Compare the five points Kant is about to make about space with the Metaphysical Exposition of the Concept of Space in the *Critique of Pure Reason* (1781/1787) A22–5 / B37–40 (AK 3:51–4 / AK 4:31–3).

36 Kant, without always drawing the same conclusions from his discussion, explicitly addresses the topic of incongruent counterparts on three other

occasions: (1) *Directions in Space* (1768) (AK 2:381–3); (2) *Prolegomena* (1783), §13 (AK 4:285–6); (3) *Metaphysical First Principles* (1786) (AK 4:483–4).

37 This could be argued for in a fashion analogous to the argument for the continuity of time (thesis 4 in the above discussion of time [AK 2:400]). Kant had already given the proof of the continuity of space in the *Physical Monadology* (1756), Proposition III (AK 1:478).

38 For a space not to be a limit of another space means that it is not the boundary of any space. On the assumption that there is no four-dimensional space, three-dimensional space (a cube or a solid) is not a boundary or limit of any space, whereas, as Kant goes on to observe, two-dimensional spaces (surfaces) are limits of solids, etc. Only solids, on the above-mentioned assumptions, will not be limits.

39 Lambert, Mendelssohn, and Schultz have in principle the same objections to this claim of Kant's as they have to its counterpart for time. See note 31 above.

40 Cf. Newton, *Principia mathematica* (1687) Book I, Scholium.

41 Cf. Leibniz, *First Truths* (ca. 1680) (Loemker, p. 269).

42 Cf. *Living Forces,* §10 (AK 1:24–5), where Kant argues that the three-dimensionality of space is a consequence of the empirical inverse-square law of attraction and that it is therefore an empirical matter as to which of various possible geometries applies to space. If this did not lead in his own mind to the suspicion in question, a similar argument which he may have had in mind occurs in Euler's *Lettres à une princesse d'Allemagne* (1768–72) (cf. the fifth letter of 5 May 1761).

43 In the Transcendental Aesthetic of the *Critique of Pure Reason* (1781/1787) A25 / B39 (AK 3:53 / AK 4:33) space is characterised as an 'infinite given'; at A32 / B47 (AK 3:58 / AK 4:37) time is said to be infinite. For time, the explanation is the same as that in the present passage: infinity is necessary for determinate duration.

44 Cf. *Critique of Pure Reason* (1787) B154 (AK 3:121), where a line is characterised as an outer (figurative) representation of time.

45 This view foreshadows the doctrine of the spatial schematisation of categorical principles in the *Critique of Pure Reason* (1781/1787) in the Third Analogy, A211–18 / B256–65 (AK 3:180–5 / AK 4:141–5). See also the argument in the second edition of the *Critique of Pure Reason* of the Refutation of Material Idealism, B274–9 (AK 3:190–3).

46 Cf. the Second Analogy in the *Critique of Pure Reason* (1781/1787) A189–211 / B 232–56 (AK 3:166–80 / AK 4:128–41).

47 Cf. *Critique of Pure Reason* (1781/1787) A142–3 / B182 (AK 3:137 / AK 4:101–2).

48 Cf. *Critique of Pure Reason* (1781/1787) B167–8 (AK 3:128–9), where Kant declares that any preformation-explanation of pure reason is unacceptable and conducive to scepticism.

49 Kant is still dealing with this problem in the Third Analogy of the *Critique of Pure Reason* (1781/1787) A211–15 / B256–62 (AK 3:180–3 / AK 4:141–3).

50 Cf. *New Elucidation* (1755), Proposition XIII (AK 1:412–16).

51 'First false statement': Kant is alluding to a fallacy mentioned by Aristotle in the *Analytica priora*, II, xvii (66a, 16–24). Aristotle there says: 'A false argument depends on the first false statement [*to proton pseudos*] in it'.

52 The doctrine of virtual presence was advocated by Euler in his *Lettres à une princesse d'Allemagne* (1768–72) (in letter of 18 November 1760). Virtual presence is defined in terms of an action which is *at* but does not *have* a location. Kant explains the difference between virtual and local presence in §27 of the present work (AK 2:414).

53 Kant offers an argument in support of this conclusion in *The Only Possible Argument* (1763) (AK 2:123–6).

54 Cf. Wolff, *Cosmologia generalis* (1731), §48 and §§60–1 (2nd edition: 1737); see also *Vernünftige Gedancken von Gott, der Welt and der Seele des Menschen* (1719), §§548–50 and §§948–50 (8th edition: 1741).

55 Cf. *New Elucidation* (1755), Proposition XIII, Application (AK 1:414).

56 Cf. Leibniz, *Monadologie* (1714), §78; see also Leibniz's letter to des Bosses of 16 June 1712 (Loemker, p. 604).

57 Cf. Malebranche, *Entretiens sur la métaphysique* (1688), Dialogue VII.

58 Kant argues for this in §30 (AK 2:418). See also *New Elucidation* (1755), Proposition X (AK 1:406–8); also *Critique of Pure Reason* (1781/1787) A182–9 / B224–32 (AK 4:124–8 / AK 3:162–6).

59 Cf. Malebranche, *De la recherche de la vérité* (1675), Book III, Part II, Chapter 6.

60 Cf. Kant's later development of the matter in the *Critique of Pure Reason* (1781/1787), The Postulates of Empirical Thought, A218–35 / B265–87 (AK 4:145–54 / AK 3:185–98).

61 Cf. Plato, *Republic*, 509d–511e; *Phaedo*, 65a–67b; *Symposium*, 211b–212a; and *Phaedrus*, 246b–249d.

62 Cf. Crusius, *Entwurf* (1745), §46.

63 A traditional proverb repeated by Kant in the *Critique of Pure Reason* (1781/ 1787) B83 (AK 3:79) and first found in Polybius, *Historia*, XXXIII, 21; see also Lucian, *Demonax*, XXVIII.

64 See note 52.

65 Kant's reference seems to be to *Letters* XCII (10 January 1761) and XCIII (13 January 1761) in the German translation (Leipzig: 1769) of Euler's *Lettres à une princesse d'Allemagne* (1768–72).

66 Kant is probably alluding to Newton, *Principia mathematica* (1687), General Scholium (2nd edition: 1713). See the fourth paragraph.

67 Cf. *A Collection of Papers* (1717) (Loemker, pp. 675–721), in particular Leibniz's Paper III, §6 (Loemker, pp. 682–3).

68 These are problems taken up again in the Antinomies of the *Critique of Pure Reason* (1781/1787), in particular at A426–43 / B454–71 (AK 3:294–307), together with Kant's solutions at A517–32 / B546–60 (AK 3:354–62).

69 The maxim is rejected by Wolff in his *Vernünftige Gedancken von Gott, der Welt und der Seele des Menschen* (1719), §39 (8th edition: 1741). Crusius, in his *Entwurf* (1745), VIII, §124, allows for one meaning of contingency which is in accord with the maxim rejected by Kant. At the same time, Crusius also allows for another meaning which is not in accord with the maxim.

70   In the Second Analogy of the *Critique of Pure Reason* (1781/1787) A189–211 / B232–56 (AK 3:166–80 / AK 4:128–41), Kant develops and defends a principle of causation universal for all objects of nature.

71   Epicurus asserts that nothing comes from nothing in his *Letter to Herodotus*, xxxviii.

72   Cf. Kant's discussion of the systematicity of principles in the appendix to the Transcendental Dialectic of the *Critique of Pure Reason* (1781/1787), especially A652 / B680 (AK 3:432).

73   See note 58.

74   See note 65.

Bibliographies of editions and translations

NEW ELUCIDATION

Editions

Principiorum primorum cognitionis metaphysicae nova dilucidatio. Königsberg: J. H. Hartung, 1755. [No further printings during Kant's lifetime.]

English translations

F. E. ENGLAND. *A New Exposition of the First Principles of Metaphysical Knowledge,* in England, 1932, pp. 211–52.

J. A. REUSCHER. *A New Exposition of the First Principles of Metaphysical Knowledge,* in Beck, 1986, pp. 56–106.

French translations

J. FERRARI. *Nouvelle explication des premiers principes de la connaissance métaphysique,* in Alquié, 1980, Vol. I, pp. 109–63.

German translations

J. H. TIEFTRUNK. *Neue Erklärung der ersten Grundsätze der metaphysischen Erkenntniss,* in Tieftrunk, 1807, Vol. IV, pp. 173–284.

J. H. VON KIRCHMANN. *Eine neue Beleuchtung der ersten Principien aller metaphysischen Erkenntniss,* in Kirchmann, 1872, Vol. I, pp. 1–51.

K. VORLÄNDER. *Eine neue Beleuchtung der ersten Prinzipien der metaphysischen Erkenntnis,* in Vorländer, 1920, Vol. V, pp. 1–52.

M. BOCK. *Neue Erhellung der ersten Grundsätze metaphysischer Erkenntnis,* in Weischedel, 1960, Vol. I, pp. 401–509.

Italian translations

R. ASSUNTO. *Nuova illustrazione dei primi principi della conoscenza metafisica,* in Carabellese, 1982, pp. 3–53.

467

PHYSICAL MONADOLOGY

Editions

Metaphysicae cum geometria iunctae usus in philosophia naturali, cuius specimen I. continet monadologiam physicam. Königsberg: J. H. Hartung, 1756. [No further printings during Kant's lifetime.]

English translations

G. RABEL. *The Benefit for Natural Philosophy of a Metaphysic Connected with Geometry* (extract only), in Rabel, 1963, pp. 31–2.

L. W. BECK. *The Use in Natural Philosophy of Metaphysics combined with Geometry. Part I: Physical Monadology*, in Beck, 1986, pp. 115–32.

French translations

S. ZAC. *Usage en philosophie naturelle de la métaphysique unie à la geometrie dont l'échantillon I. contient la monadologie physique*, in Zac, 1970, pp. 31–51.

German translations

J. H. TIEFTRUNK. *Nutzen der Verbindung der Metaphysik mit der Geometrie in der Natur-Philosophie von welcher der erste Versuch die physische Monadologie enthält*, in Tieftrunk, 1807, Vol. IV, pp. 285–316.

J. J. KIRCHMANN. *Der Nutzen einer mit der Geometrie verbundenen Metaphysik für die Natur-Philosophie. Erste Abtheilung: die physische Monadenlehre enthaltend*, in Kirchmann, 1872, Vol. I, pp. 295–318.

O. BUEK. *Über die Vereinigung von Metaphysik und Geometrie in ihrer Anwendung auf die Naturphilosophie, wovon die erste Probe die physische Monadologie bildet*, in Vorländer, 1920, Vol. VII, pp. 341–62.

N. HINSKE. *Der Gebrauch der Metaphysik, sofern sie mit der Geometrie verbunden ist, in der Naturphilosophie, dessen erste Probe die physische Monadologie enthält*, in Weischedel, 1960, Vol. II, pp. 511–63.

Italian translations

P. CARABELLESE. *Monadologia fisica*, in Carabellese, 1923, [1968, pp. 55–75].

OPTIMISM

Editions

Versuch einiger Betrachtungen über den Optimismus von M. Immanuel Kant, wodurch er zugleich seine Vorlesungen auf das bevorstehende halbe Jahr ankündigt. Den 7. October 1759. Königsberg: J. F. Driest, 1759. [Further printing: Tieftrunk, 1807, Vol. IV, pp. 351–61.]

English translations

G. RABEL. *Some Reflections on Optimism* (extract), in Rabel, 1963, pp. 40–2.

French translations

P. FESTUGIÈRE. *Considérations sur l'optimisme,* in Festugière, 1931 [1972, pp. 57–67].

J. FERRARI. *Essai de quelques considérations sur l'optimisme de M. Emmanuel Kant par lequel il annonce en même temps son cours pour le prochain semestre le 7 Octobre 1759,* in Alquié, 1980, Vol. I, pp. 165–74.

Italian translations

R. ASSUNTO. *Saggi di talune considerazioni sull' ottimismo nel quale l'autore annuncia al contempo le lezioni che terra nel prossimo semestre (1759),* in Carabellese, 1953, [1982, pp. 91–9].

FALSE SUBTLETY

Editions

Die falsche Spitzfindigkeit der vier syllogistischen Figuren erwiesen von M. Immanuel Kant. Königsberg: J. J. Kanter, 1762. [Counterfeit edition: Frankfurt; further printings in Voigt, 1797–8, Vol. II, pp. 113–44, and Tieftrunk, 1799, Vol. I, pp. 585–610.]

English translations

J. S. BECK. *The False Subtilty of the Four Syllogistic Figures Evinced,* in Beck, 1798, Vol. I, pp. 155–9.

T. K. ABBOT. *Essay on the Mistaken Subtlety of the Four Syllogistic Figures,* in Abbot, 1885, pp. 79–95.

A. RABEL. *The False Subtlety of the Four Syllogistic Figures* (extract), in Rabel, 1963, pp. 44–5.

French translations

S. ZAC. *De la fausse subtilité des quatre figures du syllogisme (1762),* in Zac, 1970, pp. 69–88.

F. COURTES. *La fausse subtilité des quatre figures syllogistiques, demontrée par Kant,* in Courtès, 1972, pp. 53–67.

J. FERRARI. *La fausse subtilité des quatre figures du syllogisme,* in Alquié, 1980, Vol. I, pp. 175–94.

Spanish translations

R. TORRETTI. *La false sutileza de las cuatro figuras del silogismo*, in *Dialogos* (Rio Piedras), Vol. VII, 1973.

THE ONLY POSSIBLE ARGUMENT

Editions

Der einzig mögliche Beweisgrund zu einer Demonstration des Daseyns Gottes. Königsberg: J. J. Kanter, 1763.

Der einzige mögliche Beweis vom Daseyn Gottes. Königsberg: J. J. Kanter, 1770.

Der einzig mögliche Beweisgrund zu einer Demonstration des Daseyns Gottes von Immanuel Kant, Königsberg, 1783 [erroneously for 1763] *Neue[r] unveränderter Abdruck.* Königsberg: J. J. Kanter, 1794.

Der einzig mögliche Beweisgrund zu einer Demonstration des Daseyns Gottes von Immanuel Kant. Leipzig: 1794.

[Further printings in: Voigt, 1797–8, Vol. II, pp. 145–288, and Tieftrunk, 1799, Vol. II, pp. 55–229.]

English translations

J. S. BECK. *The Only Possible Argument for the Demonstration of the Existence of God,* in Beck, 1798, Vol. II, pp. 217–366.

G. RABEL. *The Only Possible Argument for a Demonstration of the Existence of God* (extracts), in Rabel, 1963, pp. 51–8.

G. TREASH. *The Only Possible Basis for a Demonstration of the Existence of God,* New York: 1979.

French translations

P. FESTUGIÈRE. *L'unique fondement possible d'un démonstration de l'existence de Dieu* (1763), in Festugière, 1923, [1972, pp. 69–192].

S. ZAC. *L'unique fondement possible d'une démonstration de l'existence de Dieu,* in Alquié, 1980, Vol. I, pp. 317–435.

Italian translations

P. CARABELLESE. *L'unico argomento possibile per una dimostrazione dell'esistenza di Dio* (1762), in Carabellese, 1923, [1982, pp. 103–209].

Latin translations

F. G. BORN. *Argumentum quo, deum esse, uno potest evinci,* in Born, 1796–8, Vol. IV, pp. 428–538.

Spanish translations

J. M. QUINTANA CABANAS. *El unico fundamento posible de una demonstracion de la existencia de Dios*, in J. M. Quintana Cabanas, *Kant: Sobre Dios y la Religion*, Barcelona: 1972.

NEGATIVE MAGNITUDES

Editions

Versuch den Begriff der negativen Grössen in die Weltweisheit einzuführen von M. Immanuel Kant. Königsberg: J. J. Kanter, 1763. [Further edition: Gratz, 1797; further printings in Voigt, 1797–8, Vol. II, pp. 53–112, and Tieftrunk, 1799, Vol. I, pp. 611–76.]

English translations

D. IRVINE. *Attempt to Introduce the Conception of Negative Quantities into Philosophy*, in Irvine, 1911, pp. 117–56.

G. RABEL. *Attempt at Introducing Negative Quantities into Philosophy* (extracts), in Rabel, 1963, pp. 46–50.

French translations

R. KEMPF. *Essai pour introduire en philosophie le concept de grandeur négative*, Paris: 1972.

J. FERRARI. *Essai pour introduire en philosophie le concept de grandeurs négatives*, in Alquié, 1980, Vol. I, pp. 261–302.

Italian translations

R. ASSUNTO. *Tentativo per introdurre nella filosofia il concetto della quantità negative* (*1763*), in Carabellese, 1953, [1982, pp. 249–89].

Latin translations

G. BORN. *De conceptu quantitatum negativarum in philosophiam introducendi*, in Born, 1796–8, Vol. IV, pp. 161–99.

INQUIRY

Editions

Untersuchung über die Deutlichkeit der Grundsätze der natürlichen Theologie und der Moral. Zur Beantwortung der Frage, welche die Königl. Akademie der Wissenschaften zu Berlin auf das Jahr 1763 aufgegeben hat, in *Dissertation qui a remporté le prix proposé par l'Académie Royale des Sciences et Belles Lettres de Prusse, sur la nature, les*

471

espèces, et les degrés de l'évidence avec les pièces qui ont concouru. Berlin: Haude & Spencer, 1764. [Further printings in Voigt, 1797–98, Vol. II, pp. 479–526, and Tieftrunk, 1799, Vol. II, pp. 1–54.]

English translations

J. S. BECK. *An Inquiry concerning the Perspicuity of the Principles of Natural Theology and of Morals,* in Beck, 1798–99, Vol. I, pp. 339–85.

L. W. BECK. *An Inquiry into the Distinctness of the Principle of Natural Theology and Morals,* in Beck, 1949, pp. 261–85.

G. RABEL. *Investigation into the Evidence of the Principles of Natural Theology and Morals* (extracts), in Rabel, 1963, pp. 64–7.

D. E. WALFORD. *Enquiry concerning the Clarity of the Principles of Natural Theology and Ethics,* in Kerferd, 1968, pp. 3–35.

French translations

M. FICHANT. *Recherche sur l'évidence des principes de la théologie naturelle et de la morale,* in Fichant, 1966, pp. 25–63.

J. FERRARI. *Recherche sur l'évidence des principes de la théologie naturelle et de la morale,* in Alquié, 1980, Vol. I, pp. 215–49.

Italian translations

R. ASSUNTO. *Indagine sulla distinzione dei principi della teologia naturale e della morale,* in Carabellese, 1953, [1982, pp. 215–47].

Spanish translations

R. TORRETTI. *Sobre la nitidez de los principios de la teologia natural y la moral,* in *Dialogos* (Rio Piedras), Vol. X, 1974.

ANNOUNCEMENT

Editions

M. *Immanuel Kants Nachricht von der Einrichtung seiner Vorlesungen in dem Winterhalbenjahre von 1765–1766.* Königsberg: J. J. Kanter, 1765. [Further printing in Rink, 1800, pp. 56–70.]

English translations

G. RABEL. *Magister Immanuel Kant's Announcement of his Lectures* (extracts), in Rabel, 1963, pp. 68–71.

French translations

M. FICHANT. *Annonce du programme des leçons de M.E. Kant durant le semestre d'hiver 1765–1766*, in Fichant, 1973, pp. 65–76.

J. FERRARI. *Annonce de M. Emmanuel Kant sur le programme de ses leçons pour le semestre d'hiver 1765–1766*, in Alquié, 1980, Vol. I, pp. 511–23.

DREAMS

Editions

Träume eines Geistersehers, erläutert durch Träume der Metaphysik [Anonymous]. Königsberg: J. J. Kanter, 1766 [A1].

Träume eines Geistersehers, erläutert durch Träume der Metaphysik [Anonymous] [Title-page with rose-branch vignette]. Riga: J. F. Hartknoch, 1766 [A2].

Träume eines Geistersehers, erläutert durch Träume der Metaphysik [Anonymous] [Title-page with seated figure vignette]. Riga: J. F. Hartknoch, 1766 [A3].

[Further printings in Voigt, 1797–8, Vol. II, pp. 379–478, and Tieftrunk, 1799, Vol. II, pp. 247–346.]

English translations

E. F. GOERWITZ. *Dreams of a Spirit-Seer Illustrated by Dreams of Metaphysics*, edited with an introduction and notes by F. Sewall, London & New York: 1900.

G. RABEL. *Dreams of a Spirit-Seer Illustrated by Dreams of Metaphysics* (extracts), in Rabel, 1963, pp. 74–84.

J. MANOLESCO. *Dreams of a Spirit-Seer by Immanuel Kant and other Related Writings* [sic], with an introduction and commentary by J. Manolesco, New York: 1969.

French translations

F. COURTÈS. *Rêves d'un visionnaire expliqués par rêves métaphysiques*, Paris: 1957 [2nd edition: 1977].

B. LORTHOLARY. *Rêves d'un visionnaire expliqués par des rêves métaphysiques*, in Alquié, 1980, Vol. I, pp. 525–92.

Italian translations

P. CARABELLESE. *Sogni di un visionario chiariti con sogni della metafisica (1766)*, in Carabellese, 1923, [1982, pp. 346–405].

B. SALMONA. *Sogni di un visionario chiariti con sogni della metafisica*, Padova: 1970.

M. VENTURINI. *I sogni di un visionario spiegati con sogni del metafisica*, Milan: 1982.

Latin translations

F. G. BORN. *Somnia pneumatoptae per somnia metaphysices illustrata,* in Born, 1796–8, Vol. IV, pp. 97–160.

DIRECTIONS IN SPACE

Editions

Von dem ersten Grunde des Unterschiedes der Gegenden im Raume, in *Königsberger Frag- und Anzeigungsnachrichten.* Nos. 6, 7, & 8, Königsberg: 1768. [Further printings in Rink, 1800, pp. 71–80, and Tieftrunk, 1807, Vol. IV, pp. 71–80.]

English translations

D. IRVINE. *Concerning the First Ground of the Difference of Environs of Space,* in Irvine, 1911, pp. 157–65.

J. HANDYSIDE. *On the First Ground of the Distinction of Regions in Space,* in Handyside, 1929, pp. 17–29.

G. RABEL. *On the Primary Reason for Distinguishing Direction in Space* (extract), in Rabel, 1963, pp. 86–7.

D. E. WALFORD. *Concerning the Ultimate Foundations of the Differentiation of Regions in Space,* in Kerferd, 1968, pp. 36–43.

French translations

S. ZAC. *Du premier fondement de la différence des régions dans l'espace,* in Zac, 1970, pp. 89–98.

Italian translations

P. CARABELLESE. *Del primo fondamento della distinzione delle regioni nello spazio* (*1768*), in Carabellese, 1923, [1982, pp. 409–17].

Spanish translations

R. TORRETTI. *Sobre el fundamento primero de la differencia entre las regiones del espacio,* in *Dialogos* (Rio Piedras), Vol. VIII, 1972.

INAUGURAL DISSERTATION

Editions

De mundi sensibilis atque intelligibilis forma et principiis. Königsberg: J. J. Kanter, 1770. [Further printings in Zeitz, 1795, pp. 1–44, Voigt, 1797, Vol. III, pp. 1–63, and Tieftrunk, 1799, Vol. II, pp. 435–88.]

English translations

W. J. ECKHOFF. *Dissertation on the Form and Principles of the Sensible and Intelligible World*, in W. J. Eckhoff, *Kant's Inaugural Dissertation of 1770*, New York: 1894.

J. HANDYSIDE. *Dissertation on the Form and Principles of the Sensible and Intelligible World*, in Handyside, 1929, pp. 35–85.

G. RABEL. *On the Form and Principles of the Sensuous and Intellectual Worlds* (extracts), in Rabel, 1963, pp. 88–92.

G. B. KERFERD. *On the Form and Principles of the Sensible and Intelligible World (Inaugural Dissertation) (1770)*, in Kerferd, 1968, pp. 45–92.

J. HANDYSIDE revised by L. W. BECK. *On the Form and Principles of the Sensible and Intelligible World (Inaugural Dissertation)*, in Beck, 1986, pp. 145–88.

French translations

J. TISSOT. *De la forme et des principes du monde sensible et de l'intelligible*, Paris: 1862.

P. MOUY. *Emmanuel Kant: La dissertation de 1770*, Paris: 1942 [3rd edition: Paris: 1967].

F. ALQUIÉ. *La dissertation de 1770: De la forme et des principes du monde sensible et du monde intelligible*, in Alquié, 1980, Vol. I, pp. 623–78.

German translations

M. HERTZ (one of the respondents to Kant's *Inaugural Dissertation*). *Betrachtungen aus der Weltweisheit* [Kant describes this work as a *Copey*, by which he presumably means a paraphrase; cf. Kant's letter to Nicolai of 25 October 1778 (AK 10:135); but he also expresses dissatisfaction with the way in which his ideas had been expressed (AK 10:127, 135, and 139)], in Voigt, 1797–8, Vol. III, pp. 1–63.

J. H. TIEFTRUNK. *Von der Form und den Prinzipien der Sinnen und Verstandes-Welt*, in Tieftrunk, 1799, Vol. II, pp. 489–566.

J. H. VON KIRCHMANN. *Über die Form und die Prinzipien der sinnlichen und der Verstandes-Welt 1770*, in Kirchmann, 1870, pp. 131–76.

K. VORLÄNDER. *Über die Form und die Prinzipien der Sinnen und der Verstandeswelt*, in Vorländer, 1920, Vol. Vb, pp. 87–132.

K. REICH. *Über die Form und die Prinzipien der Sinnen und Geisteswelt*, Hamburg: 1958.

N. HINSKE. *Von der Form der Sinnen- und Verstandeswelt und ihren Gründen*, in Weischedel, 1960, Vol. V, pp. 7–107.

Italian translations

P. CARABELLESE. *La forma e i principi del mondo sensibile ed intelligibili (1770)*, in Carabellese, 1923 [1982, pp. 419–61].

A. LAMACCHIA. *La forma e i principi del mondo sensibile e del mondo intelligibile* (*Dissertazione del 1770*), Padova: 1967.

Spanish translations

R. CENAL LORENTE. *Immanuel Kant: La dissertatio de 1770 sobre la forma y los principios del mundo sensible y del intelligible*, Madrid: 1961.

Glossary

abstracted	*abgesondert*	
	abstrahirt	
abstraction	*Absonderung*	
actual	*wirklich*	(cf. real)
actuality	*Wirklichkeit*	(cf. reality)
adaptedness	*Schicklichkeit*	
	Tauglichkeit	(alt: suitability)
adequacy	*Zulänglichkeit*	
agreement	*consensus*	
	convenientia	
	Übereinstimmung	(cf. harmony)
alteration	*vicissitudo*	(cf. change)
analyse	*resolvere*	(cf. synthesise)
	zergliedern	
analysis	*analysis*	(cf. synthesis)
	Analysis	(cf. synthesis)
	Auflösung	(cf. synthesis)
	Zergliederung	(cf. synthesis)
antecedently	*antecedenter*	(cf. consequentially; alt: preceding)
apparition	*Erscheinung*	(cf. appearance; manifestation; phenomenon)
appearance	*apparentia*	(cf. phenomenon)
	Erscheinung	(cf. apparition; manifestation; phenomenon)
	phaenomenon	(occ: phenomenon)
appropriateness	*Anständigkeit*	(alt: suitability)
arbitrary[1]	*willkürlich*	(cf. product of choice; voluntary; power of choice; alt: product of will; deliberate)
argument[2]	*Beweisgrund*	(cf. demonstration; lit: ground of proof)
arrangement	*Anordung*	(cf. provision; order)
artificial	*künstlich*	(cf. product of art)
aspect	*species*	(occ. species)

balance	*aequilibrium*	
being	*ens*	(alt: entity)
	Sein	
	Wesen	(occ: essence)
boundary	*Grenze*	(cf. limit)
cancellation	*Aufhebung*	(cf. positing)
	remotio	(lit: removal)
capacity	*Fähigkeit*	(alt: faculty; ability)
certainty	*Gewissheit*	
	Sicherheit	(alt: reliability)
change	*mutatio*	(cf. alteration)
	permutatio	(cf. alteration)
characteristic mark	*Merkmal*	(alt: attribute, mark)
	nota	(alt: mark; attribute)
clear	*klar*	(cf. confused; distinct; obscure)
cluster	*Klumpe*	(alt: conglomeration; cf. mass)
cohesiveness	*Zusammenhang*	(cf. connection)
combination	*Verbindung*	
combining together	*colligatio*	
communion[3]	*Gemeinschaft*	(cf. community; society)
community	*communio*	(cf. interaction; alt: communion)
	Gemeinschaft	(cf. communion; society)
complete	*adequatus*	
	ausführlich	(cf. adequate)
	completus	
compound	*compositus*	
concept[4]	*conceptus*	
	notio	
conclusion	*Conclusion*	
	Folge	(cf. inference)
	Schlussfolge	
	Schlussatz	
	Schlussurtheil	
conflict	*conflictus*	
	repugnantia	(cf. contradiction; alt: inconsistency)
	Widerstreit	(cf. contradiction; alt: inconsistency)
confused	*verworren*	(cf. obscure)
conjunction	*colligatio*	(cf. connection)
connection	*nexus*	(cf. conjunction)
	Verknüpfung	

	Zusammenhang	(occ: cohesiveness)
conscience	*conscientia*	(cf. consciousness)
consciousness	*conscientia*	(cf. conscience)
consequence[5]	*Folge*	(cf. conclusion)
consequentially	*consequenter*	(cf. antecedently; alt: subsequently)
contradiction	*contradictio*	(cf. conflict)
	repugnantia	(alt: inconsistency)
	Widerspruch	(cf. conflict)
deception	*Betrug*	
	Täuschung	
defect	*Mangel*	(cf. deprivation)
define	*erklären*	(occ: explain)
definite	*definitus*	(cf. determinate)
definition[6]	*Definition*	
	Erklärung	(occ: explanation)
deliberate	*willkürlich*	(cf. arbitrary, product of choice, voluntary)
delusion	*Wahn*	(cf. madness, mental delusion)
demonstration[2]	*Demonstration*	(cf. argument)
deprivation	*Beraubung*	(cf. lack, defect)
	privatio	
derangement	*Verrückung*	(cf. displacement; madness; mental delusion)
determinate	*bestimmt*	(cf. determined)
	definitus	(cf. definite)
	determinatus	(cf. determined)
determination	*Bestimmung*	
	Determination	
determined	*determinatus*	(cf. determinate)
direction[7]	*Gegend*	
	Richtung	
direction, line which indicates	*Directionslinie*	
	Richtungslinie	
displacement	*Verrückung*	(cf. derangement)
disposition	*Fügung*	(alt: arrangement)
distinct	*deutlich*	(cf. clear)
effective power	*efficacia*	(alt: power to produce an effect)
entirety	*universitas*	(cf. totality; universality)
entity	*Einheit*	(cf. monad; occ: unity)
equal[8]	*gleich*	(cf. similar)

479

essence	*Wesen*	(cf. being)
existence	*Dasein*	(cf. being)
	Existenz	(cf. being)
false subtlety	*falsche Spitzfindigkeit*	(alt: sophistry)
fantasies	*Phantasterei*	
fantastical visionary	*Phantast*	
fantasy	*Phantasie*	
fill	*implere*	(cf. occupy)
	replere	(cf. occupy)
freedom	*libertas*	
	licentia	
futurition	*futuritio*	(alt: future occurrence)
ground[5]	*Grund*	
	ratio	(alt: reason)
grounded[5]	*rationatus*	(alt: consequent)
harmoniousness	*Wohlgereimtheit*	
harmonising	*convenientia*	(cf. harmony)
harmony	*harmonia*	
	Harmonie	
	Übereinstimmung	(alt: agreement)
	Zusammenpassung	(alt: agreement)
	Zussamenstimmung	(alt: agreement)
idea[9]	*Idee*	
illusion	*Blendwerk*	(cf. deception; delusion)
imagination	*Einbildung*	(cf. fantasy; imagination, faculty of)
	Phantasie	
imagination, faculty of	*Einbildungskraft*	
imagination, figment of	*Hirngeburt*	
	Hirngespenst	
	Hirngespinst	
incongruent	*discongruens*	
	incongruent	
infer	*folgern*	
	schliessen	(alt: deduce, draw a conclusion)
inference	*Folge*	(cf. conclusion)
	Folgerung	
	Schluss	
influence	*Einfluss*	
	influxus	(lit: flowing into)
inherent	*insitus*	(cf. innate)
innate	*ingenitus*	(cf. inherent)
intelligence	*intelligentia*	(cf. understanding)
intelligible	*intelligibilis*	

interaction	*commercium*	(cf: community; alt: reciprocity)
intervention	*Vorkehrung*	(alt: precautionary measure, arrangement, provision)
intuition	*Anschauung*	
	intuitus	
judgement[10]	*Urtheil*	
lack	*Mangel*	(cf. deprivation)
	absentia	
	defectus	
limit	*limes*	(cf: boundary)
	Schranke	(cf: boundary; alt: barrier; limitation)
	terminus	
limitation	*limitatio*	(cf: boundary; limit)
madness	*Wahnsinn*	(cf. derangement; mental delusion)
magnitude	*Grösse*	
	quantum	
malady	*Krankheit*	(alt: illness; sickness)
manifestation	*Erscheinung*	(cf. apparition; appearance; phenomenon)
manifold	*Mannigfaltige*	
mass	*Klumpe*	(cf. cluster; alt: conglomeration)
	Klumpen	(cf. cluster; alt: conglomeration)
	massa	
	Masse	
meaning	*Bedeutung*	
mental delusion	*Wahnwitz*	(cf: derangement; madness)
mind	*animus*	(cf: soul)
	mens	
monad	*Einheit*	(cf: entity; occ: unity)
	monas	
multiplicity	*multitudo*	
	Vielheit	
negation	*Negation*	
	Verneinung	
noumenon	*noumenon*	(cf. phenomenon)
obscure	*dunkel*	(cf. clear; confused; distinct)
opposed	*entgegengesetzt*	
	opponirt	
opposite	*Gegentheil*	

opposition	*Entgegensetzung*	
	oppositio	
	Opposition	
order	*Ordnung*	(cf. arrangement; provision)
original Being	*Urwesen*	(alt: primordial Being; archetypal Being)
originary	*originarius*	(alt: original; archetypal)
phantom	*Schattenbild*	(cf. illusion; imagination, figment of)
phenomenon	*Erscheinung*	(cf. apparition; appearance; manifestation)
place	*locus*	
	Ort	
planetary system	*Planetenbau*	
	Planetensystem	
	Planetenwelt	
posit	*ponere*	(lit: place; put)
	setzen	
posited	*positus*	(cf. position)
positing	*positio*	(cf. position)
	Position	
	Setzung	
position	*Lage*	
	positio	(cf. positing)
	positus	(cf. positing; occ: posited)
power of choice	*arbitrium*	(cf. volition; will)
	Willkür	(cf. arbitrary, voluntary, product of choice)
premiss[11]	*Vordersatz*	
	Vorderurtheil	
principle	*Grundsatz*	
product of art	*künstlich*	(cf. artificial)
product of choice	*willkürlich*	(cf. arbitrary, power of choice)
property	*Eigenschaft*	(cf. quality)
proposition[11]	*Satz*	(alt: sentence)
provision	*Anstalt*	(cf. arrangement, disposition, intervention)
	Veranstaltung	(cf. arrangement, disposition, intervention)
	Verfügung	(cf. arrangement, dis-

		position, interven-tion)
purpose	*Zweck*	(occ: end)
quality	*affectio*	
	Beschaffenheit	(cf. property; alt: state, condition, constitu-tion)
real	*real*	(cf. actual)
real ground	*Realgrund*	
real opposition	*Realentgegensetzung*	(cf. real repugnancy)
	Realopposition	
real repugnancy	*Realrepugnanz*	(cf. real opposition)
reality	*Realität*	(cf. actuality)
reasoning	*argumentatio*	
	ratiocinatio	
receptivity	*receptivitas*	
reciprocal	*mutuus*	
	reciprocus	
reference	*Beziehung*	(cf. relation)
relation	*relatio*	
	respectus	
	Verhältnis	(cf. reference)
repugnancy	*Repugnanz*	
schema	*schema*	
scheme	*Plan*	(cf: schema; alt: plan, project)
semblance	*Anschein*	
	Schein	
	species	
sensation	*sensatio*	
sense	*sensus*	
	Sinn	(cf: meaning)
sensed, what is[12]	*sensa*	
sensibility[12]	*sensualitas*	
sensible[12]	*sinnlich*	
	sensibilis	
sensitive[12]	*sensitivus*	
sensory[12]	*sensualis*	
sensory delusion	*Wahnsinn*	(cf. derangement; mad-ness; mental delu-sion)
sign	*character*	
	Zeichen	
signify	*bezeichnen*	
similar[8]	*ähnlich*	(cf. equal)
society	*Gesellschaft*	(cf. communion; com-munity)

	Societät	(cf. communion; community)
soul	*anima*	(cf. mind)
specifiable	*assignabilis*	
spirit[13]	*Geist*	(cf. soul; mind; occ: mind)
spirit[14]	*geistig*	(occ: mental)
structure	*compages*	(alt: action of binding)
syllogism	*Vernunftschluss*	(lit: inference of reason)
syllogistic	*Syllogistik*	(alt: theory of the syllogism)
synthesis	*synthesis*	(cf. analysis)
	Synthesis	(cf. analysis)
	Zusammensetzung	(cf. analysis)
synthesise	*componere*	(cf. analyse)
system of the universe	*Weltbau*	(cf. planetary system)
	Weltsystem	(cf. planetary system)
term[15]	*Hauptbegriff*	
	terminus	
thought	*cogitatio*	
totality	*omnitudo*	(cf. entirety; universality)
turning	*Drehung*	(cf. convolution)
	Wendung	
	Windung	(alt: winding)
unanalysable	*unauflöslich*	
understanding[16]	*intellectus*	(cf. intelligence; alt: intellect)
understanding, of or deriving from[16]	*intellectualis*	(alt. intellectual)
understanding, use of[16]	*intellectio*	(alt. intellection)
universality	*universitas*	(cf. entirety; totality)
use	*Nutzen*	(cf. usefulness; alt: benefit)
useful	*nützlich*	(alt: beneficial)
usefulness	*Nutzen*	(cf. use)
	Nützlichkeit	
	Nutzbarkeit	
volition	*volitio*	(cf. will; cf. power of choice)
voluntary	*willkürlich*	(cf. arbitrary; deliberate)
whole	*Ganze*	(alt: totality; entirety)
	totum	(alt: totality; entirety)
will	*volitio*	(cf. volition; cf. power of choice)

voluntas	(cf. volition; cf. power of choice)
Wille	(cf. power of will)

NOTES TO GLOSSARY

1 The English word 'arbitrary' and the German word *willkürlich* display similar patterns of ambiguity: both words originally mean issuing from, arising out of, being the product of, being governed by choice (and thus in some contexts, voluntary or deliberate); both words have also come to have the pejorative meaning capricious, willful, unrestrained, despotic. In these works Kant almost never employs the word *willkürlich* in this pejorative sense. Where the word *willkürlich* is used to qualify a *definition* (or some other linguistic phenomenon), the word has been translated by 'arbitrary' (in the sense of 'stipulative' [as in 'stipulative definition'] or of G. E. Moore's 'arbitrary verbal definition'); where the word is used to qualify an *action* it has been translated by 'voluntary' or 'deliberate' or, occasionally, 'which is the product of choice'. A linguistic note always records the occurrence of this difficult word.

2 The German word *Beweisgrund* does not need and indeed ought not to be translated literally by 'ground of proof'; it is ordinarily used in German to signify the same as the English word 'argument'. Grimm offers the Latin *argumentum* as the full definition of the term, citing the title of Kant's *Only Possible Argument* (1763) as a paradigm of its use. Lewis and Short contrast *argumentum* with *ratio:* the former appeals to *facts*, whereas the latter appeals to logical considerations. Kant contrasts *Beweisgrund* and *Demonstration:* the difference is primarily one of form: the former provides the raw data of the latter, which organises and articulates that data in accordance with the laws of logic; the informal *Beweisgrund* is thus converted into a formal demonstration which is apodeictic and certain.

3 The word *Gemeinschaft* is ambiguous: it may mean either the dynamic relation holding between things or persons (say, the gravitational attraction between things in space, or the sociability or gregariousness which holds between persons), or the resultant unity which arises from that dynamic relation (say, the system of nature in space and time, or the system of society). Kant himself draws attention to this ambiguity in the *Critique of Pure Reason* (1781/1787) A313 / B260 (AK 3:182), designating the dynamic relation by the Latin term *commercium* ('reciprocity' or 'interaction') and the resultant unity or system by the Latin term *communio* ('community'). Occurrences of this difficult word are registered in the linguistic footnotes. Occasionally, it is unclear which sense is intended by Kant, and that problem too receives comment in the linguistic footnotes.

4 *Conceptus* and *notio* are synonymous terms and have been used as such by Kant. Both terms have been translated by the single English term 'concept'. In German both Latin terms would have to be translated by *Begriff.* Reuscher, in his introduction to his translation of the *Nova Dilucidatio* (Beck, 1986, pp. 47–109), makes the following unsubstantiated claim: 'The word

notion [Reuscher's translation of *notio*] in the *New Exposition* always carries the connotation of orientation towards something there and given. It never means the merely thinkable. It is therefore a technical term whose [*sic*] distinctive feature is its existential colouring. It does not belong to the vocabulary of the purely speculative' (Beck, 1986, p. 51). Apart from the obscurity of the claims made, there is no evidence whatsoever to support the contention that *notio* is a technical term and therefore quite distinct from *conceptus*. A close examination of the text of the three Latin dissertations included in this volume reveals that these two terms are employed with the following frequencies: *New Elucidation: notio* 42, *conceptus* 6; *Physical Monadology: notio* 4, *conceptus* 0; *Inaugural Dissertation: notio* 20, *conceptus* 100. A close scrutiny of Kant's use of the two Latin terms reveals that they are employed synonymously (they are sometimes used interchangeably within the same sentence; they are sometimes linked by *vel* ('or'), and *notio* is sometimes employed explicitly of something which is *not* 'there and given' but of something 'purely speculative'. The fact that Kant employs *notio* seven times more frequently than *conceptus* in the *New Elucidation* and *conceptus* five times more frequently than *notio* in the *Inaugural Dissertation* does not document a change of preoccupation, but nothing more significant than a change of stylistic preference. Since Kant employs the two Latin terms interchangeably and since the English words 'concept' and 'notion' are *not* synonyms (the latter is much more general in meaning, for it embraces both 'concept' and 'idea' in its broadest sense), and so as not to raise unnecessary and distracting questions in the reader's mind, the single English equivalent 'concept' has been used to translate both Latin terms.

5   The two German terms *Grund* and *Folge* correspond roughly to the Latin terms *ratio* and *rationatus*, and display the same patterns of ambiguity. Both *Grund* and *ratio* are neutral in respect of being the premise of an argument, the cause of an effect, and the reason for an action; likewise, *Folge* and *rationatus* are neutral in respect of being the conclusion of an argument, the effect of a cause, or an action or choice which has been governed by a reason. In order to preserve this neutrality *Grund* has been translated by 'ground' (which may be a premise, or a cause, or a reason), and *Folge* by 'consequence' (which may be the conclusion of an argument, or the effect of a cause, or an action resulting from choice).

   Ratio signifies an explanation either of something's being the case (*ratio essendi*), or of something's coming to be the case (*ratio fiendi*), or of something's being known to be the case (*ratio cognoscendi*). The Latin term may therefore designate the cause of an event, the premise of an argument, or the reason for a belief or truth. The neutrality of the Latin term with respect to these different types of explanations contributed to (and was a product of) the conflation of causes and reasons. In order to preserve the neutrality of the term, *ratio* has been translated by 'ground' (rather than by 'reason'). The German translation of *ratio* is itself *Grund*. For the sake of consistency, the phrase *principium rationis sufficientis* (traditionally translated 'principle of sufficient reason') has been translated by 'principle of sufficient ground'. The same pattern of meanings is to be found in the term *rationatus*, which signifies that which is governed by, or is a product of, a *ratio* (the conclusion of an argument, the implication of a premise, the effect of a cause). It has normally been translated by 'that which is grounded' and sometimes by 'that which is determined by a ground'.

6 Kant employs the terms *Definition* and *Erklärung* as synonyms in the works in this volume – despite drawing a distinction between them in the *Critique of Pure Reason* (1781). The reader is referred to note 4 to *The Only Possible Argument* for further details. Both terms have thus been translated by 'definition'. Kant distinguishes between real and nominal definitions, employing the terms *Realerklärungen, Realdefinitionen,* and *Sacherklärungen* for the former, and *Nominalerklärungen, Nominaldefinitionen,* and *Worterklärungen* for the latter.

7 For the justification for the translation of *Gegend* by 'direction' (rather than 'region') see factual note 1 to the *Directions in Space* (1768).

8 For the full significance of this phrase – a *terminus technicus* – see factual note 16 to the *Directions in Space* (1768).

9 Kant employs the word *Idee* in the manner condemned in the *Critique of Pure Reason* (1781) to signify 'idea' or *Vorstellung.* It is not employed to designate Platonic ideas only. It does not yet have the narrow technical sense (pure idea of reason) which it will later assume for Kant.

10 Kant also employs the following compounds involving the word *Urtheil: Vorderurtheil* ('premise'); *Haupturtheil* ('main judgement' or 'major premise'); *Zwischenurtheil* ('intermediate judgement' or 'minor premise').

11 Kant also employs the following compounds involving the word *Satz: Obersatz* ('major premise') (cf. *Haupturtheil*); *Untersatz* ('minor premise') (cf. *Zwischenurtheil*).

12 The following words, ordered according to the frequency of their occurrence in the *Inaugural Dissertation* (indicated in brackets), require comment: *sensitivus* ('sensitive') and the adverb *sensitive* ('sensitively') [84]; *sensus* ('sense') [40]; *sensibilis* ('sensible') [17]; *sensualis* ('sensory') [12]; *sensatio* ('sensation') [10]; *sensualitas* ('sensibility') [7]; and *sensa* ('what is sensed') [4]. Of these, *sensus, sensatio,* and *sensa* present no great difficulties: *sensus* has the same meaning and displays the same pattern of ambiguities as the English word 'sense'; *sensatio* and 'sensation' are exact synonyms; *sensa* is slightly more problematic; it has been taken to signify any object of sensory experience. The words *sensitivus, sensitive, sensibilis, sensualis,* and *sensualitas* are much more difficult. It is important to bear in mind that the vocabulary of the *Inaugural Dissertation* is, in this area, much more complicated than that of the *Critique of Pure Reason,* where two words only (*sinnlich* and *Sinnlichkeit* ['sensible' and 'sensibility']) fulfil the function of the five words just listed. It is also worth noting that Kant does not anywhere in this work employ the words *sensitivitas* (although Beck's employment of the word 'sensitivity' [Beck, 1986, pp. 189 and 250] may suggest otherwise) or *sensibilitas.* The word *sensualitas* is, it is true, employed, but only on seven occasions. The term which Kant employs with by far the greatest frequency is *sensitivus* (and its adverbial form *sensitive*). On all occasions without exception they qualify or characterise what might be called 'the subjective content and the *a priori*

487

form of our experience' (intuitions and concepts, both empirical and *a priori*, the faculty of knowledge, the conditions of cognition, any thought or conception). Neither term is ever used to qualify the objects of experience (the world, or things and events in the world). It follows that the neuter plural substantival form of the word (*sensitiva*) may never be translated 'things sensitive' or 'sensitive things'; it must always be translated by a locution which refers to a content of subjective experience (for example, 'sensitive concepts' or 'sensitive representations'). Kant's use of *sensitivus* and *sensitive* is absolutely consistent. The same consistency marks Kant's use of the term *sensibilis* (which occurs far less frequently): it is always and without exception employed to qualify or characterise the objective side of experience, specifically the world or the things and events which occur in the world; it never qualifies or describes the subjective aspects of experience. The neuter plural substantival form of the term (*sensibilia*) has always been translated by 'sensible things'. Kant's retention of two quite distinct terms, *sensitivus* and *sensibilis*, with their entirely distinct and carefully observed applications, suggests that, in this area at least, Kant's idealism in the *Inaugural Dissertation* was not as radical as that of the first edition of the *Critique of Pure Reason*, where the traditional subject–object distinction is much more substantially eroded. Kant's use of the word *sensualis* is no less consistent. The term is defined at the beginning of §5 (AK 2:393) in terms of the matter of experience, namely, sensation: any cognition, concept, or intuition which contains or involves sensation is *sensualis*. The term might quite legitimately have been translated by 'empirical', but since Kant also employs *empiricus* (and since the English word 'sensual' has inappropriate connotations) it was decided to adopt 'sensory'. The cognate term *sensualitas* occurs only very rarely: three times in §3 (AK 2:392); once in §12 (AK 2:397); once in §13 (AK 2:398); and twice in §15 (AK 2:404). It is defined in §3 (AK 2:392) as 'the receptivity of the subject in virtue of which it is possible for the subject's own representative state to be affected in a definite way by the presence of some object'. From the passage at the beginning of §13 (AK 2:398): 'But things which, since they do not touch the senses, contain only the singular form of sensibility (*sensualitatis*), belong to pure intuition (that is to say, intuition which is devoid of sensation . . .)' it is clear that *sensualitas* does not, as the cognate word *sensualis* would suggest, signify simply sensory receptivity only, but rather the faculty of sensibility in general, both pure and empirical. Hence the decision to adopt 'sensibility' as the translation. The three *key* terms in Kant's discussion are *sensitivus*, *sensibilis*, and *sensualis*, and they are employed by Kant (contrary to the misleading and confusing claims made by Beck [Beck, 1986, pp. 188–9], who unfairly accuses Kant of 'much equivocation and looseness' of usage and of not always honouring the distinction between *sensualis* and *sensitivus*) with exemplary (and, it must be said, not entirely characteristic) consistency and rigour. Nonetheless Kant's decision to simplify his terminology in this area in the first *Critique* is entirely commendable, and represents a deepening of his idealist outlook.

13   The word *Geist* has a wide range of meanings, of which 'spirit' and 'mind' are the two most important in philosophical contexts. The word is used almost exclusively in the sense of 'spirit' in the *Dreams* (1766).

14 The German word *geistiger* would ordinarily be translated by 'spiritual'. The religious and moral overtones of the English word would, however, be out of place in the context of the *Dreams* (1766). Because Kant is not talking about minds as such, 'mental' would also be an inappropriate translation. In order to preserve the reference to spirits and yet exclude the religious and moral connotations which are extraneous to this work, the translator has opted for 'spirit-'.

15 Kant distinguishes *grösserer Hauptbegriff* ('major term'), *kleinerer Hauptbegriff* ('minor term') and *mittlerer Hauptbegriff* ('minor term').

16 The temptation to translate the Latin term *intellectus* by the cognate English term 'intellect' has been deliberately resisted. The adoption of such a translation would inevitably raise distracting questions in the reader's mind (for example, is Kant postulating the existence of a faculty distinct from understanding? Is Kant's silence about understanding [the word would no longer feature in the translation at all] to be taken as an indication of his denial that such a faculty exists? If not, why is he silent about it? And what is its relation to intellect?) and tempt the reader (as it has tempted some scholars) to maintain that the faculty of intellect in the *Inaugural Dissertation* is to be distinguished sharply from the later notion of the understanding (as it occurs in the *Critique of Pure Reason* [1781/1787]). What is sometimes overlooked is the fact that there is only one German equivalent of *intellectus* and that is *Verstand*. And if it is maintained that the Latin could also be translated by the German word *Intellekt*, then it must be pointed out that the word did *not exist* in Kant's day at all. (The word *Intellekt* is not listed in Grimm, nor is it listed in Campe. However, unlike Grimm, Campe does list *intellectual, intellectuell*, and *Intellectus*, though only in the supplementary volume devoted to foreign borrowings.) Accordingly, Kant *must*, as a matter of linguistic necessity, have been thinking of *Verstand* when he employs the Latin term *intellectus*. This is not, of course, to say that Kant's conception of understanding is identical in the *Inaugural Dissertation* and the *Critique of Pure Reason* (in the earlier work, understanding and reason are not distinguished, for example). The adjective *intellectualis* has not, in general, been translated by 'intellectual'. Unfortunately, there is no adjective which can be formed directly from 'understanding' (in the way that 'intellectual' is formed directly from 'intellect'); the translator has thus been constrained to employ an adjectival *phrase* to translate *intellectualis* (such as: 'belonging to the understanding', 'deriving from the understanding', or 'of the understanding'). All such occurrences of *intellectualis* have been recorded in the Linguistic Notes.

Biographical-bibliographical sketches
of persons mentioned by Kant

<hr>

AEPINUS, *Franz Maria Ulrich Theodor Hoch* (1724–1802): German physicist best known for work on electricity and magnetism. In 1757 elected to Prussian Royal Academy and to chair of physics at St. Petersburg, where he remained until he retired in 1798. Chief works: *Sermo academicus de similitudine vis electricae atque magneticae* ('Academic Discourse of the Similarity between the Forces of Electricity and Magnetism') (St. Petersburg: 1758) (German translation: *Hamburger Magazin*, Vol. XXII, 1759); *Tentamen theoriae electricitatis et magnetismi* ('An attempt at a Theory of Electricity and Magnetism') (St. Petersburg: 1759).

AESOP (ca. 570 B.C.): Greek fabulist. Probably a slave; contemporary of Solon. His fables were turned into Greek verse by Babrius and into Latin verse by Phaedrus. The most celebrated version of Aesop's fables is that of La Fontaine (q.v.).

ALEXANDER OF MACEDONIA (356–323 B.C.): Macedonian general. Born at Pella, the son of Philip II. Educated and allegedly deeply influenced by Aristotle (q.v.). Succeeded to Macedonian crown at the age of twenty upon the assassination of his father in 336 B.C. Within a decade he had created a Greek empire extending to Scythia in the north, Egypt in the south, and India in the east. It was on his return from India that Alexander fell ill and died in Babylon in June 323 B.C. at the age of thirty-two.

APOLLONIUS OF TYANA (1st century A.D.): Neo-Pythagorean sage and religious teacher. Taught that there was a supreme God, who may not be named or worshipped, but that the other gods must be revered and worshipped. Fame of Apollonius established by biography of Philostratus (q.v.) who presents him as a miracle worker. As a result he came to be revered by pious Romans of the Later Empire (Caracalla built a shrine to him; Alexander Severus revered him along with Abraham, Jesus, and Orpheus). The anti-Christian Hierocles of Nicomedia compared the miracles of Jesus and Apollonius.

ARIOSTO, *Ludovico* (1474–1533): Italian epic poet. Spent early life in Ferrara where, after public employment and service at the court of d'Este, he retired and died. Famed for his romantic epic, *Orlando furioso,* first published in 1516, but only reaching final form in 1532. Kant's knowledge of Ariosto is almost certainly mediated by Fontenelle (q.v.), who cites the Italian poet in his *Entretiens sur la pluralité des mondes* (Paris: 1686), which Kant had read and admired.

ARISTOTLE (384–322 B.C.): Greek philosopher and logician. Studied in the Academy under Plato until the latter's death in 347 B.C. Left Athens; travelled widely, engaging in biological and historical research. Returned to Athens in 335 B.C.; founded the Lyceum, of which he was head until his death. In spite of his supreme achievements in all fields of philosophy, and doubtless as a reaction against his dominance during the Middle Ages, Aristotle's reputation was eclipsed by that of Plato in the eighteenth century. For Kant, Aristotle's chief importance was as the creator of logic (in the *Categories, On Interpretation, On Sophistical Refutations, Topics, Prior Analytics,* and the *Posterior Analytics*). Kant's library contained the works of Aristotle in Greek and Latin.

ARTEMIDORUS OF EPHESUS (2nd century A.D.): Greek soothsayer. Author of *Oneirokritika* ('Interpretation of Dreams') in four books. The work is a compilation from earlier authors and affords valuable insight into ancient superstitions. The first modern edition appeared in Greek in Venice in 1518; it was then frequently republished in a variety of forms, especially during the seventeenth century.

AUGUSTINE, *Saint* (354–430): Christian theologian and philosopher. Studied and taught at Carthage; subscribed to the materialist dualism of the Manichaean philosophy. In 382 left Carthage for Rome; appointment to a professorship in Milan brought him under the influence of St. Ambrose and the spiritual monism of Plotinus. In 386 converted to Christianity; baptised in 387; ordained in 391; in 396 appointed Bishop of Hippo, where he devoted the rest of his life to the composition of numerous works of theology and philosophy, and to combating the Manichaeans, Donatists, and Pelagians. Kant's knowledge of Augustine was probably limited to his two most celebrated works: the *Confessions* and the *City of God.*

BAUMEISTER, *Friedrich Christian* (1709–85): German philosopher of the Wolffian School. Held chair of philosophy at Wittenberg; in 1736 became rector of the *Gymnasium* at Görlitz, where he spent the rest of his life. Chief works: *Philosophia definitiva* ('Comprehensive Philosophy') (Wittenberg: 1735); *Institutiones philosophiae rationalis methodo wolffiana conscriptae* ('Principles of Rational Philosophy, Composed in Accordance with the Wolffian Method') (Wittenberg: 1738); *Philosophia recens controversa complexa definitiones theoremata et quaestiones nostra aetate in controversiam vocatas* ('The Recent Philosophical Controversy, Including the Definitions, Theorems and Questions Which Have Been Called into Dispute in our Time') (Leipzig: 1738); *Historia doctrinae recentius controversae de mundo optimo* ('History of the Recently Disputed Doctrine Concerning the Best World') (Görlitz: 1741).

BAUMGARTEN, *Alexander Gottlieb* (1714–62): German philosopher of the Wolffian School; founder of aesthetics. In 1740 appointed professor of philosophy at Frankfurt-an-der-Oder, where he remained until his death. Chief works: *Metaphysica* ('Metaphysics') (Halle: 1739); *Aesthetica* ('Aesthetics') (2 vols. Frankfurt an der Oder: 1750–8); *Initia philosophiae practicae primae* ('Fundamental Principles of Elementary Practical Philosophy') (Halle: 1760); *Acroasis logica in Chr.Wolff* ('Public Logical Discourse on Christian Wolff') (Halle: 1761). Kant's library contained the following works of Baumgarten: *Metaphysica* (4th edition. Halle: 1757); *Initia* (Halle: 1760); *Acroasis logica* (Halle: 1761).

BEL, *Mathias* (1684–1749): Hungarian historian, educationalist, and theologian. Studied at Bratislava and then Halle, where he read philosophy, theology, natural science, and educational theory. Became rector of the *Gymnasium* in Bratislava, instituting reforms in the spirit of the 'educational realism' he had learned at Halle. Elected foreign member of the London Royal Society and the Prussian and St. Petersburg Royal Academies. Wrote a number of works on the language, history, and culture of his native country. His most important work (for which he was ennobled and appointed court historian to Emperor Charles VI) was *Notitia Hungariae novae historico-geographica divisa in partes quattor* ('Historical and Geographical Notes on Modern Hungary, Divided into Four Parts') (4 vols. Vienna: 1735–42).

BOERHAAVE, *Hermann* (1668–1738): Dutch physicist, chemist, botanist, and physician. Studied philosophy at Leyden and then medicine at Harderwyck. Adopted a chemical-mechanical conception of medicine. Became the incumbent of four professorships simultaneously at Leyden: from 1709 of medicine and botany, from 1714 of practical medicine, and from 1718 of chemistry. Established the fame of Leyden University and especially its School of Medicine. Boerhaave's own renown extended throughout Europe and far beyond to the Middle East and even China. Exercised a decisive influence on the practice of medicine, particularly through his students, in Edinburgh, Vienna, and throughout Germany. In 1728 elected to the Paris Academy of Sciences, and in 1730 to the London Royal Society. Towards the end of his life, Boerhaave tended to return to the vitalism of Hippocrates. Of Boerhaave's vast published output, the following are perhaps the most celebrated: *De usu ratiocinii mechanici in medicina* ('Concerning the Employment of Mechanical Reasoning in Medicine') (Leyden: 1705); *Institutiones medicae in usus annuae exercitationis domesticos* ('The Principles of Medicine for Domestic Use throughout the Year') (Leyden: 1708) [Reprinted: 1713, 1720, 1727, and 1746; translated into many European languages as well as Arabic]; *Aphorismi de cognoscendis et curandis morbis* ('Aphorisms on the Diagnosis and Cure of Illnesses') (Leyden: 1709) [Reprinted in 1715, 1728, and 1742; translated into many languages]; *Elementa chimiae quae anniversario labore docuit in publicis privatisque scholis* ('Elements of Chemistry as they are Taught Annually in Schools both Public and Private') (2 vols. Paris: 1724); *De mercurio experimenta* ('Experiments on Mercury'), in *The Philosophical Transactions of the Royal Society of London*, Nos. 430, 443, and 444 (London: 1733 and 1736) (German translation: *Hamburger Magazin*, Vol. IV, 1753).

BONNET, *Charles* (1720–93): Swiss naturalist; practised law and pursued scientific research. In 1740 discovered parthenogenesis in aphids and was elected to the Paris Royal Academy. Discovered that caterpillars and butterflies breathe through pores and was elected to the London Royal Society. Engaged in important research on the function of leaves. Weakening eyesight forced him to abandon his scientific research; turned to psychology and philosophy. Employing the Leibnizian principle of continuity, Bonnet anticipated evolutionary theory by postulating the existence of a continuous scale of beings. Also construed all mental processes as functions of physiological processes. His works include: *Considérations sur les corps organisés* (2 vols. Amsterdam: 1762–8); *Essai de psychologie, ou considérations sur les observations de l'âme, sur l'habitude et sur l'éducation* (London: 1754); *Essai analytique des facultés de l'âme* (Copenhagen: 1760).

BORELLI, *Giovanni Alfonso* (1608–79): Italian astronomer, mathematician, and physiologist. Held chairs of mathematics at Messina, Pisa, and Florence. Retired to Rome, where he enjoyed the protection and patronage of Queen Christina of Sweden. Belonged to the Cartesian tradition and was devoted in particular to mathematising physiological and medical phenomena. His study of the motion of animals is an attempt at a purely mechanical account of the matter. In addition to the important *De motu animalium* ('Concerning the Motion of Animals') (2 vols. Rome: 1680–1), Borelli also published a study of the relative strengths of the right and left eyes which initially appeared in: *Recueil des mémoires et conférences sur les arts et les sciences presentées a Monseigneur le Dauphin pendant l'année 1672* (Amsterdam: 1673) and of which a German translation was published over a century later: *Des Herrn Alphonsus Borelli Bemerkungen von der ungleichen Stärke der Augen, woraus man schliessen kann, dass das linke Auge die Objecte gemeiniglich viel deutlicher sehe als das rechte* ('Alfonso Borelli's Remarks on the Unequal Strength of the Eyes, from Which It Can Be Concluded That the Left Eye normally sees Objects Much More Clearly than the Right Eye') (*Hamburger Magazin*, Vol. XXIII, 1759).

BRAHE, *Tycho de* (1546–1601): Danish astronomer. Studied at Copenhagen and Leipzig; the patronage of Frederic II of Denmark enabled Brahe to establish two observatories, the famous *Uraniburgum* and *Stellaeburgum.* There for two decades he conducted the meticulous observations necessary for the revision of the Alphonsine Tables and for Kepler's later work. Primarily an observer and maker of astronomical instruments; also attempted a reconciliation of the Ptolemaic and Copernican systems. His published works include: *Astronomiae instauratae progymnasta* ('Introduction to the New Astronomy') (Prague: 1587–9); *Astronomiae instauratae mechanica* ('The Mechanics of the New Astronomy') (Hamburg: 1597); *Epistolarum astronomicarum libri duo* ('Two Books of Astronomical Letters') (Frankfurt: 1610).

BUFFON, *Georges-Louis Leclerc, Comte de* (1707–88): French naturalist. Studied law at Dijon; toured Italy and England with Lord Kingston. Published translation of Hales's (q.v.) *Vegetable Staticks* in 1735 and of Newton's (q.v.) *Treatise on Fluxions* in 1740. In 1739 appointed keeper of the *Jardin du Roi* and of the *Musée Royale.* There he began amassing the material for his monumental *Histoire naturelle, générale et particulière* (36 vols. Paris: 1740–88). Systematically applied the Leibnizian principle of continuity to erode the concept of rigidly distinct species and genera. Like Bonnet (q.v.) Buffon anticipated evolutionary theory.

BURNET, *Thomas* (ca. 1635–1715): Anglican theologian and divine. Author of the celebrated *Telluris theoria sacra, orbis nostri originem et mutationes generales, quas aut iam subiit aut olim subiturus est, complectens* (2 vols. London: 1681–9). Published his own English translation: *Theory of the Earth: Containing an Account of the Original of the Earth, and of all the General Changes which it hath already undergone, or is to undergo, till the Consumation of All Things* (2 vols. London: 1684–90); (German translation: *Theoria sacra telluris d.i. Heiliger Entwurff oder Biblische Betrachtung des Erdreichs, begreiffend, nebens dem Ursprung, die allgemeine Enderungen, welche unser Erd-Kreis allschon ausgestanden, und anderseits noch auszusetzen hat* [Hamburg: 1703]). The book's initial success was followed by hostile criticism from, among others, Keil (q.v.) and Buffon (q.v.). Burnet composed a second work, the *Archaeologiae Philosophicae, sive doctrina antiqua de rerum originibus libri duo* (London: 1692) which, because of its allegorical interpretation of the Genesis story of the Fall, unleashed a storm of controversy when the English translation appeared under the title *Archaeologiae Philosophicae, or, The Ancient Doctrine concerning the Original of Things* (London: 1729).

BUTLER, *Samuel* (1612–80): English satirical poet. Author of the celebrated *Hudibras* (London: 1663–78), a scurrilous attack on puritanism, bigotry and religious intolerance. The satire was loosely modelled on Cervantes's *Don Quixote.*

CHRYSIPPUS (ca. 280–206 B.C.): Stoic logician. Studied at Athens, possibly under Zeno, certainly under Cleanthes. Famed for skill as a dialectician. Refined earlier logical theory: laid foundations of propositional logic. Systematised Stoic teaching. Only fragments of the 700 treatises attributed to him survive (cf. Arnim, *Stoicorum veterum fragmenta;* see also *Diogenes Laertius*, VII, 179).

CRUSIUS, *Christian August* (1715–75): German philosopher; opponent of Leibniz and Wolff (q.v. both). Professor of theology at Leipzig from 1750. Employed the single principle of what can and cannot be thought as the criterion of truth and falsity. From this he derived the principle of contradiction (thus depriving it of its ultimate authority), and the principles of what cannot be separated and what cannot be combined. Also denied that the principle of sufficient reason (which he distinguished from the principle of determining reason) could be derived from the principle of contradiction. Crusius, distinguishing between ideal and real existence, rejected the ontological proof of the existence of God. Also rejected the Leibnizian doctrine of preestablished harmony; defended the freedom of will (or freedom of indifference). Kant, who was deeply influenced by Crusius, examined this latter thesis in the *New Elucidation.* Chief works: *Dissertatio de usu et limitibus principii rationis determinantis, vulgo sufficientis* ('Dissertation on the Use and Limits of the Principle of Determining Reason, Commonly known as the Principle of Sufficient Reason') (Leipzig: 1743); *Anweisung, vernünftig zu leben* ('Guidance to Living Rationally') (Leipzig: 1744); *Entwurf der nothwendigen Vernunftwahrheiten wiefern sie den zufälligen entgegengesetzt werden* ('Outline of the Necessary Truths of Reason, in so far as they are Opposed to Contingent Truths') (Leipzig: 1745); *Weg zur Gewissheit und Zuverlässigkeit der menschlichen Erkenntnis* ('Path to the Attainment of Certainty and Reliability in Human Knowledge') (Leipzig: 1747); *Anleitung, über natürliche Begebenheiten ordentlich und vorsichtig nachzudenken* ('Instruction on How to Reflect Correctly and Cautiously on Natural Events') (2 vols. Leipzig: 1749). Kant's library contained the following works by Crusius: *Anweisung* (2nd edition. Leipzig: 1751); *Entwurf* (2nd edition. Leipzig: 1753); *Anleitung* (Leipzig: 1749).

DARIES, *Joachim Georg* (1714–91): German jurist and philosopher. Professor of philosophy at Frankfurt-an-der-Oder (at invitation of Frederick the Great, who made him privy counsellor). Important pioneering work in field of political economy, for which he obtained recognition as an academic discipline. Accepted the mathematical method of Wolff, but opposed the doctrines of determinism and preestablished harmony, favouring instead a theory of physical influence. Chief works: *Introductio in artem inveniendi seu logicam theoretico-practicam* ('Introduction to the Art of Invention or Theoretical-Practical Logic') (Jena: 1742); *Elementa Metaphysica* ('Metaphysical Elements') (Jena: 1743); *Erste Gründe der philosophischen Sitten-*

lehre ('First Principles of the Philosophical Doctrine of Morals') (Jena: 1750); *Discourse über Natur- und Völker-Recht* ('Discourse on Natural and International Justice') (3 vols. Jena: 1762–3). Kant's library contained the following works of Daries: *Erste Gründe* (2nd edition. Jena: 1755); *Discours* (Jena: 1762–3).

DEMOCRITUS OF ABDERA (ca. 460–371 B.C.): Greek atomist philosopher. Studied under Leucippus. Postulated existence of an infinite number of atoms, which were eternal, invisible, indivisible, and differing only quantitatively in size, weight, and shape. He maintained that the original chaos of atoms resolved itself into ordered and structured worlds (of which he supposed that there were an infinite number) by virtue of the differing motions of the quantitatively differing atoms. Maintained that life arose by spontaneous generation, that the soul was material and mortal, and that perception involved physical influences. Democritus exercised a deep influence on Epicurus (q.v.), Lucretius (q.v.), Bacon, and Hobbes.

DERHAM, *William* (1657–1735): English divine and naturalist. His first major work was the celebrated *The Artificial Clockmaker* (London: 1696). Elected Fellow of the Royal Society in 1702. Contributed frequently to the *Philosophical Transactions* with papers on astronomy, meteorology, and natural history. In 1711 and 1712 Derham gave the Bayle Lectures, which were published under the title *Physico-Theology, or a Demonstration of the Being and Attributes of God from his Works of Creation* (London: 1713). The book enjoyed enormous popularity and ran to twelve editions by 1754. It was translated into many European languages including a German translation: *William Derhams . . . Physico-Theologie, oder Natur- Leitung zu Gott* (Hamburg: 1750). Encouraged by his success, he developed his theme in a second work, which proved equally popular: *Astro-Theology, or a Demonstration of the Being and Attributes of God from a Survey of the Heavens* (London: 1715; 9th edition: 1750) (German translation: *William Derhams . . . Astrotheologie, oder Himlisches Vergnügen in Gott* [Hamburg: 1732]).

DESCARTES, *René* (1596–1650): French philosopher and mathematician. Educated by Jesuits; completed period of military service; travelled widely; eventually retired from active life in 1629 and settled in Holland, where he spent twenty years engaged in philosophical and mathematical research. In 1649 accepted an invitation from Christina, queen of Sweden, to Stockholm, where he died the following year. Chief works: *Discours de la méthode* (Leyden: 1737); *Meditationes de prima philosophia, in quibus Dei exsistentia et animae immortalitas demonstratur* ('Meditations on First Philosophy, Wherein Is Demonstrated the Existence of God and the Immortality of the Soul') (Paris: 1641); *Principia philosophiae* ('Principles of Philosophy') (Amsterdam: 1644); *Les passions de l'âme* (Paris: 1649). Kant, in his 1755 *New Elucidation* and the 1763 *The Only Possible Argument*, attacks the Cartesian ontological proof of the existence of God as it is presented in the *Meditationes de prima philosophia*. Kant's library contained the following works of Descartes: *Geometria* (Leyden: 1637); *Meditationes de prima philosophia* (3rd edition. Amsterdam: 1650); *Principia philosophiae* (2nd edition. Amsterdam: 1650).

DIOGENES THE CYNIC (ca. 412–323 B.C.): Cynic philosopher. Nothing survives of his writings. Famed for his caustic wit and the asceticism of his life. The chief source of information about his life and personality: *Diogenes Laertius*, VI, ii.

EPICURUS (341–270): Greek atomist philosopher and moralist. Educated at Athens; taught at Mytilene and Lampsacus. In 306 founded a school of philosophy (known as The Garden). A prolific writer, particularly on scientific matters, though his prime concern was morality. His physics is similar to that of Democritus (q.v.), but it contains one original feature: the doctrine of the *clinamen*, which was introduced to explain the existence of compound objects and the possibility of human freedom. Epicurean moral theory has two distinctive features: its concern to eliminate fear (of nature, the gods, and the future life) and the distinction between kinetic and static pleasure. The supreme good, and indeed the supreme pleasure, is absence of pain. The Epicurean movement survived until the fourth century A.D. The classic statement of Epicureanism is found in Lucretius, *De rerum natura*, a work much admired by Kant.

ERNESTI, *Johann August* (1707–81): German classical scholar and theologian. Educated at Schulpforta; studied at Wittenberg and Leipzig. Held chairs of classical philology (1742), rhetoric (1756), and theology (1758) at the University of Leipzig. Renowned for his editions of classical writers (Cicero, Suetonius, Tacitus, Aristophanes, Homer, Callimachus, and Polybius). Also published a number of philological works. Kant, in his 1766 *Dreams of a Spirit-Seer*, refers to Ernesti's *Neue theologische Bibliothek darinnen von den neuesten theologischen Büchern und Schriften Nachrichten gegeben wird* ('New Theological Library Containing Information about the Latest Theological Books and Publications') (10 vols. Leipzig: 1760–8). Kant's library contained one work by Ernesti: *Initia doctrinae solidioris* ('First Principles of a Better Founded Doctrine') (4th edition. Leipzig: 1758).

EUCLID (fl. 300 B.C.): Greek mathematician. Founded a school at Alexandria during the reign of Ptolemy I (306–283 B.C.). Author of the famous *Elements* in thirteen books. It was to remain the undisputed classical text of geometry until the mid-nineteenth century, with the emergence of an 'away from Euclid' movement. Non-Euclidean geometries, with which

Kant was familiar (his friend Lambert developed such a system), emerged in the mid-eighteenth century.

EULER, *Leonard* (1707–83): Swiss mathematician. Studied mathematics at Basel under Jean Bernoulli. In 1727 elected to the St. Petersburg Royal Academy; also appointed successively to the chairs of physics (1730) and mathematics (1733) at the University of Saint Petersburg. In 1741 elected to the Prussian Royal Academy and, at the invitation of Frederick the Great, moved to Berlin, where for twenty-five years he published prolifically. In 1766, at the invitation of Catherine the Great, returned to St. Petersburg, where he was to spend the rest of his life. Although now completely blind, he continued to publish extensively. Arguably the greatest mathematician of his age: made important discoveries in all fields of the discipline. Also interested in the philosophical side of the subject, and especially in the nature of space and time. Foreshadowing Kant, he maintained that neither space nor time could be derived from experience or from pure intellection, though both space and time were indisputably real (being absolutely necessary to motion and mechanics). He asserted that neither space nor time could be expressed by any traditional category of philosophy. Also maintained the distinct and unique character of mathematical truth. Rejected the Leibnizian doctrine of monads on the ground of its incompatibility with the infinite divisibility of space and time. Of Euler's vast output of publications, the following are among the more important: *Mechanica, sive motus scientia, analytice exposita* ('Mechanics, or the Science of Motion, Analytically Expounded') (3 vols. St. Petersburg: 1736); *Gedancken von den Elementen der Körper* ('Thoughts concerning the Elements of Bodies') (Berlin: 1746); *Réflexions sur l'espace et le temps*, in *Mémoires de l'Académie des Sciences*, Vol. IV (Berlin: 1748); *Dissertatio de principio minimae actionis* ('Dissertation on the Principle of Least Action') (Berlin: 1753); *Theoria motus corporum solidorum seu rigidorum ex primis nostrae cognitionis principiis stabilita* ('Theory of the Motion of Solid or Rigid Bodies, based on the First Principles of our Knowledge') (Rostock: 1765); *Lettres à une princesse d'Allemagne sur quelques sujets de physique et de philosophie* (3 vols. St. Petersburg: 1768–72) (German translation: *Briefe an eine Deutsche Prinzessin über verschiedene Gegenstände aus der Physik und Philosophie. Aus dem Französischen übersetzt* [Leipzig: 1769]); Kant's library contained two works by Euler: *Mechanica* (St. Petersburg: 1736); *Vollständige Anleitung zur Differenzial-Rechnung* (Berlin: 1790) (this was the German translation of Euler's *Institutiones calculi differentialis* ['Principles of the Differential Calculus'] [Berlin: 1755]).

FONTENELLE, *Bernard le Bovier de* (1657–1757): French writer and Cartesian thinker. Did much to popularise the new astronomy of Copernicus and Kepler in his 1686 *Entretiens*. The following year, attacked Malebranche's doctrine of occasional causes. His work on oracles of the same year is a covert attack on Christianity. A close friend of Montesquieu's and well acquainted with Voltaire. Chief works: *Nouveaux dialogues des morts* (Paris: 1683), *Entretiens sur la pluralité des mondes* (Paris: 1686), *Doutes sur les causes occasionelles* (Paris: 1687), *Histoire des oracles* (Paris: 1687).

GALILEO *(Galileo Galilei)* (1564–1642): Italian mathematician, physicist, and astronomer. From 1581 studied at Pisa, where he discovered the principle underlying Huygens's (q.v.) pendulum clock by observing the regular oscillations of a hanging lamp in Pisa's cathedral. Established that all bodies, irrespective of weight, fall with the same velocity. Appointed to chair of mathematics at Pisa University in 1592. In 1609 invented a telescope powerful enough to establish that the surface of the moon was irregular, that the Milky Way consisted of stars, that Jupiter had satellites, that the appearance of Saturn seemed to change in a curious fashion (the rings were mistaken for two satellites), and that there were sun spots. In 1611 visited Rome and demonstrated his telescope. In 1613 published a letter on sunspots and championed the Copernican hypothesis. In 1616 Galileo's work was condemned as 'false and erroneous'. Retired to Florence. In 1623 the new pope, Urban VIII (a friend of Galileo's), granted him permission to write 'non-committally' on the two systems. In 1632 Galileo published his famous *Dialogi;* he was accused of breaking his agreement and forced to recant. The last eight years of his life were spent under house arrest near Florence. Completed his *Discorsi* in 1634. Chief works: *Storia e dimostrazioni intorno alle macchie solari e loro accidenti* ('History and Proofs relating to Sun-Spots and the Changes they Undergo') (Rome: 1613); *Dialoghi quattro sopra i due massimi sistemi del mondo, tolemaico e copernicano* ('Four Dialogues concerning the Two Chief Systems of the World, the Ptolemaic and the Copernican') (Florence: 1632); *Discorsi e dimostrazioni matematiche intorno a due scienze attenanti alla mecanica ed i movimenti locali* ('Discourses and Mathematical Demonstrations relating to the Two Sciences which concern Mechanics and Local Motions') (Leyden: 1638); *Epistolae tres de conciliatione sacrae scripturae cum systemate telluris mobilis* ('Three Letters concerning the Reconciliation of Holy Scripture with the System of a Moving World') (Lyons: 1649). Kant's library contained the following works by Galileo: *System cosmicum* ('Cosmic System') (Leyden: 1699); *Discursus et dimonstrationes mathematicae circa duas novas scientias pertinentes ad mechanicam et motum localem* (this was the Latin translation of the *Discorsi* [1638]).

GUERICKE, *Otto von* (1602–86): German physicist and engineer. In 1631 served as an engineer in the army of Gustavus Adolphus. Returned to civil life in his native town of Magdeburg in 1646. In 1650 invented the air pump; created partial vacuum, and discovered that light but not sound can travel through a vacuum. In 1654 conducted experiments with the so-called Magdeburg Hemispheres (emptied of air they could not be dragged apart by teams of horses). Published an account of his experiments in *Experimenta nova, ut vocant, Magdeburgica* ('New Experiments Known as the Magdeburg Experiments') (Amsterdam: 1672).

HALES, *Stephen* (1677–1761): English naturalist and chemist. An ordained priest, divided his time between his religious duties and his scientific interests. In 1718 elected Fellow of the Royal Society; in 1753 elected to the Paris Academy of Sciences for his invention of the ventilator, which had been used to good effect in French mines, hospitals, and prisons. Did important work on the circulation of the blood. His works include: *A Specimen of an Attempt to Analyse the Air by a Great Variety of Chimico-Statical Experiments*, in *Philosophical Transactions of the Royal Society*, XXXIV, pp. 264–91, and XXXV, pp. 323–31 (London: 1726–7 and 1727–8). His chief work was: *Vegetable Staticks: or an Account of some Statical Experiments on the Sap in Vegetables . . . Also a Specimen of an Attempt to Analyse Air* (2 vols. London: 1727). Buffon published his French translation of this work in 1735. Hales also published *Some Considerations on the Causes of Earthquakes* (London: 1750). Kant possessed a copy of the German translation of the *Staticks* which appeared at Halle in 1748 (*Statick der Gewächse oder angestellte Versuche mit dem Saft in Pflanzen und ihrem Wachsthum nebst Proben von der in Körpern befindlichen Luft . . .*).

HILL, *John* (ca. 1716–75): English botanist. Worked first as an apothecary; entered service of Duke of Richmond and Lord Petre, arranging their botanical collections and gathering samples. Very versatile (he wrote plays and novels, acted, practised medicine, wrote a gossip column for the *London Advertiser and Literary Gazette*, sold herbal medicines), but his lasting achievement was in the field of botany, in which he published prolifically. Among his many works, the more important are: *A General Natural History: or Descriptions of the Animals, Vegetables and Minerals of the Different Parts of the World* (London: 1748–52); *Essays in Natural History and Philosophy, Containing a Series of Discoveries by the Assistance of Microscopes* (London: 1752). Kant was probably familiar with at least some of these essays (especially no. 13) through translations which appeared in the *Hamburger Magazin.* Hill's supreme achievement was *The Vegetable System; or, a Series of Observations tending to explain the Internal Structure and the Life of Plants* (26 vols. London: 1759–75; 2nd edition: 1770–75).

HOFMANN, *Friedrich* (1660–1742): German physician and chemist. Studied medicine; quickly established reputation in chemistry. In 1693 Frederick III, Elector of Brandenburg, founded the University of Halle, and appointed Hofmann to the chair of medicine; Hofmann drew up the statutes of the School of Medicine. Elected to the Paris and St. Petersburg royal academies and to the London Royal Society. In 1709 appointed personal physician to the king of Prussia. In 1712 returned to Halle, where he spent the rest of his life. Chief works: *Medicina rationalis systematica* ('Rational and Systematic Medicine') (Halle: 1730); *Hofmanii opera omnia medico-physica cum supplementis* ('Complete Medical and Physical Works of Hofmann, Along with Supplements') (11 vols. Geneva: 1740–53).

HORACE *(Horatius Flaccus Quintus)* (65–8 B.C.): Roman poet. Educated at Rome and Athens. Supported Brutus and fought at the Battle of Philippi in the civil war following the death of Caesar. Returned to Rome: pardoned by Augustus, who would later bestow marks of favour on the poet. Virgil was introduced by him to Maecenas, who became his patron (conferring a Sabine farm on him). Divided his time between his country seat and a house in Rome. Kant much admired Horace. Chief works: *Epodes, Odes, Satires, Epistles,* and the *Art of Poetry.*

HUME, *David* (1711–76): Scottish philosopher, historian, economist, and essayist. Destined for law but turned to letters. In 1729 suffered nervous breakdown. In 1734 visited France, where he spent three years preparing the *Treatise,* which was largely ignored when it was published in 1739. The following decade was an unsettled period marked by various employments and the publication of the 1741 *Essays, Moral and Political,* the 1748 *Three Essays, Moral and Political,* the 1748 *Philosophical Essays concerning the Human Understanding,* and the 1751 *Enquiry concerning the Principles of Morals.* A settled period (1751–63) in Edinburgh followed, which saw his appointment as Keeper of the Advocates' Library in Edinburgh, which enabled Hume to indulge his interests in politics and history. His *Political Discourse* appeared in 1752, and his great *History of England from the Invasion of Julius Caesar to the Revolution of 1688* began to appear in 1754 (the sixth, final volume appeared in 1762). In 1763 visited Paris to take up a minor diplomatic post: lionised by the French. Stormy friendship with the paranoid Rousseau. In 1769 returned to Edinburgh, where he composed the posthumously published *Dialogues concerning Natural Religion.* Kant's own philosophical development was crucially affected by the problems raised by Hume's radically empiricist account of categorical notions (in particular, those of substance and causality). Hume's most important philosophical works include: *A Treatise of Human Nature, Being an Attempt to Introduce the Experimental Method into Moral Subjects* (3 vols. London: 1739–40); *Enquiry concerning the Principles of Morals* (London: 1751); *Dialogues concerning Natural Religion* (London: 1779). Kant's library contained a collected edition of Hume's works: *Vermischte Schriften* ('Collected Works') (4 vols. Hamburg: 1754–6), comprising Volume I: *Vermischte Schriften über die Handlung, die Manufacturen und die andern Quellen des Reichthums und der Macht des Staats* ('Collected Works on Trade, Industry and other Sources of the Wealth and Power of the State'); Volume II:

Philosophische Versuche über die menschliche Erkenntniss ('Philosophical Essays on Human Knowledge' – the 1748 *Philosophical Essays concerning the Human Understanding*); Volume III: *Sittenlehre der Gesellschaft* ('The Ethics of Society' – the 1751 *Enquiry concerning the Principles of Morals*); Volume IV: *Gespräche über natürliche Religion nebst einem Gespräch über den Atheismus von Ernst Platner* ('Conversations on Natural Religion, Together with a Conversation on Atheism by Ernst Platner' – the 1779 *Dialogues concerning Natural Religion*) and *Moralische und politische Versuche* ('Moral and Political Essays' – the 1741 *Essays, Moral and Political* and the 1748 *Three Essays, Moral and Political*).

HUTCHESON, *Francis* (1694–1747): Irish moral philosopher of the Shaftesbury (q.v.) school. Studied philosophy, classics, and theology at Glasgow. In 1716 returned to Ireland where he founded a dissenting academy in Dublin (only Anglicans were permitted to attend university in England and Ireland; the higher education needs of nonconformists were catered for by the so-called dissenting academies). In 1725 published his *Inquiry*, and in 1728 his *Essay*. Returned to Glasgow in 1729 as incumbent of the chair of moral philosophy. Published a number of works on the sociability of man, on moral philosophy, and on metaphysics. His chief works remained his first two: *An Inquiry into the Original of our Ideas of Beauty and Virtue; in Two Treatises, in which the Principles of the Late Earl of Shaftesbury are Explained and Defended against the Author of the Fable of the Bees; and the Ideas of Moral Good and Evil are Established, according to the Sentiments of the Ancient Moralists With an Attempt to Introduce a Mathematical Calculation in Subjects of Morality* (London: 1725) (German translation: *Untersuchung unserer Begriffe von Schönheit und Tugend in zwei Abhandlungen* ['Investigation of our Concepts of Beauty and Virtue in Two Treatises'] [Frankfurt: 1762]); *An Essay on the Nature and Conduct of the Passions and Affections, with Illustrations upon the Moral Sense* (London: 1728) (German translation: *Abhandlungen über die Natur und Beherrschung der Leidenschaften und Neigungen und über das moralische Gefühl insonderheit* ['Treatises on the Nature and Control of the Passions and Inclinations, and in particular on the Moral Feeling'] [Leipzig: 1760]). Kant's library contained the above two German translations of the 1725 *Inquiry* and the 1728 *Essay*.

HUYGENS, *Christian* (1629–95): Dutch mathematician, astronomer, and physician. Inventor of the pendulum clock. Studied mathematics at Leyden and in France. In 1655 discovered new method of lens grinding which led to the invention of a much improved telescope, by means of which he discovered the rings of Saturn (hitherto supposed to have been satellites or 'handles'). His astronomical work made him aware of the need for a more accurate method of measuring time. Employing the principle discovered by Galileo (q.v.) that the period of the oscillation of a pendulum is independent of its length, Huygens invented the pendulum clock. Presented his invention to the Dutch Estates-General in 1657, publishing an account of the mechanism, its principles, and application in 1658. In 1660 established the principles governing the collision of elastic bodies. In 1663 elected to the London Royal Society. Louis XIV appointed him Keeper of the *Bibliothèque du Roi* in 1665. During his stay in France he completed his *magnum opus*, the 1673 *Horologium oscillatorium*. In 1681 returned to Holland, where he worked at the construction of more powerful telescopes, and developed a wave theory of light. Universally recognised as one of the greatest scientific minds of his age. Chief works: *Brevis institutio de usu horologiorum ad inveniendas longitudines* ('Brief Introduction to the Use of Clocks for establishing Longitudes') (Leyden: 1658); *Systemata Saturnium sive de causis mirandorum Saturni phaenomenon et comite eius planeta novo* ('System of Saturn; or, Concerning the Causes of the Amazing Phenomena of Saturn and of its New Satellite Planet') (The Hague: 1659); *Horologium oscillatorium sive de motu pendulorum ad horologia adaptato demonstrationes geometricae* ('The Pendulum Clock; or Geometrical Demonstrations concerning the Motion of Pendulums in its Adaptation to Clocks') (Paris: 1673).

ISOCRATES (436–338 B.C.): Greek educationalist and rhetorician. Influenced by the Sophists and by Socrates (q.v.), he was a professional writer of forensic speeches. In 392 founded his celebrated school of rhetoric at Athens; it attracted students from all over the Greek world. Plato's Academy was founded shortly after, and there was rivalry between the two institutions (Plato [q.v.] criticises Isocrates in the *Phaedrus*). His extant speeches were devoted to political, moral, and educational themes; attacked the narrowness of contemporary orators, and also practitioners of eristic debate, including Plato. Construed morality in terms of enlightened self-interest, and emphasised the importance of piety and justice.

JACOBI, *Johann Friedrich* (1712–91): German cleric. Studied philosophy at Göttingen. Active as a clergyman in Hannover at the time of the publication of his *Sammlung einiger Erfahrungen und Anmerkungen über die Wärme und Kälte in freier Luft. Zusammengetragen von Herrn Johann Friedrich Jacobi* ('Anthology of Some Experiences of and Notes on Heat and Cold in the Open Air. Collected by Herr Johann Friedrich Jacobi'), in *Hamburger Magazin*, Vol. XXI (Hamburg: 1758). (Not to be confused [*pace* Alquié, Vol. I, p. 1770, 1980] with the more famous philosophical writer, Friedrich Heinrich Jacobi.)

KÄSTNER, *Abraham Gotthelf* (1719–1800): German mathematician and astronomer. Appointed to chair of mathematics at Göttingen in 1756; also appointed director of the Göttingen observatory. A man of wide learning (he knew twelve languages), he published numerous works on mathematics. Quickly established a reputation as an effective and lucid populariser of astronomy and mathematics. Kant's library contained three works by Kästner: *Vermischte Schriften* ('Selected Works') (Altenburg: 1755); *Mathematische Anfangsgründe* (4 vols. Göttingen: 1758–61); Kästner's translation from the Dutch of a work by Luloss under the title *Enleitung zur mathematischen und physikalischen Kenntniss der Erdkugel* ('Introduction to Mathematical and Physical Knowledge of the Globe') (Göttingen: 1755); *Anfangsgründe der höheren Mechanik, welche von der Bewegung fester Körper besonders die praktischen Lehre enthalten* ('First Principles of Advanced Mechanics, Containing in Particular the Practical Theories of the Motion of Solid Bodies') (Göttingen: 1758).

KEILL, *John* (1671–1721): Scottish mathematician and exponent of Newtonian physics. In 1698 published a criticism of Burnet's (q.v.) *Telluris theoria sacra* and of Whiston's (q.v.) *New Theory of the Earth*. In 1700 appointed to chair of natural philosophy at Oxford; published his celebrated *Introductio ad veram physicam seu lectiones physicae habitae in schola naturalis philosophiae academiae oxoniensis* ('Introduction to the True Physics, or Lectures on Physics Held in the School of Natural Science at the University of Oxford') (London: 1702), of which an English translation appeared, at the instigation of Maupertuis (q.v.), under the title *Introduction to Natural Philosophy* (London: 1720). This work was generally regarded as the best introduction to the new physics of Newton. In 1708 published his *Epistola in qua leges attractionis aliaque physices principia traduntur* ('Letter in Which Are Presented the Laws of Attraction and other Physical Principles'), in *Philosophical Transactions of the Royal Society*, XXXVI, 97–110 (London: 1708). It was this paper which initiated the famous dispute between Leibniz and Newton concerning the discovery of the differential calculus. In 1710 appointed to the chair of astronomy at Oxford. In 1718 published his *Introductio ad veram astronomiam seu lectiones astronomicae habitae in scola astronomica academiae oxoniensis* ('Introduction to the True Astronomy, or Lectures on Astronomy Held in the School of Astronomy at the University of Oxford') (London: 1718) (English translation: *Introduction to the New Astronomy* [London: 1721]). Kant's library contained the following edition of Keill: *Introductiones ad veram physicam et veram astronomiam. Quibus accedunt trigonometria, de viribus centralibus, de legibus attractionis* ('Introduction to the True Physics and the True Astronomy. To Which Are Added Trigonometry, on Gravitational Forces, and the Laws of Attraction') (Leyden: 1739), an edition of Keill which contained the 1702 *Introductio,* the 1718 *Introductio* and three supplementary papers.

LA FONTAINE, *Jean de* (1621–93): French poet and fabulist. Celebrated in particular for his two collections of *Fables* (Paris: 1668 and 1678), many of them based on Aesop (q.v.), Babrius, and Phaedrus.

LAMBERT, *Johann Heinrich* (1728–77): Swiss-German mathematician, astronomer, physicist, and philosopher. Compensated for the lack of a university education by voracious reading in the fields of mathematics, physics, and philosophy. Employed for a while as a private tutor and secretary. Travelled widely, quickly winning the recognition of the leading scholars and scientists of his age (including Kant); engaged in an extensive correspondence and published prolifically. In 1759 accepted an invitation from the Elector Maximilian-Joseph of Bavaria to participate in establishing the Bavarian Academy of Sciences, of which he became a founding member. Visited Berlin in 1764 and was appointed by Frederick the Great a member of the Prussian Royal Academy of Sciences. In 1765 appointed *Oberbaurat* (government surveyor), a post he held until his death. Made important contributions to the advancement of astronomy, mathematics, and philosophy. His more important publications include: *Kosmologische Briefe über die Einrichtung des Weltbaues* ('Cosmological Letters on the Structure of the Universe') (Augsburg: 1761); *Insigniores orbitae cometarum proprietates* ('The Chief Characteristics of the Orbits of the Comets') (Augsburg: 1761); *Neues Organon, oder Gedanken über die Erforschung und Beziehung des Wahren und dessen Unterscheidung von Irrthum und Schein* ('New Organon, or Thoughts on the Inquiry into and the Relation of the True and Its Distinction from Error and Illusion') (Leipzig: 1764). Kant's library contained two works by Lambert: *Die freye Perspective, oder Anweisung, jeden perspectivischen Aufriss von freyen Stücken und ohne Grundriss zu verfertigen* ('Free Perspective, or, Instructions on How, Freely and Without a Plan, to Prepare any Perspectival Outline') (Zurich: 1759); *Kosmologische Briefe* (Augsburg: 1761).

LEIBNIZ, *Gottfried Wilhelm* (1646–1716): German logician, jurist, mathematician, theologian, philosopher, historian, and diplomat. Studied law, philosophy, and mathematics; entered service of Elector of Mainz as secretary and political adviser. Spent 1672–6 in Paris on a diplomatic mission; met Malebranche (q.v.), Arnauld, and Huygens (q.v.). Member of the Paris Royal Academy. In 1673 visited London, where he met Bayle and Oldenburg, and was elected Fellow of the Royal Society. Returned to Paris: engaged in mathematical research with Huygens; discovered the differential and integral calculus. On the death of the Elector of Mainz, he entered the service of the House of Brunswick-Luneburg, acting first as librarian and then as official historian. Leibniz enjoyed the patronage of the Electress of Hanover and of her daughter, the Electress of Brandenburg, who invited him to Berlin, where he became involved in the founding of the Prussian Royal Academy of Sciences, and became its first president in 1703. That year he started work on the *Nouveaux essais*. At the invitation of the Electress of Brandenburg, Leibniz prepared a reply to Bayle's view (expressed in *Réponses aux questions d'un provincial*) that faith and reason are not reconcilable. This reply was to become the *Essais de Théodicée*. The final decade of Leibniz's life, following the death of his patroness in 1705, was taken up with the composition of the *Monadologie* and the *Principes de la nature* and with the important correspondence with Clarke on space and time. It was also overshadowed by the acrimonious dispute with Newton and the London Royal Society (which unfairly accused Leibniz of plagiarism) about the discovery of the differential calculus. Of Leibniz's enormous philosophical and mathematical output, the following works may be regarded as among the most important and the most relevant to Kant: *Dissertatio de arte combinatoria* ('Dissertation on the Art of Combinations') (Leipzig: 1666) (Loemker, pp. 73–84); *On the General Characteristic* (ca. 1679) (Loemker, pp. 221–8); *On Universal Synthesis and Analysis, or the Art of Discovery and Judgement* (1679?) (Loemker, pp. 229–34); *Two Studies in the Logical Calculus* (1679) (Loemker, pp. 235–47); *Studies in a Geometry of Situation* (including *Analysis situs*) (1679) (Loemker, pp. 235–47 and 254–8); *De veritatibus primis* ('First Truths') (ca. 1680–4) (Loemker, pp. 267–71); *Meditationes de cognitione, veritate et ideis* ('Meditations on Knowledge, Truth and Ideas'), in *Acta Eruditorum*, November 1684 (Loemker, pp. 291–5); *Nova methodus pro maximis et minimis* ('New Method for Handling Maxima and Minima'), in *Acta Eruditorum*, 1684); *Discours de metaphysique* (1686) (Loemker, pp. 303–30); *Specimen dynamicum, pro admirandi naturae legibus circa corporum vires et mutuas actiones detegendis* ('Essay on Dynamics for Admiring the Laws of Nature Concerning the Forces of Bodies and for Discovering Their Reciprocal Actions'), in *Acta Eruditorum*, April 1695; *Système nouveau de la nature et de la communication des substances aussi bien que de l'union qu'il y a entre l'âme et le corps*, in *Journal des Scavans*, June and July 1695; *De rerum originatione radicali* ('On the Radical Origination of Things') (1697) (Loemker, pp. 486–91); *Essais de théodicée sur la bonté de Dieu, la liberté de l'homme et l'origine du mal* (Amsterdam: 1710); *Principes de la nature et de la grâce*, in *L'Europe Savante*, 1714; *The Monadology* (1714) (Loemker, pp. 643–53); *A Collection of Papers which passed between the Late Learned Mr. Leibnitz and Dr. Clarke, in the Years 1715 and 1716. Relative to the Principles of Natural Philosophy and Religion* (London: 1717); *Nouveaux essais sur l'entendement humain* (Amsterdam: 1765).

LISCOW, *Christian Ludwig* (1701–60): German satiric writer. Studied law; became private tutor; held series of minor diplomatic-secretarial posts; incautious criticism of his final employer led to a period of imprisonment, after which he devoted himself to writing. His satirical writings include: *Vitrea fracta oder des Ritters Robert Clifton Schreiben an einen gelehrten Samojeden . . . auf einer gefrornen Fenster-Scheibe wahrgenommen; aus dem Englischen . . . übersetzt von Christian Ludwig Liscow* ('Broken Glass, or The Communication Written by Sir Robert Clifton to a Learned Samojed . . . and Perceived on a Frozen Window-Pane; Translated from the English [in fact composed in German] by Christian Ludwig Liscow) (Frankfurt: 1732); *Sammlung satyrischer und ernsthafter Schriften* ('Collection of Satirical and Serious Writings') (Frankfurt: 1739).

MAIRAN, *Jean-Jacques Doutous de* (1678–1771): French scientist and mathematician. Studied at Toulouse and Paris, where he settled towards 1707. Elected to the Paris Royal Academy in 1718. Wrote numerous papers on geometry, astronomy, natural history, and physics. In 1740 elected perpetual secretary to the Paris Academy of Sciences, but resigned after only three years. Elected to the French Academy in 1743. Directed the *Journal des Scavans* and corresponded with leading scientists and thinkers, including, most importantly, Malebranche (q.v.). Also a friend and correspondent to Voltaire (q.v.). His works include: *Dissertation sur la glace* (Paris: 1715); *Dissertation sur l'estimation et la mesure des forces motrices des corps* (Paris: 1741); *Lettre à Madame de Chastelet sur la question des forces vives* (Paris: 1741). Kant's library contained a German translation of the 1715 *Dissertation sur la glace* under the title *Abhandlung von dem Eisse oder physikalische Erklärung der Entstehung des Eisses* ('Treatise on Ice, or a Physical Explanation of the Genesis of Ice') (Leipzig: 1752).

MALEBRANCHE, *Nicolas de* (1638–1715): French philosopher of the Cartesian school. Studied theology at the Sorbonne. Entered the Congregation of the Oratory of Jesus. Fortuitous reading of Descartes's *Traité de l'homme* in 1664 awakened his interest in philosophy, and led to an intensive study of Descartes (q.v.). In 1674 published *De la recherche de la vérité*, which reached its fourth edition in four years. The 1680 *Traité de la nature et de la grâce* precipitated a quarrel with Bossuet and Arnauld (the 1697 *Traité de l'amour de Dieu* placated Bossuet). In 1699 elected to the Paris Academy of Sciences, having published an important paper on colour and light. Malebranche's version of Cartesianism is distinctive: he maintained that we do not know material things in themselves but only their prototypes in the mind of God (hence 'we see all things in God'); also held that the *only* efficient cause in the universe is the will of God; and that that alone explains interaction between substances, both material and mental (the celebrated doctrine of occasionalism). Chief works: *De la recherche de la vérité ou l'on traite de la nature de l'esprit, de l'homme et de l'usage qu'il doit fair pour éviter l'erreur dans les sciences* (2 vols. Paris: 1674–5; the most complete edition is that of 1714 in 4 vols.); *Traité de la nature et de la grâce* (Paris: 1680); *Méditations chrétiennes et métaphysiques* (Cologne: 1683); *Entretiens sur la métaphysique* (Rotterdam: 1688); *Traité de l'amour de Dieu* (Lyons: 1697).

MARIOTTE, *Edme* (ca. 1620–84): French scientist. Prior of St. Martin-sous-Beaune. One of the first members of the Paris Academy of Sciences, for which he published many papers on a wide range of topics including colour, sound, atmosphere, liquids, the barometer, the fall of bodies, the motion of fluids, the freezing of water, heat, and cold. Independently discovered the law known in the English-speaking world as Boyle's Law (and as Mariotte's Law in France); this discovery is explained in his *De la nature de l'air* (*Oeuvres* Vol. I). Mariotte's most important papers are contained in *Oeuvres de Mariotte* (2 vols. Leyden: 1717) (Volume I: *Traité de la percussion ou choc des corps; Essais de physique: De la végétation des plantes; De la nature de l'air; Du chaud et du froid; De la nature des couleurs;* Volume II: *Traité du mouvement des eaux et des autres corps fluides; Règles pour les jets d'eau; Nouvelle découverte touchant la vue; Traité du nivellement; Traité du mouvement des pendules; Expériences touchant les couleurs et la congélation de l'eau; Essai de logique*).

MAUPERTUIS, *Pierre Louis Moreau de* (1698–1759): French physicist, astronomer, and mathematician; discoverer of the principle of least action. Introduced Newtonian physics into France and was elected to membership of the Paris Royal Academy. In 1736 led an expedition to Lapland to measure the length of a degree along the meridian; he confirmed Newton's claim that the earth was an oblate spheroid. Elected to the London Royal Society. In 1741 visited Berlin, and was elected to the Prussian Royal Academy; in 1745 he was made its president. Maupertuis made many enemies in Berlin, and was accused of having plagiarised the principle of least action from Leibniz (q.v.); defended by Euler (q.v.) and attacked by Voltaire (q.v.) (in *Micromégas* and *La diatribe du Docteur Akakia* in 1752). In 1753 resigned his presidency and left Berlin, first for Paris and then for Basel, where he stayed with Bernoulli (q.v.) and died in 1759. His more important works include: *Discours sur les différentes figures des astres, avec une exposition des systèmes de MM. Descartes et Newton* (Paris: 1732); *Venus physique* (Paris: 1745); *Les lois du mouvement et du repos, déduites d'un principe de métaphysique* (Paris: 1746); *Essaie de philosophie morale* (Berlin: 1749); *Dissertatio inauguralis metaphysica de universali naturae systemate* ('Inaugural Metaphysical Dissertation on the Universal System of Nature') [Pseudonymously under the name Dr. Baumann] (Paris: 1751) (French translation: *Essai sur la formation des corps organisés* [Berlin: 1754]). Kant's library contained three works by Maupertuis: *Der meridian-Grad zwischen Paris und Amiens . . . woraus man die Figur der Erde herleitet, durch Vergleichung dieses Grads mit dem, so beym Polar-Zirkel gemessen worden . . .* ('The Degree of the Meridian Between Paris and Amiens . . . on Which Basis the Shape of the Earth Is Established by Comparison of this Degree with That Measured at the Polar Circle') (Zurich: 1742); *Versuch in der moralischen Weltweisheit* (Halle: 1750) ('Essay on Moral Philosophy') (German translation of the 1749 *Essai de philosophie morale*); *Versuch, von der Bildung der Körper, aus dem Lateinischen . . . übersetzt von einem Freunde der Naturlehre* ('Essay on the Formation of Bodies, Translated from the Latin by a Friend of Physics') (Leipzig: 1761) (German translation of the 1751 *Dissertatio inauguralis metaphysica*).

MEIER, *Georg Friedrich* (1718–77): German philsopher of the Leibniz-Wolff School; one of the founders of aesthetics. Studied theology and philosophy at Halle under Baumgarten, to whom he succeeded in the chair of philosophy in 1740. A popular teacher whose lectures and books did much to disseminate the ideas of Leibniz (q.v.), Wolff (q.v.), and Baumgarten (q.v.). His chief work was in the field of aesthetics (he construed the aesthetic as a form of sensible and thus confused knowledge requiring clarification by logic). Chief works: *Anfangsgründe aller schönen Künste und Wissenschaften* ('First Principles of All the Fine Arts and Sciences') (3 vols. Halle: 1748–50); *Versuch eines Lehrgebäudes von den Seelen der Thiere* ('Attempt at a Theory of the Souls of Animals') (Halle: 1749); *Vernunftlehre* ('Theory of Reason') (Halle: 1752); *Auszug aus der Vernunftlehre* ('Extract from the Theory of Reason') (Halle: 1752); *Philosophische Sittenlehre* ('Philosophical Theory of Morals') (5 vols. Halle: 1753–61); *Metaphysik* ('Metaphysics') (4 vols. Halle: 1755–9); *Versuch einer allgemeinen Auslegungskunst* ('Attempt at a Universal Art of Interpretation') (Halle: 1757). Kant's library contained two of Meier's works: *Vernunftlehre* (Halle: 1752); *Auszug aus der Vernunftlehre* (Halle: 1752).

MILTON, *John* (1608–74): English Puritan poet and political writer. His famous early poems include *On the Morning of Christ's Nativity* (1629), *L'Allegro* and *Il Penseroso* (1631) and *Comus* (1634), but his supreme achievement is *Paradise Lost* (1667; 2nd revised edition: 1674). His two other greatest works are *Paradise Regained* (London: 1671) and *Samson Agonistes* (1671). His most celebrated prose work, a defence of the freedom of the press, is *Areopagitica* (1645).

MUSSCHENBROEK, *Pieter van* (1692–1761): Dutch scientist. Studied chemistry and medicine under Boerhaave (q.v.) at Leyden. Held a series of chairs at the Universities of Duisburg, Utrecht and, finally, from 1739, Leyden; colleague of the mathematician s'Gravesande. Accidentally discovered the method for storing static electricity now known as the Leyden jar. Published prolifically in the learned journals of his day; a corresponding member of the London Royal Society, and the royal academies of Paris, Berlin, and St. Petersburg. His experimental work was chiefly in the fields of electricity, magnetism, phosphorescence, meteorology, capillary action, and the cohesion of bodies. Chief works: *Epitome elementorum physico-mathematicorum conscripta in usus academicos* ('Epitome of Physical-Mathematical Elements, Composed for the Use of Universities') (Leyden: 1726); *Introductio ad philosophiam naturalem* ('Introduction to Natural Philosophy') (2 vols. Leyden: 1762). Kant's library contained the German translation of the 1726 *Epitome elementorum: Herrn Peter Musschenbroek . . .*

Grundlehren der Naturwissenschaft, nach der zweiten lateinischen Ausgabe [*"Elementa Physicae" 1734*] *nebst einigen neuen Zusätzen des Verfassers* ('Herr Peter Musschenbroek . . . Fundamental Doctrines of Natural Science, According to the Second Latin Edition ["Elementa physicae" 1734], Together with a Number of New Additions Made by the Author Himself') (Leipzig: 1747).

NEWTON, *Sir Isaac* (1642–1727): English physicist and mathematician. Studied at Trinity College, Cambridge, of which he was elected Fellow in 1667; after the closure of the university during the Great Plague Newton withdrew to his home at Woolsthorpe, where he discovered the Binomial Theorem, and the differential and integral calculi. Returned to Cambridge; appointed Lucasian Professor of Mathematics. Devoted himself to optics. Invented the reflecting telescope. Elected Fellow of the Royal Society. Discovered that white light was a compound of lights of all the colours of the spectrum (each with its own index of refraction). Developed a corpuscular theory of light, which he later combined with the wave theory in his *Opticks*. Supreme achievement was the discovery of the Law of Gravitational Attraction. Began work on the *Principia* in 1686, and it was published in 1687. Later in life, Newton held a number of public appointments: he was Member of Parliament for the University of Cambridge (1689 and again in 1701); appointed, first, Warden (1695) and then, Master (1703) of the Mint; elected President of the Royal Society in 1703; and knighted by Queen Anne in 1705. The last part of Newton's life was overshadowed by acrimonious dispute with Leibniz (q.v.) as to who had first discovered the differential calculus – Newton erroneously charging Leibniz with plagiarism. Chief works: *Philosophiae naturalis principia mathematica* ('The Mathematical Principles of Natural Philosophy') (London: 1687); *Opticks* (London: 1704; 2nd enlarged edition: 1717). For Kant, Newton's *Principia* was for natural science what Euclid's *Elements* was for geometry. In his *Universal Natural History* Kant out-Newtons Newton by employing Newtonian principles to explain the motions and the structure of the solar system (indeed, the entire visible universe), a problem which Newton himself had been unable to solve. Kant did not, however, accept the Newtonian conception of space and time. Kant's library contained the following editions of Newton: *Principia* (Amsterdam: 1714); a Latin translation of the *Opticks* under the title *Optice sive de reflexionibus, refractionibus, inflexionibus & coloribus lucis libri tres. Latine reddidit Samuel Clarke* ('Opticks, or Three Books on the Reflection, Refraction, Inflection and Colours of Light. Translated into Latin by Samuel Clarke') (London: 1719).

NIEUWENTIJDT, *Bernard* (1654–1718): Dutch mathematician. Studied natural science and mathematics (also law and medicine). Much influenced by Descartes (q.v.) and involved in the Leibniz–Newton controversy about the origin of the differential calculus. Published a number of books on mathematics (particularly on the differential calculus); also published a criticism of Spinoza (q.v.). His most important work, which became a European best-seller, was an attempt to prove the existence of God based on an appeal to the structure of nature and natural phenomena. It bore the title *Het regt Gebruik der Wereltbeschouningen* ('The Right Employment of the Contemplation of the World') (Amsterdam: 1715). An English translation by J. Chamberlayne appeared under the title *The Religious Philosopher, or the Right Use of Contemplating the Works of the Creator . . . Designed for the Conviction of Atheists and Infidels* (3 vols. London: 1718). A French translation by Noguez appeared in 1725 under the title: *L'existence de Dieu, démontré par les merveilles de la nature; où l'on traite de la structure du corps de l'homme, des éléments, des astres et de leurs effets.*

PHILOSTRATUS, *Flavius* (ca. 170–250): Celebrated biographer of Apollonius of Tyana (q.v.). Educated at Athens; eventually settled in Rome. Induced by Empress Julia Domna (second wife of Septimus Severus) to write his *Life of Apollonius*. It is surmised that it was intended as a pagan antidote to the gospels and to impede the spread of Christianity; certainly it spread the fame of Apollonius, who is portrayed as a miracle worker. Also wrote a romanticised *Lives of the Sophists*, the *Gymnastics*, and the erotic *Epistolae*.

PLATO (427–347 B.C.): Greek mathematician and metaphysician. Deeply influenced by Pythagoras, Parmenides, and Heraclitus, but especially by Socrates (q.v.), of whom he was a pupil and disciple, and whose trial and execution he reported in the *Apology, Crito,* and *Phaedo.* Plato's early works, the so-called eristic (or Socratic) dialogues, are devoted to the attempted (but unsuccessful) definition of moral concepts. Plato's main achievements were in the fields of political philosophy (*Republic* and *Laws*), moral philosophy (*Protagoras* and *Gorgias*), and epistemology (*Theatetus* and *Sophist*). Chiefly remembered as the originator of the doctrine of ideal forms, a theory which, to judge by the *Parmenides*, Plato abandoned in later life. Aristotle (q.v.) was a pupil of his, studying at the Academy (founded by Plato in 387 B.C.) for some twenty years. Aristotle's influence, dominant throughout the Middle Ages, was eventually eclipsed by that of his mentor in the modern period. Although Kant's conception of metaphysics was incompatible with that of Plato, his epistemology may, in many respects, be construed as continuing the tradition of Platonic idealism, particularly as it was embodied by Plato in the *Theaetetus* and developed by the Cambridge Platonists (especially Cudworth) in the seventeenth century, and by Leibniz (q.v.) in the *Nouveaux essais sur l'entendement humain* (1765).

POLYBIUS (ca. 200–ca. 118 B.C.): Greek historian of Rome. After his deportation to Rome, became friend and adviser to Scipio Aemilianus (whom he probably accompanied to Spain and Africa). Witnessed the destruction of Carthage. His *Historiae* was initially intended to trace the history of Rome from the Haniballic Wars to Pydna and Roman supremacy, but the scope was later extended. Of its forty books only the first five (probably completed by 150 B.C.) survive in complete form, the rest only in fragments. Polybius's *Historiae* is a strictly political-military history with a severely didactic purpose.

POPE, *Alexander* (1688–1744): English poet, satiricist, and critic. His chief works include: *Essay on Criticism* (1711); *The Rape of the Lock* (1712); the translations of Homer (the *Iliad* [1715–20] and the *Odyssey* [1725–6]) and an edition of Shakespeare (1725). Perhaps Pope's most celebrated work is his *Essay on Man* (London: 1733–4), which served to popularise philosophical optimism; Pope's ideas owe more to Shaftesbury (q.v.) and to his friend Bolingbroke than to Leibniz (q.v.). Pope's other works include the satires, *Imitations of Horace* (1733–8), the *Epistle to Dr. Arbuthnot* (1735), and the *Dunciad* (1742–3). Kant greatly admired Pope's poetry.

RAY, *John* (1627–1705): English naturalist. Studied at Cambridge; in 1649 elected Fellow of Trinity College (resigning his fellowship in 1662 because of his unwillingness to subscribe to the Act of Uniformity). Collaborated with and benefitted from the generosity of Francis Willoughby. In 1667 elected Fellow of the London Royal Society. Published some dozen works devoted to the classification of plants, shrubs, trees, animals, insects, birds, and fish. His numerous publications include: *Historia plantarum* ('The Natural History of Plants') (3 vols. London: 1686–1704) and a philosophical work, *The Wisdom of God manifested in the Works of Creation* (London: 1691; 2nd enlarged edition: 1692; 12th edition: 1759); also worthy of mention is his *Miscellaneous Discourses concerning the Dissolution and Changes of the World* (London: 1692; 2nd edition under the title *Three Physico-Theological Discourses:* 1693).

REIMARUS, *Hermann Samuel* (1694–1768): German deistic philosopher of the Wolffian school; man of letters. Studied at Jena, and in 1727 appointed Professor of Hebrew and Oriental Languages at the *Gymnasium* in Hamburg, a post he was to occupy until his death. Reimarus's house became the focus of the literary and cultural life of Hamburg. His most important work, the celebrated *Apologie oder Schutzschrift*, published posthumously, maintains that natural and revealed religion are absolutely incompatible: all miracles (apart from Creation itself) are denied, though Reimarus maintained that the two fundamental tenets of natural religion (the existence of God and the immortality of the soul) were capable of proof by reason. Reimarus also published an important edition of *Dio Cassius* in 1750. Reimarus's works include *Abhandlungen von den vornehmsten Wahrheiten der natürlichen Religion* ('Treatises on the Chief Truths of

Natural Religion') (Hamburg: 1754; 6th edition: 1791); *Allgemeine Betrachtungen über die Triebe der Thiere, hauptsächlich über ihren Kunsttrieb* ('General Reflections on the Instincts of Animals, and in Particular Their Artistic Instinct') (Hamburg: 1762; 4th edition: 1798); *Apologie oder Schutzschrift für die vernünftigen Verehrer Gottes* ('Apology or Letter of Safe Conduct for Those Who Honour God Rationally') [Partly published by Lessing in his *Beiträge zur Geschichte und Literatur* ('Contributions to History and Literature') (1774–8) under the title *Wolfenbüttler Fragmente eines Ungenannten* ('Wolfenbüttler Fragments of One Unnamed'), and published pseudonymously partly under the name C. A. E. Schmidt in 1787 under the title *Übrige noch ungedrückte Werke des Wolfenbüttlerschen Fragmentisten* ('The Remaining yet Unprinted Works of the Wolfenbüttel Author of the Fragments') and partly under the name W. Klose in *Niedners Zeitschrift für historische Theologie* ('Niedner's Journal for Historical Theology') (1850–2)]. Kant's library contained two works by Reimarus: *Die Vernunftlehre als eine Anweisung zum richtigen Gebrauche der Vernunft in der Erkenntniss der Wahrheit, aus zwoen ganz natürlichen Regeln der Einstimmung und des Widerspruchs hergeleitet* ('The Doctrine of Reason as a Guide to the Correct Use of Reason in the Knowledge of Truth, Derived from Two Wholly Natural Rules of Agreement and Contradiction') (Hamburg: 1756); *Anhang von der verschiedenen Determination der Naturkräfte, und ihren mancherley Stufen, zur Erläuterung des zehnten Capitels* ('Appendix on the Diverse Determination of the Forces of Nature, and Their Various Levels, by Way of Elucidating the Tenth Chapter') (1762).

REINHARD, *Adolf Friedrich* (1728–83): Minor German philosopher of the School of Crusius. Studied law and theology; practised law and appointed Assessor to the *Reichskammergericht* in Wetzlar. In 1755 won the Prussian Royal Academy Philosophy Essay-Prize on the theme of Pope's optimism and its relation to that of Leibniz. Our knowledge of Reinhard is limited to a number of minor publications (of which Kant's library contained surprisingly no fewer than four). Reinhard's works include: *Adolf Friedrich Reinhards . . . vernünftige Gedanken über die Lehre von der Unendlichkeit der Welt in Ansehung der Zeit und des Raumes* ('Adolf Friedrich Reinhard's . . . Rational Thoughts on the Doctrine of the Infinity of the World in respect of Time and Space') (Leipzig: 1753); *Dissertation qui a remporté le prix proposé par l'Académie royale des sciences et belles lettres de Prusse sur l'optimisme* (Berlin: 1755); *Abhandlung von der besten Welt* ('Treatise on the Best World') (Greifswald: 1757), Reinhard's own translation of his prize-winning essay of 1755; *Vergleichung des Lehrgebäudes des Herrn Pope von der Vollkommenheit der Welt, mit dem System des Herrn von Leibnitz, nebst einer Untersuchung der Lehre von der besten Welt . . . nebst einer Abhandlung des Hrn. Bürlamaquai, von dem Willen und der Freyheit des Menschen, beydes aus dem Französischen übersetzt* ('Comparison of Mr.

Pope's Theory of the Perfection of the World with the System of Mr. Leibniz, Together with an Investigation of the Doctrine of the Best World . . . Together with a Treatise by Mr. Bürlamaquai on the Will and the Freedom of Man, both translated from the French') (Leipzig: 1757); *Disquisitio philosophica, qua ex eo, quod aliquid exsistit, demonstratur, dari ens perfectissimum, aeternum a mundo distinctum* ('Philosophical Treatise by Which It Is Demonstrated from the Fact that Something Exists That There Is a Most Perfect Being, Eternal and Distinct from the World') (Hamburg: 1761); *Betrachtungen über die Freyheit. Nebst einer Vorrede des Herrn Prof. Formey, Aus dem Französischen übersetzt, und mit dem Anhange eines Schreibens des Erz-Bischofs Fenelon über die Freyheit Gottes, zu schaffen und nicht zu schaffen . . .* ('Reflections on Freedom. Along with a Preface by Professor Formey. Translated from the French with an Appendix Consisting of a Work by Archbishop Fenelon on the Freedom of God to Create or Not to Create . . .') (Leipzig: 1762); *System der Wesen, enthaltend die metaphysischen Principien der Natur* ('The System of Beings. Containing the Metaphysical Principles of Nature') (3 vols. 1769–70). Kant's library contained four works by Reinhard: *Abhandlung der besten Welt* (Greifswald: 1757); *Disquisitio philosophica* (Hamburg: 1761); *Betrachtungen über die Freyheit* (Leipzig: 1762); *System der Wesen* (1769–70).

SAUVAGES, *François-Boissier de la Croix de* (1706–67): French physician and natural scientist. Studied medicine at Montpellier. His doctoral dissertation (*L'amour peut-il être gueri par les plantes*) established his name in 1726. In 1730 visited Paris and published a classification of illnesses, which would eventually become the 1763 *Nosologia methodica*. In 1731 appointed to the chair of medicine at Montpellier, where he introduced, in modified form, the vitalist ideas of Stahl (q.v.). Corresponded with the leading men of science of his day. His published output, both papers for the journals of the academies of Montpellier, Rouen, Toulouse, Stockholm, Paris and Berlin and books (reputedly one a year), was enormous. His most important work was *Nosologia methodica sistens morborum classes, genera et species* ('Systematic Classification of Diseases, Being a Presentation of their Classes, Genera and Species') (5 vols. Amsterdam: 1763).

SHAFTESBURY, *Anthony Ashley Cooper, 3rd Earl of* (1671–1713): English philosopher and man of letters; founder of the Moral Sense School. Early education supervised by Locke; pupil at Winchester College; education completed by Grand Tour (1687–9). Entered Parliament after period of private study, but ill health forced his resignation. In 1698 made first visit to Holland, where he met Le Clerc and other leading intellectuals. In 1699 an illicit edition of his *Inquiry* appeared. In 1700 entered the House of Lords, where he was active on behalf of the Whigs, but again ill health prevented his acceptance of high office. Made second visit to Holland in 1703. His return to England in 1704 marked the start of the period of his chief philosophical activity, which culminated with the appearance of the *Characteristicks* in 1711. Ill health drove Shaftesbury south to Naples, where he died two years later. Chief works: *Inquiry concerning Virtue, or Merit* (London: 1699); *The Moralists, A Philosophical Rhapsody* (London: 1709); *Characteristicks of Men, Manners, Opinions, Times* (3 vols. London: 1711), Volume I: *Letter concerning Enthusiasm* (1708); *Sensus Communis* (1709); *Soliloquy, or Advice to an Author* (1710); Volume II: *Inquiry* (1699); *The Moralists;* Volume III: *Miscellaneous Reflections* (and, in the second edition of 1714) *A Notion of the Historical Draught, or Tablature of the Judgement of Hercules* and *Letter concerning Design.*

SIMONIDES OF CEOS (ca. 556 – ca. 468 [?] B.C.): Greek lyric poet and epigrammatist. Spent youth on Ceos; travelled in Asia Minor; visited Athens, enjoying the favour of Hipparchos, son of Pisistratos. On the death of his patron, he went to the court of Alenas, king of Thessaly. In 489 B.C. returned to Athens, where he celebrated the events of the Persian Wars and contested the prize with Aeschylus for the best elegy on the Victory of Marathon. In 447 he was persuaded to join the court of Hieron, king of Syracuse. Hieron is supposed to have asked Simonides what he thought concerning God. Simonides asked first for one, then two, then four days, and so on, to answer the question. Hieron, puzzled by the ever-lengthening delays, asked for an explanation. Simonides is reputed to have said: 'The more I meditate on the matter, the more difficult it becomes.'

SOCRATES (470–399 B.C.): Greek philosopher, moralist, and mentor to Plato (q.v.). Devoted his life to pursuit of philosophy by employing the method of eristic debate in the hope (always disappointed) of establishing real definitions of moral concepts and with a view to demonstrating the ignorance of his opponents. Maintained that vice was a product of ignorance and therefore involuntary; that knowledge guaranteed virtue; and virtue, happiness. After a life of exemplary virtue devoted to philosophy and his duties as an Athenian citizen, he was put on trial for his life on charges of introducing new gods and corrupting the young. He was found guilty and condemned to die. Since he left no writings, we are dependent for our knowledge of his person and thought on Plato (*Apology, Crito, Phaedo,* and the early eristic dialogues) and on Xenophon (*Memorabilia, Apology,* and *Symposium*). Both Stoics and Epicureans (and indeed, much later, existentialist thinkers) drew their moral inspiration from Socrates.

SPINOZA, *Benedictus de* (1632–77): Dutch philosopher of Portuguese-Jewish extraction. Received rabbinical education, but his lack of orthodoxy led to his expulsion from the Jewish community. Earned his living by grinding lenses. Withdrew to Rijnsburg (near Leyden), and had composed the *Korte Verhandling* and the *De intellectus emendatione* by 1662; the following year he published a geometrically formulated version of Descartes's *Principia*. It was at about this time that Spinoza started work on the *Ethica* (which was completed by 1675 but not published until after Spinoza's death in 1677). The *Tractatus Theologico-Politicus* was published anonymously in 1670; its defence of the freedom of thought and religious belief and its statement of the principles of historical biblical criticism aroused great controversy. Spinoza maintained an important correspondence with Leibniz (q.v.), Oldenburg, and Huygens (q.v.). The employment of the mathematical method in philosophy – characteristic of Spinoza's *Ethica* – is the object of Kant's criticism in the *Negative Magnitudes* and the *Inquiry*.

STAHL, *Georg Ernst* (1660–1734): German chemist and physician; proponent of vitalism. Studied natural science and medicine at Jena. In 1687 became physician to the court of Saxony-Weimar. In 1694 appointed, with the support of Hofmann (q.v.), to the second chair of medicine at the newly founded University of Halle. Through his teaching, medical practise, and prolific publications, Stahl quickly established a European reputation. Moved to Berlin in 1716 to take up appointment as personal physician to the king of Prussia. In addition to championing a vitalist conception of medicine, Stahl is also remembered for his phlogiston theory of combustion. Much influenced by Leibniz (q.v.) and Wolff (q.v.). Of his numerous publications on chemistry and medicine, perhaps the most important is *Theoria medica vera, physiologiam et pathologiam tanquam doctrinae medicae partes vere contemplativas et naturae et artis veris fundamentis intaminata ratione et inconcussa experientia, sistens* ('True Medical Theory Presenting Physiology and Pathology as Also the Truly Contemplative Parts of Medical Doctrine and Secured by Reason and by Incontrovertible Experience and Based on the True Foundations of Both Art and Nature') (Halle: 1707).

SÜSSMILCH, *Johann Peter* (1707–67): German economist, demographer, statistician, and theologian. Studied medicine, botany, chemistry, and theology at Halle, and then, theology, law, and philosophy at Jena, completing his studies in 1732 with the dissertation, *De cohesione et attractione corporum* ('On the Cohesiveness and Attraction of Bodies'). Then held a variety of posts including private tutor, military chaplain, and court preacher. In 1741 published his celebrated *Die göttliche Ordnung*, which secured him election to the Prussian Royal Academy. Maupertuis (q.v.) persuaded Süssmilch to deliver some public lectures on this material. Employing statistics from registers of births, deaths and marriages, he established the existence of demographical statistical regularities and concluded that the hand of providence exercised control over seemingly accidental occurrences. His work was suggested to him by Derham's (q.v.) 1723 *Physico-Theology*. Also published important work on comparative linguistics. Chief work: *Die göttliche Ordnung in den Verhältnissen des menschlichen Geschlechts, aus der Geburt, dem Tode und der Fortpflanzung desselben erwiesen* ('Divine Order in the Relations of the Human Species, Demonstrated from the Birth, Death and Propagation of the Species') (Berlin: 1741; new enlarged edition in 2 vols.: 1761; 4th edition with a 3rd vol. drawn up by Baumann: 1775; 6th edition: 1798).

SWEDENBORG, *Emanuel* (1688–1772): Swedish scientist, theologian, and religious visionary. Studied natural science at Uppsala University. In 1710–14 visited Germany, Holland, France and, most importantly, England, where he deepened his knowledge of Newtonian physics. Upon his return to Sweden, appointed by Charles XII Assessor Extraordinary to the Royal College of Mines, a post he was to hold for thirty-one years until 1747. In 1719 ennobled for engineering services (probably of a military character) to the state (hence the change of name from Svedborg to Svedenborg – the Swedish 'en' having the same force as the French 'de'). During this period, Swedenborg published a number of works on natural science, geology, mineralogy, engineering, and zoology. About 1736 became subject to religious crises of an ecstatic nature, which in 1745, during a visit to London, culminated in a vision which convinced him that he was called upon by God to offer a new spiritual-moral interpretation of the Bible. In 1747 resigned his government assessorship and devoted himself exclusively to his new mission. His 'inner sense' was 'opened up', and access to the spirit-world was thus secured for him; his numerous publications contain extensive and elaborate reports of these spirit-dealings. The *Arcana coelestia* (the object of Kant's mockery in the *Dreams of a Spirit-Seer* [1766]) appeared in eight volumes between 1749 and 1756. His most famous work, the *De coelo . . . et de inferno* appeared in 1758. The vision of the Stockholm fire (reported by Kant in the *Dreams* [1766]) took place in 1759; the episode involving the missing receipt took place in 1761, and the episode involving the queen of Sweden possibly in the same year. Died in 1772 in London, where he was buried at the Swedish Church; his remains were removed in 1908 to Uppsala Cathedral. Chief works: *Arcana coelestia* ('Celestial Mysteries') (8 vols. London: 1749–56); *De coelo et eius mirabilibus, et de inferno* ('On Heaven and Its Wonders, and on Hell') (London: 1758); *Sapientia angelica de divino amore et de divina sapientia* ('Angelic Wisdom Concerning Divine Love and Divine Wisdom') (Amsterdam: 1763); *Sapientia angelica de divina providentia* ('Angelic Wisdom Concerning Divine Providence') (Amsterdam: 1764); *Vera christiana religio* ('The True Christian Religion') (Amsterdam: 1771).

TERENCE *(Publius Terentius Afer)* (ca. 190 – ca. 159 [?] B.C.): Roman writer of comedies. Born in North Africa; brought to Rome as a slave; served in the household of a senator, Terentius Lucanus (from whom

Terence derived his name when manumitted). Author of six extant comedies: *Andria* (166 B.C.); *Heautontimorumenos* (163 B.C.); *Eunuchus* (161 B.C.); *Phormio* (161 B.C.); *Adelphi* (160 B.C.) and *Hecyra* (160 B.C.). Apart from *Phormio* and *Hecyra,* Terence's comedies were adaptations of plays by Menander; they were particularly popular in the eighteenth century and were themselves frequently adapted by playwrights of the period.

TORRICELLI, *Evangelista* (1608–47): Italian physicist and mathematician; inventor of the barometer. Studied under Galileo's disciple and friend Benedetto Castelli at the *Collegio di Sapienza* in Rome. Torricelli, inspired by Galileo's 1638 *Discorsi sulle nuove scienze,* developed many of its principles, especially in the fields of projectile and fluid motion. In 1641 became Galileo's amanuensis for the final three months of the latter's life. On Galileo's death, appointed professor of mathematics at the Florentine Academy. In 1643 discovered the principle of the barometer (known as the Torricellian Tube) and thereby the possibility of the vacuum. Chief works: *Opera geometrica* ('Geometrical Works') (Florence: 1644), which contains the important paper *De motu gravium naturaliter accelerato* ('On the Naturally Accelerated Motion of Heavy Bodies'); *Lezzione accademiche* ('Academic Lectures') (Florence: 1715) (this posthumous work contains Torricelli's findings relating to the barometer).

ULLOA, *Antonio de* (1716–95): Spanish naval officer, traveller, and man of science. Entered the Spanish navy in 1733. Two years later, with Jorge Juan, was commissioned to accompany a Franco-Spanish expedition to South America, organised by the Paris Academy of Sciences, to measure one degree of the meridian at the equator. Geodesic operations began in Quito, Peru, in 1736. Ulloa and Juan found themselves caught up in the Anglo-Spanish war which broke out in 1740; they carried out their naval and military duties with conspicuous skill and success. The scientific expedition was eventually completed in 1744, but Ulloa was captured by an English corsair on the return journey and for a while imprisoned in England. He was released and favourably received by the London Royal Society, to which he was elected Fellow. Eventually returned to Madrid in 1746, where Ulloa and Juan prepared their reports on the expedition, the latter publishing his *Observaciones* (on the scientific matters) in 1748, and the former his *Relación historica* (on the geographical and anthropological aspects of the expedition) in the same year. Ulloa divided the rest of his life between a successful and eventful naval career (he was governor of Louisiana for a while) and travelling, exploring, and engaging in scientific research. Travelled extensively in South and North America (described in his 1772 *Noticias americanas*). Died in León in 1795. Chief works: *Relación historica del viage a la America meridional* ('Historical Account of the Journey to South America') (Madrid: 1748); *Noticias americanas, entretenimientos physico-historicos sobre la America meridional y la septentrional oriental*

('American Notes: Physical and Historical Conversations on South America and the Eastern Part of North America') (Madrid: 1772).

VIRGIL *(Publius Vergilius Maro)* (70–19 B.C.): Roman poet. Brought up in Mantua, and educated at Cremona. Studied rhetoric at Rome, and after the outbreak of the civil war, studied philosophy at Naples under the Epicurean Siro. The *Eclogues* were probably composed between 45 and 37 B.C. Formed a friendship with Maecenas and Horace (q.v.). The *Georgics* were probably completed by 29 B.C. The final years of Virgil's life were devoted to the composition of the *Aeneid* (which he may have started in 26 B.C.). In 19 B.C. he embarked on what was intended to be a three-year visit to Greece, but the visit was cut short and Virgil returned to Italy from Athens; he fell ill at Megara and died at Brundisium. Virgil's instructions to his literary executor Varius that the *Aeneid* should be destroyed if he died before its completion were over-ridden by Augustus. Virgil was buried near Naples.

VOLTAIRE, *François-Marie Arouet de* (1694–1778): French poet, dramatist, historian and philosopher. Educated by Jesuits and introduced early on to free-thinking circles. Briefly imprisoned in the Bastille for an incautious political lampoon. In 1722 published *Le Pour et le contre*, a defence of deism. In 1726 a quarrel with de Rohan led to further imprisonment and then flight to England, where he spent three years (meeting Berkeley, Bolingbroke, Pope (q.v.), and Swift). Returned to Paris in 1729, but publication of his *Lettres philosophiques sur les Anglais* in 1734 obliged him to flee the capital; he stayed with Mme de Chatelet at Cirey (near Switzerland) from 1734 to 1743. To this fruitful period belonged the composition of the *Traité de métaphysique* and the *Eléments de la philosophie de Newton* and preliminary work on the *Discours en vers sur l'homme*, the *Siècle de Louis XIV* and the *Essai sur les moeurs*. In 1743 returned to Paris and frequented Versailles and Fontainebleu; in 1746 elected to the French Academy. On the death of Mme de Chatelet in 1749, he accepted an invitation from Frederick the Great and settled in Potsdam. There he completed the *Siècle de Louis XIV* and the *Essai sur les moeurs*. His relations with Frederick became strained in 1752, the year in which he published his attacks on Maupertuis (q.v.), the president of the Prussian Royal Academy, in *Micromégas* and the *Diatribe du Docteur Akakia*. Voltaire left Prussia, and settled in Switzerland, where he composed the *Poème sur le désastre de Lisbonne* (1756) and *Candide* (1759), in which optimism is attacked. Collaborated with d'Alembert on the *Encyclopédie*. In 1760 settled at Ferney. Voltaire was now a man of great wealth. To this period belong the *Dictionnaire philosophique* (1764) and the deistic *Lettres de Memmius à Ciceron* (1771). In 1778 Voltaire returned to Paris to great popular acclaim, dying there shortly afterwards.

WARBURTON, *William* (1698–1779): English critic, theologian, and divine. Ordained in 1727 and appointed to the parish of Brant Broughton (Lincolnshire), where he remained until 1745. It was here that he composed his most celebrated work, *The Divine Legislation*, which appeared between 1738 and 1741. In 1742 won the friendship of Pope (q.v.) (whose works he was to edit and publish in 1751) with his *Vindication of Mr. Pope's Essay on Man from the Misrepresentations of Mr. de Crousaz* (London: 1742) and his *Critical and Philosophical Commentary on Mr. Pope's Essay on Man* (London: 1742). In 1747 brought out his famous edition of Shakespeare. A series of preferments led to his appointment as Bishop of Gloucester. Defended revealed religion in a number of works, but most successfully in his *A View of Lord Bolingbroke's Philosophy* (2 vols. London: 1753–63) and, in collaboration with Richard Hurd, in *Remarks on Hume's Natural History of Religion* (London: 1757). Warburton's works include: *The Divine Legislation of Moses demonstrated on the Principles of a Religious Deist from the Omission of the Doctrine of a Future State of Reward and Punishment in the Jewish Dispensation* (2 vols. London: 1738–41; 10th edition: 1846); *Julian, or a Discourse concerning the Earthquake and Fiery Eruption which Defeated that Emperor's Attempt to Rebuild the Temple at Jerusalem, in which the Reality of a Divine Interposition is Shown* (London: 1750) (German translation: *Hern Wilhelm Warburtons critische Abhandlung von dem Erdbeben und Feuerflammen . . . Aus dem Englischen übersetzt* ['Mr William Warburton's Critical Treatise on the Earthquake and Fiery Eruption . . . Translated from the English'] [Gotha: 1755]).

WHISTON, *William* (1667–1752): English mathematician and theologian. Studied at Clare College, Cambridge where he read mathematics and was appointed to a fellowship in 1693. Whiston's first book, the 1696 *New Theory of the Earth*, ran to six editions, and won the applause of Newton (q.v.) and Locke. Newton made Whiston his deputy at Cambridge, and in 1703 he succeeded Newton in the Lucasian Chair of Mathematics. While at Cambridge, Whiston published many important papers and books on mathematics, astronomy, and theology. His 1708 *Essay on the Apostolic Constitutions* maintained that the creed of the primitive church had been Arian. Whiston's heterodoxy became notorious, and in 1710 he was deprived of his chair and expelled from the university, but he continued to publish on mathematics, astronomy, and theology. His *Primitive Christianity Revived* was an attempt to vindicate his Arianism. Wrote an important biography of Samuel Clarke (1730) and a useful translation of Josephus (1737). Chief works: *A New Theory of the Earth . . . Wherein the Creation . . . Deluge and . . . Conflagration as laid in the Holy Scriptures are shewn to be Perfectly Agreeable to Reason and Philosophy. With a . . . Discourse concerning the . . . Mosaick History of the Creation* (London: 1696) (German translation: *W. W.'s Nova Telluris Theoria, das ist: Neue*

Betrachtung der Erde, nach ihrem Ursprung and Fortgang biss zur Hervorbringung aller Dinge . . . ['W. W.'s New Theory of the Earth, That Is: New Observation of the Earth, from Its Origin and Development to the Bringing Forth of All Things'] [Frankfurt: 1713]); *The Cause of the Deluge Demonstrated* . . . *Being an Appendix to the 2nd Edition of the New Theory of the Earth* (London: 1708); *Primitive Christianity Revived* (5 vols. London: 1711–12); *Astronomical Principles of Religion, Natural and Revealed* . . . *The Cause of the Deluge Demonstrated* (London: 1717); *A New Theory of the Deluge: Being a Plain Abstract of What the Author has said on that Subject in Different Treatises* (London: 1737).

WOLFF, *Christian* (1679–1754): German rationalist philosopher and chief representative of the German Enlightenment. Studied mathematics and philosophy at Jena from 1699 to 1702. His 1704 *De algorithmo infinitessimali differentiali* attracted the notice of Leibniz (q.v.), with whom Wolff entered into an important correspondence and by whom Wolff was helped to the chair of mathematics at Halle in 1706; he taught there until 1723, lecturing on mathematics, natural science and, after 1709, philosophy. To this period belongs an important series of works written, not in the customary Latin but in German; thus he played a crucial role in the formation of the German philosophical vocabulary. His success and rationalism won him many enemies in Pietist Halle. His 1721 public oration *De Sinorum philosophia practica* (maintaining that the moral precepts of Confucius were proof of the power of reason to arrive at moral truth independently of religion and revelation) unleashed a storm of controversy, which culminated in his dismissal from the university and his banishment from Prussia. Wolff was promptly offered and accepted a chair at Marburg from the Landgrave of Hesse. Wolff remained at Marburg until 1740, when Frederick II succeeded to the Prussian throne. While at Marburg Wolff published an important series of works in Latin, which made his philosophical thought accessible to thinkers outside Germany. In 1740 Wolff was reinstated as professor in the chair of law at Halle. In 1743 he was appointed rector of the university. Wolff continued to publish prolifically, but his popularity as a teacher declined. Chief works: *Vernünftige Gedanken von den Kräften des menschlichen Verstandes und ihrem richtigen Gebrauch in der Erkenntnis der Wahrheit* ('Rational Thoughts on the Powers of the Human Understanding and their Correct Employment in the Cognition of the Truth') (Halle: 1712); *Vernünftige Gedanken von Gott, der Welt und der Seele des Menschen, auch allen Dingen überhaupt* ('Rational Thoughts on God, the World and the Soul of Man, and on All Things Whatsoever') (Halle: 1719; 5th edition: 1732); *Vernünftige Gedanken von der Menschen Thun und Lassen zur Beförderung ihrer Glückseligkeit* ('Rational Thoughts on Man's Acts of Commission and Omission, with a View to Advancing His Happiness') (Halle: 1720); *Vernünftige Gedanken von dem gesellschaftlichen Leben der Menschen, und insonderheit dem gemeinen Wesen* ('Rational Thoughts on the Social Life of Man, and in Particular on Society') (Halle: 1721; 5th edition: 1740); *Vernünftige Gedanken von den Wirkungen der Natur* ('Rational Thoughts on the Operations of Nature') (Halle: 1723); *Vernünftige Gedanken von den Absichten der natürlichen Dingen* ('Rational Thoughts on the Intentions of Natural Things') (Frankfurt and Leipzig: 1724); *Vernünftige Gedanken von dem Gebrauche der Theile des menschlichen Leibes, der Thiere und Pflanzen* ('Rational Thoughts on the Employment of the Parts of the Human Body, of Animals and Plants') (Frankfurt: 1725). Of the series of Latin works published between 1728 and 1750, the most important include: *Philosophia rationalis sive logica methodo scientifica pertractata et ad usum scientiarum atque vitae aptat* ('Rational Philosophy, or Logic Treated According to the Scientific Method, and Suited to the Use of the Sciences and of Life') (Frankfurt: 1728; 3rd edition: 1740); *Philosophia prima sive ontologia* ('First Philosophy or Ontology') (Frankfurt: 1730); *Cosmologia generalis* ('Universal Cosmology') (Frankfurt: 1731); *Psychologia empirica* ('Empirical Psychology') (Frankfurt: 1732); *Theologia naturalis* ('Natural Theology') (2 vols. Frankfurt: 1736–7); *Philosophia practica universalis* ('Universal Practical Philosophy') (2 vols. Frankfurt: 1738–9); *Philosophia moralis sive ethica* ('Moral Philosophy or Ethics') (5 vols. Halle: 1750–3). Kant's library contained four works by Wolff: *Elementa matheseos universae* ('Elements of General Mathematics') (2 vols. Halle: 1713–15); *Philosophia prima* (Frankfurt: 1730); *Auszug aus den Anfangs-Gründen aller mathematischen Wissenschaften* ('Excerpt from the First Principles of All Mathematical Sciences') (Frankfurt: 1749); *Anfangs-Gründe aller mathematischen Wissenschaften* ('First Principles of All Mathematical Sciences') (new, enlarged, and revised edition: Frankfurt: 1750).

WRIGHT, *Thomas* (fl. 1740–60): English astronomer. Nothing is known of Thomas Wright (known as Wright of Durham) apart from the titles of the books on cosmology (and also Irish antiquities) which he published in the period 1740–50. Chief works: *The Use of the Globes, or the General Doctrine of the Sphere* (London: 1740); *Clavis Celestis, being the Explication of a Diagram entitled [sic] a Synopsis of the Universe, or the Visible World Epitomised* (London: 1742); *An Original Theory or New Hypothesis of the Universe founded upon the Laws of Nature, and solving by Mathematical Principles the General Phenomena of the Visible Creation; and particularly the Via Lactea. Comprised in Nine Familiar Letters from the Author to a Friend* (London: 1750).

ACKNOWLEDGEMENTS

In preparing the foregoing entries, the editor drew information from a variety of sources. The reference works which were most frequently consulted and to which the editor wishes herewith to acknowledge his indebtedness are: *Der Grosse Brockhaus* 12 vols. (Wiesbaden: 1952–7); *Biographie universelle moderne et ancienne* 83 vols. (Paris: 1811–53); *Dictionary of National Biography* 63 vols. (London: 1855–1900); *Encyclopaedia Britannica* 24 vols. (14th edition: London and New York: 1949); *Enciclopedia filosofica* 6 vols. (2nd edition: Florence: 1967); *Encyclopédie moderne* 27 vols. (Paris: 1846–51); Warda: *Kants Bücher* (Berlin: 1922) and Ziegenfuss: *Philosophen-Lexikon* 2 vols. (Berlin: 1945–50).

Index

absence, 73, 211, 229–30, 236. *See also* deficiency; deprivation; negation

abstraction, 208, 228–30, 259, 308n, 310, 366, 386–7; and negative attention, 228

action, 24, 25, 26, 28, 43, 44, 61, 62, 153, 228, 229, 236, 237, 240, 272, 274, 315, 322; and act of divine creation, 32; and chance, 26; at distance 52, 61; divine, 157, 274; ground of, 26; human, 25–7, 153; inner principle of, 38; internal, 52; morally corrupt, 28; perfect, 274; physical, 28, 153; of physical bodies, 25, 26, 43, 61; and reaction, 43, 61, 171; reciprocal, 61, 171; of substances, 43, 44, 315; universal, of spirits, 43. *See also* attraction; forces; free action; motion

actuality, 18. *See also* existence; reality

Aepinus, F. M., 224, 491; on electrical and magnetic energy, 225, 226

Aesop, 8, 491

aether, 66, 155

affirmation, form of, 267

Ahasuerus, 122

air, properties of, 141, 142, 145, 148–9

alchemy and alchemists, 8

Alexander the Great, 71, 491

algebra, certainty of, 265

all-sufficiency: of God, 83, 133, 191–4; and perfection, 194

altruism, 321

analysis, lxxii, lxxxi, 10, 195–6, 201, 240, 248, 249, 252, 253, 255, 259, 262, 263, 268, 273, 278, 356, 377, 378; ambiguity of term, 378n; of concept, 105, 196, 250, 252–3, 273; conceptual, 252; geometrical, lxix; logical, 196, 197; mathematical, lxix, 250; metaphysical, 159n; qualitative and quantitative, 378n. *See also* characteristic mark; definition; synthesis

analysis situs, xxxvii, xliv, lxix–lxx, lxxiii, lxxx, 365. *See also* incongruent counterparts; Leibniz, G. W.

animals, lxxvii, 103–4, 141, 149, 156, 157, 160, 167, 192, 221, 257–8, 314, 318; and animal machines, 314, 318; awareness among, 104; cognitive powers of, 103–4; and distinct concepts, lxxvii, 103;

generation of, 156, 157, 352; structure of, 156, 166, 167, 184

Apollonius of Tyana, 344, 491

a posteriori, xxxviii, lxxvii, 137, 282, 345, 366, 380; and argument for God's existence, xxxix, lxxxvii, 282; and end of knowledge, 344; as mode of cognition, 135. See also *a priori;* argument; God; proof

apparitions, 305, 328, 330, 335, 336, 337. *See also* appearance; illusion

appearance, 34, 56, 155, 175, 283, 351, 367, 381, 386; external, 155; of material world, 351; as opposed to reality, 34; of reality, 283, 351; union of different kinds of, 155. *See also* apparitions; illusion; *phenomenon;* reality

appetite, definition of, 257

a priori, xlii, lxxviii, 135, 282, 345, 380, 413, 415; and argument for existence of God, xxxvi, xxxix, lxxvii, lxxviii, 135, 282, 415; and end of knowledge, 344; and forms of sensibility, xxxviii, xlvii, lxx; as mode of cognition, 136. See also *a posteriori;* argument; proof; space; time

archetype, 389

argument, 195–6, 223, 347; *a posteriori*, xxxviii, lxxvii, 282; *a priori*, xxxvi, xxxix, lxxvii, lxxviii, 135, 282, 415; Cartesian, for God's existence, xl, lx, lxxv, lxxvii, 14, 15, 195–8, 201, 282; contrasted with demonstration, 111–12; direct method of, 7; for God's existence, xxxvii, xxxviii, xxxix, 15, 135, 195–6, 282, 415; ontological, lxxv; rational, 345. See also *a posteriori; a priori;* demonstration; God; proof

argumentum ab utili, 305

Ariosto, L., 346, 491–2

Aristotle, lviii, lix, 277, 329, 492; derived form, not matter, of nature from God, 165; on dreaming, 329

arithmetic, 250, 277, 390; general, 250, 255. *See also* mathematics

art, 155; of combining signs, li, 8–9; of logic, 113

Artemidorus of Ephesus, 344, 492

atheism, 'refined,' 164

INDEX

concepts (*cont.*)
of, 237; rational, 319; real grounds of,
237; of reason, 326, 397; sensitive, 386,
407, 408; sensory, 389; simple, 9, 241,
255; surreptitious, 308n, 329;
unanalysable, 119, 241, 251–3, 273; of
understanding, 158, 195, 324, 377, 387–
8, 390, 407–9, 411–14; universal, 9, 30,
173, 251, 265, 386, 389, 390, 396. *See
also* conception; idea; judgement; notion;
representation
congruence, xliv, 396; Leibniz on, lxix,
lxxx. See also *analysis situs;* incongruent
counterparts
conscience, 24, 221, 282
consciousness, 24, 26, 221, 236, 237, 259,
263, 273, 319, 320; ambiguity of term,
263; of human soul, 325; immediate
257; personal, 326
consequence, 124, 130, 151, 195, 196,
197, 231, 232, 239, 240, 241; principle
of, 34
contingency, 89, 127–8, 158, 413; of natural things, 17; and necessity, 16, 21, 127;
nominal and real characteristic marks of,
413; nominal and real definitions of,
127, 143
contradiction, principle (law) of, lxxv, 5, 9–
10, 104, 105, 123–7, 131, 211, 214,
241, 267, 268, 269, 278, 385, 394, 395,
406, 412; definition of, 9–10; and
ground of possibility, 124–5, 129; internal, 123–6; and necessary existence,
127, 282–3; as principle of identity, 9,
105; and principle of negations only, 5,
268; and time, 394, 399. *See also* opposition; repugnancy
conviction, 247
copula, 89, 119; absolute use of, 89
cosmology, 295
counterparts, 174, 370, 371. *See also* incongruent counterparts
creation, 157, 158, 200; act of, 32, 148,
175, 176; concept of, 181
critique: of rational theology, xxxix; of real
learning, 296; of reason, 297; of sound
understanding, 296; of taste, 297
Crusius, C. A., xxxvi, xxxix, xl, li, liv, lv, lix,
lx, 17, 18, 20, 30, 40, 97n, 98, 122–3,
209, 268, 269; on connections of soul
with organic body, 40; and demonstration of principle of determining ground,
13, 17, 20; on determinations of existence, 122; on distinction between absolute and hypothetical necessity, 21–2; on
distinction between real and ideal
ground, xl, 240; on divine foreknowledge, 30; on free will, 18; on human rea-

son, 267; on material and formal principles, 269; on metaphysical cognition,
267, 269; on metaphysical principles,
267, 269; method of, 267, 269; on negative attraction, 209; on truth, 269; on
what can and cannot be thought, 329
crystals, 36, 155

D'Alembert, J. L., xlix
Daries, J. G., lv, 9, 496–7; on principle of
determining ground, 20n
data, 123, 125, 133, 253, 268, 339, 354;
certain, 262; of intuition, 399; primary,
269; ultimate, 372
defect, 118, 134
deficiency, 131, 134. *See also* absence; deprivation; negation
definition, lxxii, 116–17, 133, 247–9, 253,
256–8, 261, 266, 268, 269, 295; analytic, 249, 250; arbitrary, 38; created,
lxxviii, 250, 254; distinct and complete,
lxviii; of existence, 116–17, 119, 121; formal, 117; given, 250, 254; grammatical,
249; in mathematics, 248–50, 254, 256,
264, 269, 295; in metaphysics, 180, 256,
258, 264–6, 269, 387; method of arriving at, 248–9, 258, 264; nominal, lxxviii,
126, 127, 128, 256, 258; object of, 117,
252, 256, 257; in philosophy, 248–50,
254, 256, 258, 264–5, 295; real, lxxviii,
lxxix, 90, 126, 127, 128, 256; surreptitious, 261; synthetic, lxxviii, lxxix, 248.
See also analysis
Democritus of Abdera, 345, 355, 497; and
theory of atoms, 164, 188
demonstration, 293, 322; contrasted with
argument, 111–12. *See also* argument;
proof
dependence, 380; reciprocal, of substances,
41, 401, 402, 403; of things on God, 41,
143, 152
deprivation, 130, 222, 224, 230, 236, 238;
and limitation, 16; and vice, 222. *See also*
absence; deficiency; negation
Derham, W., 199, 497
derivation, 217, 220; and absolute necessity, 16; of truths, 6
Des Bosses, B., liii
Descartes, R. xlii, 281, 497–8; on forces,
xlix; and *a priori* proof of God's existence, lxxvii, 282; on *ideas materiales,*
314n, 332; on motion of light, 12; and
ontological proof of God's existence, lx,
17
desire, 23, 26, 27, 28, 117, 134, 157, 233,
237, 238, 239, 253, 275; innate, 31; natural force of, 26; negative, 221; sensible,
81; sensual, 234n

528

power (cont.)
309, 323, 329, 347, 398; active, 193; of
choice, 28, 31, 145, 153, 160, 172, 380;
divine, 78, 79; paranormal, lxvi, lxxx,
341; of representation, 315n; of soul,
350, 352; of thought, 237, 313n, 329; of
understanding, 314, 316; of will, 314,
318, 334n, 357. See also faculties
presence, 58, 60–1, 271, 405; of God in
world, 60, 271, 410; local and virtual,
403, 410, 411
principles, lxxxi, 5, 6, 10, 255, 272, 274,
317, 339, 388, 389, 391, 396, 401, 406,
409; of all truths, 6–7, 10; of benevolence, 237; of causality, xl, xli, lxxx; of
cognition, lxxxvii, 5, 256, 267, 368, 399,
407; of coming into being, 388; of determining ground, 21; empirical, 387, 397;
first, 6, 9, 268, 273, 387, 388, 395; of
form of sensible and intelligible world,
lxxxi, 391, 398, 401; formal, 268, 269,
272, 273, 389, 391, 398; of harmony,
148, 414; of identity of indiscernibles,
lxxv, 35, 36; material and immaterial,
268–9, 273, 318; metaphysical, 267,
269, 280; of metaphysical cognition,
lxxxi, 5, 37, 267; of morality, 271, 272,
274, 284, 298; of obligation, 237, 274; of
parsimony, lxxxi; rational, 265; of reason,
277, 324, 368; of reduction, 408; spurious, 407, 409; subreptic, 414; of sufficient ground, li, lxxv, 5, 11, 20, 21, 34,
53, 197; of taste, 277; universal, 6, 266,
391. See also rules
proof, 16–17, 135, 160, 174, 198, 200, 250,
282–3, 305, 309; a posteriori, xxxviii,
lxxvii, 282; a priori, xxxvi, xxxix, lxxvii,
lxxviii, 135, 282, 415; Cartesian, xl, lx,
lxxv, 14, 15, 195–7, 201, 282; from contingency, 201, 283; cosmological, 199,
200; of general rules of syllogism, 91; in
geometry, 260; logically complete, 132;
mathematical, 159; metaphysical, 159,
250; moral, 159. See also argument; demonstration
properties, 132, 139, 144, 160, 196, 199,
295; divine, 80, 130, 132, 196; essential,
135; general, 259; inner, 309; of matter,
142, 143, 178, 309n; real, 130; of space,
57, 137, 139, 144, 208, 397, 398; universal, 142. See also attributes; characteristic
mark; mark
proposition(s), 6, 7, 9, 253, 254; capable of
proof, 253; certain, 247; demonstrable
and indemonstrable, 104, 105, 252, 253,
268, 269; empirical, 247; of geometry,
396; negative and affirmative, 6, 7, 8, 10,
95, 267, 268; simple, 6; of syllogism,

94–5, 104; true, 13; universal, 268, 396.
See also judgement; principles
provision, 139–41; individual, 140–1, 148,
161, 162, 163, 168, 172, 173, 175, 198;
perfect, of nature, 177; special, 177, 317;
supernatural, 152, 184
psychology, 219; empirical, 295, 296, 390;
and phenomena of inner sense, 390; rational, 295, 388
purpose, 99, 100, 139, 145, 150, 151, 156,
183, 192; ultimate, 139; of universe, 145
Pyrrhonism, 281

quality, lxix, 73, 278, 279, 280, 309, 323;
negative, 209; of objects, 389; sensible,
279; of sensible things, 390; of space,
lxix–lxx. See also magnitude; quantity
quantity, 56, 278, 279, 280, 390; arithmetical, 278; geometrical, 278–9; limits of,
279; non-extended, 280; notion of, 278,
280; of space, 399. See also magnitude;
number; quality

ratiocinium hybridum, 92, 93, 95, 96. See
also syllogism
ratiocinium purum, 92. See also syllogism
Ray, J., 147n, 513
reality, 72–4, 124, 127, 130, 132, 198, 234,
366; absolute, 32, 34; appearance of,
283, 351; degrees of, 72, 73, 74, 124;
ground of, 72n; infinite and finite, 74;
inherent, 32n; limit of, 73; magnitude of,
73; and negation, 73; objective, 394; as
opposed to appearance, 34; and perfection, 73–4, 127, 134; sum of, 73, 234,
235, 236; supreme, 72n, 129; of time,
394. See also actuality; appearance; illusion; matter; world(s)
reason, 103, 104, 161, 165, 297, 298, 307,
309, 320, 338, 339, 343, 344, 347, 356,
359, 371, 379, 397, 412; concepts of, 326,
397; deception of, 347; foundation of human, 268; human, 199, 267, 268, 359;
idea of, 378; illusory arguments of, 347;
laws of, 379, 399, 407; limits of human,
354, 355, 399; principles of, 268, 277,
324; pure, 379; and understanding, lxxvi,
109, 291–2; unity of, 322; use of, 406. See
also mind; soul; spirit; understanding
reflection: abstract, 251; metaphysical, 258;
philosophical, 173, 251
regularity, 139, 158, 166, 169, 170, 187,
189, 191, 192. See also harmony; order;
uniformity
Reimarus, H. S., 229, 513–14; on natural
religion, 200
Reinhard, A. F., lv, lvi, lvii, 514–15; on
optimism, 73, 77